SPRINGER PUBLISHING

D1066620

GET THE MOST FROM YOUR BOOK

SPRINGER PUBLISHING
CONNECT™

VOUCHER CODE:

PY4LGFT4

Online Access

Your print purchase of *The Professional Practice of Rehabilitation Counseling, Third Edition,* includes **online access via Springer Publishing Connect**™ to increase accessibility, portability, and searchability.

Insert the code at https://connect.springerpub.com/content/book/978-0-8261-3904-7 today!

Having trouble? Contact our customer service department at cs@springerpub.com

Instructor Resource Access for Adopters

Let us do some of the heavy lifting to create an engaging classroom experience with a variety of instructor resources included in most textbooks SUCH AS:

INSTRUCTOR'S MANUAL

POWERPOINTS

TEST BANK

Visit **https://connect.springerpub.com/** and look for the **"Show Supplementary"** button on your **book homepage** to see what is available to instructors! First time using Springer Publishing Connect?
Email **textbook@springerpub.com** to create an account and start unlocking valuable resources.

The Professional Practice of Rehabilitation Counseling

Michael T. Hartley, PhD, CRC, is an associate professor in the Counseling Program, Department of Disability and Psychoeducational Studies at the University of Arizona. His scholarly interests lie in the professionalization of rehabilitation counseling, including the application of ethical principles. Much of his work has targeted distributive justice issues, and therefore, his scholarship on ethical obligations has focused on the importance of promoting resilience and advocating against ableism or the preference for able-bodiedness. Dr. Hartley has collaborated on research grants and was the primary investigator on recent grant-funded research projects focused on developing innovative interventions to support resilience among military veterans with spinal cord injuries. He has also worked to support youth with disabilities during the school-to-work transition to increase resilience and decrease dropout. In the area of advocacy, he has been involved in leadership and research collaborations with Centers for Independent Living to teach and empower individuals with disabilities to advocate for themselves. Rooted in the concept of self-advocacy, his research on advocacy has emphasized the use of digital technology as a way for individuals who have experienced marginalization to reclaim power and control over their environments. Finally, his research on salient ethical issues in contemporary rehabilitation counseling practice was used to guide recent revisions to the 2017 Commission on Rehabilitation Counselor Certification Code of Ethics, developed by a taskforce on which he served. He recently joined as coauthor of the fifth edition of *Ethics and Decision Making in Counseling and Psychotherapy* (2021). Dr. Hartley is knowledgeable about the profession and professional practice of rehabilitation counseling and is committed to defining and better preparing rehabilitation counselors to work ethically and effectively with persons with disabilities.

Vilia M. Tarvydas, PhD, CRC (Ret.), is a professor emerita of counselor education at the University of Iowa. She has worked in rehabilitation practice in traumatic brain injury and physical rehabilitation and as a rehabilitation counselor educator for over 40 years. Her scholarly works and national and international presentations have concentrated on the areas of ethics, ethical decision-making, and professional governance and standards. She has published extensively in these areas, and, aside from this text, she is coauthor of *Ethics and Decision Making in Counseling and Psychotherapy* (2021), a revised fifth edition of her earlier book, *Ethical and Professional Issues in Counseling.* Dr. Tarvydas has had a career-long involvement in counseling professionalization, ethics, and credentialing. She served as chair of the Iowa Board of Behavioral Science Examiners and its Disciplinary Committee. She served on the American Counseling Association (ACA) Licensure Committee for many years and was a member of the Oversight Committee for the joint American Association of State Counseling Boards/ACA 20/20 initiative. She also has had extensive experience in counselor certification, having served for 8 years with the Commission on Rehabilitation Counselor Certification (CRCC) as vice-chair and secretary, on the Examination and Research Committee, and as chair of the Ethics Committee. Dr. Tarvydas is a past president of three national professional organizations: the National Council on Rehabilitation Education, the American Rehabilitation Counseling Association, and the American Association of State Counseling Boards. She has been a member of the ACA Ethics Committee and the American Occupational Therapy Association's Judicial Council. She was a member of the ACA Task Force on Revision of the Code of Ethics that produced the 2005 ACA Code of Ethics. She chaired the groups that developed the 1987 unified *Code of Professional Ethics for Rehabilitation Counselors* and served on the task force that drafted the 2002 CRCC Code of Professional Ethics. She was the chair of the CRCC Task Force on Code Revision that produced the 2010 Code. She served on the Council for Accreditation of Counseling and Related Educational Programs Board of Directors from 2014 to 2019.

The Professional Practice of Rehabilitation Counseling

Third Edition

Editors

Michael T. Hartley, PhD, CRC
Vilia M. Tarvydas, PhD, CRC

 SPRINGER PUBLISHING

First Springer Publishing edition 978-0-8261-0738-1 (2011); subsequent edition 2017

Springer Publishing Company, LLC
11 West 42nd Street, New York, NY 10036
www.springerpub.com
connect.springerpub.com/

Acquisitions Editor: Rhonda Dearborn
Compositor: Exeter Premedia Services Private Limited

ISBN: 978-0-8261-3903-0
ebook ISBN: 978-0-8261-3904-7
DOI: 10.1891/9780826139047

SUPPLEMENTS:
Instructor Materials:

 A robust set of instructor resources designed to supplement this text is located at http://connect.springerpub.com/content/book/978-0-8261-3904-7. Qualifying instructors may request access by emailing **textbook@springerpub.com.**

Instructor's Manual ISBN: 978-0-8261-3906-1
Instructor's Test Bank ISBN: 978-0-8261-3907-8
Instructor's PowerPoints ISBN: 978-0-8261-3905-4

Printed by LSI

Library of Congress Cataloging-in-Publication Data

Names: Hartley, Michael T., editor. | Tarvydas, Vilia M., editor.
Title: The professional practice of rehabilitation counseling / editors,
    Michael T. Hartley, PhD, CRC, Vilia M. Tarvydas, PhD, CRC.
Description: Third edition. | New York, NY : Springer Publishing Company,
    [2023] | Includes bibliographical references and index.
Identifiers: LCCN 2022022584 (print) | LCCN 2022022585 (ebook) | ISBN
    9780826139030 (paperback) | ISBN 9780826139047 (ebook)
Subjects: LCSH: Rehabilitation counseling. | Vocational rehabilitation.
Classification: LCC HD7255.5 .P76 2022 (print) | LCC HD7255.5 (ebook) |
    DDC 362.4/0486--dc23/eng/20220512
LC record available at https://lccn.loc.gov/2022022584
LC ebook record available at https://lccn.loc.gov/2022022585

Contact sales@springerpub.com to receive discount rates on bulk purchases.

Printed in the United States of America.

Contents

Contributors

Mary Barros-Bailey, PhD, Intermountain Vocational Services, Inc., Boise, Idaho

Terrilyn Battle, PhD, LCMHC-A, LCAS-R, CRC, Assistant Professor, Master of Arts in Counseling, Stockton University, Hammonton, New Jersey

Kevin Bengtson, PhD, CRC, Senior Instructor, Rehabilitation Counseling Health and Community Studies, Western Washington University, Everett, Washington

Nicole L. Birri, EdD, Training Specialist, Department of Special Education, University of Illinois Urbana-Champaign and the Illinois Center for Transition and Work, Champaign, Illinois

Ashley J. Blount, PhD, Assistant Professor, Department of Counseling, College of Education, Health, and Human Sciences, University of Nebraska Omaha, Omaha, Nebraska

Susanne M. Bruyère, PhD, Director and Professor of Disability Studies, Yang-Tan Institute on Employment and Disability, ILR School, Cornell University, Ithaca, New York

Fong Chan, PhD, Norman L. and Barbara M. Berven Professor of Rehabilitation Psychology (Emeritus), Department of Rehabilitation Psychology and Special Education, University of Wisconsin–Madison, Madison, Wisconsin

Martha H. Chapin, PhD, CRC, Professor Emerita, Department of Addictions and Rehabilitation Studies, East Carolina University, Greenville, North Carolina

Xiangli Chen, PhD, MPH, Kessler Foundation, East Hanover, New Jersey; Research Assistant Professor, Department of Physical Medicine and Rehabilitation, Rutgers New Jersey Medical School, Newark, New Jersey

Patrick Corrigan, PsyD, Distinguished Professor and Associate Dean of Research in the Institute of Psychology, Illinois Institute of Technology, Chicago, Illinois

R. Rocco Cottone, PhD, CFT, University of Missouri Distinguished Professor, Department of Education Sciences and Professional Programs, University of Missouri–St. Louis, St. Louis, Missouri

Noel Estrada-Hernández, PhD, CRC, Professor of Rehabilitation Counseling, Department Executive Officer for Counselor Education, The University of Iowa, Iowa City, Iowa

Glacia Ethridge, PhD, LCMHCA, LCAS-A, CRC, NCC, Associate Professor, Department of Counseling, North Carolina Agricultural and Technical State University, Greensboro, North Carolina

Michael Gerald, PhD, LCMHC (Utah), LMHC (Iowa), CRC, Assistant Professor, Special Education and Rehabilitation Counseling, Utah State University, Logan, Utah

Margaret K. Glenn, EdD, CRC, Professor, School of Counseling and Well-Being, College of Applied Human Sciences, West Virginia University, Morgantown, West Virginia

Chelsea E. Greco, PhD, Postdoctoral Research Associate, Department of Kinesiology and Community Health, University of Illinois Urbana–Champaign, Champaign, Illinois

Michael T. Hartley, PhD, CRC, Associate Professor and Codirector of the Doctoral Program in Counselor Education and Supervision, Department of Disability and Psychoeducational Studies at the University of Arizona, Tucson, Arizona

Kanako Iwanaga, PhD, CRC, LPC, Assistant Professor, Department of Rehabilitation Counseling, Virginia Commonwealth University, Richmond, Virginia

Sara P. Johnston, PhD, MPH, CRC, Adjunct Professor, Department of Clinical Counseling and Mental Health, School of Health Professions, Texas Tech University Health Sciences Center, Lubbock, Texas

Stephen M. Kwiatek, PhD, Postdoctoral Research Associate, University of Illinois Urbana-Champaign and the Illinois Center for Transition and Work, Champaign, Illinois

Carla Kundert, MS, CRC, Illinois Institute of Technology, Chicago, Illinois

Trent Landon, PhD, CRC, Assistant Professor, Department of Special Education and Rehabilitation Counseling, College of Education, Utah State University, Logan, Utah

Michael J. Leahy, PhD, CRC, LPC, University Distinguished Professor Emeritus, Office of Rehabilitation and Disability Studies, Department of Counseling, Educational Psychology and Special Education, College of Education, Michigan State University, East Lansing, Michigan

Robin Wilbourn Lee, PhD, LPC/MHSP, NCC, ACS, Professor, Professional Counseling Program, Womack Educational Leadership Department, Middle Tennessee State University, Murfreesboro, Tennessee

Lisa López Levers, PhD, CRC, NCC, LPCC-S, LPC, Professor Emerita, Department of Educational Foundations and Leadership; School of Education, Duquesne University, Pittsburgh, Pennsylvania

William Ming Liu, PhD, Professor and Chair, Counseling, Higher Education, and Special Education, College of Education, University of Maryland, College Park, Maryland

Irmo Marini, PhD, Professor, School of Rehabilitation, The University of Texas Rio Grande Valley, Edinburg, Texas

Henry McCarthy, PhD, CRC, LPC, Professor Emeritus, Department of Clinical Rehabilitation and Counseling, Louisiana State University Health Sciences Center, New Orleans, Louisiana

Elias Mpofu, PhD, DEd, Professor, Rehabilitation and Health Services, University of North Texas, Denton, Texas, and Honorary Professor, University of Sydney, Camperdown, Australia, and Visiting Professor, University of the Witwatersrand, Johannesburg, South Africa

Ngonidzashe Mpofu, PhD, Assistant Professor and Clinical Rehabilitation Counseling Program Coordinator, Department of Counseling, Idaho State University, Pocatello, Idaho

Patricia Nunez, MA, CRC, CDMS, CCM, Director, Claim Supply Management, CNA, Brea, California

Vanessa M. Perry, PhD, CRC, Associate Professor of Practice, Department of Disability and Psychoeducational Studies, The University of Arizona, Tucson, Arizona

Rigel Macarena Pinon, PhDc, PhD Candidate, School of Rehabilitation, The University of Texas Rio Grande Valley, Edinburg, Texas

Toni Saia, PhD, CRC, Assistant Professor, Department of Administration, Rehabilitation, and Postsecondary Education, San Diego State University, San Diego, California

Matthew C. Saleh, JD, PhD, Research Associate, Yang-Tan Institute on Employment and Disability, ILR School, Cornell University, Ithaca, New York

Jared C. Schultz, PhD, CRC, Professor and Chair, Department of Rehabilitation Counseling, College of Health Professions, Virginia Commonwealth University, Richmond, Virginia

David Staten, PhD, Professor, Rehabilitation Counseling, South Carolina State University, Orangeburg, South Carolina

David R. Strauser, PhD, Professor, College of Applied Health Sciences, University of Illinois at Urbana–Champaign and the Illinois Center for Transition and Work, Champaign, Illinois

D. George Strauser, MS, Doctoral Student, College of Applied Health Sciences, University of Illinois Urbana-Champaign, Champaign, Illinois

Connie Sung, PhD, LPC, CRC, Associate Professor, Department of Counseling, Educational Psychology and Special Education, Michigan State University, East Lansing, Michigan

Vilia M. Tarvydas, PhD, CRC, Professor Emerita, Faculty Director, I-SERVE, College of Education, Department of Counselor Education, The University of Iowa, Iowa City, Iowa

Amanda B. Tashjian, PhD, CRC, LPC (Arizona, Michigan), LCPC (Illinois), Associate Professor of Practice, Department of Disability and Psychoeducational Studies, The University of Arizona, Tucson, Arizona

Rebecca L. Toporek, PhD, Professor, Department of Counseling, San Francisco State University, San Francisco, California

Emre Umucu, PhD, CRC, Assistant Professor, Department of Counseling, Educational Psychology and Special Education, Michigan State University, East Lansing, Michigan

Laura A. Villarreal, MS, CRC, Doctoral Student, School of Rehabilitation, The University of Texas Rio Grande Valley, Edinburg, Texas

Jia Rung Wu, PhD, CRC, LPC, Assistant Professor, Department of Counselor Education, Northeastern Illinois University, Chicago, Illinois

Rana Yaghmaian, PhD, CRC, Associate Professor and Department Chair, Counselor Education, Portland State University, Portland, Oregon

Stephen A. Zanskas, PhD, CRC, LPC, Associate Dean, College of Education, The University of Memphis, Memphis, Tennessee

Foreword

You only have what you give. It's by spending yourself that you become rich.
—Isabel Allende

Rich is a word that describes not only the history but also the contributions of rehabilitation counseling to the broader counseling profession and to the many lives of individuals with disabilities around the world. Although there is more work to be done, today individuals with disabilities can enter competitive education and work environments, live a life of independence and inclusion, access and participate in our modern society, and live a life of physical and mental health wellness. Almost certainly, many of these individuals with disabilities have been served by a rehabilitation counselor.

The professional history of rehabilitation counseling has been characterized by many fundamental questions surrounding the identity of a rehabilitation counselor. As very well detailed by Hartley and Tarvydas in this present edition of *The Professional Practice of Rehabilitation Counseling*, the counseling profession has taken steps to recognize that indeed *rehabilitation counselors are counselors* and that rehabilitation counseling is an important specialty area within the counseling profession. Historically, rehabilitation counselors identified as part of the larger counseling profession yet remained separate and distinct with our Council on Rehabilitation Education (CORE) accreditation process. Over time, our counseling curriculum began to mirror the general counseling requirements of Council for Accreditation of Counseling and Related Educational Programs (CACREP). However, the separate accreditation process by CORE separated rehabilitation counselors from the rest of the counseling world. This limited employment opportunities for our graduates. Despite multiyear efforts to unify rehabilitation counseling with the counseling profession, challenges remained for our graduates to become licensed professional counselors—due to having the "wrong" program accreditation.

One of the most important steps in the process to demonstrate *rehabilitation counselors are counselors* was the historic merger between CORE and CACREP. This merger materialized after thoughtful consideration of both CORE and CACREP Boards of Directors. The merger began with an affiliation agreement in 2013, that lead to a merger agreement in 2015, which was completed in 2017. The CORE Board determined the benefits of the merger were clear and significant for the profession of rehabilitation counseling, students, programs, and persons with disability. As you can imagine, "letting go" of CORE did not have 100% support from all rehabilitation counselors, but the benefits of the merger led many to support the merger. We both, within our leadership roles, spent quite a bit of time talking through the terms of the merger, and how we could best communicate to our respective memberships and programs what this merger would mean. We also had the benefit of significant feedback from leaders such as the editors of this text and some of the authors. Ultimately, the CORE/CACREP merger enhanced training for all counselors by making accessible disability-related concepts and paradigms to other counseling specialty areas. It also served to provide more visibility to the work done by rehabilitation counselors in nontraditional rehabilitation settings such as schools, trauma centers, veterans affairs, and the private sector and within the psychiatric and mental health care systems.

Readers will find that the main pillars of this new edition are the unification of the counseling profession and the full integration of rehabilitation counseling within CACREP. The position adopted in this text does not call for the abandonment of the traditional practice of rehabilitation counseling with its emphasis on vocational, medical, and psychosocial aspects of disability, case management, independent living, and assistive technology. Rather, the position adopted in this text integrates these traditional concepts within the framework of advocacy, diversity, empowerment, recovery, and the clinical counseling practices embraced by psychiatric rehabilitation and mental health professionals.

The chapters in this text have been written by forward-thinking individuals who represent the core values, knowledge base, and traditions of rehabilitation counseling as a specialty and counseling as our profession. Many of these scholars and leaders have contributed significantly through their service to many counseling professional organizations (e.g., American Counseling Association, American Rehabilitation Counseling Association, National Rehabilitation Association, National Rehabilitation Counseling Association, and the National Council on Rehabilitation Education), accrediting bodies (e.g., CORE and CACREP), certification bodies (Commission on Rehabilitation Counselor Certification [CRCC] and National Board for Certified Counselors), and licensure boards (e.g., American Association of State Counselor Licensure Boards). At the same time, they were making important scholarly contributions to the specialized knowledge base of rehabilitation counseling.

We invite educators, students, and practitioners all to read and reflect on the current standing of rehabilitation counseling as presented in this text. Rehabilitation counseling is many things, including, but not limited to, (a) the second-largest specialty within the counseling profession; (b) a professional practice that has grown in global interest; (c) a specialty area that demonstrates a unique understanding and integration of concepts related to physical disabilities, mental illness, and diversity, equity, and inclusion; and (d) a specialty area that prepares qualified counseling professionals to assist those individuals who have been marginalized by health and/or social inequities. Chapters included in this edition present contemporary and seminal literature on the foundations of the rehabilitation counseling practice, including an overview of private-sector practice; information on the disability experience, with particular attention to family relations, and disability rights; and a detailed account of perennial and emerging professional roles and competencies. Special attention is given to key aspects of practice, including advocacy and social justice, psychiatric rehabilitation, counseling and mental health issues, assessment, vocational and career development, case management, ethics, and the use of technology (e.g., telemedicine) within service delivery.

On a personal note, we both know Vilia Tarvydas as well as Dennis Maki, the founding editor of this textbook, and we would like to recognize their leadership, advocacy, and passion for rehabilitation counseling. Thanks for all those years of professional service, for being there in the front lines regardless of how hard the battle was. Michael Hartley, you are the future. We count on your leadership and vision to help us write the newest chapters in our professional history. A work of this magnitude requires the knowledge and expertise of many scholars, and we want to thank all the chapter contributors. It has been an honor to have read and followed their scholarly work and professional contributions.

As former leaders within the profession we are humbled and honored to present to you, the reader, our reflections and commentary on this visionary and much-needed work. Finally, we invite you to continue to *spend* rehabilitation counseling's assets to create a world that is unique, diverse, equitable, and inclusive or in the words of Isabelle Allende, *"rich."*

Noel Estrada-Hernández, PhD, CRC
President, NCRE, 2015–2016

Patricia Nunez, MA, CRC, CDMS, CCM
President, NRCA, 1991–1992
President, ARCA, 2006–2007
President, CORE, 2013–2017
Member, CORE/CACREP Merger Leadership Team

Preface

We welcome you to the third edition of *The Professional Practice of Rehabilitation Counseling*. More accurately this volume is the fifth edition of this foundational text on rehabilitation counseling, titled in previous editions as the *Handbook of Rehabilitation Counseling* and *Rehabilitation Counseling: Profession and Practice*. This longevity is a testament to the ongoing need to provide a text that is linked firmly to the structures and identity of both rehabilitation counseling and the counseling profession. Over the years, these editions have documented the incredible history, knowledge, and skill sets that are unique to rehabilitation counseling's trailblazing role in working with and serving all types of people with disabilities. The current title of this text is the same as the last edition, maintaining the structure and format of that edition yet with new and timely content to address more broadly psychiatric rehabilitation and mental health counseling as practiced by rehabilitation counselors. The opening chapter describes in detail the organization of the text and the content that has been included throughout subsequent chapters.

The information in this text has been developed by some of the strongest scholars in the field. The contributing authors are experts on their respective topics, and we are fortunate to have put together such a remarkable group of leaders in the field. We have taken pains to invite the addition of strong emerging scholars where warranted so that these areas reflect strong cross-generational perspectives as well. In each chapter, the authors have provided clear lines of inductive and deductive reasoning to provide clear takeaway points, allowing us to both understand our past and look to the future. In doing so, our intent is to memorialize the history and philosophy of rehabilitation counseling while simultaneously assimilating new research and knowledge from breakthroughs in neuroscience and pharmacology, innovations in digital communication and technology, and shifts in the economy and social milieu. In other words, without throwing out the baby with the bathwater, we believe that the knowledge and tools used by rehabilitation counselors today should not be the same as 10 years ago.

Rehabilitation counseling as well as the profession of counseling are in a state of change. To our knowledge, no versions of introductory texts have emerged that directly address the significant changes in the nature of practice since the last edition of this text in 2017. It is a daunting task to predict what will happen in the field moving forward, because of unprecedented changes both within the profession and society more broadly. Although we do not claim to know the future, we believe a clear understanding of our history and philosophy will allow current and future students, educators, and practitioners to have a fairly good sense of a rewarding future for themselves as well as their clients.

Editing this text has continued to be a remarkable journey, reassuring us that rehabilitation counselors will continue to have a wide range of professional opportunities because of their unique training, expertise, and emphasis on disability as a civil rights issue. With this in mind, we have intentionally attempted to capture the rich history and diversity of rehabilitation counseling practice. We hope that readers will respond with excitement to reflecting on the past while simultaneously imagining the futures that excellence in professional practice in rehabilitation counseling may bring them. We also hope that they will take to heart the knowledge and wisdom that our authors have sought to impart to them to guide them on this journey. Finally, we encourage students new to the profession to try to place yourselves in the lived experiences of people with disabilities and explore the richness our value-laden practices and philosophies can bring to assist and partner with them. You may also discover the passion of the rehabilitation movement and the satisfaction that can come from a career devoted to the truly meaningful work that rehabilitation counselors can do. We have been careful to make the content as accessible as possible for readers new to the field. **For qualified instructors who adopt this text, we alert you to the very fine ancillaries to this book, including PowerPoint slides, learning activities, Internet resources, and a test item bank. Requests for these ancillaries can be made by e-mail (textbook@springerpub.com).**

Michael T. Hartley
Vilia M. Tarvydas

Acknowledgments

A work such as this requires the support and hard work of many individuals. First and foremost, we are grateful to the chapter authors who found time to write these chapters amid their many other responsibilities and commitments. This work was undertaken during the particularly trying times of our global pandemic and related social upheavals, and done with great professionalism and grace. All these authors have generously shared their wisdom and inspired us through their contributions to this text. Many of them have shared the struggles, work, and hopes for improving rehabilitation counseling with us over the years—and for that, all of us in rehabilitation counseling will be forever grateful. We also wish to thank Rhonda Dearborn, our editor at Springer Publishing Company, who was supportive in the face of looming deadlines, and Kirsten Elmer and the adroit editorial team helping us produce the highest-quality text possible.

It will become apparent when reading this text that the professionalization efforts of rehabilitation counseling are greater than any single individual. With this in mind, we would like to acknowledge the presidents of the National Council on Rehabilitation Education (NCRE), the National Rehabilitation Counseling Association (NRCA), and the American Rehabilitation Counseling Association (ARCA) for their leadership and outstanding contributions to the profession over the years. In addition to honoring these remarkable individuals, we hope to inspire our fellow professionals to follow in their footsteps and continue to guide the profession and practice of rehabilitation counseling through service and leadership.

As educators, we want to express our heartfelt gratitude to the countless students whose questions and interests have caused us to remain thoughtful and passionate about the improvement of the practice and professional evolution of rehabilitation counseling. Teaching is one of the most rewarding occupations imaginable when there is genuine care and respect between teachers and students. We hope we have been gracious enough to personally express our thanks to the many students we have worked with and learned from. It is one of the most rewarding aspects of being an educator.

A final acknowledgment is to our friends and family, who have motivated and sustained us to be thoughtful scholars; the book would not have been possible without your love and support.

Instructor Resources

A robust set of resources designed to supplement this text is available. Qualifying instructors may request access by emailing textbook@springerpub.com.
Available resources include:

- Instructor's Manual
  - Example Syllabus
  - Chapter Overviews
  - Learning Objectives
  - Discussion Questions
  - Class Activities
  - Internet Resources
- Test Bank
- Chapter-Based PowerPoint Presentations

 A robust set of instructor resources designed to supplement this text is located at **http://connect.springerpub.com/content/book/978-0-8261-3904-7.** Qualifying instructors may request access by emailing **textbook@springerpub.com.**

CHAPTER 1

Rehabilitation Counseling: A Specialty Practice of the Counseling Profession

MICHAEL T. HARTLEY AND VILIA M. TARVYDAS

LEARNING OBJECTIVES

After reading this chapter, you should be able to:

- *Describe the diverse professional practice of rehabilitation counseling as a specialty of the counseling profession.*
- *Summarize the progression and professionalization of rehabilitation counseling and its relation to the broader field of counseling.*
- *Explain psychiatric rehabilitation as a bridge between traditional rehabilitation counseling and mental health counseling as practiced by rehabilitation counselors.*
- *Evaluate emerging trends and planned initiatives within the counseling profession that are affecting the professional practice of rehabilitation counseling.*

CACREP STANDARDS

CACREP 2016 Core: 2F1.a, 2F1.b, 2F1.d, 2F1.g, 2F1.k, 2F1.h
CACREP 2016 Specialties:
 Clinical Rehabilitation Counseling: 5D1.a, 5D1.f, 5D2.a, 5D.2.b., 5D.2.c., 5D2.g, 5D2.k, 5D2.u, 5D2.v
 Rehabilitation Counseling: 5H1.a, 5H1.f, 5H2.a, 5H2.b, 5H2.f, 5H2.i, 5H2.k, 5H2.n, 5H2.p, 5H3.j

INTRODUCTION

Welcome to your introductory text on the history and evolution of the *Professional Practice of Rehabilitation Counseling*—what it is and how to do it. Rehabilitation counseling is a dynamic *specialization* of the broader profession of counseling. In fact, rehabilitation counseling was one of the first counseling specialties around which the broader profession of counseling coalesced (Leahy et al., 2010). However, at different points in time, rehabilitation counseling has trended toward separate professional status, which weakened its relationship to the broader profession of counseling (Thomas & Parker, 1981). These debates often have centered on which core identity underlies rehabilitation counseling—counseling or rehabilitation (Leahy et al., 2011). While both identities are important, professionalization efforts since the 1990s have led to counseling as the core identity. This shift has been complex and involved a multi-year alignment process, codified through the 2017 merger of the two major accreditation bodies of Council on Rehabilitation Education (CORE) and the Council for Accreditation of Counseling and Related Educational Programs (CACREP).

To embrace a core identity as counselors is not incompatible with, or disrespectful to, the rehabilitation counselors (RCs), who identify with rehabilitation and choose to work in areas of practice that are not titled counselor or are not primarily counseling in function. The fact that RCs do more than counsel does not compromise their primary affiliation with the counseling profession, nor does it diminish other essential functions. Indeed, counseling practitioners from other specialties like mental health counseling and school counseling also perform a broad range of services such as assessment, career guidance, case management, and consultation. The fact that rehabilitation counselors (RCs) and other counseling specialties engage in roles and functions other than affective counseling does not weaken their relationship to the counseling profession.

From our perspective, rehabilitation counseling is the process of counseling persons with disabilities—often in rehabilitation settings. Therefore, this text is guided by the "conviction that counseling is the core profession with which rehabilitation counseling is linked" (Maki & Tarvydas, 2012). This view is dialectical, not dichotomous. In other words, we take a "this/and" rather than an "either/or" perspective. Identification with the counseling profession does not diminish the rehabilitation identity that is linked heavily with vocational rehabilitation, insurance rehabilitation, forensics, independent living, and psychosocial adjustment to disability; rather, it incorporates these traditions and strengthens our focus on advocacy, recovery, and clinical counseling that have been more characteristic of psychiatric rehabilitation. In this text, we view psychiatric rehabilitation, a long-standing area of service to persons with severe and persistent mental illness, as a bridge to understand the intersection between traditional rehabilitation and mental health counseling as practiced by RCs. Similarly, we remind rehabilitation counseling educators and practitioners that persons with severe and persistent mental illnesses are persons with disabilities—they need, are entitled to, and respond to the full range of well-honed rehabilitation counseling interventions and advocacy that our field has developed over its long and successful history and evolution. This is especially true in contemporary times when mental illness and distress are accelerating problems, yet the systems providing care often are disjointed, underfunded and lack a robust community-based intervention and support system.

Embracing the broadest scope of practice, it is our position that rehabilitation counseling has contributed to the evolution of mental health counseling, one of the fastest growing aspects of counseling. The ability to diagnose and provide mental health services is an expertise necessary for new rehabilitation counseling graduates who will need to gain licensure and often employment in behavioral health. This development is consistent with the evolution of rehabilitation counseling. Indeed, RCs have served individuals with psychiatric disabilities within the Vocational Rehabilitation (VR) system since the 1940s and contributed their advanced expertise to provide innovative treatment models to assist people with psychiatric disabilities to manage mental health symptoms as well as polysubstance abuse (Corrigan, 2016). Through the lens of psychiatric rehabilitation, the ideas and information contained in this text provide a necessary structuring of rehabilitation counseling around a clear point of view on its identity and credentials that includes the diagnosis and treatment of mental health and substance abuse problems. Therefore, we provide information about the profession of counseling and rehabilitation counseling's relationship to it in this text. We are making a choice in the timeworn debate about whether rehabilitation counseling at its core is essentially counseling or case management (Patterson, 1957).

To be clear, this text is premised on the fact that *rehabilitation counselors are counselors.* By this statement, we mean that rehabilitation counseling does not meet the historical or

BOX 1.1 REFLECTION ACTIVITY: PROFESSION VERSUS OCCUPATION

What is the difference between an occupation and a profession? Consider the difference between someone trained as a line cook and someone who is a master chef. A cook is usually described as someone who prepares and cooks a particular type of food, while a master chef is someone who has undergone specialized training and demonstrated advanced skills. In this way, the chef is expected to have the knowledge and skills to cook many different types of cuisine even though they may specialize in a particular type of cuisine. Using the analogy of a master chef, consider the ways in which RCs are trained to practice professional counseling yet also possess specialized expertise in rehabilitation. What does the analogy of a master chef mean for the education and training of RCs?

sociological definition of a separate and distinct profession with its own unique accreditation and certification standards (Rothman, 1987). As a result, in this text, we honor the history and philosophy of rehabilitation counseling while simultaneously assimilating trends and planned initiatives impacting the profession of counseling. Additionally, we address emerging ethical and cultural issues that have impacted the practice of rehabilitation counseling directly, such as the novel coronavirus (COVID-19), the economic downturn, the Black Lives Matter movement, and violence toward groups who have been marginalized. It is our view that the foundational philosophy and skills of rehabilitation counseling must evolve, allowing RCs to address the needs of groups of people who have been marginalized and who often experience a variety of disabling conditions. The emphasis on supporting people across environments and life areas affected by physical, social, and political realities is a powerful perspective. An important aspect of this text is to situate how the foundational knowledge and tools used by RCs must continue to evolve. Readers should reflect on the difference between an occupation and profession in Box 1.1.

WHAT IS REHABILITATION COUNSELING?

Rehabilitation counseling is one of most exciting and diverse specializations of the counseling profession. The Commission on Rehabilitation Counselor Certification (CRCC, 2016) has defined rehabilitation counseling as supporting "persons with physical, mental, developmental, cognitive, and emotional disabilities to achieve their personal, career, and independent living goals in the most integrated setting possible" (p. 1). By necessity, rehabilitation counseling is based on a person–environment fit, and a successful rehabilitation outcome is not the result of working with the individual alone but rather of understanding the reciprocal interaction between the individual and their environment. Therefore, rehabilitation counseling is the counseling specialty that "assists persons with disabilities in adapting to the environment, assists environments in accommodating the needs of the individual, and works toward full participation of persons with disabilities in all aspects of society, especially work" (Szymanski, 1985, p. 3).

Over the last century, the need for RCs and their expertise in disability, mental health, and employment has continued to grow exponentially. In 2018, there were 120,000 RCs practicing in the United States, with an anticipated 10% increase of 12,000 more in the next decade (United States Department of Labor, 2020). In addition, the field of mental health counseling is expected to add more than 30,000 jobs and grow approximately 20% in the next decade. This growth further increases the demand for those RCs who are trained in the area of clinical rehabilitation counseling and clinical mental health counseling. As one of the largest counseling specialties, the CACREP (2018) reported 1,342 students graduated from accredited rehabilitation counseling programs in 2018. The work that RCs do is aligned clearly with the definition of counseling as "a professional relationship that empowers diverse individuals, families, and groups to accomplish mental health, wellness, education, and career goals" (Kaplan et al., 2014, p. 368). At the same time, RCs have unique expertise in the area of disability, employment, and mental health.

Jane Myers (2012) was an esteemed leader of the counseling profession who began her career with a degree in rehabilitation counseling. In the preface to an earlier edition of this text, she described rehabilitation counseling "at the forefront in creating sustained positive change in the holistic wellbeing of persons with disabilities . . . to be effective advocates and change agents for themselves, their families, their communications and society" (p. xvi). Focused on providing ethical and effective counseling to individuals with disabilities, RCs have continued to promote disability rights as a set of competencies within the broader profession of counseling. As a recent example, the Disability-Related Counseling Competencies (DRCC) were developed by the American Rehabilitation Counseling Association (ARCA) and endorsed by the American Counseling Association (ACA) Governing Council in 2019. Aligned with the ACA *Code of Ethics* and *Multicultural and Social Justice Counseling Competencies*, the DRCC are aspirational guidelines to assist all counselors in better understanding and recognizing "disability as a part of personal identity and cultural diversity and in affirmation of their professional commitment to social justice" (Chapin et al., 2018, p. 1). The DRCC is the latest example of RCs promoting disability competencies within the broader profession of counseling.

Leahy and Szymanski (1995) noted that rehabilitation counseling is unique among the counseling specialties because it emerged out of state and federal legislation. Following the American Civil War, the United States government compensated military veterans disabled during their military service (Sales, 2007). This development was a significant shift as services for individuals with disabilities previously were provided through local communities and religious organizations. By the early 1900s, there was a need for more government services because the Industrial Revolution had shifted the United States economy from small, self-sustaining rural communities to unskilled laborers living in a growing number of large urban cities (Gladding & Newsome, 2018). The Industrial Revolution led to compulsory education (requiring children to attend school) and vocational education (assisting citizens with employment) as well as a growing number of workplace injuries. In 1911, the first Workers' Compensation law signified that the United States government was beginning to protect the rights and safety of workers by requiring employers to compensate injured employees (Rubin et al., 2016). Massive casualties in World War I and a significant number of veterans returning to civilian life with a disability led to rehabilitation services funded by the government. Soon after, the 1920 Smith–Fess Act established the Vocational Rehabilitation (VR) system to serve the rehabilitation needs of civilians with disabilities. Rehabilitation counseling grew out of the societal changes of the early 1900s.

With rehabilitation counseling's 100-year history, Sales (2007) argued that its practice evolved from paternalism to empowerment. **Paternalism** is the notion that people in positions of power make "benevolent" decisions that remove the decision making and choice of individuals (Hartley, Tarvydas, et al., 2021). The early practice of rehabilitation counseling was guided by policies and practices characterized as paternalistic because decisions were made for clients. A paternalistic orientation compromised the autonomy of individuals with disabilities "by dictating changes that are believed to reflect their best interests" (Keferl et al., 2004, p. 8). An important shift occurred in the 1970s when independent living emerged as an approach to promote community integration and inclusion as well as the self-determination of individuals with disabilities. Moving away from paternalism, RCs recognize that professional power is "rooted in a system that, in order to maintain itself, depends on clients who are powerless" (Sales, 2007, p. 3). Rather than looking for deficits and making decisions for clients, rehabilitation counseling is rooted in client autonomy, defined as "the rights of clients to be self-governing within their social and cultural framework" (CRCC, 2017). In practice, respect for autonomy is about recognizing the client as the expert on their own life with the RC supporting their potential for growth. This dominant philosophical orientation is very strong in the tradition of rehabilitation counseling. It provides a unique, distinguishing groundwork for strong attention to self-determination, advocacy, and social justice as foundational principles guiding the practice of rehabilitation counseling.

With a focus on disability and empowerment, the professional competencies associated with rehabilitation counseling have become increasingly diversified over the years. RCs continue to practice in traditional settings such as vocational rehabilitation and workers compensation that require extensive knowledge of career development and employment. Additionally, RCs practice in psychiatric rehabilitation, mental health, and substance abuse settings, where diagnosis of mental disorders is a prominent responsibility. It is also true that RCs educated with rehabilitation skills and knowledge can provide a unique and valuable contribution to the diagnostic process. They can make diagnoses from a rehabilitation-informed stance, attending more fully to the diagnostic criteria related to daily functioning, with concern about the stigmatizing potential of diagnoses, and a focus on assets the client possesses that will be important in the treatment plan. With complementary knowledge in clinical counseling, career development, and responses to disability, RCs perform functions such as case management, advocacy, consultation, and assessment. In fact, some RCs specialize in forensic services, "conducting evaluations and/or reviews of records and conduct[ing] research for the purpose of providing unbiased and objective expert opinions via case consultation or testimony" (CRCC, 2017, p. 18). With such a broad range of knowledge and skills, rehabilitation counselors often are trained as a counseling generalist with unique rehabilitation knowledge and skills that apply across multiple settings.

While RCs possess a wide range of knowledge and skills, it is their focus on individuals with disabilities as competent, capable, and valuable that historically has differentiated them from other counselors. Individuals with disabilities are one of the fastest growing minority groups in the United States, with 61 million Americans having a disability (Kraus et al., 2018; Okoro et al., 2018). In fact, one in four adults in the United States self-reported having a disability (Okoro et al., 2018). Disability is inherently diverse, including but not limited to physical (e.g., spinal cord injury or epilepsy), sensory (e.g., blindness or deafness), developmental (e.g., intellectual or autism), cognitive (e.g., traumatic brain injury or learning disability), emotional or psychological (e.g., schizophrenia or substance abuse), and chronic illness (e.g., HIV/AIDS or cancer). The experience of disability is as unique as humans are, and RCs provide services to individuals across the life span, including children, adolescents, young adults, and older adults. Therefore, RCs must understand disability from a developmental perspective, considering variation due to client experience and the ecological context (Marini et al., 2018; Smart, 2019). At the heart of rehabilitation counseling is a multi-dimensional understanding of disability as a natural part of life. This viewpoint of disability is important in avoiding the over-medicalization of disability.

RCs understand disability as much more than a medical condition. As an example, legislation such as the Americans with Disabilities Act (ADA, 1990) has defined **disability** as a physical or mental impairment that substantially limits one or more major life activities, a person who has a history or record of such an impairment, or a person who is perceived by others as having such an impairment. More than just a medical condition, this definition includes major life activities and environmental factors, including social perceptions of disability. Similar to the ADA's definition of disability, RCs view disability from a holistic lens that includes medical, functional, environmental, social, and cultural dimensions. Embracing disability as a natural and common aspect of what it means to be human, rehabilitation counseling is rooted in the idea that people with disabilities are not fundamentally different to those without disabilities. Indeed, rehabilitation counseling has thus evolved to provide services to people who do not meet the definition of having a diagnosable disability (Jenkins & Strauser, 1999). While RCs clearly possess advanced knowledge in disability and rehabilitation concepts, this specialized training does not mean that they are no longer counselors any more than the specialized training received by cardiologists means that they are no longer physicians (Thomas & Parker, 1981).

Unfortunately, people with disabilities have been treated differently by society because of the social prejudice of ableism. Slesaransky-Poe and García (2014) defined **ableism** as the "belief that disability in and of itself makes one in some way lesser—less deserving of respect, a good education, membership in the community, equal treatment . . . and opportunities to have inclusive, self-fulfilling, and productive lives" (p. 76). Ableism is a way to rationalize who is valuable and worthy in society and thus deeply rooted in the types of problematic belief systems underpinning anti-Blackness, eugenics, misogyny, colonialism, imperialism. and capitalism (Lewis, 2022). To be clear, a person does not have to have a disability to experience ableism. This conclusion is possible because ableism is not based on actual ability. Rather, ableism is the misrepresentation of disability; like false representations of gender and race are rooted in racism and sexism. Part of diversity, inclusion, and equity, Berne (2017) observed that "one cannot look at the history of U.S., slavery, the stealing of indigenous lands, and U.S. imperialism without seeing the way that white supremacy leverages ableism to create a subjugated 'other' that is deemed less worthy/abled/smart/capable" (p. 149). Disability always has been entangled with oppression, and thus, RCs always have engaged in social justice work to offset the social and economic disadvantage associated with disability (Hartley & Tarvydas, 2013).

Across the world, people with disabilities are the poorest of the poor (Yeo & Moore, 2003). In the United States, for example, individuals with disabilities are two to five times more likely to live in poverty than individuals without disabilities (Stapleton et al., 2005). Individuals with disabilities make up 47% of working-age adults in poverty in this country, and more than 50% of those who experience poverty for more than 36 months (She & Livermore, 2009). However, not all impairments result in the same level of disability or disadvantage. The social experience of disability differs for men and women, middle-class White and nondominant minority communities, and heterosexual and lesbian, gay, bisexual, and transgender people (Davis, 2021; Hunter et al., 2020). Racial and ethnic differences continue to exist in the VR system (Yin et al., 2021). For this reason, Crenshaw's (1989) concept of **intersectionality** is critical to understand that people's multiple social identities can overlap with unique but varied experiences of privilege and oppression even among people with disabilities. In this text, we highlight the ways that rehabilitation counseling has worked to promote of a more inclusive society by increasing opportunities and services for all groups of people with disabilities. Discussions in this text also provide background information for understanding how the RCs understanding for marginalization, disadvantage, and intersectionality associated with ableism relate to the contemporary issues of diversity, inclusion, and cultural competence that are occurring in our society and professions.

The environmental focus of rehabilitation counseling fits well with trends in healthcare and behavioral health. Currently there is a growing awareness of **social determinants of health** as nonmedical factors that influence health outcomes. For instance, food insecurity is experienced disproportionately by individuals with disabilities contributing to negative health outcomes (Fleming et al., 2020). Other examples include a lack of safe housing and access to transportation as well as the traumatic effects of racism, discrimination, and violence experienced by some groups of people. With high rates of trauma, there is a significant need for all counselors to practice **trauma-informed care** focused on recovery and resilience for those individuals and families impacted by trauma. According to the Substance Abuse and Mental Health Services Administration (SAMHSA, 2014a), trauma is a result of events or circumstances that are physically or emotionally harmful with "lasting adverse effects on the individual's functioning and mental, physical, social, emotional, or spiritual well-being" (p. 7). Unfortunately, research has found that 60% to 70% of the U.S. general population have experienced a traumatic event, with 20% to 30% developing posttraumatic stress disorder as a result (Kessler et al., 1995). Rehabilitation counseling has long been concerned with social and environmental factors impacting the health and quality of life among individuals with disabilities, including the significant role that trauma can play.

Rehabilitation counseling has long recognized the complexities of multiple or co-occurring disabilities (Sales, 2007). In medicine, **comorbidity** is the co-occurrence of mental and physical disorders in the same person. A national comorbidity study reported that 68% of adults with a diagnosable mental health disorder also had a chronic illness or disability (Kessler et al., 2005). In particular, there has been a high rate of substance use disorders (SUD) among individuals with disabilities (Chan et al., 2009). While SUD can occur with any disability, the term **dual diagnosis** is the co-occurrence of SUD with a mental disorder, such as depression and anxiety. Similarly, it is also true that individuals who experience the onset or worsening of a disability, such as a spinal cord injury or blindness, may also experience a mental health condition, such as depression or anxiety, as part of the adaptation and adjustment process (Marini et al., 2018). RCs specialize in providing services to individuals with multiple disabilities, which has necessitated knowledge of each disability as well as the potential interactive effects on the individual's experience and functioning. With its holistic understanding of people, the practice of rehabilitation counseling fits well with **integrative health** focused on the whole person, including connections between the body, mind, spirit, and community.

In today's behavioral health system, RCs and mental health counselors are increasingly similar with respect to the clients served, employment settings, knowledge requirements, and counseling techniques. Additionally, if we consider it imperative for the field of rehabilitation counseling to address the needs of people with disabilities, rehabilitation counseling must be firm in continuing to pursue the education, credentials, and access to settings in which those with psychiatric disabilities are served. It could be argued that in our contemporary society, people with psychiatric disabilities have great need for expert application of rehabilitation and recovery approaches (Corrigan & Lam, 2007). However, in order to assert our continued place in the practice of behavioral and mental health ethically, RCs must have education and professional preparation standards that embrace and integrate all the necessary elements to practice responsibly and with skill and respect. For example, stronger attention to such areas as evidence-based practices and the diagnosis and treatment of psychiatric disorders are necessary. Research on the knowledge necessary to practice rehabilitation counseling has indicated an increased need for preservice and continuing education in counseling, mental health, and substance abuse (Leahy et al., 2009). Aligned with psychiatric rehabilitation, we are proud to highlight the necessary knowledge, skills, and attitudes in this text whereby RCs may confidently announce: "I am a counselor who works with people who have disabilities"—whether the disability is mental illness, substance abuse, some other type of disability, or coexisting disabilities.

WHAT IS PSYCHIATRIC REHABILITATION?

Psychiatric rehabilitation emerged in the 1960s as a result of the deinstitutionalization movement whereby hundreds of thousands of individuals with significant psychiatric disabilities were "discharged from long-stay psychiatric hospitals into the community, and others were never institutionalized" (Mueser, 2016, p. vii). Pioneering and effective psychiatric rehabilitation programs and models evolved. A highly respected psychiatric rehabilitation program was developed at Boston University by Dr. Bill Anthony and his colleagues that evolved out of the broader rehabilitation and recovery traditions (Anthony et al., 1990). Anthony is clear that this psychiatric rehabilitation model was based on traditional rehabilitation counseling philosophies and practices. RCs always have found it in their mission to work with those people who experience the greatest stigma and biggest barriers to living their lives with a disability. At this point in our history, people with psychiatric disorders would certainly be the group most in need of professionals who carry this perspective and have the requisite skills to assist them (Corrigan & Lam, 2007). Therefore, with the appropriate and necessary training to provide mental health services, RCs increasingly are prepared as practitioners of mental health counseling, clinical rehabilitation, or psychiatric rehabilitation.

Today, mental illness is a leading cause of disability in the United States and across the world (McAlpine & Warner, 2002; Murray & Lopez, 1996). Koch et al. (2016) summarized the prevalence of mental illness in the United States as one in five (18.5%) adults, with approximately 10 million (4.2%) individuals in 2013 meeting the criteria for a serious mental illness (SAMHSA, 2014b). A **psychiatric disability** is identified when an individual with a serious mental illness is unable to perform major life activities in particular life contexts, such as work, community participation, and independent living (Sánchez et al., 2016). With unemployment rates as high as 80% to 90% (Goldberg et al., 2001), it is not surprising that individuals with serious mental illness are the largest disability group served by state–federal VR, constituting 32.2% of the cases in a study by Rosenthal et al. (2007). At the same time, individuals with psychiatric disabilities have the lowest success rates in VR, with fewer than 15% obtaining competitive employment (Anthony, 1993). It is our position that rehabilitation counseling practice must evolve and become better at addressing the vocational, independent living, and psychosocial needs of people with psychiatric disabilities, not only in the state–federal VR system (Lusk et al., 2016) but also in our healthcare and behavioral health systems of care (Sheehan & Lewicki, 2016).

As a unifying paradigm to consolidate vocational rehabilitation, clinical rehabilitation, and mental health counseling, psychiatric rehabilitation is consistent with the overall philosophy and practice of rehabilitation counseling (Olney & Gill, 2016), especially the recovery-based focus on health and wellness (Swarbrick & Nemec, 2016). As such, it has most frequently been associated with services to persons who have serious and/or persistent mental illness; as opposed to being an intervention associated with acute, or mild to moderate, forms of mental disorders. Focused on a continuum of mental health, the work done by RCs fits with a **wellness model of mental health** focused on client strengths and "a holistic view of wellness across many areas of life, including physical, emotional, mental, spiritual, relational, vocational, financial, and sexual realms" (Young & Cashwell, 2017, p. 8). As part of a wellness approach to mental health, RCs have developed unique expertise to promote employment, independent living, and quality of life related to living well with a disability. Therefore, RCs can play a significant role in the creation of a recovery-orientated behavioral health system as called for by the U.S. Surgeon General and the SAMHSA (U.S. Department of Health and Human Services, 1999, 2005).

Recovery was defined by Anthony (1993) as a "deeply personal process of changing one's attitudes, values, feelings, goals, skills, and/or roles. . . . Recovery involves the development of new meaning and purpose in one's life as one grows beyond the catastrophic effects of mental illness" (p. 15). Rather than focusing on a "cure" for mental health symptoms, a **recovery-orientated perspective** emphasizes "self-determination and such normal life pursuits as education, employment, sexuality, friendship, spirituality, and voluntary membership in faith and other kinds of communities beyond the limits of the disorder and of the mental health system" (Davidson et al., 2009, p. 1111). Similar to how RCs work with individuals with spinal cord injury, recovery does not refer to the restoration of spinal cord function or ability to walk but rather to the rights of individuals to "access and join in with those elements of community life the person chooses, and to be in control of his or her life and destiny, even and especially while remaining disabled" (Davidson et al., 2009, p. 15). Even when individuals continue to experience mental health symptoms, Davidson et al. (2009) denoted "being *in* recovery" as containing and minimizing the disruptive impact of mental illness on an individual's personal, vocational, and independent living goals (p. 11). Aligned with the core values

BOX 1.2 LEARNING ACTIVITY: RECOVERY-ORIENTATED CARE

Visit the SAMHSA Recovery and Recovery Support (https://www.samhsa.gov/find-help/recovery). Review the description of a recovery-oriented care and recovery support systems to help people with mental and substance use disorders manage their conditions successfully. How does the description of rehabilitation counseling in this chapter fit with a recovery-orientated system of care? In what ways can the unique expertise and holistic focus of rehabilitation counseling be a model for improving our current behavioral health system?

of rehabilitation counseling, Deegan (1988) described a recovery-orientated behavioral health system whereby individuals' mental illness does not "get rehabilitated" in the way that cars "get tuned up" or appliances "get repaired," but instead the focus is on "recovering a new sense of self and of purpose within and beyond the limits of the disability" (p. 11). Readers should review Box 1.2 to consider ways that recovery-oriented systems of care can can improve our current behavioral health system.

Ultimately concerned with empowerment and self-determination, the involvement of RCs in the delivery of behavioral and mental health services is an opportunity for people with psychiatric disabilities to be assisted by professionals who bring advanced skills and a commitment to advocacy. The philosophy and practice of rehabilitation counseling fits with the SAMHSA (2012) principles of recovery: (a) hope, (b) person-driven, (c) many pathways, (d) holistic, (e) peer support, (f) relational, (g) culture, (h) addresses trauma, (i) strengths/responsibility, and (j) respect. These recovery principles overlap with the principles of the Psychiatric Rehabilitation Association (2018) to support the autonomy and self-determination of individuals with mental health and substance abuse disorders (Peterson & Olney, 2020). To be clear, the concept of recovery is in full alignment with the philosophy and practice of rehabilitation counseling, and thus, RCs can serve as leaders among the counseling specialties in promoting a recovery-orientated behavioral health system of care.

REHABILITATION COUNSELING AS A SPECIALTY OF THE COUNSELING PROFESSION

Rehabilitation counseling has a long history of leadership within the counseling profession. American Rehabilitation Counseling Association (ARCA) was established in 1958 as one of the earliest membership divisions of the organization that later became the American Counseling Association. The counseling profession is unique because specialty areas emerged in response to societal needs, followed by a more unified profession of counseling almost a century later (Leahy et al., 2016). Specializations are common when a profession is too broad for every practitioner to be trained sufficiently to provide high-quality services in all areas; however, the specializations of rehabilitation counseling, school counseling, and community mental health counseling emerged separately until changes in our society and health care system required a more unified counseling profession in the 1990s (Myers, 1995). This unusual sequence has led to the counseling profession being described as a confederation of separate but affiliated counseling organizations with special interests that function more or less independently (Shaw & Mascari, 2018). Today, the legal ability to practice counseling and to be reimbursed for the provision of counseling services has become contingent on the designation of counseling as a profession, including parallel structures of credentialing across the various specialties.

Completed on July 1, 2017, a significant milestone was the merger between the two major accrediting bodies, Council on Rehabilitation Education (CORE) and Council for Accreditation of Counseling and Related Educational Programs (CACREP). Historically, the CORE established education standards for rehabilitation counseling education programs, while CACREP regulated the education standards for other counseling specialties. The merger was preceded by the formal acknowledgment of CORE as an affiliate of CACREP by the ACA to support graduates of rehabilitation counseling education programs having access to state licensure. Today, the CACREP accreditation in Clinical Rehabilitation Counseling has made graduates of these programs eligible for licensure at the independent level of clinical practice as professional counselors.

Since the CORE–CACREP merger, new questions have emerged about rehabilitation counseling, such as how the knowledge, skills, and attitudes of rehabilitation counseling complement those of mental health counseling. One source of confusion is that the CACREP (2016) standards have two different accreditations related to the practice of rehabilitation counseling: (a) Rehabilitation Counseling and (b) Clinical Rehabilitation Counseling. The Rehabilitation Counseling accreditation was designed for education programs that prepare graduates to work in the areas of vocational rehabilitation, forensics, insurance rehabilitation, and worker compensation. The standards for the Rehabilitation Counseling accreditation were developed by the CORE and adopted by the CACREP with the merger. However, the newer Clinical Rehabilitation Counseling accreditation was designed by the CACREP to mirror a great number of standards with the accreditation in Clinical Mental Health Counseling and its emphasis on diagnosis and treatment of mental disorders. An important aspect of this text is to situate the history that led up to these two accreditations.

The standards of practice specific to RCs also are continuing to evolve. CRCC currently is engaged in the process of revising the *Code of Ethics for Professional Counselors* (CRCC, 2017; hereafter referred to as the *Code*). Defining the professional practice of rehabilitation counseling, the *Code* is a living document with ongoing research conducted every 5 years to review its "relevancy to present practice and for potential revision" (Saunders et al., 2009, p. 81). The new *Code* is scheduled for release in 2023 to regulate the practice of the 16,000 practitioners who hold the Certified Rehabilitation Counselor (CRC) credential (CRCC, 2022). Additionally, the CRCC has begun the process of conducting a new role and function study, or Job Task Analysis (JTA), to delineate the specific knowledge and skill competencies required for effective rehabilitation counseling practice. The findings and specific data from the new JTA will further define the practice of rehabilitation counseling, including test specifications for the Certified Rehabilitation Counselor Examination (CRCE) to obtain the Certified Rehabilitation Counselor (CRC) credential. These initiatives continue the long-standing tradition of research on ethical and effective practice that has marked rehabilitation counseling as a leader among the various counseling specializations.

Rehabilitation counseling has contributed to counseling gaining recognition as a profession. Ritchie (1990) made the claim that counseling was not a profession—yet. At the time, only 32 states had counselor licensure laws. Arguing the need for more legal recognition and professional autonomy, Ritchie based the claim on the comparison of counseling to commonly accepted criteria of professions, such as (a) services that are unique and valued by society, (b) foundational knowledge that directly inform practice, (c) extensive specialized and uniform training, (d) enforceable codes of ethics, and (e) legal recognition and broad authority over practice. As a counterpoint, Feit and Lloyd (1990) arrived at a different conclusion, arguing that counseling already had met the criteria of a profession in 1990, pointing to a growing trend of counselor licensure laws in the majority of states. With that said, Feit and Lloyd also noted ongoing tensions within and outside of counseling, quoting Goode (1960) that "no occupation . . . becomes a profession without struggle, just as no specialty develops inside a profession without antagonism" (p. 902). Since the 1990s, counselor licensure laws have been passed in all 50 states. At the same time, internal disputes among the counseling specialties and external claims of encroachment by related disciplines like psychology have remained. Experts in the sociology of professions have long noted that it is not unusual for professions to go through cycles of evolution and devolution depending on the internal state of the profession, as well as the needs and orientations in the society more broadly (Emener & Cottone, 1989; Gardner et al., 2001).

Historically, there have been tensions between the ACA representing the interests of counselors generally, and specialty divisions concerned with encroachment on what they have viewed as their own sovereignty. After decades of friction, two of the specialty divisions, the ASCA and the AMHCA, dissolved their affiliation as official divisions of ACA in 2019 and 2020, respectively. These decisions stemmed from long-standing concerns regarding the ACA's inability to advocate for the unique needs of school and mental health counselors while also remaining faithful to their mission of supporting the other smaller and less politically powerful ACA divisions and counseling specialty areas. The result is that the American Mental Health Counselors Association (AMHCA) and the American School Counselor Association (ASCA) no longer have a formal representative on the ACA's Governing Council, structured so each division and regional branch has a vote on issues of shared governance.

Rehabilitation counseling and the other counseling specialties are at a critical junction. The ACA has become a powerful voice for all counselors. Focused on lobbying and legislative advocacy, the ACA is engaged in considerable advocacy and government lobbying. As an example, the ACA has been lobbying for the passage of the Mental Health Access Improvement Act (https://www.counseling.org/government-affairs) publicly. This act would amend a problematic oversight of the current Medicare law. Specifically, the Act would recognize licensed professional counselors as approved providers who can be reimbursed for providing mental health services to individuals aged 65 and older through Medicare. Another example is that the ACA recently funded the development of an Interstate Compact, which when enacted would make it much easier for licensed counselors to practice across state lines while also protecting public health and safety of citizens through the current system of state licensure (https://counselingcompact.org). The compact is gaining approval by individual states, with strong indication that counselors in those states will have access to practice in other compact member states, either in person or via telehealth. Hopefully, the compact will further protect counselors from outside political pressure from other professionals.

One ongoing professional challenge has been the fact that psychiatrists and psychologists have continued to argue for the sole authority to diagnose and treat mental disorders. In 2019, the Michigan Psychological Association proposed a guideline to deny over 10,000 LPCs the right to diagnose mental disorders and be reimbursed for providing psychotherapy services to their 150,000 clients (Roelofs, 2019). The Michigan licensure law was vulnerable because it had language prohibiting professional counselors from conducting diagnostic tests even though the law had always been interpreted as allowing counselors to diagnose using clinical interviews (Roelofs, 2019). Advocacy efforts by the ACA and the AMHCA protected the rights of professional counselors in Michigan, and the licensure law was changed to establish the requirements and qualifications for counselors to continue to diagnosis and provide psychotherapy. While ultimately a positive outcome, such incidents are a reminder that the counseling profession is not immune to forces that would act to de-professionalize counseling.

Although counseling has achieved the status of a profession, Emener and Cottone (1989) described **de-professionalization** as the process by which a gainful activity loses professional status. All professions must navigate societal changes in ways that maintain their professional status. Otherwise, there is a risk of de-professionalization. Gardner et al. (2001) offered examples of professions that have experienced de-professionalization, including the once highly respected field of journalism, which lost professional status due to a lack of public trust. Teaching is another example where state and federal laws, such as

No Child Left Behind, limited the professional autonomy of teachers by restricting what content they could teach. As a final example, the rise of managed care has contributed to physicians losing autonomy by only being able to prescribe a course of treatment that was reimbursable by insurance. These examples illustrate that even well-established professions face threats of de-professionalization.

The counseling profession is still relatively young by many standards of professionalism. With this in mind, Gerig (2018) described several sources of confusion that have made professionalization challenging. First, the verb *to counsel* is a synonym for *guidance*, *consultation*, and *advisement* that has contributed to counselor and counseling being used in occupational titles such as sales counselor and camp counselor. These occupations are very different from a professional counselor who has earned a 60-credit master's degree and can practice psychotherapy. A second source of confusion is that the provision of mental health counseling, also called psychotherapy, is not unique to a single profession but, rather, shared among professions who treat mental health and SUDs by psychological means. With significant overlap to the clinical work of psychologists and clinical social workers, counselors are unique because of their emphasis on both pathology and wellness from the framework of normal human development (Gerig). Perhaps the biggest source of confusion has been within the counseling profession itself because of the generic title of counselor, qualified by specialties such as addiction, career, college and student affairs, marriage and family, mental health, school, and rehabilitation. Furthermore, counselor licensure titles have varied across states in their use of terms such as *LPC* (Licensed Professional Counselor) and *LHMC* (Licensed Mental Health Counselor) . Moving forward, Gerig recommended more unified language to define what it means to be a professional counselor, often influenced by trends in professional credentialing.

PROFESSIONAL CREDENTIALING

Credentialing has defined and regulated the academic qualifications and clinical training necessary to become an RC. This text is predicated on creating the most robust practitioner: a licensed mental health or professional counselor with a certification in rehabilitation counseling. Thus, we advocate for the licensure of the counseling generalist and for certification of the rehabilitation specialist. It is our belief that RCs must have robust careers available to them, with access to all positions and work for which they are qualified, and the ability to experience new opportunities, mobility, and advancement throughout a long-term career. It is also important that as persons with disabilities integrate into other life areas, they have the option to receive services from a counselor with unique expertise in disability and how it does (or does not) affect the life challenge the client wishes to address. As part of understanding the career ladder in rehabilitation counseling, it is important to understand accreditation, certification, and licensure as distinct forms of credentialing:

- **Accreditation** is a mechanism review educational programs to demonstrate quality assurance that the education and training of professional counselors is consistent across the country.
- **Certification** is a mechanism to ensure an individual counselor has obtained and demonstrated the knowledge, attitudes, and skills to specialize in unique employment settings, with particular client populations, and/or to implement specialized techniques.
- **Licensure** is a governmentally sanctioned credential to protect the public safety by assuring that citizens are served by qualified providers. Licensure is regulated by individual states; thus, individuals who are not licensed in a state may be prohibited from engaging in professional activities that include counseling if both the title of counseling and its practice are written into the licensure law.

In the past, highly regulated and supervised work environments historically have been exempt from state licensure and national certification requirements, including the state–federal VR system. However, it has become increasingly difficult to convince the public and other professionals that RCs employed in exempt settings are trained sufficiently to provide professional counseling services without state licensure and national certification requirements. As a comparison, consider that physicians who worked in hospitals were initially exempt from medical licensure, yet over time licensure became a requirement for all physicians regardless of setting (Remley, 2012). It is thus critical that RCs graduate from properly accredited educational programs, obtain certification, and continue to become licensed, especially if engaged in the provision of mental health and substance abuse counseling. While professional credentialing is being driven by the labor market, it is also a form of validating the practitioner's professional identity.

IDENTITY OF REHABILITATION COUNSELORS AS COUNSELORS

The underlying premise of this text is one of professional identity. The professional identity of an RC as a counselor has been formally endorsed by the major professional organizations and leaders in the field. As George Wright (1980) pointed out, "counseling is inherent in rehabilitation counseling: this is a nontransferable obligation of the rehabilitation counselor . . . the ultimate professional responsibility for the function of counseling cannot be delegated" (p. 55). The identity of RCs as counselors was endorsed formally in 2005 by professional organizations within the Rehabilitation Counseling Corsortium (RCC), including (a) CORE, (b) CRCC, (c) ARCA, (d) National Rehabilitation Counseling Association (NRCA), (e) National Council on Rehabilitation Education (NCRE), (f) Canadian Association of Rehabilitation Professionals (CARP), (g) International Association of Rehabilitation Professionals (IARP), and (h) American Deafness and Rehabilitation Association (ADARA). The following definition of **rehabilitation counseling** was established and adopted by these organizations:

> A rehabilitation counselor is a counselor who possesses the specialized knowledge, skills, and attitudes needed to collaborate in a professional relationship with persons with disabilities to achieve their personal, social, psychological, and vocational goals. (RCC, 2005)

Clearly supporting the identity of RCs as counselors, credentialing in rehabilitation counseling have mirrored the standards of other counseling specializations.

In an effort to unify the various counseling specializations, rehabilitation counseling organizations, including ARCA, NRCA, CORE, and CACREP, were involved in the decade-long 20/20 Initiative (Kaplan et al., 2014). The 20/20 Initiative was organized by the ACA and the American Association of State Counseling Boards (AASCB) to facilitate the unification of the counseling profession and foster collaborative dialogue and promote a more unified counseling profession.

Efforts such as the 20/20 Initiative are critical to the ability of RCs to be reimbursed by third-party health insurance for the provision of counseling services. Indeed, a driving force behind the 20/20 Initiative was a stronger collective voice on Capitol Hill to compete with the lobbying efforts of social work and psychology. The lobbying efforts of the counseling profession have resulted in legislation to assure Medicare reimbursement for counselors, the hiring of counselors into the Veterans Administration (VA), and increasing mental health counseling within elementary and secondary schools (ACA, 2016). Furthermore, the counseling profession has successfully lobbied to have counselors that meet certain criteria reimbursed for the provision of counseling services by the U.S. Department of Defense under TRICARE health insurance services (Federal Register, 2014). The significance of TRICARE is that RCs can work with mental health centers, agencies, and organizations as well as the VA and veteran organizations as long as they obtain and maintain the necessary credentials to become independent service providers, generally seen as being an LMHC. RCs can play a critical role in improving the delivery of counseling and rehabilitation services to all individuals with disabilities, especially those served in our behavioral and mental healthcare systems.

EMERGING TRENDS

It is an exciting time to be a RC. Rehabilitation counseling has been rated as the 10th most meaningful job in America (Smith, 2015), as well as the highest paid counseling specialization in a survey by the ACA (2014), with an average annual salary of $53,561. Part of the reason for the higher salaries is the wide range of employment opportunities for RCs, including working in for-profit insurance and forensic settings. The types of people served by RCs, their residual assets and limitations that impact their quality of life, and their successful integration into their responsibilities and communities has continued to expand (see the chapters in Part III). As such, the parameters of the scope of practice of rehabilitation counseling are evolving to meet the changing needs of society and the individuals whom it serves, as reflected in the growth and diversity in employment opportunities and professional functions (see the chapters in Part IV). Finally, there is a growing awareness and appreciation of individuals within the context of their culture, as well as the advances of technology and a broadening research base for best practices. These developments require an increasingly broad set of professional competencies reflected in more intense preservice preparation and commitment to ongoing continuing education (see the chapters in Part V). With this demand in mind, this text seeks to highlight emerging areas of importance while still providing the most up-to-date information about more traditional aspects of rehabilitation counseling practice.

Counselors previously were restricted from employment in behavioral and mental health settings because the prevention and intervention of mental illness such as anxiety or depression, substance abuse and other addictions, were protected by the traditions and credentials of psychiatry and psychology. Yet the scope of practice for counselors licensed as independent practitioners by state counselor licensure laws now includes the legal ability to diagnose and treat mental health and substance abuse disorders. As a result, trends in employment indicate job growth in behavioral and mental health settings, particularly with the expansion of services available to individuals following the signing of the Affordable Care Act. RCs also are being called upon to work with wounded veterans as they return from Iraq and Afghanistan toward their medical and vocational reintegration (Frain et al., 2013). Today's veterans' "signature injuries" are cognitive and emotional injuries, calling on those who serve them to add strong mental health counseling skills to serve those recovering from primarily traumatic brain injuries and psychiatric disorders (Isham et al., 2010). Sadly, the history of rehabilitation counseling reflects the never-ending stream of wars and military actions that occur and underscore the rehabilitation needs of our military members and veterans. With these trends in mind, we have included a chapter on psychiatric rehabilitation in this introductory text to highlight the substantial evidence-based research supporting the effectiveness of psychosocial interventions provided by rehabilitation counselors.

The professional landscape of rehabilitation counseling has changed globally as well. More and more international students are studying rehabilitation counseling in the United States and returning to their home countries to educate and practice rehabilitation counseling. With an increased focus on international rehabilitation, the *International Classification of Functioning, Disability and Health (ICF)* model has become an essential complement to the *Diagnostic and Statistical Manual (DSM)*. RCs historically have relied on the *ICF* and its emphasis on environments and contexts to understand mental health symptoms. The fact that the *DSM* and *ICF* are increasingly complementary is consistent with psychiatric rehabilitation. This edition of the textbook more robustly addresses the expansion of international rehabilitation, including an emphasis on the *ICF* model in the chapter on assessment. Furthermore, a global perspective is infused throughout the chapters, especially in the chapter on disability in a global context.

Another trend is the way that digital technologies are transforming the way people gather information and communicate, including the delivery of counseling services (Hartley & Bourgeois, 2020). While there is great potential in using emerging digital technologies to deliver professional rehabilitation counseling services, there are also numerous legal and ethical challenges. Technological conglomerates such as Talkspace (https://www.talkspace.com) and BetterHelp (https://www.betterhelp.com) are driving the delivery of online counseling services despite the fact that both have had ethical complaints filed because of threats to client confidentiality and safety (Hartley, Tarvydas, et al., 2021). Furthermore, the increasing use of mental health apps and text messaging may cause confusion among the public about what actually constitutes professional counseling. With technology becoming integral to the therapeutic work counselors do, counselors must engage in the development and application of counseling technologies and distance counseling services in ways that assist, not replace counselors. A focus on emerging counseling technologies is included in relevant chapters of this text and highlighted in the chapter on technology.

Finally, there is a growing understanding of disability as a cultural identity within the counseling profession. Historically, rehabilitation counseling has been the counseling specialization that has worked to offset the social and economic disadvantages associated with disability. Outside of rehabilitation counseling, only 1% of the articles published in counseling journals have addressed disability over the last 30 years (Woo et al., 2016). Although topics of multiculturalism and diversity have increased over the years, the same cannot be said for disability (Rivas, 2020). A study by Priester et al. (2008) found disability to be addressed in only 25% of multicultural counseling course syllabi. In a study of counseling students' perceptions, more than half reported disability received less attention than other cultural identities (Deroche et al., 2020). Worse, simulation exercises such as sitting in a wheelchair often perpetuate medicalized rather than sociopolitical understandings of disability. In response, RCs have been promoting disability as a valued cultural identity through best practice guidelines like the DRCC (Chapin et al., 2018). With a focus on intersectionality and disability as a valued cultural identity, this text considers the evolving nature of what is considered to be a disability (see Chapter 9). Readers should reflect on how their own understanding of rehabilitation counseling and what they hope to see happen in the next 5 to 10 years in Box 1.3.

CONCLUSION

Rehabilitation counseling as well as the profession of counseling are in a state of change. While change can create uncertainty, it is our position that current changes offer opportunities for the professional practice of rehabilitation counseling to evolve and grow. In this chapter, we intentionally have introduced concepts that will be further expanded on

BOX 1.3 REFLECTION ACTIVITY

Rehabilitation counseling offers robust professional practice opportunities, allowing individual practitioners to specialize in diverse areas. Reflect on the major concepts introduced in this chapter. How has your understanding of rehabilitation counseling grown or changed from reading this chapter? From your perspective, what are the most important trends in rehabilitation counseling and the counseling profession right now? What do you hope to see happen over the next 5 to 10 years, and how will this impact your own professional practice?

in later chapters. As you read the chapters in this introductory text, we encourage you to envision how foundational knowledge and tools used by RCs must continue to evolve in response to emerging societal and cultural trends.

CONTENT REVIEW QUESTIONS

1. What are the definitions of *counseling* and *rehabilitation counseling*?
2. In what ways has the specialty of rehabilitation counseling been a leader within the counseling profession?
3. What are the commonly accepted criteria of a profession and the concept of de-professionalization?
4. What are emerging trends and issues affecting rehabilitation counseling as a specialty area of the counseling profession?

REFERENCES

American Counseling Association. (2014). *2014 state of the profession: Counselor compensation*. http://www.counseling.org

American Counseling Association. (2016). *Government affairs*. http://www.counseling.org

Americans With Disabilities Act of 1990. (1990). Pub. L. No. 101-336, 104 Stat. 328.

Anthony, W. A. (1993). Recovery from mental illness. *Psychosocial Rehabilitation Journal*, *16*(4), 11–23. https://doi.org/10.1037/h0095655

Anthony, W. A., Cohen, M., & Farkas, M. (1990). *Psychiatric rehabilitation*. Center for Psychiatric Rehabilitation.

Berne, P. (2017). Skin, tooth, and bone – the basis of our movement is people: A disability justice primer. *Reproductive Health Matters*, *25*(50), 149–150. https://doi.org/10.1080/09688080.2017.1335999

Chan, F., Cardoso, E., & Chronister, J. (2009). *Psychosocial interventions for people with chronic illness and disability*. Springer.

Chapin, M., McCarthy, H., Shaw, L., Bradham-Cousar, M., Chapman, R., Nosek, M., Peterson, S., Yilmaz, Z., & Ysasi, N. (2018). *Disability-related counseling competencies. ARCA*. https://www.counseling.org

Commission on Rehabilitation Counselor Certification. (2016). *Rehabilitation counseling*. http://www.crccertification.com/pages/rehabilitation_counseling/30.php

Commission on Rehabilitation Counselor Certification. (2017). *Code of professional ethics for rehabilitation counselors*.

Commission on Rehabilitation Counselor Certification. (2022). *Code of Ethics public comments 2022*. https://www.surveymonkey.com/r/53SCCF9

Corrigan, P. (2016). *Principles & practice of psychiatric rehabilitation* (2nd ed.). Guilford.

Corrigan, P. W., & Lam, C. (2007). Challenging the structural discrimination of psychiatric disabilities. *Rehabilitation Education*, *21*(1), 53–58.

Council for Accreditation of Counseling and Related Educational Programs. (2016). *2016 CACREP standards*. https://www.cacrep.org/for-programs/2016-cacrep-standards

Council for Accreditation of Counseling and Related Educational Programs. (2018). *Annual report 2018*. http://www.cacrep.org/wp-content/uploads/2019/05/CACREP-2018-Annual-Report.pdf

Crenshaw, K. (1989). Demarginalizing the intersection of race and sex. *University of Chicago Legal Forum*, 139–167.

Davidson, L., Tondora, J., Staeheli Lawless, M., O'Connell, M. J., & Rowe, M. (2009). *A practical guide to recovery-oriented practice*. Oxford University Press. https://doi.org/10.1093/oso/9780195304770.001.0001

Davis, L. J. (Ed.). (2021). *The disability studies reader* (5th ed.). Routledge.

Deegan, P. E. (1988). Recovery. *Psychosocial Rehabilitation Journal, 11*, 11–19.

Deroche, M. D., Herlihy, B., & Lyons, M. L. (2020). Counselor trainee self-perceived disability competence. *Counselor Education and Supervision, 59*(3), 187–199. https://doi.org/10.1002/ceas.12183

Emener, W. G., & Cottone, R. R. (1989). Professionalization, deprofessionalization, and reprofessionalization of rehabilitation counseling according to criteria of the professions. *Journal of Counseling and Development, 67*, 576–581.

Federal Register. (2014). *TRICARE certified mental health counselors.* https://www.federalregister.gov

Feit, S. S., & Lloyd, A. P. (1990). A profession in search of professionals. *Counselor Education and Supervision, 29*(4), 216–219. https://doi.org/10.1002/j.1556-6978.1990.tb01160.x

Fleming, A. R., Phillips, B. N., & Hanna, J. L. (2020). Are you getting enough to eat? Addressing food insecurity in rehabilitation clients. *Rehabilitation Counseling Bulletin, 63*(4), 224–234. https://doi.org/10.1177/0034355219886654

Frain, M., Bishop, M., Tansey, T., Sanchez, J., & Wijngaarde, F. (2013). Current knowledge and training needs of certified rehabilitation counselors to work effectively with veterans with disabilities. *Rehabilitation Research, Policy, and Education, 27*(1), 2–17. https://doi.org/10.1891/2168-6653.27.1.2

Gardner, H., Csikszentmihalyi, M., & Damon, W. (2001). *Good work.* Basic Books.

Gerig, M. S. (2018). *Foundations for clinical mental health counseling* (2nd ed.). Pearson.

Gladding, S. T., & Newsome, D. W. (2018). *Clinical mental health counseling in community and agency settings* (5th ed.). Pearson.

Goldberg, R. W., Lucksted, A., McNary, S., Gold, J. M., Dixon, L., & Lehman, A. (2001). Correlates of long-term unemployment among inner-city adults with serious and persistent mental illness. *Psychiatric Services, 52*(1), 101–103. https://doi.org/10.1176/appi.ps.52.1.101

Goode, W. J. (1960). Encroachment, charlatanism, and the emerging profession: Psychology, sociology, and medicine. *American Sociological Review, 25*, 902–914. https://doi.org/10.2307/2092933

Hartley, M. T., & Bourgeois, P. (2020). The commission on rehabilitation counselor certification code of ethics: An emerging approach to digital technology. *Rehabilitation Research, Policy, and Education, 34*(2), 73–85. https://doi.org/10.1891/RE-19-04

Hartley, M. T., & Tarvydas, V. M. (2013). Rehabilitation issues, social class and counseling. In W. Liu (Ed.), *Oxford handbook of social class in counseling psychology* (pp. 218–228). Oxford University Press.

Hartley, M. T., Peterson, D., & Fennie, C. (2021). Technology ethics and distance counseling. In C. C. Cottone, V. M. Tarvydas, & M. T. Hartley (Eds.), *Ethics and decision making in counseling and psychotherapy* (5th ed., pp. 351–376). Springer.

Hartley, M. T., Tarvydas, V. M., & Saia, T. A. (2021). Rehabilitation counseling. In C. C. Cottone, V. M. Tarvydas, & M. T. Hartley (Eds.), *Ethics and decision making in counseling and psychotherapy* (5th ed., pp. 209–234). Springer.

Hunter, T., Dispenza, F., Huffstead, M., Suttles, M., & Bradley, Z. (2020). Queering disability: Exploring the resilience of sexual and gender minority persons living with disabilities. *Rehabilitation Counseling Bulletin, 64*(1), 31–41. https://doi.org/10.1177/0034355219895813

Isham, G. J., Basham, K. K., Busch, A. B., Cassimatis, N. E. G., Moxley, J. H. III., Pincus, H. A., & Tarvydas, V. M. (2010). *Provision of mental health services under TRICARE.* Institute of Medicine.

Jenkins, W., & Strauser, D. R. (1999). Horizontal expansion of the role of the rehabilitation counselor. *Journal of Rehabilitation, 65*(1), 4–9.

Kaplan, D. M., Tarvydas, V. M., & Gladding, S. T. (2014). 20/20: A vision for the future of counseling. *Journal of Counseling and Development, 92*, 366–372.

Keferl, J. E., La Forge, J., & Toriello, P. J. (2004). Who gets to choose. *Journal of Applied Rehabilitation Counseling, 35*(3), 8–13.

Kessler, R. C., Chiu, W. T., Demler, O., Merikangas, K. R., & Walters, E. E, *et al.* (2005). Prevalence, severity, and comorbidity of 12-month DSM-IV disorders in the National Comorbidity Survey Replication. *Archives of General Psychiatry, 62*(6), 617–627. https://doi.org/10.1001/archpsyc.62.6.617

Kessler, R. C., Sonnega, A., Bromet, E., Hughes, M., & Nelson, C. B. (1995). Posttraumatic stress disorder in the National Comorbidity Survey. *Archives of General Psychiatry, 52*(12), 1048–1060. https://doi.org/10.1001/archpsyc.1995.03950240066012

Koch, L. C., Carey, C. D., & Lusk, S. L. (2016). Introduction to the special issue on psychiatric reha-bilitation. *Rehabilitation Research, Policy, and Education, 30*(3), 198–203. https://doi.org/10.1891/2168-6653.30.3.198

Kraus, L., Lauer, E., Coleman, R., & Houtenville, A. (2018). *2017 disability statistics annual report.* University of New Hampshire.

Leahy, M. J., Muenzen, P., Saunders, J. L., & Strauser, D. (2009). Essential knowledge domains underlying effective rehabilitation counseling practicKnowledge domains underlying effective rehabilitation counseling practiceDomains Underlying Effective Rehabilitation Counseling Practice. *Rehabilitation Counseling Bulletin, 52*(2), 95–106. https://doi.org/10.1177/0034355208323646

Leahy, M. J., Rak, E., & Zanskas, S. A. (2016). A brief history of counseling and specialty areas of practice. In M. Stebnicki & I. Marini (Eds.), *Professional counselor's desk reference* (2nd ed., pp. 3–8). Springer Publishing.

Leahy, M. J., & Szymanski, E. M. (1995). Rehabilitation counseling: Evolution and current status. *Journal of Counseling & Development, 74*(2), 163–166. https://doi.org/10.1002/j.1556-6676.1995.tb01843.x

Leahy, M. J., Tarvydas, V. T., Conner, A., & Landon, T. (2010). Rehabilitation counseling. In S. Nassar-McMillan & S. G. Niles (Eds.), *Developing your identity as a professional counselor* (1st ed.). American Counseling Association.

Leahy, M. J., Tarvydas, V. M., & Phillips, B. N. (2011). Rehabilitation counseling's phoenix project. *Rehabilitation Research, Policy & Education, 25*(1/2), 5–14. https://doi.org/10.1891/2168-6653.25.1.5

Lewis, T. L. (2022). *Working definition of ableism: January 2022 update.* https://www.talilalewis.com/blog

Lusk, S. L., Koch, L. C., & Paul, T. M. (2016). Recovery-oriented vocational rehabilitation ser-vices for individuals with co-occurring psychiatric disabilities and substance abuse disorders. *Rehabilitation Research, Policy, and Education, 30*(3), 243–258. https://doi.org/10.1891/2168-6653.30.3.243

Maki, D. R., & Tarvydas, V. M. (2012). Rehabilitation counseling: A specialty practice of the coun-seling profession. In D. R. Maki & V. M. Tarvydas (Eds.), *The professional practice of rehabilitation counseling* (pp. 3–16). Springer.

Marini, I., Glover-Graf, N. M., & Millington, M. J. (2018). *Psychosocial aspects of disability: Insider per-spectives and counseling strategies* (2nd ed.). Springer. https://doi.org/10.1891/9780826180636

McAlpine, D. D., & Warner, L. (2002). *Barriers to employment among persons with mental illness.* Rutgers University. http://www.dri.illinois.edu/research/p01-04c/final_technical_report_p01-04c.pdf

Mueser, K. T. (2016). Foreword. In P. Corrigan (Ed.), *Principles and practice of psychiatric rehabilitation: An empirical approach* (2nd ed., pp. vii–viii). Guilford Press.

Murray, C., & Lopez, A. (Eds.). (1996). *The global burden of disease.* Harvard University.

Myers, J. E. (1995). Specialties in counseling: Rich heritage or force for fragmentation? *Journal of Counseling & Development, 74*(2), 115–116. https://doi.org/10.1002/j.1556-6676.1995.tb01833.x

Myers, J. E. (2012). Foreword. In D. R. Maki & V. M. Tarvydas (Eds.), *The professional practice of reha-bilitation counseling* (pp. xv–xvii). Springer Publishing.

Okoro, C. A., Hollis, N. D., Cyrus, A. C., & Griffin-Blake, S. (2018). Prevalence of disabilities and health care access by disability status and type among adults—United States, 2016. *MMWR. Morbidity and Mortality Weekly Report, 67*(32), 882–887. https://doi.org/10.15585/mmwr.mm6732a3

Olney, M. F., & Gill, K. J. (2016). Can psychiatric rehabilitation be CORE to CORE? *Rehabilitation Research, Policy, and Education, 30*(3), 204–214. https://doi.org/10.1891/2168-6653.30.3.204

Patterson, C. H. (1957). Counselor or coordinator? *Journal of Rehabilitation, 25*(2), 9–10.

Peterson, S., & Olney, M. (2020). An examination of CACREP curriculum standards from a psychiat-ric rehabilitation recovery model perspective. *Rehabilitation Research, Policy, and Education, 34*(4), 222–234. https://doi.org/10.1891/RE-19-17

Priester, P. E., Jones, J. E., Jackson-Bailey, C. M., Jana-Masri, A., Jordan, E. X., & Metz, A. J. (2008). An Analysis of Content and Instructional Strategies in Multicultural Counseling Courses. *Journal of Multicultural Counseling and Development, 36*(1), 29–39. https://doi.org/10.1002/j.2161-1912.2008.tb00067.x

Psychiatric Rehabilitation Association. (2018). *Core principles and values.* https://www.psychrehabassociation.org/about/core-principles-and-values

Rehabilitation Counseling Consortium. (2005). *Rehabilitation counselor and rehabilitation counseling definitions.* CRCC.

Remley, T. P. (2012). Evolution of counseling and its specializations. In D. Maki & V. Tarvydas (Eds.), *The professional practice of rehabilitation counseling* (pp. 17–38). Springer Publishing.

Ritchie, M. H. (1990). Counseling is not a profession-yet. *Counselor Education and Supervision, 29*(4), 220–227. https://doi.org/10.1002/j.1556-6978.1990.tb01161.x

Rivas, M. (2020). Disability in counselor education. *International Journal for the Advancement of Counselling, 42*, 366–381. https://doi.org/10.1007/s10447-020-09404-y

Roelofs, T. (2019, October). *New law shields 10,000 Michigan counselors from limits to their practice.* https://www.bridgemi.com/michigan-health-watch/new-law-shields-10000-michigan-counselors-limits-their-practice

Rosenthal, D. A., Dalton, J. A., & Gervey, R. (2007). Analyzing vocational outcomes of individuals with psychiatric disabilities who received state vocational rehabilitation services: a data mining approach. *The International Journal of Social Psychiatry, 53*(4), 357–368. https://doi.org/10.1177/0020764006074555

Rothman, R. A. (1987). *Working: Sociological perspectives.* Prentice Hall.

Rubin, S., Roessler, R., & Rumrill, P. (2016). *Foundations of the vocational rehabilitation process* (7th ed.). Pro-Ed.

Sales, A. (2007). *Rehabilitation counseling: An empowerment perspective.* Pro-Ed.

Sánchez, J., Rosenthal, D. A., Chan, F., Brooks, J., & Bezyak, J. L. (2016). Relationships between world health organization *international classification of functioning, disability and health* constructs and participation in adults with severe mental illness. *Rehabilitation Research, Policy, and Education, 30*(3), 286–304. https://doi.org/10.1891/2168-6653.30.3.286

Saunders, J. L., Barros-Bailey, M., Chapman, C., & Nunez, P. (2009). Rehabilitation counselor certification. *Rehabilitation Counseling Bulletin, 52*(2), 77–84. https://doi.org/10.1177/0034355208325077

Shaw, L. R., & Mascari, J. B. (2018). History and evolution of counseling and rehabilitation counseling. In V. M. Tarvydas & M. T. Hartley (Eds.), *The professional practice of rehabilitation counseling* (2nd ed., pp. 51–70). Springer.

She, P., & Livermore, G. (2009). Long-term poverty and disability among working-age adults. *Journal of Disability Policy Studies, 19*(4), 244–256. https://doi.org/10.1177/1044207308314954

Sheehan, L., & Lewicki, T. (2016). Collaborative documentation in mental health. *Rehabilitation Research, Policy, and Education, 30*(3), 305–320.

Slesaransky-Poe, G., & García, A. (2014). Social construction of difference. In D. Lawrence-Brown & M. Sapon-Shevin (Eds.), *Condition critical* (pp. 66–85). Teachers College Press.

Smart, J. (2019). *Disability across the developmental lifespan* (2nd ed.). Springer.

Smith, J. (2015, July 23). *The 13 most meaningful jobs. Business Insider.* http://www.businessinsider.com/most-meaningful-jobs-in-america-2015-7

Stapleton, D. C., O'Day, B., & Livermore, G. A. (2005). *Dismantling the poverty trap.* Cornell Institute for Policy Research, Rehabilitation Research and Training Center.

Substance Abuse and Mental Health Services Administration. (2012). *SAMHSA's working definition of recovery.* https://store.samhsa.gov/sites/default/files/d7/priv/pep12-recdef.pdf

Substance Abuse and Mental Health Services Administration. (2014a). *SAMHSA's concept of trauma and guidance for a trauma-informed approach.* http://store.samhsa.gov/product/SAMHSA-s-Concept-of-Trauma-and-Guidance-for-a-Trauma-Informed-Approach/SMA14-4884

Substance Abuse and Mental Health Services Administration. (2014b). *Substance use and mental health estimates from the 2013 National Survey on Drug Use and Health: Overview of findings.* http://www.samhsa.gov/data/sites/default/files/NSDUH-SR200-RecoveryMonth-2014/NSDUH-SR200-RecoveryMonth-2014.htm

Swarbrick, M., & Nemec, P. B. (2016). Supporting the health and wellness of individuals with psychiatric disabilities. *Rehabilitation Research, Policy, and Education, 30*(3), 321–333. https://doi.org/10.1891/2168-6653.30.3.321

Szymanski, E. M. (1985). Rehabilitation counseling: A profession with A vision, an identity, and A future (Presidential address). *Rehabilitation Counseling Bulletin, 29*, 2–5.

Thomas, K. R., & Parker, R. M. (1981). Promoting counseling in rehabilitation settings. *Journal of Applied Rehabilitation Counseling, 12*(2), 101–103. https://doi.org/10.1891/0047-2220.12.2.101

U.S. Department of Health and Human Services. (1999). *Mental health: A report of the Surgeon General.* U.S Department of Health and Human Services.

U.S. Department of Health and Human Services. (2005). *Transforming mental health care in America: Federal action agenda: First steps.* SAMHSA.

United States Department of Labor. (2020). *Bureau of Labor Statistics.* http://www.bls.gov/ooh/community-and-social-service/rehabilitation-counselors.htm

Woo, H., Goo, M., & Lee, M. (2016). A content analysis of research on disability. *Journal of Multicultural Counseling and Development, 44*(4), 228–244.

Wright, G. N. (1980). *Total rehabilitation.* Brown.

Yeo, R., & Moore, K. (2003). Including disabled people in poverty reduction work. *World Development, 31,* 571–590.

Yin, M., Pathak, A., Lin, D., & Dizdari, N. (2021). Identifying racial differences in vocational rehabilitation services. *Rehabilitation Counseling Bulletin,* 1–12. https://doi.org/10.1177/00343552211048218

Young, J. S., & Cashwell, C. S. (2017). *Clinical mental health counseling.* Sage.

CHAPTER 2

History and Evolution of Counseling and Rehabilitation Counseling

MARGARET K. GLENN AND ROBIN WILBOURN LEE

LEARNING OBJECTIVES

After reading this chapter, you should be able to:

- Describe historical events and legislation that have shaped the fields of counseling and rehabilitation counseling.
- Explain the difference between an occupation and profession, including the role that professional organizations have had in the evolution of counseling and rehabilitation.
- Outline the professionalization processes of credentialing, accreditation, certification, and licensure.
- Discuss current trends, and how these trends are projected to impact the future of counseling and rehabilitation.

CACREP STANDARDS

CACREP 2016: 2F1.a, 2F1.d, 2F1.e, 2F1.f, 2F1.g, 2F1.h, 2F1.i
CACREP 2016 Specialties:
   Clinical Rehabilitation Counseling: 5D1.a, 5D1.c
   Rehabilitation Counseling: 5H1.a, 5H2.a, 5H2.i

INTRODUCTION

On the 11th hour of the 11th day of the 11th month of 1918, the armistice halting the *War to End All Wars* was signed. The battlefields went quiet. But, for many, the din and impact of war would endlessly reverberate, disrupting their lives forever.

Over 200,000 soldiers returned home from World War I with physical, cognitive, and psychological wounds, a catastrophic dividend in exchange for their military service. Many found themselves unable to participate fully and independently in their homes, communities, and places of work because of their disabilities. Charitable organizations responded to their needs, creating rehabilitation centers to facilitate recovery. The centers were soon overrun with veterans needing services.

With President Woodrow Wilson's approval, the federal government—a system that more commonly had provided subsistence payments supporting the status quo—responded in a new way by offering government-funded rehabilitation services and vocational training. The passage of the Soldiers Rehabilitation Act of 1918 led to the hiring of the earliest rehabilitation counselors (RCs) to help World War I veterans navigate the process of returning to civilian life with a disability. Poorly prepared for their new role in supporting individuals with disabilities, many of the veterans saw the early RCs as remote and nonresponsive (Maloney, 2017). Despite this inauspicious beginning, the intent was noble, and vocational rehabilitation services were quickly expanded to serve civilians with the passage of the Smith–Fess Act of 1920. These early pieces of legislation signaled the beginning of the professional practice of rehabilitation counseling.

Fast-forward 100 years. It is now 2020.

On the June 2, 2020, we celebrated the 100th anniversary of the Smith–Fess Act, a moment in time when a presidential signature started the civilian vocational rehabilitation system. From its humble beginnings, rehabilitation counseling has evolved into a multidisciplinary practice that blends an emphasis on civil rights and advocacy with clinical services related to client care and treatment. For over a century, RCs have supported people with disabilities to achieve independence, full participation in society, and purpose and economic security through employment.

Rehabilitation counseling has the distinction of being one of the oldest specialties around which the counseling profession coalesced (Leahy et al., 2010). The definition of a rehabilitation counselor has always included counseling with an emphasis on addressing the needs of people with all different types of disabilities, ages, and multicultural backgrounds. The focus on supporting individuals with disabilities has always integrated the concept of independence across work, career, and independent living goals.

This chapter addresses the historical evolution of the counseling profession and the specialty area of rehabilitation counseling. Specifically, we review the political and social issues and decisions that influenced the history and evolution of the RC over the last century. As we journey through the evolution of rehabilitation counseling, we observe a profession with commendable depth and breadth of scope because of its dual expertise in both counseling and rehabilitation

Counseling represents the art of rehabilitation counseling. The counseling aspects refer to the fact that RCs must thoroughly understand counseling theories, principles, and techniques to apply therapeutic skills and interventions to support individuals to adjust to their disabilities. The art of counseling is about knowing when to apply the wide range of therapeutic skills and interventions at the RCs, making an educated guess as to what approaches will work best with a client in each moment, remaining open and flexible to changing the approach as necessary. To be effective and ethical practitioners, RCs must understand and adhere to ethical principles that underpin their counseling practice. Perhaps most importantly, RCs must possess a passion for helping people maximize their potential.

If counseling represents the art of rehabilitation counseling practice, then rehabilitation represents the science. The rehabilitation aspects refer to the fact that RCs must understand how disability and all aspects of a person's world interface. Specifically, RCs must know the cause and course of physical and mental disabilities and the functional limitations that may result from both. Additionally, they must be knowledgeable about accommodation and universal design strategies to promote the inclusion of people with disabilities in all aspects of society, in community life, education, and housing, as well as employment. RCs possess extensive expertise about the world of work, including essential duties, qualifications, and expectations, and the ability to convey those qualifications and expectations to their clients and employers. Moreover, they must coordinate services with various interdisciplinary rehabilitation providers to ensure a timely provision of services. Rehabilitation is a dynamic, multifaceted process.

The dual identity and expertise in counseling and rehabilitation have created challenges in the development of a consensus definition of rehabilitation counseling. According to

BOX 2.1 DIVERSE AREAS OF PRACTICE

Today, RCs fill various roles in a variety of venues, including state and federal vocational rehabilitation agencies, community rehabilitation programs, and private rehabilitation firms. Within the state–federal agencies, roles include rehabilitation counselor, administrator, job placement specialist, business services specialist, and transition counselor for youth with disabilities. In community rehabilitation centers, they work as vocational evaluators and employment specialists. In private rehabilitation, their practice focuses on forensic rehabilitation services including, life care planning and expert testimony in social security hearings. In behavioral and mental health agencies and addiction treatment facilities, they work as counselors, care coordinators, or treatment specialists. In high schools, they work as transition counselors and in institutions of higher learning as access specialists or counselors in student counseling centers. What areas of practice are you most interested in pursuing?

Leahy and Tarvydas (2001), one model views rehabilitation counseling as "a separate and autonomous professional, organizationally aligned with other related rehabilitation disciplines"; in contrast, "the other model views the rehabilitation profession as a specialty area of counseling, organizationally aligned with other related counseling groups" (p. 3). Historically, RCs have enjoyed prominence within both the counseling and rehabilitation disciplines (Leahy et al., 2011).

Rehabilitation counseling was born out of the veteran and civilian vocational rehabilitation systems. Over the last century, the knowledge and skills associated with rehabilitation counseling have continued to evolve, offering great potential to enhance other counseling specialties that address behavioral health, mental health, and substance use disorders. The broadening scope of practice in rehabilitation counseling will continue as the number of people with disabilities grows, and they seek equity in access to services and opportunities (see Box 2.1).

This chapter is dedicated to honoring and contributing to this evolution of rehabilitation counseling as a specialty area of the counseling profession. Studying history helps us understand how things came to be and provides the data and worldview necessary to create new laws, theories, and practices that may transform the lives of people with disabilities. It also gives us a sense of identity that comes from discovering how those in counseling and rehabilitation responded to larger historical events and how emerging professionals can build on their legacy. This chapter lays the groundwork for emerging professional to build a legacy for themselves and future generations. The Reflection Activity in Box 2.2 lays the foundation for you to engage in contemplation of what our history and emerging future means for you and how to build on what you learn.

BOX 2.2 REFLECTION ACTIVITY

Become the leaf that knows it is part of a tree. We invite you to take a journey of discovery, engaging with the content of this chapter. As you read this chapter, use a journal to record your thoughts and feelings as we wander through the last 100 years of our profession's evolution. As part of forming your professional identity, focus on identifying what tree(s) you are connected to as a distinct leaf on that tree. As a starting place, close your eyes and visualize yourself in 5 years. *How do you define a rehabilitation counselor? How do you see RCs operating in the future? What challenges will emerge?* Write down your thoughts in your journal.

THE EVOLUTION OF A PROFESSION

Our first task is to analyze what it means for an occupation to evolve into a profession. For many of us, it is hard to imagine a time when the modern Western concept of a "professional" did not exist. The concept of a professional emerged from the influence of premodern European society and traditional works of healing, education, law, engineering, and finance, to name a few. The second half of the 20th century brought with it an explosion in the variety and sheer numbers of professions or "white collar" workers that exist. Over time, the definition of a professional took on specific meaning. Counseling scholars such as Ritchie (1990) and Feit and Lloyd (1990) pointed to commonly accepted criteria of professions such as specialized training, enforceable codes of ethics, broad authority over practice, and services valued by society. Similar to medicine and law, the profession of counseling has evolved to include the criteria necessary to become a profession.

The professionalization of counseling and rehabilitation from an occupation into a profession has been complex (Emener & Cottone, 1989). In this chapter, we explore the distinct expertise involved in rehabilitation counseling, the expansion of knowledge over time, the influence of education and professional associations, and the role of certification and licensure. Understanding the history of counseling and rehabilitation will guide you through the evolutionary process that has led us to this moment in time. We can then identify the issues that are present and important to the ongoing evolution and future of counseling and rehabilitation.

White et al. (1966) defined **professionalization** as the process by which an occupation moves toward a more formal and organized state of having more control over the work activities. For an occupation to move toward professionalization, the following steps must occur:

- Development of a unique professional identity.
- Establishment of professional associations.
- Implementation of systematic educational programs.
- Creation of accreditation standards to self-govern educational programs.
- Development of a code of professional ethics.
- Requirement of certification and licensure by state and federal governments.
- Promotion of public interest to gain support from governing bodies.

In the following sections, we use these steps to explore the history and evolution of counseling and rehabilitation.

DEVELOPMENT OF A UNIQUE PROFESSIONAL IDENTITY

Our first step in understanding the development of rehabilitation counseling is to examine the dual professional identities—counseling and rehabilitation. This task can be a bit tricky because of how much overlap there is with related helping professions such as social work and psychology. Yet, each of these professional groups has established a distinct body of expertise that has public value. Usually, societal recognition of professional expertise involves individuals performing the work and gaining knowledge and skills as they go, which then gets translated into formal training for future professionals. That was true for RCs who have enjoyed prominence in both counseling and rehabilitation, detailed in the following sections.

Counseling

Counseling is a relatively young profession even though people have been doing it for centuries. Indeed, people have always needed counseling to deal with transitions in their lives and other difficulties. Early forms of counseling often came from individuals requesting advice or support from family or community members rather than profession-ally trained counselors.

The counseling profession typically is referred to as an interdisciplinary field, born out of the work of teachers and social reformers who were focused on humanitarian concerns. Three historical events influenced the emergence of counseling as a profession: (a) the impact of the Industrial Revolution of the 1800s, (b) the influx of immigrants to the United States, and (c) mandatory public schooling for children. These factors led to a shift in the late 1800s and early 1900s from rural, agrarian communities that were self-sufficient to large urban cities that required more regulation regarding social support services, appro-priate housing, and safe work environments (Aubrey, 1977). Reform also began in the public schools to improve conditions for children, many of whom were forced to be wage earners.

Focused on the evolving needs of individuals in society, the interdisciplinary nature of the counseling profession is reflected in the fact that specialties such as school, rehabili-tation, college, and mental health counseling emerged first, followed by a more unified profession (Myers, 1995). These specialties emerged to address societal change and pro-mote the welfare of individuals in need, particularly around vocational and education guidance. By the early 1900s, there were several influential counseling-related profession-als who shaped the counseling field, beginning with Jesse B. Davis, Frank Parsons, and Clifford Beers.

Jessie B. Davis was a leader in the field of vocational guidance in the late 1800s and early 1900s. As a school administrator, he was concerned about the vocational and social problems of his students and created the first systematic vocational guidance program (Aubrey, 1977). Many consider him to be the first school counselor in the United States (Pope, 2009).

Frank Parsons is widely considered the father of counseling. In 1908, Parsons founded the Vocational Bureau in Civic Service House in Boston, which promoted vocational guid-ance (Aubrey, 1977). Parsons developed the first theory of career development focused on three factors: (a) knowledge of work, (b) knowledge of self, and (c) then matching the two. Parsons wrote *Choosing a Vocation,* which influenced many other guidance pro-grams. Although Parsons was not an educator, he influenced the work of Stratton Brooks, a Boston superintendent, who worked to develop guidance practices in local schools (Leahy et al., 2009).

Clifford Beers is recognized as an advocate who focused attention on the difficult conditions of mental health facilities. Beers was institutionalized several times in his life due to mental illness. In 1908 he wrote *A Mind That Found Itself,* which described the deplorable conditions he experienced firsthand as a patient. His work seeded the men-tal hygiene movement in the United States, including advocacy groups that exist today (Gladding, 2018).

As the counseling profession continued to evolve, E. G. Williamson is credited with developing the first comprehensive theory of counseling in the 1930s. He moved coun-seling out of the world of pure vocational guidance when he modified Parson's theory to use with students and people who were unemployed. Williamson's trait and factor theory emphasized a directive, counselor-centered approach, identifying traits (i.e., aptitudes, interests, personality, achievements) integrated to form factors (individual characteristics; Gladding, 2018).

In the 1940s and 1950s, Carl Rogers developed his non-directive therapeutic technique now referred to as person-centered, built on the establishment of trust in the counseling relationship. He also promoted counseling as a tool for people with all types of develop-mental problems (Gerig, 2014). This is just one way the field of psychology influenced counseling to move beyond addressing education and employment issues.

In 1963, President John K. Kennedy signed the Community Health Act. This was a sig-nificant shift away from institutional care to community-based care for individuals with disabilities. It was John F. Kennedy's belief that community-based treatment was a viable alternative to hospitalization that created a significant demand for what become community and mental health counselors (Miguel, 2018). The 1960s paved the way for counseling to emerge as a unique profession with its focus on social justice and community-based services.

In celebration of this rich history, counselors today focus on fostering optimal health and well-being with the goal of helping people live life more fully (Myers et al., 2000). In this way, counselors focus on the whole person. Rehabilitation counseling fits with the following definition of counseling endorsed by the American Counseling Association (ACA) "Counseling is a professional relationship that empowers diverse individuals, families, and groups to accomplish mental health, wellness, education, and career goals" (Kaplan et al., 2014, p. 368).

Rehabilitation

Rehabilitation was very much a part of the humanitarian efforts that responded to major economic and social upheavals in the first half of the 1900's. The Soldier Rehabilitation Act of 1918 (Public Law 65–178) created a new conceptual framework for how to support people with disabilities. Instead of just providing veterans with disabilities money to live on, there was a shift to funding vocational training and rehabilitation services to promote gainful employment. The rehabilitation or reconstruction programs provided training for jobs to match their new and different abilities (Bonfiglioli Stagni et al., 2015; RCEP 7, 2004).

Around this same time, the Industrial Revolution became associated with unsafe working conditions that resulted in significant workplace injuries. Work safety was a key issue given the rise in workplace accidents in manufacturing, as well as in the agricultural industry. New York passed the first worker's compensation law in 1910 to provide support and rehabilitation services for injured workers. By 1920, 44 states had followed suit (Economic History Association, n.d.).

By 1920, the focus on gainful employment held such value that President Woodrow Wilson signed the Smith–Fess Act (Civilian Vocational Rehabilitation Act) to establish the civilian vocational rehabilitation program. One hundred years later, the public vocational rehabilitation system is still in existence, serving a more diverse population than ever before. Both the civilian and veteran systems of vocational rehabilitation continue to have an influence on the evolution of rehabilitation counseling.

The 1930s were an era of disasters in the United States, not all natural. The stock market crash in 1929 ended an era of prosperity and we entered the Great Depression (History .com, n.d.). Vocational rehabilitation was part of the series of programs enacted by the New Deal legislation that funded public work projects and financial reform between 1933 and 1939. The New Deal once again shifted the perception of need. It focused attention on providing people with the resources they needed to be successful, rather than expecting everyone to live up to the unrealistic expectations of American individualism (Constitutional Rights Foundation, 2021). With this shift, the field of rehabilitation was playing a bigger part.

During World War II, vocational rehabilitation found a new champion, President Franklin Roosevelt, who was no stranger to disability. In 1944, he directed his secretary of war to ensure that "no overseas casualty [should] be discharged from the armed forces until he has received the maximum benefit of hospitalization and convalescent facilities, which must include physical and psychological rehabilitation, vocational guidance, prevocational training, and resocialization" (Marble, 2008, p. 55). Toward the end of the war, the Veteran's Administration hospitals were established under the guidance of physicians Howard Rusk and Henry Kessler. A boost for the fledgling field of rehabilitation medicine, evolving into the comprehensive, multidiscipline approach rehabilitation maintains today (Berkowitz, 1981). Rehabilitation counselors became part of that team, most currently serving eligible Service members and Veterans with service-connected disabilities through the Vocational Rehabilitation and Employment program (U.S. Department of Veterans' Affairs, 2015).

During the 1960s, RCs became part of Lyndon Johnson's War on Poverty. Vocational rehabilitation services were expanded to serve people disadvantaged and economically impacted by alcoholism, lack of educational opportunities, and/or prison records. The expansion of who was eligible to receive these services allowed RCs to develop innovative practices that eventually resulted in more people with severe and multiple disabilities receiving services. Later amendments to the Vocational Rehabilitation Act addressed the needs of people with intellectual and mental health disabilities, migratory workers, family members, youth with disabilities, and persons disadvantaged by reasons of age, level of vocational attainment, ethnicity, or other factors. All these changes led to expansion of the depth and breadth of the professional practice of rehabilitation counseling.

There have also been evolutionary changes in the perspective of and advocacy for civil rights for people with disabilities. The Rehabilitation Act of 1973 (PL 93–112) promoted the civil rights of those with disabilities, including the right to nondiscrimination in the workplace (U.S. Equal Employment Opportunity Commission, 1973). The 1992 Rehabilitation Act Amendments (Pl 102–569) emphasized empowering people with disabilities in choosing their own goals and developing their own rehabilitation programs. The tide was turning. Vocational rehabilitation was no longer viewed as a response to addressing the needs of people impacted by major economic upheavals. The new stance was one of advocacy, promoting actions that lead to universal access and economic opportunities for people with disabilities.

These federal laws have continued to influence the evolution of the public and private sectors of rehabilitation, while also being influenced by those in the field. Throughout, the specific expertise of RCs remained centered on supporting people with disabilities in achieving their highest level of independence and engagement in the world. That intention evolved into a broader and deeper definition through the 1990s, 2000s, 2010s, and 2020s.

The 1990s ushered in the Americans with Disabilities Act, a significant victory for disability activists and the work of rehabilitation. Guided by the assumption of ability, the 1992 Amendments to the Rehabilitation Act made substantial adjustments to the federal/ state program of vocational rehabilitation. One of the more empowering components was the concept of **informed choice**, rehabilitation counselors became mentors for people with disabilities as they made choices for their futures (Revell, n.d.). The 1992 amendments also added "the term **'transition services'** means a coordinated set of activities for a student, designed within an outcome-oriented process, that promotes movement from school to post school activities." This change started the expansion of rehabilitation counseling efforts into the world of youth with disabilities. In 2022, one finds rehabilitation counselors working with youth from the age of 14 and up in preemployment transition services. Those services include job-placement counseling, work-based learning experiences, counseling on opportunities in comprehensive transition or postsecondary educational programs, workplace readiness training to develop social skills and independent living, and instruction in self advocacy (WINTAC, 2016).

The Workforce Innovation and Opportunity Act (WIOA) was signed into law on July 22, 2014. It was designed to reform the public workforce system, which included vocational rehabilitation. They joined other state workforce agencies to align their core workforce development programs (U.S. Department of Labor, n.d.). The expected outcome was a coordinated effort to meet the needs of the job seeker and employers, including people with disabilities. Rehabilitation counselors continued to develop their skills in coordinating services on behalf of consumers and advocating for access to workforce programs.

As we review these decades, we might simplify the journey with the statement –"from soldiers to students." Yet, there is so much more in between that has created a rich tapestry that is the rehabilitation counselor. And there is so much more to be learned in the

BOX 2.3 REFELCTION ACTIVITY

Over time, the practice of rehabilitation counseling, particularly in public vocational rehabilitation agencies, has been called upon to address economic crises, impacts of disasters and wars. Throughout all these challenges it has expanded the definition of disability. Think forward to emerging types of disabilities. Is "long COVID" a significant health issue which can now be considered a disability under Titles II and III of the ADA? What other healthcare or economic or issues are creating strain on local and national resources? How would RCs best serve these needs?

subsequent chapters of this textbook. As you engage in the reflective activity in Box 2.3, review what you have learned about emerging disabilities and how many health concerns have been redefined.

Philosophical Approaches in Counseling and Rehabilitation

The philosophical underpinnings for counseling and rehabilitation have evolved over time, influenced by the events we have discussed so far. Today, the counseling profession can be distilled into four common areas of emphasis: (a) focus on wellness, (b) strategies that facilitate a developmental process, (c) commitment to early intervention and prevention, and (d) using strengths-based approaches to empowering individuals, couples, and families to identify and solve their problems (Remley & Herlihy, 2010). These guiding beliefs are consistent with the values and beliefs of rehabilitation counseling. In fact, RCs learned these values through their work with individuals with disabilities and vocational rehabilitation.

With the passage of the 1973 Rehabilitation Act amendments and shift toward disability rights and community living, the emphasis and term "vocational" was removed from the rehabilitation counselor's title, reflecting the expanding holistic focus of their work (MacDonald & Shim, 1976). As opposed to a singular focus on employment, rehabilitation became an integrated process, addressing the whole person. Disability impacts all aspects of a person's life and crosses all cultural, social, economic, and gender arenas in the general population. As a result, it has required a philosophical approach focused on those facts.

The groundwork for the 1973 Rehabilitation Act was laid during the 1960s, a decade known for civil rights activism. People with disabilities and RCs joined the larger movement of other groups to demand the right to access, inclusion, and integration. Societal views of disability had long been associated with limitation, with the belief that the disability itself was responsible for a person's inability to engage in what are considered typical roles, such as in education, work, and relationships (Hahn, 1985).

The shift to disability rights was powerful. The counselor–client relationship shifted from a paternalistic orientation with the counselor having all the power to a more egalitarian relationship between counselor and client (MacDonald & Shim, 1976). The perceived impact of disability on a person's life moved away from the medical model to a social–environmental perspective (Habeck & Fuller, 1985). This shift in perspectives is often referred to as the sociopolitical or minority model, whereby people with disabilities are viewed as a minority group experiencing discrimination (Smart, 2016).

The social justice emphasis of counseling and rehabilitation has waxed and waned over the years (Lancaster et al., 2015), although it has taken on renewed energy in the last decade. For rehabilitation, it was the growth of the disability civil rights movement of the 1970's and 1980's that fueled the inclusion of a social justice or disability focus. Counseling stepped up more recently, responding to the mental health needs of marginalized people.

Advocacy and attention to social justice are now required competencies for all counselors, including RCs (CACREP, 2021).

ESTABLISHMENT OF PROFESSIONAL ASSOCIATIONS

Building on professional identity, the second task on our journey to understand the professionalization of counseling and rehabilitation is professional associations. In many ways, professional associations are the "boots on the ground" for both the professionals and their clients. Associations play a central role in advocacy for the profession through innovation and research, communication and coalition building, and professional development opportunities. The development of the counselor's professional identity, in general and as specializations, has been and continues to be influenced by the work and leadership of professional associations and their members.

Rehabilitation counseling has numerous professional associations that operate at the international, national, and state levels. So many options create a challenge for RCs in deciding which to join. There is considerable overlap and similarities across many of the associations, yet when you view their work from an evolutionary lens, some differences appear. We discuss them in the following sections.

American Counseling Association

The American Counseling Association is a nonprofit organization focused on the growth and enhancement of the counseling profession (ACA, n.d.-b). ACA was originally created out of a recognized need for one voice to represent the counseling profession. It is the world's largest association exclusively representing professional counselors in various practice settings. As a professional organization, the ACA was formed in 1952 when four independent organizations joined together: National Vocational Guidance Association, the National Association of Guidance and Counselor Trainers, the Student Personnel Association for Teacher Education, and the American College Personnel Association (ACA, n.d.-a). The outcome was the establishment of the American Personnel and Guidance Association Two name changes later, in 1992 it became the ACA. It has also become an organization of counseling professional whose vision, mission, and values reflect the power and responsibility one has as a counselor in today's world. Those statements can be found in Box 2.4. Take a moment and reflect on the Learning Activity in

BOX 2.4 OPERATIONAL PRINCIPLES OF THE AMERICAN COUNSELING ASSOCIATION

Vision Statement. "Every person has access to quality professional counseling to thrive."

Mission Statement. "Promote the professional development of counselors, advocate for the profession, and ensure ethical, culturally-inclusive practices that protect those using counseling services."

Values/What We Believe "Counseling is a professional relationship that empowers diverse individuals, families, and groups to accomplish mental health, wellness, education, and career goals. ACA is an educational, scientific, and professional organization whose members work in a variety of settings and service in multiple capacities. The values that individual professional counselors hold are complemented by the following values of ACA: Diversity, Equity, & Inclusion; Integrity, Proactive Leadership; Professional Community & Relationships; Scientific Practice & Knowledge; and Social Justice & Empowerment."

BOX 2.5 LEARNING ACTIVITY

The core values of the American Counseling Association are expanded on in the following chart. They are designed to complement individual professional counselors' value systems. Review the chart and consider the following questions:

What would be your "bumper sticker" say to describe your beliefs about what it means to be an RC? What values are most important to you as a counseling professional? What would you want to share with your clients about what you believe?

Box 2.5 and the content in Table 2.1 The American Counseling Association's Strategic Plan: Core Values Chart. As you read these, reflect on your personal values statement. Then create your "bumper sticker" in Box 2.6.

Today, the ACA strives to promote "public confidence and trust in the counseling profession so that professionals can further assist their clients and students in dealing with the challenges life presents" (ACA, n.d.-b). ACA members now exist throughout the United States and in 50 other countries. The organization offers them networking opportunities through 19 divisions and 56 branches. For a full list, visit www.counseling.org/about-us/divisions-regions-and-branches/divisions We explore the one most relevant to our discussion, the American Rehabilitation Counseling Association.

American Rehabilitation Counseling Association

American Rehabilitation Counseling Association (ARCA) was founded in 1957, signaling rehabilitation counseling as one of the oldest recognized specialties of the counseling profession. The membership of ARCA consists of rehabilitation counseling practitioners, educators, and students who are "concerned with improving the lives of people with disabilities. Its mission is to enhance the development of people with disabilities throughout their life span and to promote excellence in the rehabilitation counseling profession" (ARCA, n.d.).

ARCA is deeply committed to advocacy and inclusion of people with disabilities in all areas of life. In 2019, the ACA Governing Council approved ARCA's recommended *Disability-Related Counseling Competencies* (DRCC; counseling.org/knowledge-center/competencies). The goal of the DRCC is for counselors and counselor training programs to support the attainment of disability "competencies among all counselors, in recognition of disability as a part of personal identity and cultural diversity and in affirmation of their professional commitment to social justice" (Chapin et al., 2018, p.1).

National Rehabilitation Association

One of the first recognized rehabilitation associations was the National Rehabilitation Association (NRA). In 1923, administrators of state vocational rehabilitation agencies conceptualized and developed this independent association of rehabilitation service personnel. Until 1928, employment with a state vocational rehabilitation agency was required for membership. That year they invited private-sector rehabilitation professionals to join as members, uniting private and public rehabilitation staff. Their purpose was to join forces in advocating for the vocational rehabilitation program and the emerging profession that included, but was not limited to, RCs.

In the 1930s the NRA prioritized its advocacy efforts toward legislation to renew the state/federal program of vocational rehabilitation and growing the program to meet the needs of individuals with disabilities. This expansion continued as the membership grew and state chapters were authorized in 1950 and divisions in 1957. In the 1970s, NRA was

TABLE 2.1 American Counseling Association Strategic Plan: Core Values Chart

Our Values	The "Bumper Sticker"	What Does It Mean?	Samples of How We Live These Values Today
Diversity, Equity & Inclusion	*Everyone counts. Everyone has opportunity. Everyone welcomed.*	We value every person for the differences of identity, ideas, and interests they bring, and we actively work to engage with those people and their differences.	▪ We go beyond inclusion to ensure diverse people are engaged and "at the table" ▪ Seek diverse representation of counselling practices ▪ The ACA seeks leadership and membership that represents the spectrum of identities in our community ▪ Social justice is a lens used in all our decision-making
Integrity	*Our word is our bond.*	We will be honest, transparent and aligned with our values through communication, advocacy and action-always.	▪ Protection of client confidentiality ▪ Transparency in financial decision-making processes ▪ Client needs are always our primary concern ▪ We consistently follow our Codes of Ethics
Proactive Leadership	*If you're not leading. You're following.*	We will be at the front of the profession, leading the way. We will create a vision for the profession and take action to turn it into reality.	▪ Thought leadership in the mental health arena ▪ Excellence in staff and business operations ▪ Award-winning publications ▪ Advocating for counselors and counseling at the federal, state, and local levels.
Professional Community & Relationships	*The power of people.*	We create opportunities for real and virtual networking, collaboration, and lifelong learning.	▪ Members believe that the ACA is a place to belong ▪ The ACA branches, regions, divisionsl and the national organization work together in the exchange of ideas ▪ The ACA is one organization with multiple experience opportunities in branches, regions. and divisions and as a national association ▪ Multigenerational mentoring

(continued)

TABLE 2.1 American Counseling Association Strategic Plan: Core Values Chart (*continued*)

Our Values	The "Bumper Sticker"	What Does It Mean?	Samples of How We Live These Values Today
Scientific Practice & Knowledge	*Knowledge is power.*	We ground our profession and our work in evidence-based methodologies and practices.	■ We promote peer-reviewed research ■ We publish *The Journal of Counseling and Development* ■ Pursuit of best practice in pedagogy, instruction, and in our practice
Social Justice & Empowermwnt	*Human rights are right.*	We will stand with and for every person in pursuit of high-quality mental healthcare and wellness.	■ Policy statements that advocate for the protect all humans ■ Socially conscious investing of our assets ■ We advocate for licensure portability, imporves access to counseling, fair pay for counsellors, independent practice, and scope of practice ■ Wellness approach to counseling is unique to our profession

Source: Reprinted with permission from https://www.counseling.org/about-us/about-aca/our-mission

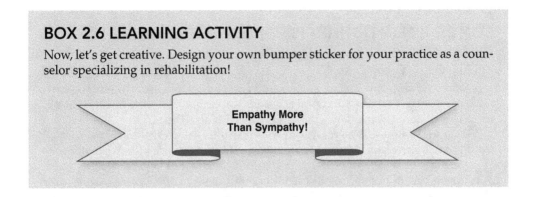

BOX 2.6 LEARNING ACTIVITY

Now, let's get creative. Design your own bumper sticker for your practice as a counselor specializing in rehabilitation!

Empathy More
Than Sympathy!

successful in fighting a legal battle known as the "Florida test case" in support of the provisions of the Rehabilitation Act of 1973, almost bankrupting the organization in the process. In 2007, NRA member Dru Fentem was responsible for the designation of March 22, 2007 as National Rehabilitation Counselor Day in honor of the day in 1983 when the term "qualified rehabilitation counselor" was inserted into the language of the Rehabilitation Act. (NRA, n.d.)

Today, NRA has state chapters in seven regions across the country and numerous divisions. Those divisions include the NAMRC and the RCEA. The RCEA is a more recent addition to the NRA family and is its largest division. The division focuses on providing counselor educators and counselors research resources to stay current on contemporary issues in the field. The following is a discussion of another, more longstanding association that started as a division of NRA and now operates independently.

National Rehabilitation Counseling Association

In 1958, the National Rehabilitation Counseling Association (NRCA) became a division of the NRA; however, divisional status has changed through the years, dictated by the needs of the field. At present, it is a freestanding organization with the mission statement: "To facilitate the fulfillment of human potential and to promote global understanding of inclusivity" (NRCA, n.d). In 2019, the NRCA board reaffirmed the philosophical statement that "rehabilitation counseling is a profession, rather than any particular skill area within the context of general counseling or guidance, that transcends the variety of employment settings, for example, state-federal, veterans, mental health, community based, substance abuse, or hospital programs" (Kirk & La Forge, 1995, p. 47). Reflect on the distinction of what the leadership of NRCA views as important to your practice, as shown in Box 2.7.

International Association of Rehabilitation Professionals

The private rehabilitation industry evolved into a body of rehabilitation professionals moving into new practice settings that were different than the public sector agencies and institutions. The International Association of Rehabilitation Professionals (IARP)'s mission statement focuses on "strengthening the community of rehabilitation professionals over the course of a lifetime." It accomplishes this goal by providing educational opportunities, promoting quality research and publications, and influencing legislative, regulatory, and policy issues (IARP, 1999).

At present, the IARP has 28 chapters in various states and Canada, as well as one for members at large. The professional interest sections address Forensics, Life-care Planning, Rehabilitation and Disability Case Management, Social Security Vocational Expert, and

BOX 2.7 OPERATIONAL PRINCIPLES OF THE NATIONAL REHABILITATION ASSOCIATION

Mission Statement: To provide exemplary leadership through social advocacy and legislation, advance cultural awareness and competence across communities, promote excellence in research and practice, and support professionals engaged in the employment and independence of individuals with disabilities.

Vision and Values: A commitment to advancing the professional practices of rehabilitation driven by culturally-competent, ethical, evidence-based and accountable practices so that individuals with disabilities would be regarded and valued as full members of our society. These individuals deserve equal access, expression of choice, and security of freedom within our communities when engaging in all aspects of life (NRA, n.d.)

Vocational Rehabilitation Transition Services. In addition, its Foundation for Life Care Planning Research funded numerous research projects from 2002 to 2016. It was then reincorporated in affiliation with the IARP as the Foundation for Life Care Planning and Rehabilitation Research. Professional associations in counseling and rehabilitation are important to the growth of the profession and the well-being of those we serve. Which one(s) to join is the first question posed to you in the Box 2.8 Learning Activity Exploring Your Professional Identity through Engagement in Professional Organizations. How to use your talents in the work of the association is your next challenge.

SYSTEMATIC EDUCATIONAL PROGRAMS

One of the elements of the development of a profession is that it requires a high degree of education and specific expertise. As we continue our quest to explore the evolution of the fields of counseling and rehabilitation, our next step is to explore the origins and

BOX 2.8 LEARNING ACTIVITY

Exploring Your Professional Identity through Engagement in Professional Organizations

Visit and review the associations' websites listed below. Determine which is a best fit for your interests:·

- ACA https://www.counseling.org/about-us/about-aca
- ARCA http://www.arcaweb.org
- IARP https://connect.rehabpro.org
- NRA https://www.nationalrehab.org
- NRACA https://nationalrehabcounselingassciation.wildapricot.org

Once you have chosen an association, how would you go about joining? Getting involved as a volunteer is the hallmark of a professional counselor, so what committees, special sections, or other activities would interest you? What are you passionate about? Are you a natural organizer? A person who is comfortable talking to strangers? Interested in attending a conference and volunteering at the registration desk? Would you like to learn advocacy skills? Find a mentor? Develop leadership skills? Learn more about strategic planning? Educating legislators?

Go ahead and volunteer! Give them a call or send an email outlining your interest and how you think you can be of help.

development of their educational programs. As early as 1909, the Boston School Board, in partnership with the Boston Vocational Bureau founded by Frank Parsons, designed and offered training for teachers to learn vocational counseling skills (Savickas, 2011). Based on their success, Meyer Bloomfield, the director of the Vocational Bureau after Frank Parsons's death, recognized the importance of going beyond school in-service events. He believed that for counseling to become a profession, a crucial step would be a dedicated university department, allowing counseling to be a formalized program of study. In 1911, Bloomfield offered the first university course on counseling during Harvard University's summer term. Additional courses on vocational guidance were offered at the University of Chicago, Columbia University, and the University of Missouri–Columbia. Bloomfield is credited with founding the first department of counselor education, the Department of Vocational Guidance, at Boston University in 1914 (Savickas, 2011).

In the 1950s, the Vocational Rehabilitation Act Amendments of 1954 (PL 565) provided funding for the creation of master's-level training programs in rehabilitation counseling. Initially, seven universities were awarded funding to design and implement programs. The rationale for such unprecedented action came from the growing awareness of the need for trained specialist to serve at the core of the state–federal service delivery system, the RC. That person needed the skillset to facilitate the process of psychosocial adaptation to disability for those engaged in vocational rehabilitation as well as coordinate the myriad of services available for them as they worked toward employment and independence (Jenkins et al., 1998). The position was both counselor and case manager.

The ongoing, growing need for qualified rehabilitation counselors has led to the implementation of over 100 accredited master's-level rehabilitation counseling specialization programs (CACREP, 2021). Many counselors have gone on to pursue further certifications in a variety of areas, including vocational evaluation, forensic rehabilitation, life care planning, to name a few. They have also pursued doctoral programs in rehabilitation areas to expand the capacity for postsecondary education and research related to counseling and rehabilitation.

In addition to supporting the implementation of graduate study, the U.S. Rehabilitation Services Administration (RSA) awards funding for scholarships through the Rehabilitation Long Term Training Program - Vocational Rehabilitation Counseling (84.129B) that "supports projects that provide training in areas of personnel shortages to increase the number of personnel trained to provide vocational rehabilitation services to individuals with disabilities" (Rehabilitation Long Term Training Program – Vocational Rehabilitation Counseling, 85 Fed. Reg, 2020, p. 17548). In fiscal year 2020, the RSA issued new grant awards to 33 institutions of higher education throughout the United States totaling $6,361,294.55 in funding (RSA, n.d). The relationship between this funding and the content of academic preparation programs in rehabilitation counseling cannot be overlooked. Since the beginning, when the primary intent of these programs was to produce graduates who would work in the state-federal system of vocational rehabilitation, there has been a close association between academia and vocational rehabilitation agencies. The field has since diversified leading, in turn, to a shift in emphases within graduate education programs. Today, some rehabilitation counselor education programs focus on knowledge and skillsets aligned with traditional vocational rehabilitation, while others emphasize a focus on integrating clinical rehabilitation counseling with the provision of mental health counseling services.

Benefits of Graduate Education in Counseling and Rehabilitation

A series of studies investigating the relationship of education and experience to outcomes achieved by individuals with disabilities in vocational rehabilitation have demonstrated the effectiveness of graduate rehabilitation counselor training. Research conducted by Szymanski and colleagues suggested that clients with severe disabilities achieved better outcomes when working with counselors with graduate degrees in rehabilitation counseling or related degrees than those without this focused education (Szymanski, 1991; Szymanski & Danek, 1992; Szymanski E. & Parker R., 1989). In 2006, Frain and colleagues published the results of a meta-analysis of studies that addressed employment outcomes to answer the question—"What is the benefit of a rehabilitation counselor having a rehabilitation counseling master's degree?" (p. 10). They reported that individuals with disabilities who worked with counselors who held master's degrees in rehabilitation counseling had better employment outcome results than those with counselors who had other degrees.

Based on research demonstrating the effectiveness of graduate training in rehabilitation counseling, federal regulations specific to the Comprehensive System of Personnel Development (CSPD) in vocational rehabilitation established the concept of a qualified RC in 1997. These regulations were and continue to be focused on "ensuring that personnel have a 21st-century understanding of the evolving labor force and the needs of individuals with disabilities means that personnel have specialized training and experience that enables them to work effectively with individuals with disabilities to assist them to achieve competitive integrated employment and with employers who hire such individuals" (34 CFR § 361.18 CSPD, 2018, p. 308).

So, education makes a difference. Individuals with disabilities deserve access to "sophisticated professionals," a term used by Rubin and Roessler (2001) to describe how counselors must operate to be effective. They need a diverse set of skills and knowledge as well as the ability to work within a multifaceted service delivery system.

Knowledge and Skill Requirements for Rehabiliation Counselors

The knowledge and skill domains that comprise graduate education in rehabilitation counselor are based a long history of role and function studies. In 1969, Muthard and Salamone published findings from an investigation of counselors working in vocational rehabilitation programs. They identified counseling and guidance; planning, recording, and placement; and professional growth, public relations, developing resources, reporting, and other administrative duties. In 1984, Rubin continued this line of research by further verifying the unique and varied role of certified RCs in a variety of work settings.

Over the years, the duties and responsibilities of counselors in rehabilitation have increased and become more complex. For instance, in the early 2000s, Leahy et al. (2003) identified six domains perceived by certified rehabilitation counselors as important for contemporary practice. These include (a) career counseling, assessment, and consultation; (b) counseling theories, techniques, and applications; (c) rehabilitation services and resources; (d) case and caseload management; (e) healthcare and disability systems; and (f) medical, functional, and environmental implications of disability. Rehabilitation counseling has been a leader among the counseling specialties in research on professional competencies.

CREATION OF ACCREDITATION STANDARDS TO SELF-GOVERN EDUCATIONAL PROGRAMS

Building upon the effectiveness of graduate education in rehabilitation counseling, our overview of the professionalization of counseling and rehabilitation now moves to the accreditation standards. According to the Council for Higher Education (CHEA), "accreditation is a process used by higher education to scrutinize colleges, universities and educational programs for quality assurance and quality improvement" (CHEA, n.d.-a). The accreditation process in the United States is administered by not-for-profit organizations that have adopted a specific purpose related to the field of study. The CHEA (2008) described two types of accreditors: (a) organizations that provide evaluations of entire institutions, such as regional institutions, faith-based accreditors, and private career accreditors, and (b) organizations that provide specialized evaluations of specific programs of study (e.g., education, law, medicine, or business). However, the evaluation process has common elements such as comprehensive assessments by the institution or program under review (i.e., self-study), peer reviews, including a site visit, and evaluation based on a set of accredited standards, which typically are developed by the accrediting organization in conjunction with the professional specializations.

According to CHEA (2016), the purposes for accreditation are as follows:

- Assuring Quality. Accreditation is the primary means by which colleges, universities and programs assure academic quality to students and the public.
- Access to Federal Funds. Accreditation of institutions and programs is required for students to gain access to federal funds such as student grants and loans and other federal support.
- Easing Transfer. Accreditation of institutions and programs is important to students for smooth transfer of courses and programs among colleges and universities.
- Engendering Private Sector Confidence. Accredited status of an institution or program is important to employers when evaluating credentials of job applicants and providing financial support to current employees seeking additional education. It is taken into account by corporations, foundations and individuals making private donations to higher education.

Historically, there were two accreditation bodies for professional counselors.

Council for the Accreditation of Counseling and Related Educational Programs

In 1981, the Council for the Accreditation of Counseling and Related Educational Programs (CACREP) was established to develop educational standards in training counselors. CACREP has been seen as "the national standard for counseling programs . . . [which] has set the profession on a path toward clear counselor identity through its process of preparation program accreditation" (Mascari & Webber, 2013, p. 16).

The CACREP is recognized by CHEA as a program accreditor and currently "accredits over 900 master's and doctoral degree programs in counseling and its specialties offered by 416 colleges and universities across the United States" (CHEA, n.d.-b). The specializations include addiction counseling; career counseling; clinical mental health counseling; clinical rehabilitation counseling; college counseling and student affairs; marriage, couple, and family counseling; school counseling; and rehabilitation counseling (CACREP, 2022). It also accredits doctoral-level counselor education and supervision programs.

The CACREP has been integral in the development of the counseling profession, working closely with associations and certifying bodies. One element of the professionalization process requires a "high degree of education and expertise specific to the profession" (White et al., 1966, p. 502). The CACREP fulfilled this requirement in the professionalization of counseling.

Council on Rehabilitation Education

The original accrediting body for rehabilitation counseling programs was the Council on Rehabilitation Education (CORE). In the 1970s, there was a need for uniform standards to train RCs, so the government funded a research center to investigate the creation of an accreditation entity to do so (Geist, n.d.). This initiative led to the incorporation of CORE in 1972. Over time, the work was overseen by a board of directors composed of representatives of external organizational bodies. The membership of these organizational bodies represented the accredited rehabilitation counseling programs and other stakeholders such as consumers and related professional organizations (Shaw & Kuehn, 2008). The board guided policy and formalized program reviews and recommendations.

Accreditation bodies are both regulatory and developmental by nature, the balance between the two can differ greatly from one organization to another. CORE's approach was more developmental in nature, providing educational programs the opportunity to learn and improve while still monitoring compliance (Shaw & Kuehn, 2008).

Over the decades, the number of accredited graduate educational programs increased, and standards underwent multiple revisions in response to changes in the field. In particular, the 2001–2002 standards revisions were a significant shift, reflecting the growth in type of populations served and the expansion of RCs roles and responsibilities. The desire for graduates to meet evolving expectations of state counseling licensure boards was also reflected in the changes. In addition, the CORE accreditation standards were revised to reflect and mirror the categories of the CACREP. These structural changes were controversial, the attempt to require a minimum of 60 semester credit hours instead of 48 specifically bringing forward the most dissension. The shift was in direct response to the fact that most counselor licensing boards were requiring 60 credit hours (Shaw & Kuehn, 2008). The ever-expanding knowledge base required of the RC also appeared to require more educational programming than could be provided in the traditional 48-hour program (Leahy et al., 2003). Despite this evidence, CORE voted to retain the 48 hours with an amendment to address the requirement that programs identify an additional 12 hours for those students wishing to qualify for licensure (CORE, 2004).

In 2002, CORE began a strategic action committing the organization to collaborate with other organizations when it was found to be mutually beneficial (Maki, 2005, as cited in Shaw & Kuehn, 2009). These collaborations included the Rehabilitation Counseling Consortium organized by the Commission on Rehabilitation Counselor Certification, the American Counseling Association 20/20 Visioning initiative, and collaboration with the CACREP, which initiated discussions of a merger between CORE and CACREP (Shaw & Kuehn, 2008).

Council for Accreditation of Counseling and Related Education Programs and Council on Rehabilitation Education Merger History

The CACREP and CORE had a long, complicated, yet respectful history. This solid relationship, ongoing collaboration, and two merger attempts finally led to a successful merger in 2017. Prior to the official merger, the CACREP and CORE worked closely together, offering joint site visits for programs that offered the rehabilitation specialization but also included coursework in clinical mental health counseling. By offering mental health coursework, graduates from these rehabilitation programs would qualify for licensure in states that did not license graduates with traditional rehabilitation counseling degrees.

The first attempt to merge began in 2012 with the recognition that both groups could join to benefit the profession by offering one accrediting body. Discussions included a name change to Council for Accreditation of Counselor Education, which demonstrated a commitment to a unified profession and accreditation process furthering the goal of parity for all counselors regardless of their area of specialization (CACREP, 2019b).

The second merger attempt came about as part of the *20/20: A Vision for The Future of Counseling*. This project, sponsored by the ACA and the American Association of State Counseling Boards, created a group of 31 counseling-related organizations that collaborated over a span of eight years (2005–2013) with the goal of promoting the needs of professional counselors, advancing the counseling profession, and engaging in profession-wide strategic planning (ACA, n.d.-d). The project focused the following areas: (a) Principles for Unifying and Strengthening the Profession, (b) Consensus Definition of Counseling, and (c) Building-Blocks-to-Portability-Project. Part of the task for the Building-Blocks-to-Portability-Project group was to focus on "licensure scope of practice and licensure education requirements endorsed by the counseling profession" (ACA, n.d.-c). To address this task, the Education Requirements Work Group was developed with the tasks "determining the common educational goals and outcomes for the education of license-eligible counselors" (Kaplan & Kraus, 2018, p. 225).

Although much of the 20/20 Vision project was successful, one element was not. The Educational Work Group recommended one counseling accrediting body. However, they were unable to agree as to which group that would be—the CACREP or CORE. According to Kaplan (2013), "delegates reaffirmed their statement from the San Francisco conference that having a single educational accrediting body would be a clear benefit for the counseling profession but could not come to a consensus on the proposal from the education workgroup" (as cited in Kaplan & Kraus, 2018, p. 226).

Following the 20/20 Vision project discussions, the CACREP and CORE collaborated again to resolve some of the continued issues surrounding counseling accreditation and licensure. In 2013, an historic affiliation agreement was developed and entered into by and between both organizations with CORE becoming a corporate affiliate of CACREP (ACA, 2021). The agreement included the option for rehabilitation programs to apply for accreditation under the newly formed CACREP Clinical Rehabilitation Counseling standards, which were licensed to and implemented by CORE. Programs were reviewed jointly by CACREP and CORE. An additional aspect of the agreement was that CORE and CACREP would continue to accredit other programs within their respective scopes of practice.

In July 2015, CACREP and CORE announced that the two organizations had signed a Plan for Merger Agreement, which finally would lead to the identification of one, unified accreditation body for the counseling profession (CACREP, 2015). The agreement included several aspects important to the success of the merger, including (a) development of a task force to ensure the infusion of disability concepts into the CACREP core curriculum standard; (b) the opportunity for each organization to submit a pool of candidates to join the respective boards as representatives of each organization; (c) adoption of rehabilitation counseling standards into the 2016 CACREP standards; (d) agreement by CACREP to honor all CORE accredited programs and their cycles until October 2023, giving programs ample time to meet the new standards and accreditation process; and (e) the allowance of faculty who were teaching in CORE-accredited programs to be considered as CACREP core faculty (personal communication, S. Fernandez, December 15, 2021).

It is important to acknowledge that the merger was met with some skepticism within the rehabilitation community. However, as time passes and relationships are built, Dr. Fernandez believes that the merger will be seen as a positive factor with the progression of the accreditation process, and thus the counseling field as a whole. She noted positive aspects of the merger, including a dedicated, informed CACREP staff member supporting the programs, as well as more access to information regarding the accreditation process.

Accreditation Standards Moving Forward

CACREP (2021) is engaged in the lengthy process used to revise educational standards for all counselors, with the target date of July 2024 for new standards to go into effect. In spring 2019, the CACREP Standards Revision Selection Committee began the process of identifying and selecting members of the 2024 SRC. At the July 2019 CACREP board of directors meeting, the SRC committee members were approved with careful attention to ensuring representation from the various specializations, including rehabilitation counseling (CACREP, 2021, October 18). The charge of this committee was to review the current CACREP standards and revise or develop new standards. The charges included infusing disability concepts into the eight core curricular areas, those required of all counselor education programs regardless of specialty. While it can be argued that all counselors need to possess a basic level of disability competence (Deroche et al., 2020), the degree to which disability content is covered in the Common Core is nowhere near the education and training that has historically defined rehabilitation counseling (Peterson & Olney, 2020). This position would seem to argue for the ongoing need for specialty training that provides advanced knowledge and skills in rehabilitation counseling, with an enriched understanding of individuals with disabilities and their families by the entire profession.

It is too soon to know the final version of the 2024 CACREP standards. For instance, it appears that the CACREP will not maintain the 2016 structure of having two different accreditations of Rehabilitation Counseling and Clinical Rehabilitation Counseling. Furthermore, for a period of time, a number of Clinical Rehabilitation Counseling programs had been co-accredited under Clinical Mental Health Counseling. While there is considerable overlap between the 2016 standards for Clinical Rehabilitation and Clinical Mental Health, co-accreditation may cease to be available moving forward. Accreditation standards should evolve in response to the needs of society and clients served. The following proposed rehabilitation counseling specialization standards offer a comprehensive look at the breadth and depth of knowledge today's graduates need to be effective and ethical practitioners:

- Classification, terminology, etiology, functional capacity, and prognosis of disabilities.
- Effects of the onset, progression, and expected duration of disability on clients' holistic functioning.
- Individual response to disability, including the role of families, communities, and other social networks.
- Impact of disability on sexuality.
- Strategies to enhance adjustment to disability.
- Effects of socioeconomic trends, public policies, stigma, access, and attitudinal barriers as they relate to disability.
- Principles of independent living, self-determination, and informed choice.
- Rehabilitation service delivery systems, including housing, independent living, case management, educational programs, and public/proprietary vocational rehabilitation programs.
- Benefit systems used by individuals with disabilities, including, but not limited to, Social Security, governmental monetary assistance, workers' compensation insurance, long-term disability insurance, and veterans' benefits.
- Rehabilitation counseling services within the continuum of care, such as inpatient, outpatient, partial hospitalization and aftercare, and the rehabilitation counseling services networks.
- Career- and work-related assessments, including job analysis, work-site modification, transferrable skills analysis, job readiness, and work hardening.
- Role of family, social networks, and community in the provision of services for and treatment of people with disabilities.
- Skills analysis, job readiness, and work hardening in regards to accessibility, Americans with Disabilities Act compliance, and accommodations.
- Evaluation and application of assistive technology with an emphasis on individualized assessment and planning.
- Career development and employment models and strategies for achieving and maintaining meaningful employment for people with disabilities.
- Strategies to analyze work activity and labor-market data and trends to facilitate the match between an individual with a disability and targeted jobs.

- Consultation and collaboration with employers regarding the legal rights and benefits of hiring individuals with disabilities, including accommodations, universal design, and workplace disability prevention.
- Techniques to promote self-advocacy skills of individuals with disabilities.
- Facilitating client knowledge of and access to community and technology services and resources.
- Strategies to advocate for persons with disabilities.

For more information, visit https://www.cacrep.org/SRC-2023.

DEVELOPMENT OF A CODE OF PROFESSIONAL ETHICS

In addition to educational standards, regulation of professional practice is the hallmark of a profession. The next step in our journey is the development of professional ethics. Counseling and rehabilitation professionals are expected to operate within their professional and personal scopes of practice. There are also specific values and principles that guide their thoughts and behaviors, leading to the adoption of a professional code of conduct. Professional associations and certification bodies have developed formalized codes of professional ethics to ensure RCs uphold the standards of their profession to protect the clients they serve and the profession. The following two codes of ethics are the most recognized within counseling and rehabilitation.

American Counseling Association Code of Ethics

In 1961, the American Personnel and Guidance Association (APGA), now called the ACA, developed the first ethical guidelines for counselors. The document was five pages long and included a preamble and seven sections (General, Counseling, Testing, Research & Publication, Consulting & Private Practice, Personnel Administration and Preparation for Personnel Work). The code is updated every 7 to 10 years, with the most recent code being adopted in 2014 by the ACA Governing Council. The revision process typically takes an average of 3 years to update.

The 2014 ACA Code of Ethics includes the following sections: Preamble and Purpose; The Counseling Relationship; Confidentiality and Privacy; Professional Responsibility; Relationships with Other Professionals; Evaluation, Assessment, and Interpretation; Supervision, Training, and Teaching; Research and Publication; and Distance Counseling, Technology, and Social Media.

To download a copy of the ACA Code of Ethics and review other resources, visit https://www.counseling.org/knowledge-center/ethics.

Commission on Rehabilitation Counselor Certification Code of Professional Ethics

In 1987, the Commission on Rehabilitation Counselor Certification (CRCC) Board of Directors approved the CRCC Code of Ethics for CRCs. It was not modified until 2001, when the results of a job analysis identified significant changes in the practice of rehabilitation counseling. A thorough review was completed, and the revision process led to a revised Code of Professional Ethics approved by the CRCC board of directors.

The code has since undergone two additional reviews and revisions, in 2010 and 2017. The revisions have focused on specific areas of specialization in rehabilitation as well as emerging ethical concerns. For example, in 2010, CRCC expanded the section addressing forensic and indirect services. More CRCs were becoming involved in this new venue of forensics. It was also noted that CRCC acknowledged that it received permission to adopt parts of the ethics codes published by the ACA and the IARP (Nunez, 2011). The popularity of social media led to specific guidelines that were included in the 2017 revision of the code. Advances in technology have created standards in distance education and telehealth, unfamiliar concepts only 30 years ago.

The 2017 CRCC Code of Professional Ethics includes the following sections containing enforceable standards: The Counseling Relationship; Confidentiality, Privileged Communication, and Privacy; Advocacy and Accessibility; Professional Responsibility; Relationships with Other Professionals and Employers; Forensic Science; Assessment and Evaluation; Supervision, Training, and Teaching; Research and Publication; Technology, Social Media, and Distance Counseling; Business Practices; and Resolving Ethical Issues. If one reviews the ACA and CRCC Codes, there are many commonalities between the two.

To download a copy of the CRCC Professional Code of Ethics, visit https://crccertification.com/code-of-ethics-4.

REQUIREMENT OF CERTIFICATION AND LICENSURE

As part of ensuring the ethical and effective practice of rehabilitation counseling, it is important to understand the emergence of certification and licensure as part of the professionalization of counseling and rehabilitation. The evolution of a profession calls for mechanisms to regulate the practice of its practitioners and, in most cases, that means certification and/or licensure. There are numerous credentials available to RCs, and students need to consider their career trajectory and what credentials may be required to accomplish those goals. Two leading certification organizations are the CRCC and the National Board for Certified Counselors (NBCC).

Commission on Rehabilitation Counselor Certification

The creation of Commission on Rehabilitation Counselor Certification (CRCC) officially began in 1963 when the Professional Standards Committee of NRCA proposed a professional certification for rehabilitation counselors and an associated governing body (Livingston, 1979). In 1969 the Professional Relations Committee of the ARCA and the External Relations Committee of the NRCA proposed a joint committee with membership from the two groups to conduct a role and function analysis of rehabilitation counseling based on the work being performed in the field (Leahy & Holt, 1993).

In 1973, the ARCA/NRCA created the Joint Committee on Rehabilitation Counselor Certification. It was incorporated in January 1974 and renamed the Commission on Rehabilitation Counselor Certification. The certification examination was field-tested in 1974 and 1975, and 1,965 practitioners qualified for certification. Ongoing refinements to the exam are informed by empirical research and job analyses.

In 1980, the Certified Rehabilitation Counselor (CRC) certification program became accredited by the National Commission for Certifying Agencies and now undergoes reaccreditation every 5 years. For its first three decades, the governing body of the commission included representatives appointed by other rehabilitation counseling organizations. Currently, the commission is governed by an independently elected board of directors.

The designation of the CRC credential provides a counselor with a professional identity, a *Scope of Practice for Rehabilitation Counseling* that defines the services provided, and ensures the public that they are practicing in accordance with the *Code of Professional Ethics for Rehabilitation Counselors* (CRCC, 2021). The CRCC also provides practitioners in the field of rehabilitation a process to become vocational evaluation specialists, and most recently, they have added a National Certified Rehabilitation Leadership Certification. They advocate for the recognition of the CRCC exam to state licensing boards and provide educational opportunities to meet the required professional development hours.

National Board for Certified Counselors

The National Board for Certified Counselors (NBCC) is a not-for-profit organization that offers credentialing for counseling professionals. The NBCC was formed following an APGA Special Committee on Registry which conducted an examination of the current registry and certifying organizations (Stone, 1985). Based on needs assessments and input from prominent leaders in the field, the APGA recommended the committee move forward with developing a general national certification process. In 1982, the NBCC was incorporated as an independent organization from the APGA rather than an extension based on legal recommendations. With a general credential, the NCC, the NBCC was able to avoid any competition with other credentialing bodies, one of which was the CRCC.

The NBCC's goal is to "ensure that counselors who become board certified have achieved the highest standard of practice through education, examination, supervision, experience, and ethical guidelines" (NBCC, n.d.). Although NBCC's primary purpose is as a certification organization, the organization broadened its purpose to include additional responsibilities focused on advancing counseling profession and enhancing mental health on a global scale.

NBCC also administers the Certified Clinical Mental Health Counselor (CCMHC) credential. The National Certified Counselor (NCC) credential, and a passing score on the National Counselor Examination (NCE), is a prerequisite and there are specific course content requirements, including nine semester or 15 quarter hours of clinical training in supervised field experience. In addition to education and supervision expectations, applicants must pass the National Clinical Mental Health Counseling Examination (NCMHCE). The exam is comprised of simulations that assess the applicant's clinical problem-solving ability, including identifying, analyzing, diagnosing and treating clinical problems. Ten mental health case studies cover assessment and diagnosis, counseling and psychotherapy, as well as administration, consultation, and supervision.

Counselor Licensure

One of the important elements of professionalization is licensure by state governments (White et al., 1966). According to the International Certification and Reciprocity Consortium, **licensure** is a process whereby a state grants a practitioner the "legal authority to practice a profession within a designated scope of practice" International Certification & Reciprocity Consortium (n.d). Understanding the licensure process is important to the career of any counselor who is providing direct services. Licensure laws are established by states to allow the practice of counseling (Bergman, 2013).

Until the 1970s there was no licensure available for counselors in the United States. The number of educated counselors operating private practices was growing, often competing with helping professionals such as social workers and psychologists. By 1972, the American Psychological Association had implemented a plan to establish practice laws in every state, and it was well underway. State boards undertook aggressive enforcement measures. In turn, counselors began calling on their professional associations to address their right to practice. Thomas Sweeney, a leading advocate for counselor licensure, was asked to chair the first PGA/ACA licensure committee (Myers et al., 2002).

In the meantime, the number of cease-and-desist orders from state psychology boards were increasing. In one instance, a counselor who held a doctorate in counseling as well as postgraduate preparation in advanced psychological testing was arrested in Ohio on a felony charge for practicing psychology without a license. His case was dismissed by the judge without a ruling, but it could not remove the extreme distress experienced by the defendant (Kress & Barrio Minton, 2015). The ruling that did open the opportunity for licensure for counselors came in *Weldon v. Virginia State Board of Psychological Examiners* (1972). The judge ruled that counseling was a separate profession from psychology and

BOX 2.9 LEARNING ACTIVITY

Checking Licensing Opportunities

Visit the state licensure board website of a state where you are interested in working and learn about the requirements for licensure as a professional counselor. You can find the state counseling board information on the NBCC's website on state licensure boards at https://www.nbcc.org/search/stateboarddirectory. You are also urged to cross-check information with the official state website since requirements change periodically. This may not be an easy task.

Look for the rule and regulations as opposed to the statutes or laws. When you access the licensure regulations, search for the three Es—education, experience, exams. While education and exams expectations may be clear, supervised experience requirements may be less clear. Be sure to locate any rules and regulations related to rehabilitation counseling. If they are not on the website, call or email the staff of the licensing board.

required its own regulatory process (Vacc & Loesch, 2000). After 33 years of advocacy, all 50 states, as well as the District of Columbia and Puerto Rico, now offer licensure for professional counselors. Virginia was the first state adopt licensure laws in 1976, and California was the final state in 2009. Yet our work toward ensuring equal access for counselors across specializations is not over.

To obtain licensure, states require a minimum of a master's degree in counseling or a related field, with almost all states requiring a 60-semester hour degree. With this educational requirement, we again see the importance of the CACREP, as most states base the educational requirements on the CACREP content standards (e.g., eight core content areas). All states require individuals graduate from an accredited program, holding either a regional accreditation or a counseling-specific accrediting body such as the CACREP. Some now require that applicants for licensure must have graduated from a CACREP-accredited program, and more states are likely to follow. These requirements are very similar to those in the fields of psychology and social work.

In addition to an MA degree in counseling, a second requirement for licensure is postgraduate supervised clinical experience, ranging from 2,000 to 3,000 hours. Other experience parameters states may include are a certain number of direct versus indirect hours, a designated time period to obtain the hours, and a qualified supervisor as defined by the state. Additionally, a common requirement for licensure is passing a designated counseling-related exam. Depending on the state, multiple exams may be required. This may include a jurisprudence exam based on the rules and regulations that govern the licensure process and ethical guidelines developed by the profession. Exams that may be recognized by states include the CRCC, the NCE, and the NCMHCE, among others. Make sure you are meeting the educational and related requirements as you move through graduate study or otherwise prepare for becoming a licensed professional counselor in the state in which you plan to practice. Box 2.9 provides the resources you need to do a deep-dive investigation now. Develop a resilient professional portfolio by checking out other states as well.

GAINING SUPPORT FROM GOVERNING BODIES

The final and ongoing step in the professionalization process is recognition from society and governmental bodies. The fields of counseling and rehabilitation have grown as their value to the public intensifies. This often occurs as major economic and social upheavals increase the need for counseling and rehabilitation services. In recent years, the need for rehabilitation counseling services has moved beyond the confines of our national boundaries and across the globe (Heyward & Honderich, 2016).

In the United States and across the world, RCs are recognized for their commitment to social justice as it relates to access for people with disabilities and their advocacy efforts conducted in partnership with those in the disability community (CRCC, 2021). As common as disability is, not many people know how to talk about it or how to interact with people who have disabilities. And that includes counselors. Until most recently, disability was missing in the conversations of diversity, equity, and inclusion. Embedding rehabilitation in the larger world of counseling allows for an infusion of awareness about what is missing in counselor education and training around disability (Stuntzner & Hartley, 2014). Expertise gained because of our immersion in the world of disability can infuse decades of experience and knowledge into counselor education, training, advocacy, and research. Prioritizing this dialogue is essential.

The roles, functions, and opportunities that exist in counseling and rehabilitation will continue to expand. According to the latest statistics provided by the Centers for Disease Control and Prevention, one out of every four adults in the United States has a disability that impacts one or more major life activities. That 25% represents approximately 61 million people across six disability types, including mobility, cognition, hearing, vision, independent living, and self-care (Okoro et al., 2018). These statistics do not include children and youth with disabilities, so more than 3 million additional individuals with disabilities who are younger than 18 will be added (Young & Crankshaw, 2021). Even if the statistics did not include people with mental health and substance use disorders, this population is likely to continue to be the largest minority population in the United States. Counselors with a focus on rehabilitation have the unique preparation, knowledge, and skills to both serve this population and advocate for competency and inclusion in the larger world of counseling. Additionally, the United States is a kaleidoscope of ethnicities, races, ages, sexual orientations, religions, spiritual practices, and socioeconomic statuses. Rehabilitation counseling is an area in which professionals will find the enjoyment of lifelong learning and a myriad of ways to express their expertise and talents to serve others.

The larger world of opportunity for rehabilitation counseling indeed *is* the world. According to the World Health Organization (WHO), there are approximately 2.4 billion people living with a health condition that can benefit from rehabilitation. Recently, WHO (2022) launched a Rehabilitation 2030 initiative focused on the need for strengthening health systems and calls for "all stakeholders worldwide to come together to work on different priority areas, including: improving leadership and governance; developing a strong multidisciplinary rehabilitation workforce; expanding financing for rehabilitation; and improving data collection and research on rehabilitation" (WHO response, para. 2). What better source for this humanitarian effort than professionals trained in counseling and rehabilitation? Professionals practiced in using evidence-based counseling strategies to address the biopsychosocial needs of a multicultural population of people with disabilities from across the life span and professionals also versed in the process of rehabilitation, empowering people to make informed choices, utilize community resources, and advocate for access and accommodations that ensure their inclusion and full participation in the life of those communities. Practitioners who know their history, thus able to draw on the collective memories of those who, in various capacities, have actively contributed to the development of this dynamic profession and can move forward making their own contributions in an exponential fashion. The Learning Activity in Box 2.10 will help you navigate planning for a resilient and engaging professional future.

CONCLUSION

As long as people with disabilities do not have universal access, need counselors with training and experience in the biopsychosocial needs of people living with disability, and

BOX 2.10 LEARNING ACTIVITY

Building a Resilient Future

As you have read this chapter, what did you discover? If I asked you to describe resilient career in counseling and rehabilitation, what would it look like? *Merriam-Webster* defines resilience as "an ability to recover from or adjust easily to misfortune or change. What do you want to start building in your portfolio to navigate a successful and engaging career in counseling and rehabilitation?

Here are four strategies (Joubert, 2021) to consider:

1. Embrace lifelong learning
2. Cultivate a robust professional network
3. Actively manage your career
4. Look toward the future

Go back through your journal and incorporate what you discovered into these strategies. Keep modifying them throughout your life. "The future depends on what you do today." —Mahatma Gandhi

need assistance to navigate the comprehensive, multifaceted world of rehabilitation; there will be a need for RCs. This specialization in counseling is a rich mix of unique talents that are woven into the creation of a counselor like no other. It is imperative that RCs embrace their history, learn from it and use the information to strategically design the future of the profession. It is also essential that they value themselves and identify avenues of opportunities that will arise over the next decades to serve people who live with disabilities or are otherwise disadvantaged in a way that makes a difference. RCs must rise to the cause and make history happen!

CONTENT REVIEW QUESTIONS

1. What factors have made the development of a consensus definition of rehabilitation counseling difficult to achieve?
2. Where do counseling and the rehabilitation counseling specialization stand in meeting the criteria associated with occupation and profession?
3. What commonalities are found in a review of the history of the fields of counseling and rehabilitation counseling? How have political decisions and changing labor-market expectations led to diverse areas of practice in rehabilitation counseling?
4. What roles have educational systems played in the production of qualified RCs?
5. How did the licensure movement lead to actions to promote unification of the counseling profession?

REFERENCES

American Counseling Association. (2021, July 30). *Core to become corporate affiliate of CACREP. Counseling today.* https://ct.counseling.org/2013/07/core-to-become-corporate-affiliate-of-cacrep

American Counseling Association. (n.d.-a.). *Our history.* https://www.counseling.org/about-us/about-aca/our-history

American Counseling Association. (n.d.-b.). *Our vision and mission: ACA's strategic plan.* https://www.counseling.org/about-us/about-aca/our-mission

American Counseling Association. (n.d.-c.). *State licensing of professional counselors. ACA*. https://
www.counseling.org/knowledge-center/licensure-requirements/overview-of-state-licensing-of
-professional-counselors

American Counseling Association. (n.d.-d.). *20/20: A vision for the future of counseling.ACA*. https://
www.counseling.org/about-us/about-aca/20-20-a-vision-for-the-future-of-counseling

American Rehabilitation Counseling Association. (n.d.). *Overview*. http://www.arcaweb.org

Aubrey, R. F. (1977). Historical development of guidance and counseling and implications for the
future. *The Personnel and Guidance Journal, 55*(6), 288–295. https://doi.org/10.1002/j.2164-4918
.1977.tb04991.x

Bergman, D. M. (2013). The role of government and lobbying in the creation of a health profession:
The legal foundations of counseling. *Journal of Counseling & Development, 91*(1), 61–67. https://
doi.org/10.1002/j.1556-6676.2013.00072.x

Berkowitz, E. D. (1981). The federal government and the emergence of rehabilitation medicine.
Historian, 43(4), 530–545. https://doi.org/10.1111/j.1540-6563.1981.tb00607.x

Bonfiglioli Stagni, S., Tomba, P., Viganò, A., Zati, A., & Benedetti, M. G. (2015). The first world war
drives rehabilitation toward the modern concepts of disability and participation. *European Journal
of Physical and Rehabilitation Medicine, 51*(3), 331–336.

Chapin, M., McCarthy, H., Shaw, L., Bradham-Cousar, M., Chapman, R., Nosek, M., Peterson, S.,
Yilmaz, Z., & Ysasi, N. (2018). *Disability-related counseling competencies*. American Rehabilitation
Counseling Association.

Commission on Rehabilitation Counselor Certification. (2021). *Rehabilitation counselor scope of practice*. https://crccertification.com/scope-of-practice

Comprehensive System of Personnel Development. Fed. Reg. 361.18. (2018). [361: 306–309].

Constitutional Rights Foundation. (2021). *BRIA 14 3 a how welfare began in the United States*. https://
www.crf-usa.org/bill-of-rights-in-action/bria-14-3-a-how-welfare-began-in-the-united-states
.html

Council for Higher Education Accreditation. (2008). *Accreditation and the Higher Education Opportunity
Act of 2008*. https://www.chea.org/accreditation-and-higher-education-opportunity-act-200845

Council for Higher Education Accreditation. (2016). *Fact Sheet #1: Profile of accreditation*. https://
www.chea.org/profile-accreditation

Council for Higher Education Accreditation. (n.d.-a.). *About accreditation. Accreditation & recognition*.
Retrieved February 4, 2022, from. https://www.chea.org/about-accreditation

Council for Higher Education Accreditation. (n.d.-b.). *Counsel for accreditation of counseling and related
educational programs– (CACREP)*. https://www.chea.org/council-accreditation-counseling-and
-related-educational-programs

Council for the Accreditation of Counseling and Related Educational Programs. (2015, July).
CACREP/core merger information. http://cacrepdev.wpengine.com/wp-content/uploads/2017/
05/Press-Release-on-Merger-7-20-15.pdf

Council for the Accreditation of Counseling and Related Educational Programs. (2019b, October
1). *Spring 2012 CACREP connection. CACREP*. Retrieved February 4, 2022, from. https://www
.cacrep.org/newsletter/spring-2012-connection/#news

Council for the Accreditation of Counseling and Related Educational Programs. (2021, October 18).
CACREP 2024 standards draft 2. CACREP. https://www.cacrep.org/news/cacrep-2024-standards
-draft-2

Council for the Accreditation of Counseling and Related Educational Programs. (2022). *Counseling
specialties*. https://www.cacrep.org/counseling-specialities

Council on Rehabilitation Education. (2004). *Accreditation manual for rehabilitation counselor education
programs*. Author.

Deroche, M. D., Herlihy, B., & Lyons, M. L. (2020). Counselor trainee self-perceived disability competence. *Counselor Education and Supervision, 59*(3), 187–199. https://doi.org/10.1002/ceas.12183

Economic History Association. (n.d.). *History of Workplace Safety in the United States, 1880–1970*.
https://eh.net/encyclopedia/history-of-workplace-safety-in-the-united-states-1880-1970

Emener, W. G., & Cottone, R. R. (1989). Professionalization, deprofessionalization, and reprofessionalization of rehabilitation counseling according to criteria of the professions. *Journal of Counseling
and Development, 67*, 576–581.

Feit, S. S., & Lloyd, A. P. (1990). A Profession in Search of Professionals. *Counselor Education and Supervision, 29*(4), 216–219. https://doi.org/10.1002/j.1556-6978.1990.tb01160.x

Gerig, M. S. (2014). *Foundations for clinical mental health counseling* (2nd ed.). Pearson.

Gladding, S. (2018). *Counseling: A comprehensive profession* (8th ed.). Pearson.

Habeck, R., & Fuller, T. (1985). Special Issue: Rehabilitation counseling: Orientations to practice. *Journal of Applied Rehabilitation Counseling, 16*(3), 43–47. https://doi.org/10.1891/0047-2220.16.3.43

Hahn, H. (1985). *Toward a politics of disability: definitions, disciplines, and policies.* https://www.independentliving.org/docs4/hahn2.html

Heyward, K., & Honderich, E. (2016). Establishing a professional international counseling identity. *Counseling Today.* https://ct.counseling.org/2016/10/establishing-professional-international-counseling-identity/#:~:text=Namely%2C%20counseling%20identity%20spans%20the%20globe%20and%20transcends,exist%20in%20terms%20of%20application%20%28e.g.%2C%20theoretical%20preferences%29

History.com. (n.d.). *The 1960's history.* https://www.history.com/topics/1960s/1960s-history

International Association of Rehabilitation Professionals. (1999). *Mission, vision, and goals.* https://rehabpro.org/page/mission_vision_goals

International Certification & Reciprocity Consortium. (n.d.). *Licensure vs. certification. IC&RC - Licensure vs Certification.* Retrieved December 16, 2021, from. https://internationalcredentialing.org/lic-cert

Jenkins, W. M., Patterson, J. B., & Szymanski, E. M. (1998). Philosophical, historical and legislative aspects of the rehabilitation counseling profession. In R. M. Parker & E. M. Szymanski (Eds.), *Rehabilitation counseling: Basics and beyond* (3rd ed., pp. 1–40). Pro-Ed.

Joubert, S. (2021, February 2). *Career resilience: What it is and how to build it.* https://www.northeastern.edu/graduate/blog/how-to-build-career-resilience

Kaplan, D. (2013). *20/20: A vision for the future of counseling delegates meeting notes.* Archives of the American Counseling Association.

Kaplan, D. M., & Kraus, K. L. (2018). Building blocks to portability: Culmination of the 20/20 initiative. *Journal of Counseling & Development, 96*(2), 223–228. https://doi.org/10.1002/jcad.12195

Kaplan, D. M., Tarvydas, V. M., & Gladding, S. T. (2014). 20/20: A vision for the future of counseling. *Journal of Counseling and Development, 92*, 366–372.

Kirk, F., & La Forge, J. (1995). The national rehabilitation counseling association. *The Journal of Rehabilitation, 61*(3), 47. https://go.gale.com/ps/i.do?id=GALE%7CA17631745&sid=googleScholar&v=2.1&it=r&linkaccess=abs&issn=00224154&p=HRCA&sw=w&userGroupName=anon%7E3eb97c

Kress, V. E., & Barrio Minton, C. A. (2015). Thomas Sweeney: A visionary leader and advocate for the counseling profession. *Journal of Counseling & Development, 93*(1), 114–118. https://doi.org/10.1002/j.1556-6676.2015.00187.x

Lancaster, C., Dominguez, D., Lopez, S., Garcia, R., & Constantin, D. (2015). *Enacting social justice through the advocacy competencies, Article 61, VISTAS Online.* https://www.counseling.org/docs/default-source/vistas/article_617d5a22f16116603abcacff0000bee5e7.pdf?sfvrsn=e34c422c_4

Leahy, M. J., Chan, F., & Saunders, J. L. (2003). Job functions and knowledge requirements of certified rehabilitation counselors in the 21st century. *Rehabilitation Counseling Bulletin, 46*(2), 66–81. https://doi.org/10.1177/00343552030460020101

Leahy, M. J., & Holt, E. (1993). Certification in rehabilitation counseling: History and process. *Journal of Applied Rehabilitation Counseling, 24*(4), 5–9. https://doi.org/10.1891/0047-2220.24.4.5

Leahy, M., Rak, E., & Zanskas, S. (2009). A brief history of counseling and specialty areas of practice. In M. Stebnicki & I. Marini (Eds.), *The professional counselor's desk reference* (pp. 3–8). Springer.

Leahy, M. J., & Tarvydas, V. M. (2001). Transforming our professional organizations: A first step toward the unification of the rehabilitation counseling Profession. *Journal of Applied Rehabilitation Counseling, 32*(3), 3–8. https://doi.org/10.1891/0047-2220.32.3.3

Leahy, M. J., Tarvydas, V. M., & Phillips, B. N. (2011). Rehabilitation counseling's phoenix project. *Rehabilitation Research, Policy & Education, 25*(1/2), 5–14. https://doi.org/10.1891/2168-6653.25.1.5

Leahy, M. J., Tarvydas, V. T., Conner, A., & Landon, T. (2010). Rehabilitation counseling. In S. Nassar-McMillan & S. G. Niles (Eds.), *Developing your identity as a professional counselor* (1st ed.). American Counseling Association.

Livingston, R. H. (1979). The history of rehabilitation counselor certification. *Journal of Applied Rehabilitation Counseling, 10*(3), 111–118. https://doi.org/10.1891/0047-2220.10.3.111

MacDonald, C., & Shim, N. (1976). The rehabilitation counselor: Provider of service. *Educational Perspectives, 15*(4), 15–18.

Maloney, W. (2017, December 21). *Re: World War I: Injured veterans and the disability rights movement. Library of Congress.* https://blogs.loc.gov/loc/2017/12/world-war-i-injured-veterans-and-the-disability-rights-movement

Marble, S. (2008). *Rehabilitating the wounded: historical perspective on Army policy. Office of Medical History, Office of the Surgeon General.* https://apps.dtic.mil/sti/pdfs/ADA483626.pdf

Mascari, J. B., & Webber, J. (2013). CACREP accreditation: A solution to license portability and Counselor Identity problems. *Journal of Counseling & Development, 91*(1), 15–25. https://doi.org/10.1002/j.1556-6676.2013.00066.x

Miguel, M. (2018). The history of mental health counseling. *History News Network.* https://history-newsnetwork.org/article/169522

Myers, J. E. (1995). Specialties in counseling: Rich heritage or force for fragmentation? *Journal of Counseling & Development, 74,* 115–116. https://doi.org/10.1002/j.1556-6676.1995.tb01833.x

Myers, J. E., Sweeney, T. J., & White, V. E. (2002). Advocacy for counseling and counselors: a professional imperative. *Journal of Counseling & Development, 80*(4), 394–402. https://doi.org/10.1002/j.1556-6678.2002.tb00205.x

Myers, J. E., Sweeney, T. J., & Witmer, J. M. (2000). The wheel of wellness counseling for wellness: A holistic model for treatment planning. *Journal of Counseling & Development, 78*(3), 251–266. https://doi.org/10.1002/j.1556-6676.2000.tb01906.x

National Board for Certified Counselors. (n.d.). *About us. NBCC.* Retrieved February 4, 2022, from https://www.nbcc.org/about

National Rehabilitation Association. (n.d.). *Our mission and history.* https://www.nationalrehab.org/our-mission-and-history

National Rehabilitation Counseling Association. (n.d.). *Mission.* https://nationalrehabcounselingassciation.wildapricot.org/NRCA-mission

Nunez, P. (2011, August 4). Ethics in rehabilitation counseling. *Counseling Today.* https://ct.counseling.org/2011/08/ethics-in-rehabilitation-counseling/#:~:text=The%20CRCC%20Code%20of%20Professional%20Ethics%20for%20Rehabilitation,be%20addressed%20within%20the%20context%20of%20ethical%20practice

Okoro, C. A., Hollis, N. D., Cyrus, A. C., & Griffin-Blake, S. (2018). Prevalence of disabilities and health care access by disability status and type among adults – United States, 2016. *Morbidity and Mortality Weekly Report, 67,* 882–887. https://doi.org/10.15585/mmwr.mm6732a3

Peterson, S., & Olney, M. (2020). An examination of CACREP curriculum standards from a psychiatric rehabilitation recovery model perspective. *Rehabilitation Research, Policy, and Education, 34*(4), 222–234. https://doi.org/10.1891/RE-19-17

Pope, M. (2009). Jesse Buttrick Davis (1871–1955): Pioneer of Vocational Guidance in the Schools. *The Career Development Quarterly, 57*(3), 248–258. https://doi.org/10.1002/j.2161-0045.2009.tb00110.x

Rehabilitation Continuing Education Program, Region 7, University of Missouri. (2004). *The history of rehabilitation. The Public Mandate: A Federal Overview.* https://mn.gov/mnddc/parallels2/four/rehab_act/rehab1.html

Rehabilitation Long Term Training Program – Vocational Rehabilitation Counseling, 85 Fed. Reg. (2020), *61,* 17548–17555.

Rehabilitation Services Administration. (n.d.). *Rehabilitation training-long-term.* https://rsa.ed.gov/about/programs/rehabilitation-training-long-term

Remley, T., & Herlihy, B. (2010). *Ethical, legal, and professional issues in counseling* (3rd ed.). Pearson.

Revell, G. (n.d.). *PL 102–569: The rehabilitation act amendment of 1992. The rehabilitation research and training center on supported employment, virginia commonwealth university's supported employment technical assistance center, and the United Cerebral Palsy Association, Inc.* https://mn.gov/mnddc/parallels2/pdf/90s/93/93-TRA-VCU.pdf

Ritchie, M. H. (1990). Counseling is not a profession—yet. *Counselor Education and Supervision, 29*(4), 220–227. https://doi.org/10.1002/j.1556-6978.1990.tb01161.x

Rubin, S. E., & Roessler, R. T. (2001). *Foundations of the vocational rehabilitation process* (5th ed.). Pro-Ed.

Savickas, M. L. (2011). The centennial of counselor education: Origin and early development of a discipline. *Journal of Counseling & Development, 89*(4), 500–504. https://doi.org/10.1002/j.1556 -6676.2011.tb02848.x

Shaw, L. R., & Kuehn, M. D. (2008). Rehabilitation counselor education accreditation: History, structure, and evolution. *Journal of Applied Rehabilitation Counseling, 39*(4), 69–76. https://doi.org/10 .1891/0047-2220.39.4.5

Smart, J. (2016). *Disability, society, and the individual* (3rd ed.). PRO-ED.

Stone, L. A. (1985). National Board for Certified Counselors: History, relationships, and projections. *Journal of Counseling & Development, 63*(10), 605–606. https://doi.org/10.1002/j.1556-6676.1985 .tb00639.x

Szymanski, E. M. (1991). Relationship of level of rehabilitation counselor education to rehabilitation client outcome in Wisconsin Division of Vocational Rehabilitation. *Rehabilitation Counseling Bulletin, 35,* 23–37.

Szymanski, E. M., & Danek, M. M. (1992). The relationship of rehabilitation counselor education to rehabilitation outcome: A replication and extension. *Journal of Rehabilitation, 58*(1): 49–56.

Stuntzner, S., & Hartley, M. T. (2014). *Disability and the counseling relationship: What counselors need to know.* In Ideas and research you can use: VISTAS 2014. https://www.counseling.org

Szymanski E., M., & Parker R., M. (1989). Relationship of rehabilitation client outcome to level of rehabilitation counselor education. *Journal of Rehabilitation, 55*(4), 32–36.

U.S. Department of Labor. (n.d.). *Workforce innovation and opportunity act.* https://www.dol.gov/ agencies/eta/wioa

U.S. Department of Veterans' Affairs. (2015). Federal benefits for Veterans, dependents and survivors, chapter 3 vocational rehabilitation and employment (VR&E). https://www.va.gov/opa/ publications/benefits_book/benefits_chap03.asp

U.S. Equal Employment Opportunity Commission. (1973, September 26). *Rehabilitation Act of 1973 (original text).* https://www.eeoc.gov/rehabilitation-act-1973-original-text

Vacc, N. A., & Loesch, L. C. (2000). *Professional orientation to counseling* (3rd ed.). Brunner-Routledge.

White, R. F., Vollmer, H., & Mills, D. (1966). Professionalization. *Administrative Science Quarterly, 11*(3), 502. https://doi.org/10.2307/2391173

Workforce Innovation Technical Assistance Center. (2016). *Work-based learning experiences.* https:// www.who.int/news-room/fact-sheets/detail/rehabilitation

World Health Organization. (2022). *WHO response.* Rehabilitation. https://www.who.int/news -room/fact-sheets/detail/rehabilitation

CHAPTER 3

Concepts and Models

HENRY McCARTHY AND TONI SAIA

LEARNING OBJECTIVES

After reading this chapter, you should be able to:

- *Describe five fundamental philosophical values that characterize rehabilitation counselors (RCs) and how they approach their work.*
- *Explain at least eight different models of disability that analyze how disability has been perceived, interpreted, and responded to in society.*
- *Express basic understanding of how the various concepts and perspectives presented affect the practice of rehabilitation counseling.*
- *Summarize each of these concepts: awareness, accessibility, accommodation, advocacy, allyship.*

CACREP STANDARDS

The following CACREP Standards are addressed in this chapter:
CACREP 2016 Core: 2F1.d, 2F1.e, 2F2.b, 2F2.d, 2F2.h, 2F3.h, 2F3.i, 2F5.b, 2F5.f
CACREP 2016 Specialties:
 Clinical Rehabilitation Counseling: 5D1.a, 5D1.b, 5D1.c, 5D2.b, 5D2.k, 5D2.m, 5D2.p, 5D3.c, 5D3.e
 Rehabilitation Counseling: 5H1.a, 5H1.b, 5H1.d, 5H1.e, 5H2.c, 5H2.e, 5H2.f, 5H2.n, 5H3.e., 5H3.f, 5H3.g, 5H3.j, 5H3.m

INTRODUCTION

Ideas and beliefs about disability are as old as human beings' ability to observe and compare each other. As society evolved, so too did the concept of disability. By the early 1900s, the profession of rehabilitation counseling emerged to provide vocational and psychosocial services for citizens who have disabilities to earn a living and pursue a career. Approximately 50 years later, during the zenith of the civil rights era in America, persons with disabilities (PWD) joined the tide of Black, feminist, and gay liberation movements to demand changes in how they were treated by society. Today, rehabilitation counseling practice is rooted in civil rights concepts and laws that emphasize how to serve PWDs with dignity and respect while also engaging in advocacy to promote a more equitable, accessible, and inclusive society.

This chapter is designed in three main sections. The first section describes fundamental philosophical values that characterize rehabilitation counselors (RCs) and how they approach their work. The next two sections delineate four *traditional models* of disability, followed by six *unconventional models* of disability. Readers will notice that some of the references in this chapter are not recent or not the latest edition of that publication. This choice was purposeful in order to recognize classic insights on perennial issues or to provide an historical vantage point from which the concepts and models developed. Such sources are still shaping the field.

All the chapter's concepts and resources are woven together to describe the complex and evolving context within which the practice of rehabilitation counseling operates. However, the majority of the observations and recommendations in this chapter apply to all counselors because the specialty of rehabilitation counseling is an integral part of the counseling profession. Please take the "clay" of all that is presented in this chapter and shape it for your best understanding and application of the knowledge and sensitivity needed to be effective as counselors, advocates, and allies in collaborating with PWDs in their journeys of holistic development in their chosen careers and communities.

VALUES AND PERSPECTIVES UNDERGIRDING REHABILITATION COUNSELING

Values are crucial to informing our identity and guiding our behavior as individuals, groups, and organizations. Making values explicit to the public and real in our efforts to live by them should be an ongoing process that reinforces the meaningfulness of the values. Reflecting and acting on our values also serve as methods of professional self-monitoring and continued improvement. Beatrice Wright was a groundbreaking scholar whose insights and writings have been among the most prominent influences in the history of the profession of rehabilitation counseling. Wright (1959) articulated several essential guidelines for rehabilitation practitioners that have endured as part of our profession's guiding conscience and ethical compass. In Wright (1983), she elaborated and explained her foundational list of 20 *"value-laden beliefs and principles."* McCarthy (2011) included an interview with Wright wherein she emphasized the ongoing need for professionals to review, critique, adapt, and embrace our values in practice. Specifically, Wright recommended that within the credentialing process, to become a certified or licensed rehabilitation practitioner, candidates should be given a list of their profession's value base and asked if "there are any values that could be added or omitted and to explain their view, as a way of ensuring serious consideration of values," and in order to continually "revise the value-laden beliefs and principles based on suggestions made by candidates" (McCarthy, 2011, p. 77). The following explanation of RCs' core values benefits from the cumulative work of Wright and several other thought leaders of our profession.

Person–Environment Interaction

Several theorists and researchers who contributed to the early development of rehabilitation counseling were influenced by the **field theory** of Lewin et al. (1936). Lewin was a social psychologist who postulated the functional formula, $B = f(P \times E)$. That is, he argued that in order to understand human behavior (B), we need to realize that it is a function (f) of the interaction ($\times$) between aspects of the person (P) and forces in the surrounding context or environment (E). This interactionist proposition seems like common sense today, but it was avant-garde at that time when behavior was believed to be determined predominantly by the abilities, emotions, genes, motives, and vulnerabilities that existed within the person. For detailed explanations of how the early rehabilitation scholars (e.g., R. Barker, T. Dembo, G. Leviton, B. Wright) applied field theory's interest in environmental factors to conceptualizing the experience of disability, see Dunn (2015), Livneh et al. (2014), and McCarthy (2011, 2014).

The environment has been important in other theories that address the consequences of having a disability. Vash and Crewe (2004) discussed how the disability experience is likely to be affected by various aspects of the environment. They classified it into two spheres: the **cultural context** (including societal attitudes, technological developments, and political philosophies, such as free enterprise versus socialist economies) and the **immediate environment** (including family characteristics, regional differences, and residence in home versus institutional settings). There are also notable examples of applied research in career development, work adjustment, and mental health that have focused on the fit between person and environment (e.g., Lofquist & Dawis, 1969, 1991; Moos, 1974). Thus, RCs are more likely than many of their counterparts in other disciplines to attend to the influences of the environment—both its resources and its barriers. Nonetheless, the attention given to the environment is still not equal to the focus on the person. There continues to be a strong bias toward assessing and trying to change the person, to the comparative neglect of exploiting the positives and modifying the negatives in the environment, as explained by Groomes and Olsheski (2002), McCarthy (2014), and Wright and Lopez (2005).

Strengths-Based Practice

An **asset-oriented approach** (e.g., Atkins, 1988) or **strengths-based orientation** (e.g., Galassi & Akos, 2007) of uncovering and reinforcing the advantageous aspects in both the person and the situation is the widely endorsed current expectation for RCs. Today, taking a purposefully positive approach is fairly common in the social sciences, as reflected in the popularity of the positive psychology movement (Chou et al., 2013) and wellness programs. However, there continues to be a tension between these positive approaches and much of medical practice. A prominent characteristic of the medical professions is focusing primarily or exclusively on the pathology or the problem, in order to prevent or cure disease with military aggressiveness, such as "conquering cancer." The zeal that drives the problem-oriented approach in medicine to treat disability tends to direct insufficient attention to the positive elements in the person and context. In response, for many decades rehabilitation counseling has espoused (a) an optimistic perspective on the achievable potential of people with disabilities to lead satisfying and successful lives; (b) a focus on building up the skills and potential that remain after the changes that were brought on by a chronic illness, injury, or other significant loss; and (c) an emphasis on utilizing the client's situation and broader environment for supportive resources.

Coping attitudes and behaviors have long been demonstrated by PWDs and encouraged by RCs. Today, coping is often referred to by the term **resilience**: "the process of, capacity for, or outcome of successful adaptation despite challenging or threatening circumstances" (Masten et al., 1990, p. 426). Although it is widely accepted intellectually, taking such an approach requires persistent attention because of what has been called the **fundamental negative bias** by Wright (1988). She explained with many eye-opening examples how this tendency in the way humans process information leads to giving more attention and weight to salient negative stimuli, such as the stigma and misfortune often assumed to be associated with a disability. With similar arguments about unconscious reactions to disability, Hahn (1993) cogently hypothesized that two major contributors to strained interaction (and eventual negative attitudes) are stimulated when able-bodied people encounter a person with a visible disability. These apprehensions are **aesthetic anxiety** (discomfort at being close to disfigured appearance) and **existential anxiety** (unconscious threat felt to one's own safety or existence by seeing disability and associating it with accidents and trauma). Thus, practitioners can easily but unconsciously be thrown off center, which may lead them to underestimate the capability of PWDs, unless they consciously apply a strengths-based approach.

Holistic Perspective

In facilitating their clients' long-term integration into community life, RCs employ a multidimensional **holistic approach** to explore and embrace the whole person and all the relevant circumstances. Depending on the client's preferred focus and possible limitations set by the service agency, an appropriate rehabilitation counseling assessment could explore many aspects of the person's life, including the following domains (each exemplified with a few representative components):

- Vocational (career aspirations, work history, volunteer experience)
- Social (family roles, support networks, community participation)
- Psychological (attitudes about coping, self-perceptions, affect about the future)
- Disability-related (functional capacity, accommodations, disability-management skills)
- Cognitive (communication skills, academic performance, problem-solving style)
- Health-related (insurance coverage, medications, wellness practices)
- Sexual (level of technical information, current satisfaction, safety-related concerns)
- Recreational (exercise routines, hobbies, access to community venues)
- Cultural/spiritual (core values, cultural identity, sense of hopefulness)

Not all domains will generate issues an individual client wishes to address or resources that can be marshaled to fulfill desired goals. Often, the declared needs of the client may be beyond the scope of a single agency and a referral to another provider is necessary.

RCs demonstrate a holistic orientation when they explore the client's comprehensive **quality of life (QOL)**, which is the subjective, multidimensional evaluation of relevant positive and negative aspects of a person's life. When RCs provide direct services, such as enhancing clients' resilience to cope with crises and daily stressors, or assist them in starting a meaningful career path, they are directly promoting clients' subjective QOL. The holistic approach, the advancement of clients' QOL, and the mission of RC practice are mutually reinforcing in many ways (e.g., Bishop et al., 2008; Chan et al., 2009; Hartley, 2011; Livneh, 2016). The concepts and practices referred to in counseling as the wellness model are another example of a holistic approach. A popular version is the wheel of wellness model developed by Myers and Sweeney (2008) and Witmer and Sweeney (1992). These authors defined **wellness** as "a way of life oriented toward optimal health and well-being in which body, mind, and spirit are integrated by the individual to live more fully within the human and natural community" (Myers et al., 2000, p. 252). Nested concentric circles compose the model's graphic representation of five proposed life tasks (Spirituality, Self-Direction, Work and Leisure, Friendship, Love). The spokes of the wheel identify 12 subtasks that include various patterns of behavior and methods of adjustment, such as problem-solving and creativity, sense of humor, nutrition, self-care, and cultural identity. The wellness model is favored quite widely among the current frameworks for counseling. Its content and process are clearly holistic, affirmative, and interactive.

Collaborative and Interdisciplinary Partnerships

As early as the original edition of her classic book, Wright (1960) proposed and explained the necessity of counselors' collaborating with *clients as comanagers* of their rehabilitation plan. At the time, that was a revolutionary recommendation to advance. Currently, that philosophy of actively involving stakeholders in activities that affect their health and welfare is infused in most human services. Some well-established procedures formalize and ensure the solicitation of clients' input and continuing contributions to their process of **habilitation** (acquiring knowledge and life skills as a developmental process) or **rehabilitation** (relearning lost skills or developing compensatory strategies after the onset of disability). One such process is the **Individualized Education Plan (IEP)**. This document is created annually for students with a disability in primary and secondary schools if they are eligible for accommodations and support services. The team that discusses, determines, and implements the needed services includes the student, parent or advocate, and the school staff directly involved such as teacher(s),the counselor, and needed therapists. The counterpart document developed collaboratively by each new client in many VR programs and the counselor is the **Individualized Plan for Employment (IPE)**. Clients not only discuss and sign the plan but also are expected to write down their input in their own words. An analogous instrument for the senior stage of life, the **Individualized Plan for Retirement (IPR)**, was proposed and delineated by Hershenson (2015).

The use of an **interdisciplinary team**, a group of professionals with different expertise working to provide multidisciplinary services, has been a primary model for the delivery of comprehensive rehabilitation services, especially in large clinical settings. Thus, RCs employed in hospitals and clinics may coordinate with any of these team members: physiatrists (medical doctors specializing in physical medicine and rehabilitation), psychiatrists, neurologists, orthopedists, nurses, psychologists, occupational therapists, physical therapists, and speech–language therapists. The expectation of effective **interprofessional collaboration** has been reinforced in employment settings and preservice training programs by institutional and educational accreditation standards. RCs who work in vocational programs have an essential partner in employers, sometimes called their "second client." By providing training, paid jobs and work experience, local businesses and industries fulfill the occupational goals of the clients. In addition, employers have their own needs which many RCs are qualified to satisfy. The needs of employers as rehabilitation's *corporate clients* include assistance and consultation on topics such as (a) determining appropriate physical and procedural accommodations for their employees who require them (new hires as well as long-term employees with recently acquired functional limitations), (b) developing policies and procedures to ensure compliance with applicable laws governing nondiscrimination in employment, and (c) staff training on disability diversity, stress management, and strategies for optimizing safety and wellness in the workplace. Similarly, RCs employed in the private sector and the workers' compensation system provide direct vocational services to a varied clientele: (a) case management of workers with acquired disabilities, (b) expert testimony for court systems, and (c) detailed life care plans for attorneys representing catastrophically injured clients. All these professionals who advise, consult, or collaborate with RCs are important colleagues in the rehabilitation process. Nevertheless, the primary partner should be the individual client seeking our services.

Promotion of Dignity and Human Rights

Two significant indicators of the social disparities experienced by the disability community are persistently higher unemployment rates and lower rates of graduation from high school and beyond. Higher rates of poverty and social isolation are additional indices of the second-class citizenship experienced by many people with disabilities. To redress these problems of inequity, it is important that counselors provide the types of services that will enable clients to succeed academically and vocationally because they are prepared to resist the factors that have contributed to these negative statistics. One resource to strengthen practitioners' provision of such effective services is the Disability-Related Counseling Competencies (DRCCs), which were developed by the American Rehabilitation Counseling Association (ARCA) and endorsed by the American Counseling Association (ACA) as aspirational, best-practice guidelines for all counselors (Chapin et al., 2018). The DRCCs are organized into five domains, with the indicated number of individual guidelines in each: A.1–15: Understanding and Accommodating the Disability Experience; B.1–16: Advocacy for PWDs and Support of Their Self-Advocacy; C.1–16: The Counseling Process and Relationship; D.1–7: Testing and Assessment; E.1–17: Working with or Supervising PWDs in School, Employment, Community, and Clinical

Settings. Consistent with the DRCCs, the following are a set of practical intervention pathways, structured around our *five strategic A's* (awareness, accessibility, accommodation, advocacy, allyship) and designed to promote dignity and human rights by enhancing the delivery of counseling and inclusion services to PWDs.

Awareness

Essential to developing a thorough awareness of inequity against people with disabilities is an understanding of the concept of **ableism**. Like institutional racism and sexism, ableism is a form of systemic oppression that "places value on people's bodies and minds based on societally constructed ideas of normality, intelligence, excellence, desirability, and productivity . . . determining who is valuable and worthy" (Lewis, 2021, para. 1–2). It is called ableism because it establishes performance requirements not on individual needs and rights but on idealized expectations associated with "able-bodied" appearance, performance, and preferences. It is systemic because it is so ingrained and taken for granted in society's norms. Evidence of ableism can be uncovered by questioning and deconstructing established practices and performance standards set by the dominant, nondisabled majority. This involves (a) becoming informed, observant, and sensitive to what is going on in your organization and community that prevents equitable treatment of people with disabilities; (b) honestly examining existing policies, attitudes, assumptions, expectations, or requirements that everything should be done the "normal" or usual way; and (c) remembering that not all barriers are concrete and visible, so it is necessary to look broadly and reflect deeply on possible problems with the status quo.

The DRCCs directly address the concept of ableism, requiring that all counselors "validate and collaboratively problem-solve client concerns about their experiences of oppression and ableism" (Chapin et al., 2018, A.6). Experiences of oppression can be subtle or overt. A subtle form of ableism could be addressing the American Sign Language (ASL) interpreter instead of talking directly to the client or person with the hearing loss. More overt examples of ableism include constructing buildings without accessible elevators or ramps. Whether subtle or overt, the larger point is that all counselors must be aware of ableism and how it has contributed to the unequal treatment of PWDs in society, including our education, rehabilitation, and healthcare systems.

Accessibility

The term **accessibility** is used in regular conversation to refer to how easy it is to enter and move about a location or to obtain, use, and experience something. It has acquired heightened applicability to rehabilitation counseling since we have become more aware and concerned that many settings or experiences are not easily (or not at all) approachable by or available to PWDs. When raised awareness reveals situations of disparity in need of change, it is important to investigate what the possible contributing factors are. Careful analysis of the aspects of the situation and listening to the complaints of those who have been marginalized or excluded should help identify whether there are *physical, procedural, or attitudinal barriers* that prevent or complicate access and full participation. Are there features of the natural or built environment that constitute physical barriers? Are there requirements in the process of participation that create procedural barriers? Are there assumptions or beliefs held by gatekeepers or peers in the situation that communicate attitudinal barriers that make some people feel unwelcome, mistreated, or denied equal opportunity? Reducing these barriers requires honesty about oneself and listening to the marginalized group, as well as commitment and creativity, to assess and then increase accessibility as appropriate. The term **universal design** refers to intentionally creating, in the development of products and structures, those characteristics and options that will maximize accessibility by the greatest number of users (e.g., Iwarsson & Ståhl, 2003; Null, 2014). Actually, most architectural or environmental features that promote access and convenience for PWDs improve those functional criteria for the public as well. Ramps and automatic doors, for example, help all of us when we are transporting heavy loads. The concept of accessibility is addressed throughout the DRCCs, including the need to "advocate for the accessibility of all spaces in their organization . . . the parking lot, building entrance, waiting area, restrooms, offices, and meeting rooms" (Chapin et al., 2018, A.11). The DRCCs offer direct guidance to help counselors "promote decisions and actions that make mental health, medical, and wellness services accessible to PWDs within their community" (Chapin et al., 2018, B.14) and "make efforts to ensure the accessibility of technology used for distance counseling, websites, social media sites, software, and computer applications" (Chapin et al., 2018, C.2).

Accommodation

There is considerable overlap both in concept and in practical examples between accessibility and accommodation. Ideally, accessibility from a universal design perspective would mean there is no need for individualized accommodation. Instead, environments would be proactively designed with options and flexibility to meet the needs of all people, thus affirming disability as a natural part of life. Since universal design is often not yet the case, **accommodation** consists of a variety of options and strategies that substitute or compensate for the different or specifically limited abilities of PWDs. Examples include (a) work-from-home opportunities or the option to participate virtually, (b) providing adaptive equipment or resources, such as screen-reading software or sign-language interpreters, and (c) substituting alternatives for accomplishing requirements, such as allowing a job coach to train a new employee on-site or offering a low-distraction testing environment. From a legal perspective, the phrase **reasonable accommodation** is the extent of adjustments and modifications that a responsible organization such as a business or school should be expected to provide to a qualified individual with a disability. The term *reasonable* was purposefully not delineated by any list of specific examples or formula. Rather, the laws and regulations provide some guidance and criteria to be considered when accommodation requests are individually negotiated and determined. Beyond legal requirements, it is important that all counselors create accommodations when they will make the difference in whether PWDs can receive services or actively and conveniently participate.

Counselors can use the DRCCs to guide their identification of appropriate accommodations for PWDs (Chapin et al., 2018). As an example, standard C.8 encourages counselors to ask about and provide accommodations, as necessary, for the effective delivery of individual and group counseling services to PWDs. Standard D.4 identifies various issues to explore as counselors determine if and how accommodations should be provided during the administration of tests and assessments. While accommodations seek to remove barriers for PWDs, it is important to point out that accessibility does not guarantee an equitable experience. For example, the very process of having to request an accommodation puts the onus of that negotiation on the PWD. Rather than addressing disability only from a reactive or legal-compliance standpoint, it is important for organizations to send the message proactively that PWDs are welcome as clients, coworkers, customers, or partners in their enterprises. In recent years, the novel coronavirus pandemic created increased access for people with disabilities via telehealth, work from home, and virtual participation in community events; these are all accommodations that consistently had been denied to PWDs for years (Saia et al., 2021). We advocate that these types of accommodations will remain post-pandemic to ensure equity and integration of PWDs in all aspects of community life.

Advocacy

The term **advocacy** refers to multiple ways of achieving change where it is needed. Three types of advocacy are (a) **individual advocacy** to empower a particular person, (b) **self-advocacy** when one is fighting a cause on behalf of oneself or one's community, and (c) **systems advocacy** to generate improvement on an institutional or societal level (such as effecting a policy change that benefits a class of people). Advocacy comes from Latin words meaning to speak up or use your voice to advance a cause. Accordingly, many modes of advocacy have to do with verbal communication: giving talks to educate stakeholders about an injustice, writing letters to controlling authorities, lobbying legislators, creating public service announcements, and participating in a boycott or protest march. Other ways of promoting a message or cause are to conduct research, solicit resources and supporters, monitor enforcement of equal-opportunity laws, and sponsor demonstration projects of innovative practices. These actions can serve to validate the need or instigate the desired change. Many other means of effecting advocacy can be chosen to fit with the agenda and the preferred style of the advocate or self-advocate.

Kiselica and Robinson (2001) discussed several qualities and skills that facilitate the process of effective advocacy. These include the ability to maintain a multisystems perspective; the ability to use individual, group, and organizational change strategies; a willingness to compromise; an awareness of the impact of your personality on others; and the ability to adjust your style in order to be an effective change agent. Internationally, the declaration and protection of **human rights** are major sociopolitical goals pushed by advocates for women, children, and other marginalized sectors of society, such as PWDs, as articulated in the 2006 UN CRPD. Umeasiegbu et al. (2013) provided informative analyses of this policy document and its comparison with counterpart laws in the United States and several other countries.

Social justice has become the contemporary term to refer to counseling and advocacy strategies focused on human rights. The goal is to reduce the impact of deprivation, discrimination, and oppression in the lives of clients and in the communities where they reside by eliminating the root causes and manifestations of the injustices. This agenda is relatively new for our profession and ought to be more fully infused into our curricula and ethical codes. That effort will require honest self-reflection and serious analysis and critique of our professional practices. Harley et al. (2007, p. 44) cogently advised us to "critically examine the power dynamics of the rehabilitation counseling approach to service . . . identify new ways of entering into a reciprocal relationship in the community . . . teaching and learning about social justice are not destinations . . . they are processes of continuous growth and understanding."

Advocacy is an essential part of counseling, and that importance is reinforced by the DRCCs, especially Section B (Chapin et al., 2018). Examples include B.4 Recognize and constructively confront misinformation and biases about PWDs when interacting with other professionals, students, supervisees, consumers, and the public, and B.5 Inform clients about their right to due process and mechanisms for reporting discrimination or unfair treatment. Advocacy is a call to action and a set of skills that must be learned. The DRCCs can help counselors by providing actionable guidelines to engage in advocacy in ways that are consistent with the CRCC (2017) *Code of Ethics*, including the need for advocacy competence and client consent. The decision to advocate is the client's choice, and a critical aspect of the DRCC standards is for counselors to listen to and be guided by PWDs and their recognized allies.

Allyship

As anyone who has genuine experience in long-term advocacy work knows, you need allies outside of your activist group to support your campaign for change. To become an ally for disability rights, counselors need to understand how the dominant culture has intentionally and unintentionally treated marginalized groups of individuals with disabilities as less capable. In a monograph dedicated to **allyship**, Scholz et al. (2021, p. 454) warned that allyship "is not a passive undertaking. Arguably, the first step involves awareness of the self in relation to those who are marginalized . . . It can be useful to identify a more experienced ally who can act as a mentor." Forber-Pratt et al. (2019) explained ways that allyship is demonstrated when rehabilitation providers embrace disability identity development and engagement with their clients. Targeting a broader audience, McCarthy (2021) discussed how all of us, whether helping professionals or laypersons, can become informed by engaging with the lived experience of PWDs and then contribute as allies to various causes promoting disability justice. Highlighting the importance of openness and shared communication, Ladau (2021, p. 3) wrote that "nondisabled and disabled people alike have more to learn about how to make the world . . . more inclusive. . . . If the disability community wants a world that's accessible, then we must make ideas and experiences of disability accessible to the world." To be truly effective and ethical in pursuing social justice or any of the other missions of rehabilitation counseling, it is essential to approach the process with humility and to do the work collaboratively. Most directly, this can be done by getting input and feedback from the least powerful stakeholders who are most affected. This approach is consistent with the phrase captured by Charlton (1998): "Nothing about us, without us" (p. 3). Another option for obtaining guidance on becoming a useful ally or team member is Standard E.17: Seek supervision or consultation to avoid abuse of privilege and power in the counselor–client relationship.

The five strategic A's presented in this section offer actionable steps to increase opportunities and full participation for PWDs in their community. This process involves proactive work by RCs to ensure spaces and activities are designed with disabilities in mind and implemented through collaborative work between RCs and PWDs. In all that we do as RCs, it is important to center the experiences of affected stakeholders by listening to and involving PWDs in the process from the start. This goal can be accomplished by inviting PWDs to (a) provide feedback on the physical and procedural accessibility of an organization, (b) share their experiences related to accommodations, and (c) facilitate collaborative advocacy efforts. These strategies not only validate disability as a natural part of life but can also improve the sense of empowerment PWDs experience throughout the counseling process. The five A's should serve as a mnemonic device to remind us of the major tasks of our roles and ethical duties as RCs. Now that you have read the explanations of the strategic A's, apply your understanding of them by completing the exercise described in Box 3.1.

TRADITIONAL MODELS OF HOW DISABILITY HAS BEEN PERCEIVED AND TREATED

This section explains four different models that describe how people have perceived disability from ancient times to the present day. The models in this section are presented in the order in which they emerged historically. They vary in their acceptability as useful conceptual frameworks. However, they all have some contemporary connection to the

BOX 3.1 REFLECTION ACTIVITY

FIVE STRATEGIC A's

Demonstrate your understanding of the five strategic A's (awareness, accessibility, accommodation, advocacy, allyship) by describing, for each of them, one specific way that you would try to implement that goal or strategy, in order to address a need in your school, job, or community.

experience of disability and the provision of rehabilitation services. Overall, these models represent the perspectives of the outsider or professional or scholar—looking as an unaffected observer at disability and its interfaces with the world. The main value of these **models of disability** is to examine critically how diverse perspectives on the origin and meaning of disability shape personal, professional, organizational, and societal responses to people who have, or are perceived to have, a disability. The reader should understand that the presentations of the various conceptual models are not meant as an evaluation of specific programs or services.

The Moral Model

The moral interpretation of disability is represented by a diverse accumulation of beliefs (whether explicitly expressed or unconsciously internalized), most of which are rooted in traditional thinking in some cultures and religions. The **moral model** views disability as a symbolic attribute of the person that demands an explanation. If the disability is perceived positively, then the individual is revered as blessed with special powers. For example, this was the case with certain people who were blind in ancient Greek and Roman civilizations, where it was deduced that because they could not see in the physical world, they were believed to have keen powers to "see" in the metaphysical realm. Therefore, they were brought into the inner sanctum of the emperor to serve as advisers and predictors of the future. Even today, it is not uncommon for people to believe that people who are blind inherently have alternate sensory powers rather than understanding that greater reliance on and increased practice using nonvisual cues can strengthen other sensory modalities. Much more frequently, disabilities were reacted to with fear, stigmatization, ostracism, or death by infanticide. Typically, it was assumed that the disability was an outward sign that evil had befallen the family or sin had been committed. In different cultures or circumstances, the person blamed was either the person bearing the disability, the mother or both parents, or some ancestor.

The moral model is no longer a common interpretation of disability as it was in past centuries. Indeed, such beliefs may seem so superstitious in today's scientific knowledge environment that they are considered nonexistent. But "primitive" beliefs can remain subliminally implanted in the depths of cultural consciousness and can result in imposition of stigma and shame, which are often internalized by people on whom such are imposed, however subtly. Some recent examples of these misconceptions include the perception that HIV, the virus that causes AIDS, emerged as punishment for "choosing the gay lifestyle" over heterosexuality and that people with biochemically based psychiatric disorders are "possessed by evil spirits." Psychiatric and behavioral conditions are more often stigmatized and considered the person's fault, compared to orthopedic and sensory disabilities. Perhaps the best descriptions of the contemporary (and more secular) version of this moral model are given in books by Susan Sontag (1978, 1989). She criticized some perspectives on disease and the metaphorical language used at that time in discussing its origins (especially cancer and the AIDS "plague"). Her discussions demonstrate how this metaphorical language reinforces the phenomenon of **blaming the victim** by shaming the character of those who acquire the disease. As an example, substance use traditionally has been viewed as a moral failing, and addicted individuals are shamed as "degenerates" for their behavior. This perspective misinterprets addiction as a weakness of character or will power. Accordingly, the treatment was often punitive or redemptive.

The Medical Model

The conceptual framework known as the **medical model** is arguably the most dominant and culturally infused of the models we will discuss. The medical model views disability as contained within the person as a result of an organic impairment in the body that is probed and prodded for diagnostic and treatment purposes. The role of the medical professional is to cure the disabling condition or reduce it to the closest approximation of "within normal limits." The person with a disability is expected to be compliant and unquestioning. On the macro level, the miracles of modern medicine have resulted in tremendous strides in saving lives, extending the life span, and increasing the level of residual function after the onset of a host of diseases, injuries, and congenital abnormalities. Overall, individuals with a significantly disabling condition are more likely to agree that they are physically better off due to medical science than they would be without its interventions. Psychosocially, however, the process of having a person single-mindedly focus on "fixing" something that is a permanent part of your identity and adapted lifestyle can have lasting and stigmatizing side effects. This phenomenon can be true regardless of how good the professional's intention is and how beneficial (functionally or cosmetically) the outcome is. Many people born with a disability that required extensive treatments feel that the medical improvement came to them at a high psychological price in terms of depleted sense of self-worth, a loss of dignity, and being treated as undesirable. For this reason, the medical model has also been called the "individual pathology" or "personal defect" model because it disparages disability, in both indirect and explicit ways, rather than seeing disability as part of the spectrum of human variation. Additional concerns about the negative impact of the dominance of the medical model on psychotherapeutic practices are summarized cogently and succinctly by Vash and Crewe (2004).

Another particularly problematic assumption of the medical model is that the credentialed expertise of the professional is more valid and important than the preferences, direct experience, and learned lessons of the PWD. This creates a tension between the *perspectives of the outsider versus the insider* (who personally experiences both the challenges and the growth opportunities from disability). Marshak and Seligman (1993) pp. 1–19 and Wright, 1983, 1988; Wright & Lopez, 2005) provide many explanations of undesirable effects of the discrepancies between these experiential worlds of insider consumers versus outsider providers. Despite better sensitivity training of healthcare professionals and more assertiveness among clients than in the past, their inherent differences in power (that get reinforced by the medical model) can distance professionals from understanding what is going on inside the client, cognitively and emotionally. Discrepancies in perceptions and priorities can affect the therapeutic process and outcome negatively, thus demanding that professionals engage in honest reflection and self-monitoring to address the resulting conflicts, which are often covert (Wright, 1987). For further critique and examples of the paradoxically negative impact of the helping professions, interested readers are referred to Schriner and Scotch (2001), Scotch (1988), and Szymanski and Trueba (1994).

The Labor-Market Economic or Vocational Model

The basic tenet of the **labor-market economic model** is that inability to work defines one as disabled. This tenet presents a conundrum, because many people who have a disability either are employed successfully or know that they are capable of working. Thus, there is no simple, direct relationship between disability and employability. This model's main strategy is to rely on primarily medical assessments to determine the existence, extent, and projected time span of a disability and its limiting impact on a person's functional capacity to perform work tasks. Thus, some scholars call it the **functional limitations model** or *vocational rehabilitation model*. Based on the data from the medical/vocational evaluation or functional capacity assessment, a person is determined to be fully or partially capable of working or defined as disabled and provided disability income to replace the lost or unrealized income from a job. Usually, if disability income is approved, so is government-subsidized health insurance (Medicare or Medicaid), because in the United States, most people obtain health insurance as a benefit of their job, although this has recently begun to change.

Despite the value of their intended purpose, some regulatory features of disability benefits programs have created problems. Two major ones are explained briefly. First, the system has developed too rigid a diagnostic dichotomy: one can versus cannot work. In reality, most human characteristics are differentiated more realistically along a continuum of capacities. It would have been wiser practice for disability determinations to be made by assessing *actual work performance* more validly and creatively. Such assessments might include samples of behavior when assistive devices, accommodating strategies, or work-site modifications were used that could eliminate or reduce the impact of the specific functional limitation(s) associated with the particular disability. Second, some PWDs have ongoing needs for medical treatments and/or personal attendant services that are provided by a single package of government-subsidized disability benefits. For such individuals, the system creates a difficult motivational dilemma called a *financial disincentive to work*. Many such beneficiaries are eager to work for a salary and give up the income portion of their government benefit, but they do not seek employment because they cannot afford to lose certain medical or long-term attendant services provided as disability benefits that would not be covered by any employer's health insurance plan.

The Ecological Model or Biopsychosocial Model

Comprised of domains of interdependent components, the **ecological model** is a multidimensional and more humanistic expansion of the medical model. Engel (1980) and others called it the **biopsychosocial (BPS) model** because they saw illness as a function of more than an impaired body (the biological component). They recognized the integral importance of additional factors that contributed to disease or dysfunction—and to its remediation. These included an array of individual psychological characteristics (e.g., feelings, preferences, beliefs, compliance behaviors), as well as various social factors. The latter can encompass variables ranging from the closely surrounding context to broad societal forces. An inherent characteristic of the BPS model is an appreciation that the various components are interconnected in ways that can change as the person develops and responds to new experiences. Thus, the model depicts a system of relevant variables that not only interact with but also mutually influence each other. Accordingly, *systems model* is another term used by some authors (e.g., Cottone, 1987) to refer to this framework. Although some authors in psychology (e.g., Bronfenbrenner, 1979; Moos, 1979) and rehabilitation counseling (e.g., Hershenson, 1998; Szymanski, 1998) have used the term *ecological* in their publication titles and explanations of this conceptual perspective, it is not yet a common descriptor in our field. Nonetheless, we prefer the label "ecological model" because it more clearly emphasizes the dynamic, interconnected web of influence of the components on each other and on the synthesized outcome.

Another reason why we prefer the more concise term *ecological* for this model is that it has continued to expand, as various authors argue for the specification of new components. Those who have added a *cultural* component and critique to the BPS model include Molina (1983), Jackson et al. (2003), and Hatala (2012). There is also a growing movement of scholars and practitioners who argue for incorporating the *spiritual* dimension of clients' lives and concerns in any holistic approach to counseling (Bruno, 1999; McCarthy, 1995, 2007; Mijares, 2014; Nosek & Hughes, 2001; Stebnicki, 2016; Vash, 1994). In 2009, the Association for Spiritual, Ethical, and Religious Values in Counseling developed and approved a list of spirituality competencies for counselors (www.counseling.org/knowledge-center/competencies). If these advancements were to become broadly accepted, we would then be using the elongated term, the *biopsychosocial-cultural-spiritual model*.

The ecological model is the most popular and pervasive in current clinical and research endeavors. A prime example of this point is the **International Classification of Functioning, Disability and Health (ICF**; World Health Organization, 2001; also see Peterson, 2016). ICF is the product of a global effort to devise a universal system for measuring the impact of disability on a person (the clinical application) and, more frequently, on a national or regional population (the public health research application). One notable quality of the ICF is that it conceptualizes the constructs of *disability* and *health* not as a dichotomy but as a continuum. Another is that it provides a multidimensional structure for categories of personal and environmental variables, each with multiple components and sublevels. However, a close examination of the substructure of this assessment tool does expose a definite preponderance of personal function and disability variables, compared to its identification of potentially influential environmental variables (McCarthy, 2014, pp. 4–5). For a more balanced application of the ICF and the ecological model, readers should review Millington (2016) excellent explanation of the paradigm of **community-based rehabilitation (CBR)** focused on enhancing the lives of PWDs within their support systems and communities.

UNCONVENTIONAL MODELS FOR UNDERSTANDING THE DISABILITY EXPERIENCE

This section explains six newer models, presented in historical order, that propose alternative interpretations and responses to the ideas and issues that disabilities present. The models in this section are changing how the disability experience is understood and appreciated. However, because they have emerged rather recently, the later ones have not benefited from as much time in the marketplace of ideas to be developed and discussed. In large measure, these models represent the perspectives of the insiders to the disability experience or innovative thinkers, as they look out at the world and its interface with disability and work to revise and optimize that relationship. Before describing these six innovative disability models, it is worth mentioning another conceptual framework, developed by disability studies scholars and called *critical disability theory* (CDT). Like critical pedagogy and critical race theory, CDT is another descendant of *critical theory*, a sociological school of research and thought that originated in the early 20th century in Germany and that focused on changing society through critiquing the conditions of its marginalized sectors. It took almost a century for CDT's development to emerge in English-speaking academia. Like the unconventional models of disability, CDT represents another variant in the expansion and refinement of ways of fathoming the personal experience and societal issues of disability, hopefully in ever more enlightened and equitable ways. In their CDT-based critique of the counseling profession, Emir Öksüz and Brubaker (2020, p. 165) built on the work of its original proponent; specifically, they explained: "Hosking (2008) outlined a framework for CDT as a means of systematic evaluation. . . .The seven elements of Hosking's framework include models of disability, multidimensionality, valuing diversity, rights, voices of disability, language, and transformative politics." The importance of each of these elements is acknowledged in this chapter, and the first element is critically examined by our deconstructing models of disability.

The Social Model

Perhaps the most dramatic shift in thinking about disability over the past 50 years is represented by the **social model** of disability. This viewpoint strongly opposes the medical model's narrow and oppressive definition of disability as a problem within the person and the consequent solution as correcting or changing the person with a disability. From the social model perspective, the problem is not paralyzed legs but environments, buildings, and transportation systems that are not accessible to wheelchairs. The problem is not the inability of a person to see, hear, or stand for extended periods of time. It is the discriminatory refusal of people in the workplace to allow PWDs to perform the job duties in an accommodated way and with the assistive devices that enable them.

At least as early as Barker (1948), there were scholarly propositions suggestive of the social model of disability, noting a "minority parallel" with regard to biased preconceptions of and unjust discrimination against PWDs similar to what happens from racism against ethnic groups. Thus, some scholars refer to this framework as the **minority model**. The term *social model* first appeared in a book by Oliver (1983), a British disability activist and scholar, and it has endured primarily through ongoing discourse within academia and professions concerned about disability issues. However, it was the **independent living (IL) movement** to promote community integration and inclusion, as well as the self-determination of individuals with disabilities in the United States, that became the public and powerful engine for implementing this paradigm shift in analyzing disability. The leaders of the IL movement demonstrated that they were not "confined to a wheelchair" (an erroneous phrase often used to describe people who actively use wheelchairs as their regular mode of mobility). Rather, they were confined by unnecessary physical barriers and social policies or expectations that kept them in the parental homes where they were raised or in the nursing homes where they were placed, secluded from mainstream life. Readers are strongly encouraged to learn about the IL movement and the movers and shakers who started and further fueled it. The most extensive source is the Oral Histories/ Archives project on Disability Rights and Independent Living Movement (www.bancroft.berkeley.edu/collections/drilm/index.html). Other informative and interesting accounts include Charlton (1998), Davis (2015), Fleischer and Zames (2011), McCarthy (2003), McMahon and Shaw (2000), and Pelka (2012). Inspired by the wave of civil rights movements in the 1960s and 1970s by African American, feminist, and gay activists, early disability rights self-advocates forged their own personal liberation and public policy agendas and successes. Accordingly, we believe a clearer descriptor for the perspective known as the social model is the **self-determination philosophy** of the IL movement or the **civil rights model** of disability. Others choose to highlight the social power dynamics of this model and call it the politics of disability (e.g., Hahn, 1985; Stubbins, 1988) or the **sociopolitical model** (e.g., Smart & Smart, 2006).

To capture the impact that the unconventional models are having on our thinking about disability—from its psychosocial meaning to its pragmatic management—let's consider the concept of independence. It is perhaps the most common goal believed to represent "successful adaptation" to disability. The **Functional Independence Measurement (FIM) system** is a clinical and research tool most used to assess the current functioning of patients with physical disabilities in hospital rehabilitation programs (Uniform Data System for Medical Rehabilitation, 1997; www.rehabmeasures.org/lists/rehabmeasures/dispform .aspx?id=889). This tool is grounded in the medical model because it was designed to record therapeutic progress and to justify requests to health insurers to pay for further treatments in the program by nurses and allied health therapists, who are the professionals designated to complete the FIM form. It measures how independently a PWD can perform ADLs such as bathing, dressing, toileting, talking, and walking. The rating scale for each activity ranges from 1 (*total assistance*) to 7 (*complete independence*). The instructions for assigning someone a score of 7 read: "All of the tasks making up the activity are typically performed safely, without modification, assistive devices, or aids, and within a reasonable amount of time; no helper required." By this criterion, most PWDs would never reach a score of independence, so they remain perceived and labeled as dependent. In contrast to the stringent, ableist FIM criteria is the broad concept of independence as defined by the social model and expressed by PWDs who endorse the philosophy of the IL movement: "independence . . . does not imply being able to survive without the help of other people or assistive devices; it simply means *freedom of decision making and the power of self-determination*" (Vash & Crewe, 2004, p. 46). As an example, consider people with high-level quadriplegia (i.e., lacking neuromuscular control of all four limbs). The FIM system would categorize them as having "complete dependence" because they require "total assistance" (i.e., help from assistive devices or an aide to perform ADLs). However, if they embrace the ideology of the social model, the same people would define themselves (and should be understood by others) as independent, once they obtain the supervisory skills and financial ability to hire and manage their personal assistants. They claim independence when they are in control of the people and equipment that they use to accomplish their ADLs, go where they want, and do what they choose—how and when they desire. Their chosen path to independence requires social and cognitive skills, not physical ones. These include learning how to secure and supervise reliable caregivers; mastering the complicated regulations so that they can satisfy the eligibility criteria and obtain support services from the disability benefits system, advocating for health policies and work incentives that will provide the funds to pay for the extra costs of these services, or cultivating a support system that will assist you either with the ADLs or with recruiting and managing personal assistants.

The Disability Pride and Culture Model

An often-unacknowledged alternative in this collection of conceptual frameworks is the **disability pride and culture model**. There are lots of similarities in the perspectives of those who embrace this model and those who assert the social or civil rights model. Differences are primarily in (a) how and when the models developed historically and (b) their chosen emphases. At the risk of reducing the contrasts to a few phrases, one could say that the construct of **disability culture** emerged from ideological, psychological, and sociological discourse in academia and the arts, starting around 1990. Significant references and resources on disability culture include Brown (2003), Linton (1998), and Riddell and Watson (2003). By comparison, the rights model grew out of political engagement and "in the streets" activism for pragmatic changes in social policy and community access, starting in the 1960s with the IL movement. Perusing the following two selected websites will also help readers grasp the commonalities and differences between disability culture organizations (e.g., www.instituteondisabilityculture.org) and disability rights organizations (e.g., www.adapt.org). The academic discipline of **disability studies** and its flagship organization, the Society for Disability Studies (www.disstudies.org), are the main engines of scholarship and mentoring that have successfully promoted both of these models of disability. Unfortunately, outside of the realms of disability studies and the insider-perspective scholarship of the activist disability community, there has been far too little inclusion of disability as a cultural identity and marginalized status, within the publications and programs of counselor education, multiculturalism, and social justice (e.g., see Connor, 2012; Rivas, 2020).

Gill (1997) and Forber-Pratt and Zape (2017) have summarized much of the relevant research within the behavioral sciences that has focused on individual development of disability identity, and they proposed their own stage-based theories thereof. Bogart (2015) reported that level of disability identity predicted positive mental health effects. **Disability pride** is hypothesized to be one component of **disability identity** and to consist of four affective–cognitive elements (Putnam, 2005). These are (a) "claiming" disability (a term that contrasts with the typical therapeutic goal of "accepting" one's disability); (b) seeing impairments as a natural part of the human condition; (c) believing disability is not inherently negative, although it is frequently interpreted so; and (d) experiencing disability as creating the consciousness of a cultural minority group. She says feelings of disability pride "run counter to social and cultural beliefs that disability is tragedy and that persons with physical or mental disabilities would rather not be who they are" (Putnam, 2005, p. 191). Actually, there are three distinguishable subpopulations of the disability pride model that share fundamental commonalities but usually operate within their own networks. One group is composed primarily of people with obvious physical disabilities. For them, wheelchair access and accommodations for blindness have been major issues; assertive personalities and communication skills have been their notable strengths. This group is predominant among the trailblazers and current participants in the IL movement and adapted competitive sports, such as the Paralympics. There are several publications that reflect this community's perspectives and agendas. Prominent among them is the monthly magazine, *New Mobility*, that publishes interesting, provocative, and pragmatic articles.

A second group whose identity is rooted in disability pride is the **Deaf culture**, made up of people whose primary language is ASL. (Note that *deaf* is the common adjective and diagnostic label for persons with a significant hearing impairment, whereas *Deaf*, with a capital "D," refers to the subgroup of that population who psychosocially self-identify with that culture.) They view deafness as a communication difference that engenders group cohesiveness, not a deficit to be corrected. Because their condition typically is not apparent initially, this population does not have the annoying experience of immediate reactions of being avoided, stared at, or given unwanted help that many people with visible physical disabilities have to handle. Instead, they experience significant isolation from mainstream culture because ability to communicate fluently in ASL among the hearing population is very rare.

People with chronic mental illness or past psychiatric histories comprise a third group demonstrating disability pride. Typically, they do not encounter the physical or communication barriers just described. However, they bear the persistent brunt of the deepest discrimination from the general population, in the form of social stigma, fearful rejection, and unreasonable or cruel treatment, even in allegedly therapeutic institutions. Schrader et al. (2013) explained the evolution in this community's self-advocacy priorities to promote a broader culture of madness that "emphasized the connections between madness and art, theater, spirituality, and a valuable sensitivity to individual and collective pain . . . supports interventions that target the social exclusion, poverty, trauma, and grief that contribute to distress and block positive adaptation" (pp. 62–63).

The Interdependence or Social-Capital Model

Rugged individualism and personal autonomy are strongly ingrained in American mythology and cultural socialization. This embrace of individual independence is so powerful that even concepts or approaches that promote interdependent relationships are sometimes described as un-American. A current example of this is the ideological conflict between personal freedom versus community safety regarding COVID-19 vaccinations and wearing masks indoors to protect public health during a deadly pandemic. This "survival of the fittest" form of ableism is most likely to hinder and harm PWDs and other marginalized communities. Disability activists and scholars (e.g., Wendell, 1997) have explained how a culture that reinforces interdependence would greatly improve the lives of PWDs. Nonetheless, much of the work of (re)habilitation disciplines has focused on the goal of a*chieving independence*, albeit with reference to *community participation* or *social inclusion* as one ultimate index of that goal. A few scholars in disability and rehabilitation studies have critiqued this focus on independence, and instead argued the goal should be to strengthen skills and values of interdependence for everyone's benefit. We believe the work of these scholar-advocates should be recognized as the **interdependence model**.

Condeluci (1995) centered interdependence as the essential conceptual framework and strategic goal for improving the quality of life of PWDs. He proposed supplementing the core services of independent living programs with enhancements that he called the four *interdependent* services that programs serving PWDs should provide. These educational services target (a) *role competency* (practice in being a friend, neighbor, consumer, and citizen), (b) *control of supplemental supports* (learning to manage services one needs, such as from an ASL interpreter, rather than having it controlled by an agency case manager), (c) *relationship building* (developing connections that integrate once-devalued people into their communities), and (d) *creating cultural change* (advocating for causes that would improve community life for PWDs). White et al. (2010) likewise strongly recommended expansion of the independent living paradigm and programs by adding services to strengthen consumers' interdependence. They argued that when people can "freely choose their arenas for community participation, including education, employment, recreation, and civic engagement . . . people with disabilities will no longer be mere occupants in *the* community—rather they will be vital contributors to *their* communities" (p. 238).

In addition to elevating interdependence, Condeluci's research with colleagues adopted the closely related construct, **social capital**, that has a well-developed history in sociological research on social determinants of physical, emotional, and vocational well-being. Discourse on social capital was popularized by the scholarship of Putnam (2000), who defined it as "connections among individuals—social networks and the norms of reciprocity and trustworthiness that arise from them" (p. 19). Condeluci et al. (2008) asserted that: "relationships, friendships and the associated 'habits of the heart' . . . are the building blocks for not only social capital, but also for the primary goals associated with rehabilitation: working, living and engaging in community." Subcomponents of the concept of social capital include social support systems, degree of social trust, diversity of friendships, informal socializing, and civic participation.

Because PWDs traditionally have experienced more isolation and less social appreciation, Dimakos et al. (2016) argued that this conceptual approach is especially important for problem-solving issues of community access and inclusion. Proponents of this model utiliize counseling interventions to support PWDs to not only increase their social capital but also critique the restrictiveness of many community resources. In this way, the model is similar to the ecological model in that it provides a framework for exploring barriers and resources at both the personal and community levels, as well as their interactive processes and effects.

The Disability Justice Model

Social justice has emerged as an umbrella term to refer to a spectrum of aspirations and activities to redress inequities experienced by marginalized sectors of society. Prominent examples of campaigns by such groups that are raising awareness and organizing actions to promote equity include: *racial justice* for those who identify as BIPOC; *environmental justice* to achieve equitable distribution of the socio-economic benefits and environmental consequences of manufacturing and other commercial activity; and *LGBTQ+ justice* for people who are gender-fluid or gender-nonconforming in their identity or behavior. Similar to these other movements, **disability justice** (DJ) is focused on removing systemic barriers to the realization of human rights, social inclusion, and self-determination of PWDs by their community. The DJ movement is dedicated to uplifting and amplifying the voice and experience of those most marginalized, within society and the disability community itself (Piepzna-Samarasinha, 2018). The disability justice model is the conceptual lens through which disabled activists examine the cumulative effects of ableism, sexism, classism, and other forms of oppression on the disability experience (Berne et al., 2018). Such a dynamic perspective regarding multiple aspects of a person's identities, their interaction, and the impact on how a person is perceived and treated is known as **intersectionality**. Coined by Crenshaw (1991), this term was used originally to describe the experience of Black womanhood. Being Black and being female are separate aspects of identity, but she argued that neither can be considered in isolation. A succinct argument for an intersectional analysis of ableism is presented in a book by a group of disabled activists and artists called Sins Invalid (2019, p. 18): "A single-issue civil rights framework is not enough to explain the full extent of ableism and how it operates in society. We can only truly understand ableism by tracing its connections to hetero-patriarchy, white supremacy, colonialism, and capitalism." In addition to its theoretical discourse, this book provides a glossary, milestones in the DJ movement, and practical information on diverse topics.

A repeated rallying cry of the DJ movement is a commitment to cross-disability and cross-movement solidarity for collective liberation with a vision of beauty and inclusion for all bodies and minds. Briefly, we'll mention three relevant and varied resources. Project LETS (Let's Erase The Stigma; https://projectlets.org/mission) is a national network of mutual-aid support systems, composed of folks with diverse experiences of disability, trauma and mental health. Among other services, this network creates alternatives to their peers' being jailed or institutionalized due to a mismanaged crisis episode. *Care Work: Dreaming Disability Justice* by Piepzna-Samarasinha (2018) is a thought-provoking compilation of critical analyses and liberating strategies that many DJ activists, allies, and scholars would benefit from reading. Taking an historical perspective of disability movements up through contemporary DJ groups, McCarthy (2021) showcased numerous organizations and resources that are making an impressive impact in reducing disability disparities and empowering their community.

The Technology Model

Technology's impact on PWDs has been substantial, ranging from lifesaving to lifestyle-expanding. The philosophical questions and engineering opportunities within the human–technology interface can get even more intriguing when disability is added to the mix of relevant factors. The practical aspects of this interface have a very respected evidence base in the innovative research and product development conducted in the fields of assistive technology (e.g., Lenker & Paquet, 2003) and rehabilitation engineering (see www.resna.org). In an unpublished presentation, Daniels (2009) contrasted three paradigms for understanding disability that she labeled as (a) *individual defect*, (b) *human rights*, and (c) *eco-tech* models. The first two were her renditions of the medical model and social model, respectively. The third could be considered an alternative version of the ecological model, but it was delineated so distinctively around technology to warrant designation and explanation as its own **technology model** of disability. She presented her comparisons cogently and succinctly by posing and answering the following *model-defining questions*. Because the other two models have already been discussed, only her abbreviated answers to the defining questions for the eco-tech model are given (in parentheses) to explain the main ideas and implications of the technology model.

- *Where is the problem?* (the interface between individuals and the environment)
- *What is the source of the problem?* (a lack of fit between the variation in human capabilities and the requirements in the environment)
- *How is the solution defined?* (odification of the interface to achieve a better fit)
- *What solution strategies are used?* (improvements in technology, integrated delivery systems, knowledge transfer, market research, and systems design)
- *How does society benefit?* (more effective and efficient performance; more individual choice and control)
- *Who are the experts?* (engineers, technologists, designers, manufacturers, users)
- *What are the consequences for the individual?* (identification with the engineer role; motivation to create high-performance scenarios)

Daniels's brief answers to the last defining question highlight the psychologically divergent impacts for people with disabilities that the different conceptual models would generate. For the individual-defect model, she listed these disempowering consequences: internalization of a deviant role, acceptance of inferior status, and endless effort to overcome in order to be socially acceptable. In sharp contrast, application of the eco-tech model leaves PWDs feeling energized and liberated. In particular, it is noteworthy that Daniels listed users as one of the experts in her delineation of this model. The work of Bennett et al. (2018) on assistive technology (AT) strongly endorses this point. Specifically, they argued (and illustrated through several case studies) that (a) AT design and use are necessarily collaborative processes and (b) more openly appreciating the often-understated roles and contributions of PWDs would improve AT design and utilization. Their work is influenced by their disability-affirmative awareness that sensitizes practitioners and researchers not to perpetuate implicit devaluation of their partners with a disability. For example, they wrote that "since interdependence considers everyone mutually reliant, it asserts that people with and without disabilities are equal . . . regardless of whether they are assisting, being assisted, or doing both" (p. 165). Indeed, if we reflect honestly and deeply, we will recognize that we are all interdependent, but as Ki'tay Davidson (quoted in Bennett et al., 2018, p. 161) explained: "The difference between the needs that many disabled people have and the needs of people who are not labeled as disabled is that non-disabled people have had their dependencies normalized."

The topic of technology related to PWDs is discussed more fully in Chapter 21. Nonetheless, to reinforce concepts presented in this chapter, we will summarize one example of a well-developed application of the technology model. The website for the Matching Person and Technology (MPT) Assessment Process (www.matchingpersonan dtechnology.com/index.html) provides a wealth of information on this approach, its various tools, and published evaluation research. MPT has a definite mission to collaborate with the user in all phases of the processes of assessment, selection, training, and adoption of AT. Due attention is given to psychological, physical, and technical factors of potential influence (Scherer & Craddock, 2002). For example, MPT measures attitudinal and physical characteristics of the multifaceted environment where the technology will be used, as well as personal preferences and capacities of the user. Another strength of this resource is its diversity of applications to (a) the needs of consumers with either physical or mental disabilities and (b) different performance domains, such as education, employment, and independent living (Kirsch & Scherer, 2009).

The Consumer-Economic Model

Perceiving PWDs as a growing market niche heretofore disregarded or unimagined by the retail industry is the premise of the **consumer-economic model**. This is a perspective that has not been discussed in the counseling or rehabilitation literature. To date, this model almost exclusively has appeared in the media of a sector of the disability community. One good, brief explanation is provided in a blog posted (January 16, 2012) on the Audio Accessibility website (www.audioaccessibility.com/news/2012/01/economic-model-of -disability). Rather than starting with a focus on reducing the disadvantages of perceiving disability as a medical problem or functional deficit or stigmatized status deserving of legislative protection from unjust treatment, this perspective begins with positive expectations about PWDs. It positions these individuals as typical, active adults: consumers in search of better products, having money to spend, wanting to go on vacation, and bringing along their friends and family. Furthermore, it openly acknowledges that by effectively responding to the purchase desires and consumer needs of PWDs, business and industry also benefit. This is true not only in terms of their increased revenue but also in terms of their learning ways of becoming a more inclusive and responsive business in a diverse and assertive consumer population. In contrast, the mission of traditional human service organizations is assumed and expressed to be serving the good of the client only. Indeed, this belief is enshrined in the primary ethical principle of **beneficence** (i.e., to do good) that counselors and other helping professionals are obligated to follow. Certainly, service organizations provide benefits to many clients on a daily basis. However, these helping organizations and the practitioners who staff them also gain advantages from their professional work—financial, psychological, and social advantages. Interested readers are referred to Szymanski et al. (2012) pp. 375–381 for a thought-provoking presentation on this dilemma of the formal, bureaucratic relationship between professionals and clients in the "business of disability."

BOX 3.2 LEARNING ACTIVITY

Review the section on the technology model and the set of questions that Daniels (2009) posed and answered to describe that model. Choose one of the other models of disability presented and answer each of the eight questions with respect to your chosen model.

The expressed goal of the consumer-economic model is to create an inclusive culture through appealing to the growing population of PWDs and their loved ones as a competitive advantage in the marketplace. The proponents of this perspective rely on the principles of universal design, economic integration through market forces, and facilitated participation in all domains of living as the strategies for achieving social inclusion. People with disabilities are targeted as one of the groups of humanity to be included; therefore, they should be cultivated as desired consumers. Although its conceptual framework and mission are broader, this model to date has been applied primarily to the tourism and recreation business. Proponents of this model distinguish their positive and productive marketing approach from the punitive and disengaging enforcement strategy of the civil-rights model of disability. For example, they argue: "The shortcoming of the social model is that change has been driven as compliance . . . a cost that society demands of a business. . . . At that point it . . . just becomes another problem for organizations . . . and is handed to their risk management departments" (Travability, 2011, pp. 3–4). In contrast, the consumer-economic model encourages the disability community to promote itself as an eager win-win partner, and it has begun to gain more attention and understanding from the corporate sector. Whereas once the voices and interests of PWDs were restricted to small-scale publications or organizations dedicated specifically to expressing their message or advancing their agendas, they are now beginning to be recognized in the mainstream media and marketplace (Rucker, 2016). As the disability community becomes more appreciated by corporations, it is crucial that they not treat this population sector of PWDs as a homogeneous entity. It is a diverse population, with many intragroup differences in priorities and preferences. You have just absorbed a large amount of material that explains the many ways that disability has been conceptualized, debated, and deconstructed over time, by those with a professional interest in the lives of PWDs, as well as by the general public. To help you apply and reinforce an example of that learning, complete the exercise explained in Box 3.2. When you have finished that activity and are ready to engage in an analytic review of salient concepts from the entire chapter, do the reflective exercise described in Box 3.3.

CONCLUSION

This chapter delineated the value-based orientations of the rehabilitation counseling process. It also presented a diversity of conceptual frameworks that have shaped the complex context of societal expectations and structures within which RCs and PWDs work together. Part of the complexity was highlighted in the contrast between traditional and

BOX 3.3 LEARNING ACTIVITY

Prepare an essay or outline for a class discussion that identifies three concepts or points presented in the chapter that you find (a) *easy to embrace* and three concepts/ points that you (b) *do not agree with or do not understand*. Explain your reasons for your response to each of the six items you selected.

unconventional models for understanding disability on both personal and societal levels. Being an effective and empathic counselor for diverse clientele, including PWDs, within rehabilitation or any other specialty, is an ongoing, relational process. Publications by authors who write cogently from their perspectives as insiders to the disability experience are especially useful for the nondisabled community's understanding of and relations with PWDs. Three particularly engaging resources on this topic are Klimitas (2011), Ladau (2021), and the work of Olkin (1999), whose article (Olkin, 2016, p. 222) succinctly advised professionals thus: "as most therapists cannot become truly culturally competent in disability, they need to be culturally aware, informed, and receptive." Schrader et al. (2013) recommended that human service professionals: "suspend their assumptions about . . . clients' experiences (i.e., assumptions of disease, distress, and impairment)" in order to engage with clients in "deeper explorations of the desirable but neglected aspects of clients' experiences and personhood to facilitate individualized processes of meaning-making" (p. 63). That quote is an inviting message with which to conclude our discussion of these conceptual models of the varied ways that disability has been interpreted and managed by society, too often to the disregard and detriment of experienced insiders. Although the authors were speaking specifically about psychiatric survivors, the advice is an apt caveat for all counselors working with people who have any unusual differences and stigmatized characteristics. We encourage you to continue exploring the yin and yang of theory and practice, questioning and applying conceptual models and direct experience to guide your mutual learning and collaborative work with PWDs and colleagues, now and in the future. We welcome your feedback, suggestions, and constructive critiques.

CONTENT REVIEW QUESTIONS

1. What are the core values discussed in the chapter that reflect the cumulative work of Wright and several other thought leaders of our profession?
2. What are the five strategic A's presented in this chapter, and how can they be used to offer actionable steps to increase opportunities and full participation for PWDs in their community?
3. What are the four traditional models of disability that describe how people have perceived disability from ancient times to the present day?
4. What are six newer models of disability that propose alternative interpretations and responses to the ideas and issues that disabilities present?

REFERENCES

Atkins, B. (1988). An asset-oriented approach to cross-cultural issues: Blacks in rehabilitation. *Journal of Applied Rehabilitation Counseling*, 19(4), 45–49. https://doi.org/10.1891/0047-2220.19.4.45

Barker, R. G. (1948). The social psychology of physical disability. *Journal of Social Issues*, 4(4), 28–35. https://doi.org/10.1111/j.1540-4560.1948.tb01516.x

Bennett, C. L., Brady, E., & Branham, S. M. (2018). Interdependence as a frame for assistive technology research and design, Conference session 4. *ASSETS '18: Proceedings of the 20th International ACM SIGACCESS Conference on Computers and Accessibility*. https://doi.org/10.1145/3234695.3236348

Berne, P., Morales, A. L., Langstaff, D., & Invalid, S. (2018). Ten principles of disability justice. *WSQ: Women's Studies Quarterly*, 46(1–2), 227–230. https://doi.org/10.1353/wsq.2018.0003

Bishop, M., Chapin, M. H., & Miller, S. (2008). Quality of life assessment in the measurement of rehabilitation outcome. *Journal of Rehabilitation*, 74(2), 45–55.

Bogart, K. R. (2015). Disability identity predicts lower anxiety and depression in multiple sclerosis. *Rehabilitation Psychology*, 60(1), 105–109. https://doi.org/10.1037/rep0000029

Bronfenbrenner, U. (1979). *The ecology of human development: Experiments by nature and design.* Harvard University Press.

Brown, S. E. (2003). *Movie stars and sensuous scars: Essays on the journey from disability shame to disability pride.* iUniverse, Inc.

Bruno, R. (1999). Buddhism plus disability: One "step" closer to Nirvana. *New Mobility, 10*, 32–37. http://www.angelfire.com/electronic/awakening101/ada-buddhism.html

Chan, F., Tarvydas, V., Blalock, K., Strauser, D., & Atkins, B. J. (2009). Unifying and elevating rehabilitation counseling through model-driven, diversity-sensitive evidence-based practice. *Rehabilitation Counseling Bulletin, 52*(2), 114–119. https://doi.org/10.1177/0034355208323947

Chapin, M., McCarthy, H., Shaw, L., Bradham-Cousar, M., Chapman, R., Nosek, M., Peterson, S., Yilmaz, Z., & Ysasi, N. (2018). *Disability-related counseling competencies.* ARCA. https://www.counseling.org/docs/default-source/competencies/arca-disability-related-counseling-competencies-final-version-5-15-19.pdf?sfvrsn=c376562c_6

Charlton, J.. (1998). *Nothing about us without us: Disability oppression and empowerment.* University of California Press. https://doi.org/10.1525/9780520925441

Chou, C. C., Chan, F., Chan, J. Y. C., Phillips, B., Ditchman, N., & Kaseroff, A. (2013). Positive psychology theory, research, and practice. *Rehabilitation Research, Policy, and Education, 27*(3), 131–153.

Commission on Rehabilitation Counselor Certification. (2017). *Code of professional ethics for rehabilitation counselors.* https://crccertification.com/wp-content/uploads/2021/03/CRC_CodeEthics_Eff2017-FinaLnewdiesign.pdf

Condeluci, A. (1995). *Interdependence: The route to community.* GR Press, Inc.

Condeluci, A., Ledbetter, M. G., Ortman, D., Fromknecht, J., & DeFries, M. (2008). Social capital: A view from the field [Editorial]. *Journal of Vocational Rehabilitation, 29*(3), 133–139.

Connor, D. (2012). Does disability now sit at the table(s) of social justice and multicultural education? *Disability Studies Quarterly, 32.* https://doi.org/10.18061/dsq.v32i3.1770

Cottone, R. R. (1987). A systemic theory of vocational rehabilitation. *Rehabilitation Counseling Bulletin, 30*, 167–176.

Crenshaw, K. (1991). Mapping the margins: Intersectionality, identity politics, and violence against women of color. *Stanford Law Review, 43*(6), 1241–1299. https://doi.org/10.2307/1229039

Daniels, S. (2009). *Paradigms of disability. Workshop presented at the Louisiana.* State University Health Sciences Center, Department of Rehabilitation Counseling.

Davis, L. J. (2015). *Enabling acts.* Beacon Press.

Dimakos, C., Kamenetsky, S. B., Condeluci, A., Curran, J., Flaherty, P., Fromknecht, J., Howard, M., & Williams, J. (2016). Somewhere to live, something to do, someone to love: Examining levels and sources of social capital among people with disabilities. *Canadian Journal of Disability Studies, 5*(4), 130, 18. https://doi.org/10.15353/cjds.v5i4.317

Dunn, D. (2015). *The social psychology of disability.* Oxford University Press.

Emir Öksüz, E., & Brubaker, M. D. (2020). Deconstructing disability training in counseling: A critical examination and call to the profession. *Journal of Counselor Leadership and Advocacy, 7*(2), 163–175. https://doi.org/10.1080/2326716X.2020.1820407

Engel, G. L. (1980). The clinical application of the biopsychosocial model. *The American Journal of Psychiatry, 137*(5), 535–544. https://doi.org/10.1176/ajp.137.5.535

Fleischer, D., & Zames, F. (2011). *The disability rights movement.* Temple University Press.

Forber-Pratt, A. J., Mueller, C. O., & Andrews, E. E. (2019). Disability identity and allyship in rehabilitation psychology. *Rehabilitation Psychology, 64*(2), 119–129. https://doi.org/10.1037/rep0000256

Forber-Pratt, A. J., & Zape, M. P. (2017). Disability identity development model: Voices from the ADA-generation. *Disability and Health Journal, 10*(2), 350–355. https://doi.org/10.1016/j.dhjo.2016.12.013

Galassi, J. P., & Akos, P. (2007). *Strengths-based school counseling: Promoting student development and achievement.* Lawrence Erlbaum.

Gill, C. J. (1997). Four types of integration in disability identity development. *Journal of Vocational Rehabilitation, 9*(1), 39–46. https://doi.org/10.3233/JVR-1997-9106

Groomes, D., & Olsheski, J. (2002). Continued exploration of the psychosocial adaptation to disability research frontier. *Rehabilitation Education, 16*(2), 213–226.

Hahn, H. (1985). Toward a politics of disability. *Social Science Journal, 22*(4), 87–105.

Hahn, H. (1993). The political implications of disability definitions and data. *Journal of Disability Policy Studies*, 4(2), 41–52. https://doi.org/10.1177/104420739300400203

Harley, D. A., Alston, R. J., & Middleton, R. A. (2007). Infusing social justice into rehabilitation education. *Rehabilitation Education*, 21(1), 41–52.

Hartley, M. T. (2011). Examining the relationships between resilience, mental health, and academic persistence in undergraduate college students. *Journal of American College Health*, 59(7), 596–604. https://doi.org/10.1080/07448481.2010.515632

Hatala, A. R. (2012). The status of the "biopsychosocial" model in health psychology: Towards an integrated approach and a critique of cultural conceptions. *Open Journal of Medical Psychology*, 01(4), 51–62. https://doi.org/10.4236/ojmp.2012.14009

Hershenson, D. (1998). Systemic, ecological model for rehabilitation counseling. *Rehabilitation Counseling Bulletin*, 42(1), 40–50.

Hershenson, D. (2015). The individual plan for retirement: A missing part of plan development with older consumers. *Rehabilitation Counseling Bulletin*, 59(1), 9–17.

Hosking, D. L. (2008). Critical disability theory. In *Conference presentation]. 4th Biennial Disability Studies Conference*. Lancaster University.

Iwarsson, S., & Ståhl, A. (2003). Accessibility, usability and universal design--positioning and definition of concepts describing person-environment relationships. *Disability and Rehabilitation*, 25(2), 57–66. https://doi.org/10.1080/dre.25.2.57.66

Jackson, J. S., Antonucci, T. C., & Brown, E. (2003). A cultural lens on biopsychosocial models of aging. In P. Costa & I. Siegler (Eds.), *Recent advances in psychology and aging* (pp. 221–241). JAI Press.

Kirsch, N. L., & Scherer, M. J. (2009). Assistive technology for cognition and behavior. In R. G. Frank, M. Rosenthal, & B. Caplan (Eds.), *Handbook of rehabilitation psychology* (2nd ed., pp. 273–284). American Psychological Association. https://doi.org/10.1037/15972-000

Kiselica, M., & Robinson, M. (2001). Bringing advocacy counseling to life. *Journal of Counseling and Development*, 79(4), 387–397.

Klimitas, K. (2011). *Looking up*. Arthur Hardy Publishing.

Ladau, E. (2021). *Demystifying disability: What to know, what to say, and how to be an ally*. Ten Speed Press.

Lenker, J. A., & Paquet, V. L. (2003). A review of conceptual models for assistive technology outcomes research and practice. *Assistive Technology*, 15(1), 1–15. https://doi.org/10.1080/10400435.2003.10131885

Lewin, K., Heider, F., & Heider, G. M. (1936). *Principles of topological psychology*. McGraw-Hill.

Lewis, T. (2021, January 1). *Working definition of ableism*. https://www.talilalewis.com/blog/january-2021-working-definition-of-ableism

Linton, S. (1998). *Claiming disability*. New York University Press.

Livneh, H. (2016). Quality of life and coping with chronic illness and disability: A temporal perspective. *Rehabilitation Counseling Bulletin*, 59(2), 67–83. https://doi.org/10.1177/0034355215575180

Livneh, H., Bishop, M., & Anctil, T.. (2014). Modern models of psychosocial adaptation to chronic illness and disability as viewed through the prism of Lewin's field theory: A comparative review. *Rehabilitation Research, Policy, and Education*, 28(3), 126–142. https://doi.org/10.1891/2168-6653.28.3.126

Lofquist, L. H., & Dawis, R. V. (1969). *Adjustment to work: A psychological view of man's problems in A work-oriented society*. Appleton-Century-Crofts.

Lofquist, L. H., & Dawis, R. V. (1991). *Essentials of person-environment-correspondence counseling*. University of Minnesota Press.

Marshak, L. E., & Seligman, M. (1993). *Counseling persons with physical disabilities: Theoretical and clinical perspectives*. Pro-Ed.

Masten, A. S., Best, K. M., & Garmezy, N. (1990). Resilience and development. *Development and Psychopathology*, 2, 425–444.

McCarthy, H. (1995). Understanding and reversing rehabilitation counseling's neglect of spirituality. *Rehabilitation Education*, 9(2–3), 187–199.

McCarthy, H. (2003). The disability rights movement: Experiences and perspectives of selected leaders in the disability community. *Rehabilitation Counseling Bulletin*, 46(4), 209–223.

McCarthy, H. (2007). Incorporating spirituality into rehabilitation counseling and coping with disability. In O. Morgan (Ed.), *Counseling and spirituality: Views from the profession* (pp. 202–229). Lahaska Press, Houghton Mifflin.

McCarthy, H. (2011). A modest Festschrift and insider perspective on Beatrice Wright's contributions to rehabilitation theory and practice. *Rehabilitation Counseling Bulletin, 54*(2), 67–81. https://doi .org/10.1177/0034355210386971

McCarthy, H. (2014). Cultivating our roots and extending our branches: Appreciating and marketing rehabilitation theory and research. *Rehabilitation Counseling Bulletin, 57*(2), 67–79.

McCarthy, H. (2021). Self-advocacy and ally-advocacy for disability justice. *Disability, CBR & Inclusive Development, 32*(2), 160–178.

McMahon, B. T., & Shaw, L. (2000). *Enabling lives: Biographies of six prominent Americans with disabilities.* CRC Press.

Mijares, S. G. (2014). *Modern psychology and ancient wisdom: Psychological healing practices from the world's religious traditions* (2nd ed.). Routledge, Taylor & Francis. https://doi.org/10.4324/ 9781315808925

Millington, M. J. (2016). Community-based rehabilitation: Context for counseling. In I. Marini & M. Stebnicki (Eds.), *The professional counselor's desk reference* (pp. 111–116). Springer.

Molina, J. A. (1983). Understanding the biopsychosocial model. *International Journal of Psychiatry in Medicine, 13*(1), 29–36. https://doi.org/10.2190/0uhq-bxne-6ggy-n1tf

Moos, R. H. (1974). *Evaluating treatment environments.* Wiley-Interscience.

Moos, R. H. (1979). Social–ecological perspectives on health. In G. C. Stone, F. Cohen, & N. E. Adler (Eds.), *Health psychology: A handbook* (pp. 259–275). Jossey-Bass.

Myers, J. E., & Sweeney, T. J. (2008). Wellness counseling: The evidence base for practice. *Journal of Counseling & Development, 86*(4), 482–493. https://doi.org/10.1002/j.1556-6678.2008.tb00536.x

Myers, J. E., Sweeney, T. J., & Witmer, J. M. (2000). The wheel of wellness, counseling for wellness. *Journal of Counseling and Development, 78*(3), 251–266.

Nosek, M., & Hughes, R. (2001). Psychospiritual aspects of sense of self in women with physical disabilities. *Journal of Rehabilitation, 67*(1), 20–25.

Null, R. L. (2014). *Universal design: Principles and models.* CRC Press.

Oliver, M. (1983). Social work with disabled people. https://doi.org/10.1007/978-1-349-86058-6

Olkin, R. (1999). *What psychotherapists should know about disability.* Guilford.

Olkin, R. (2016). Disability-affirmative therapy. In I. Marini & M. Stebnicki (Eds.), *The professional counselor's desk reference* (pp. 215–223). Springer.

Pelka, F. (2012). *What we have done: An oral history of the disability rights movement.* University of Massachusetts Press.

Peterson, D. B. (2016). The international classification of functioning, disability & health: Applications for professional counseling. In I. Marini & M. Stebnicki (Eds.), *The Professional counselor's desk reference* (2nd ed., pp. 329–336). Springer.

Putnam, R. (2000). *Bowling alone.* Simon & Schuster.

Putnam, M. (2005). Conceptualizing disability: Developing a framework for political disability identity. *Journal of Disability Policy Studies, 16*(3), 188–198.

Piepzna-Samarasinha, L. L. (2018). *Care work: Dreaming disability justice.* Arsenal Pulp Press.

Riddell, S., & Watson, N. (2003). *Disability, culture and identity.* Routledge, Taylor & Francis.

Rivas, M. (2020). Disability in Counselor Education: Perspectives from the United States. *International Journal for the Advancement of Counselling, 42*(4), 366–381. https://doi.org/10.1007/s10447-020 -09404-y

Rucker, A. (2016). Is ad land really changing? *New Mobility, 27*, 26–31.

Saia, T., Nerlich, A. P., & Johnston, S. P. (2021). Why not the "new flexible"? The argument for not returning to "normal" after COVID-19. *Rehabilitation Counselors and Educators Journal, 11*(1), 1–10. https://doi.org/10.52017/001c.28332

Scherer, M., & Craddock, G. (2002). The assessment of assistive technology outcomes, effects and costs. *Technology and Disability, 14*(3), 125–131. https://doi.org/10.3233/TAD-2002-14308

Scholz, B., Gordon, S. E., & Treharne, G. J. (2021). Special issue introduction – working towards allyship: Acknowledging and redressing power imbalances in psychology [Special Issue Introduction]. *Qualitative Research in Psychology, 18*(4), 451–458. https://doi.org/10.1080/ 14780887.2021.1970358

Schrader, S., Jones, N., & Shattell, M. (2013). Mad pride: reflections on sociopolitical identity and mental diversity in the context of culturally competent psychiatric care. *Issues in Mental Health Nursing*, 34(1), 62–64. https://doi.org/10.3109/01612840.2012.740769

Schriner, K., & Scotch, R. K. (2001). Disability and institutional change. *Journal of Disability Policy Studies*, 12(2), 100–106. https://doi.org/10.1177/104420730101200207

Scotch, R. K. (1988). Disability as the basis for a social movement: Advocacy and the politics of definition. *Journal of Social Issues*, 44(1), 159–172. https://doi.org/10.1111/j.1540-4560.1988.tb02055.x

Sins Invalid. (2019). *Skin, tooth, and bone: The basis of movement is our people* (2nd ed.). https://www.flipcause.com/secure/reward/OTMxNQ==

Smart, J. F., & Smart, D. W. (2006). Models of Disability: Implications for the Counseling Profession. *Journal of Counseling & Development*, 84(1), 29–40. https://doi.org/10.1002/j.1556-6678.2006.tb00377.x

Sontag, S. (1978). *Illness as metaphor*. Farrar, Straus & Giroux.

Sontag, S. (1989). *AIDS and its metaphors*. Farrar, Straus & Giroux.

Stebnicki, M. (2016). Integrative approaches in counseling and psychotherapy: Foundations of mind, body, and spirit. In I. Marini & M. A. Stebnicki (Eds.), *The Professional counselor's desk reference* (2nd ed., pp. 593–604). Springer.

Stubbins, J. (1988). The politics of disability. In H. E. Yuker (Ed.), *Attitudes toward persons with disabilities* (pp. 22–32). Springer.

Szymanski, E., & Trueba, H. T. (1994). Castification of people with disabilities. *Journal of Rehabilitation*, 60(3), 12–20.

Szymanski, E. (1998). Career development, school-to-work transition, and diversity: An ecological approach. In F. Rusch & J. Chadsey (Eds.), *Beyond high school: Transition from school to work* (pp. 127–145). Wadsworth.

Szymanski, E., Parker, R. M., & Patterson, J. B. (2012). Beyond the basics: The sociopolitical context of rehabilitation counseling practice. In R. M. Parker & J. B. Patterson (Eds.), *Rehabilitation counseling: Basics and beyond* (5th ed., pp. 369–384). Pro-Ed.

Travability. (2011). *Occasional Paper no.4: An economic model of disability*. http://travability.travel/Articles/economic_model_3.pdf

Umeasiegbu, V. I., Bishop, M., & Mpofu, E. (2013). The conventional and unconventional about disability conventions. *Rehabilitation Research, Policy, and Education*, 27(1), 58–72.

Uniform Data System for Medical Rehabilitation. (1997). *Guide for the use of the uniform data set for medical rehabilitation, Version 5.0*. State University of New York at Buffalo.

Vash, C. L. (1994). *Personality and adversity*. Springer.

Vash, C. L., & Crewe, N. M. (2004). *Psychology of disability* (2nd ed.). Springer.

Wendell, S. (1997). Toward a feminist theory of disability. *The Disability Studies Reader*, 260, 243–256.

White, G. W., Lloyd Simpson, J., Gonda, C., Ravesloot, C., & Coble, Z. (2010). Moving from Independence to Interdependence: A Conceptual Model for Better Understanding Community Participation of Centers for Independent Living Consumers. *Journal of Disability Policy Studies*, 20(4), 233–240. https://doi.org/10.1177/1044207309350561

Witmer, J. M., & Sweeney, T. J. (1992). A holistic model for wellness and prevention over the life span. *Journal of Counseling & Development*, 71(2), 140–148. https://doi.org/10.1002/j.1556-6676.1992.tb02189.x

Wright, B. A. (1960). *Physical disability--A psychological approach*. Harper & Row. https://doi.org/10.1037/10038-000

Wright, B. A. (1983). *Physical disability - A psychosocial approach* (2nd ed.). Harper & Row. https://doi.org/10.1037/10589-000

Wright, B. A. (1987). Human dignity and professional self-monitoring. *Journal of Applied Rehabilitation Counseling*, 18(4), 12–14.

Wright, B. A. (1988). Attitudes and the fundamental negative bias. In H. E. Yuker (Ed.), *Attitudes toward persons with disabilities* (pp. 3–21). Springer.

World Health Organization. (2001). *ICF: International classification of functioning, disability, and health*. https://icd.who.int/dev11/l-icf/en

Wright, B. A. (Ed.). (1959). *Psychology and rehabilitation*. APA. https://doi.org/10.1037/10539-000

Wright, B. A., & Lopez, S. J. (2005). Widening the diagnostic focus: A case for including human strengths and environmental resources. In C. R. Snyder & S. J. Lopez (Eds.), *Handbook of positive psychology* (pp. 26–44). Oxford University Press.

CHAPTER 4

Rehabilitation Counseling Professional Competencies

MICHAEL J. LEAHY AND MICHAEL T. HARTLEY

LEARNING OBJECTIVES

After reading this chapter, you should be able to:

- *Appraise the scope of practice for rehabilitation counseling and explain why it is important to the discipline.*
- *Describe how empirical research has provided an evidence-based foundation for the role and function as well as knowledge and skill competency requirements underlying effective practice.*
- *Evaluate how this research about role and function and knowledge and skill competency requirements has been translated to inform practice over the years within rehabilitation counseling.*

CACREP STANDARDS

CACREP 2016 Core: 2F1.b, 2F1.e, 2F5.j, 2F8.a, 2F8.b, 2F8.e, 2F8.i
CACREP 2016 Specialties:
 Clinical Rehabilitation Counseling: 5D1.a., 5D2.a., 5D2.b., 5D2.c., 5D2.d
 Rehabilitation Counseling: 5H1.a, 5H1.b, 5.H2.a, 5H2.i, 5H2.p, 5H3.a, 5H3.d

INTRODUCTION

Rehabilitation counseling has been a leader in research on professional competencies among the counseling specializations. Underlying the practice of any discipline or professional specialty area is the delineation of specific knowledge and skill competencies required for effective service delivery. Job analysis, job task analysis, role and function, professional competency, critical incident, and knowledge validation research are all terms that describe a process whereby the professional practice of rehabilitation counseling has been systematically studied. These research efforts over the past five decades have identified and described the critical functions and tasks, or knowledge and skills, associated with the effective delivery of services to individuals with disabilities (Leahy, 2012). The findings from these research efforts also have been translated to empirically inform the discipline's scope of practice and professional identity, as well as the rehabilitation counseling preservice training curricula, academic accreditation standards, and practitioner certification at the national level.

Among the various professionals (e.g., physiatrists, psychologists, social workers, medical case managers) who may provide services to individuals with disabilities during their individual rehabilitation processes, the Rehabilitation Counselor (RC) represents a unique professional who plays a central role in the extra-medical phase of the rehabilitation process, for individuals with both acquired and congenital disabilities (Wright, 1980). Rehabilitation counseling emerged as a full-time occupation more than 100 years ago. Unlike the beginnings of other counseling specialties and health-related occupations, rehabilitation counseling was mandated as a specific work role through federal legislation (Smith-Fess Act, 1920), which established the public or state–federal rehabilitation program in this country. In the years following this landmark legislation, rehabilitation counseling practice in the public and private sectors evolved and expanded to provide a comprehensive array of vocational and independent living services to an ever-increasing adult population of people with a wide range of physical and mental disabilities (Leahy & Szymanski, 1995).

Although the occupational status of rehabilitation counseling was established in the 1920s, it was not until the mid-1950s, with the passage of the 1954 Vocational Rehabilitation Act Amendments, that the discipline embarked on a series of significant ongoing developments (e.g., establishing preservice education, professional associations, code of ethics, regulation of practice) that have led over time to the professionalization of practice in this country and, to some extent, internationally. Initially, rehabilitation counselors (RCs) were a varied group of practitioners in terms of educational background and professional competencies. Today, as a result of the professionalization process over the past 60 years, RCs represent a group of professionals with a much higher degree of commonality in relation to preservice preparation, practice, and professional identity than at any previous time in our professional history.

The purpose of this chapter is to review those aspects of the discipline that serve to both uniquely identify and provide the foundation for rehabilitation counseling practice in today's health and human services environment. Particular attention is devoted to discussion of the scope and research-based foundation of practice. This chapter provides a foundation for a deeper understanding of the nature of rehabilitation counseling practice. Specific professional functions and competencies are presented in greater detail in Parts IV and V of this book.

SCOPE OF PRACTICE

Rehabilitation counseling has been described as a process in which the counselor works collaboratively with the client to understand existing problems, barriers, and potentials in order to facilitate the effective use of personal and environmental resources for career, personal, social, and community adjustment following disability (Jaques, 1970). In carrying out this multifaceted process, RCs must be prepared to assist individuals with disabilities in adapting to the environment, assist environments in accommodating the needs of the individual, and work toward the full participation of individuals in all aspects of society, with a particular focus on career aspirations (Szymanski, 1985). RCs differ from other counseling specialties because of their focus on disability with an emphasis on addressing environmental barriers impeding the well-being of individuals with disabilities. Given the history of **paternalistic** attitudes toward individuals with disabilities in society, RCs have sought to navigate their unique position of having expertise in counseling and rehabilitation, while also not abusing their roles and power as "experts" that would contribute to people with disabilities as diseased, broken, and in need of fixing (Hartley et al., 2021; Sales, 2007).

Over the years, the fundamental role of the RC has evolved with the subsequent functions and required knowledge and skill competencies of the RC expanding as well (Jaques, 1970; Rubin & Roessler, 1995; Wright, 1980). Regardless of variations in their practice settings and client populations, most RCs (a) assess needs, (b) establish a work-ing alliance with the individual to develop goals and individualized plans to meet iden-tified needs, and (c) provide or arrange for the therapeutic services and interventions (e.g., psychological, medical, social, behavioral), including job-placement and follow-up services. Throughout this individualized process, counseling skills are considered an essential component of all activities. It is the specialized knowledge of disabilities and of environmental factors that interact with disabilities, as well as the range of knowl-edge and skills required in addition to counseling, that differentiates RCs from social workers, other types of counselors (e.g., mental health counselors, school counselors, career counselors), and other rehabilitation practitioners (e.g., vocational evaluators, job-placement specialists) in today's service delivery environments (Jenkins et al., 1992; Leahy & Szymanski, 1995).

Utilizing the long-standing tradition in rehabilitation counseling research of studying the role and functions of qualified practitioners, in 1994 the Commission on Rehabilitation Counselor Certification (CRCC, 1994) led a national professionalization initiative to develop the discipline's official scope of practice statement, which was adopted by all the major professional and regulatory organizations in rehabilitation counseling (See Box 4.1). This statement is consistent with available empirical research and necessary to explicitly identify the scope of practice for the public, clients, related professionals, and regulatory bodies. The overall importance of this statement cannot be overemphasized. It stands as the official statement that describes the professional practice of the discipline

BOX 4.1 REFLECTION ACTIVITY: SCOPE OF PRACTICE

Rehabilitation counseling is a systematic process which assists persons with phys-ical, mental, developmental, cognitive, and emotional disabilities to achieve their personal, career, and independent living goals in the most integrated setting pos-sible through the application of the counseling process. The counseling process involves communication, goal setting, and beneficial growth or change through self-advocacy, psychological, vocational, social, and behavioral interventions. The specific techniques and modalities utilized within this rehabilitation counseling process may include, but are not limited to, the following:·

- Assessment and appraisal·
- Diagnosis and treatment planning
- Career (vocational) counseling
- Individual and group counseling treatment interventions focused on facilitating adjustments to the medical and psychosocial impact of disability
- Case management, referral, and service coordination
- Program evaluation and research
- Interventions to remove environmental, employment, and attitudinal barriers
- Consultation services among multiple parties and regulatory systems
- Job analysis, job development, and placement services, including assistance with employment and job accommodations
- Provision of consultation about and access to rehabilitation technology

After reading this CRCC scope of practice statement for rehabilitation counselors, in what ways is the rehabilitation counselors' scope of practice similar and different to other counseling specialties?

Source: Reproduced with permission from Commission on Rehabilitation Counselor Certification. (n.d.). *Rehabilitation counselor scope of practice.* https://www.crccertification. com/crc-crcc-scope-of-practice.

across clinical practice settings and the specific techniques and modalities typically used to address the needs of the clients engaged in a working alliance with the RC.

The professional scope of practice is important because it describes what an RC is permitted to do, provided they have acquired the required knowledge and skills in their personal educational and training process. However, rather than a false dichotomy of completely competent to incompetent to perform all the tasks and functions, RCs are ethically bound to practice within their individual competence boundaries based on their unique knowledge, abilities, and skills (Cottone et al., 2021). Since there is more variance in job functions within rehabilitation counseling than other counseling specialties, it is important for RCs to differentiate their individual scopes of practice based on their own unique education, training, and supervised practice. Thus, readers are encouraged to review the official scope of practice (see Box 4.1) and reflect on the roles and tasks that they are most drawn to performing in their own practice. This analysis may help to intentionally seek out the training and supervision needed to ensure competence in these particular areas.

RESEARCH-BASED FOUNDATIONS OF PRACTICE

There is an extensive research-based foundation for the roles and functions performed by RCs extending back to the 1950s. Over the past 60 years, through various research methods, an extensive body of knowledge has been acquired that has empirically identified the specific competencies and job functions important to the practice of rehabilitation counseling. This long-standing emphasis on the development and ongoing refinement of a research-based foundation has served to define and validate the rehabilitation counseling scope of practice. It also distinguishes it from other counseling specialties that are also seeking to define and validate their scope of professional practice. These research efforts have provided the discipline with evidence of construct validity of rehabilitation counseling knowledge and skill areas (Leahy, 2012; Leahy et al., 2013, 2019; Szymanski, Leahy, et al., 1993).

The professional competencies underlying rehabilitation counseling are not static and have evolved in response to emerging cultural, legislative, and credentialing changes within our society and healthcare system. Over time, the major tasks performed by RCs have expanded as evident from empirically derived descriptions of practice. **Role and function studies** are an empirical approach for identifying the work requirements of specific functions by detailing the tasks and responsibilities that must be performed within and across work settings. While role and function studies have documented what RCs do, there also is a need to understand the knowledge and skills necessary to effectively and ethically perform the major tasks. Sometimes, the knowledge required to perform these functions is more indirectly assessed and inferred on the basis of the described functions and tasks. In contrast, **knowledge validation studies** are a data-driven approach to define the knowledge domains and skill sets needed to perform the major tasks with a focus on importance and preparedness within and across particular work settings. The legacy of research on both role and functions as well as knowledge and skills has directly informed accreditation and certification bodies that regulate the professional competencies of RCs. Roessler and Rubin (1992), in their historic review of major studies (Emener & Rubin, 1980; Leahy et al., 1987; Rubin et al., 1984), concluded that RCs have a diverse role requiring many skills if they are to assist individuals with disabilities effectively to improve the quality of their lives. They also concluded that the role of the RC could be described fundamentally as encompassing the following functions or job task areas: (a) assessment, (b) affective counseling, (c) vocational (career) counseling, (d) case management, and (e) job placement.

In the years that have passed, service settings have continued to diversify and the delivery of rehabilitation counseling services has continued to evolve, to address not only the changing needs of people with disabilities, but also to keep pace with advances in medicine, technology, and new knowledge generation and translation in practice settings. Recognizing and understanding these changes are important and consistent with the continued professionalization of rehabilitation counseling, including professional credentialing requirements. Used as empirical grounding for the scope of practice for RCs, findings from a knowledge validation study by Leahy et al. (1993) were translated directly by accreditation and regulatory bodies to education and training standards. Furthermore, an examination of job functions and knowledge requirements by Leahy et al. (2003) provided direct evidence of major job functions of RCs such as vocational counseling, counseling interventions, and case management as well as corresponding knowledge domains such as career counseling, counseling theories, techniques, and applications, and case and caseload management.

Building upon these seminal studies, the role and function study by Leahy et al. (2013) examined the major tasks performed in today's rapidly changing practice environments. See Box 4.2 for a description of the major job function domains and associated subdomains (Job Placement and Vocational Assessment and Career Counseling; and Counseling, Psychosocial Interventions, and Case Management; and Demand-Side Employment and Workers' Compensation and Forensic Services) that are important for rehabilitation counseling across clinical practice settings. **Domain** is the term used to describe an area of similar job function or knowledge. They tend to be broad areas of practice. The **subdomains** within each domain provide a more specific description of the professional tasks or knowledge and skill associated with the domain.

Leahy et al. (2013) found corresponding empirical support that the following 10 knowledge domains represent the core knowledge and skill requirements of RCs across practice settings: (a) assessment, appraisal, and vocational evaluation; (b) job development, job placement, and career lifestyle development; (c) vocational consultation and services for employers; (d) case management, professional roles and practices, and utilization of community resources; (e) foundations of counseling, professional orientation and ethical practice, theories, social and cultural issues, and human growth and development; (f) group and family counseling; (g) mental health counseling; (h) medical, functional, and psychosocial aspects of disabilities; (i) disability management; and (j) research, program evaluation, and evidence-based practice. A complete listing of the knowledge domains and subdomains is provided in Box 4.3.

Taken together, Box 4.2 and Box 4.3 represent the findings from the comprehensive study of the diverse roles and knowledge associated with the specialized practice of rehabilitation counseling. Subsequently, there has been one additional knowledge validation study by Leahy et al. (2019) that further supported the core knowledge domains of: (a) rehabilitation and mental health counseling, (b), employer engagement and job placement, (c) case management, (d) medical and psychosocial aspects of chronic illness and disability, (e) research methodology and evidence-based practice, and (f) group and family counseling. However, an accompanying updated role and function study is needed to link these knowledge domains to the direct tasks and functions performed by RCs. With that point in mind, readers are directed to the information in Box 4.2 and Box 4.3. An important take-away message is that RCs perform many different tasks and functions.

Ideally, future research on the professional competencies underlying rehabilitation counseling practice will build upon the existing evidence with an eye toward areas of expanding practice. Perhaps most important, it is important to understand that RCs are not trained for one job or work setting but, rather, are prepared to be robust professionals who can perform diverse tasks and functions across a wide range of settings. Later chapters in Parts IV and V of this book present greater detail about these professional functions and competencies.

BOX 4.2 REFLECTION ACTIVITY: JOB FUNCTIONS RELATED TO REHABILITATION COUNSELING

Job Placement and Vocational Assessment and Career Counseling

Job Placement

- Instruct clients in preparing for the job interview (e.g., job application, resumé preparation, attire, interviewing skills).
- Instruct clients in developing systematic job-search skills.
- Respond to employer biases and concerns regarding hiring people with disabilities.
- Inform clients of job openings suitable to their needs and abilities.
- Monitor clients' postemployment adjustment to determine the need for additional services.
- Provide prospective employers with appropriate information on clients' work skills and abilities.
- Use supportive counseling techniques to prepare clients for the stress of the job search.
- Use local resources to assist with placement (e.g., employer contacts, colleagues, state employment service).
- Develop mutually agreed-on vocational counseling goals.
- Apply knowledge of assistive technology in job accommodation.
- Identify hidden job leads and customized jobs/employment opportunities.
- Provide information to help clients answer other individuals' questions, including employers, about their disabilities.
- Identify and arrange for functional or skill remediation services for clients' successful job placements.
- Understand the applications of current laws affecting the employment of individuals with disabilities.
- Discuss clients' vocational plans when they appear unrealistic.
- Recommend modifications of job tasks to accommodate clients' functional limitations.
- Determine the level of intervention necessary for job placement (e.g., job club, supported work, on-the-job training).
- Counsel clients to select jobs consistent with their abilities, interests, and rehabilitation goals.
- Discuss with clients labor market conditions that may influence the feasibility of entering certain occupations.
- Identify educational and training requirements for specific jobs.
- Recommend occupational and/or educational materials for clients to explore vocational alternatives and choices.

Vocational Assessment and Career Counseling

- Integrate assessment data to describe clients' assets, limitations, and preferences for rehabilitation planning purposes.
- Make logical job, work area, or adjustment training recommendations based on comprehensive client assessment information.
- Use behavioral observations to make inferences about work personality characteristics and adjustment.
- Counsel with clients regarding educational and vocational implications of test and interview information.

(continued)

BOX 4.2 REFLECTION ACTIVITY: JOB FUNCTIONS RELATED TO REHABILITATION COUNSELING (*CONTINUED*)

- Interpret diagnostic information (e.g., tests vocational and educational records, medical reports) to clients.
- Select evaluation instruments and strategies according to their appropriateness and usefulness for a particular client.
- Match clients' needs with job reinforcers and clients' aptitudes with job requirements.
- Identify clients' work personality characteristics to be observed through an on-the-job evaluation or simulated work situation.
- Administer appropriate standardized tests for assessment purposes.
- Assess clients' readiness for gainful employment.
- Assess the significance of clients' disabilities.
- Review medical information with clients to determine vocational implications of their functional limitations.

Occupational Information Analysis

- Classify local jobs using the *DOT* and O*Net or other classification systems.
- Utilize occupational information such as the *DOT, Occupational Outlook Handbook,* and other publications.
- Analyze the tasks of a job.
- Use computer-based assessment, counseling, and job-matching systems in the rehabilitation process.
- Apply labor-market information influencing the task of locating, obtaining, and progressing in employment.
- Identify transferable work skills by analyzing clients' work history and functional assets and limitations.

Counseling, Psychosocial Interventions, and Case Management
Counseling

- Clarify for clients mutual expectations and the nature of the counseling relationship.
- Adjust counseling approaches or styles according to clients' cognitive and personality characteristics.
- Employ counseling techniques (e.g., reflection, interpretation, summarization) to facilitate client self-exploration.
- Identify one's own biases and weaknesses, which may affect the development of a healthy client relationship.
- Develop a therapeutic relationship characterized by empathy and positive regard for the client.
- Identify social, economic, and environmental forces that may present barriers to a client's rehabilitation.
- Counsel clients to help them appreciate and emphasize their personal assets.
- Counsel with clients to identify emotional reactions to disability.
- Recognize psychological problems (e.g., depression, suicidal ideation) requiring consultation or referral.
- Assist clients in terminating counseling in a positive manner, thus enhancing their ability to function independently.
- Use assessment information to provide clients with insights into personal dynamics.

(continued)

BOX 4.2 REFLECTION ACTIVITY: JOB FUNCTIONS RELATED TO REHABILITATION COUNSELING (*CONTINUED*)

- Apply psychological and social theory to develop strategies for rehabilitation intervention.
- Work with clients to prepare rehabilitation plans with mutually agreed-on interventions and goals.
- Confront clients with observations about inconsistencies between their goals and their behavior.

Psychosocial Interventions

- Counsel with clients using group methods for psychosocial and vocational adjustment problems.
- Provide psychological counseling to clients regarding sexuality and disability issues.
- Counsel with clients' families to provide information and support positive coping behaviors.
- Use behavioral techniques such as shaping, rehearsal, modeling, and contingency management.
- Explore clients' needs for individual, group, or family counseling.
- Assist clients in verbalizing specific behavioral goals for personal adjustment.
- Conduct group activities and programs such as job clubs, vocational exploration groups, or job-seeking skills groups.
- Supervise new counselors and/or practicum or internship students in rehabilitation counseling activities.
- Develop acceptable client work behavior through the use of behavioral techniques.
- Assist clients in understanding stress and in utilizing mechanisms for coping.
- Diagnose and identify treatment options for mental health issues.
- Participate with advocacy groups to promote rehabilitation programs.

Case Management

- Collaborate with other providers so that services are coordinated, appropriate, and timely.
- Coordinate activities of all agencies involved in a rehabilitation plan.
- Monitor client progress.
- Attend team conferences.
- Explain the services and limitations of various community resources to clients.
- Establish meaningful working alliances with the clients served.
- Refer clients to appropriate specialists and/or for special services.
- Identify and challenge stereotypic views toward people with disabilities.
- Determine clients' ability to perform independent living activities.
- Obtain regular client feedback regarding the satisfaction with services delivered and suggestions for improvement.
- Assist clients to identify needs and request accommodations or supports to address functional limitations.
- Teach problem-solving skills to clients.
- Determine appropriate community services for clients' stated needs.

Demand-Side Employment and Workers' Compensation and Forensic Services
Demand-Side Employment

(continued)

BOX 4.2 REFLECTION ACTIVITY: JOB FUNCTIONS RELATED TO REHABILITATION COUNSELING (*CONTINUED*)

- Research and secure funding, community resources, and support needed for community reentry.
- Provide benefits counseling to Social Security beneficiaries seeking vocational rehabilitation (VR) services.
- Promote public awareness and legislative support of rehabilitation programs.
- Train clients' coworkers/supervisors regarding work and disability issues.
- Provide consultation to employers regarding accessibility and issues related to Americans with Disabilities Act (ADA) compliance.
- Evaluate and select facilities that provide specialized care services for clients.
- Market rehabilitation services to businesses and organizations.
- Act as an advocate for the client and family with third-party payers and service providers.
- Contact vendors in order to purchase adaptive/accommodative equipment.
- Negotiate financial responsibilities for client rehabilitation with the referral source and/or sponsor.
- Use social networking in the rehabilitation and placement process.
- Negotiate with employers or labor union representatives to reinstate/rehire an injured worker.
- Utilize demand-side employment strategies related to hiring, return to work, and retention.
- Conduct a review of the rehabilitation literature on a given topic or case problem to identify the research-based evidence of effectiveness of various treatment or intervention options.
- Make sound and timely financial decisions within the context of caseload management in your work setting.
- Apply evidence-based research results to professional practice.
- Apply principles of rehabilitation legislation to daily practice.

Workers' Compensation and Forensic Services

- Understand insurance claims processing and professional responsibilities in workers' compensation.
- Provide expert opinion or testimony regarding employability and rehabilitation feasibility.
- Document all significant client vocational findings in a manner sufficient for legal testimony or records.
- Discuss return-to-work options with the employer.
- Conduct labor market analyses.
- Report to referral sources regarding progress of cases.
- Obtain a release for a return to work from the treating physician.
- Obtain written reports regarding client progress.

Evidence-Based Foundation of Practice

The historic evidence-based foundation of practice has been useful in identifying both the common professional ground (competency areas) shared with the profession of counseling, and the uniqueness of rehabilitation counseling among related rehabilitation disciplines (e.g., vocational evaluators, job placement specialists) and other counseling specialties (e.g., career counselors, school counselors, mental health counselors). This process of further defining the area of occupational competence is a normal sequence in the

BOX 4.3 REHABILITATION COUNSELING KNOWLEDGE DOMAINS AND SUBDOMAINS

Assessment, Appraisal, and Vocational Evaluation

- The tests and evaluation techniques available for assessing clients' needs
- Psychometric concepts related to measurement
- Interpretation of assessment results for rehabilitation planning purposes
- Computer-based job-matching systems
- Computer-based and online assessment tools

Job Development, Job Placement, and Career and Lifestyle Development

- Theories of career development and work adjustment
- Vocational implications of functional limitations associated with disabilities
- Methods and techniques used to conduct labor market surveys
- Transferable skills analysis
- Occupational and labor market information
- Job analysis
- Ergonomics, job accommodations, and assistive technology
- Job readiness, including seeking and retention skills development
- Job placement and job development strategies
- Job modification and restructuring techniques
- Demand-side employment issues related to hiring, return to work, and retention
- Services available from one-stop career centers

Vocational Consultation and Services for Employers

- The workplace culture, environment, and business terminology
- Marketing strategies and techniques for rehabilitation services
- Employer development for job placement
- Consultation process with employers related to management of disability issues in the workplace
- Educating employers on disability-related issues

Case Management, Professional Roles and Practices, and Utilization of Community Resources

- Principles of caseload management
- Case management tools
- The case management process, including case finding, planning, service coordination, referral to and utilization of other disciplines, and client advocacy
- Case recording and documentation
- Professional roles, functions, and relationships with other human services providers
- Techniques for working effectively in teams and across disciplines
- Health promotion and wellness concepts and strategies for people with chronic illness and disability
- The services available for a variety of rehabilitation populations, including people with multiple disabilities
- Techniques for working with individuals who have limited English proficiency
- Negotiation, mediation, and conflict resolution strategies
- Advocacy processes needed to address institutional and social barriers that impede access, equity, and success for clients

(continued)

BOX 4.3 REHABILITATION COUNSELING KNOWLEDGE DOMAINS AND SUBDOMAINS (*CONTINUED*)

- Human resources practices, diversity in the workplace, and workplace supports for people with disabilities
- Programs and services for specialty populations
- Organizational structure of rehabilitation counseling practice settings
- Social Security programs, benefits, work incentives, and disincentives
- Services available through client advocacy programs
- Community resources and services for rehabilitation planning
- Supported employment strategies and services
- School-to-work transition for students with disabilities
- Financial resources for rehabilitation services
- Independent living services
- Health care benefits and delivery systems
- Laws and public policy affecting individuals with disabilities

Foundations of Counseling, Professional Orientation and Ethical Practice, Theories, Social and Cultural Issues, and Human Growth and Development

- Individual counseling theories
- Individual counseling practices and interventions
- Human growth and development
- Societal issues, trends, and developments
- Diversity and multicultural counseling issues
- Theories and techniques of clinical supervision
- Clinical problem-solving and critical-thinking skills
- Internet-based counseling tools and resources
- Risk management and professional ethical standards
- Ethical decision-making models and processes

Group and Family Counseling

- Family counseling theories
- Family counseling practices and interventions
- Group counseling theories
- Group counseling practices and interventions

Mental Health Counseling

- Behavior and personality theory
- Techniques for individuals with psychological disabilities
- Dual diagnosis and the workplace
- Human sexuality and disability issues
- Substance abuse and treatment
- Treatment planning for clinical problems
- Knowledge of the current version of the *Diagnostic and Statistical Manual of Mental Disorders*

Medical, Functional, and Psychosocial Aspects of Disabilities

- Medical aspects and implications of various disabilities
- Medical terminology
- Rehabilitation terminology and concepts
- The psychosocial and cultural impact of disability on the individual

(*continued*)

BOX 4.3 REHABILITATION COUNSELING KNOWLEDGE DOMAINS AND SUBDOMAINS (*CONTINUED*)

- The psychosocial and cultural impact of disability on the family
- Environmental and attitudinal barriers for individuals with disabilities
- The functional capacities of individuals with disabilities
- Implications of medications as they apply to individuals with disabilities
- Individual and family adjustment to disability
- Appropriate medical intervention resources
- Work conditioning or work hardening resources and strategies

Disability Management

- Disability prevention and management strategies
- Managed care concepts
- Insurance programs
- Workers' compensation laws and practices
- Forensic rehabilitation

Research, Program Evaluation, and Evidence-Based Practice

- Historical and philosophical foundations of rehabilitation counseling
- Program evaluation procedures for assessing the effectiveness of rehabilitation services and outcomes
- Research databases for locating empirically validated interventions
- Rehabilitation research literature related to evidence-based practice
- Research methods and statistics
- Evidence-based practice and research utilization
- Evidence-based psychiatric rehabilitation practices
- Systematic review/meta-analysis

professionalization process for any occupation seeking public recognition. With this idea in mind, the empirically derived descriptions of the RC's role, function, and knowledge have assisted the discipline in a number of important ways.

First, the extensive research base has helped to support the scope of practice and professional identity of the RC by empirically defining the uniqueness of the discipline and by providing evidence in support of the construct validity of its knowledge base. Rehabilitation counseling clearly is aligned with the counseling profession. At the same time, strong empirical support has differentiated the scope of practice for rehabilitation counseling from other counseling specializations. It also provides evidence that counseling skills are critical, including the ability to diagnose and provide mental health counseling services. It is the specialty knowledge of disability that separates rehabilitation counselors from other counseling specializations.

Second, the research base has been used extensively in the development of accreditation standards and preservice educational curricula in order to provide graduate training in areas of knowledge and skill critical to practice across major employment settings. The long-standing emphasis on a research-based foundation to practice has contributed greatly to the rehabilitation counseling field's leadership role in the establishment and ongoing refinement of graduate educational program accreditation. The role and function as well as knowledge validation studies have directly informed accreditation standards for rehabilitation counseling programs. Rehabilitation counseling education programs were accredited through CORE until the 2017 merger with the CACREP. The majority of knowledge and skills required by CORE, and more recently by the CACREP, were viewed as essential for effective practice by directors of state–federal vocational rehabilitation

(VR) agencies as reported by Chan et al. (2017). Moving forward, accreditation standards need to account for the diverse practice of rehabilitation counseling as reflected in the research literature with a focus on the counseling knowledge and skills associated with the best client outcomes.

Third, research on rehabilitation counseling competencies has defined individual practitioner certification through the CRCC (CRCC, 2021; Leahy, 2009). Consequently, research on the critical functions and knowledge underlying ethical and effective practice is used by the CRCC to regularly review the test specifications used to guide the certification examination (Leahy, Muenzen, et al., 2009). For instance, findings from Leahy et al. (2013) were used by the CRCC to examine and set test specifications for future versions of the CRC examination, and to empirically define the nature of professional practice of rehabilitation counseling more generally. Furthermore, research on professional competencies has defined eligibility requirements for who can sit for the Certified Rehabilitation Counselor Examination (CRCE). Specifically, for students graduating from nonaccredited programs in rehabilitation counseling, the CRCC (2019) *Certification Guide* requires content in core areas such as medical and psychosocial aspects of disability as well as career development and techniques of counseling as supported by research.

In sum, the research base on rehabilitation counseling has provided empirical support for the unique, but varied role and functions as well as the knowledge base underlying ethical and effective practice. It also has contributed further empirical evidence in relation to the content and construct validity of the knowledge domains. Over the past 30 years, multiple large-scale national research initiatives (Leahy et al., 1993, 2003, Leahy, Muenzen, et al., 2009, Leahy et al., 2013) have identified and defined the specific competencies and job functions important to the practice of rehabilitation counseling and the achievement of positive outcomes with the clients they serve. Each successive replication and extension of this line of inquiry has added to the evidence-based foundation of practice (DePalma, 2002) in terms of underlying knowledge dimensions essential for effective rehabilitation counseling. These studies and prior research efforts (e.g., Berven, 1979; Emener & Rubin, 1980; Harrison & Lee, 1979; Jaques, 1959; Leahy et al., 1987; Muthard & Salomone, 1969; Rubin et al., 1984; Wright & Fraser, 1975) have provided the discipline with consistent empirically based evidence of an established and mature discipline that is able to respond appropriately to the evolutionary demands and pressures of a dynamic human service field (Leahy et al., 2013, 2016).

Knowledge Translation

Knowledge translation is discussed later in this book in Chapter 19 ("Evidence-Based Practice and Research Utilization") as the process by which research facilitates more effective clinical practice. There is a long history of knowledge translation in rehabilitation counseling, including a series of studies investigating the relationship between rehabilitation counselor education and service delivery outcomes. These studies provide consistent support for the position that RCs, as qualified providers, need to obtain preservice training at the graduate level in rehabilitation counseling or a closely related field prior to practice. Studies of the New York (Szymanski & Parker, 1989), Wisconsin (Szymanski, 1991), Maryland (Szymanski & Danek, 1992), and Arkansas (Cook & Bolton, 1992) state Vocational Rehabilitation (VR) agencies demonstrated that counselors with master's degrees in rehabilitation counseling achieved better outcomes with clients with severe disabilities than did RCs with unrelated master's or bachelor's degrees. In another group of studies, involving RCs from a variety of employment settings, preservice education was linked to the RCs, perceived (self-assessed) level of competency. Shapson et al. (1987) and Szymanski, Linkowski, et al. (1993) demonstrated that counselors with master's degrees in rehabilitation counseling perceived themselves to be more competent or better prepared in critical knowledge and skill areas of rehabilitation counseling than did counselors with unrelated preservice preparation (Leahy & Szymanski, 1995).

More recently, Van Houtte (2013) found evidence that graduate education in rehabilitation counseling had a significant positive effect on client outcomes as well as decreased expenditures in the New Jersey VR system. In other words, formally trained RCs provided more effective services that directly improved the efficacy and fiscal health of the entire VR system. Furthermore, a national study by Sherman et al. (2017) found that master's degree requirements in rehabilitation counseling were associated with more effective outcomes for clients with the most severe disabilities. Specifically, in states with an order of selection that prioritized services to clients with the most significant disabilities, master's degree counselors outperformed those with a bachelor's degree. Finally, Mackay et al. (2020) found that having a master's degree in rehabilitation counseling was associated with better client employment outcomes in the Utah VR system. Specifically, RCs outperformed those with a bachelor's degree in terms of high-quality placements associated with clients obtaining full-time employment and a living wage. In a meta-analysis of research outcomes Frain et al. (2006) estimated that 20,000 more individuals with disabilities would be employed each year with an estimated cost savings of $225,000 per RC if all public VR counselors held a master's degree in rehabilitation counseling.

There is clear evidence supporting the effectiveness of rehabilitation counseling training and practice (Fleming et al., 2013; Pruett et al., 2008), including the critical role of counseling skills (McCarthy, 2015). A majority of RCs still practice in the public, private, and not-for-profit rehabilitation sectors. However, RCs also practice in independent living centers, employee assistance programs, hospitals, clinics, mental health organizations, public school transition programs, and employer-based disability prevention and management programs. Although setting-based factors may affect the relative emphasis or importance of various RC functions or may introduce new specialized knowledge requirements for the RC, there remains a great deal of communality in the role and function among RCs regardless of practice setting (Leahy et al., 1987, 1993, Leahy, Muenzen, et al., 2009, Leahy et al., 2013). One aspect that is often affected by these various settings is the wide variation in job title used by RCs.

Much more than a job title, it is the specialized knowledge of disabilities and environmental factors that interact with disabilities, as well as the range of knowledge and skills required in addition to counseling, that differentiate RCs from other types of counselors and human service providers. Although the RC job title is used in the majority of settings, one can also find the use of the titles "rehabilitation consultant" or "case manager" among today's RCs in practice. As one advances up the career ladder within these various settings, RCs can assume supervisory, management, and administrative roles within these various organizations. Saunders et al. (2009) reported that approximately half of CRC were employed under the title of RC, with others employed under titles such as counselor, evaluator, and specialist. RCs also work in substance abuse and mental health centers and seek state licensure often using the title of (licensed) professional counselor.

Another aspect of variation in competencies among practicing RCs is the degree to which they specialize their practices. One particularly useful model for viewing this issue was developed by DiMichael (1967), who suggested a two-way classification of horizontal and vertical specialization. In DiMichael's model, **horizontal specialization** refers to RCs who restrict or specialize their practice with a particular disability group (e.g., deaf, blind, head injury, substance abuse) that requires a significant amount of specialized knowledge or skill, specific to the type of disability. **Vertical specialization,** in contrast, occurs when RCs attend to only one function in the rehabilitation process (e.g., assessment or job placement) in their work with clients. Vocational evaluators and job placement specialists are examples of vertical specialists in this model. Additionally, any of the functions and tasks described in Box 4.4 could be examples of vertical specialization. Alternatively, examples of horizontal specialization may include specializing in

BOX 4.4 REFLECTION ACTIVITY

Review the detailed list of job and knowledge domains in Boxes 4.2 and 4.3. Write down the job and knowledge domains that you are most and least drawn to. Is there a pattern in the job domains you are most and least interested in? What might this inform your future professional practice, and how can you maximize professional development opportunities to gain the competence necessary to perform these tasks ethically and effectively? Where and how might your role and scope of practice differ as well as overlap from related professionals such as social workers and psychologists? How do you communicate the unique philosophy and approach of rehabilitation counseling to clients, colleagues, and supervisors?

providing services to different types of disability groups, such as psychiatric disabilities as discussed in Chapter 20 (Psychiatric Rehabilitation) of this book. Even within such disability groups, there is a great deal of diversity that may require further horizontal specialization. The diverse practice of rehabilitation counseling means that RCs can specialize in many different areas. Additionally, Jenkins and Strauser (1999) argued for the horizontal expansion of RCs beyond any disability type, pointing to the fact that RCs also serve people who do not meet the definition of having a disability.

Finally, rehabilitation is an interdisciplinary practice, and there are numerous related professional groups that contribute to the rehabilitation process and complement the role and services provided by the RC. In addition to vocational evaluators and job placement specialists, who can assist the RC and client at critical stages in the rehabilitation process (assessment and job placement), other supportive resources include psychiatrists, physicians, and physiatrists; physical and occupational therapists; psychologists; work adjustment trainers; job coaches; and various vocational training personnel. Quite often, a critical aspect of the RC's role is the coordination of services provided by these various professionals within the context of a multidisciplinary team approach to effectively address the multifaceted needs of the client in the rehabilitation process.

CONCLUSION

Rehabilitation counseling is a professional discipline and specialty area of counseling. It has had a rich history of professionalization. Although the occupation has been in existence for over 100 years, we have witnessed significant growth and development of this specialty area of practice over the past few decades. This chapter provides several important conclusions. First, the official scope of practice defines the diverse job tasks and functions that serve to both uniquely identify and provide the foundation for rehabilitation counseling practice. Second, the long history of empirical research has provided the evidence-based foundation for the evolution of accreditation and certification, and ultimately the professional practice of rehabilitation counseling. Third, RCs possess a wide range of knowledge and skills and perform many different roles and functions. It is important that RCs remain cognizant of their own areas of competence based on education, training, and supervised practice. Finally, research has found that graduate-level training in rehabilitation counseling is associated with better client outcomes, especially for individuals with the most severe disabilities. Today, there are more RCs practicing in a variety of employment settings than at any time in our history, and the future market for these types of trained professionals looks excellent.

CONTENT REVIEW QUESTIONS

1. What is the scope of practice and definition of rehabilitation counseling, as a specialty area of counseling practice?
2. What are the basic roles and functions of the RC in practice?
3. What types of knowledge and skill areas are required to practice effectively within the discipline?

REFERENCES

Berven, N. L. (1979). The role and function of the rehabilitation counselor revisited. *Rehabilitation Counseling Bulletin, 22,* 84–88.

Chan, F., Tansey, T. N., Chronister, J., McMahon, B. T., Iwanaga, K., Wu, J.-R., Chen, X., Lee, B., Bengtson, K., Umucu, E., Flowers, S., & Moser, E. (2017). Rehabilitation counseling practice in state vocational rehabilitation and the effect of the workforce innovation and opportunity act (WIOA). *Journal of Applied Rehabilitation Counseling, 48*(3), 20–28. https://doi.org/10.1891/0047 -2220.48.3.20

Commission on Rehabilitation Counselor Certification. (1994). *CRCC certification guide.* Author.

Commission on Rehabilitation Counselor Certification. (2019). *CRC certification guide.* http://crccer- tification.com/wp-content/uploads/2021/01/CRCCertificationGuideCRCCertificationGuide -2021.pdf

Commission on Rehabilitation Counselor Certification. (2021). *CRCC role and function study.* https:// crccertification.com/crcc-role-and-function-study

Cook, D., & Bolton, B. (1992). Rehabilitation counselor education and case performance: An inde- pendent replication. *Rehabilitation Counseling Bulletin, 36,* 37–43.

Cottone, C. C., Tarvydas, V. M., & Hartley, M. T. (2021). *Ethics and decision making in counseling and psychotherapy* (5th ed.). Springer Publishing.

DePalma, J. A. (2002). Proposing an evidence-based policy process. *Nursing Administration Quarterly, 26*(4), 55–61. https://doi.org/10.1097/00006216-200207000-00010

DiMichael, S. G. (1967). New directions and expectations in rehabilitation counseling. *Journal of Rehabilitation, 33*(1), 38–39.

Emener, W. G., & Rubin, S. E. (1980). Rehabilitation counselor roles and functions and sources of role strain. *Journal of Applied Rehabilitation Counseling, 11*(2), 57–69. https://doi.org/10.1891/0047 -2220.11.2.57

Fleming, A. R., Del Valle, R., Kim, M., & Leahy, M. J. (2013). Best practice models of effective voca- tional rehabilitation service delivery in the public rehabilitation program: A review and synthesis of the empirical literature. *Rehabilitation Counseling Bulletin, 56*(3), 146–159. https://doi.org/10 .1177/0034355212459661

Frain, M. P., Ferrin, J. M., Rosenthal, D. A., & Wampold, B. E. (2006). A meta-analysis of rehabilitation outcomes based on education level of the counselor. *Journal of Rehabilitation, 72*(1), 10.

Harrison, D. K., & Lee, C. C. (1979). Rehabilitation Counseling Competencies. *Journal of Applied Rehabilitation Counseling, 10*(3), 135–141. https://doi.org/10.1891/0047-2220.10.3.135

Hartley, M. T., Tarvydas, V. M., & Saia, T. A. (2021). Rehabilitation counseling. In C. C. Cottone, V. M. Tarvydas, & M. T. Hartley (Eds.), *Ethics and decision making in counseling and psychotherapy* (5th ed., p. 209). Springer Publishing.

Jaques, M. E. (1959). *Critical counseling behavior in rehabilitation settings.* University of Iowa, College of Education.

Jaques, M. E. (1970). *Rehabilitation counseling: Scope and services.* Houghton Mifflin.

Jenkins, W., & Strauser, D. R. (1999). Horizontal expansion of the role of the rehabilitation counselor. *Journal of Rehabilitation, 65*(1), 4.

Jenkins, W., Patterson, J. B., & Szymanski, E. M. (1992). Philosophical, historic, and legislative aspects of the rehabilitation counseling profession. In R. M. Parker & E. M. Szymanski (Eds.), *Rehabilitation counseling: Basics and beyond* (2nd ed., pp. 27–55). Pro-Ed.

Leahy, M. J. (2009). Prologue: Rehabilitation counseling credentialing: Research practice and the future of the profession. *Rehabilitation Counseling Bulletin, 52*(2), 67–68.

Leahy, M. J. (2012). Qualified providers of rehabilitation counseling services. In D. R. Maki & V. M. Tarvydas (Eds.), *The professional practice of rehabilitation counseling* (pp. 193–211). Springer Publishing.

Leahy, M. J., Chan, F., Iwanaga, K., Umucu, E., Sung, C., Bishop, M., & Strauser, D. (2019). Empirically derived test specifications for the certified rehabilitation counselor examination: Revisiting the essential competencies of rehabilitation counselors. *Rehabilitation Counseling Bulletin, 63*(1), 35–49. https://doi.org/10.1177/0034355218800842

Leahy, M. J., Chan, F., & Saunders, J. (2003). Job functions and knowledge requirements of certified rehabilitation counselors in the 21st century. *Rehabilitation Counseling Bulletin, 46*(2), 66–81. https://doi.org/10.1177/00343552030460020101

Leahy, M. J., Chan, F., Sung, C., & Kim, M. (2013). Empirically derived test specifications for the CRC examination. *Rehabilitation Counseling Bulletin, 56*(4), 199–214.

Leahy, M. J., Muenzen, P., Saunders, J. L., & Strauser, D. (2009). Essential knowledge domains underlying effective rehabilitation counseling practice. *Rehabilitation Counseling Bulletin, 52*(2), 95–106. https://doi.org/10.1177/0034355208323646

Leahy, M. J., Rak, E., & Zanskas, S. A. (2016). A brief history of counseling and specialty areas of practice. In M. Stebnicki & I. Marini (Eds.), *Professional counselor's desk reference* (2nd ed., pp. 3–8). Springer Publishing.

Leahy, M. J., Shapson, P. R., & Wright, G. N. (1987). Rehabilitation practitioner competencies by role and setting. *Rehabilitation Counseling Bulletin, 31*, 119–131.

Leahy, M. J., & Szymanski, E. M. (1995). Rehabilitation Counseling: Evolution and Current Status. *Journal of Counseling & Development, 74*(2), 163–166. https://doi.org/10.1002/j.1556-6676.1995.tb01843.x

Leahy, M. J., Szymanski, E. M., & Linkowski, D. C. (1993). Knowledge importance in rehabilitation counseling. *Rehabilitation Counseling Bulletin, 37*, 130–145.

Mackay, M. M., Dunn, J. P., Suedmeyer, E., Schiro-Geist, C., Strohmer, D. C., & West, S. L. (2020). Rehabilitation counselor degree type as a predictor of client outcomes: A comparison of quantity versus quality in closure rates. *Rehabilitation Counseling Bulletin, 63*(2), 91–101. https://doi.org/10.1177/0034355218806378

McCarthy, A. K. (2015). Relationship between rehabilitation counselor efficacy for counseling skills and client outcomes. *Journal of Rehabilitation, 80*(2), 3.

Muthard, J. E., & Salomone, P. (1969). The roles and functions of the rehabilitation counselor. *Rehabilitation Counseling Bulletin, 13*, 81–168.

Pruett, S. R., Swett, E. A., Chan, F., Rosenthal, D. A., & Lee, G. K. (2008). Empirical evidence supporting the effectiveness of vocational rehabilitation. *Journal of Rehabilitation, 74*(1), 56.

Rubin, S. E., & Roessler, R. T. (1995). *Foundations of the vocational rehabilitation process* (4th ed.). Pro-Ed.

Sales, A. (2007). *Rehabilitation counseling: An empowerment perspective.* Pro-Ed.

Roessler, R. T., & Rubin, S. E. (1992). *Case management and rehabilitation counseling: Procedures and techniques* (2nd ed.). Pro-Ed.

Rubin, S. E., Matkin, R. E., Ashley, J., Beardsley, M. M., May, V. R., Onstott, K., & Puckett, F. D. (1984). Roles and functions of certified rehabilitation counselors. *Rehabilitation Counseling Bulletin, 27*, 199–224.

Saunders, J. L., Barros-Bailey, M., Chapman, C., & Nunez, P. (2009). Rehabilitation counselor certification. *Rehabilitation Counseling Bulletin, 52*(2), 77–84. https://doi.org/10.1177/0034355208325077

Shapson, P. R., Wright, G. N., & Leahy, M. J. (1987). Education and the attainment of rehabilitation competencies. *Rehabilitation Counseling Bulletin, 31*, 131–145.

Sherman, S. G., Meola, C. C., Eischens, P., Scroggs, L. B., & Leierer, S. (2017). Factors influencing state-federal vocational rehabilitation agency consumers. *Journal of Rehabilitation, 83*(4), 51.

Smith-Fess Act. (1920). *Pub, L,* 66.

Szymanski, E. M. (1985). Rehabilitation counseling: A profession with a vision, identity, and a future. *Rehabilitation Counseling Bulletin, 29*, 2–5.

Szymanski, E. M. (1991). The relationship of the level of rehabilitation counselor education to rehabilitation client outcome in the Wisconsin Division of Vocational Rehabilitation. *Rehabilitation Counseling Bulletin, 35*, 23–37.

Szymanski, E. M., & Danek, M. M. (1992). The relationship of rehabilitation counselor education to rehabilitation client outcome: A replication and extension. *Journal of Rehabilitation, 58*, 49–56.

Szymanski, E. M., & Parker, R. M. (1989). Relationship of rehabilitation client outcome to level of rehabilitation counselor education. *Journal of Rehabilitation, 55*, 32–36.

Szymanski, E. M., Leahy, M. J., & Linkowski, D. C. (1993). Reported preparedness of certified counselors in rehabilitation counseling knowledge areas. *Rehabilitation Counseling Bulletin, 37*, 146–162.

Szymanski, E. M., Linkowski, D. C., Leahy, M. J., Diamond, E. E., & Thoreson, R. W. (1993). Validation of rehabilitation counseling accreditation and certification knowledge areas: Methodology and initial results. *Rehabilitation Counseling Bulletin, 37*, 109–122.

Van Houtte, E. M. (2013). The effects of level of counselor education on client outcomes in the public vocational rehabilitation system of New Jersey. *Rehabilitation Research, Policy, and Education, 27*(4), 234–245. https://doi.org/10.1891/2168-6653.27.4.234

Wright, G. N. (1980). *Total rehabilitation.* Little, Brown.

Wright, G. N., & Fraser, R. T. (1975). *Task analysis for the evaluation, preparation, classification, and utilization of rehabilitation counselor track personnel (Wisconsin Studies in Vocational Rehabilitation Monograph no. 22, Series 3).* University of Wisconsin.

CHAPTER 5

Professional Credentialing

STEPHEN A. ZANSKAS

LEARNING OBJECTIVES

After reading this chapter, you should be able to:

- *Describe the role of credentialing in expanding career opportunities for professional rehabilitation counselors (RCs).*
- *Distinguish the purposes of and the difference between accreditation, certification, and licensure.*
- *Identify the professional associations associated with rehabilitation counseling.*
- *Understand the credentialing challenges confronting RCs, including changes in the legislative foundation, licensure requirements, and behavioral health and third-party insurance reimbursement.*

CACREP STANDARDS

CACREP 2016 Core: 2F1.d, 2F1.f, 2F1.g
CACREP 2016 Specialties:
   Clinical Rehabilitation Counseling: 5D1.a, 5D2.a, 5D2.r, 5D2.t, 5D2.v
   Rehabilitation Counseling: 5H1.a, 5H2.a, 5H2.j, 5H2.n, 5H2.o, 5H2.p

INTRODUCTION

Rehabilitation counseling is a dynamic counseling specialization with a rich history that is experiencing tremendous growth and transition. The Bureau of Labor Statistics (BLS, 2021) projects that the employment of rehabilitation counselors (RCs) will grow by 10% between 2020 and 2030, about average for all occupations. However, this projection is conservative, as many RCs have worked under other job titles since the 1980s, including employment as mental health counselors in community and behavioral healthcare settings (Dew & Peters, 2002; Goodwin, 2006; Stebnicki, 2009). As employment opportunities have expanded, so too has the regulatory role of credentialing. It is thus critical that RCs understand the regulatory role of professional credentialing to have the broadest scope of practice possible.

    The good news is that RCs are accustomed to practicing in a rapidly changing labor market (Leahy, 2009; Leahy, Chan, et al., 2012; Stebnicki, 2009; Zanskas & Leahy, 2007). Over the years, a variety of social and labor-market trends have impacted rehabilitation counseling with respect to practice, setting, and service delivery (Hershenson & McKenna, 1998; Leahy et al., 2003; McClanahan & Sligar, 2015; Stebnicki, 2009; Zanskas & Leahy, 2007). These trends have included evolving knowledge and skill requirements, legislative changes, and behavioral health and insurance reimbursement, all of which have had a significant impact on the credentialing of RCs (Emener & Cottone, 1989; Hershenson & McKenna; Leahy et al., 2003; Leahy, Chan, et al., 2012; McClanahan & Sligar; Shaw et al., 2006; Stebnicki; Tarvydas et al., 2009; Zanskas & Leahy). In other words, RCs have a long history of navigating labor-market changes, including more recent changes that are occurring within the broader counseling profession.

The counseling profession is in a state of change, and the credentialing mechanisms of accreditation, certification, and licensure are as relevant to the process of professionalization of counseling as ever before (Emener & Cottone, 1989). With rehabilitation counseling recognized as an official specialization of the counseling profession, it is an exciting time to be a RC because it is rife with opportunity. As a gateway to professional practice, RCs interested in maximizing their employment opportunities must understand professional credentialing. As rehabilitation counseling and the counseling profession continue to mature, the requirements for professional credentialing will become both more restrictive and important for an individual practitioner's ability to practice professional counseling.

Credentialing is the establishment of minimum standards, qualifications, and/or requirements necessary to practice professional counseling. As part of the professionalization of counseling, the credentialing process serves two fundamental purposes: (a) control of the profession and (b) public recognition of the profession (Tarvydas et al., 2009). This chapter is intended to assist RCs to understand professional credentialing and the factors influencing the practice of rehabilitation counseling. In order to accomplish this objective, the credentialing mechanisms of accreditation, certification, and licensure as well as the role of professional associations and legislative changes are discussed. As credentialing continues to grow, it is imperative that RCs understand both the basics and emerging trends and planned initiatives.

ACCREDITATION

Accreditation is the process that organizations or educational programs undergo to demonstrate the fact that they have met predetermined criteria and standards. Rather than being at the individual practitioner level, accreditation is at an institutional or organizational level. According to the Council for Higher Education Accreditation (CHEA), accreditation in higher education is intended to "ensure that appropriate and effective teaching, support, assessment and learning resources are provided for students; that the learning opportunities provided are monitored; and that the provider considers how to improve them" (CHEA, n.d, p. 3). In this way, accreditation of rehabilitation counselor education (RCE) programs is an evaluation process whereby an academic program completes a self-study and then undergoes an external peer-reviewprocess, which usually includes an on-site visit (Urofsky, 2013). Accreditation is the main way RCE programs show that high-quality training is being done to prepare new counselors for the field.

Graduation from an accredited educational program is often the first step in obtaining the professional credentials to become a counselor. This is because accreditation distinguishes that the graduate has obtained the education and fundamental counseling skills and knowledge prior professional practice (Tarvydas et al., 2015). A benefit of graduating from an accredited educational program is that graduates often are automatically eligible "to apply for certification and licensure through curriculum equivalency provisions" (Tarvydas et al., 2015, p. 17). Graduates of nonaccredited counseling programs may submit documentation to demonstrate the completion of equivalent educational standards; however, there is no guarantee that the nonaccredited program's educational standards will be accepted. The reality is that a graduate from a nonaccredited program will need to submit copious amounts of documentation, including all syllabi and sometimes even key assignments. In contrast, graduates of accredited programs have had this work done for them, with recognition that their program curriculum was aligned with national accreditation standards. Historically, there have been two primary accreditation bodies for counseling specializations: the Council on Rehabilitation Education (CORE) and the Council for Accreditation of Counseling and Related Educational Programs (CACREP).

Council on Rehabilitation Education

Understanding accreditation begins with CORE because it was the first accreditation body for professional counselors. The impetus for CORE emerged when a group of professionals in the field of rehabilitation counseling met in 1969 to discuss the need for a more standardized process for training RCs. By 1972, CORE (n.d) was formally incorporated with a board that included the following five rehabilitation professional organizations:

- American Rehabilitation Counseling Association (ARCA)
- International Association of Rehabilitation Facilities, later renamed the American Rehabilitation Association
- Council of State Administrators of Vocational Rehabilitation (CSAVR)
- Council of Rehabilitation Counselor Educators, which later became the National Council on Rehabilitation Education (NCRE)
- National Rehabilitation Counseling Association (NRCA)

Throughout its history, CORE (n.d) developed and regulated educational standards for the accreditation of graduate programs in rehabilitation counseling and undergraduate rehabilitation education programs as well as standards for other academic-based rehabilitation programs.

Officially recognized by the CHEA and the ASPA, CORE's board of directors came from diverse rehabilitation-related organizations. Some of these organizations changed over time, but CORE continued to be made up of diverse rehabilitation organizations including representation and leadership from individuals with disabilities (Shaw & Kuehn, 2009). In 2013, CORE was encouraged by the CHEA to change its board away from only organizational representatives to include no more 12 and no fewer than 9 at-large members, including public members who applied to serve on the board. This shift was important because it created more access for diverse representation on the board by creating more equity in terms of who could serve on the board and set policy around the training requirements for RCs.

Over the years, CORE conducted systematic reviews of its standards to assure that they continued to be relevant and firmly grounded in research (Leahy & Tansey, 2008). As the first accreditation body in counseling, its educational standards for RCs represents a critical part of the long history of professionalization of counseling, including the foundation of rehabilitation counseling practice (Berven, 1979; Emener & Rubin, 1980; Jaques, 1959; Leahy et al., 2003; Leahy, Muenzen, et al., 2009; Leahy et al., 1987, 1993; Muthard & Salamone, 1969; Wright & Fraser, 1975). Stated another way, rigorous empirical knowledge on the training needs of RCs contributed to a unique professional identity among the various counseling specialties, including research on preservice training and graduate program curricula that has shaped accreditation standards (Leahy, 2012). While the master's degree in rehabilitation counseling has long been a terminal degree for clinical counseling practice, CORE also maintained an undergraduate registry.

A **registry** is a less restrictive process than accreditation because while an academic program submits information about its program, there is no external evaluative review process. To address the regulation of undergraduate programs in rehabilitation education, CORE changed its commission structure in July 2008. The Committee on Undergraduate Education (CUE) became the Commission on Undergraduate Standards and Accreditation (CUSA). A few years later, the graduate and undergraduate commissions merged, going from two commissions to one commission for both graduate and undergraduate programs. Today, undergraduate programs in rehabilitation are accredited by the Committee on Rehabilitation Accreditation (CoRA) through the Commission on Accreditation of Allied Health Programs (CAAHEP, n.d.). A primary reason is that regulation of undergraduate programs became less connected with the graduate programs in rehabilitation counseling as a result of the CORE–CACREP merger in 2017.

With the CORE–CACREP merger,, undergraduate programs were able to remain on a registry under CACREP following the merger; however, there was no momentum to develop a more formal accreditation process through CACREP. The CACREP Undergraduate Rehabilitation Registry (URR) has been inactive, and its future remains uncertain (J. Gunderman, personal communication, February 7, 2022). While CORE had not accredited doctoral degrees, the merger with CACREP meant that doctoral degrees in rehabilitation counselor education started to become accredited in counselor education and supervision. Before we discuss the CORE–CACREP merger, it is important to overview CACREP.

Council for Accreditation of Counseling and Related Educational Programs

Similar to CORE, the mission of the CACREP is to promote the professional competence of counseling and related practitioners through (a) the development of preparation standards, (b) the encouragement of excellence in program development, and (c) the accreditation of professional preparation programs (CACREP, n.d). The CACREP originally was established through a partnership between the Association for Counselor Education and Supervision (ACES) and the American Personnel and Guidance Association (now known as the ACA) in 1981. As part of monitoring the training of professional counselors, the CACREP requires that accredited programs submit "comprehensive assessment plans and document assessment of student learning outcomes for the specific curricular standards" (Urofsky, 2013, p. 10).

The CACREP accredits master and doctoral programs in counseling and its specialties that are offered by colleges and universities in the United States and throughout the world. Specialty programs accredited by CACREP (n.d), include programs in Addictions Counseling; Career Counseling; Marriage, Couple, and Family Counseling; School Counseling; Student Affairs and College Counseling; Clinical Mental Health Counseling; Clinical Rehabilitation Counseling, Rehabilitation Counseling; and School Counseling. In addition to having more than 600 accredited counseling and counseling specialty programs, the CACREP maintains an IRCEP that meets basic standards of program quality and assists in preparation for the accreditation process (Erford, 2014).

Accredited by the CHEA, the CACREP has a board of directors made up of 13 to 15 members. Of those members, eight must be counselor educators, at least two must be counseling practitioners, and at least two must be public members. Historically, the CACREP board has consisted of counselor educators from across the counseling specialty areas. Leading up to the merger agreement between the CACREP and CORE, the CACREP agreed that two of its board members should represent the profession of rehabilitation counseling in two areas: (a) clinical rehabilitation and the (b) rehabilitation. The clinical rehabilitation accreditation was developed by the CACREP, while the Rehabilitation accreditation was based on the accreditation standards developed by CORE.

The CACREP undertakes a standards revision for its programs about every 8 years to improve its accredited programs and make sure its standards remain relevant. The current revision of the CACREP Standards is of critical importance to RCs. Areas of standards that govern infusion of disability content into the curriculum for all counselors, the definition of who is eligible to serve as a faculty member in RCE programs, and even the name of the specialty standards are being determined (Peterson & Olney, 2020). Currently, the CACREP has maintained two different accreditations for RCs: (a) Rehabilitation Counseling and (b) Clinical Rehabilitation Counseling. The Rehabilitation

Counseling accreditation prepare graduates to work in the areas of vocational rehabilitation, forensics, insurance rehabilitation, and worker compensation, while the Clinical Rehabilitation Counseling accreditation is broader in that it mirrors Clinical Mental Health Counseling. It is too soon to know what will happen with the current revision process and whether there will be two different accreditations for RCs. The last update on the revision process and draft standards was during the fall of 2020, and in March 2021, the Standards Revision Committee posted the first draft of the proposed revision. The CACREP Standards Revision Committee is maintaining its agenda and continuing to work on its revision, slated for completion in 2024 (CACREP, 2021).

The Council on Rehabilitation Education and the Council for Accreditation of Counseling and Related Education Programs Merger

On July 30, 2017, CORE dissolved and on July 1, 2017, CACREP began to carry on the mission of both organizations (CORE, 2015). On that date, all CORE-accredited programs became CACREP-accredited programs. The merger between CORE and the CACREP was long sought after with the intent of moving the counseling profession forward by creating one counseling accreditation organization. As outlined in the CORE–CACREP press release dated July 20, 2015, the organizations stated that their vision for a unified counseling profession was better realized through a merger of both the organizations.

CORE and the CACREP had been in dialogue for decades leading up to the 2017 merger. As far back as 2002, CORE voted to establish a task force to explore a written agreement with the CACREP to unify and promote the counseling profession. A task force was formed and a written MOU for merger was developed between the two organizations. In 2007, the CACREP board voted to accept the agreement, whereas the CORE board chose not to vote on the MOU due to concerns about the CACREP's requirements for faculty and program credit hours (48 vs. 60); thus, the merger failed. Dialogue continued between the two organizations, and on July 12, 2013, CORE became a corporate affiliate of CACREP and began a process to administer both CORE's traditional RC standards and the clinical RC standards owned by the CACREP (CORE, 2013). In 2014, each of the organizations elected a member to serve on the other's board of directors (CORE, 2014). The following year, in 2015, CORE and the CACREP signed a plan of merger agreement, and in 2016, it was announced that PhD programs in rehabilitation counseling would become eligible for accreditation under the CACREP.

Individuals and professional organizations have had diverse opinions on the merger. Although some organizations, such as the National Council on Rehabilitation Education (NCRE, 2015), went on record to support the merger, other organizations and RCs have had mixed reactions. The merger is a clear example of the professionalization of rehabilitation counseling within the broader counseling profession, yet whenever professions strive to control and regulate who can practice, there is often pushback from others who believe they have equivalent training, education, and competence. As an example, the 2009 CACREP Standards established minimum standards for core faculty that included two types of stipulations that were carried over to the 2016 Standards (Urofsky et al., 2009). First, new faculty hired after July 1, 2013, had to "have earned a doctoral degree in counselor education and supervision . . . preferably from a CACREP-accredited program, or have been employed as full-time faculty members in a counselor education program for a minimum of one full academic year before July 1, 2013" (2016, p. 6). Second, at least half of the credit hours taught during any calendar year must be taught by a minimum of three faculty members who identified as counselor educators (CACREP, 2016). The intent of these standards was to enhance the professionalization of counseling by ensuring that primary or "core" counselor education faculty possessed a clear identity as professional counselors. However, faculty who do not met these criteria cannot be considered "core," which was perceived by some to be overly restrictive and may have negatively impact the quality of RC training programs (Peterson & Olney, 2020). With the CACREP currently engaged in a revision of their policies and standards, many RCs are watching intently to see if these regulations will be changed in the 2024 Standards.

CERTIFICATION

Certification is a credentialing process developed by a group in order to foster the group's professional identity and define their specialty area of practice. The relationship between accreditation and certification is complex, with some certifications available only to graduates of a certain type of accredited education program or programs determined to be equivalent by the certification body. However, certification usually occurs after a student has graduated from an accredited education program, although sometimes certification exams are used within education programs as a comprehensive exit exam.

The purpose of certification is to ensure that counseling practitioners have the knowledge, skills, and experience necessary to practice nationally and in specialty practice settings. Certification in counseling is similar to that in other professions, "such as medical doctors, who are licensed by their state to practice general medicine, yet apply for board certifications to demonstrate their expertise in a specialty field (i.e., allergist, cardiologist, endocrinologist)" (Tarvydas et al., 2015, p. 18). Certification organizations hold their certificants accountable to peer-reviewed standards and have codes of ethics by which their certificants must abide. Certification is a voluntary process that is often critical to the hiring and selection of practitioners who wish to specialize. In certain practice settings, practitioners are required to hold certifications. Certification bodies typically require continuing education at various intervals so that those who are certified can stay current in the field in order to maintain their certification. The two primary certification bodies in our field are the Commission on Rehabilitation Counselor Certification (CRCC) and the National Board for Counselor Certification (NBCC).

Commission on Rehabilitation Counselor Certification

Incorporated in 1974, the Certified Rehabilitation Counselor Certification (CRCC) is the oldest established credentialing body in the counseling profession (Saunders et al., 2008). Since 1980, the CRCC has been accredited by the National Commission for Certifying Agencies (NCCA). Currently, the CRCC has more than 17,000 certified rehabilitation counselors (CRCs) in the United States (CRCC, n.d). In addition to the flagship CRC credential, the CRCC has created other CRC certifications and designations in the past, including the Canadian Certified Rehabilitation Counselor CCRC, Certified Rehabilitation Counselor-Master Addictions Counselor (the CRC–MAC), and Certified Rehabilitation Counselor-Clinical Supervisor (the CRC-CS). All these certifications eventually became supported in maintenance mode only with no active applications being accepted.

The CRCC also has maintained certifications from other organizations that are no longer offered. For instance, the Commission on Certification of Work Adjustment and Vocational Evaluation Services (CCWAVES) offered three active certifications: Certified Vocational Evaluation (the CVE) from 1981 to 2008, Certified Work Adjustment (the CWA) from 1981 to 1990, and Certified Career Assessment Associates (the CCAA) from 1997 to 2002. CCWAVES started in 1981 and used the CRCC's Foundation for Rehabilitation Education and Research (FRER) for administrative services. CCWAVES stopped using FRER for administrative services in the early 1990s, when it left to obtain services from

BOX 5.1 ART OF REHABILITATION COUNSELING

Search online for *The Art of Rehabilitation Counseling* (https://www.youtube.com/watch?v=FqfeY3EZBKQ) created by the CRCC. What are some examples of the unique abilities and qualifications of CRCs as described in the video? What makes rehabilitation counselors unique from other counseling specialty areas?

entities in California, Colorado, and Virginia before returning to FRER in 1999. CCWAVES discontinued the active application/exam process for the CVE in 2008 and dissolved on April 1, 2009, at which time the maintenance of credentials was turned over to the CRCC.

Initially, the CRCC governance included a 17-member board of directors: 15 of the board members were appointed by professional associations in the field of rehabilitation, in addition to one public member and one at-large member. Today, the board is composed of four elected officers, one student director, one public member not affiliated with the profession of rehabilitation counseling, and six additional directors. This change was important to allow all qualified individuals interested in director or committee positions could submit applications through an annual call. The applications then are vetted using a competency/constituency model to allow for the greatest diversity possible in directors and committee members, thus representing individuals in the field of rehabilitation. Many activities of the CRCC are handled by standing committees. These committees such as the Executive, Ethics, Finance and Audit, Governance, and Standards and Exam Committees. Ad hoc committees are used for special assignments, such as revising the code of ethics that governs the CRC credential.

Eligibility to become a CRC requires a master's degree in rehabilitation counseling or a closely related field and supervision from a professional who has their CRC. There are various categories under which individuals who seek certification can apply, and those categories have changed slightly over the years to assure that all qualified individuals who meet the requirements can sit for the exam. The Certified Rehabilitation Counselor Examination (CRCE) is a 175-item exam consisting of questions across 10 knowledge domains, which are further defined into subdomains. One part of the exam tests counseling knowledge, whereas the other part of the exam tests the applicants' knowledge of rehabilitation and disability issues. In order to pass the exam, applicants must pass both sections of the exam. In 2008, the CRCC began offering its exam in a computer-based format. A number of university rehabilitation counseling programs now utilize the CRC exam as the comprehensive examination for their programs.

The CRCC *Code of Professional Ethics for Rehabilitation Counselors* was first developed in 1987 and has been revised about every 5 years since then. The ethical code has four primary objectives: protecting the public by describing ethical behavior, establishing ethical principles as guidelines for professional behavior, providing a foundation for professional behavior and decision-making, and providing a basis for professional sanction of unethical behavior (CRCC, 2017).

To assist CRCs in staying involved with their profession, the CRCC created an online community. The CRCC community includes a networking platform it calls "Engage," which is open to those interested in learning about the rehabilitation counseling profession. Additionally, the CRCC offers "Aspire," an online job board that connects rehabilitation professionals to employers looking to hire qualified RCs. Finally, CRCC has an "e-university," an online learning community where RCs can take courses for CE. The site allows counselors who complete the training modules to have their CE credits automatically uploaded to their individual CRCC continuing education file (CRCC, n.d.).

National Board for Certified Counselors

Incorporated in 1982, the National Board for Certified Counselors (NBCC) is an independent certification body with more than 62,000 certified counselors in more than 40 countries (NBCC, 2016a). The NBCC, as an organization, parallels the CRCC in terms of continuing education, ethics, examination, and fostering professional identity. Accredited by NCCA, the NBCC has a president, who is the chief executive officer, and a board of directors. The major functions of the NBCC are to establish and monitor a national certification system, identify those counselors who have obtained certification, and maintain a register of those counselors (NBCC, 2016a). The entry-level and flagship certification offered by the NBCC is the National Certified Counselor (NCC). In addition, the NBCC offers three additional specialty certifications: Certified Clinical Mental Health Counselor (CCMHC), Master's Addition Counselor (MAC), and National Certified School Counselor (NCSC).

Eligibility to become an NCC includes a master's degree in counseling or related degree. The NCE is a 200-item test used to assess the knowledge and abilities determined to be important for providing effective counseling (NBCC, 2016b). The NCE was first used in 1983 and has been used widely as the exam for state counselor licensure as well as for the NCC credential. Once an individual passes the NCE, they become eligible for to take additional examinations in a number of specialty areas, including school counseling, clinical mental health and addictions counseling. Each of these specialty certifications requires additional educational, experience, and examination requirements. The NBCC also has its own code of ethics, which governs the behavior of all nationally certified counselors.

One of the specialty areas is the Certified Clinical Mental Health Counselor (CCMHC), which requires applicants to pass the National Clinical Mental Health Counseling Examination (NCMHCE). The NCMHCE consists of 10 simulated clinical mental health counseling cases covering three content areas: assessment and diagnosis, counseling and psychotherapy, and administration, consultation, and supervision. Each simulation involves five to eight sections including both information-gathering and decision-making questions. The information-gathering sections assess the test taker's ability to gather appropriate clinical data required to evaluate a situation or to make a decision. Decision-making sections assess the test taker's ability to solve clinical problems by utilizing data to make judgments and decisions (NBCC, 2016a). The NCMHCE is another exam used for state licensure in some states and in the military health systems (NBCC, 2016b). As the profession continues to mature, we anticipate that the NCMHCE will become more influential in the regulation of counselors who engage in the diagnosis and treatment of mental health disorders.

LICENSURE

Licensure is not to be confused with certification. Only licensure legally governs professional counseling practice in particular jurisdictions, such as individual states (Hosie, 1995). Historically, the licensure of RCs has been perceived as crucial to our professionalization and legally providing the ability to practice counseling (Barros-Bailey et al., 2009; Brubaker, 1977; Cottone, 1985; Hardy et al., 1982; Leahy, 2002; Stebnicki, 2009; Tarvydas & Leahy, 1993; Tarvydas et al., 2009; Trolley & Cervoni, 1999;). As early as 1977, Brubaker

BOX 5.2 CERTIFICATIONS

Use the internet to investigate the certification requirements associated with the CRC, the NCE, and the NCMHCE. Reflect on the benefits and limitations of each certification in relation to your career goals. Which certification is most aligned with your career goals? Why?

expressed that licensing requirements would professionalize our discipline. Despite this long-standing recognition of the importance of licensure, with few exceptions rehabilitation counseling was a late entrant into the counselor licensure movement (Tarvydas & Leahy, 1993; Tarvydas et al., 2009). This lag was due, in part, to professional identity issues of whether RCs were counseling specialists or rehabilitation specialists (Tarvydas & Leahy, 1993; Tarvydas et al., 2009). Additionally, vocational RCs working for the state–federal vocational rehabilitation system have often been, historically, exempted from counselor licensure because they worked for the government (ACA, 2016).

Licensure is a form of public recognition, representing one of the hallmarks of professional legitimization (Rothman, 1987). State counselor licensure laws establish the minimum level of competence necessary to protect the public from harm (ACA, 2016; Tarvydas & Leahy, 1993; Tarvydas et al., 2009; Wheeler & Bertram, 2019). Presently, all 50 states, the District of Columbia, Guam, and Puerto Rico have passed statutes to regulate the title, practice, or title and practice of professional counselors (AASCB, 2021). Each of these 53 governmental bodies has established a regulatory board, often referred to as a licensure board, with oversight over the profession of counseling within its jurisdiction. Licensure is a state's right, and thus, these regulatory boards are responsible for developing the rules and regulations governing the practice of professional counseling, issuing licenses, handling complaints, and enforcing the laws (Stebnicki, 2009; Tarvydas & Leahy, 1993; Tarvydas et al., 2009; Wheeler & Bertram, 2019). Ultimately, licensure boards define the scope of practice for a profession in their respective states. It is important to understand the connections between licensure with accreditation and certification. Many states have written in accreditations like the CACREP, requiring that applicants have graduated from a CACREP-accredited or equivalent master's degree. Additionally, states require a national certification exam offered by the NBCC and the CRCC as well as jurisprudence examinations regarding the laws of the respective state. According to the ACA (2016, p. 7), the following national examinations are among the most frequently required:

- **NCE:** Administered by the NBCC, this is the exam most commonly used by states in the credentialing process.
- **NCMHCE:** Also administered by the NBCC, this examination focuses more specifically on mental health practice, and is used by a number of states for licensure.
- **CRCE:** Administered by the CRCC, the passage of this exam also is accepted in some states for meeting testing requirements for licensure.

The NCE is the most common exam written into licensure laws, followed by the CRCE. The CRCE is recognized in roughly 16 states: Arizona, California, District of Columbia, Illinois, Iowa, Michigan, North Carolina, Oregon, Pennsylvania, West Virginia, Wisconsin, and Wyoming. Alaska, Minnesota, and accept the CRC examination through departmental policy (CRCC, n.d.).

The shift to a 60-credit MA degree in rehabilitation counseling was a response to states requiring 60 graduate credits to become licensed as a professional counselor. Today, the CACREP accreditation in Clinical Rehabilitation Counseling has served to ensure RCs have access to licensure while raising new questions about professional identity because of the additional CACREP accreditation in Rehabilitation Counseling. Whether RCs are counselors first with a specialization in rehabilitation or rehabilitation specialists remains a point of contention. However, these debates are largely academic as the CORE/CACREP merger provides clear evidence of the future direction and opportunities for RCs as counselors who specialize in rehabilitation (Zanskas, 2017).

Title and Practice Licensure Laws

Each state has its own licensure law with states choosing to regulate the title, practice, or both. **Title protection** establishes and restricts the use of specific titles for professional counselors who have met education, training, and experiential requirements (ACA, 2016; Tarvydas &

Leahy, 1993; Tarvydas et al., 2009 Wheeler & Bertram, 2019). According to ACA (2016), the most commonly used title for independent licensure is LPC. Other commonly used titles include LMHC, LCPC, LPCC, LCMHC, and LMHP. In terms of the evolution of counselor licensure laws, states have generally evolved from title to practice or a combination of title and practice protection. Presently, only six states have title-only protection (ACA, 2016). Furthermore, many state have added an associate level for licensure to designate individuals licensed for the purpose of gaining experience required for licensure and who must work under the direct supervision of an independent licensed professional.

While the title used by professional counselors is important, it is the practice of counseling that is written into licensure laws that is most important. **Practice protection** refers to the scope of practice written into the licensure law that prohibits individuals who have not obtained a license from performing the functions of a professional counselor in that state. Because practice protection extends to what a counselor does rather than merely the title the counselor utilizes, it provides the most protection for consumers. According to the ACA (2016), 32 states have both title and practice acts. Of the 32 states with title and practice acts, 27 states and the District of Columbia include career counseling in their scope of practice, and 12 of these states also specifically mention rehabilitation counseling.

There has been considerable variation across different states, which is further becoming more uniform with time. According to the American Association of State Counseling Boards, (AASCB, 2021), the majority of states require a master's degree in counseling (although some accept degrees in a related field), a degree from an accredited university or program, completion of an examination, and on average, 3,000 hours of post-master's experience. Most states also require new graduates to complete a 60-credit-hour counseling-related graduate degree (ACA, 2016). Despite progress toward uniformity, counselor licensure laws remain confusing because of the array of different definitions and rules regulating the title, definition, scope of practice, educational requirements, and postgraduate supervision requirements for counselors (ACA, 2016; Mascari & Webber, 2013; Tarvydas & Leahy, 1993; Tarvydas et al., 2009; Wheeler & Bertram, 2019). These state-by-state differences, in conjunction with regulatory bodies' inconsistent recognition of other regulatory bodies' standards for licensure, historically have limited portability and counselor mobility (Kaplan, 2012).

Licensure Portability and Reciprocity

License portability represents the single most important issue for LPCs. **Portability** refers to a licensed counselor's ability to relocate to other states and retain the privilege of practicing the profession. **Reciprocity**, an older term, refers to state regulatory boards recognizing and accepting an LPC license obtained in another state. Many states have adopted an "equal or exceeds" standard regarding licensure. In other words, most states will accept the applicant's license held and obtained in another state provided the standards of that state meet or exceed their state requirements. **Endorsement** is another term related to licensure portability. Endorsement is a process used to grant a license to an applicant licensed in another state at an equivalent license designation in another jurisdiction.

Licensure portability has long been a goal of the counseling profession and advocated for by the CACREP. In 2006, the AASCB, an organization made up of state licensure boards, collaborated with the ACA to conduct a series of meetings over a number of years titled "20/20: A Vision for the Future of Counseling" (Bobby, 2013). This group worked on core principles common to the counseling profession, such as professional identity, unification of the profession, the definition of counseling, and a common set of counseling standards (Kaplan & Gladding, 2011). The 20/20 Initiative working group agreed on a common definition of a counseling as "a professional relationship that empowers diverse individuals, families, and groups to accomplish mental health, wellness, education, and career goals" (Kaplan et al., 2014, p. 368). During 2007, an attempt at a merger between CORE and the CACREP failed to materialize. In September 2010, the U.S. VA approved a decision to recognize LPCs as those professionals who graduate from a CACREP-accredited program and are qualified to work with clients who have mental health issues. In 2010, the IOM (IOM, 2010) put forth a similar recommendation for those working with veterans in the TRICARE system in the U.S. DoD. At the time, the IOM report suggested that to provide mental health counseling services to military veterans, professional counselors needed to have graduated from a 60-hour CACREP-accredited clinical mental health program. The IOM report contributed to the development of the CACREP accreditation in Clinical Rehabilitation Counseling, which mirrored many of the standards of Clinical Mental Health Counseling.

An encouraging development in counselor license portability is the **Counseling Compact** (Marsalek, 2021; National Center for Interstate Compacts, n.d.). The compact is an interstate contract among states that would allow professional counselors licensed and living in a state to practice in other states without requiring multiple licenses (National Center for Interstate Compacts, n.d.). The Counseling Compact will go into effect once enacted into law in 10 states. At the time of this writing, the states of Georgia and Maryland have adopted the Counseling Compact (Marsalek, 2021). Legislative adoption of the compact is pending in the states of Florida, Nebraska, North Carolina, Ohio, and Tennessee (Marsalek, 2021). Professional counselors who meet the universal licensure requirements established in the compact would be able to obtain the privilege to practice in member states (National Center for Interstate Compacts, n.d). The benefits of the compact include counselor mobility, increased availability of counselors, improving the continuity of care while traveling or following relocation, and the creation of a shared database of LPCs expediting the granting of licensure privileges as well as allowing member states to share investigative and disciplinary data increasing public protection (National Center for Interstate Compacts, n.d.).

Prior to the introduction of an Interstate Compact, there have been previous attempts to provide a path to licensure portability, such as the NCLEP. The NCLEP 1.0 was originally introduced in 2017 (The National Portability Taskforce, 2019), and updated as 2.0 in 2019. A significant aspect component of NCLEP 2.0 was to strongly encourage states to adopt a minimum 60-credit hour master's degree for initial associate counselor licensure with more consistent requirements for an Independent Clinical and Supervised Practice License. NCLEP 2.0 initially was endorsed by AASCB, as well as the ACES, the AMHCA, and the NBCC (The National Portability Taskforce, 2019).

NCLEP 2.0 outlines two options for licensure through endorsement. Applicants in the first option are able to demonstrate that they meet all the requirements for licensure endorsement in the receiving state (The National Portability Taskforce, 2019). Applicants in the second endorsement option must have been licensed as a mental health counselor for at least 3 years before their application for endorsement, are not undergoing professional discipline, have completed the receiving state's background checks, and a jurisprudence or equivalent examination (The National Portability Taskforce, 2019). Additionally, applicants in the second option must also meet one of these requirements (The National Portability Taskforce, 2019): (a) have been licensed to practice independently in another jurisdiction on or before December 31, 2014; (b) possess the NCC credential; and (c) earned a graduate-level degree in counseling from a regionally accredited program by January 1, 2025. After January 1, 2025, applicants under the second option must possess a graduate-level degree from a CACREP-accredited program.

Since counselor licensure will continue to evolve and change, RCs are advised to research the licensure requirements in their current state of residence and in any state to which they might consider relocating. Aspiring professional RCs are encouraged to discuss their career plans with faculty or other mentors and contact licensure boards in order to prepare for potential practice in another state. Even though most professional RCs never plan on moving to another state, there are many reasons for relocation throughout a career and lifetime. In our mobile society, relocation is often unanticipated. Exercising personal due diligence, undertaking broad academic preparation, and engaging in dialogue

BOX 5.3 LEARNING ACTIVITY: COUNSELOR LICENSURE BOARD ACTIVITY

Form a mock state counselor licensure board to discuss the benefits and limitations of portable title and practice legislation across states. With a classmate, assume a role on the state counseling licensure board or be assigned to develop arguments to persuade the board to adopt the exact same title and practice legislation as other states or tailor the title and practice to the needs of citizens in that state. What are the benefits and limitations of having similarities and/or differences across the title and practice of professional counseling?

with mentors will assist prospective professional RCs and established professionals to prepare for the complexities of practicing in another state.

REHABILITATION COUNSELING PROFESSIONAL ASSOCIATIONS

Rehabilitation counseling has a rich, diverse history of many different professional associations. As the field of rehabilitation counseling and counseling continues to unify, there may be increased pressure for the field's professional associations to do the same. Leadership in associations will be looking ahead at the challenges and opportunities of maintaining membership and seeking out ways to attract new members. Typically, common benefits of membership have included awards and grants, journals and newsletters, conferences and continuing education, advocacy and lobbying, and access to unique benefits such as discounted liability insurance. In this section, readers are provided with an introduction to the major rehabilitation counseling associations.

American Rehabilitation Counseling Association

The ARCA was founded in 1958 as one of the first divisions of the American Counseling Association (ACA). According to its website, the ARCA's mission is to enhance the development of people with disabilities throughout the life span and to promote best practices in the rehabilitation counseling profession. To do so, the ARCA's goal is to provide leadership that encourages excellence in rehabilitation counseling practice, research, consultation, and professional development (ARCA, n.d.). The ARCA publishes a scholarly journal, the *Rehabilitation Counseling Bulletin* in addition to its newsletter (Erford, 2014). Organizationally, the ARCA bills itself as an organization of rehabilitation counseling practitioners, educators, and students who are concerned with improving the lives of people with disabilities. Philosophically, the association believes that RCs are counselors with specialized training and expertise in providing counseling and other services to people with disability. One of the ARCA's primary goals is to increase public awareness of rehabilitation counseling and to extend its influence by encouraging members to become involved in the association's outreach and educational efforts (McCarthy, 2020). Other goals include helping members develop their leadership skills through participation in the ARCA's organizational activities and to work with state officials to develop appropriate licensure requirements (ARCA, n.d.).

National Rehabilitation Counseling Association

Founded in 1958, the NRCA was a division of the NRA until the organizations parted ways in 2005. As stated in its original constitution, the purpose of the NRCA is to provide standards of professional conduct and performance for its members (Kirk & LaForge, 1995; Mundt, 1986). The NRCA was involved in the professionalization of landmarks within the rehabilitation counseling profession, including collaborations with the ARCA and other associations. On October 26, 2005, the NRA board of directors voted to withdraw divisional status for NRCA, then a division of the NRA, due to ongoing failure to comply with the NRA constitution and bylaws. This action was effective as of November 1, 2005. As a professional association, the NRCA seeks to improve RC effectiveness through professional meetings and conferences, support research in the field, and provide to its members the *Journal of Applied Rehabilitation Counseling*. In October 2016, theNRCA sent an email to its membership notifying them that the NRCA would officially end all daily office operations as of October 27, 2016 (Sherman, personal communication, December 2016). The NRCA participated in merger discussions with the RCEA and the NRA, although the MOU expired without agreement at the end of 2018 (Zanskas, personal communication, December 2018).

Rehabilitation Counselors and Educators Association

In 2006, after the NRCA and the NRA broke ties with each other, the RCEA was developed to replace the NRCA. In the winter of 2007, the RCEA's first journal came out. The journal continues to be a mix of gray matter (news and views) and peer-reviewed research and conceptual articles. As stated in its bylaws, the RCEA promotes, through its journal and training opportunities, continuing activities to ensure that those in the field of rehabilitation stay up to date about their profession. Public information, as well as continuing education, is recognized as a responsibility of a professional group. The national RCEA is organized to develop, improve, strengthen, and enhance professional standards and performance within the field of rehabilitation counseling. The RCEA is governed by a board of directors and continues to be a division of the NRA. As such, it falls under the constitution of the NRA. The RCEA has affiliated state chapters of its organization in many states in the United States.

National Council on Rehabilitation Education

The NCRE was formed in 1955 as a professional organization for rehabilitation educators. The NCRE (n.d) is governed by a board of directors that includes officers, regional representatives, and international representative and a student representative. The NCRE has a committee structure, including the Council of Past Presidents, nominations, membership, research, and awards. The purpose of the organization, according to its bylaws, is to "promote the improvement of supports and services available to individuals with disabilities and/or chronic illnesses through quality rehabilitation and research" (NCRE, n.d.). The NCRE hosts two conferences annually, a fall and a spring conference. The fall conference features representatives from the RSA and usually is held in the greater District of Columbia area. The NCRE publishes a scholarly journal called *Rehabilitation Research, Policy, and Education*, in addition to its newsletter.

International Association of Rehabilitation Professionals

The IARP is a global association for professionals in private rehabilitation. According to the IARP's bylaws, its mission is to promote competent rehabilitation, disability management, and return-to-work services on behalf of people with disabilities and the economically disadvantaged; support business development; and influence policies that affect private rehabilitation services (IARP, 2016). The IARP is governed by a board of directors with representatives from different sections such as forensic, life care planning, rehabilitation and disability case management, Social Security, and VR transition services. The IARP structure includes director positions for marketing/membership and education. The IARP's paid staff includes directors in the following areas: executive, technology, meetings, and education. The organization hosts conferences and has online educational offerings in addition to an awards and recognition program, job bank, and publications. The IARP's official journals include *The Rehabilitation Professional*, known as *RehabPro*, and the *Journal of Life Care Planning* for members of that section of the organization (IARP, 2016). The IARP hosts professional conferences geared to the private rehabilitation professional. IARP has a code of ethics for its members, which was last amended in 2007, and has standards of practice for life care planners, case management, and vocational/placement.

COORDINATING ASSOCIATIONS

Attempts to unify the rehabilitation counseling organizations began with the Alliance for Rehabilitation Counseling, originally formed by ARCA and NRCA in 1994 (Leahy & Tarvydas, 2001). Although considerable progress was made through the dedicated efforts of leaders in our field, the alliance dissolved in 2002 (Leahy, 2009). Since that time, numerous initiatives have come and gone that have unsuccessfully merged the various associations yet have served to bring together important collaborations. One possible explanation for the inability to unify rehabilitation counseling organizations can be attributed to one of our greatest strengths, our diversity. As reflected in this chapter, there are many organizations that have been developed to represent a specific sector of rehabilitation. Organizationally, each association would need to have a vision of what is essential and what it as an organization could surrender to merge and serve the greater rehabilitation counseling community and the people we serve.

Another notable collaboration was the RCC to collaborate on credentialing and professional issues in 2005 (Leahy, 2009). In 2014, representatives of rehabilitation organizations met to address the future of the rehabilitation counseling profession. As a result of this dialogue, eight rehabilitation organizations established the Rehabilitation Counseling Coalition (2014) to renew strategic planning efforts and advance the profession. Member organizations include the ABVE, the ARCA, the CSAVR, the IARP, the NASPPR, the NCRE, the NRA, and the RCEA. Although well intended, the impact of this coalition remains uncertain.

Prior to the RCC, there had been numerous other attempts to unify the various rehabilitation counseling professional organizations. For instance, the ARCA and the NRCA formed the Alliance for Rehabilitation Counseling in 1994. In 2005, the NRCA withdrew from the NRA and in 2006, the NRA replaced the NRCA with the RCEA. Subsequently, in October 2016, NRCA members voted to merge with the NRA and the RCEA, thereby unifying the field (Angela Price, personal communication, October 20, 2016). Although well intended, the attempt to reunite the three organizations was unsuccessful (F. Schroeder, personal communication, December 2018). Today, there are fewer members of all associations, as membership numbers in all professional membership organizations as well as rehabilitation counseling have continued to decline in the 21st century, leading to potentially less political clout for the field (Leahy et al., 2011).

The most recent example of coordinating associations is the Rehabilitation Counseling Leadership Forum (RCLF), chartered in January 2020 (C. Anderson, personal communication, November 11, 2021). The collaborating organizations included the RCEA, the NCRE, the CSAVR, the CRCC, and the ARCA. Intended as a time-limited collaboration, the goals of the RCLF include identifying the critical issues in rehabilitation counseling, developing a plan to address and inform these issues, promoting professional unification, and promoting the milestones of the public VR program, disability rights, and legislation. Intended as a short-term affiliation, the RCLF continues to work towards these goals.

> ## BOX 5.4 PROFESSIONAL MEMBERSHIPS
>
> Reflect on the importance of membership and active participation in professional rehabilitation counseling associations. Choose a professional association and research the mission and purpose of the organization. What are the benefits of being a member? How does the organization fit with your professional goals?

LEGISLATIVE INFLUENCES

Historically rehabilitation counseling is a profession created by legislative mandate. Today, regardless of setting, the practice of professional rehabilitation counseling is heavily influenced by state and federal legislation. Both experienced and aspiring rehabilitation counselors need to keep informed about legislative developments, understand how these acts might impact their practice, and whenever needed, advocate for legislation that is favorable to our profession and those who we serve. Two major federal influences on the practice of RCs in behavioral health and public rehabilitation are summarized next.

TRICARE

TRICARE is the military healthcare insurance system that covers 9.4 million beneficiaries (TRICARE, 2016a). Beneficiaries of TRICARE include uniformed service members, retired service members, and their families. In 2006, the DoD reported to Congress that LPCs lacked uniform pre-practice training, education, and experience standards to provide the level of care that the DoD mandates for its beneficiaries. Subsequently, in 2010, an IOM report regarding the provision of mental health services under TRICARE recommended that licensed counselors graduating from CACREP-accredited programs in mental health counseling who had also passed the NCMHCE should be allowed to practice independently under TRICARE.

On July 17, 2014, the DoD published the Final Rule regarding the TCMHC (ACA, 2014). It was considered a precedent-setting act in establishing national criteria for LPCs to receive third-party reimbursement. This ruling was a key component in the ACA's effort to demonstrate parity among those providing mental health services. The Final Rule also established a 5-year (rather than 5-month) transition period for meeting education, examination, and supervised clinical practice criteria to January 1, 2017. The Final Rule allows LPCs who meet the following criteria to operate as independent practitioners under TRICARE (TRICARE, 2016b):

1. Possess a master's degree or higher from a mental health counseling program accredited by CACREP and passage of the NCE for licensure and certification
2. Possess a master's degree or higher in counseling from a regionally accredited institution and passage of the NCMHCE
3. Complete a minimum of 2 years' post post–master's degree supervised mental health counseling, including at least 3,000 hours of supervised clinical practice and 100 hours of face-to-face supervision.

Another provision of the Final Rule allowed those LPCs in the Supervised Mental Health Counselor (SMHC) category to continue indefinitely. Only physicians may supervise or refer to an SMHC. As originally drafted, counselors in this category would have no longer been able to practice within TRICARE.

Advocacy by the ACA resulted in the insertion of a broad grandparenting clause that affords LPCs more time to meet the TRICARE transition requirements originally included in The Final Rule until 2027 (ACA, 2015). The amended language is part of the House version of the 2016 NDAA, the legislation that sets the policy and rules for the nation's armed forces. Passage of these revisions would enable an LPC who possesses a master's degree in counseling from an institution that is regionally accredited, or has accreditation from the CACREP, in a 48- or 60-credit-hour program, that has been licensed and practiced in good standing for at least 5 years in their respective state to be certified as an independent practitioner.

The VA revised the standards for licensed professional counselors to specifically include graduates of CACREP-accredited clinical rehabilitation counseling programs on April 3, 2018 (Veterans Affairs, 2018). However, due to the curricular differences between traditional and clinical rehabilitation counseling programs, graduates from traditional rehabilitation counseling programs do not meet the new standards even though both counseling concentrations currently are accredited by the CACREP (Veterans Affairs, 2018).

WORKFORCE INNOVATION AND OPPORTUNITY ACT

The passage of the WIOA, which became public law in 2014, appeared to reverse the progress toward the professionalization of RCs in the state–federal VR system (WIOA, 2014). Master's degrees were mandated for RCs employed in the state–federal VR system in 1992. Despite this mandate, by 2004, 30% to 50% of all public VR counselors still did not have a graduate degree (Chan, 2003). Explanations for the difficulties that states had recruiting and retaining qualified counselors have ranged from salary disparities (Chan, 2003; Frain et al., 2006; McClanahan & Sligar, 2015) to work environments that were incongruent with counselor preparation and expectations (Lustig & Strauser, 2008, 2009; Zanskas & Strohmer, 2010). Regardless of the explanation, according to the comments in the Workforce Investment Act VR Final Rule (34 C.F.R. Parts 361, 363, & 397 Stat. 982, 2016), prospective RCs are only required to have a bachelor's degree in a field closely related to VR, such as VR counseling, social work, psychology, disability studies, business administration, human resources, special education, supported employment, customized employment, or economics.

The rehabilitation counseling community expressed concern about the diminution of standards for RCs in the state–federal VR system. However, the intent of the act was to establish a minimum rather than a maximum academic standard for both VR professionals and paraprofessionals. According to the comments in the Workforce Investment Act VR Final Rule, "there is nothing in the Act or these final regulations to preclude a DSU from continuing to hire VR professionals and paraprofessionals that satisfy the higher standard" (2016, p. 162). As with other legislation, the impact of this law requires monitoring to determine the need for reform.

CONCLUSION

Rehabilitation counseling is a specialty area of counseling that offers tremendous career and employment opportunities. Never have RCs had access to so many employment settings. Rehabilitation counseling has a rich history with more than 60 years of preservice education, pioneering both academic program accreditation and national certification for practitioners in the counseling profession. However, the environment for RCs is undergoing momentous change, and the discipline cannot remain viable by resting on past accomplishments. Although the creation of the clinical RC specialty increases licensing opportunities for graduates of the 60-credit-hourdegree programs, it also raises new questions about our professional identity. The myriad of professional associations contributes to the public's confusion, ability to recognize, and understanding of our discipline. It is a new era, and dynamic leadership is necessary to strategically navigate the intricacies of the future. Many of the founding visionaries who contributed to our professionalization are retiring. New leadership is required, and this represents one of the biggest challenges for our discipline and opportunities for you as a professional.

CONTENT REVIEW QUESTIONS

1. What is the overall purpose of credentialing? Define and give examples of accreditation, certification, and licensure.
2. What are the similarities and differences between licensing and certification as distinct forms of credentialing?
3. What are the differences between title and practice licensure laws?
4. How can portability and the Counseling Compact impact LPCs?
5. What is the primary certification body for rehabilitation counseling?
6. What are examples of professional associations in rehabilitation counseling?
7. How have professional associations been instrumental in the evolution of the rehabilitation counseling profession?
8. What are the challenges and current legislative influences on contemporary rehabilitation counseling practice?

REFERENCES

American Association of State Counseling Boards. (2021). *Licensure portability*. http://www.aascb .org/aws/AASCB/pt/sp/licensure

American Counseling Association. (2014). *Final TRICARE rules more beneficial to Licensed Professional Counselors* [Press release]. http://www.counseling.org/news/news-release-archives/by-year/ 2014/2014/07/18/final-tricare-rules-more-beneficial-to-licensed-professional-counselors

American Counseling Association. (2015). *More LPCs to be included under new TRICARE language* [Press release]. http://www.counseling.org/news/updates/2015/05/12/more-lpcs-to-be -included-under-new-tricare-language

American Counseling Association. (2016). The center for counseling practice, policy and research. In *Licensure requirements for professional counselors: A state-by-state report 2016 edition*. http://www .arcaweb.org

American Rehabilitation Counseling Association. (n.d.). *Overview*. http://www.arcaweb.org

Barros-Bailey, M., Benshoff, J. J., & Fischer, J. (2009). Rehabilitation Counseling in the Year 2011. *Rehabilitation Counseling Bulletin, 52*(2), 107–113. https://doi.org/10.1177/0034355208324262

Berven, N. L. (1979). The role and function of the rehabilitation counselor revisited. *Rehabilitation Counseling Bulletin, 22*, 84–88.

Bobby, C. L. (2013). The evolution of specialties in the CACREP standard. *Journal of Counseling and Development, 91*(1), 35–43.

Brubaker, D. R. (1977). Professionalization and Rehabilitation Counseling. *Journal of Applied Rehabilitation Counseling, 8*(4), 208–217. https://doi.org/10.1891/0047-2220.8.4.208

Bureau of Labor Statistics. (2021, September 8). *Rehabilitation counselors: Occupational outlook handbook*. U.S. Bureau of Labor Statistics. https://www.bls.gov/ooh/community-and-social-service/ rehabilitation-counselors.htm

Chan, T. (2003). *Recruiting and retaining professional staff in VR agencies: Some preliminary findings from the RSA evaluation study*. American Institutes for Research.

Commission on Accreditation of Allied Health Education Programs. (n.d.). *Committee on Rehabilitation Accreditation*. https://www.caahep.org/CORA.aspx

Commission on Rehabilitation Counselor Certification. (2017). *Code of professional ethics for rehabilitation counselors*. Author.

Commission on Rehabilitation Counselor Certification. (n.d.). *Website*. https://www.crccertification .com

Cottone, R. R. (1985). The need for counselor licensure: A rehabilitation counseling perspective. *Journal of Counseling & Development, 63*(10), 625–629. https://doi.org/10.1002/j.1556-6676.1985 .tb00647.x

Council for Accreditation of Counseling and Related Educational Programs. (2016). *2016 CACREP standards*. www.cacrep.org/wp-content/uploads/2012/10/2016-CACREP-Standards.pdf

Council for Accreditation of Counseling and Related Educational Programs. (n.d.). *Vision and core values*. http://www.cacrep.org/about-cacrep

Council for Higher Education Accreditation. (n.d.). *Principles*. http://chea.org/userfiles/CIQG/Principles_Papers_Complete_web.pdf

Council on Rehabilitation Education. (2013). *CORE press release* [Press release].

Council on Rehabilitation Education. (2014). *CACREP and its affiliate CORE move forward with accreditation reviews for clinical rehabilitation counseling programs* [Press release].

Council on Rehabilitation Education. (2015). *CORE/CACREP merger agreement signed* [Press release]. Author.

Council on Rehabilitation Education. (n.d.). *What is CORE: Structure and function*. http://core-rehab.org/whatiscore

Dew, D. W., & Peters, S. (2002). Survey of master's level rehabilitation counselor programs: Relationship to public vocational rehabilitation recruitment and retention of state vocational rehabilitation counselors. *Rehabilitation Education, 16,* 61–65.

Emener, W. G., & Cottone, R. R. (1989). Professionalization, deprofessionalization, and reprofessionalization of rehabilitation counseling according to criteria of the professions. *Journal of Counseling and Development, 67,* 576–581.

Emener, W. G., & Rubin, S. E. (1980). Rehabilitation counselor roles and functions and sources of role strain. *Journal of Applied Rehabilitation Counseling, 11*(2), 57–69. https://doi.org/10.1891/0047-2220.11.2.57

Erford, B. (2014). *Orientation to the counseling profession*. Pearson.

Frain, M., Ferrin, J., Rosenthal, D., & Wampold, B. (2006). A meta-analysis of rehabilitation outcomes on education level of the counselor. *Journal of Rehabilitation, 72*(1), 10–18.

Goodwin, L. R. (2006). Rehabilitation counselor specialty areas offered by rehabilitation counselor education programs. *Rehabilitation Education, 20*(2), 133–143. https://doi.org/10.1891/088970106805074485

Hardy, R. E., Luck, R. S., & Chandler, A. L. (1982). Licensure of rehabilitation counselors and related issues. *Rehabilitation Counseling Bulletin, 25,* 157–161.

Hershenson, D. B., & McKenna, M. A. (1998). Trends affecting rehabilitation counselor education. *Rehabilitation Education, 12,* 277–288.

Hosie, T. W. (1995). Counseling specialties: A case of basic preparation rather than advanced specialization. *Journal of Counseling & Development, 74*(2), 177–180. https://doi.org/10.1002/j.1556-6676.1995.tb01847.x

Institute of Medicine. (2010). *Provision of mental health services under TRICARE*. http://www.nap.edu/openbook.php?record_id=12813

International Association of Rehabilitation Professionals. (2016). *Bylaws*. http://www.rehabpro.org/about-iarp/bylaws

Jaques, M. E. (1959). *Critical counseling behavior in rehabilitation settings*. University of Iowa.

Kaplan, D. (2012, January). *Licensure reciprocity: A critical public protection issue that needs action*. Paper presented at the American Association of State Counseling Boards Conference.

Kaplan, D. M., & Gladding, S. T. (2011). A vision for the future of counseling: The 20/20 principles for unifying and strengthening the profession. *Journal of Counseling & Development, 89*(3), 367–372. https://doi.org/10.1002/j.1556-6678.2011.tb00101.x

Kaplan, D. M., Tarvydas, V. M., & Gladding, S. T. (2014). 20/20: A vision for the future of counseling. *Journal of Counseling and Development, 92,* 366–372.

Kirk, F., & LaForge, J. (1995). The national rehabilitation association. *The Journal of Rehabilitation, 61*(3), 47–50.

Leahy, M. J. (2002). Professionalism in rehabilitation counseling: A retrospective review. *Journal of Rehabilitation, 26*(2), 99–109.

Leahy, M. J. (2009). Rehabilitation counseling credentialing: Research, practice, and the future of the profession. *Rehabilitation Counseling Bulletin, 52*(2), 67–68.

Leahy, M. J. (2012). Qualified providers of rehabilitation counseling services. In D. R. Maki & V. M. Tarvydas (Eds.), *The professional practice of rehabilitation counseling* (pp. 193–211). Springer.

Leahy, M. J., Fong, C., & Saunders, J. L. (2003). Job functions and knowledge requirements of certified rehabilitation counselors in the 21st century. *Rehabilitation Counseling Bulletin, 46*(2), 66–81. https://doi.org/10.1177/00343552030460020101

Leahy, M. J., Muenzen, P., Saunders, J. L., & Strauser, D. (2009). Essential knowledge domains underlying effective rehabilitation counseling practice. *Rehabilitation Counseling Bulletin, 52*(2), 95–106. https://doi.org/10.1177/0034355208323646

Leahy, M. J., Shapson, P. R., & Wright, G. N. (1987). Rehabilitation practitioner competencies role and setting. *Rehabilitation Counseling Bulletin, 31*, 119–131.

Leahy, M. J., Szymanski, E. M., & Linkowski, D. C. (1993). Rehabilitation counseling: Evolution and current status. *Journal of Counseling & Development, 74*(2), 163–166. https://doi.org/10.1002/j.1556-6676.1995.tb01843.x

Leahy, M. J., & Tansey, T. N. (2008). The impact of CORE standards across the rehabilitation educational continuum. *Rehabilitation Education, 22*(3), 217–225. https://doi.org/10.1891/088970108805059309

Leahy, Michael J., & Tarvydas, V. M. (2001). Transforming our professional organizations: a first step toward the unification of the rehabilitation counseling profession. *Journal of Applied Rehabilitation Counseling, 32*(3), 3–8. https://doi.org/10.1891/0047-2220.32.3.3

Leahy, M. J., Tarvydas, V. M., & Phillips, B. N. (2011). Rehabilitation counseling's phoenix project: re-visiting the call for unification of the professional associations in rehabilitation counseling. *Rehabilitation Research, Policy, and Education, 25*(1), 5–14. https://doi.org/10.1891/2168-6653.25.1.5

Leahy, M. J., Chan, F., Sung, C., & Kim, M. (2012). Empirically derived test specifications for the Certified Rehabilitation Counselor Examination. *Rehabilitation Counseling Bulletin, 56*(4), 199–214. https://doi.org/10.1177/0034355212469839

Lustig, D. C., & Strauser, D. R. (2008). The relationship between degree type, certification status, and years of employment and the amount of time spent on rehabilitation counseling tasks in state—federal vocational rehabilitation. *Rehabilitation Counseling Bulletin, 52*(1), 28–34. https://doi.org/10.1177/0034355208319999

Lustig, D. C., & Strauser, D. R. (2009). Rehabilitation counseling graduate students' preferences for employment: Agreement between actual and perceived job tasks of state-federal vocational rehabilitation counselors. *Rehabilitation Counseling Bulletin, 52*, 179–188.

Marsalek, D. N. (2021, April 5). *Counseling compact update.* ACA Governmental Affairs Blog. https://www.counseling.org/news/aca-blogs/aca-government-affairs-blog/aca-government-affairs-blog/2021/04/05/counseling-compact-update

Mascari, J. B., & Webber, J. (2013). CACREP Accreditation: A Solution to License Portability and Counselor Identity Problems. *Journal of Counseling & Development, 91*(1), 15–25. https://doi.org/10.1002/j.1556-6676.2013.00066.x

McCarthy, H. (2020). Advocacy to invigorate rehabilitation counseling professional associations: A reflective inquiry and suggested action goals. *Rehabilitation Counseling Bulletin, 63*(3), 179–186. https://doi.org/10.1177/0034355219864649

McClanahan, M. L., & Sligar, S. R. (2015). Adapting to WIOA minimum education requirement for vocational rehabilitation counselors. *Journal of Rehabilitation, 81*(3), 3–8.

Mundt, P. (1986). The National Rehabilitation Counseling Association. *Journal of Rehabilitation, 52*(3), 51–53.

Muthard, J. E., & Salamone, P. (1969). The roles and functions of the rehabilitation counselor. *Rehabilitation Counseling Bulletin, 13*, 81–168.

National Board for Certified Counselors. (2016a). *About NBCC.* http://www.nbcc.org/footer/AboutNBCC

National Board for Certified Counselors. (2016b). *National counselor examination for licensure and certification.* NBCC comment. http://www.nbcc.org/exam/nationalcounselorexaminationforlicensureandcertification

National Center for Interstate Compacts. (n.d.). *Counseling Compact.* https://counselingcompact.org

National Council on Rehabilitation Education. (n.d.). *The national council on rehabilitation education overview.* https//:ncre.org/ncre-overview/bylaw

National Council on Rehabilitation Education. (2015). *CACREP accreditation made available to doctoral programs in rehabilitation counselor education.* http://cacrepdev.wpengine.com/wp-content/uploads/2012/10/Press-Release-10.-22.-15.pdf

The National Portability Taskforce 2019. (2021, September 17). *A toolkit for state counseling boards: Portability standards for counselors.* http://www.aascb.org/aws/AASCB/asset_manager/get_file/390200?ver=7972

Peterson, S., & Olney, M. (2020). An examination of CACREP curriculum standards from a psychiatric rehabilitation recovery model perspective. *Rehabilitation Research, Policy, and Education, 34*(4), 222–234. https://doi.org/10.1891/RE-19-17

Rehabilitation Counseling Coalition. (2014). *Public announcement of the Rehabilitation Counseling Coalition (RCC).* Press release. http://rehabcea.org/article/rehabilitation-counseling-coalition -rcc-officially-announced

Rothman, R. A. (1987). *Working: Sociological perspectives.* Prentice Hall.

Saunders, J. L., Barros-Bailey, M., Chapman, C., & Nunez, P. (2008). Rehabilitation counselor certification: moving forward. *Journal of Applied Rehabilitation Counseling, 39*(4), 12–18. https://doi.org/ 10.1891/0047-2220.39.4.12

Shaw, L., & Kuehn, M. D. (2009). Rehabilitation counselor education accreditation, history, structure, and evolution. *Rehabilitation Counseling Bulletin, 52*(2), 69–76.

Shaw, L., Leahy, M. J., Chan, F., & Catalano, D. (2006). Contemporary issues facing rehabilitation counseling. *Rehabilitation Education, 20*, 163–178.

Stebnicki, M. A. (2009). A call for integral approaches in the professional identity of rehabilitation counseling. *Rehabilitation Counseling Bulletin, 52*(2), 133–137. https://doi.org/10.1177/ 0034355208324263

Tarvydas, V., Hartley, M. T., & Gerald, M. (2015). Professional credentialing. In M. Stebnicki & I. Marini (Eds.), *Professional counselors' desk reference* (2nd ed, pp. 17–22). Springer Publishing.

Tarvydas, V., & Leahy, M. J. (1993). Licensure in rehabilitation counseling: A critical incident in professionalization. *Rehabilitation Counseling Bulletin, 37*(2), 92–108.

Tarvydas, V., Leahy, M. J., & Zanskas, S. (2009). Judgment deferred: Reappraisal of rehabilitation counseling movement toward licensure parity. *Rehabilitation Counseling Bulletin, 52*(2), 85–94.

The National Portability Taskforce. (2019, September 17). *20201 A toolkit for state counseling boards: Portability standards for counselors.* http://www.aascb.org/aws/AASCB/asset_manager/get_ file/390200?ver=7972

TRICARE. (2016a). *Facts and figures.* http://www.tricare.mil/About/Facts?sc_database=web

TRICARE. (2016b). *Mental health counselor provider requirements.* https://www.tricare-west.com/ content/hnfs/home/tw/prov/benefits/benefits_a_to_z/mental_health/mhc_requirements .html

Trolley, B. C., & Cervoni, A. B. (1999). New millennium employment reflections for rehabilitation counselors: A follow-up study. *Rehabilitation Education, 13*(4), 335–347.

Urofsky, R. I. (2013). The Council for Accreditation of Counseling and related educational programs. *Journal of Counseling and Development, 91*(1), 6–14.

Urofsky, R. I., Bobby, C., & Pope, V. (2009). The CACREP 2009 standards. *Counseling Today,* May, 68–69.

Veterans Affairs. (2018). *Staffing. from the VA Handbook 5005/106, Part II, Appendix G43.* Retrieved on October 7, 2021, from. https://www.va.gov/vapubs/viewPublication.asp?Pub_ID=942& FType=2

Wheeler, A. M., & Bertram, B. (2019). *The counselor and the law: A guide to legal and ethical practice* (8th ed.). American Counseling Association.

Workforce Innovation and Opportunity Act. (2014). Pub. L. No. 113–128.

Workforce Investment Act. (2016). VR Final Rule, 34 C.F.R. pts. 361, 363, & 397 Stat. 982.

Wright, G. N., & Fraser, R. T. (1975). *Task analysis for the evaluation, preparation, classification, and utilization of rehabilitation counselor track personnel* (Wisconsin Studies in Vocational Rehabilitation Monograph no.22, Series 3). University of Wisconsin.

Zanskas, S. A. (2017). Stewardship, the accreditation merger, and opportunities for growth. *Journal of Applied Rehabilitation Counseling, 48*(3), 16–19. https://doi.org/10.1891/0047-2220.48.3.16

Zanskas, S. A., & Leahy, M. (2007). Preparing rehabilitation counselors for private sector practice within a core accredited generalist educational model. *Rehabilitation Education, 21*(3), 205–214. https://doi.org/10.1891/088970107805059715

Zanskas, S., & Strohmer, D. C. (2010). Rehabilitation counselor work environment: Examining congruence With prototypic work personality. *Rehabilitation Counseling Bulletin, 53*(3), 143–152. https://doi.org/10.1177/0034355209359812

CHAPTER 6

Disability Policy and Law

MATTHEW C. SALEH AND SUSANNE M. BRUYÈRE

LEARNING OBJECTIVES

After reading this chapter, you should be able to:

- Recognize the array of laws that govern and impact the provision of Vocational Rehabilitation (VR) services.
- Review the specific provisions of laws related to improved employment outcomes for people with disabilities.
- Analyze the implications of this legislation for VR and mental health counseling, practice, training, and research.

CACREP STANDARDS

CACREP 2016 Core: 2F1.g, 2F1.i
CACREP 2016 Specialties:
   Clinical Rehabilitation Counseling: 5D2.r, 5D2.p, 5D2.w, 5D3.e
   Rehabilitation Counseling: 5H1.a, 5H1.f, 5H1.l, 5H1.n, 5H1.m, 5H3.m

INTRODUCTION

Although counseling focuses on the one-on-one relationship between the counselor and the client, services are provided within a context of state and national legislation and regulation that can have a significant influence. As well as being motivators for both service provider and recipient, service availability and outcomes are governed and influenced by a myriad of individual intersecting laws. The purpose of this chapter is to identify a selection of these laws, discuss their provisions, and know why these might be of interest to counselors—particularly those providing services to people with disabilities, including mental health disabilities. Implications for the counseling profession, specifically the specialization of rehabilitation counseling, clinical rehabilitation counseling, and mental health counseling, are presented as well. Employment is the focus of this chapter, as work is a means to economic and social independence, as well as enhanced personal self-confidence and community participation. Access to employment for people with disabilities is a significant key to building a more inclusive society, one that not only contributes to an individual's economic self-sufficiency, but also enables that individual to have a higher quality of life (QOL). In addition, with the increasing incidence of mental health-related conditions in U.S. society (National Institute of Mental Health,

2020), and especially during the novel coronavirus (COVID-19) pandemic (Brooks et al., 2020; Embregts et al., 2020), attention to how these laws protect individuals and influence workplace policies and practices is imperative for service delivery.

Because improved employment outcomes are a primary focus of rehabilitation counseling, this chapter concentrates on laws that support and intersect with employment for people with disabilities. This is a worthy focus, as people with disabilities remain significantly disadvantaged in the employment arena. The ability to work and earn a living is an important contributing factor to individual overall QOL and economic independence, and many of the laws discussed in this chapter are designed to protect and increase opportunities for meaningful and safe employment. People with disabilities experience half the employment participation rates of those without disabilities. In 2018, an estimated 38% of noninstitutionalized working-age (21–64) people with a disability—regardless of gender, race, ethnicity, or education level—were employed, compared to 80% of those without disabilities (Erickson et al., 2020). This translates to significant economic disparities: In 2018, the median annual income for households with at least one working-age person with a disability was $46,900, compared to $74,400 for households that do not have any person with disability (Erickson et al., 2020). A lower median household income translates to a significantly higher percentage of people with disabilities in the United States living below the poverty line (26% compared to 10% of those without disabilities; Erickson et al., 2020).

The following laws have been selected for discussion in this chapter because of their relevance to employment of people with disabilities and those with mental health conditions and their related importance to rehabilitation counseling practice: the Rehabilitation Act of 1973 as amended, the Americans with Disabilities Act (ADA) of 1990 as amended; the Family and Medical Leave Act (FMLA); the Uniformed Services Employment and Reemployment Rights Act (USERRA); the Vietnam Era Veterans Readjustment Assistance Act (VEVRAA); the Workforce Innovation and Opportunity Act (WIOA) of 2014 and its predecessor, the Workforce Investment Act (WIA) of 1998; the Ticket to Work and Work Incentives Improvement Act (TWWIIA) of 1999; workers' compensation laws; the Health Insurance Portability and Accountability Act (HIPAA) of 1996; the Patient Protection and Affordable Care Act (ACA) of 2010; the Mental Health Parity and Addiction Equity Act (MHPAEA) of 2008; and the Genetic Information Nondiscrimination Act (GINA) of 2008. We also briefly update considerations under two laws (the ADA and the Rehabilitation Act) to review federal guidance related to the COVID-19 pandemic, clarifying how these laws pertain to safety procedures, accommodations, medical testing, and other unique aspects of the pandemic.

These laws span more than 40 years, including important recent developments. Readers will learn about workplace disability nondiscrimination requirements in both public and private work settings, disability disclosure and confidentiality issues in employment, specific employment protections afforded to veterans with disabilities, service delivery systems, and emerging issues such as genetic testing and health care considerations as they intersect with Vocational Rehabilitation (VR) systems.

OVERVIEW OF SELECT DISABILITY LAWS

Rehabilitation Act of 1973

Vocational Rehabilitation

Title I of the Rehabilitation Act, as modified by the 1992 and 1998 amendments and by the WIOA of 2014, deals with the state–federal VR system, which provides employment support to individuals with disabilities. The goal of this federal law is to assist states with the operation of "comprehensive, coordinated, effective, efficient, and accountable" VR programs (29 U.S.C. § 720(a)(2)). These programs involve both public- and private-sector services, including vocational assessment, career counseling, job training, job development and placement, assistive technology, supported employment, and follow-along services. In the event that state resources are not sufficient to serve all eligible parties, the Rehabilitation Act mandates that states first provide services to those individuals with the most significant disabilities. Although state VR agencies have discretion in determining which conditions constitute **most significant disabilities**, this term generally refers to individuals with "a severe physical or mental impairment that seriously limits one or more functional capacities (such as mobility, communication, self-care, self-direction, interpersonal skills, work tolerance, or work skills) whose vocational rehabilitation can be expected to require multiple [VR] services over an extended period of time" (34 C.F.R. § 361.5(c)(30)).

Every year, the state and federal VR program serves approximately 1.2 million individuals with disabilities and places approximately 230,000 consumers into competitive employment (Rehabilitation Services Administration, 2016). The funding for the VR service delivery system was more than $3.7 billion in federal fiscal year 2021 (U.S. Department of Education and Rehabilitation Services, 2020).

The 2014 WIOA amendments to Title I of the Rehabilitation Act included the replacement of the preference for preparing people with disabilities for "gainful employment" with a preference for "competitive integrated employment" (§ 100(a)(2)). Under the new definitions implemented by the WIOA, all individuals with disabilities are presumed to be employable. Placement in a competitive integrated employment setting at a prevailing wage rate for at least 90 days is considered a successful final outcome in the Act.

Previously, certain uncompensated vocational outcomes, including homemaker and unpaid family worker, were accepted as legitimate VR closures for individuals deemed unable to seek competitive employment. The new final regulations for the WIOA have eliminated uncompensated employment as a successful outcome for state VR systems, and place significant limitations on the payment of subminimum wages to workers with disabilities (U.S. Department of Education, 2014, 2016). In place of such outcomes, the Final Rule incorporated additional new outcome targets involving supported and customized employment alternatives into the definition of VR employment outcomes.

Other important amendments included initiatives to further integrate VR programs and workforce development systems, common outcomes measures across VR programs to ensure accountability, a new focus on "transition" VR services for youth with disabilities, and efforts to allocate program funding toward "21st-century" work-based learning needs. The WIOA introduced accountability measures for programs covered under the act, including accountability measures related to the program participant rates of unsubsidized employment, median earnings, postsecondary credentials and secondary diplomas, participation in skills training programs leading to postsecondary credential or employment, and core program effectiveness in serving employers (§ 116(a)(2)).

Employment Discrimination

Title V of the Rehabilitation Act of 1973 is the precursor to modern disability law as codified in the ADA, prohibiting discrimination against people with disabilities in the federal employment sector (Rubin & Roessler, 2001). Here, we discuss a few of the sections in Title V, which prohibit employment discrimination by federal agencies, contractors, and programs. The topic of nondiscrimination in private employment will be covered in the subsequent sections discussing Title I of the ADA. The Rehabilitation Act's standards for determining what constitutes employment discrimination mirror those of the ADA and are discussed at length in the next section.

Section 501 of the Rehabilitation Act requires affirmative action and nondiscrimination by executive branch agencies. Section 503 requires the same for federal contractors and subcontractors, applying generally to federal contracts of $10,000 or more, whereas contractors with 50 or more employees and contracts of $50,000 or more are required to implement compliant affirmative action programs. Section 504 prohibits exclusion, discrimination, and/or denial of benefits in activities or programs receiving federal financial assistance or administered by an executive agency (including duty to accommodate, program accessibility, effective communication mediums, and accessible new construction and alterations). Section 508 provides accessibility standards and guidelines for federal agencies in the development, procurement, maintenance, and use of electronic and information technologies. Although Title V of the Rehabilitation Act is important for prohibiting discrimination on the basis of disability by the federal government, federal contractors, and recipients of federal financial assistance, it also served as a valuable model for Title II of the ADA, which extended these protections to state- and local government–funded programs.

In August 2013, new final regulations were released for Section 503 of the Rehabilitation Act, establishing a nationwide "aspirational goal" of 7% for federal contractors and subcontractors hiring people with disabilities. Although not a quota, the new goal requires appropriate outreach and recruitment activities, along with data collection, reporting, and accountability measures for demonstrating effective outreach activities (Rudstam et al., 2014). The new 503 regulations coincided with new rules for the VEVRAA, which similarly set an annual hiring benchmark of 8% for hiring veterans in disability categories, adjusted for regional and industry-specific workforce demographics. The VEVRAA and other veteran employment legislation are discussed later in this chapter.

To aid affirmative action, the 503 regulations require contractors to invite applicants to self-identify as having a disability during the pre- and post-offer phases, using a standardized U.S. Department of Labor (DOL), Office of Federal Contract Compliance Programs (OFCCP, 2014) form. Self-identification must be completely voluntary and no penalty may be imposed for nondisclosure. All records of disclosure must remain confidential and separate from other personnel records. Moreover, disclosure information may not be used for hiring, promotion, or termination decisions, but rather is for the sole purpose of aggregate assessment of employer outreach, recruitment, employment, and accessibility efforts. The U.S. Equal Employment Opportunity Commission (EEOC) released specific guidance clarifying that this "invitation to self-identify" does not violate the ADA's restrictions on pre- and post-offer medical inquiries so long as it is used for affirmative action rather than hiring and employment decisions (EEOC, 2015).

Despite the new regulatory framework, disability disclosure remains a complex issue for employers and employees alike: common barriers to employee self-identification include perceived risk of being fired, losing healthcare benefits, limiting promotion opportunities, unsupportive management, and risk of being treated or viewed differently by coworkers and supervisors (von Schrader et al., 2013).

Americans With Disabilities Act of 1990

The ADA is the seminal piece of federal legislation addressing disability in the workplace. While passing the ADA in 1990, the U.S. Congress called attention to the fact that approximately 43 million Americans had one or more physical or mental disabilities, a number that was expected only to escalate as the age of the U.S. population continued to increase (42 U.S.C. § 12101). By 2010, this figure had risen to an estimated 56.7 million people—19% of the total U.S. population (U.S. Census Bureau, 2012). The ADA reached out to the millions of Americans working in nonfederal employment and extended to them the protections enjoyed by federal employees.

Definition of Disability

Title I of the ADA provides that no covered employer shall discriminate against a qualified individual with a disability on the basis of their disability with respect to job application procedures, hiring, advancement, compensation, job training, or other privileges of employment. The definition of **disability** in the ADA mirrors that contained in the Rehabilitation Act: "(1) a physical or mental impairment that substantially limits one or more of the major life activities of such individual, (2) a record of such an impairment, or (3) being regarded as having such an impairment" (42 U.S.C. § 12102(1)).

Regarding the phrase **major life activities**, the ADA specifically includes functions such as caring for oneself, performing manual tasks, walking, seeing, hearing, breathing, speaking, learning, reading, concentrating, communicating, and thinking. A major life activity also includes the operation of a major bodily function, such as the functions of the immune system, normal cell growth, and the functions of the respiratory, circulatory, endocrine, or neurological systems—to name a few examples (42 U.S.C. § 12102). The ADA Amendments Act (ADAAA) broadened the definition of "major life activities" in a number of ways, including adding the **major bodily functions** category, providing a nonexhaustive list of both major life activities and major bodily functions, and prohibiting consideration of the ameliorative effects of **mitigating measures** (e.g., medication, assistive technologies) in determining whether an individual meets the definition of disability under the law (U.S. Department of Labor Office of Federal Contract Compliance Programs, 2016). The one exception to the "mitigating measures" rule is the use of eyeglasses or contact lenses, the ameliorative effects of which may be considered.

In order for an impairment to qualify as an ADA disability, it must substantially limit a major life activity or bodily function, meaning that the individual is unable to perform— or is significantly limited in the ability to perform—the function or activity as compared with an average person in the general population. One cannot consider mitigating measures when determining whether an impairment substantially limits a major life activity. Thus, an individual who ameliorates the effects of his or her impairment with medication, and as a result experiences few symptoms of the impairment while taking the medication, would nevertheless have an ADA disability if, among other things, the impairment substantially limits a major life activity or bodily function in its unmitigated state.

One important contribution of the ADAAA is that it significantly broadened coverage for psychiatric disabilities under the Prong 1 and 2 ADA definition of disability ("actual" or "record of" disability), most notably by recognizing that episodic impairments that "substantially limit one or more major life activities" are entitled to coverage, and by prohibiting consideration of the ameliorative effects of mitigating measures like medication or therapy (42 U.S.C. § 12102(1)(A)-(E)). This was important in a legal sense, because psychiatric disabilities are "less linear in progression than physical illness . . . tend to be more erratic, less predictable, and more sudden. . . . Many mental illnesses tend to be episodic, following a kind of ebb and flow one rarely sees in physical illness" (Parikh, 2004, pp. 742–43). The ADAAA did, however, provide an exemption for employers under the Prong 3 definition ("regarded as" having a disability), if the disability in question was (or was perceived to be) "transitory and minor" in nature (29 C.F.R. § 1630.15).

The definition of disability under the ADA as originally codified in 1990 initially proved problematic, with the U.S. Supreme Court issuing a series of opinions that dramatically changed the way the ADA is interpreted and who qualified as a person with a disability under the Act, limiting the broad meaning intended by the legislature (National Council on Disability, 2004). In response to the Court's limitations, Congress passed the ADAAA of 2008, which explicitly rejected the narrow judicial constructions of the ADA in favor of the broad coverage that was the original intent of the Act (EEOC, 2008). Although the ADAAA retained the basic definition of disability from the ADA, it specifically overturned judicial holdings that narrowed the definition of disability and overemphasized the effect of mitigating measures such as medications or assistive devices in determining whether an individual meets the definition of having a disability (EEOC, 2011).

Subsequent empirical analysis of ADAAA litigation outcomes found that summary judgments for employers on the basis of a lack of disability status were down significantly since the passage of the ADAAA (Befort, 2013). However, the study also demonstrated that an increase in rulings that an individual is not "qualified for" employment has occurred since the passage of the ADAAA, seeming to indicate that judicial unease with disability discrimination and with reasonable accommodation claims persist nonetheless (Befort, 2013).

Determining Who Is Qualified to Work

In addition to having a disability as defined, individuals must be **qualified** for the position in question—with or without reasonable accommodation. If an applicant or employee cannot perform an essential function of the job, even with reasonable accommodation, then the ADA does not apply and the individual in question is not protected against discrimination. In other words, the ADA does not obligate employers to hire, promote, or provide any other privilege of employment to an individual who simply cannot perform the essential functions of the job. Nevertheless, this requirement protects the employee or applicant against an employer that might otherwise screen out individuals with disabilities based on stereotypes regarding those persons' abilities. Ideally, if employers base their employment decisions on the essential functions of the job rather than marginalized ones, they should be able to determine whether an individual is truly qualified for the position at issue.

Essential functions are those that are not marginal tasks. A job function may be essential if (a) the position exists solely for the performance of such function, (b) there are a limited number of employees available among whom the job function can be distributed and shared, or (c) the function is highly specialized and the employee was hired specifically because of their expertise.

Reasonable Accommodation

Provided that an individual who is otherwise qualified for a position has a mental or physical impairment that substantially limits a major life activity, then the ADA obligates the employer to reasonably accommodate them (42 U.S.C. § 12112). An employer therefore engages in **unlawful discrimination** if (a) the employer fails to provide reasonable accommodation to a qualified individual with a disability and (b) that failure denies the applicant or employee an employment opportunity.

A **reasonable accommodation** is any modification or adjustment to a job, employment practice, or work environment that makes it possible for a qualified individual with a disability to participate in the job application process, perform the essential functions of a job, and/or enjoy benefits and privileges of employment equal to those enjoyed by similarly situated employees without disabilities (EEOC, 2002). Examples of reasonable accommodations include job restructuring, workspace modification, modifying work schedules or instituting flexible work schedules, providing adaptive or assistive equipment, and modifying the job application process or company policies.

Generally, the applicant or employee bears the burden of notifying the employer of the need for accommodation, whether in writing or in the course of conversation. In some circumstances, however, the employer should initiate the process of determining a reasonable accommodation. Specifically, employers should inquire whether an accommodation is necessary when: they know that the employee's or applicant's disability exists and they know or have reason to know that the disability is causing problems in the workplace that can be corrected with a reasonable accommodation.

The ADAAA and its accompanying regulations reaffirmed that the duty to provide reasonable accommodations applies to only two of the **three qualifying prongs** for meeting the definition of disability ("actual" or "record of" disability but not "regarded as" having a disability; EEOC, 2011). Under the "regarded as" prong, an employee may be perceived by an employer as having a disability even where there is no actual qualifying impairment or "record of" that employee having a disability. Although being "regarded as" having a disability meets the ADA definition of disability, the accompanying protections apply primarily to issues of employment discrimination (e.g., failure to hire, termination, failure to promote, harassment, and so forth). An employee who meets the definition of disability under the "regarded as" prong is entitled to ADA protections but is usually not entitled to reasonable accommodations under the act (EEOC, 2011).

Undue Hardship

The duty of an employer to provide reasonable accommodation is limited by the doctrine of **undue hardship,** which means significant difficulty or expense to the employer (42 U.S.C. § 12112). When determining whether a proposed accommodation would constitute an undue hardship, the employer examines factors such as its financial resources, its size, and the impact that the proposed accommodation would have on the operation of the facility. As one might imagine, employers often identify cost as the source of undue hardship (Olsheski & Schelat, 2003, p. 64). When this is the case, the employer should grant the employee or applicant the option of contributing the burdensome portion of that accommodation cost. This arrangement preserves the employment opportunity for the employee or applicant while bringing the employer's cost of accommodation within a reasonable price range.

Input from rehabilitation counseling professionals can be an integral part of the accommodation process. "The most successful accommodations are not developed when the employer operates independently of all others. Rather, they tend to be the product of the efforts of many individuals, including supervisors, union officials, health care workers, rehabilitation counseling professionals, occupational therapists, physical therapists, and ergonomists, among others" (Olsheski & Schelat, 2003, p. 65). Ideally, the accommodation process is one of give-and-take among the employer, the employee or applicant, and the relevant professionals. If there is more than one potential reasonable accommodation, the employer may select which one to implement.

Direct Threat

The ADA does allow an employer to exclude from employment any individual who poses a "direct threat" to workplace safety or to health (42 U.S.C. § 12113(b)). A **direct threat** is a significant, as opposed to slightly increased, risk of substantial harm to the health or safety of the individual or others that cannot be eliminated or reduced by reasonable accommodation (EEOC, 1997). This determination depends on an assessment of the present ability of the employee or applicant to perform job functions, considering reasonable medical opinion based on the best available medical knowledge or other objective evidence. The employer should consider the following factors and apply them equally to all employees and applicants, regardless of disability, when determining the presence of a direct threat: (a) the duration of the risk, (b) the nature and severity of the potential harm, (c) the likelihood that the potential harm will occur, and (d) the imminence of the potential harm (EEOC, 1997).

Medical Testing

The ADA limits the use of pre- and postemployment medical examinations and inquiries as an additional means of preventing employers from basing employment decisions on disability-related stereotypes (42 U.S.C. § 12111). During the initial application stage, an employer may ask any applicant about their professional qualifications for the job and/or ability to perform the essential functions of the job but may not ask any questions regarding the applicant's health, medical history, or history of workers' compensation claims (Rubin & Roessler, 2001). For example, questions with respect to the number of days an applicant was absent in a prior job due to illness or whether the applicant is taking any prescription medication would be prohibited. In addition, no medical examination of any kind is allowed during the preemployment stage. Examinations that are not medical, per se, such as the measurement of an applicant's performance of relevant physical criteria would be allowed, provided that medical measurements such as blood pressure and heart rate are not obtained during or after such test (Rubin & Roessler, 2001).

Acknowledging that it is not always easy to determine whether an examination or inquiry is *medical*, the U.S. EEOC provided guidance outlining certain considerations in making this determination, including whether it is administered by, or has results interpreted by, a healthcare professional or someone trained by a healthcare professional; it is given in a medical setting or uses medical equipment; it is designed to reveal an impairment to physical or mental health; the employer is trying to determine the applicant's physical or mental health or impairments; it is invasive (e.g., drawing of blood, urine, or breath); it measures an applicant's physiological responses to performing the task (EEOC, n.d.-b).

Once the employer has extended an offer of employment to the applicant, however, the employer may condition such offer upon a medical exam or responses to medical inquiries, provided that such exams or inquiries are required for all entering candidates in that job category. If the employer screens out an applicant due to the presence of a disability, it must show that such a decision was "job-related and consistent with business necessity" (42 U.S.C. § 12112(d)). The ADA provides that employers must keep any employee medical information or medical histories that it receives in separate medical files and treat all such information as a confidential medical record (42 U.S.C. § 12112; EEOC, n.d.-a). More than 10 million workers sign authorizations every year, before the commencement of their employment, for the release of medical records (Rothstein & Talbott, 2007).

It is useful to note that the GINA of 2008, discussed later in this chapter, provides additional prohibitions against medical inquiries by employers (such as requests for family medical history), and prohibits employers from requesting, requiring, or purchasing medical records or personal/family medical data (§ 202(a)–(b); EEOC, 2013).

Corresponding State Disability Law

Although Title I of the ADA applies only to employers having 15 or more employees, disability nondiscrimination legislation enacted by states may be more expansive. For example, New York (N.Y. Exec. Law § 292), California (Cal. Gov. Code § 12926) and other states have passed disability nondiscrimination legislation applicable to employers having fewer than 15 employees. Therefore, individuals who would be unable to file a claim against an employer under the ADA due to the small size of the employer's business should determine whether their claim is nevertheless viable under state law. RCs should familiarize themselves with the disability laws that are applicable in the states in which they practice.

Accommodating Individuals With Psychiatric Disabilities

The prevalence of mental disorder in the United States is quite high. In 2019, there were an estimated 51.5 million adults aged 18 or older in the United States with some type of mental illness, representing 20.6% of all U.S. adults (National Institute of Mental Health, 2020). That same year, there were an estimated 13.1 million adults aged 18 or older in the United States with a "serious mental illness," representing 5.2% of all U.S. adults (National Institute of Mental Health, 2020). The labor force participation rate of individuals with mental health disabilities has consistently lagged behind not only that of employees without disabilities but also that of all employees with a disability in general. According to the 2002 NHIS data, the employment rate of people aged 25 to 61 with mental illness was 37.1%—lower than that of people with physical impairments (43.8%) and those with sensory impairments (58.6%). A more recent analysis estimated an approximately 80% unemployment rate for Americans with mental health disabilities (National Alliance on Mental Illness, 2014). For comparison, in 2013 the employment rate for working-age people (21–65) with "any disability" was 34.5%, whereas the rate for people without any disability was 76.8% (Erickson et al., 2020). Not surprisingly, the workplace accommodation of individuals with psychiatric disabilities presents unique issues and leads to unique problems that merit separate discussions.

The ADA accommodation process encourages employers and employees to share information with each other. The employer has the right to request information regarding the nature of that disability so that it may make an informed decision regarding the accommodation request. Because psychiatric disabilities are often invisible or episodic, the employer may need to ask more questions and/or require reasonable documentation in order to determine an appropriate accommodation. Employees are encouraged to communicate with their employer in order to assist the employer in selecting the most effective accommodation. These forces, which strongly favor the disclosure of information regarding a psychiatric disability, run counter to an opposing force: the stigma of having a psychiatric disability. That stigma could cause the employer to assume, often incorrectly, that the individual with a psychiatric disability poses a significant risk to the health and safety of other individuals in the workplace, due in part to stereotypical beliefs about the association of psychiatric disability and violent behavior (Rubin & Roessler, 2001).

Some of the legal complexities related to preventing workplace discrimination for individuals with mental health disabilities include the episodic nature of many mental health conditions, the frequently shifting professional consensus on what constitutes a mental health condition, and the legal inconsistencies in the duty to accommodate where employers are unaware of the existence of a disability (Kaminer, 2016). Faced with the stigma of psychiatric disability, some rehabilitation counseling professionals have advised clients against disclosing prior hospitalizations to employers (Campbell, 1994). This would prevent an employee from obtaining ADA accommodation, however, because employers need not provide any accommodation for individuals with disabilities of which the employer is unaware (42 U.S.C. § 12112).

In contrast, the ADA confidentiality provisions forestall employers from sharing any information regarding an employee's psychiatric condition with fellow workers. If coworkers question the employer about an individual with a psychiatric disability, employers may not disclose that they are providing a reasonable accommodation to any particular individual, and they should state instead that they are "acting for legitimate business reasons or in compliance with federal law" (EEOC, 1997). In that respect, an employee need not be concerned that the opinion of their coworkers will be influenced by knowledge of their psychiatric condition.

Updated Federal Guidance on Employment Discrimination During the COVID-19 Pandemic

The public health emergency presented by the COVID-19 pandemic created concern among employers related to how they could implement appropriate, disability-inclusive safety and accommodations procedures without running afoul of the Rehabilitation Act and ADA's provisions, which we discussed earlier. To address these concerns, the Equal Employment Opportunity Commission (EEOC) issued guidance during the pandemic to guide employers on topics related to (a) reasonable accommodations, (b) medical testing, (c) medical inquiries, (d) confidentiality, (e) retaliation, and other topics (EEOC, 2020a, 2020b). One goal of this guidance was to reiterate that the employment discrimination guidelines from the Rehabilitation Act and the ADA still apply during the pandemic, but also would be aligned with Centers for Disease Control and Prevention's and state/local public health authority's evolving guidelines and suggestions about steps employers should take to maintain workplace safety (EEOC, 2020a). Some examples of topics outlined in this guidance include (a) that during a pandemic, employers may ask employees who call in sick if they are experiencing COVID-19 symptoms, so long as confidentiality measures in line with federal antidiscrimination law are followed; (b) that the administration of COVID-19 screening and temperature tests, which under the ADA and the Rehabilitation Act must be "job related and consistent with business necessity," are by definition permitted because individuals with the virus pose a "direct threat" to the health of others; (c) that employers may screen job applicants for symptoms of COVID-19 after making a conditional job offer, whether or not the applicant has a disability, as long as it does so for all entering employees in the same type of job; and (d) clarifying that the EEO rules for retaliation based on exercising rights related to workplace discrimination still apply, even if the complaint involves employer practices related to COVID-19 health and safety measures (EEOC, 2020a).

Family and Medical Leave Act

The FMLA (29 U.S.C. §§ 2601–2654), which went into effect in 1993, allows eligible employees up to 12 weeks of leave for family or medical reasons during any 12-month period. Its purpose is different from that of the ADA, in that the FMLA seeks to provide reasonable leave opportunities for all eligible employees, rather than focusing on creating equal employment opportunities for qualified employees (Lipnic & DeCamp, 2007). An employee may have a condition, however, that qualifies them for FMLA leave, and leave may be a reasonable accommodation under the ADA. As such, rehabilitation counseling professionals must strive to understand both the manner in which these two statutes overlap and the manner in which they appear, at times, to conflict.

The FMLA applies to fewer employers than the ADA—only those employers with 50 or more employees rather than 15 or more. It specifically allows 12 weeks of unpaid leave for any one or more of the following reasons: the birth of a child; the care of a newborn child; the placement of a child with the employee through adoption or foster care and the care of such child; the care of the employee's spouse, son, daughter, or parent with a serious health condition; or a serious health condition of the employee that causes the employee to be incapable of performing one or more of the essential functions of their job. The FMLA also allows 26 weeks of unpaid leave for an employee's next of kin who is a member of the Armed Forces (including the National Guard or Reserves) or, in some cases, a veteran who is undergoing medical treatment, recuperation, or therapy; is otherwise in outpatient status; or is otherwise on the temporary disability retired list for a serious injury or illness.

FMLA **serious health conditions** are illnesses, injuries, impairments, or physical or mental conditions that involve inpatient care or continuing treatment by a health care provider. FMLA serious health conditions and ADA disabilities are not mutually exclusive categories. If an employee must visit a doctor twice and stay out of work for 4 days due to an illness, the FMLA applies (Postol, 2002). By contrast, a condition must normally be long term and substantially limiting with respect to a major life activity to constitute an ADA disability (Postol, 2002). Although under the ADA an employer has no obligation to provide an accommodation if it would impose an "undue burden," such is not the case with FMLA leave.

An employer who desires to know the medical reason behind the requested leave may, in accordance with the FMLA, request evidence of the employee's "serious health condition" by means of an FMLA certification form (U.S. Department of Labor, 2009a). This form seeks information pertaining solely to the health condition that is the basis for the leave request. ADA medical inquiries are limited by a different standard—that is, the inquiry must be job-related and consistent with business necessity. The EEOC has noted that an employer medical inquiry using the FMLA certification form will not violate the ADA medical inquiry standard (EEOC, 2000). Regardless, a more recent study has revealed employer problems in this area, as some employers grant FMLA requests that they deem to be of questionable reliability without additional inquiry out of fear of violating employee rights under the ADA (Lipnic & DeCamp, 2007).

Many issues also have arisen with respect to the option of light-duty work. Under the FMLA, an employer may offer light-duty work as an option in lieu of or in addition to leave, but may not compel the employee to select light-duty work. Some employers may perceive this as an obstacle to the employee's return to work. If the employee selects a light-duty option, the time spent doing that work does not count against their FLMA leave entitlement (Lipnic & DeCamp, 2007). In contrast, under the ADA, an employer may offer light-duty work as a reasonable accommodation for an injured worker who is returning to work. Any employee who accepts such accommodation, and who also possesses rights under the FMLA with respect to a serious health condition, reserves the FMLA right to be restored to the same or an equivalent position to that which they held at the commencement of the leave period.

The FMLA was amended in 2008 to clarify the rights of military personnel and their families to take and use FMLA leave (U.S. Department of Labor, 2009b). The new regulations specifically incorporated additional military family leave entitlements, including up to 26 weeks of leave during a 12-month period to care for a covered service member recovering from a serious injury or illness incurred in the line of duty on active duty (U.S. Department of Labor, 2009b). In 2013, additional regulations were issued clarifying that the definition of a "serious injury or illness" was expanded to include injuries or illnesses existing before the beginning of active duty, but aggravated during military service (U.S. Department of Labor, Wage and Hour Division, 2013).

Veterans Employment Legislation

Veterans have enjoyed reemployment rights since the creation of the Selective Training and Service Act of 1940. In 1994, however, the U.S. Congress passed the USERRA, which is now the principal statute dealing with the employment and reemployment of members of the uniformed services (38 U.S.C. §§ 4301–4334). Although many provisions of the USERRA are similar to those that were included in the 1940 law (Quinn, 2005), the USERRA provides broader coverage in order to encourage noncareer service in the military by minimizing disadvantages to civilian careers, minimizing the disruption of the lives of service members and their employers' businesses by facilitating prompt job reinstatement, and reducing discrimination on the basis of service in the military (38 U.S.C. § 4301(a)).

More specifically, the USERRA requires that employers must give employees time off from work for active military duty, prohibits employers from discriminating against employees or applicants based on military service, and provides that employers must reinstate their employees returning from up to 5 years of leave for service in the uniformed services—subject to certain limitations. Employers must also restore all benefits to their returning service members, treating time spent on leave as time worked. Finally, employers cannot fire returning service members without good cause for up to 1 year after their return from active duty.

The USERRA is applicable to every employer, whether private or public. Even foreign businesses incorporated abroad must comply with the USERRA if a U.S. employer controls the foreign business. With respect to veterans, those who separate from a uniformed service under other than honorable conditions will not be eligible for the USERRA privileges and protections.

According to the U.S. Bureau of Labor Statistics (BLS, 2016), in August 2015 approximately 4.3 million veterans had a service-related disability, including 33% of Gulf War II–era veterans, and about 20% of all veterans. Despite legislative efforts to support and promote the employment and reemployment of American veterans via USERRA, veterans have experienced unemployment rates close to those of nonveterans in recent years (U.S. Department of Labor, 2010). This may be due, in part, to the inadequate knowledge of USERRA on the part of the employers, the employees, or both (U.S. General Accounting Office, 2005). Rehabilitation counseling professionals should be aware of the expansive protections available to veterans under the USERRA in order to best advise clients and employers regarding the rights of veterans with disabilities.

In 2010, Congress passed the Veterans Benefits Act, which provided additional benefits and programs aimed at enhancing employment opportunities and small business programs, among other initiatives, and clarified the USERRA's prohibition of wage discrimination against veterans.

Additionally, the VEVRAA prohibits federal contractors and subcontractors from engaging in employment discrimination against protected veterans, and requires affirmative action steps in the recruitment, hiring, promotion, and retention of veterans. In August 2013, the U.S. DOL published new regulations for the VEVRAA. Although the VEVRAA provisions previously applied to all federal contracts and subcontracts of $25,000 or more, the new regulations updated the rule, so it now applies only to contracts of $100,000 or more. The new regulations require federal contractors to establish annual hiring benchmarks for protected veterans using benchmark data provided by the OFCCP's "Benchmark Database" (https://ofccp.dolesa.gov/errd/VEVRAA.jsp). Under the new regulations, contractors must invite applicants to self-identify as protected veterans at the pre-offer and post-offer phases.

Workforce Investment Act (1998) and Workforce Innovation and Opportunity Act (2014)

Although the WIOA of 2014 overrides its predecessor, the WIA of 1998, it is important to provide an overview of the WIA for context. The WIA was a continuation and improvement of the VR services portion of the Rehabilitation Act. The goal of the WIA was to require states to coordinate federally funded employment and training services, including those in Title V of the Rehabilitation Act, into a single, comprehensive, **One-Stop System** (U.S. General Accounting Office, 2003), thereby creating a new and improved workforce investment system.

The WIA was designed to streamline the old system, in which parties sought services from a variety of sources in what could be a costly and confusing process (Hager & Sheldon, 2001). Instead, the WIA designated 17 categories of programs as mandatory partners with the One-Stop System, including Veterans Employment and Training Services, adult literacy programs, Department of Housing and Urban Development–administered employment and training, and U.S. DOL-administered employment training for migrant workers, Native Americans, youths, and dislocated workers.

Any person who could demonstrate a physical, mental, or learning disability that creates a substantial impediment to his or her ability to work was eligible for WIA services. People qualified to receive Social Security Income or Social Security Disability Insurance (SSDI) were presumed to be eligible, provided that they sought WIA services for the purpose of obtaining employment (Hager & Sheldon, 2001). Similar to requirements under the Rehabilitation Act, VR agencies were required to provide services according to an order of selection if agency resources were inadequate to serve every individual seeking employment.

The role of the VR agency is to assist individuals with disabilities in making informed choices with respect to their desired employment outcomes and the services necessary to achieve such goal. VR agencies assist eligible individuals in developing a written Individualized Plan for Employment (IPE). A VR agency may deny services to any individual whom it deems cannot benefit from them. The WIA mandated a presumption that individuals with disabilities are capable of employment, but a VR agency may rebut that presumption if it shows by clear and convincing evidence that the individual cannot benefit from services. To this point, the VR agency must provide the individual with trial work experiences of "sufficient variety and over a sufficient length of time to determine" whether the individual may benefit from services (29 U.S.C. § 722(a)(2)(B)).

WIA faced challenges in achieving the complete integration of the workforce investment systems that existed prior to the WIA (under the Rehabilitation Act) and the One-Stop System. For example, both systems continued to maintain separate administrations, and in some states, the systems are located in completely separate state agencies (Bruyère et al., 2010). Part of the challenge arose from the fact that WIA attempted to integrate VR—a specialized field—into the broader workforce development system. In 2002, the Social Security Administration (SSA) and the U.S. DOL jointly launched their **Disability Program Navigator**, a resource aimed at connecting individuals with disabilities to appropriate VR services (www.doleta.gov/disability/new_dpn_grants.cfm).

Then, in July 2014, the WIOA was signed into law, and took effect a year later on July 1, 2015. As a reauthorization of the WIA, the WIOA supersedes the WIA and WIA's amendments to the Rehabilitation Act, aiming to help job seekers access education, training, and support services necessary for success in the 21st-century labor market while matching employers with skilled workers needed for global economic competition (U.S. Department of Labor, Employment and Training Administration, 2015). Importantly, the WIOA takes steps to further align and integrate state VR programs with other core programs of the workforce development system, through unified strategic planning, common performance accountability measures, and one-stop delivery.

Efforts to streamline the workforce development system include (a) implementing common outcome measures for federal workforce programs, including six performance indicators for adults and six for youth served under the Rehabilitation Act; (b) smaller, more strategic state/local workforce development boards; (c) integration of intake, case management, evaluation, and reporting systems; and (d) elimination of the sequence of services to allow local boards to meet each unique individual's needs. Local boards are empowered under the act to customize services for region-specific workforce needs. As described later, the WIOA supports access to real-world education and workforce development opportunities for job seekers in the system (e.g., work-based learning, incumbent worker, customized training, pay-for-performance contracts).

The WIOA improves services to youth with disabilities by increasing opportunities for this population to practice workplace skills, exercise self-determination in career interests, and obtain work-based experience. At least 15% of federal program funds for VR agencies must now be set aside for preemployment transition services to students with disabilities. The WIOA's job-driven programs emphasize employer engagement in matching employers with skilled individuals, including through a wider array of work-based learning opportunities under the VR program (e.g., apprenticeships and internships; Employer Assistance and Resource Network, 2014). As discussed previously in the Rehabilitation Act section of this chapter, new final regulations in 2016 updated the definition of VR outcomes in the WIOA Title IV (programs authorized by the Rehabilitation Act), finalizing a shift from "gainful employment" to "competitive integrated employment" for people with disabilities, and specifying that "customized employment" constitutes a valid employment outcome.

The new **competitive integrated employment** terminology reflects the federal government's shift toward emphasizing integrated employment opportunities and pay that is commensurate with that of workers without disabilities in similar occupations, with similar training, experience, and skills (Title IV, § 404(5)). The ODEP recently described this shift, which it characterized as states "mov[ing] forward to implement policies that focus on integrated, community-based employment earning at or above the minimum wage as the first option for individuals with intellectual and other developmental disabilities . . . [in] employment first states, sheltered employment with subminimum wages and non-work 'day activities' are no longer acceptable employment outcomes" (U.S. Department of Labor, 2009a). The final regulations specify common performance accountability measures for core state workforce development systems, and place substantial new restrictions on subminimum wage employment outcomes.

Ticket to Work and Work Incentives Improvement Act

The TWWIIA (Pub. L. No. 106–170, 113 Stat. 1860), enacted in 1999, was designed to provide beneficiaries and recipients of Supplemental Security Income (SSI, SSDI, or both) the incentives and supports that they need to prepare for, attach to, or advance in work. It also expanded options for continuing healthcare coverage benefits during recipients' transition to work and eliminating the disincentive to work for recipients of SSI or SSDI cash benefits that arose when such individuals lost their eligibility to receive benefits due to participation in work activities.

The Ticket-to-Work and Self-Sufficiency Program, found in Subtitle A of Title I of the TWWIIA, replaced the Social Security Administration's (SSA's) existing VR system with an outcome-based, market-driven program. It created a system in which all eligible beneficiaries receive a **Ticket to Work** (TTW): a voucher that the beneficiary may deposit with a service provider (otherwise known as an **Employment Network** [EN]) in order to receive employment services, which may include case management, work incentives planning, supported employment, career planning, career plan development, vocational assessment, job training, and other services like those available under state and federal VR programs discussed earlier (42 U.S.C. § 1320b-19(e)(5)).

The Ticket Program is purely voluntary on the part of the beneficiary. The beneficiary may decide whether to use the ticket, may select a desirable EN from among an array of choices, and may at any time retrieve the ticket from the EN if they feel that the EN's employment services are not adequate. Service providers, either private or public organizations, that provide employment support services to assist an SSA beneficiary or recipient in preparing for, obtaining, or remaining at work may elect to become ENs. A state VR agency may be part of numerous ENs in any given state, but the statute requires each EN to be part of an agreement with a VR before referring a beneficiary to the designated state VR agency. ENs may also choose the preferred system of payment for services, either (a) outcome payments for those months in which the beneficiaries do not receive benefits due to work activity (up to 60 months) or (b) reduced outcome payments in addition to payments for helping the beneficiary achieve certain employment milestones. VRs have the additional option of electing to receive payment under a cost-reimbursement option.

Initial studies of the success of the Ticket Program following its rollout revealed low participation rates among potential beneficiaries due to an inadequate and inefficient payment system and the lack of adequate marketing, incentive, technical assistance, and training (Stapleton et al., 2008; Ticket to Work and Work Incentives Advisory Panel, 2004). In response to these findings, the SSA revised the Ticket Program regulations with the goal of improving program participation rates. The revisions took effect in late 2008, and included additional financial incentives for community service providers to participate in the program. One type of new financial incentive is **milestone payments**, payments triggered earlier in the employment process, for part-time and lower paying outcomes, and based on gross earnings (rather than reduced by the value of SSA work incentives received by the beneficiary). In recognizing that disability beneficiaries need longer term employment supports as they move toward self-sufficiency, the new regulations also established the **Partnership Plus** option, which allows participants served under the traditional cost-reimbursement program with state VR programs to continue access to individualized employment services through an EN, following their case closure with the state VR program.

Early empirical analyses provide only limited evidence of improved participant outcomes following the 2008 revisions: while the number of participating EN providers and program participants has increased, and while benchmark data for benefits forgone and termination of benefits for work have gone up, such benchmarks pertain to TTW participants and nonparticipants alike, leaving questions as to the long-term efficacy of the revisions (Livermore et al., 2012; Schimmel et al., 2013).

Title II of TWWIIA governs the provision of healthcare services to workers with disabilities. This section of the law attempted to reduce the disincentives to employment for people with disabilities posed by the threat of loss of healthcare benefits by encouraging states to improve access to health care coverage available under Medicaid (Goodman & Livermore, 2004). Under this provision, new optional eligibility groups are established, creating two new Medicaid Buy-In eligibility categories; the period of premium-free Medicare Part A eligibility is extended; and protection for certain individuals with Medigap is required. The U.S. DHHS, through the U.S. Centers for Medicare and Medicaid Services, administers the healthcare provisions.

Workers' Compensation

Workers' compensation programs, which exist in each of the 50 states, the District of Columbia, and the U.S. territories, provide protections for employers and employees with respect to work-related injuries. Additional related federal laws are the Federal Coal Mine Health and Safety Act, the Longshore and Harbor Workers' Compensation Act, and the Federal Employers' Liability Act. Rehabilitation counseling professionals will regularly interact with these laws, as they impact the return-to-work process for most individuals with disabilities.

Prior to the development of workers' compensation laws, employees, on one hand, had little recourse against employers in the event of a work-related injury, and many faced destitution resulting from occupational injuries or diseases. On the other hand, with respect to the few cases in which injured employees succeeded in suing their employers for negligence, employers faced the prospect of being ordered to pay injured employees large sums, and were thus subjected to unpredictable financial risk.

Workers' compensation remedies these two problems. First, it created a "no-fault approach" to occupational injury and disease, in which a worker would be eligible for disability benefits if they could show that the injury or disease was work-related. Second, workers' compensation statutes limited employer liability by insulating them from negligence suits, provided that the employers paid for the no-fault workers' compensation benefits prescribed by statute (Spieler & Burton, 1998). The benefits available under workers' compensation law include medical care, disability payments, rehabilitation services, survivor benefits, and funeral expenses. In addition, benefits for temporary incapacity, scarring, and permanent impairment of specific body parts are typically included. The job and benefit protections available under the FMLA and, to an extent, under the ADA, are not available under workers' compensation law.

Initially, workers' compensation laws did not focus on returning injured workers to the workplace. A remarkable shift in workers' compensation law occurred during the latter half of the 20th century. These changes brought an increased focus on disability management and return-to-work options and thus brought the goals of workers' compensation more closely in line with those of state and federal disability discrimination laws (Spieler & Burton, 1998). The distinctive philosophies underlying workers' compensation and disability discrimination law give rise to somewhat conflicting perspectives of individuals with disabilities and their interaction with the workplace. Although the ADA focuses on the removal of barriers to employment through accommodations in the workplace, workers' compensation views impairments as causing work limitations. Thus, workers' compensation laws may require an employee to emphasize the limitations caused by their disability in order to be eligible for benefits, but those very statements may, at the same time, be detrimental to an ADA accommodation request (Geaney, 2004).

Rehabilitation counseling professionals may better assist individuals with disabilities and their employers if they possess a solid understanding of workers' compensation laws and the manner in which they interact with ADA and FMLA protections. Specific areas of concern include (a) whether an injured worker also qualifies as having an ADA disability or has a serious medical condition under the FMLA; (b) how the ADA rules regarding medical inquiries impact an applicant with a history of occupational injury or disease; (c) whether an employee with a history of occupational injury or disease poses a direct threat to himself or herself or coworkers under the ADA; (d) ADA accommodations available to individuals injured in the workplace, including the development of light-duty positions; and (e) the impact of exclusive remedy provisions under workers' compensation laws on an employee's rights under other disability statutes (EEOC, 1996). Although an employer bears the ultimate responsibility of determining whether an employee is ready to return to work, the employer may seek the advice of an RC or other specialist in order to understand an employee's specific functional limitations or abilities when returning to work.

Health Insurance Portability and Accountability Act

HIPAA (42 U.S.C. §§ 1320d–1320d-8) governs the disclosure of medical information by covered entities. A **covered entity** is a health plan, healthcare provider, or health care clearinghouse. Based on this definition, employers generally do not qualify as covered entities under HIPAA. Thus, HIPAA rules would not apply to any "**return-to-work notes**—medical information provided to substantiate requests for employee benefits such as short-term disability, long-term disability, FMLA requirements, job accommodation requests, or medical information for compliance with ADA" (DiBenedetto, 2005). The confidentiality of the medical information in such records would remain protected, however, by the confidentiality rules contained within the ADA and the FMLA, as previously mentioned.

The greater impact of HIPAA on the practice of rehabilitation counseling, however, involves the situation in which an occupational health provider qualifies as a health care provider or business affiliate under HIPAA. The regulations implementing HIPAA broadly define a **healthcare provider** as one who "furnishes, bills, or is paid for health care in the normal course of business" (45 C.F.R. § 160.103). *Healthcare* means care, services, or supplies related to the health of an individual. Healthcare includes, but is not limited to, the following: (a) preventive, diagnostic, therapeutic, rehabilitative, maintenance, or palliative care, and counseling, service, assessment, or procedure with respect to the physical or mental condition, or functional status, of an individual or that affects the structure or function of the body and (2) the sale or dispensing of a drug, device, equipment, or other item in accordance with a prescription (45 C.F.R. § 160.103)

All covered entities must comply with HIPAA's **Privacy Rule** (Standards of Privacy for Individually Identifiable Health Information, 45 C.F.R. pt. 160 and subpts. A and E of pt. 164) in order to safeguard individually identifiable medical information (referred to as **protected health information** or PHI) that it handles or transmits. Generally, the covered entity may provide PHI to the individual to whom it belongs and may use such information for its own treatment, payment, and healthcare operations. Otherwise, covered entities may use PHI only as required by law or with the written authorization of the individual to whom it belongs.

HIPAA further requires that covered entities tailor their uses and disclosures of PHI, other than those to the subject individual or with their authorization, so that it uses or discloses only the minimum amount of information necessary to meet the purpose of that use or disclosure (45 C.F.R. § 164.502).

Interestingly, the Privacy Rule contains a direct reference to **psychotherapy notes**, which are considered unique from other healthcare records. Psychotherapy notes document the content of conversations during a private counseling session, but do not include medical information such as medications, diagnoses, symptoms, and treatment plans (45 C.F.R. § 164.501). Psychotherapy notes or process notes are distinguishable from the medical record, or official records. The differentiation is that progress notes are related to treatment plan, progress, test results, or diagnosis, whereas psychotherapy notes instead focus on the counselor's impression, questions, observations, thought, and feelings about the session.

The Privacy Rule provides that covered entities must obtain the subject individual's permission to use or disclose psychotherapy notes except when using such notes for the treatment of that individual or for other specified circumstances generally pertaining to the training of the covered entity, the need to protect the health or safety of that individual or others in the community, or where necessitated by law (45 C.F.R. § 160.508(a)(2)). The Privacy Rule applies with general uniformity to all PHI, but special protections are afforded to psychotherapy notes because of their potential to contain particularly sensitive information and the fact that they are not typically used in treatment, payment, or healthcare operations (U.S. Department of Health and Human Services, 2014). This is why, with few exceptions (e.g., reporting of abuse and "duty to warn"), covered entities are required to obtain the patient's authorization prior to a disclosure of psychotherapy notes for any reason (45 C.F.R. § 164.508(a)(2)).

HIPAA also contains a **Security Rule** (Security Standards for the Protection of Electronic Protected Health Information, 45 C.F.R. pt. 160 and subpts. A and C of pt. 164), which sets forth the standards to which covered entities must adhere in order to maintain the confidentiality and integrity of PHI that is stored or transferred electronically. After a covered entity identifies any potential risks to its PHI, it must then adopt appropriate administrative, physical, and technical safeguards.

Business associates also are drawn within the umbrella of HIPAA legislation. HIPAA defines a **business associate** as a person or entity that provides services to a covered entity or performs functions or activities for a covered entity that involve the use or disclosure of PHI (45 C.F.R. § 160.103). The concept of a business associate was developed to prevent covered entities from shirking their responsibilities under HIPAA by simply outsourcing certain aspects of their businesses to noncovered entities. Under the HIPAA Privacy Rule, covered entities may release certain PHI to a business associate only if they obtain the business associate's written assurance that it will safeguard the PHI and assist the covered entity in complying with the Privacy Rule (45 C.F.R. § 164.502(e)).

Most recently, the Health Information Technology for Economic and Clinical Health (HITECH) Act (42 U.S.C. § 17921 *et seq.*) updates HIPAA obligations by requiring both business associates and covered entities to notify an individual if the confidentiality or integrity of that individual's PHI has been compromised. The HITECH Act also extends the application of many of the HIPAA privacy and security regulations that originally applied only to covered entities to business associates as well. As of the date of this publication, although the Office of Civil Rights of the U.S. DHHS had not yet enacted the final rules implementing the HITECH Act, the interim rules were in full force and effect.

In conclusion, any individual planning to practice in the area of rehabilitation counseling or counseling in general must become educated regarding HIPAA in order to determine the extent to which they must comply with its rules and regulations. For those who are unsure whether they fall within the scope of HIPAA, they may certainly choose, nevertheless, to voluntarily implement the practices described in the Privacy Rule and the Security Rule as a means of protecting the privacy of their clients and maintaining the confidentiality of information to which they have access.

Patient Protection and Affordable Care Act of 2010

The 2010 Patient Protection and Affordable Care Act (ACA) refers to two pieces of legislation: the ACA (Pub. L. No. 111–148) and the Health Care and Education Reconciliation Act (Pub. L. No. 111–152). In combination, these statutes seek to enhance health care security in the United States through efforts to expand coverage, hold insurance companies accountable, increase consumer choice, lower healthcare costs, and improve the overall quality of care (U.S. Department of Health and Human Services, 2010). Commentators have noted that the ACA represents the most extensive regulatory and legal changes to the U.S. healthcare system since the passage of Medicare and Medicaid in 1965 (Manchikanti et al., 2011). In June 2012, the U.S. Supreme Court upheld all provisions of the ACA except for the mandated expansion of Medicaid eligibility for low-income adults by state governments; as to this latter, the court held that states opting out of the Medicaid expansion could not be penalized by a loss of federal funding to their existing Medicaid programs. Many states have nevertheless opted into the Medicaid expansion, with the most recent tally being 32 states opting in (including Washington, D.C.) and 19 opting out (Kaiser Family Foundation, 2015).

One persistent issue facing state VR agencies is how to manage and maximize state and federal funding to pay for services and supports (including health-related services). The ACA implements substantial new potential funding sources for such services, and contains important provisions that increase access to private health insurance, such as removing preexisting conditions from insurance eligibility determinations and expanding eligibility for the receipt of health care through Medicaid programs, depending on states' willingness to participate (Silverstein, 2012). Essential health benefits (EHB)—including rehabilitative and habilitative services—may therefore be more readily available to VR service recipients as a result of the ACA.

Because individuals with disabilities tend to have lower rates of employment, and lower rates of employer-sponsored health insurance, healthcare and health insurance issues intersect heavily with the VR context (Croft & Parish, 2012). The ACA directly impacts access to health care by expanding Medicaid eligibility criteria, setting aside additional federal funds for states opting to expand their Medicaid programs to allow coverage of adults younger than 65 with an income up to 133% of the federal poverty level, as well as children at that income level (U.S. Centers for Medicare andMedicaid Services, 2015). Therefore, for states that have opted in to the Medicaid expansion, free or low-cost health coverage is available to people with incomes below a certain threshold, regardless of disability, financial resources, family status, and other designations that would previously have been factored into eligibility determinations (U.S. Centers for Medicare andMedicaid Services, 2015). Finally, the ACA provides the option for state-level expansion of community VR services such as vocational supports and case management, allowing participating states to offer such services through their regular state Medicaid plans without seeking a waiver, for individuals with incomes up to 300% of the maximum SSI payment and who also have a high level of need (Croft & Parish, 2012).

Mental Health Parity and Addiction Equity Act of 2008, as Amended

The Mental Health Parity and Addiction Equity Act (MHPAEA) of 2008 is a federal law that generally prohibits large group health plans (e.g., employer "self-funded" or purchased group plans from "large" employers)[i] and health insurance issuers that provide mental health or substance use disorder benefits from imposing benefit limitations (e.g., annual or lifetime dollar limits, financial requirements like deductibles and copayments, and treatment limitations like number of visits) that are less favorable than those placed on other medical or surgical benefits (Pub. L. 110–343). In 2010, the MHPAEA was amended by the ACA (discussed earlier) to also apply to individual health insurance coverage. While, the MHPAEA does not require large-group health plans or health insurance issuers to cover mental health or substance use disorder benefits, and as such, its requirements only apply to covered entities who choose to include such benefits, the ACA did expand such coverage by requiring coverage of mental health and substance use disorder services as one of 10 EHB categories in non-grandfathered individual and small-group plans. Additionally, under the MHPAEA, standards for medical necessity determinations and reasons for any denial of benefits relating to mental health and substance use disorder benefits must be disclosed upon request. In 2014, implementing regulations further described that the application of the "substantially all/predominant test" for benefits parity to six different classifications of benefits (inpatient in-network, inpatient out-of-network, outpatient in-network, outpatient out-of-network, emergency, prescription drug), provided examples of permissible and impermissible cumulative financial requirements, and distinguished between quantitative and nonquantitative treatment limitations (e.g., medical management and preauthorization limitations), for which covered entities are prohibited from applying additional requirements than are comparably applied to other types of medical benefits (78 Fed. Reg. 68239). The final regulation eliminated an exception that allowed for different nonquantitative treatment limitations "to the extent that recognized clinically appropriate standards of care may permit a difference."

Genetic Information Nondiscrimination Act of 2008

Enacted in 2008, GINA prohibits employers from discharging, refusing to hire, or making other decisions related to the terms and privileges of employment based on an employee's genetic information (42 U.S.C. § 200ff-1). GINA also bars employers from using genetic information to classify employees in such a way as to decrease their employment opportunities or to otherwise negatively affect their employment status. GINA was passed in response to mounting fears among Americans that employers could discriminate against them based on the improper use of genetic information. Such fears inhibited the use of genetic testing and raised issues regarding the viability of finding willing subjects for future genetic research (Appelbaum, 2010).

The definition of **genetic information** in GINA is broad enough that it covers genetic tests performed both on an employee/applicant and on their family members because the test results of family members could adversely affect the employee/applicant's risk status. In the absence of a formal genetic test, a family medical history may, in and of itself, constitute genetic information if it reveals the presence of genetically linked diseases among family members. Medical providers and health professionals should therefore

---

[i]The Protecting Affordable Coverage for Employees Act amended the definition of small employer in section 1304(b) of the Affordable Care Act and section 2791(e) of the Public Health Service Act to mean generally an employer with 1 to 50 employees, with the option for states to expand the definition of small employer to 1 to 100 employees. ERISA also defines a "small employer" as one with 50 or fewer employees.

omit both types of information when responding to an employer's request for medical information or documentation.

Regardless of efforts by health professionals to redact or omit genetic information contained in records that are being provided to employers, family medical information may be interspersed throughout the records and therefore be challenging to completely remove (Relias Media, 2010). Questions abound regarding whether medical providers and health professionals have "the time, inclination, or even ability to carefully redact genetic information from patient records," particularly with the increasing prevalence of electronic health record systems (Hoffman, 2010). Even assuming that medical providers and health professionals do have adequate time and ability to redact genetic information from records, it may be best for medical professionals to heed the recent warning of Marcia Scott, MD, affiliated with the Department of Psychiatry at Harvard Medical School: "because a family history is a necessary part of any evaluation, we all need to be aware that the pen and computer have become dangerous instruments" (Scott, 2010, p. 634). When questions regarding genetic testing arise, health professionals should ensure that their patients/clients are aware of GINA and understand its protections (Appelbaum, 2010).

There is no overlap in coverage between GINA and the FMLA. Instead, GINA specifically excludes from its coverage any family medical history that an employer requests or requires in order to comply with the FMLA.

IMPLICATIONS FOR COUNSELING PRACTICE

Many rehabilitation counseling, clinical rehabilitation counseling, and other mental health professionals work within the state VR service delivery system governed by the Rehabilitation Act, and are likely knowledgeable about these services. However, for those who are employed outside this system, being knowledgeable about available services for referral purposes is imperative, as is knowledge of the interface with other workforce development systems afforded by the WIA. Similarly, for those providing services to Social Security recipients, veterans, or those impacted by an occupational injury, awareness of the TWWIIA, the USERRA, the VEVRAA, workers' compensation laws, HIPAA, and the ACA is a necessity. Without this knowledge, counselors will not be able to direct their clients to the services for which they are eligible, or guide their vocational choices in light of available benefits that may affect decisions about income-earning capacity and benefits eligibility, as well as the health benefits and health record confidentiality provisions that afford protections.

The purpose of this chapter is to provide a broad overview of select pieces of legislation that impact the employment of people with disabilities, either through the creation and implementation of employment services for people with disabilities or the protection of their employment rights. In the remainder of this chapter, the implications of these laws for rehabilitation and general counseling practice, training, and research are discussed.

The laws described here have implications for counseling practice in that they govern the provision of VR services and provide protections against workplace discrimination for both applicants and employees with disabilities. However, the summarized legislation and regulations are important to all counselors, even outside the VR context, who work with individuals with disabilities and mental health conditions. Counseling professionals providing employment services to people with disabilities should know that these laws exist, be very familiar with the services they make available, and be knowledgeable about the rights and protections that people with disabilities are afforded in the employment process.

Support of employment disability nondiscrimination policy and practice is a part of every rehabilitation, clinical rehabilitation, and mental health counseling professional's role. The opportunity to execute this responsibility comes daily, in moving people toward the employment application process and in coaching them on ways to maximize their employment retention and advancement. In addition, counselors have a role that they can provide in informing employers and workplace agents such as HR professionals about the provisions of these laws and how these regulations should inform the design of disability-inclusive workplace HR policies and practices.

Doing this effectively requires that practitioners be knowledgeable about the protections against discrimination and the requirements of accommodations (including leaves) provided by the ADA, the FMLA, workers' compensation laws, and newly emerging laws such as GINA. They should also be aware of common HR practices around these laws and related practices (Erickson et al., 2014). Coaching on disclosure issues can also be informed by knowledge of the confidentiality requirements of these laws, as well as the related provisions afforded by HIPAA. Finally, knowledge of the intersection between the new healthcare and community services provisions of the ACA can prove essential for VR practitioners, who deal on a daily basis with a population that has historically struggled to gain adequate access to healthcare and community services. These issues may be even more complex to navigate for those with psychiatric disabilities, where disclosure can be a particularly challenging issue, so heightened attention to the implications for this population is imperative.

Counseling Professional Education

The importance of being knowledgeable about these laws for effective rehabilitation counseling service delivery has been already presented. It is imperative that information about these laws be an expected part of core coursework requirements in counselor preparation. Inclusion in select related courses, such as those on legislation related to people with disabilities, is most appropriate. But, in addition, this information is also relevant to courses such as rehabilitation counseling scope of practice; history, systems, and philosophy of rehabilitation; disability benefits systems; employer consultation and disability prevention; workplace culture and environment; and vocational consultation and job-placement strategies.

Perhaps not as obvious, however, are the implications of this knowledge for the preparation of counselors in fulfilling their professional roles as workplace educators and policy advocates. Not only rehabilitation and mental health services clients, but the employers who hire them, as well as policy makers at the local and state level, must be informed about the provisions for employment disability nondiscrimination, confidentiality of medical information, access to employment services, application process and workplace accommodation, and other rights that these laws provide. Rehabilitation, clinical rehabilitation, and mental health counseling professionals have a role to play in this community education process. Providing information to the **demand side** of the employment equation—that is, viewing things from the perspective of employers—to address HR strategists and build a convincing business case for employers will be vital (Barrington et al., 2014). Likewise, knowledge of how these laws are being interpreted and implemented by HR managers and hiring committees should become a part of preservice training (Nazarov & von Schrader, 2014). Only if HR students and practitioners are informed, as part of their preservice and postgraduate educational processes, about the laws and roles they can play will these outcomes be realized in their professional practices.

Needed Related Research

Finally, there is a significant need for rehabilitation counseling researchers to become partners in policy formulation and evaluation efforts (Nazarov et al., 2014). Far too often, this discipline is all but absent from policy discourse when such laws are being formulated. RCs' disciplinary preparation and field-based practice experiences make them exceedingly valuable potential allies in this process, as well as in the evaluation of these laws once implemented. Rehabilitation education should provide students with the necessary information to be able to maximally utilize these laws to support effective rehabilitation counseling service delivery. They must also convey in this educational process the responsibility that future rehabilitation counseling practitioners have to be on-the-ground policy advocates and policy analysts.

As discussed in the overview of particular laws, in many cases the impact of these laws on increasing employment outcomes for people with disabilities is as yet unknown or unclear. Rehabilitation counseling researchers are needed who are able to work alongside economists, policy analysts, and others in determining the impact of the WIOA, the TWWIIA, and workers' compensation legislation in improving initial hiring and the return to work for people with disabilities. Similarly, RCs should be applying their unique analytical lens in determining whether employment disability nondiscrimination and accommodation provisions are currently designed in a way to minimize marginalization and maximize inclusion. They also should commit to seeking publishing outlets outside their field to share their findings beyond the rehabilitation community with other participants in the employment process (Karpur et al., 2014). It is a tremendous opportunity for these specialized professionals to contribute to the policy arena.

CONCLUSION

Counseling often focuses on the one-on-one relationship between the counselor and the client; however, state and federal legislation protects the legal rights of individuals with disabilities in our society. With this in mind, this chapter focused on the legislation most relevant to the employment and civil rights of people with disabilities. Laws and legislation are significant for promoting a more inclusive society, one that not only contributes to an individual's economic self-sufficiency but also enables that individual to have a higher quality of life.

CONTENT REVIEW QUESTIONS

1. How does the Vocational Rehabilitation Act of 1973 as amended assist states with the operation of comprehensive, coordinated, and effective VR services?
2. What effect did the WIOA's amendments to the Rehabilitation Act have on the types of employment outcomes that are permitted in state VR programs?
3. What are the specific provisions of the ADA of 1990 as they relate to employer requirements to make reasonable accommodations for an applicant or employee with a disability?
4. How might the requirements of the ADA and the FMLA intersect?
5. Why should rehabilitation professionals be familiar with the provisions of the USERRA and the VEVRAA?
6. What might be the strengths and weaknesses of the provision of services to people with disabilities through the workforce development system provided for under the WIOA?
7. Which challenges to employment faced by Social Security beneficiaries was the TWWIIA designed to address?
8. How might the ADA and the provisions of state workers' compensation laws intersect?
9. What are the rehabilitation counseling practice implications of HIPAA, GINA, and the ACA?
10. What are the mental health counseling practice implications for the ADA, HIPAA, and the ACA?

LEARNING ACTIVITY

Choose one of the current legislative acts discussed in the chapter that you are interested in researching. Search online to provide the following information: (a) When was the legislation passed and what was going on in the United States, (b) What is the purpose of the legislative act, (c) What does it regulate or fund, and (d) How might knowing the legislative act help you in your future practice?

REFERENCES

Appelbaum, P. S. (2010). Law & psychiatry: Genetic discrimination in mental disorders. *Psychiatric Services, 61*, 338–340.

Barrington, L., Bruyère, S., & Waelder, M. (2014). Employer practices in improving employment outcomes for people with disabilities. *Journal of Rehabilitation Research, Policy and Education, 28*(4), 208–224.

Befort, S. F. (2013). An empirical analysis of case outcomes under the ADA Amendments Act. *Washington and Lee Law Review, 70*, 2027–2071.

Brooks, S. K., Webster, R. K., Smith, L. E., Woodland, L., Wessely, S., Greenberg, N., & Rubin, G. J, *et al.* (2020). The psychological impact of quarantine and how to reduce it: rapid review of the evidence. *Lancet (London, England), 395*(10227), 912–920. https://doi.org/10.1016/S0140-6736(20)30460-8

Bruyère, S., VanLooy, S., & Golden, T. (2010). Legislation and rehabilitation professionals. In S. Flanagan, H. Zaretsky, & A. Moroz (Eds.), *Medical aspects of disability: A handbook for the rehabilitation professional* (4th ed., pp. 669–686). Springer.

Campbell, J. (1994). Unintended consequences in public policy: Persons with Psychiatric Disabilities and the Americans with Disabilities Act. *Policy Studies Journal, 22*(1), 133–145. https://doi.org/10.1111/j.1541-0072.1994.tb02186.x

Croft, B., & Parish, S. L. (2012). Care integration in the Patient Protection and Affordable Care Act: implications for behavioral health. *Administration and Policy in Mental Health, 40*(4), 258–263. https://doi.org/10.1007/s10488-012-0405-0

DiBenedetto, D. V. (2005). *HIPAA not always is applicable to occ-health. Occupational Health Management.* https://www.ahcmedia.com/articles/84802-hipaa-not-always-is-applicable-to-occ-health

Embregts, P. J. C. M., van den Bogaard, K. J. H. M., Frielink, N., Voermans, M. A. C., Thalen, M., & Jahoda, A. (2020). A thematic analysis into the experiences of people with a mild intellectual disability during the COVID-19 lockdown period. *International Journal of Developmental Disabilities*, 1–5. https://doi.org/10.1080/20473869.2020.1827214

Employer Assistance and Resource Network. (2014). Workforce Innovation and Opportunity Act of 2014 (WIOA). http://askearn.org/refdesk/Disability_Laws/WIOA

Erickson, W., Lee, C., & von Schrader, S. (2020). *2018 disability status report: United States.* http://www.disabilitystatistics.org

Erickson, W. A., Schrader, S. von, Bruyère, S. M., VanLooy, S. A., & Matteson, D. S. (2014). Disability-inclusive employer practices and hiring of individuals with disabilities. *Rehabilitation Research, Policy, and Education, 28*(4), 309–328. https://doi.org/10.1891/2168-6653.28.4.309

Geaney, J. H. (2004). The relationship of workers' compensation to the Americans with Disabilities Act and Family and Medical Leave Act. *Clinics in Occupational and Environmental Medicine, 4*(2), vi, . https://doi.org/10.1016/j.coem.2004.02.001

Goodman, N., & Livermore, G. (2004, July 28). *The effectiveness of Medicaid Buy-In programs in promoting the employment of people with disabilities. Briefing paper prepared for the Ticket to work and work incentives advisory panel of the social security administration.* https://www.scribd.com/document/1947561/Social-Security-Buy-in-20paper-20Goodman-Livermore-20072804r

Hager, R. M., & Sheldon, J. R. (2001). *State and federal vocational rehabilitation programs: Services and supports to assist individuals with disabilities in preparing for, attaching to, and advancing in employment.* http://digitalcommons.ilr.cornell.edu/cgi/viewcontent.cgi?article=1218&context=edicollect

Hoffman, S. (2010). Employing E-health: The impact of electronic health records on the workplace. *Kansas Journal of Law and Public Policy, 19*, 409.

Kaiser Family Foundation. (2015). *Status of state action on the Medicaid expansion decision.* http:// kff.org/health-reform/state-indicator/state-activity-around-expanding-medicaid-under-the -affordable-care-act/

Kaminer, D. N. (2016). Mentally ill employees in the workplace: Does the ADA Amendments Act provide adequate protection? *Health Matrix, 26*, 205–253.

Karpur, A., VanLooy, S. A., & Bruyère, S. M. (2014). Employer practices for employment of people with disabilities: A literature scoping review. *Rehabilitation Research, Policy, and Education, 28*(4), 225–241. https://doi.org/10.1891/2168-6653.28.4.225

Lipnic, V. A., & DeCamp, P. (2007). *Family and medical leave act regulations: A report on the Department of Labor's request for information.* http://digitalcommons.ilr.cornell.edu/key_workplace/315

Livermore, G. A., Hoffman, D., & Bardos, M. (2012, September 24). *Ticket to work participant characteristics and outcomes under the revised regulations.* Mathematica Policy Research Institute.

Manchikanti, L., Caraway, D., Parr, A. T., Fellows, B., & Hirsch, J. A. (2011). Patient protection and affordable care act of 2010: Reforming the health care reform for the new decade. *Pain Physician, 1;14*(1;1), E35–E67. https://doi.org/10.36076/ppj.2011/14/E35

National Alliance on Mental Illness. (2014). *Road to recovery: Employment and mental illness.* Author. http://www.nami.org/work

National Council on Disability. (2004). *Righting the Americans with Disabilities Act.* Author. http:// www.ncd.gov/publications/2004/Dec12004

Nazarov, Z. E., & von Schrader, S. (2014). Comparison of employer factors in disability and other employment discrimination charges. *Rehabilitation Research, Policy, and Education, 28*(4), 291–308. https://doi.org/10.1891/2168-6653.28.4.291

National Institute of Mental Health. (2020). *Statistics: Any disorder among adults.* https://www.nimh .nih.gov/health/statistics/prevalence/any-mental-illness-ami-among-us-adults.shtml

Nazarov, Z. E., Erickson, W. A., & Bruyère, S. M. (2014). Rehabilitation-related research on disability and employer practices using individual-based national and administrative data sets. *Rehabilitation Research, Policy, and Education, 28*(4), 242–263. https://doi.org/10.1891/2168-6653 .28.4.242

Olsheski, J., & Schelat, R. (2003). Reasonable job accommodations for people with psychiatric disabilities. In D. Moxley & J. Finch (Eds.), *Sourcebook of rehabilitation and mental health practice* (pp. 61–76). Kluwer Academic Publishers.

Parikh, M. (2004). Burning the candle at both ends, and there is nothing left for proof: The Americans with Disabilities Act's disservice to persons with mental illness. *Cornell Law Review, 89*(3), 721–762.

Postol, L. (2002). Sailing the employment law Bermuda Triangle. *Labor Lawyer, 18*, 165–192.

Quinn, M. (2005). Uniformed Services Employment and Reemployment Rights Act (USERRA)— broad in protections, inadequate in scope. *University of Pennsylvania Journal of Labor & Employment, 8*, 237.

Rehabilitation Services Administration. (2016). *Frequently asked questions.* https://rsa.ed.gov/faqs .cfm

Relias Media. (2010). *Are you compliant with genetic screening law?.* https://www.ahcmedia.com/ articles/19028-are-you-compliant-with-genetic-screening-law

Rothstein, M. A., & Talbott, M. K. (2007). Compelled authorizations for disclosure of health records: magnitude and implications. *The American Journal of Bioethics, 7*(3), 38–45. https://doi.org/10 .1080/15265160601171887

Rubin, S. E., & Roessler, R. T. (2001). *Foundations of the vocational rehabilitation process.* Pro-Ed.

Rudstam, H., Golden, T. P., Gower, W. S., Switzer, E., Bruyere, S., & Van Looy, S. (2014). Leveraging new rules to advance new opportunities: Implications of the Rehabilitation Act Section 503 new rules for employment service providers. *Journal of Vocational Rehabilitation, 41*(3), 193–208. https://doi.org/10.3233/JVR-140713

Schimmel, J., Stapleton, D., Mann, D. R., & Phelps, D. (2013, July 25). *Participant and provider outcomes since the inception of ticket to work and the effects of the 2008 regulatory changes.* Mathematica Policy Research Institute.

Scott, M. (2010). Family history and GINA. *Psychiatric Services, 61*(6), 634. https://doi.org/10.1176/ ps.2010.61.6.634a

Silverstein, B. (2012). *Funding health-related VR services: The potential impact of the Affordable Care Act on the use of private health insurance and Medicaid to pay for health-related VR services.* Institute for Community Inclusion.

Spieler, E. A., & Burton, J. F. (1998). Compensation for disabled workers: Workers' compensation. In T. Thomason, J. Burton, & D. Hyatt (Eds.), *New approaches to disability in the workplace* (pp. 205–244). Industrial Relations Research Association.

Stapleton, D., Livermore, G., Thornton, C., O'Day, B., Weathers, R., Harrison, K., & Wright, D. (2008). *Ticket to work at the crossroads: A solid foundation with an uncertain future (Report submitted to the Social Security Administration Office of Disability and Income Support Programs). Mathematica Policy Research Institute.* Mathematica Policy Research Institute. https://www.ssa.gov/disabilityresearch/ttw4/TTW_Rpt4_508_vol1r.pdf

Ticket to Work and Work Incentives Advisory Panel. (2004). *The crisis in EN participation: A blueprint for action.* Social Security Administration.

U.S. Bureau of Labor Statistics. (2016). *Employment situation of veterans summary.* http://www.bls.gov/news.release/vet.nr0.htm

U.S. Census Bureau. (2012). *Nearly 1 in 5 people have a disability in the U.S Census Bureau reports.* https://www.census.gov/newsroom/releases/archives/miscellaneous/cb12-134.html

U.S. Centers for Medicare and Medicaid Services. (2015). *Medicaid expansion & what it means for you.* https://www.healthcare.gov/medicaid-chip/medicaid-expansion-and-you

U.S. Department of Education and Rehabilitation Services. (2020). *Fiscal year 2021 budget request.*

U.S. Department of Education. (2014). *The Workforce Innovation and Opportunity Act: Overview of Title IV: Amendments to the Rehabilitation Act of 1973.* https://www2.ed.gov/about/offices/list/osers/rsa/publications/wioa-changes-to-rehab-act.pdf

U.S. Department of Education. (2016, June 30). *Final regulation: State vocational rehabilitation services program; State supported employment services program; limitations on use of subminimum wage.* http://www2.ed.gov/about/offices/list/osers/rsa/wioa-vr-final-rule.pdf

U.S. Department of Health and Human Services. (2010). Patient Protection and Affordable Care Act: requirements for group health plans and health insurance issuers under the Patient Protection and Affordable Care Act relating to preexisting condition exclusions, lifetime and annual limits, rescissions, and patient protections. *Federal Register, 75,* 37187–37241.

U.S. Department of Labor. (2009a). *Military family leave provisions of the FMLA (Family and Medical Leave Act): Frequently asked questions and answers.* Author. http://www.dol.gov/whd/fmla/finalrule/MilitaryFAQs.pdf

U.S. Department of Labor. (2009b). *Frequently asked questions and answers about the revisions to the Family and Medical Leave Act.* http://www.dol.gov/whd/fmla/finalrule/NonMilitaryFAQs.pdf

U.S. Department of Health and Human Services. (2014). *HIPAA privacy rule and sharing information related to mental health.* http://www.hhs.gov/hipaa/for-professionals/special-topics/mental-health

U.S. Department of Labor Office of Federal Contract Compliance Programs. (2016). *The ADA Amendments Act of 2008: Frequently asked questions.* https://www.dol.gov/ofccp/regs/compliance/faqs/ADAfaqs.htm

U.S. Department of Labor, Employment and Training Administration. (2015). *Obama administration seeks public comment on proposed rules to implement the Workforce Innovation and Opportunity Act.* https://www.dol.gov/newsroom/releases/eta/eta20150691

U.S. Department of Labor, Wage and Hour Division. (2013). *Side-by-side comparison of current/final regulations.* https://www.dol.gov/whd/fmla/finalrule/comparison.htm

U.S. Department of Labor. (2010). *Bureau of labor statistics, economic news release: Employment situation of veterans—2009.* http://www.bls.gov/news.release/vet.nr0.htm

U.S. Equal Employment Opportunity Commission. (1996). *EEOC enforcement guidance: Workers' compensation and the ADA.* No.915.002. https://www.eeoc.gov/policy/html

U.S. Equal Employment Opportunity Commission. (1997, March 25). *Enforcement guidance on the Americans with Disabilities Act and psychiatric disabilities (no.915.002).* https://www.eeoc.gov/policy/docs/psych.html

U.S. Equal Employment Opportunity Commission. (2000, July 27). *Enforcement guidance: Disability-related inquiries and medical examinations of employees under the Americans with Disabilities Act (no.915.002).* https://www.eeoc.gov/policy/docs/guidance-inquiries.html

U.S. Equal Employment Opportunity Commission. (2002). *Enforcement guidance on reasonable accommodation and undue hardship under the Americans with Disabilities Act.* https://www.eeoc.gov//policy/docs/accommodation.html#privileges

U.S. Equal Employment Opportunity Commission. (2008). *Notice concerning the Americans with Disabilities Act (ADA) Amendments Act of 2008.* http://www.eeoc.gov/ada/amendments_notice.html

U.S. Equal Employment Opportunity Commission. (2011). *Questions and answers on the final rule implementing the ADA Amendments Act of 2008.* http://www.eeoc.gov/laws/regulations/ada_qa_final_rule.cfm

U.S. Equal Employment Opportunity Commission. (2013). *Press release: Fabricut to pay $50,000 to settle EEOC disability and genetic information discrimination lawsuit.* https://www.eeoc.gov/eeoc/newsroom/release/5-7-13b.cfm

U.S. Equal Employment Opportunity Commission. (2015). *EEOC opinion on invitation to self-identify.* https://www.dol.gov/ofccp/regs/compliance/sec503/Self_ID_Forms/OLC_letter_to_OFCCP_8-8-2013_508c.pdf

U.S. Equal Employment Opportunity Commission. (2020a). *What you should know about COVID-19 and the ADA, the Rehabilitation Act, and other EEO laws.* https://www.eeoc.gov/wysk/what-you-should-know-about-covid-19-and-ada-rehabilitation-act-and-other-eeo-laws

U.S. Equal Employment Opportunity Commission. (2020b). *Pandemic preparedness in the workplace and the Americans with Disabilities Act.* https://www.eeoc.gov/laws/guidance/pandemic-preparedness-workplace-and-americans-disabilities-act

U.S. Equal Employment Opportunity Commission. (n.d.-a.). *ADA enforcement guidance: Preemployment disability-related questions and medical examinations.* https://www.eeoc.gov/policy/docs/medfin5.pdf

U.S. Equal Employment Opportunity Commission. (n.d.-b.). *Facts about the Americans with Disabilities Act.* http://www.eeoc.gov/facts/fs-ada.html

U.S. General Accounting Office. (2003). *Workforce Investment Act: One-stop centers implemented strategies to strengthen services and partnerships, but more research and information sharing is needed.* http://www.gao.gov/new.items/d03725.pdf

U.S. General Accounting Office. (2005). *Military personnel: Federal management of service member employment rights can be further improved.* http://www.gao.gov/new.items/d0660.pdf

U.S. Office of Federal Contract Compliance Programs, Department of Labor. (2014). *Section 503 regulations frequently asked questions.* https://www.dol.gov/agencies/ofccp/faqs/section-503

von Schrader, S., Malzer, V., & Bruyère, S. (2013). Perspectives on disability disclosure: The importance of employer practices and workplace climate. *Employee Responsibilities and Rights Journal, 26,* 237–255. http://link.springer.com/article/10.1007/s10672-013-9227-9-#page-1

CHAPTER 7

The Person With Disability

IRMO MARINI, RIGEL MACARENA PINON, AND LAURA A. VILLARREAL

LEARNING OBJECTIVES

After reading this chapter, you should be able to:

- *Evaluate from a historical perspective how persons with various disabilities have been treated and perceived in order to understand how some of those societal attitudes continue to exist today.*
- *Recognize the daily nuances those with disabilities experience in negotiating their lived environment including societal attitudes, physical barriers, financial constraints and access to healthcare, transportation, and accessible housing.*
- *Apply and analyze the psychosocial impact of oppression, social inequity, and its impact on an individual's quality of life (QOL) and life satisfaction.*
- *Recognize some of the most common adjustment or adaptation theories to disability.*
- *Interpret the basic impact of optimizing health and wellness regarding exercise and discuss research pertaining to existing barriers.*
- *Evaluate and analyze the psychosocial benefits of adaptive aids and durable medical equipment, briefly discussing types of aids and the impact on one's independence.*

CACREP STANDARDS

CACREP 2016 Core: 2F3.f, 2F3.g, 2F4.b
CACREP 2016 Specialties:
  Clinical Rehabilitation Counseling: 5D1.c, 5D2.h, 5D2.k, 5D2.m, 5D2.o, 5D2.p, 5D2.s
  Rehabilitation Counseling: 5H1.d, 5H1.e, 5H1.f, 5H2.c, 5H2.d, 5H2.e, 5H2.f, 5H3.e

INTRODUCTION

The first author of this chapter is an "insider" living with a C5–C6 tetraplegia for the past 40 years from a hockey injury. As such, this chapter conveys aspects of his experience as a once able-bodied athlete until age 23, who is spending the rest of his life in a wheelchair paralyzed from the chest down. The word *insider* is used here to differentiate between "outsiders" or those who do not have a disability (Hart et al., 2003; McCord et al., 2016; Wright, 1983). The difference is significant in that research generally has shown that those who live with a disability view themselves and the world around them much differently than outsiders who attempt to perceive what having a disability must be like. Many outsider assumptions are erroneously based on myths and misconceptions propagated by various forms of media, significant others, and their own perceptual biases. These assumptions often project how outsiders might feel if they were blind, in a wheelchair, deaf, or had some other disability. Outsider opinions generally rate those with disabilities as being less happy, having a poor quality of life (QOL), and having poor life satisfaction, while insiders generally report higher ratings in those respective domains (Dunn & Brody, 2008; Hart et al., 2003; McCord et al., 2016; Marini, 2018a).

The intent of the present chapter is to provide readers with a more accurate perception of living with various disabilities by combining several insider perspectives with empirical research to capture what life is often like living with a disability. In doing so, we discuss the unique and various lived experiences of those with disabilities. This description includes daily interactions of individuals with disabilities negotiating their life space or living environment. While disability has a biological component, it is societal perceptions or attitudes that most impact those with disabilities. Therefore, we explore what living with a disability means in terms of relationships, employment, and full participation in society. Functioning largely as a cultural minority in society, persons with disabilities must adapt, adjust, and respond to differing daily situations they encounter with outsiders who do not have disabilities. The reader will find that while many people with disabilities optimize their health and fully participate in society, others unfortunately succumb to the oppressive and often exclusionary attitudes, physical barriers, and negative perceptions of disability found in the dominant culture.

HISTORICAL TREATMENT OF DISABILITY

Like the historical treatment of African Americans and other ethnic minority cultures in the United States, it is important to understand disability history in order to see where we are today (Baynton, 2001; Marini, 2018b; Nguyen-Finn, 2018). Without this context, one is left to wonder how attitudes toward individuals with disabilities are formed (Livneh, 1991; Marini, 2018a). At present, attitude research has suggested that persons with disabilities are often perceived as incapable, helpless, asexual, pitied, admired, need to be cared for, and often treated as second-class citizens (Coco, 2010; Mackelprang & Salsgiver, 2009; Olkin, 1999; Smart, 2009).

Prior to the 19th century, persons with various disabilities were often subjected to brutal treatment dating back to the Greek and Roman eras. This reaction included torture, being burned at the stake, exorcised for demon possession, imprisoned, forced into inhumane asylums, and ostracized or segregated from the public (Marini, 2018b; Smart, 2009). Such treatment was often justified because persons with certain disabilities were viewed as abominations of God for having sinned as well as economic burdens and threats to the social welfare of the community.

Sometime after Charles Darwin's 1859 controversial book, *On the Origin of Species*, introduced the concept of natural selection, there was a growing interest in understanding disability as part of human evolution. Herbert Spencer's divisive theory of *survival of the fittest* contributed to *social Darwinism* and the *eugenics movement*. The hypothesis drawn from eugenics was that if persons with disabilities (perceived as the weaker species) were allowed to conceive children with a nondisabled partner, this would eventually lead to diluting the stronger species and ultimately humanity's extinction (Carlson, 2009; Largent, 2002; Pearson, 1995).

As a result of this fervent thinking, the eugenics movement gained power during the early 20th century in the U.S. with sterilization, it ultimately culminated in Hitler's Nazi Germany policies in 1939 and its extermination of citizens with disabilities (Gallagher, 1995). Although the eugenics movement largely died down in the 1950s, proponents of eugenics and such thinking still exist today (Lynn & Vanhanen, 2002; Lynn & Van Court, 2004; Singer, 1995). Indeed, current debates on whether systemic racism exists often reflect eugenics and social Darwinism that contribute to the social injustices endured by African

Americans and other minorities. Much like these denials of systemic racism, so, too, do persons with disabilities have to contend with systemic discrimination (Marini, 2018c).

LIVED EXPERIENCE OF PERSONS WITH DISABILITIES

Persons with disabilities are often discussed as a homogeneous group. However, there are literally hundreds of diverse disability conditions that essentially fall into four categories: (a) physical disability (i.e., paralysis, amputation), (b) sensory disability (i.e., blindness, deafness), (c) emotional disability (i.e., psychiatric illness), and (d) cognitive disability (i.e., traumatic and organic brain injury). Living with one or more of these conditions is uniquely different in terms of how individuals function as well as how they are treated and perceived by others in society. Regardless of medical condition and resulting functional limitations, how persons with disabilities negotiate their community is dependent largely on physical and attitudinal barriers.

In the United States, legislation such as the Americans with Disabilities Act (ADA) has mandated greater community participation and social inclusion. Indeed, the ADA and other legislation have directly led to greater access for persons with disabilities in travel, public access like restaurants, theaters, and sporting events, and employment. From an outsider perspective, one would think that persons with disabilities are no longer excluded from society; however, for many insiders, the proverbial glass is still half-empty. This perspective is supported by the hundreds if not thousands of ADA lawsuits that are filed by individuals with disabilities annually. Examples of such lawsuits include discrimination in the workplace through not being rightfully hired, promoted, or wrongfully terminated; inaccessible public venues, such as seating having the poorest line of sight in stadium-style movie theaters; and airlines and bus lines refusing to make accessible transportation. Successful lawsuits have improved what was minimal compliance with the ADA, while other companies continue to shirk the law (; Blackwell et al., 2001; West, 1991).

Pinon et al. (2021) performed a content analysis of 278 letters to the editor of *New Mobility* magazine (read primarily by persons with physical disabilities) from 2013 to 2019. They found nine common issues that continue to be experienced by persons with physical disabilities. The most frequently topic (17% of the letters) pertained to anger and frustration readers expressed over inadequate and expensive healthcare, a lack of disability knowledge and negative healthcare worker attitudes, and limited access to ADA equipment such as an accessible scale and examination table for wheelchair users in hospitals and doctors' clinics. Letter writers also complained about limited Medicaid/Medicare and private insurance coverage whereby consumers had to settle for medical equipment that differed from what their physician and occupational therapist had prescribed. Finally, approximately 10% of the letter writers expressed anger and frustration over the lack of physical accessibility encountered at hotels, restaurants, parks, sports venues, and movie theaters (Graf et al., 2009; Marini et al., 2009).

Accessibility is also a problem for persons with visual disabilities, who share a similar frustration when it comes to the availability of braille menus at restaurants, monitoring for elevators and crosswalks, as well as accessibility issues in the workplace. For instance, A. Olvera (personal communication, September 28, 2021) discussed her frustration dealing with insurance companies after losing her sight. It took her more than 4 years to finally receive disability payments as her condition worsened. She indicated she fell into a deep depression and lost motivation. She was unable to continue in her job and had to take a different job for minimum wage. She expressed how the Health and Human Services personnel were always rude to her, making her feel awful as though she was asking for assistance for things that they did not think she needed. Her parents were unsupportive as well, and she had to rely on her own teenage children to drive her to and from appointments as well as filling out paperwork. She has since gone on to do well once these issues were settled. However, she said initially dealing with community agencies was chaotic.

Persons who are deaf or hard of hearing also experience challenges. C. Cantu (personal communication, September 27, 2021) noted how people's lack of patience in communicating with her coupled with her need for extra time to learn information has been a challenge. Her major frustrations have included a lack of resources and the closed-minded attitudes of others regarding persons who are deaf. Despite such challenges, she nevertheless is currently obtaining her graduate degree in rehabilitation counseling. She described her daily experiences of having to remind people to look at her when talking and provide PowerPoints, written notes, and clear directions and having to helping them understand that persons who are deaf or hard of hearing often have problems with grammar and must rewrite messages to get them straight.

As a final example, persons with severe and persistent mental illness (SMI) are considered to have an invisible disability and are often discriminated against or treated poorly by those who are aware of their disability. With high rates of unemployment among those with SMI, if there are no significant others for financial support, becoming homeless has become the norm (Tsai et al., 2021; Tsai & Huang, 2019). Still for others with SMI who display erratic or violent behavior in public, prisons have become a holding place for 20% to 40% of those with a diagnosed mental illness who are vulnerable to inhumane treatment (Nakic et al., 2021). Cowles and Washburn (2005) note that despite civil rights legislation to provide adequate treatment for juveniles and adults with SMI while incarcerated, such psychological treatment is almost nonexistent. To the contrary, persons with SMI who act up in prison are often isolated and sometimes sexually exploited at the hands of violent offenders (Wolff et al., 2007).

COMMUNITY LIVING WITH A DISABILITY

Despite the daily hassles and periodic barriers persons with various disabilities experience, research suggests that many insiders report a good quality of life (QOL) and life satisfaction depending on their condition and community resource assistance (Kellett et al., 2021). However, this research has to be viewed looking through the lens of insiders, rather than outsiders. Using Maslow (1970) revised hierarchy of needs, Kellett and colleagues conducted a qualitative study of 1566 participants and obtained feedback at 6-, 12-, and 24-month time intervals from individuals with disabilities who had transitioned from an institution into community living. The researchers found that participants reported a high quality of life and global life satisfaction that improved significantly over time. They also found that when persons with disabilities reported problems with healthcare coverage, assistive technology, transportation options, and low income in meeting basic needs, their level of satisfaction went down.

Bishop (2005) differentiated between subjective versus objective QOL. **Subjective QOL** pertains to how one perceives their life, support from others, health, and satisfaction. **Objective QOL** is tied more directly to such measures as material wealth, employment, or marriage. As such, persons without disabilities or outsiders generally view the lives of those with disabilities/insiders as poor, whereas persons with disabilities perceive their lives more favorably (Kellett et al., 2021). Persons with disabilities generally view their lives from a more subjective QOL, while those without disabilities place more weight on an objective QOL perspective.

A second aspect of living with a disability is interdependence and interactions between individuals with their environment or community. Proponents of somatopsychology theorize that our behavior is a result of how we view ourselves and how we perceive others view us (Lewin, 1935). Persons with disabilities who perceive themselves to be in an unfriendly community are less likely to go out and more likely to feel isolated and lonely and experience sadness and anxiety (DiTommaso & Spinner, 1997; Li & Moore, 1998). Conversely, those with a disability who perceive themselves as having good family and social support are less likely to experience loneliness. Furthermore, being financially stable to afford durable medical and adaptive equipment, such as a wheelchair-accessible van, and possessing personality traits like internal locus of control and perseverance are associated with more successful adaptation to disability (Kellett et al., 2021; Marini, 2018d).

INDIVIDUAL RESPONSES TO DISABILITY

An individual's response to disability depends on several factors. A plethora of literature exists regarding how individual personality traits impact how one copes, responds, adapts, or adjusts to disability (Marini, 2018e). This section addresses the first author's experience with tetraplegia for over 40 years and his extensive scholarship on the topic. In addition, we have solicited lived experiences personal communications from persons who are deaf or blind.

There are numerous theories of adaptation to disability. Adapting or responding to disability involves an overlapping combination of several of these existing theories (Marini, 2018d). Some theorists believe that for those with acquired disabilities, there is a stage-like process similar to the stages of grief that are associated with major life transitions (Livneh, 1991). Proponents of the stage theory believe individuals will reach a final stage of adaptation and acknowledgment, while others will get stuck in a stage or regress to an earlier stage. Other theorists propose a recurrent or integrated model of adaptation, asserting that the human response to disability is too complex for a linear stage theory (Kendall & Buys, 1998).

The recurrent or integrated model of adaptation is premised on the notion that the initial experience of disability may involve emotional turmoil, which will then slowly reset into a pattern of emotional stability over time. The recurrent or integrated model of adaptation is based, in part, by Beck's (Beck, 1967; Beck & Weishaar, 1989) cognitive theory and the concept of **cognitive schema**. This concept involves a pattern of thoughts and behaviors that includes preconceived ideas we have about ourselves and the world, organizing our reality to fit our beliefs. Following a traumatic injury that drastically changed one's lifestyle, many individuals will cling to their old schema of self. Wright (1983) used the term **as-if behavior**—behaving as if the severity of their disability is not real. These individuals instead contradict, deny, and refute any cognitions of the loss of their previous way of life to fit our preconceived preinjury selves. Kendall and Buys (1998) asserted that individuals mourn and yearn for their past life by dwelling on all the activities they used to do. However, once realizing that they can no longer deny the permanency of their disability, they may become depressed, anxious, and feel hopeless about their situation. It is only after they begin to adapt to their new lifestyle that they begin looking forward and refrain from looking back on what they no longer can do. The current authors indicate that to make this future time-oriented shift, the individual must (a) search for new meaning living with a disability, (b) attempt to master or control their environment, and (c) define and protect their new disability self. The authors acknowledge that there will be periodic setbacks that cause individuals to experience periods of sorrow and despair regarding what they have lost (see Box 7.1).

Finally, the ecological theorists consider other factors outside of individual traits that can positively or negatively impact one's response or adaptation to disability. These theorists consider not only individual traits but also the importance of external factors regarding the interdependence each of us has with factors outside of our direct control. These external or environmental forces are equally important because if we perceive they are not in our control and impose barriers to our development, they can negatively affect us personally (DiTommaso & Spinner, 1997; Li & Moore, 1998; Vash & Crewe, 2004).

BOX 7.1 REFLECTION ACTIVITY

Of the numerous types of known disabilities that if you had to choose, which one would you choose to have, and which one would you be most fearful of having and why? Then consider which of your five senses you perceive that is quality of life and overall life satisfaction would be severely compromised.

Examples could include being well-qualified for jobs yet chronically unemployed due to employer discrimination. Similarly, having continual negative experiences of rejection in attempting to form romantic relationships. In addition, if there are no community support systems to provide such resources as financial aid, transportation, interpreters, or personal attendant care, these obstacles to our self-growth may begin to build up and repress an individual's ability to thrive following a trauma (Kellett et al., 2021; Marini et al., 2009).

Ecological theorists view human behavior as a function of how we view ourselves as well as how we perceive others to view us (Vash & Crewe, 2004). The first author, who is an insider with tetraplegia, opines that there are aspects of each of these three overlapping theories that impact one's ability to eventually thrive after a traumatic disability, or conversely succumb or surrender trying to move forward emotionally, mentally, and behaviorally. In this way, one's predisposed personality and coping traits will have an impact on how an individual responds to disability (Marini, 2018d; Marini, 2018e). Individual traits such as resilience, hardiness, perseverance, past coping strategies, perceived health, optimism, hope, extroversion, sense of humor about oneself, subjective well-being, internal locus of control, spirituality, perceived QOL, happiness, family support, and self-determination have been found to be some of the central factors that are part of an individual's ability to adapt or respond well to an adventitious or traumatic disability (Diener & Lucas, 1999; Marini, 2018e; Seligman & Csikszentmihalyi, 2000; Seligman, 2002; Snyder & Lopez, 2002; Steel et al., 2008). From the lens of positive psychology, individuals who set and succeed at their goals, are optimistic of their future, perceive they are in control or responsible for their own growth, have strong family and/or significant other support, can persevere through adversity, feel strengthened by their faith, and are happy and satisfied with their quality of life are key factors to successful adaptation (Seligman & Csikszentmihalyi, 2000).

For the first author, after becoming paralyzed from the chest down in his early 20s, he did not want to live what he perceived as a meaningless life. Rather than collecting a meager monthly disability check and vicariously watching everyone else live their lives, he returned to college to earn a PhD and has thrived since his accident, crediting the strong support of his wife and family. For him, key elements to thriving were setting goals and accomplishing each one, spousal support, earning an income, and community support and resources, including vocational rehabilitation services, an available paratransit system, integrated wheelchair-accessible apartments, adequate healthcare, and attendant care. His experience mirrors that of the Kellett et al. (2021) study's participant findings.

OPTIMIZING ONE'S HEALTH AND FUNCTIONING

The number of people living with a disability worldwide is growing, especially in the United States (Kraus, 2016; Rosenberg et al., 2011) with approximately 52 million Americans reporting at least one disability (Carmona et al., 2010). Persons with disabilities (PWDs) can experience a wide range of physical, emotional, cognitive, and sensory functional limitations (Jeong & Yu, 2018). Nevertheless, despite etiology, people living with disabilities also encounter unique physical (Okoro et al., 2018) and psychosocial issues (Richardson et al., 2017b).

Researchers have found that PWDs are much less physically active than their nondisabled counterparts and report a higher number of secondary conditions, which in many instances are largely preventable (i.e., fatigue, weight gain, type 2 diabetes, and chronic pain; Kinne et al., 2004; Sharon-David et al., 2021). This situation is troublesome to health experts. Secondary conditions significantly deteriorate an individual's overall health and quality of life, further restricting functioning and independence (Bolin et al., 2015; Lexell, 2000; Ravesloot et al., 1998; Rejeski & Focht, 2002). These conditions include cardiovascular diseases such as coronary artery disease, musculoskeletal issues, and hypertension (Matcham et al., 2016; Okrainec et al., 2004). Cardiovascular disease is a common result of obesity (Piatt et al., 2016) and inactive lifestyles (Carroll et al., 2014; Cooper & Quatrano, 1999; Ginis et al., 2010). Researchers have found that such inactivity also creates a higher risk of developing depression, anxiety, and low self-esteem as well as loneliness and social withdrawal (Mazur, 2008; Turner et al., 2006; Richardson et al., 2017c; Villanueva-Flores et al., 2017). Thomas (2004) cited that the physical and societal barriers that continue to exist and are experienced by PWDs are a form of social inequity and oppression. The term **disablism** pertains to social oppression that people with disabilities encounter in the form of social isolation or restriction of activity, resulting in negatively affecting their physical, psychological, and overall well-being (Berghs et al., 2021; DiTommaso & Spinner, 1997; Li & Moore, 1998; Kellett et al., 2021). Tough et al. (2017) found these variables to collectively decrease overall social and psychological well-being (i.e., depression and anxiety), accounting for approximately 47% of the annual medical expenses in the present U.S. economy (Hoffman et al., 1996). Cooper and Quatrano (1999) noted that medical expenditures are 42% higher for persons who are obese, accounting for $147 billion annually in healthcare costs.

The value of physical activity in improving health and wellness among people with physical disabilities is evident. Nonetheless, most people with disabilities do not exercise enough to meet the minimal requirements necessary to gain the mental and physical health benefits from regular exercise (Carroll et al., 2014; Malone et al., 2012). Despite efforts aimed at the prevention or reduction of risk factor education associated with poor health and chronic disease (e.g., cardiovascular disease, stroke, obesity and type 2 diabetes), health disparities still exist among specific racial and ethnic minority groups (Han et al., 2009; Nelson, 2002; Wilson, 2009). This problem is more prevalent among people with disabilities, who have consistently been an underserved group (Cervantes & Hodge, 2019). A lack of physical activity and other health risk behaviors are associated with lower health-related QOL, higher risk of death and disability, and the restricted ability to carry out regular activities of daily living (World Health Organization, 2007), such as maintaining a job and an active social life (Brooks, 1984; Brandon, 1985; Nosek, 1997).

Researchers have found that the absence of physical activity is a major factor contributing to one's deteriorating aerobic capabilities, strength, fatigue, and flexibility, resulting in limited functional capabilities (Cardinal & Spaziani, 2003; Lawrence & Jette, 1996; Miller, 1995). Relatedly, researchers show lower scores of overall health and decreased QOL when dealing with secondary conditions (Figoni et al., 1998; Brownson et al., 2001). Increased weight may be more problematic for people living with impairments than for the nondisabled population, and people with disabilities are more likely to be obese than the general population (Cervantes & Hodge, 2019; Weil et al., 2002). A study that measured the height and weight of 306 adults with disabilities found that 62% of these individuals were classified as obese and that 22% of those participants fell within the category of being extremely obese (Rimmer & Wang, 2005). Interestingly, participants self-reported obesity was a contributing factor to their disability and 55% reported having diabetes, arthritis, and a previous stroke prior to further medical complications. This information is troubling considering people with disabilities are at risk for the same weight-related chronic conditions experienced by the general population; however, they also are predisposed to developing more severe chronic medical conditions associated with disability (Kinne et al., 2004; Rasch et al., 2008).

Durstine et al. (2000) posited several subtle lifestyle changes including exercise may reduce the likelihood of cancer, heart diseases, strokes, and diabetes by 20% to 30%, and increase life span by 3 to 5 years. Although lack of activity and poor diet contribute to chronic illness and disability for those without disabilities as well as a higher mortality rate, the epidemic obesity the United States has yet to be curtailed. For those individuals with disabilities, these mostly preventable chronic health conditions are often amplified.

Unfortunately, like the rest of America, many persons with disabilities report that they essentially have never incorporated regular exercise into their daily lives. Vang et al. (2020) found that of their 74 study participants with spinal cord injury (SCI), 72% indicated finding it difficult to motivate themselves to exercise regularly. For those who worked, they reported that there was just not enough time to exercise. Many of these participants had also never been involved in competitive sports or noncompetitive activities such as aerobics, strength building, meditation, or yoga. Similar findings have been expressed by other researchers as well (Borodulin et al., 2016; Kehn & Kroll, 2009; Ottomanelli et al., 2013).

Unfriendly Fitness Centers

Persons with physical disabilities have long perceived that fitness centers are largely inaccessible to them in terms of available adaptive exercise equipment as well as having unfriendly customer service. Vang et al. (2020) found that of their 74 SCI participants, 87% perceived fitness managers or instructors as having little or no knowledge about exercises for persons with SCI, 77% perceived owners did not want to spend funds on accessible equipment, and 67% of those who had gone to a fitness center found there was no accessible equipment. Similar results have been shared by numerous other researchers (; Anderson et al., 2017; Hwang et al., 2016; Richardson et al., 2017a, 2017b, 2017c; Rimmer et al., 2004). An added barrier to those who do desire to exercise is their complaint that purchasing their own accessible equipment is too expensive, particularly for those collecting disability benefits. Other individuals have noted that the severity of their disability is too restrictive for them to be able to participate in any type of exercise (Vang et al., 2020).

Several researchers who have studied the exercise barriers for persons with disabilities, also have discussed proposed solutions in making fitness centers or disability friendly (Richardson et al., 2017a, 2017; Rimmer & Rowland, 2008). Important measures include educating fitness owners and instructors about accessible disability equipment and working with persons with physical sensory disabilities, changing policies and procedures for centers to address this population, and education that addresses any myths or misconceptions about persons with disabilities. In addition, fitness center personnel can be assisted in developing tailored exercise programs and health promotion lifestyles including diet for this population (Froehlich et al., 2002; Rimmer et al., 2004; Weil et al., 2002). If fitness center personnel can be made aware of the health benefits of exercise for persons with disabilities, they may be more apt to make their centers more accessible.

Finally, a lack of access to exercise and recreational resources is not limited to fitness centers. Persons with disabilities also cited the lack of access to fitness trails, state parks, playgrounds, pools and adequate seating options at sports venues (Cardinal & Spaziani, 2003; Figoni et al., 1998; Miller, 1995). Aside from the health benefits of incorporating some type of exercise opportunities be it fitness centers or state parks, the impact on QOL and life satisfaction has been studied extensively for those with and without disabilities. Denying persons with disabilities this right to engage in public life that subsequently improves one's mental well-being is just another example of social inequity.

ADAPTIVE AIDS AND ASSISTIVE TECHNOLOGY

The lived experience of having a disability would not be complete without discussing the psychosocial impact of assistive technology and durable medical equipment that enhances the functional independence and spontaneity of those with disabilities. The number of PWDs constitutes about 12% of the population (Krahn et al., 2015) and as such, there has been a growing need for technology that improves their quality of life. Many people, such as older adults with age-acquired disabilities depend on family members and friends for assistance as well as assistive devices to perform their ADLs (Horowitz et al., 2006). In fact, a common way to increase functional independence in PWDs is to implement the use of adaptive aids or assistive technology (De-Rosende-Celeiro et al., 2019). According to the International Classification of Functioning (ICF, n.d), the definition of **assistive technology** is "any product, instrument, equipment or technology adapted or specially designed for improving the functioning of a disabled person" (ICF, n.d). Regardless of the disability or type of assistive technology, the overall goal is to promote functional independence (Lancioni & Singh, 2014).

When referring to assistive devices, it is important to consider the concept of QOL as they are intricately related. QOL has expanded in its definition over the years, and it has transitioned from a concept that defines emotional, physical, and social well-being into "specific dimensions of life for specific groups of people," in this case the PWD. QOL as defined by Petry et al. (2005) is a "multi-element structure consisting of different domains." However, PWDs may experience complex and specific needs, such as varying degrees of disability or types of disability that make it difficult to judge what constitutes their QOL. Ultimately, regardless of the level of adaptive technology or complexity of the adaptive aids they provide, they offer essential behavioral and functional advantages as such technologies decrease the negative impact of disabilities (Bauer et al., 2011; Brown et al., 2009; Reichle, 2011; Shih, 2011).

Types of Assistive Technology

It is beyond the scope of this chapter to delve into a comprehensive exploration of the thousands of assistive devices and durable medical equipment that assist persons with disabilities to become more independent and spontaneous in their lives. However, we briefly explore some of them here and refer readers to the many books on the topic of such technology (Bryant & Bryant, 2022; Scherer, 2002, 2007). It is first important to differentiate between low versus high tech solutions, and several examples are provided for each noting that the differences between the two is largely based on cost.

Low-tech solutions are relatively inexpensive, with most costing less than $100. Examples for persons with hand mobility or finger dexterity impairments may include button hooks, wrist splints that hold kitchen utensils such as a spoon or fork, and removable showerhead hoses with related mobility impairments. For persons who are visually impaired, many utilize large print phones, voice-activated kitchen appliances, alarms, and watches, and magnifying enhancers. For persons who are deaf or hard of hearing, strobe light alarms, closed caption on devices, and strobe-light telephones are often employed.

High-tech solutions typically are more expensive exceeding $100 and sometimes cost tens of thousands of dollars. For persons with mobility impairments, powered reclining/standing /tilt wheelchairs, exoskeletons, modified vehicles for someone with quadriplegia or paraplegia to drive, and environmental control units that control most home electrical appliances (e.g., TV, door locks, kitchen appliances, lights, or air-conditioning) are available. For those with hearing impairments, there are cochlear implants, Bluetooth hearing aids, and looping systems that might offer assistance. And for those with visual impairments, voice-activated book readers, ORcams (glasses that read written signs, billboards, mall advertisements, out in the community) may be useful. These types of technology assist persons with various disabilities not only to be more independent, but also to engage with their communities and hence improve the QOL and life satisfaction for these individuals.

Inclusion of Clients in Assistive Technology Selection

Scherer (2002) and Scherer et al. (2007) emphasized the crucial importance of including clients with disabilities in the purchase of assistive devices. She described how consumers who are not included in the selection of assistive device purchases often will not use or abandon the device for various reasons, such as it is too complicated to use, it is too cumbersome, or it does not fit properly. Perhaps one of the most obvious examples of device abandonment is prosthesis abandonment. Persons with one or more extremity amputations have been known to not use the prosthesis because it was too heavy, bulky, or simply unattractive in appearance. Individuals also may abandon devices purchased for them by well-meaning therapists because they do not like the color, or the device draws too much attention to their disability. It is important for rehabilitation counselors to include clients in exploring the ever-increasing growing number of assistive technology and durable medical equipment that can improve their lives.

Psychosocial Impact of Assistive Technology

The most important aspect of assistive technology for persons with disabilities is the psychological and sociological impact it has on their QOL, life satisfaction, attitudes, self-esteem, and self-worth. The first author with tetraplegia, who is able to drive his own adapted van from his wheelchair, stresses the QOL and freedom that spontaneity brings to his life because of the ability to come and go whenever he wishes. Without such a means of mobility, there would be little opportunity to decide to go to with theater, a restaurant, some other social function, or work because of having to rely on others for a ride. The freedom to be spontaneous to do what you want when you want cannot be overstated.

The resulting impact of being able to function more independently not only improves one's QOL and life satisfaction but also restores a sense of self-esteem and self-worth. This improvement results from being more independent and not having to succumb to societal expectations that people with disabilities are helpless and incapable of managing their own lives (Marini, 2018b). Kendall and Buys (1998) proposed an Integrated Model of Adaptation to Disability in which they proposed three critical components of successful adjustment to disability. One of these three components is an individual's perception of mastery over their environment. Assistive technology and durable medical equipment enhance an individual's mastery or control by allowing them to become more functionally independent at home, work, and in their community. A second component of the model is gaining autonomy over decisions in one's life, and similarly, assistive technology and durable medical equipment accomplish exactly that for persons with disabilities.

Finally, we would be remiss if we did not discuss the ongoing barriers that frustrate persons with disabilities (see Box 7.2). A critical barrier is the excessive cost and restrictions in purchasing the technology one needs to rely upon for autonomy, control, and mastery of their environment. Several qualitative studies have repeatedly noted the frustration of limited insurance policies, whether they be private or public like Medicaid or Medicare, in denying or curtailing the permission to purchase adaptive equipment (Graf et al., 2009; Marini et al., 2009; Pinon et al., 2021). When persons with disabilities are denied or restricted to purchase lower cost assistive technology that does not fully meet their needs, the resulting impact on their psychosocial adjustment impedes not only their QOL but life satisfaction in general.

BOX 7.2 REFLECTION ACTIVITY

Ask yourself: How might you feel if you were told by an insurance company that the adaptive equipment you wanted was not covered on your insurance, but a less expensive piece of equipment was available despite the fact that it was not what you needed? Specifically, if you were a wheelchair user who needed a hoist or lift to get you in/out of bed and you lived in a small apartment in a small bedroom and you wanted a track ceiling left but the company told you you qualified for a Hoyer lift that really would be cumbersome and not enough space for you to do your transfers. If you are unfamiliar with these types of lifts, Google them looking for picture images.

Ask yourself: What if you were a teenager who could drive your own modified van with a lift but did not have the finances to purchase such a vehicle? Since teenagers have a critical developmental need to be part of a peer group, your able-bodied friends ask you to restaurants, theaters, and concerts all the time, but your city does not have accessible transportation, or if it does, it may take an hour or two for them to pick you up. How might you eventually start to feel by not having the means to spontaneously go out with your friends and enjoy community life?

CONCLUSION

Ultimately, the lived experiences of persons with various disabilities and how successfully they may or may not adapt to disability depends on several mitigating factors. These factors include individual personality traits and temperament, available access to community resources, adequate insurance for health and assistive technology needs, and other environmental or external forces that either support or stifle one's response to disability. When persons with disabilities can find themselves on an equitable playing field of having all the appropriate resources (Kellett et al., 2021), they generally will thrive and experience a good QOL and life satisfaction. However, when they are thwarted or blocked in the variety of ways we have discussed in this chapter, a positive lived experience will not be fully realized.

CONTENT REVIEW QUESTIONS

1. How does the historical treatment and perceptions of those with disabilities compare or contrast to how persons with disabilities are currently viewed by society today?
2. What are some of the challenges to how persons with physical, sensory, cognitive, and emotional disabilities navigate their environment and potential barriers?
3. What is the psychological and health impact of a lack of accessible fitness centers, and what can be done about it?
4. What are the mental health benefits of having access to assistive technology, transportation, and durable medical equipment?
5. What are some of the current barriers to living a full life for persons with disabilities may have on their mental health and adaptation to disability?

REFERENCES

Anderson, C., Grant, R. L., & Hurley, M. V. (2017). Exercise facilities for neurologically disabled populations - Perceptions from the fitness industry. *Disability and Health Journal, 10*(1), 157–162. https://doi.org/10.1016/j.dhjo.2016.09.006

Bauer, S. M., Elsaesser, L. J., & Arthanat, S. (2011). Assistive technology device classification based upon the World Health Organization's International Classification of Functioning, Disability and Health (ICF). *Disability and Rehabilitation. Assistive Technology, 6*(3), 243–259. https://doi.org/10.3109/17483107.2010.529631

Baynton, D. C. (2001). Disability and the justification of inequality in American history. In P. K. Longmore, & L. Umansky (Eds.), *The new disability history: American perspectives,* (pp. 33–57). New York University Press.

Beck, A. T. (1967). *Depression: Causes and treatment.* University of Pennsylvania Press.

Beck, A. T., & Weishaar, M. (1989). Cognitive therapy. In A. Freeman, K. M. Simon, L. E. Beutler, & H. Arkowitz (Eds.), *Comprehensive handbook of cognitive therapy* (pp. 21–36). Plenum.

Berghs, M., Atkin, K., Graham, H., Hatton, C., & Thomas, C. (2021). Implications for public health research of models and theories of disability: a scoping study and evidence synthesis. *Public Health Research, 4*(8), 1–166. https://doi.org/10.3310/phr04080

Bishop, M. (2005). Quality of life and psychosocial adaptation to chronic illness and acquired disability: A conceptual and theoretical synthesis. *Journal of Rehabilitation, 71*(2), 5–13.

Blackwell, T. M., Marini, I., & Chacon, M. (2001). The impact of the Americans With Disabilities Act on independent living. *Rehabilitation Education, 15*(4), 395–408.

Bolin, J. N., Bellamy, G. R., Ferdinand, A. O., Vuong, A. M., Kash, B. A., Schulze, A., & Helduser, J. W. (2015). Rural healthy people 2020: New decade, same challenges. *The Journal of Rural Health, 31*(3), 326–333. https://doi.org/10.1111/jrh.12116

Borodulin, K., Sipilä, N., Rahkonen, O., Leino-Arjas, P., Kestilä, L., Jousilahti, P., & Prättälä, R. (2016). Socio-demographic and behavioral variation in barriers to leisure-time physical activity. *Scandinavian Journal of Public Health, 44*(1), 62–69. https://doi.org/10.1177/1403494815604080

Brandon, J. E. (1985). Health promotion and wellness in rehabilitation services. *Journal of Rehabilitation, 51*(4), 54.

Brooks, N. A. (1984). Opportunities for health promotion: Including the chronically ill and disabled. *Social Science & Medicine (1982), 19*(4), 405–409. https://doi.org/10.1016/0277-9536(84)90198-9

Brown, R. I., Schalock, R. L., & Brown, I. (2009). Quality of life: Its application to persons with intellectual disabilities and their families-introduction and overview. *Journal of Policy and Practice in Intellectual Disabilities, 6*(1), 2–6. https://doi.org/10.1111/j.1741-1130.2008.00202.x

Brownson, R. C., Baker, E. A., Housemann, R. A., Brennan, L. K., & Bacak, S. J. (2001). Environmental and policy determinants of physical activity in the United States. *American Journal of Public Health, 91*(12), 1995–2003. https://doi.org/10.2105/ajph.91.12.1995

Bryant, D. P., & Bryant, B. R. (2022). *Assistive technology for people with disabilities* (2nd ed.). Pearson Education Inc.

Cardinal, B. J., & Spaziani, M. D. (2003). ADA compliance and the accessibility of physical activity facilities in western Oregon. *American Journal of Health Promotion, 17*(3), 197–201. https://doi.org/10.4278/0890-1171-17.3.197

Carlson, E. (2009). Three generations, no imbeciles: Eugenics, the Supreme Court, and Buck v Bell. *Quarterly Review of Biology, 84*(2), 178–180.

Carmona, R. H., Giannini, M., Bergmark, B., & Cabe, J. (2010). The surgeon general's call to action to improve the health and wellness of persons with disabilities: Historical review, rationale, and implications 5 years after publication. *Disability and Health Journal, 3*(4), 229–232. https://doi.org/10.1016/j.dhjo.2010.07.004

Carroll, D. D., Courtney-Long, E. A., Stevens, A. C., Sloan, M. L., Lullo, C., Visser, S. N., Fox, M. H., Armour, B. S., Campbell, V. A., Brown, D. R., Dorn, J. M., & Centers for Disease Control and Prevention (CDC). (2014). Vital signs: Disability and physical activity--United States, 2009-2012. *MMWR. Morbidity and Mortality Weekly Report, 63*(18), 407–413.

Cervantes, C. M., & Hodge, S. R. (2019). Health disparities among men with disabilities and functional limitations. *In Men's Health Equity* (pp. 376–394). Routledge.

Coco, A. P. (2010). Diseased, maimed, mutilated: categorizations of disability and an ugly law in late nineteenth-century Chicago. *Journal of Social History, 44*(1), 23–37. https://doi.org/10.1353/jsh.2010.0025

Cooper, R. A., & Quatrano, L. A. (1999). Research on physical activity and health among people with disabilities: A consensus statement. *Journal of Rehabilitation Research & Development, 36*(2), 142–154.

Cowles, C. A., & Washburn, J. J. (2005). Psychological consultation on program design of intensive management units in juvenile correctional facilities. *Professional Psychology, 36*(1), 44–50. https://doi.org/10.1037/0735-7028.36.1.44

De-Rosende-Celeiro, I., Torres, G., Seoane-Bouzas, M., & Ávila, A. (2019). Exploring the use of assistive products to promote functional independence in self-care activities in the bathroom. *PloS One, 14*(4), e0215002. https://doi.org/10.1371/journal.pone.0215002

Diener, E. & Lucas, S. (1999). Personality and subjective well-being. In E. Diener & N Schwartz (Eds.), *Well-being: The foundations of hedonic psychology* (pp. 213–229). Russell Sage Foundation.

DiTommaso, E., & Spinner, B. (1997). Social and emotional loneliness: A re-examination of weiss' typology of loneliness. *Personality and Individual Differences, 22*(3), 417–427. https://doi.org/10.1016/S0191-8869(96)00204-8

Dunn, D. S., & Brody, C. (2008). Defining the good life following acquired physical disability. *Rehabilitation Psychology, 53*(4), 413–425. https://doi.org/10.1037/a0013749

Durstine, J. L., Painter, P., Franklin, B. A., Morgan, D., Pitetti, K. H., & Roberts, S. O. (2000). Physical activity for the chronically ill and disabled. *Sports Medicine, 30*(3), 207–219. https://doi.org/10.2165/00007256-200030030-00005

Figoni, S. F., McClain, L., Bell, A. A., Degnan, J. M., Norbury, N. E., & Rettele, R. R. (1998). Accessibility of physical fitness facilities in the Kansas City metropolitan area. *Topics in Spinal Cord Injury Rehabilitation, 3*(3), 66–78.

Froehlich, A. K., Nary, D. E., & White, G. W. (2002). Identifying barriers to participation in physical activity for women with disabilities. *SCI Psychosocial Process, 15*(1), 21–29.

Gallagher, H. G. (1995). *By trust betrayed: Patients, physicians, and the license to kill in the Third Reich.* Vandamere.

Ginis, K. A., Jetha, A., Mack, D. E., & Hetz, S. (2010). Physical activity and subjective well-being among people with spinal cord injury: A meta-analysis. *Spinal Cord, 48*(1), 65–72. https://doi.org/10.1038/sc.2009.87

Graf, N. M., Marini, I., & Blankenship, C. (2009). 100 Words about disability. *Journal of Rehabilitation, 75*(2), 25–34.

Han, H. R., Lee, J. E., Kim, J., Hedlin, H. K., Song, H., & Kim, M. T. (2009). A meta-analysis of interventions to promote mammography among ethnic minority women. *Nursing Research, 58*(4), 246–254. https://doi.org/10.1097/NNR.0b013e3181ac0f7f

Hart, T., Whyte, J., Polansky, M., Millis, S., Hammond, F. M., Sherer, M., Bushnik, T., Hanks, R., & Kreutzer, J. (2003). Concordance of patient and family report of neurobehavioral symptoms at 1 year after traumatic brain injury. *Archives of Physical Medicine and Rehabilitation, 84*(2), 204–213. https://doi.org/10.1053/apmr.2003.50019

Hoffman, C., Rice, D., & Sung, H. Y. (1996). Persons with chronic conditions. Their prevalence and costs. *JAMA, 276*(18), 1473–1479.

Horowitz, A., Brennan, M., Reinhardt, J. P., & Macmillan, T. (2006). The impact of assistive device use on disability and depression among older adults with age-related vision impairments. *The Journals of Gerontology. Series B, Psychological Sciences and Social Sciences, 61*(5), S274-80. https://doi.org/10.1093/geronb/61.5.s274

Hwang, E. J., Groves, M. D., Sanchez, J. N., Hudson, C. E., Jao, R. G., & Kroll, M. E. (2016). Barriers to Leisure-Time physical activities in individuals with spinal cord injury. *Occupational Therapy in Health Care, 30*(3), 215–230. https://doi.org/10.1080/07380577.2016.1183180

International Classification of Functioning. (n.d.). *Introduction.* https://www.physio-pedia.com/International_Classification_of_Functioning,_Disability_and_Health_(ICF)

Jeong, J., & Yu, J. (2018). Prevalence and influencing factors of metabolic syndrome among persons with physical disabilities. *Asian Nursing Research, 12*(1), 50–55. https://doi.org/10.1016/j.anr.2018.02.001

Kehn, M., & Kroll, T. (2009). Staying physically active after spinal cord injury: A qualitative exploration of barriers and facilitators to exercise participation. *BMC Public Health, 9*(1), 1–11. https://doi.org/10.1186/1471-2458-9-168

Kellett, K., Ligus, K., & Robison, J. (2021). "So Glad to Be Home": Money follows the person participants' experiences after transitioning out of an institution. *Journal of Disability Policy Studies,* 104420732110435. https://doi.org/10.1177/10442073211043519

Kendall, E., & Buys, N. (1998). An integrated model of psychosocial adjustment following acquired disability. *Journal of Rehabilitation*, 64, 16–20.

Kinne, S., Patrick, D. L., & Doyle, D. L. (2004). Prevalence of secondary conditions among people with disabilities. *American Journal of Public Health*, 94(3), 443–445. https://doi.org/10.2105/ajph .94.3.443

Krahn, G. L., Walker, D. K., & Correa-De-Araujo, R. (2015). Persons with disabilities as an unrecognized health disparity population. *American Journal of Public Health*, 105 Suppl 2, S198-206. https://doi.org/10.2105/AJPH.2014.302182

Kraus, L. (2016). *2015 Disability statistics annual report. a publication of the rehabilitation research and training center on disability statistics and demographics*. Institute on Disability, University of New Hampshire.

Lancioni, G. E., & Singh, N. N. (2014). *Assistive technologies for people with diverse abilities (Autism and Child Psychopathology Series)*. Springer Science Business Media. https://doi.org/10.1007/978-1 -4899-8029-8

Largent, M. (2002). The greatest curse of the race: Eugenic sterilization in Oregon 1909–1983. *Oregon Historical Quarterly*, 103(2), 188–209.

Lawrence, R. H., & Jette, A. M. (1996). Disentangling the disablement process. *The Journals of Gerontology. Series B, Psychological Sciences and Social Sciences*, 51(4), S173-82. https://doi.org/10 .1093/geronb/51b.4.s173

Lewin, K. (1935). *A dynamic theory of personality*. McGraw-Hill.

Lexell, J. (2000). Neurological disorders: The potential of exercise to improve activities of daily living. *Exercise and Sport Sciences Reviews*, 91(6631/2802), 80–84.

Li, L., & Moore, D. (1998). Acceptance of disability and its correlates. *The Journal of Social Psychology*, 138(1), 13–25. https://doi.org/10.1080/00224549809600349

Livneh, H. (1991). On the origins of negative attitudes toward people with disabilities. In R.P. Marinelli & A. E. Dell Orto (Eds), *The psychological & social impact of disability* (pp. 111–138). Springer.

Lynn, R., & Van Court, M. (2004). New evidence of dysgenic fertility for intelligence in the United States. *Intelligence*, 32(2), 193–201. https://doi.org/10.1016/j.intell.2003.09.002

Lynn, R. & Vanhanen, T. (2002). *IQ and the wealth of nations*. Praeger Publishers.

Mackelprang, R. W., & Salsgiver, R. O. (2009). The meaning and history of disability in society. In R. W. Mackelprang & R. O. Salsgiver (Eds.), *Disability: A diversity model approach in human service practice* (pp. 3–29).

Malone, L. A., Barfield, J. P., & Brasher, J. D. (2012). Perceived benefits and barriers to exercise among persons with physical disabilities or chronic health conditions within action or maintenance stages of exercise. *Disability and Health Journal*, 5(4), 254–260.

Marini, I. (2018a). Societal attitudes and myths about disability: Improving the social consciousness. *Psychosocial aspects of disability: Insider perspectives and strategies for counselors* (pp. 33–62). Springer.

Marini, I. (2018b). The history of treatment toward people with disabilities. In I. Marini, N. M. Graf, & M. J. Millington (Eds.), *Psychosocial aspects of disability: Insider perspectives and strategies for counselors* (2nd ed., pp. 3–32). Springer.

Marini, I. (2018c). *Social justice, oppression, and disability: Counseling those most in need. Psychosocial aspects of disability: Insider perspectives and strategies for counselors* (pp. 415–436). Springer.

Marini, I. (2018d). *Theories of adjustment and adaptation to disability. Psychosocial aspects of disability: Insider perspectives and strategies for counselors* (pp. 133–167). Springer. https://doi.org/10.1891/ 9780826180636

Marini, I. (2018e). *Thriving versus succumbing to disability: Psychosocial factors and positive psychology. Psychosocial aspects of disability: Insider perspectives and strategies for counselors* (pp. 329–357). Springer.

Marini, I., Bhakta, M. V., & Graf, N. (2009). A Content analysis of common concerns of persons with physical disabilities. *Journal of Applied Rehabilitation Counseling*, 40(1), 44–49. https://doi.org/10 .1891/0047-2220.40.1.44

Maslow, A. H. (1970). *Motivation and personality* (3rd ed.). Addison Wesley Longman, Inc.

Matcham, F., Norton, S., Scott, D. L., Steer, S., & Hotopf, M. (2016). Symptoms of depression and anxiety predict treatment response and long-term physical health outcomes in rheumatoid arthritis: secondary analysis of a randomized controlled trial. *Rheumatology*, 55(2), 268–278.

Mazur, E. (2008). Negative and positive disability-related events and adjustment of parents with acquired physical disabilities and of their adolescent children. *Journal of Child and Family Studies, 17*(4), 517–537. https://doi.org/10.1007/s10826-007-9171-0

McCord, C. E., Elliott, T. R., Berry, J. W., Underhill, A. T., Fine, P. R., & Lai, M. H. C. (2016). Trajectories of happiness 5 years following medical discharge for traumatic disability: Differences between insider and outsider perspectives. *Journal of Happiness Studies, 17*(2), 553–567. https://doi.org/10.1007/s10902-014-9610-8

Miller, P. D. (1995). *Fitness programming and physical disability.* Human Kinetics.

Nakic, M., Stefanovics, E. A., Rhee, T. G., & Rosenheck, R. A. (2021). Lifetime risk and correlates of incarceration in a nationally representative sample of U.S. adults with non-substance-related mental illness. *Social Psychiatry and Psychiatric Epidemiology.* https://doi.org/10.1007/s00127-021-02158-x

Nelson, A. (2002). Unequal treatment: Confronting racial and ethnic disparities in health care. *Journal of the National Medical Association, 94*(8), 666–668.

Nguyen-Finn, K. (2018). History of treatment toward persons with psychiatric disabilities. In I. Marini & M. Stebnicki (Ed.), *The psychological and social illness and disability* (pp. 29–47). Springer.

Nosek, M. A. (1997). Women with disabilities and the delivery of empowerment medicine. *Archives of Physical Medicine and Rehabilitation, 78*(12 Suppl 5), S1-2. https://doi.org/10.1016/s0003-9993(97)90214-8

Okoro, C. A., Hollis, N. D., Cyrus, A. C., & Griffin-Blake, S. (2018). Prevalence of disabilities and health care access by disability status and type among adults - United States, 2016. *MMWR. Morbidity and Mortality Weekly Report, 67*(32), 882–887. https://doi.org/10.15585/mmwr.mm6732a3

Okrainec, K., Banerjee, D. K., & Eisenberg, M. J. (2004). Coronary artery disease in the developing world. *American Heart Journal, 148*(1), 7–15. https://doi.org/10.1016/j.ahj.2003.11.027

Olkin, R. (1999). *What psychotherapists should know about disability.* Guilford Press.

Ottomanelli, L., Barnett, S. D., & Goetz, L. L. (2013). A prospective examination of the impact of a supported employment program and employment on health-related quality of life, handicap, and disability among Veterans with SCI. *Quality of Life Research, 22*(8), 2133–2141. https://doi.org/10.1007/s11136-013-0353-5

Pearson, W. R. (1995). Comparison of methods for searching protein sequence databases. *Protein Science, 4*(6), 1145–1160. https://doi.org/10.1002/pro.5560040613

Petry, K., Maes, B., & Vlaskamp, C. (2005). Domains of quality of life of people with profound multiple disabilities: The perspective of parents and direct support staff. *Journal of Applied Research in Intellectual Disabilities, 18*(1), 35–46. https://doi.org/10.1111/j.1468-3148.2004.00209.x

Piatt, J. A., Nagata, S., Zahl, M., Li, J., & Rosenbluth, J. P. (2016). Problematic secondary health conditions among adults with spinal cord injury and its impact on social participation and daily life. *The Journal of Spinal Cord Medicine, 39*(6), 693–698. https://doi.org/10.1080/10790268.2015.1123845

Pinon, R. M., Marini, I., Antol, D. L. (2021). Every day lived experiences of persons with physical disabilities: Implications for rehabilitation counselors. *Directions in Rehabilitation Counseling.* 31(10), 17–30.

Rasch, E. K., Hochberg, M. C., Magder, L., Magaziner, J., & Altman, B. M. (2008). Health of community-dwelling adults with mobility limitations in the United States: prevalent health conditions. Part I. *Archives of Physical Medicine and Rehabilitation, 89*(2), 210–218. https://doi.org/10.1016/j.apmr.2007.08.146

Ravesloot, C., Seekins, T., & Young, Q. R. (1998). Health promotion for people with chronic illness and physical disabilities: The connection between health psychology and disability prevention. *Clinical Psychology & Psychotherapy, 5*(2), 76–85. https://doi.org/10.1002/(SICI)1099-0879(199806)5:2<76::AID-CPP156>3.0.CO;2-5

Reichle, J. (2011). Evaluating assistive technology in the education of persons with severe disabilities. *Journal of Behavioral Education, 20*(1), 77–85. https://doi.org/10.1007/s10864-011-9121-1

Rejeski, W. J., & Focht, B. C. (2002). Aging and physical disability: On integrating group and individual counseling with the promotion of physical activity. *Exercise and Sport Sciences Reviews, 30*(4), 166–170.

Richardson, E. V., Smith, B., & Papathomas, A. (2017a). Crossing boundaries: The perceived impact of disabled fitness instructors in the gym. *Psychology of Sport and Exercise, 29*, 84–92. https://doi.org/10.1016/j.psychsport.2016.12.006

Richardson, E. V., Smith, B., & Papathomas, A. (2017b). Disability and the gym: Experiences, barriers and facilitators of gym use for individuals with physical disabilities. *Disability and Rehabilitation, 39*(19), 1950–1957. https://doi.org/10.1080/09638288.2016.1213893

Richardson, E. V., Smith, B., & Papathomas, A. (2017c). Collective stories of exercise: Making sense of gym experiences with disabled peers. *Adapted Physical Activity Quarterly, 34*(3), 276–294. https://doi.org/10.1123/apaq.2016-0126

Rimmer, J. H., Riley, B., Wang, E., Rauworth, A., & Jurkowski, J. (2004). Physical activity participation among persons with disabilities: Barriers and facilitators. *American Journal of Preventive Medicine, 26*(5), 419–425.

Rimmer, J. H., & Rowland, J. L. (2008). Health promotion for people with disabilities: Implications for empowering the person and promoting disability-friendly environments. *American Journal of Lifestyle Medicine, 2*(5), 409–420. https://doi.org/10.1177/1559827608317397

Rimmer, J. H., & Wang, E. (2005). Obesity prevalence among a group of Chicago residents with disabilities. *Archives of Physical Medicine and Rehabilitation, 86*(7), 1461–1464.

Rosenberg, D. E., Bombardier, C. H., Hoffman, J. M., & Belza, B. (2011). Physical activity among persons aging with mobility disabilities: Shaping a research agenda. *Journal of Aging Research, 2011*, 1–16. https://doi.org/10.4061/2011/708510

Scherer, M. J. (2002). *Assistive technology: Matching devices and consumers for successful rehabilitation.* American Psychological Association. https://doi.org/10.1037/10420-000

Scherer, M. J. (2007). *Living in the state of stuck: How technology impacts the lives of people with disabilities* (4th ed.). Brookline Books.

Scherer, M., Jutai, J., Fuhrer, M., Demers, L., & Deruyter, F. (2007). A framework for modelling the selection of assistive technology devices (ATDs). *Disability and Rehabilitation. Assistive Technology, 2*(1), 1–8. https://doi.org/10.1080/17483100600845414

Seligman, M. E. (2002). *Authentic happiness: Using the new positive psychology to realize your potential for lasting fulfillment.* Free Press.

Seligman, M. E., & Csikszentmihalyi, M. (2000). Positive psychology. An introduction. *The American Psychologist, 55*(1), 5–14. https://doi.org/10.1037//0003-066x.55.1.5

Sharon-David, H., Siekanska, M., & Tenenbaum, G. (2021). Are gyms fit for all? A scoping review of the barriers and facilitators to gym-based exercise participation experienced by people with physical disabilities. *Performance Enhancement & Health, 9*(1), 100170. https://doi.org/10.1016/j.peh.2020.100170

Shih, C. H. (2011). Assisting people with developmental disabilities to improve computer pointing efficiency through multiple mice and automatic pointing assistive programs. *Research in Developmental Disabilities, 32*(5), 1736–1744. https://doi.org/10.1016/j.ridd.2011.03.002

Singer, P. (1995). *Rethinking life and death.* Oxford University Press.

Smart, J. (2009). *Disability, society, and the individual.* Pro-ED.

Snyder, C. R., & Lopez, S. J. (2002). The future of positive psychology: A declaration of independence. In C. R. Snyder & S. J. Lopez (Eds.), *Handbook of positive psychology* (pp. 751–767). Oxford University Press.

Steel, J. L., Gamblin, T. C., & Carr, B. I. (2008). Measuring post-traumatic growth in people diagnosed with hepatobiliary cancer: Directions for future research. *Oncology Nursing Forum, 35*(4), 643–650. https://doi.org/10.1188/08.ONF.643-650

Thomas, C. (2004). How is disability understood? An examination of sociological approaches. *Disability & Society, 19*(6), 569–583. https://doi.org/10.1080/0968759042000252506

Tough, H., Siegrist, J., & Fekete, C. (2017). Social relationships, mental health and wellbeing in physical disability: A systematic review. *BMC Public Health, 17*(1), 1–18. https://doi.org/10.1186/s12889-017-4308-6

Tsai, J., & Huang, M. (2019). Systematic review of psychosocial factors associated with evictions. *Health & Social Care in the Community, 27*(3), e1–e9. https://doi.org/10.1111/hsc.12619

Tsai, J., Jones, N., Szymkowiak, D., & Rosenheck, R. A. (2021). Longitudinal study of the housing and mental health outcomes of tenants appearing in eviction court. *Social Psychiatry and Psychiatric Epidemiology, 56*(9), 1679–1686. https://doi.org/10.1007/s00127-020-01953-2

Turner, R. J., Lloyd, D. A., & Taylor, J. (2006). Physical disability and mental health: An epidemiology of psychiatric and substance disorders. *Rehabilitation Psychology, 51*(3), 214–223. https://doi.org/10.1037/0090-5550.51.3.214

Vang, C., Cuevas, S., Graf, N., & Marini, I. (2020). Exercise experiences and barriers among individuals with spinal cord injury. *Rehabilitation Research, Policy, and Education, 34*(3), 190–205. https://doi.org/10.1891/RE-19-09

Vash, C. L. & Crewe, N. M. (2004). *Psychology of disability* (2nd Ed.). Springer.

Villanueva-Flores, M., Valle, R., & Bornay-Barrachina, M. (2017). Perceptions of discrimination and distributive injustice among people with physical disabilities. *Personnel Review, 46*(3), 680–698. https://doi.org/10.1108/PR-04-2015-0098

Weil, E., Wachterman, M., McCarthy, E. P., Davis, R. B., O'Day, B., Iezzoni, L. I., & Wee, C. C. (2002). Obesity among adults with disabling conditions. *JAMA, 288*(10), 1265. https://doi.org/10.1001/jama.288.10.1265

West, J. (1991). *The Americans with Disabilities Act: From policy to practice.* Milbank Memorial Fund.

Wilson, D. K. (2009). New perspectives on health disparities and obesity interventions in youth. *Journal of Pediatric Psychology, 34*(3), 231–244. https://doi.org/10.1093/jpepsy/jsn137

Wolff, N., Blitz, C. L., & Shi, J. (2007). Rates of sexual victimization in prison for inmates with and without mental disorders. *Psychiatric Services, 58*(8), 1087–1094. https://doi.org/10.1176/ps.2007.58.8.1087

World Health Organization. (2007). *International Classification of Functioning, Disability, and Health: Children & Youth Version: ICF-CY.* World Health Organization.

Wright, B. A. (1983). *Physical disability - A psychosocial approach (2nd ed.).* HarperCollins. https://doi.org/10.1037/10589-000

CHAPTER 8

Family and Relationship Issues

R. ROCCO COTTONE

LEARNING OBJECTIVES

After reading this chapter, you should be able to:

- *Illustrate a historical backdrop related to the psychomedical framework of traditional vocational rehabilitation (VR) as compared to the systemic-relational view of the rehabilitation process (a fully relationship-oriented perspective of rehabilitation).*
- *Show a perspective of clients as embedded within the network of relationships and the rehabilitation counselor (RC) as a social agent facilitating interface of client and rehabilitation systems.*
- *Reconstruct the rehabilitation process as a social process*
- *Describe the role and influence of the family system in rehabilitation, including all stages of the rehabilitation process (even placement in jobs or community living).*
- *Describe the adaptation process of families addressing disabilities, including defining the caregiver stages of adjustment*
- *Defend that the role of the RC is that of family advocate who ideally encourages and seeks rehabilitation counseling education and training in family therapy and social systems theory.*

CACREP STANDARDS

CACREP 2016: 2F3.a, 2F3.f, 2F4b, 2F5.b
CACREP 2016 Specialties
   Clinical Rehabilitation Counseling: 5D1.b, 5D1.c, 5D2.a, 5D2.f, 5D2.0
   Rehabilitation Counseling: 5H2.c

INTRODUCTION

Rehabilitation does not occur in a vacuum. Many people are involved in the rehabilitation process, including family members of the individual with a disability and any number of friends, acquaintances, and professionals. A relational perspective embraces the involvement of other people in a person's rehabilitation. Understanding the involvement of others in the rehabilitation process is crucial if a rehabilitation counselor (RC) hopes to gain a perspective of the rehabilitation process from a larger social system point of view. There have been recent efforts to recognize the importance of family and relationship issues in rehabilitation counseling (Millington & Marini, 2015a). However, rehabilitation counseling is a counseling specialty that has been closely and historically aligned with the non-relational psychomedical paradigm of mental health services (Cottone & Emener, 1990).

The psychomedical paradigm of mental health services is a framework for conceptualizing client problems. It is also a framework for identifying and implementing methods of problem-solving. The focus of the psychomedical paradigm is the individual person—the person with a diagnosed medical condition. The individual is viewed as an independent focus of treatment (Cottone & Emener, 1990). Prior to the late 1970s and early 1980s, RCs focused on individual clients, serving them outside of family or other larger influential social systems. Clients were viewed as individuals (somewhat isolated from their social contexts) with problems that derived from their physical and mental conditions. Disability was first and foremost a matter of limitations deriving from a medical problem. Until recently, little emphasis was placed on identifying, researching, or treating social factors that affected a client's adaptation (Millington et al., 2015). Millington et al. (2015), lamenting the medical orientation of rehabilitation counseling, stated:

> The medical model has no active role for the family. . . . When the science is reductive, the social network is invisible and the issues of family are not recognized. For all the good intent, the medical model falls short for all rehabilitation professions, but particularly for rehabilitation counseling. (pp. 4–5)

The social systems or relational model of rehabilitation intervention is just beginning to get focused attention in the field. There have been divergent and persistent calls for recognition of family and relational issues affecting both clients and the profession, and the social systems theory, rather than the psychomedical paradigm, appears to be highly applicable to the need for family intervention. In other words, the social systems model is relational in nature and interactive, because it is concerned with the influence of other individuals in the rehabilitation process, even to the degree to which systems of relationships (organizations, families, groups) are analyzed and addressed in the rehabilitation process.

Because, historically, rehabilitation counseling was closely associated with vocational issues, many of the early rehabilitation assessment and intervention methods were consistent with the vocational trait-factor movement (Kosciulek, 1993; Kosciulek & DeVinney, 2004), an approach that emphasized methods for fitting the peg (client) into the best hole (job). The trait-factor approach dates back to Parsons (1909) and the vocational choice movement. Trait-factorism held that a client could be viewed as having job-relevant characteristics (in a classic psychological and physical sense). Matching the client's positive and negative characteristics to a job and a work context was thought to be the best and easiest way to find a place for the client to work and to earn a living. Clients thereby could become productive members of society.

Rehabilitation counseling, based on trait-factor philosophy and grounded in the psychomedical paradigm, was a conglomeration of methods that were used to assess and to treat clients. For example, vocational assessment focused on identifying traits. Psychological traits (such as intelligence, aptitudes, and interests) and physical skills (such as finger dexterity, speed of processing, physical mobility, and strength) were identified, assessed, and matched to jobs in the marketplace. In the late 1970s and early 1980s, some theoreticians began to identify and to challenge the trait-factor or psychomedical framework, arguing that such a framework was less than ideal for addressing issues associated with disability. Notably, the psychosocial movement in rehabilitation, as best represented by the work of Wright (1983) and Stubbins (1977), began to recognize and conceptualize the social (along with the psychological) aspects of disability. Stubbins (1984) further challenged the status quo, as he was the first to argue for a more social systemic understanding of disability. Stubbins argued for expanding the definition of VR to include "social systems factors" (p. 375).

Soon after the call by Stubbins (1984) for a systemic understanding of the rehabilitation process, the first comprehensive theory of VR was developed to challenge the historical psychomedical framework of rehabilitation counseling. Cottone (1987) developed his systemic theory of VR. The impetus for the development of this theory was the recognition that family issues were influential to the success of rehabilitation efforts, but they were largely ignored in rehabilitation programming. In those days, the individual written rehabilitation plan used in the state–federal program had no place to address family-relevant issues. Cottone, an RC with training in family therapy, began to realize that family involvement was crucial to rehabilitation success and that family factors were related to or could be predictive of rehabilitation outcomes (Cottone, Handelsman, et al., 1986). Other authors and theorists also expressed the need to address family issues in rehabilitation (e.g., Power & Dell Orto, 1986). The client's family system began to be viewed as a network of relationships that was influential in the rehabilitation process. Cottone also took the position that the rehabilitation system could be conceptualized as a network of relationships, and that counselors could be viewed as social agents who were conduits for the larger social factors addressed at the interface between the counselor and the client being served in the state–federal or any rehabilitation service delivery system. From a purely relational viewpoint, the counselor–client relationship was crucial, because it represented a linkage of two systems: the client's system and the rehabilitation service delivery system. Rehabilitation outcomes could then be viewed as predictable based on the ease of interface of involved systems (Cottone & Cottone, 1986; Cottone, 1987; Cottone et al., 1988). If a client came from a supportive family, showed social capacity, and could communicate in a healthy way, there was likely a place that could be found for that person to work, regardless of skills or abilities. In contrast, a client connected to an unhealthy family or other system (e.g., the drug culture) showing poor social skills, (e.g., poor grooming and unusual interaction) and poor communication skills would likely be expelled from the rehabilitation program, even if the client had work-related skills (Cottone & Cottone, 1986; Cottone et al., 1988). Expulsion from the program typically occurred as (a) case closure when the client was socially deficient and a poor risk or (b) case closure after the client was put through a number of remediation measures (evaluation or personal adjustment programs) that acted more like social screening programs than rehabilitation interventions (Cottone & Cottone, 1986; Cottone et al., 1988). Those clients who survived screening were able to show some social capacity; those who did not fit socially (e.g., those who broke the rules) were clearly identified and prevented from receiving further services. It could be argued that too little rehabilitation and remediation were occurring and too much screening was occurring. Cottone et al. (1988) concluded that in cases of nonphysical disabilities (e.g., emotional, intellectual, or behavioral disabilities), vocational evaluators were making decisions about clients using data that were primarily social and interpersonal in making recommendations about client readiness for employment. The authors further concluded:

> Psychological evidence, allegedly gathered for employability decision making, appears to play a lesser role. The results of this study bring into question the nature of the vocational evaluation process as presently conceived within a psychomedical framework. (p. 50)

In effect, the state–federal VR system could be viewed as a social mechanism for screening the socially deviant from entry into the work world. This is a stunning conclusion that contradicts the intent of compassionate treatment of people with disabilities; it also shows bias in the system related to those with disabilities that affect social capacity. If the system is screening out the socially challenged, how can this be viewed as "rehabilitation?"

Reconceptualizing the rehabilitation process as a social process requires rehabilitation professionals to at least acknowledge the influence of family and other relevant social systems on rehabilitation outcomes. Even if RCs do not adopt a purely social perspective, as recommended by Cottone's (1987) systemic theory of VR, they must acknowledge the influence of relational systems on the outcomes of rehabilitation programming, or they will blindly provide services always identifying failure as an individual client problem (e.g., poor motivation). Consider that a client who appears poorly motivated in the

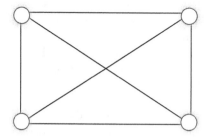

FIGURE 8.1 A system of four people is six relationships—each line represents a relationship; each circle represents a person.

rehabilitation system might be the most motivated drug pusher on the street. Motivation, from a relational standpoint, is always viewed in context.

Family relationships and family dynamics will play a major role in the rehabilitation process and rehabilitation outcomes. Nichols and Kosciulek (2014), in a qualitative study of victims of traumatic brain injury, found that, "not surprisingly family members were noted most frequently as social interaction partners and the self-assessments of participants [clients] were appreciably framed by family roles. From several individuals' perspective, the injury had brought the family closer together" (p. 25). Adaptation to disability is not just an individual issue. Families, too, adjust to disability, and the dynamics of the family may be significantly influenced by the presence of a mental or physical condition or some combination of conditions that affect family members as well as the individual with the disability. This chapter fully acknowledges the influence of relational factors in the rehabilitation process, but focuses primarily on the effect of disability from the perspective of the family. Adaptation to both disability and the rehabilitation process is addressed also.

THE FAMILY AS A SYSTEM

A system is a network of relationships—a "set of elements standing in interaction" (von Bertalanffy, 1968). Relationships (the interactions between people) are the focus of systems theory (Cottone, 1992). A system of three people is three relationships. A system of four people is six relationships (see Figure 8.1), and a system of five people is 10 relationships (see Figure 8.2).

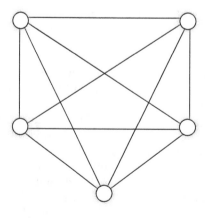

FIGURE 8.2 A system of five people is 10 relationships—each line represents a relationship; each circle represents a person.

The relationships are viewed as the crucial elements in a system. For a family of four in which one individual has a disability, each member is in a relationship with each other. Each relationship is influenced by the disability. Although all family members experience the presence of the disability in the family through relationships, in some families parents may be the primary caregivers. In families with an absent parent, siblings may be significantly involved in daily activities with family members with disabilities. Spouses or partners of adults with disabilities are often involved. The interaction among family or household members around the disability is important to note, as the family not only has a history of adjustment dynamically to the presence of the disability but also will have to adjust to changes in the family routine around the client's rehabilitation.

FAMILY ADAPTATION TO DISABILITY

The Importance of Family

Millington and Marini (2015b) made the case that "family is the touchstone of client identity, a source of client power, and the core of the client's social support network" (p. 87). If there is an intact family system (whether the family is nuclear, extended, biological, blended, or culturally defined), and the family is involved with the individual with a disability, then most likely there has been significant family adaptation to the disability itself. Some disabilities are **congenital** (e.g., inherited conditions evident at birth) and they have been with the family since the beginning of the individual's life with a disability. Other disabilities are **acquired**, such as those that result from trauma (e.g., physical injury, traumatic brain injury). Some are **developmental** or reveal themselves at different stages (e.g., intellectual impairment). Some are **progressive**, which means that typically they are inherited but they worsen with time; in these instances, the individual may have had some normal developmental period (e.g., certain muscular dystrophies, arthritis, dementia). Regardless of the type or onset of a condition, the intact family system must adjust. Family members must adapt to the disease process (if there is one) and to the personal limitations that exist or develop over time (see Box 8.1).

Family Challenges

Not only does a disability affect the family, but the family also affects the disability, with families, individuals, and social institutions interacting (Seligman & Darling, 2007). Unfortunately, not all families faced with debilitating disease or impairment stay together. Sometimes, parents of children with disabilities divorce or abandon their children. Anecdotally, divorce rates among parents of children with disabilities have been estimated to be as high as 80% (often estimated unreliably; see the review and conclusion of Sobsey (2004), who found a range of divorce estimates, leading to some confusion as to a reliable estimate). Divorce creates a complicated circumstance for remaining caregivers, as their share of the "load" increases with the lower number of committed caregivers. Generally, research shows that the percentage of children with disabilities in single-parent households exceeds the percentage of children without disabilities. Regardless of the presence and commitment of one or both parents, or of spouses or partners of individuals with disabilities, families of individuals with disabilities need help. Extended family members sometimes become involved. Sometimes, loving friends make special efforts to assist families in need. Reporting in a 1996 published survey, Burke (2008) indicated that "the need for help and assistance in the families surveyed was overwhelming; over 60 percent of families indicated this need" (p. 48). Siblings often take a caregiver role; Burke indicated that parents reported that siblings of a child with a disability were involved directly in care 75% of the time (one study reported involvement as high as 80%). Some families are able to afford assistance or obtain government assistance to hire others to

BOX 8.1 A PERSONAL EXPERIENCE

The reader should know that I had a child with a disability, and I have experienced family adjustment to disability in my own family, and have observed the adjustments of my clients to their concerns. My son, Torre, passed at age 20. He was diagnosed at age 2 with Duchenne muscular dystrophy, a genetic disorder that is fatal, usually affecting males and taking young boys around the age of 20. The moment of diagnosis was one of the most powerful moments affecting my life, my wife's life, and the lives of my other children. Torre's condition was genetic and progressive. He had several early years of normal development. At the end of his life he was in a wheelchair and needed near total assistance with most daily activities. At the end, he still had partial use of his hands, so he could still use a computer mouse and drive his wheelchair with a joystick. He could not support his own weight and he was not strong enough to turn in bed. As his condition progressed, the family had to adjust. The adjustment in this case was slow and followed the course of the disease. Each of us had to learn to accommodate our needs to ensure that Torre's needs were met. It may sound burdensome at some level. However, because Torre was a lovable and loved young man, in many ways it was a pleasure to be with him and to assist him. My wife and I made a commitment to provide him and the other children with a rich and full life. Although there was a clear commitment to someone we loved, it was also clear that sometimes relationships were strained and our lifestyles were affected. Since Torre's diagnosis, we have worked extensively with individuals and families facing muscular dystrophy (primarily through contacts with the Muscular Dystrophy Association and the Parent Project—Muscular Dystrophy). For those families that stay together, the process appears similar.

care for, watch over, or supervise the individual with the disability. The greater the network of support, the greater the likelihood that the individual with the disability will find meaning in life and will seek and cooperate with means of rehabilitation. Even with support, families of individuals with disabilities face similar challenges. Case-Smith (2007) reported that parenting a child with a chronic medical condition was associated with several challenges, including (a) managing and scheduling caregiver responsibilities, (b) feeling the burden of "always having to be there," (c) experiencing negative effects on the caregiver's outside career trajectory/plans, (d) addressing compromises in dealing with external service providers (e.g., schools, pharmacies, insurance companies, resource and rehabilitation agencies), (e) maintaining a social life outside the home, and (f) maintaining a self-identity.

Certainly, the challenge to families is magnified when there are external forces that further compound stress. For example, the COVID-19 pandemic created a major reordering of household activities, as family members had to adjust to living in close quarters, sometimes dealing with or fearing infection from the virus, and with little recourse to methods to relieve stressors by activities outside the home. In some cases, the fear or reality of death, especially for people with compromised health, is a looming concern. The mental health consequences on families will likely be addressed by mental health professionals for years following such a major upheaval. Counselors must be prepared to acknowledge and address these concerns, especially when family relations are already stressed by the impact of disability (see Box 8.1). Counselors can anticipate compounding stressors will manifest themselves in times of public health crises, natural catastrophes, economic upheaval, or political upheaval, as examples. Families with a member with a disability may have fewer options than other families when confronted by the effect of external stressors.

Family Caregivers and Stages of Caregiver Adjustment

Committed parents tend to be incredible caregivers, often sacrificing their own needs for the needs of their children. It is also the case that when the disability is acquired in adulthood, spouses and loving partners often accept the caregiver role. The toll on caregivers can be serious with serious disabilities; totally debilitating conditions, such as amyotrophic lateral sclerosis or Huntington's disease (fatal disorders with serious downward health trajectories, sometimes with death looming within a matter of years); or conditions that permanently affect a family member negatively (e.g., brain damage and quadriplegia). Millington and Marini (2015b) stated: "Family care is characterized by deep emotions, shared history, shared intimacy, and reciprocity. It is qualitatively different from the formal care of professionals. Caring is networked in the family system and orchestrated in its delivery through every family role" (pp. 88–89).

Debilitating progressive diseases or serious permanent loss of function are some of the most difficult situations for families to face (Frain et al., 2015). Caregivers in these circumstances appear to go through some predictable **stages**. First, upon diagnosis of the loved one, there is a sincere commitment to the love and care of the affected individual. Caregivers embrace the client and they formally commit to be there for the client, no matter what is faced. This is the *commitment stage*. The second stage is the *resource identification stage*, as the caregiver and family members collect resources (both personal and other resources) in order to make a difficult situation tolerable. There is much activity in this stage as the caregiver begins to identify resources, other helpers, family supports, community and church assistance, support from associations of others faced with similar circumstances, and financial supports (in the form of government assistance for rehabilitation or disability benefits). The third stage is the *plateau stage*, where often well-intended others begin to withdraw support and caregivers begin to face daily routines with limited assistance and limited or depleted resources. The fourth stage is the *exhaustion stage*. At this stage, caregivers begin to recognize that they cannot do it all—that they are overwhelmed even with the support they receive from others. They begin to feel neglected themselves and feel that their own needs are not being met. Anger may begin to set in, and they begin to ask, "Why?" They are often faced with their own career stressors, management of a home or other family members, household issues, financial issues, and a lack of sleep. The fifth stage is the *confusion stage*. Caregivers actually find themselves wishing it were over, which is frightening to them, because in some cases that would mean that their loved one would be gone. They cannot see the end. They feel a sense of hopelessness. They also feel the competing interest of self and loved one. They begin to feel real loss in their own lives, while at the same time recognizing the loss experienced by the loved one. They are torn and do not feel that they have a way out. The sixth stage is the *recommitment stage*. This typically comes near the end of the life of the affected individual, at a point of near-permanent stabilization, or at the end of the caregiver's formal commitment. Caregivers appear to rally at this stage, drawing on all their remaining resources as they recommit to the care and well-being of the individual with the disability. They are then committed until the end. Counseling through this process is crucial, as both the disability-affected individual and the caregiver face very serious social, physical, and psychological challenges.

If clients are lucky enough to stabilize and have the capacity to work or live independently, then family members and caregivers will face a transition when rehabilitation services become available.

FAMILY ADAPTATION TO THE REHABILITATION PROCESS

Routines in families with an individual with a disability appear to be fairly structured. Roles also appear to emerge over time and with experience. Consider transportation as an example. An individual in a wheelchair may be pushed by one member to a vehicle, then assisted by another to enter the car or to operate a lift or ramp, and then secured in the vehicle by another family member. So something as typical as transportation often calls for a clear separation of roles and responsibilities in family accommodation to the unique requirements of transporting an individual in a wheelchair. Family members tend to fall into these roles as the family learns to address the limitations of the individual with the disability. These roles tend to crystallize and, at best, make life a little more predictable and orderly. At worst, the roles may become rigid and unyielding. Rehabilitation efforts always call for change, and family routines typically will be disrupted.

When a counselor develops a rehabilitation plan with a client, it is always wise to explore how the client's routine will change, and how family members will be required to adjust. The more resistant the family members are to change, the more likely it is that rehabilitation efforts will fail. For example, requiring a client to attend on-the-job training when in the past the family's routine was established around the client staying at home, is a major change. In this case, the family members will have to adjust to what can be a burdensome task in adhering to a new schedule. In family systems theory, a change in routine may be interpreted as a disruption in the family **homeostasis**, the dynamic equilibrium of family interactions around the routines that have been well established in the home (Goldenberg & Goldenberg, 2008). Technically, it disrupts the homeostatic **set point**—the rules for family operation—just like leaving the door open on a very hot day disrupts the temperature in an air-conditioned home with a set point of 72°F. Disruption of a routine is equivalent to pushing the family to establish new family rules and requiring new family roles to emerge around the new rules. Classic systems theory teaches that family homeostasis tends toward stability, not change; there are often relationship dynamics that tend to work to reestablish the equilibrium (von Bertalanffy, 1968). Counselors must be alert to such factors and they must not simply identify the client as "the culprit" if problems arise related to issues such as attendance, punctuality, and full engagement in the rehabilitation process. The client's apparent "resistance" may be the evidence of systemic dynamics designed to reassert the family's homeostatic process—to reestablish or maintain the old and once functional rules and roles.

Counselors would be wise to adopt a **family practice model** of rehabilitation (Lewis, 2015). A family practice model involves the counselor anticipating, planning, and participating in full family involvement in the rehabilitation process. Clients should not just be provided services with the expectation that an intact family system will not be affected or involved. Building the family into the process is recommended, so that the family is not left to its own means of addressing the "rough spots" along the way.

FAMILY ADAPTATION TO JOB PLACEMENT AND COMMUNITY LIVING

Dosa et al. (2007) stated that "in 2004, employment rates for the 14 million U.S. adults who have a disability (7.9% of adults age[s] 18–64) were substantially lower than for adults who do not have a disability (19% vs 77%)" (p. 615). Dosa et al. went on to report a poverty rate of 28% for individuals with disabilities, versus 9% for individuals without disabilities. Certainly, VR professionals have a very important role in assisting individuals with disabilities in job training, development, and placement.

The family is an economic unit, and for those individuals with disabilities in a position to support (or to help support) a family, employment is very important. In many cases, the moment of first meaningful employment, or a return to meaningful employment, will be welcomed by family members, especially when the family has been deprived of adequate resources, perhaps due to the disability. Therefore, motivated work-capable clients in a healthy support system will tend to appreciate work opportunity, as gainful employment may mean establishing (or returning to) a better family life. Work also may prove to be personally fulfilling for the individual with the disability and lead to increased social

BOX 8.2 CASE CONCEPTUALIZATION: A PERSON WITH PHYSICAL LIMITATIONS

Consider the case of a 50-year-old man who is referred to rehabilitation due to physical limitations. Medical records establish that he has a serious ankle problem that prevents him from standing at a job without support. When interviewed, the man complains of a myriad of symptoms, and also of pain that is debilitating in other parts of his body. The state agency rehabilitation counselor sends him for medical evaluations to evaluate the pain that is not clearly associated with the ankle issue. The medical evaluations of the client came back with no physical findings (signs) of a condition that would limit the client to the degree the client subjectively reports. An evaluating physician raises the prospect of a conversion reaction or somatoform disorder (a psychological condition that produces a mental conclusion of disability in the absence of physical correlates). At exams, the man acted impaired far beyond what would be expected based on the objective medical findings. The rehabilitation counselor arranged a meeting with the client's family to address his client's status and explained to the family that the client was limited only by a serious ankle condition, which could be accommodated at a work site. The family members (his wife and teenage children) reacted with disbelief and tried to convince the RC that the man's problem was pervasive and would not allow him to work. The client's global complaints were accepted as a "truth" within the family system and accommodated by the family members. They viewed him as totally physically disabled and unable to fully perform his activities of daily living. A prediction can be made about the chances of a failed rehabilitation effort based on the family members' reactions. VR in this case will likely fail, unless the family adjusts to the idea that the client could return to work. It might require a mental evaluation of the client to address possible somatoform issues, and it might require family counseling to ensure that the family members understand the man's capability to return to work. To continue to work to rehabilitate this client without family involvement likely will lead to a dead-end, as homeostatic forces within the family will counter any individual rehabilitation effort. With family counseling, there is the prospect of a successful effort. The family's activities could be reordered to accommodate the working client's family member. Logic would dictate that the family members would be happy to hear that a family member was not seriously limited from gainful employment. However, the reaction of the family in this example supports a conclusion of unhealthy crystallized roles and rules that will need to be addressed in counseling. When a counselor encounters a family dynamic that is counter to rehabilitation efforts, then family counseling must be considered a necessary part of the rehabilitation plan.

connections, as in American society, workers are valued as productive members of society. For such clients, it will appear that the family is rallying around final rehabilitation efforts, and job placement and retention will be cause for celebration.

For individuals who do not appear motivated to find employment, even after extensive rehabilitation programming, it is incumbent upon the RC to assess the systemic dynamics that may be affecting what appears to be the client's poor motivation (see Box 8.2). **Motivation**, from a systemic perspective, is a reflection of activity within the social matrix; it is not inside the personality of the client. It is too easy to simply label a client as unmotivated and to close a demanding rehabilitation case. Often there are social factors, family dynamics, or other factors that may be pivotal to successful job placement and job retention. For example, the family may be losing Social Security benefits (either supplemental Security Income [SSI] or Social Security Disability Insurance [SSDI]). Such a loss may affect the financial stability of the household significantly, or temporary benefits may be lost (e.g., worker's compensation). The employment of one family member may affect the employment or routines of another family member adversely, for example, when the family has limited means of transportation and vehicle sharing is required. Alternatively, the absence of the individual with a disability in the home may create a void in the lives of those who have been actively involved in caregiving in the home, creating some role confusion. All these factors may be influential at the point of job placement. When family dynamics appear to interfere with the final stages of job placement, then the astute counselor must be willing to analyze possible relational pressures and to address those concerns in a way that will facilitate the final stages of worker placement.

It is often surprising to early-career rehabilitation professionals when everything looks positive for employment after an otherwise successful rehabilitation program, and then something happens at the end of a rehabilitation program that appears to sabotage the job placement effort. Especially when families are involved, those kinds of experiences may indicate the failure of the RC to take into account, address, or ameliorate systemic dynamics inconsistent with successful rehabilitation and employment of the individual with the disability.

Similar dynamics may operate when community living is a goal. Removal of the client from the household of a family of origin will significantly affect relationships in the household. Counselors must be alert to family dynamics when household members appear to resist a client's independence. This reaction may be just like the empty-nest syndrome that most couples experience when the last child leaves the household. Families with an individual with a disability experience a change in routine and roles when a formerly dependent person is transitioned to a new living or working situation. It is important for RCs to be sensitive and responsive. RCs can help ensure smooth transitions, and their role as family counselors or family advocates is never clearer than at these times.

COUNSELING FAMILIES OF INDIVIDUALS WITH DISABILITIES

Is there a valuable role for RCs as family therapists for families of individuals with disabilities? Generally, family health and adaptation have played secondary roles in the rehabilitation process. The focus of rehabilitation counseling has been the well-being and adaptation of the person with the disability consistent with the psychomedical paradigm. But RCs are mental health professionals, and to ignore or neglect the needs of the family is to view the client in isolation. A purely psychomedical approach to rehabilitation is potentially at the expense, or to the detriment, of family members closely involved with the client.

The 2016 Council on the Accreditation of Counseling and Related Educational Programs, under the category of "contextual dimensions" of the specialty of clinical rehabilitation counseling, lists the "role of family, social networks, and community in the provision of services for and treatment of people with disabilities" (p. 24) as a standard (2015). The accrediting body for rehabilitation counseling acknowledges the importance of social factors in rehabilitation.

Kosciulek (2004) has argued that the impact of disability is "at least as great for families as for the affected person, and family members are often more distressed than the person with the disability" (p. 264). He further stated that "family members themselves are a high-risk group for physical, emotional, and social difficulties. Families require help in their own right and not only as a by-product of the counseling or rehabilitation process with the family member with the disability" (Kosciulek, 2004, p. 264). But how much help can RCs offer? Most RCs do not have adequate training to do marital and family therapy. It takes more than a course on systems theory and a course on family counseling to work competently and ethically with families. Counselors who have an interest in focusing on family issues must seek additional comprehensive training through coursework, continuing education, and supervised experience under the watchful eye of a trained family

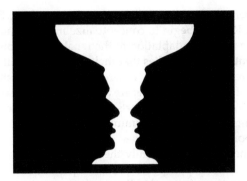

FIGURE 8.3 The Gestalt diagram—two twins facing each other versus a vase.

therapist. This expectation is asking much, because it constitutes additional specialty training for already highly trained specialists in counseling.

Short of cross-training to a second specialty, it is incumbent on rehabilitation counseling generalists to acquaint themselves with the systemic-relational paradigm of mental health services (Cottone, 2012). The systemic-relational paradigm focuses exclusively on defining the nature of problems and solutions as embedded in relationships. At its extreme, it is mutually exclusive to the psychomedical paradigm at the foundation of rehabilitation programs, which focuses on the individual client and individual stakeholders in the rehabilitation process. You cannot see people and focus on relationships at the same time. It is like the classic Gestalt diagram of the vase and the two twin faces—you see the vase if you focus on the middle of the diagram, but you see the twins if you look to one side or the other (see Figure 8.3).

Systems theory focuses on the middle between two people (like looking at the vase). It does not focus on people—their traits, abilities, interests, or skills. It looks at each person as fitting within some context. **Good fit** means finding a special place within some social network; **bad fit** means the person will appear out of sync with other individuals within a social network. Counselors ideally facilitate good fit for the client in some healthy social context. The systemic-relational framework requires counselors to be mindful of how relationships affect mental health and especially the specific behaviors of the client within the family and larger systemic contexts. It helps counselors see the big picture.

One way that RCs can begin to acquaint themselves with relational influences on the rehabilitation process is first to acknowledge the influence of relationships on their own adaptation. This acknowledgment usually is fairly easy, because most counselors will readily admit that when personally they felt most unhealthy mentally, they were enmeshed in relationships that were unhealthy. If one is in a healthy, loving network, it is easy to feel and act comfortably. Enmeshment in a sick relationship system, on the other hand, will likely negatively affect the person's mental health dramatically. Recognizing the influence of relationships on mental health is an easy first step. Of course, it is important for the RCs to acquaint themselves with some literature on family adaptation and/or stress when faced with a member with a disability.

Some theorists have likened the family reaction to the diagnosis of a child with a disability to the bereavement process (e.g., Cobb & Warner, 1999). After the initial shock of the diagnosis, families may go through a period of denial, anger, and bargaining until some level of coping is achieved. The message in such analyses is that the adaptation process is not easy.

Related to connecting theory to practice, Kosciulek et al. (1993) "Resiliency Model of Family Stress, Adjustment, and Adaptation" is a good place for RCs to start. This model is built on prior works that addressed: "(a) Illness and disability as potential family stressors, (b) family resistance resources (e.g., economic, psychological), (c) the family's appraisal of a disability, and (d) coping patterns designed to protect the family from breakdown and facilitate adjustment to disability" (Kosciulek, 2004, p. 265). By recognizing family reactions to disability, RCs can begin to conceptualize means to address such stress in a way that facilitates the family's adaptation to the rehabilitation process. Although rehabilitation may represent hope to families that their loved ones will achieve some level of independence, it still represents change. Where there is relationship change, all parties connected to the web of involved relations are affected, for better or for worse. The more resistance that is met by rehabilitation efforts within families, the more likely there will be dramatic adjustments necessary to accommodate changes; in those cases, family intervention would be important.

If an RC is not trained to provide family therapy interventions, then it is incumbent on the RC to refer families to appropriately trained professionals who will understand and work within the context of the rehabilitation programs. Many not-for-profit agencies provide family counseling services for little or no charge, and sometimes there are special considerations given to families with a member affected by a disabling condition. Knowing and developing family treatment resources should be a normal part of any RC's job when family issues are addressed in the rehabilitation process.

Typically, family therapy occurs with all household members present, or as many as will participate. Usually, it is acceptable to have up to five or six family members in a session. More than five or six participants become unwieldy and may challenge even the most skilled family therapist (because 10 relationships are interacting in a family of five). Thus, maintaining some control of the sessions becomes difficult when more relationships are present in the session.

Family counselors typically will analyze the relationship dynamics during sessions, viewing problems primarily within their social contexts (Goldenberg & Goldenberg, 2008; Nichols, 2006). They tend to be less interested in the individual behaviors, traits, or abilities of clients, and more interested in interactional patterns that have developed around specific family activities. Family therapists have many names for the patterns of interaction observed during sessions, such as "enmeshed," "disengaged," "symmetrical," "escalating," and "complementary" relationships. Each pattern has predictable consequences for individuals involved in the pattern. The intention of family counseling for rehabilitation clients typically is to strengthen family relationships and interactions that are supportive or facilitative of the natural transition experienced by successful rehabilitation clients.

Classic systems interventions always involve at least two people. Consider a family where parents have had to be extensively involved in their child's care. The child now is a young adult and is participating in a rehabilitation program. Thus, a family counselor might address how a mother and father of a young adult rehabilitation client might spend their time together or alone (in a healthy way) while the rehabilitation client is outside the home involved in rehabilitation programs. In this case, the intent would be to strengthen the marital bond, so that one or both parents do not become or remain enmeshed with the adult child rehabilitation client, potentially in a way that may interfere with the rehabilitation program. The astute family counselor, then, is always addressing relational dynamics and will intervene, where otherwise relational influence might seem tangential to a counselor trained exclusively in the psychomedical paradigm.

There are a number of family therapy theories or approaches that may be used by a trained family therapist (see Gladding, 2019; Goldenberg & Goldenberg, 2008). Entire college graduate courses are offered that survey the well-known family therapy approaches of people, such as Virginia Satir, Murray Bowen, Carl Whitaker, Salvador Minuchin, Jay Haley, Nathan Ackerman, and others. RCs should at least acquaint themselves with the major family therapy theorists so that they may speak and act intelligently on these matters when working closely with a family therapist. In fact, the Council for Accreditation of Counseling and Related Educational Programs (CACREP, 2009, 2015) standards for accreditation of educational programs for counselors require some basic introduction to family dynamics and interventions.

Ideally, family therapy will be viewed as a support for rehabilitation efforts. It may be adjunctive, but the effects may be very positive in those cases where there is active family involvement in the lives of family members with disabilities. From a purist systems perspective, involving family in the rehabilitation process is crucial to rehabilitation success and to the long-term healthy adaptation of clients.

Identifying a qualified family therapist is as easy as assessing their credentials. Those who are trained typically in counselor education programs will likely affiliate with the International Association for Marriage and Family Counseling (IAMFC), which is a division of the American Counseling Association (ACA). The IAMFC has actively pursued establishment of a viable, credible, and valuable credential in family therapy, and members of the IAMFC have established the National Credentialing Academy (NCA) for certified family therapists (CFTs). The NCA has established standard coursework and experience requirements for mental health professionals to qualify as a CFT. RCs interested in seeking training in family counseling would do well to contact the NCA for information and standards for certification. The older, more established American Association for Marriage and Family Therapy (AAMFT) has set requirements for what they define as "clinical membership," which constitutes a certification of sorts. The AAMFT's standards are high, and there has been some tension between the AAMFT and the ACA, as the AAMFT has abandoned the use of the title "counselor," and some AAMFT members have argued that counseling and family therapy are separate professions. The ACA has taken the position that marriage and family counseling is a counseling specialty. So, in a sense, there are two professional organizations vying for the allegiance of those who would identify themselves as marriage and family counselors/therapists. Regardless, if a family counselor is a CFT or a clinical member of the AAMFT, it is likely that they have met stringent training and supervision requirements in the areas of couples, marital, and family treatment.

CONCLUSION

This chapter has addressed relationship and family issues in rehabilitation counseling. Although rehabilitation counseling theory and practice have been closely and historically aligned with the psychomedical paradigm of mental health services, rehabilitation theoreticians and practitioners are now recognizing the influence of relationships on the rehabilitation process. The influence of relationships in rehabilitation may be reflective of the rehabilitation system itself, and the role the rehabilitation system plays within the larger free enterprise system in American society. It may also reflect the influence of intact family systems that may directly influence the behavior of clients being served by rehabilitation systems. A systemic theory of VR, the first comprehensive and coherent theory of VR to challenge the traditional rehabilitation model, addresses the relationship interface of clients and rehabilitation systems in conceptualizing and providing rehabilitation services and programs. The systemic perspective represents a call for recognition of relationship influences on the behavior of clients and professionals. It may act as an impetus for RCs to educate themselves on the relational way of viewing clients in the context of rehabilitation programs.

For clients with intact families, recognition of the influence of the family on the individual with a disability is important (see Box 8.3). RCs also must be sensitive to the adjustment of the family to (a) the disability, (b) rehabilitation efforts, and (c) job placement and community living. Some families may be more resilient facing disability; others may struggle. Some families adjust more easily to rehabilitation programs and goals; others may be resistant. By understanding family dynamics and the challenges faced by family members, RCs may be able to conceptualize the social and systems factors that may potentially affect rehabilitation outcomes, including job placement.

BOX 8.3 REFLECTION ACTIVITY

Social systems theory implies that mental health and the quality of relationships within which we are enmeshed are correlative, meaning they are associated. Consider a time when you were most emotionally upset. What was happening in your social network at that time? Were there tense or unhealthy relationships affecting your emotional status? Was there an interpersonal crisis? Was someone mistreating you are doing something harmful to you? Were you in a conflict with one or more other persons? Social systems theory teaches that we are emotionally a product of the relationships that surround us.

Social systems theory implies that if we are harmed by relationships, we can be healed by relationships. Consider a time when one or more persons treated you in a way that was very healing to you—a time when the person's ethical, loving, care made you feel good, healthy, and emotionally stable, even in light of painful past relational experiences. What was the nature of the healing relationship? Can you identify the relationship factors that most affected you in a positive way?

Since counseling is a relationship, doesn't it make sense that relationship theory should be prominent in rehabilitation theory and methods of treatment? Shouldn't relationship theory and methods prevail in conceptualizing the client relationship with a rehabilitation counselor?

RCs should be educated about social systems theory and family therapy. Although cross-training in family therapy would be ideal, RCs must at least be willing to obtain continuing education and appropriate training to identify relationship factors imping-ing on the rehabilitation process. In cases in which family or other relationship factors negatively affect the client, RCs must be able to intervene or to seek, to recommend, or to engage appropriate family relationship treatment. Both the families and the individuals with disabilities deserve no less.

CONTENT REVIEW QUESTIONS

1. How does social systems theory reconceptualize the rehabilitation process?
2. What is the family role in the rehabilitation process?
3. What is the role of the RC addressing family issues during the rehabilitation process?
4. How is the family affected by the rehabilitation process?
5. How is the rehabilitation process affected by family dynamics?

REFERENCES

Burke, P. (2008). *Disability and impairment: Working with children and families.* Jessica Kingsley.

Case-Smith, J. (2007). Parenting a child with a chronic medical condition. In A. E. Dell Orto & P. W. Power (Eds.), *The psychological and social impact of illness and disability* (5th ed., pp. 310–328). Springer Publishing.

Cobb, H. C., & Warner, P. (1999). Counseling and psychotherapy with children and adolescents with disabilities. In H. T. Prout & D. T. Brown (Eds.), *Counseling and psychotherapy with children and adolescents: Theory and practice for school and clinical settings* (3rd ed., pp. 401–426). Wiley.

Cottone, R. R. (1987). A systemic theory of vocational rehabilitation. *Rehabilitation Counseling Bulletin, 30,* 167–176.

Cottone, R. R. (1992). *Theories and paradigms of counseling and psychotherapy.* Allyn & Bacon.

Cottone, R. R. (2012). Paradigms of counseling and psychotherapy. www.smashwords.com/books/view/165398

Cottone, R. R., & Cottone, L. P. (1986). A systemic analysis of vocational evaluation in the state-federal rehabilitation system. *Vocational Evaluation and Work Adjustment Bulletin, 19* 47–54.

Cottone, R. R., & Emener, W. G. (1990). The psychomedical paradigm of vocational rehabilitation and its alternatives. *Rehabilitation Counseling Bulletin, 34,* 91–102.

Cottone, R. R., Grelle, M., & Wilson, W. C. (1988). The accuracy of systemic versus psychological evidence in judging vocational evaluator recommendations: A preliminary test of a systemic theory of vocational rehabilitation. *Journal of Rehabilitation, 54,* 45–52.

Cottone, R. R., Handelsman, M. M., & Walters, N. (1986). Understanding the influence of family systems on the rehabilitation process. *Journal of Applied Rehabilitation Counseling, 17*(2), 37–40. https://doi.org/10.1891/0047-2220.17.2.37

Council for the Accreditation of Counseling and Related Educational Programs. (2009). *2009 CACREP standards.* https://www.cacrep.org/wp-content/uploads/2017/07/2009-Standards.pdf

Council for the Accreditation of Counseling and Related Educational Programs. (2015). *2016 CACREP standards.* https://www.cacrep.org/for-programs/2016-cacrep-standards/

Dosa, N. P., White, P. H., & Schuyler, V. (2007). Future expectations: Transition from adolescence to adulthood. In M. L. Batshaw, L. Pellegrino, & N. J. Roizen (Eds.), *Children with disabilities* (6th ed., pp. 613–622). Paul H. Brookes.

Frain, M., Bishop, M., Frain, J., Frain, J., Tansey, T., & Tschopp, M. K. (2015). The family role in progressive illness. In M. M. J.& M. I. (Eds.), *Families in rehabilitation counseling: A community based rehabilitation approach* (pp. 171–191). Springer.

Gladding, S. T. (2019). *Family therapy: History, theory, and practice* (7th ed.). Pearson/Merrill Prentice Hall.

Goldenberg, H., & Goldenberg, I. (2008). *Family therapy: An overview* (7th ed.). Thomson Brooks/Cole.

Kosciulek, J. F. (1993). Advances in trait-and-factor theory: A person x environment fit approach to rehabilitation counseling. *Journal of Applied Rehabilitation Counseling, 24*(2), 11–14. https://doi.org/10.1891/0047-2220.24.2.11

Kosciulek, J. F. (2004). Family counseling. In F. Chan, N. L. Berven, & K. R. Thomas (Eds.), *Counseling theories and techniques for rehabilitation health professionals* (pp. 264–281). Springer Publishing.

Kosciulek, J. F., & DeVinney, D. J. (2004). The trait-factor approach. In F. Chan, N. L. Berven, & K. R. Thomas (Eds.), *Counseling theories and techniques for rehabilitation health professionals* (pp. 211–223). Springer Publishing.

Kosciulek, J. F., McCubbin, M. A., & McCubbin, H. I. (1993). A theoretical framework for family adaptation to head injury. *Journal of Rehabilitation, 59*(3), 40–45.

Lewis, T. (2015). Managing the rehabilitation environment around families. In M. J. Millington & I. Marini (Eds.), *Families in rehabilitation counseling: A community-based rehabilitation approach* (pp. 267–283). Springer Publishing.

Millington, M. J., Jenkins, B. C., & Cottone, R. R. (2015). Finding the family in rehabilitation counseling. In M. J. Millington & I. Marini (Eds.), *Families in rehabilitation counseling: A community-based rehabilitation approach* (pp. 1–20). Springer Publishing.

Millington, M. J., & Marini, I. (2015a). *Families in rehabilitation counseling.* Springer Publishing.

Millington, M. J., & Marini, I. (2015b). Family care and support. In M. J. Millington & I. Marini (Eds.), *Families in rehabilitation counseling: A community-based rehabilitation approach* (pp. 87–107). Springer Publishing.

Nichols, M. P. (2006). *Family therapy: Concepts and methods.* Pearson/Allyn & Bacon.

Nichols, J. L., & Kosciulek, J. (2014). Social interaction of individuals with traumatic brain injury. *Journal of Rehabilitation, 80*(2), 21–29.

Parsons, F. (1909). *Choosing a vocation.* Houghton-Mifflin.

Power, P. W., & Dell Orto, A. E. (1986). Families, illness and disability: The roles of the rehabilitation counselor. *Journal of Applied Rehabilitation Counseling, 17*(2), 41–44.

Seligman, M., & Darling, R. B. (2007). *Ordinary families, special children: A systems approach to childhood disability.* Guilford.

Sobsey, D. (2004). Marital stability and marital satisfaction in families of children with disabilities: Chicken or egg? *Developmental Disabilities Bulletin, 32,* 62–83.

Stubbins, J. (Ed.). (1977). *Social and psychological aspects of disability.* Pro-Ed.

Stubbins, J. (1984). Vocational rehabilitation as social science. *Rehabilitation Literature, 45*(11–12), 375–380.

von Bertalanffy, L. (1968). *General systems theory: Foundations, development, applications.* George Braziller.

Wright, B. A. (1983). *Physical disability - A psychosocial approach* (2nd ed.). Harper & Row.

CHAPTER 9

The Disability Rights Community

MICHAEL T. HARTLEY AND TONI SAIA

LEARNING OBJECTIVES

After reading this chapter, you should be able to:

- *Review the history of the independent living movement as well as the emergence of disability studies, culture, and identity.*
- *Recognize the fight for disability rights within the context of a larger cultural identity movement.*
- *Identify the core tenets of the independent living movement and corresponding services provided by Centers for Independent Living (CILs).*
- *Review the emergence of the academic field of disability studies as a sociopolitical critique of the dominant cultural discourse of disability.*
- *Evaluate the power of disability culture as championing complex identities of people with disabilities.*

CACREP STANDARDS

CACREP 2016 CORE: 2F2.a, 2F2.b, 2F2.d, 2F2.e, 2F2.h, 2F3.f, 2F3.h, 2F3.i, 2F5.k
CACREP 2016 Specialties
   Clinical Rehabilitation Counseling: 5D1.b, 5D1.c, 5D2.k, 5D2.o, 5D2.p
   Rehabilitation Counseling: 5H1.a, 5H1.d, 5H1.e, 5H1.b, 5H1.c, 5H1.e., 5H1.f, 5H1.n, 5H3.e, 5H3.f, 5H3.j

INTRODUCTION

Rehabilitation counselors (RCs) work with "persons with physical, mental, developmental, cognitive, and emotional disabilities to achieve their personal, career, and independent living goals in the most integrated setting possible" (CRCC, 2016, p. 1). Focused on self-determination and empowerment, RCs have a long history of supporting people with disabilities to function well in different environments (Marini et al., 2018; Sales, 2007). In rehabilitation counseling, a successful outcome is not the result of working with the individual alone but rather of understanding the reciprocal interaction between the individual and their environment (Hershenson, 1998; Kosciulek, 1993). With an environmental focus, rehabilitation counseling services have been an important mechanism for offsetting the social and economic disadvantages associated with disability (Bruyère, 2000; Chubon, 1992; Kilbury et al., 1992). By partnering with the Disability Rights community, RCs can continue to promote a more inclusive society by increasing opportunities and services for people with disabilities.

In rehabilitation counseling practice, there are three models that construct disability from three different points of view: (a) the medical or disease model, (b) the functional limitations or economic model, and (c) the sociopolitical or minority model, also known as the social model (Smart, 2015), as posited by the Disability Rights community (Shakespeare & Watson, 1997). In contrast to the medical model focus on pathology and cure, the social model views disability as a social, political, intellectual, and ideological issue (Davis, 2021; Linton, 1998). What is more, although issues of access and accessibility are often addressed by the functional limitations model, the reality is that societal prejudice is rarely considered (Smart, 2015). Thus, the social model is distinct from the medical and functional limitations models because of its critique of the social prejudice of **ableism,** defined as discrimination against people with disabilities and preference for able-bodiedness. Weber, a disability activist, noted that ableism has created a meta-narrative whereby "society perceives disabled persons to be damaged, defective, and less socially marketable than non-disabled persons," in essence causing the painful perception that there is something fundamentally wrong with having a disability (cited in Haller, 2010, p. iii). Aligned with the Disability Rights community, the focus of the social model in rehabilitation counseling has centered on "anti-discrimination legislation, independent living and other responses to the social oppression" often experienced by people with disabilities (Shakespeare, 2013, p. 216).

Since rehabilitation counseling practice borders the medical community and the Disability Rights community, "rehabilitation counselors are in a position to situate the medical and social model perspectives as mutually constitutive, rather than oppositional" (Tarvydas et al., 2012, p. 242. RCs have a long history of listening to and partnering with people with disabilities and as a result are in a unique position among the disciplines of medicine and counseling (Jenkins et al., 1992). Although they must be knowledgeable and adept at synthesizing medical information, the overarching goal is to promote empowerment and self-determination from a social model perspective (Bolton & Brookings, 1998; Frain et al., 2009; Kosciulek, 2005). Rather than being entrenched in the social model, RCs have the ability to traverse borders and mediate viewpoints that are often in opposition. In rehabilitation counseling practice, contact zones (Pratt, 1991) are areas where the medical and Disability Rights communities intersect. They are an important place for student learning. *Contact zones* are social spaces where the perspectives of subordinate cultural groups often resist or even mediate dominant beliefs.

Psychiatric rehabilitation represents one such important contact zone, where rehabilitation counseling practice borders the perspectives of the medical community and the Disability Rights community. The goal of psychiatric rehabilitation is not to *cure* mental illness but rather to help individuals learn how to manage their mental health symptoms, "including understanding the nature and treatment of their mental illness" (Corrigan, 2016, p. 133). A successful outcome is the social negotiation of *recovery* and *hope* within the context of an individual's life (Davidson et al., 2009). Without being a contradiction, psychiatric rehabilitation seeks to minimize the disruptive effects of mental health symptoms, while also embracing depression, anxiety, delusions, and hallucinations as part of the *normal* human experience. Regardless of the type of disability, the core message is that RCs must be well versed in medical understandings as well as evolving social conceptions of disability for which the Disability Rights community advocates.

The Disability Rights community is an assemblage of diverse disability-specific groups with parallel histories that have coalesced into a larger "sense of disability as collectively shared status and experience" (Longmore & Umansky, 2001, pp. 4–5). Disability activism has existed for centuries; however, until the 1970s, there was never a broad-based Disability Rights community in the United States. Rather, "disability groups typically formed around disability-specific categories," often competing for scarce material resources (Longmore, 2003, p. 109). Since the 18th century, the Deaf community has campaigned to protect sign as an authentic language, seeking political and economic support for signing schools in Europe and America, including Gallaudet University (Baynton, 1996; Lane, 1984). As early as the 1940s, the Blind community rallied to form a political lobby in the United States (Koestler, 1975; Matson, 1990). Countless other disability-specific groups, such as individuals with physical disabilities (Byrom, 2001; Longmore & Goldberger, 2003), cognitive and learning disabilities (Noll & Trent, 2004; Trent, 1994), and psychiatric disabilities (Beers, 1908; Porter, 1989) have fought long and hard for inclusion in education, employment, and community living. Of course, disability-specific organizations, political interests, and agendas have remained (Longmore, 2003). Yet, since the 1970s there has been a collective view, expressing that individuals with disabilities should have a say in healthcare policies and practices, as best captured by Charlton (1998) in the widely adopted slogan: "Nothing About Us, Without Us" (p. 3).

An important moment when the Disability Rights community coalesced was April 5, 1977 (Longmore, 2003; Shapiro, 1993), when the American Coalition of Citizens with Disabilities (ACCD) organized simultaneous protests in nine cities across the United States, including Denver, New York, and San Francisco, to demand implementation of Section 504 of the 1973 Rehabilitation Act (Barnartt & Scotch, 2001; Longmore, 2003). Captured in the YouTube documentary *Power of Section 504* (see Box 9.1), scholars have noted that it was during these protests that cross-disability identification first emerged, representing a critical transformation in the consciousness of people with disabilities (Barnartt, 1996; Longmore, 1995). Longmore (2003), quoting San Francisco activist Owen, explained that "people went into that building with some kind of idealism, but they didn't have much knowledge of other disabilities" (p. 110). Prior to that point, the histories of disability-specific groups were distinct yet similarly characterized by experiences of cultural devaluation (Longmore & Umansky, 2001; Scotch, 1988). As with other social justice movements, such as the women's movement and the gay and lesbian movement, the fight for equal employment, greater political participation, and better community services represented the platform for a larger cultural movement (Oliver, 1990).

Since the 1970s, the Disability Rights movement has continued to evolve. In recent years, it has emerged to embrace unique and complex understandings of the experience and intersection of disability with other cultural identities such as race, gender, and sexuality (Piepzna-Samarasinha, 2018). Crenshaw's (1989) concept of **intersectionality** is foundational to understanding that every person has several identities. Furthermore, each identity is a site of privilege and oppression. **Disability Justice** as a framework is about moving "together as people with mixed abilities, multiracial, multi-gendered, mixed class, across the orientation spectrum—where no body/mind is left behind" (Berne et al., 2018, p. 229). The Disability Justice movement is important because many of the early leaders of the Disability Rights movement were White, even though the movement was modeled after the 1960s civil rights movement for racial equality (Middleton et al., 1999). Centering the lives of Black, Brown, queer, and trans members alongside those of white activists and artists, Piepzna-Samarasinha (2018) described Disability Justice as concerned with the

BOX 9.1 LEARNING ACTIVITY

It is important to understand the history and evolution of the Disability Rights movement. Search online to locate and watch the video *The Power of 504* on YouTube. It captures media coverage of the 1977 protests to demand implementation of Section 504 of the 1973 Rehabilitation Act. After watching the video, consider the following: (a) What were your immediate thoughts and reactions to the documentary? and (b) In what ways have issues of disability and inclusion changed and/or remained the same?

struggle of navigating life when there are multiple sources of oppression, captured by the phrase "To Exist is to Resist" (p. 24).

With this in mind, RCs need to understand the rich history of the Disability Rights community to become effective practitioners. Indeed, even well-intentioned RCs can inadvertently contribute to the perceptions of people with disabilities as diseased, broken, and in need of fixing if they act without an understanding of this perspective as embraced by the Disability Rights community (Baker, 2009; Bricher, 2000; Donoghue, 2003; Illich et al., 2005). Understanding the Disability Rights community will prepare RCs to situate disability within sociopolitical contexts and thus be more empathetic and respectful of people with disabilities (Conyers, 2003). This chapter discusses some of the complexities of the Disability Rights community, including the emergence of the independent living movement, disability studies, and disability culture, in order to prepare practitioners to locate rehabilitation within the broader experience of disability.

INDEPENDENT LIVING MOVEMENT

The concept of **independent living** emerged out of the 1959 deinstitutionalization movement, in which millions of individuals with disabilities were released from institutions and others were never institutionalized (DeJong, 1979; Nosek et al., 1992). As both a philosophy and an approach to disability rights, **independent living** is a movement to promote community integration and inclusion as well as the self-determination of individuals with disabilities in society. The Rehabilitation Services Administration (RSA) funded the first Center for Independent Living in the 1960s (using the acronym CIL or ILC) because of the social and political activism of students with physical disabilities in Berkeley, California (DeJong, 1979; Switzer, 2003). Ed Roberts a group of students with disabilities led forced to live in a hospital infirmary because there was no accessible student housing. They exerted their right to participate in society and attend college during a time when very few people with significant physical disabilities lived independently in the community, let alone attended college (Shapiro, 1993). Roberts's self-advocacy efforts were a catalyst for the independent living movement because he demanded inclusion in mainstream life. Initially funded to serve college students, CILs quickly shifted to serve nonstudents, and CILs were created in large urban cities (Switzer, 2003).

Designed by activists, CILs were an important training ground for political and social activism, including participation in the April 5, 1977 protests demanding implementation of the Rehabilitation Act Amendments of 1973 (Switzer, 2003). Due to conservative political threats to withdraw funding, CILs began to emphasize individual services over large-scale activism in the 1980s (Longmore, 2003; Varela, 2001). As a consequence, those who believed that large-scale activism was the way to create societal change left CILs and formed groups that were not dependent on governmental funding, such as the American Disabled for Adaptive Public Transportation (Johnson, 2003; Scotch, 1988). In the 1980s, with the exodus of many activists and increased government oversight, CILs increasingly were run by professionals without disabilities (Longmore). In response to complaints from the Disability Rights community, the 1986 Amendments to the Rehabilitation Act of 1973 required that 51% of CIL staff and board of directors consist of people with disabilities (Nosek et al., 1992). Today, CILs must be run by people with disabilities and as a result, many CILs have returned to social and political activism while also providing individual services.

Embedded within local communities, CILs are a critical resource to support the local needs of people with disabilities to live independently. CILs provide information and referral for accessible housing, transportation, and community services, such as personal care assistants and sign language interpreters (Frieden, 2001; Richards & Smith, n.d.). Using a peer-based self-help model, they also provide counseling and independent skill training to help people with disabilities become more independent (Cole, 2001; Saxton,

2001; Shreve, 1991). Distinct from other services, CILs provide advocacy to promote a dominant culture that is more welcoming and inclusive for people with disabilities. Distinct from other services, rather than providing direct services to the individual, CIL advocacy confronts inaccessible environments and negative social attitudes toward disability. This work is grounded in a social model perspective that serves to exaggerate disability and even construct disability (Smart, 2015).

CILs provide two types of advocacy: individual and large-scale social and political advocacy (Richards & Smith, n.d.). **Individual advocacy** supports the self-determination of individuals to obtain necessary support services from other community agencies, such as state–federal VR (Zola, 2001). **Social and political advocacy** is broader, and advocacy may focus on accessible housing and transportation in society to help a wide range of people with disabilities (Varela, 2001). Although all CILs in the United States are legally mandated to provide all these services, not all CILs have the same resources. Each one is unique in terms of funding, staff, and the local communities served (Frieden, 2001; Nosek et al., 1992). In addition, different services may be more or less important in different communities, and CILs are designed to be responsive to the needs of local communities. For instance, rural communities often struggle with a lack of transportation; as a result, rural CILs may be focused particularly on providing accessible transportation (Schwab, 2001).

It is important to understand the underlying philosophy of CILs beyond just considering services. A basic premise of CILs is that people with disabilities are experts on living with their disabilities (Crewe & Zola, 2001). Unlike other rehabilitation services, CILs are run by people with disabilities who themselves have been successful in establishing independent lives (DeJong, 1979). Most traditional rehabilitation programs were built on the medical model of service delivery, but CILs were the first to use the social model of disability to help individuals with disabilities achieve and maintain independent lifestyles (Nosek et al., 1992). Thus, CILs were revolutionary in defining disability as primarily a social (rather than a medical) issue, this perspective is a unique and important development in service delivery (DeJong, 1979). Early leaders of CILs were primarily individuals with physical disabilities (McCarthy, 2003), and the underlying philosophy of independent living has been fundamental to the advocacy efforts of many other disability groups.

The Mad Pride movement emerged in the 1970s and was named to signify the need for the "reversal of standard pathological connotations with madness" (Lewis, 2013, p. 115). Mad Pride has had its own historic leaders, such as Elizabeth Packard (1868) and Clifford Beers (1908), yet the movement as it is known today emerged from the self-advocacy efforts of Leonard Frank (see Farber, 1993) and Judi Chamberlin (1977). In the early 2000s, leaders of the independent living and Mad Pride movements advocated alongside one another to oppose the selection of Dr. Satel (2000) to the New Freedom Commission. This opposition was because of her outspoken position in favor of involuntary commitment and treatment laws as well as the discontinuation of peer-run programs. At the center of the debate was the 1999 *Olmstead* Supreme Court decision that upheld the "integration mandate" of the 1990 Americans with Disabilities Act (ADA, 1990), requiring that states expand the infrastructure and funds to support the full inclusion of individuals with disabilities in the community (Davidson et al., 2009, p. 2). Arguing against "diagnostic labeling and treatment—which all too often come in the form of forced or manipulated hospitalizations, restraints, seclusions, and medication" (Lewis, 2013, p. 116), the protesters wanted to raise awareness of the disproportionally low funding for mental health services: States were spending 30% *less* on mental health in 1997 than they did in 1955 when accounting for inflation (Bernstein, 2001; Davidson et al., 2009). Justin Dart, an early leader of the independent living movement, spoke about the issue of *No Forced Treatments Ever* for individuals with psychiatric disabilities (Lewis, 2013; Oakes, 2002) because it violated the principle of "Nothing About Us, Without Us" (Charlton, 1998, p. 3). The collaborative advocacy efforts of the independent living and Mad Pride activists persuaded the New Freedom Commission that the "mental health system is fundamentally broken, that it needs extensive overhaul (not just piecemeal reform), and . . . consumers must be protected from unjust incarceration and the use of seclusion and restraints" (Lewis, 2013, p. 127). In other words, the civil rights of individuals with mental illness must be protected at all times.

There are clear benefits to understanding the independent living movement's emphasis on disability as a civil rights issue. Perhaps the most significant benefit is to advance a more inclusive and welcoming society for individuals with disabilities. With increasingly high caseloads and limited resources, many RCs do not have the time or resources to work with clients to explore the effects of environmental factors on their experience of disability. If RCs do not have the time or resources, referrals to CILs and other consumer-run organizations, such as Critical Psychiatric Network (www.criticalpsychiatry.co.uk) and Mind Freedom (www.mindfreedom.com) may promote the self-advocacy efforts of individuals with disabilities (Hartley et al., 2015). Like other self-help movements, consumer-run programs provide a safe haven for individuals with disabilities to express themselves, offering a place to share experiences and realize that they are not alone (Saxton, 2001; Shreve, 1991; Zola, 2001). Furthermore, consumer-run programs have been a powerful voice in confronting inaccessible environments and negative social attitudes toward disability. RCs share a value on advocacy, social justice, and independent living. In fact, RCs who have personal experience with disability may want to pursue careers with consumer-run organizations. Similar to other work settings, interested RCs should consult relevant organizations, such as the National Council on Independent Living (https://ncil.org/), the Association of Programs for Rural Independent Living (https://www.april-rural. org/), and RI International (www.riinternational.com).

DISABILITY STUDIES

Although the independent living movement has informed the Disability Rights community greatly, it is also important to understand the academic field of **disability studies**, which offers a sociopolitical critique of the dominant cultural discourse of disability (Davis, 2021; Linton, 1998). Rather than transforming society through protests and legislation, disability studies seek to change society through critical analysis of meanings that are taken for granted. As an academic field of inquiry, the field of disability studies has come a long way in a short time (Cushing & Smith, 2009). Prior to the 1980s, "academic interest in disability was confined almost exclusively to conventional, individualistic medical explanations" (Barnes et al., 2002, p. 3). Initially based in the United Kingdom, by the 1980s disability studies courses were being taught in the United States. The first American disability studies journal, *Disability Studies Quarterly*, was published by the Society for Disability Studies (Barnes et al., 2002). Initially disability studies movement was rooted in the social sciences, especially sociology; however, in the late 1980s, there was a shift toward a humanities approach to cultural reevaluation (Barnes et al., 2002). The field's focus moved beyond a critique of the social forces of oppression that shaped the lives of people with disabilities. The goal became to assemble a collective body of knowledge that theorizes and historicizes deafness or blindness or disability in similarly complex ways to the way race, class, and gender (Davis, 2021).

The number of disability studies programs and courses exploded in the 1990s and 2000s (Cushing & Smith, 2009). However, many of the courses and degrees offered remained in the social sciences and allied health fields, although this positioning was incongruent with the social model of disability (Linton, 1998). Some scholars argued that healthcare professionals were listening to a disability studies perspective, while others were concerned that the field was being diluted and influenced by medical perspectives (Cushing & Smith; Linton). To distinguish disability studies programs rooted in the social model of disability, RCs should be able to recognize humanities-based language, curriculum, and worldview; a social model paradigm will emphasize power relations and subjectivity. As with other cultural identity studies, a second wave of disability studies scholars moved to postmodern theories. This development allowed for the complexity of multiple and shifting identities and differentiating the experiences of disabilities for men and women, middle-class White and nondominant minority communities, and heterosexual and lesbian, gay, bisexual, and transgender people.

In the same way scholarship on race has turned its attention to Whiteness and intersectionality, Davis (2021) noted that disability studies is focused less on the construction of disability than on the construction of normalcy because the problem is the way that normalcy is constructed to create the *problem* of the disabled person. According to Berne et al. (2018), disability always has been entangled with oppression: "One cannot look at the history of US slavery, the stealing of indigenous lands, and US imperialism without seeing the way that white supremacy leverages ableism to create a subjugated 'other' that is deemed less worthy/abled/smart/capable" (p. 149). Similar to other cultural studies, disability studies advances a critique of language use that depends on defining some groups of people as normal contrasted against the abnormal. This pattern establishes how people with disabilities are defined as different or *othered*. Relatedly, the term *essentialized* refers to discourse practices that reduce a group of people who are different into a single salient trait rather than viewing the full complexity of an individual. The basic tenets of disability studies extend from and contribute to the Disability Rights community.

The primary mission of disability studies is to examine the meaning of disability through an analysis of the experiences of people with disabilities in social, political, and cultural contexts (Davis, 2021). Disability studies challenges the notion of disability as primarily a medical category studied and treated by specialists in fields such as rehabilitation counseling that often reinforce the positioning of people with disabilities as abnormal (Linton, 1998). Indeed, disability studies scholars have argued that the ways in which disability is discussed provide a lens to see how disability is understood within our larger society. For instance, ableism has been associated with racism and sexism in terms of who is valuable and worthy in society (Berne et al., 2018). Scholars have noted how ableism has been used to justify inequality for people with disabilities and other groups of people, including women, African Americans, and immigrants (Baynton, 2013; Block et al., 2001). For instance, women were considered inferior physically, intellectually, and psychologically and were not considered worthy of citizenship or equal employment until the women's suffrage movement (Baynton, 2013). Furthermore, a common mid-19th-century justification of slavery in the United States was that African Americans lacked sufficient intelligence to participate on an equal basis in society (Baynton, 2013). In fact, a fictional mental illness termed drapetomania was constructed to explain the reason African American slaves wanted to escape slavery. Extending back to early immigration policies in the United States, traces of eugenics can be found in anti-immigration debates describing immigrants as feeble-minded and prone to mental health issues (Baynton, 2013). In all these cases, ableism has been constructed to justify inequitable treatment.

There are three important aspects of the positioning of people with disabilities as abnormal. First, at the root of reframing disability is the use of language (Linton, 1998). Disability studies recognizes the underlying messages conveyed through language as a discourse system and thus shifts from medical discourse to disability as a social, political, intellectual, and ideological issue. Words such as *confined* to a wheelchair or *suffering* from mental illness represent a conceptual link to discourse of disability as deviance and thus mischaracterize disability as something that is inherently bad. Additionally, words that avoid disability as a valid cultural identity are equally problematic through the lens of disability studies. Ladau (2021), a disability rights activist, noted that euphemisms such as *challenged, handicapable, differently abled* and *special needs* intentionally obscure any real meaning. Avoiding the word disability ignores an important aspect of being human, analogous to someone saying they do not see skin color, which can be disempowering, patronizing, and even hurtful. While there is no consensus among the Disability Rights community, many disability studies scholars tend to use **identify-first language** (e.g., disabled person) rather than **person-first language** (e.g., person with a disability) to reinforce

BOX 9.2 LEARNING ACTIVITY: DISABILITY LANGUAGE

The Teacher Leaders for Inclusion Project (https://www.lead4inclusion.com) has a module on the difference between person-first and identity-first language (https://www.lead4inclusion.com/theshifttoidentity-firstlanguage). Review the module and consider whether you typically use person-first or identity-first language? Does it depend on the context? Why might you choose to use one or the other within your professional practice?

and celebrate disability as a positive and valid human identity (Dunn & Andrews, 2015). With that said, each person may have their own preference with respect to identity- versus person-first language (see Box 9.2).

Second, popular media have reinforced disability stereotypes. Such stereotypes have described people with disabilities as "pitiable and pathetic, objects of violence, sinister and evil, a curiosity, super-cripple, objects of ridicule, their own worst enemy, a burden, sexually abnormal, incapable of participating fully in community life, and normal life" (Barnes & Mercer, 2001, p. 519). Disability studies scholars have critiqued the effects of popular media on the perception of disability, especially Hollywood films glorifying assisted suicide, such as *Whose Life Is it Anyway?*, *The Sea Inside*, *Million Dollar Baby*, and *You Before Me*. The concern is that these films perpetuate **existential anxiety** (i.e., fear of the fragility of the nondisabled person's own body) and **aesthetic anxiety** (i.e., fear of appearances that look different) while discounting the high quality of life experienced by many individuals with severe disabilities (Hahn, 1988). In response to Hollywood films glorifying assisted suicide, the group *Not Dead Yet* has questioned the dominant cultural narrative of who has worth in our society (Johnson, 2003). Extending from horrific examples of forced sterilizations and mercy killings, there are still problematic and inaccurate cultural messages regarding the societal assumption of low quality of life for individuals with severe disabilities (Brockley, 2001).

Third, extending from language and stereotypes, the underlying cultural narratives of what it means to have a disability are being reexamined. Disability studies seek to change society through critical analysis of meanings that are taken for granted, such as who is expected to participate in society. In the past, individuals with disabilities were removed from society. For instance, hospitals and institutions were used to warehouse individuals with disabilities in deplorable conditions (Grob, 1994). An example is the 1972 exposé of the Willowbrook State School (www.geraldo.com/page/willowbrook). Furthermore, readers may be surprised to know that U.S. legislation, commonly known as the "Ugly Laws," restricted the public appearance of individuals with physical disabilities because they were considered offensive and frightening (Schweik, 2008). Conversely, more recent U.S. legislation such as the Olmstead Act now supports the rights of people with disabilities to live in the community. The bad news is that inaccessible environments continue to be a distributive justice problem for people with disabilities. **Distributive justice** is concerned with the socially just allocation of resources, including who has access to those resources. As an example, approximately 90% of homes are built without consideration of people with physical and sensory disabilities (Smith et al., 2008). From the lens of disability studies, inaccessible homes reflect a social prejudice that people with disabilities are still not fully included in society.

RCs can benefit from immersing themselves in the disability studies critique of disability as a disease or ailment. Central to contemporary rehabilitation counseling practice is to move away from overmedicalized understandings of disability, and the related risk of paternalistic or ill-informed interactions with their disabled clients. For instance, an individual with a disability is likely to become suspicious and resentful if a counselor only sees the individual as a *patient* while ignoring the person's other life roles, such as child, parent, romantic partner, worker, student, and so on (Baker, 2009; Bricher, 2000). With respect to mental health, there is a need to embrace the embodiment of mental difference without perpetuating **mentalist** beliefs (Price, 2013), a form of ableism "directed against people who are perceived as not having all of their mental faculties intact—people considered, for example to be mad, irrational, or insane" (Davidson et al., 2009, p. 24). Regardless of the type of disability, the development of a therapeutic relationship and working alliance are critical to rehabilitation practice (Lustig et al., 2002; Stuntzner & Hartley, 2014). An RC who understands the depth of the disability experience from a disability studies perspective will be able to communicate with and situate an individual's experiences, values, and attitudes in social, political, and cultural contexts more effectively.

DISABILITY CULTURE

Disability culture stems from the sociopolitical critique of disability studies and the services and philosophies of the independent living movement. **Disability culture** is best understood as a social movement that champions "a sense of common identity and interests that unite disabled people and separate them from their nondisabled counterparts" (Barnes & Mercer, 2001, p. 522). In other words, it is the celebration of complex identities of disability that intersect with gender, race, and sexuality by promoting effective and creative narratives of individuals with disabilities living fulfilling lives. With the disability studies shift toward the humanities, disability culture emerged as a response to the widespread cultural devaluation of disability. Beginning in the late 1980s, advocates of disability culture pointed to the need for a politicized identity for people with disabilities that resisted the marginalizing narratives of the dominant culture (Longmore, 1995). Disability culture is about a shared identity around possibility and choice.

According to Brown (2001), "disabled people have forged a group identity. We share a common history of oppression and a common bond of resilience. We generate art, music, literature, and other expressions of our lives and our culture, infused from our experience" (p. 49). In contrast to the eugenics view that people with disabilities were biologically inferior, disability culture is a "lived interrogation" of the idea that disability is primarily a medical condition. The essence of disability culture is the celebration of the lived experience of disability as uniquely beautiful and shaped by a person's particular social and cultural identity (Conyers, 2003). Perhaps most important, disability culture is a social movement intended to unite a broad cross section of people with disabilities (Gill, 1995). As part of the Disability Rights community, disability culture is not about a single disability-specific group but rather a larger, universalistic approach to disability as a cultural identity.

Defining disability culture is difficult. Not even the Disability Rights community has agreed on a common language or description of acculturation (Peters, 2000). Embodied in art, music, literature, and other expressions, disability culture celebrates the ways in which people with disabilities view themselves (Brown, 2001). A well-known story is that of Christy Brown, an Irish author, painter, and poet who had severe cerebral palsy. Brown's autobiography *My Left Foot* is a complex portrayal of a very talented individual with multiple identities intersecting with disability, class, religion, gender, and sexuality in the mid-20th century. In a review of the film, Longmore (2003) noted that Christy Brown's story is important because it is not an essentialized depiction of an individual with a disability as tragic or heroic. Rather, it captures the larger theme of people with disabilities who "fight bias and battle for control of their lives and insist that they will make their mark on the world" (Longmore, 2003, p. 130). Memorable scenes from the narrative include the ways in which the family's limited economic situation and working-class worldview influenced Brown's perception of disability and rehabilitation, including the use of a wheelbarrow as a wheelchair. For RCs, it is not possible or useful to separate the experience of disability from contextual experiences of gender, sexuality, religion, ethnicity, and class. Rather, they need to embrace the concept of disability culture as the unique intersection of disability with other contextual experiences.

One critique of the film version of *My Left Foot* is that the actor who played Christy was able-bodied. Moving away from able-bodied actors playing disability, more current examples of disability culture include the show *Special*, written by and starring Ryan O'Connell. He is a self-identified disabled actor who shared his experiences navigating life as gay and disabled man. Furthermore, documentaries such as the acclaimed *Crip Camp* offered real-life examples of the authentic lives of individuals with disabilities that embody disability culture. Aptly noted by Ladau (2021), "rather than non-disabled people pretending to be us or imaging our experiences, let's aim for a world in which disabled people are fixtures in every part of the media, so stories about us are meaningfully told by us" (p.137).

Today, social media have become a preferred interface to "organize disability-rights actions, let others know about disability related news, promote events, or just find like-minded disability rights advocates" (Haller, 2010, p. 5). The emergence of popular social media tools, such as Twitter, Facebook, YouTube, blogs, and wikis, has led to a surplus of individuals using digital technologies and social media as platforms for media authorship (Brandt, 2009). For example, Baggs countered misconceptions that individuals with autism lack personhood in the YouTube video *In My Own Language*. As another example, Withers described what it is like to experience symptoms, such as depersonalization and hallucinations, and strategies for coping that include her dog: "if the animal doesn't react to the hallucination, then it's probably not real, she says" (Chen, 2016, p. 1) in the YouTube channel *Rachel Star Schizophrenic*. Dispelling myths about the lived experience of disability, YouTube channels by *Squirmy and Grubs* address myths about inter-abled marriage, while *Segarra* explores the intersection of disability with other cultural identities. Humor is a particularly powerful avenue to promote social change, as is the case of Young in the YouTube video *I'm not Your Inspiration* and Moon in the YouTube video *I Got 99 Problems*. As a final example, in the YouTube series *My Gimpy Life*, Sherer shared the awkwardness of navigating Hollywood in a wheelchair humor. In each case, first-person, authentic perspectives on disability are contributing to the notion of disability as a valid social and cultural identity.

Today, the Internet has allowed people to form a sense of community that previously was not possible offline (Dobransky & Hargittai, 2021), including the evolution of disability culture and what it means to have a disability. Twitter examples include @*DisVisability* and @*PhilosopherCrip* with hashtags such as #*BlackDisabledLivesMatter*, #*InaccessabilityMeans*, #*ItsAccessibleButjust*, #*CripTheVote*, and #*NoBodyIsDisposable*. Facebook examples include *Critical Disability Studies, Disabled Feminist, Crutches and Spice, Spinal Cord Injury USA*, and *MobileWomen*. Instagram is another platform with diverse representations of disability including @*andrewgurza* and @*chellaman* who share perspectives on the lived experience of disability as it intersects with other cultural identities. Finally, blogs offer rich, firsthand experiences of disability, with *Leaving Evidence* and *Rooted in Rights* becoming an important resource. These works are available for anyone wanting to learn about disability through works intentionally published by people who wish to share information and perspectives about the lived experience of disability (see Box 9.3).

In rehabilitation counseling practice, social media and authentic images of disability may assist individuals with disabilities to respond in successful and creative ways to disability concerns. Complex narratives of disability may be used in the way that bibliotherapy has been incorporated into counseling practice for decades: to understand and promote the therapeutic needs of clients (Marrs, 1995). By offering authentic representations of disability, social media have the potential to counter the negative images often found in the dominant cultural discourse. In fact, the future of rehabilitation counseling practice may involve helping clients identify healthy and supportive Twitter feeds as well as therapeutic blogs that can assist individuals to respond creatively to disability concerns (Hartley et al., 2015, 2016). It is particularly important for RCs to be exposed to disability culture because it seeks to change society by expressing the lived experience of disability through art, music, and literature (Brown, 2001). The larger point is that an understanding

BOX 9.3 REFLECTION ACTIVITY

Search online and select a blog or vlog authored by a person with a disability. You can choose one of the examples cited in this chapter, although readers are encouraged to search on their own. What is the focus of the content? For instance, is the emphasis on societal barriers or personal challenges associated with the disability? Alternatively, is the emphasis on life hacks and developing creative and effective responses to living with a disability? How might the blog or vlog reflect or not reflect the concept of Disability Culture as described in this chapter? How might reading personal reflections on disability help RCs better understand the varied lived experience of disability?

of disability culture will lead to an approach to disability that questions the misrepresentation of disability in the dominant culture and encourages RCs to value the social and emotional experience of disability.

ONGOING CONSIDERATIONS

As in other specialized health fields, the medical model of disability traditionally has been the central focus of rehabilitation counseling research and policy decisions. As a consequence, many in the Disability Rights community have viewed this knowledge base as "oppressive" (Bricher, 2000, p. 781). Over the years, the growing body of literature that moved away from the traditional medical model and toward the social model is seen as a positive response to the Disability Rights community (Armstrong & Fitzgerald, 1996; Carluccio & Patterson, 2001; Kosciulek, 1999, 2000; McCarthy, 2003). However, if RCs are to incorporate the social model, further dialogue is needed between RCs and the Disability Rights community. In developing such a dialogue, several ongoing issues must be addressed.

To collaborate with the Disability Rights community, RCs need to understand that the choice of language is never value-neutral, but rather represents an approach to understanding disability. In order to establish therapeutic relationships with individuals with disabilities, RCs need to move beyond simply adopting language. They must consider underlying messages conveyed through language and the consequences to which each leads. While professional disciplines like rehabilitation counseling recommend person-first language (e.g., individual with a disability), the Disability Rights community often uses identity-first language (e.g., disabled person) to denote disability as a positive cultural identity status. Both person-first language and identity-first language have a place within rehabilitation counseling practice, and thus, the use of language must be considered in terms of intent, interpretation, and positionality (Dunn & Andrews, 2015). For instance, individuals with disabilities may intentionally use identity-first language with healthcare professionals to convey the ways in which disability is a core identity rather than a medical condition to be treated. Furthermore, while it may be inappropriate for a nondisabled person to use insider language such as crip culture, such language may be commonplace within the Disability Rights community. It is important that RCs be comfortable discussing language as well as understanding the underlying messages conveyed through language. RCs need to consider language not only in direct communication with clients and consumers but also through the language used in marketing and websites.

Related to disability language, RCs need to understand the ways that disability is a valued human identity. The concept of **disability identity** is the sense of self and feelings of connection to and solidarity with a broader disability community. Rather than a medical view of disability as a deficit, disability identity can help individuals adapt and thrive, including the successful navigation of social pressures and societal stigmas (Murugami, 2009). While each individual is unique, it is important that RCs recognize disability identity as a fluid

BOX 9.4 REFLECTION ACTIVITY

Search online for the TED Talk by Maggie Little on bioethics and the human body available on YouTube (https://www.youtube.com/watch?v=-h0qnGKYjPY). After watching the video, reflect on the following questions. In your opinion, what factors have influenced what is considered a disability or not a disability across human history? What does this tell us about the concept of disability? In your opinion, what is an example of a disability today that may not have been viewed as a disability 100 years ago? What changed? In your opinion, what is an example of something that may become a disability in the future that is not considered a disability today? What will change?

and continuous process based on the sociopolitical climate in which a person lives (Corker, 2001). Disability identity and pride historically have coalesced when a political issue has threatened the Disability Rights community. Similar to the 1970s' protests to demand implementation of the Rehabilitation Act, disability identity and pride were clearly visible during the 2017 protests to counter potential cuts to Medicaid funding (Stein, 2017). This threat was viewed as an attempt to "kill sick and disabled people by ending Medicaid, the Affordable Care Act, and the ADA" (Piepzna-Samarasinha, 2018, p. 24). Images and narratives of the 2017 protests mirrored those from the 1970s with quotes from journalists such as "These are issues of life and death. Freedom or incarceration. And disabilities advocates are rising to the challenge" (Stein, line 20–21). Central to understanding the Disability Rights movement is the fact that disability identity and pride are antidotes to combatting internalized ableism and shame (Shakespeare, 1996).

The concept of disability is evolving. Right now, the long-term impact of the novel coronavirus (COVID-19) is relatively unknown with people experiencing potentially lifelong respiratory, cardiovascular, neurological, gastrointestinal, and musculoskeletal impairments, leading to loss of functioning and the onset of disability (Umucu et al., 2021; Wong et al., 2021). Furthermore, what is considered a disability has evolved over time. As an example, the lived experience of autism has been a long-term part of human history, yet only in the past half century has autism been recognized as a disability. In our increasingly digital society, disability studies scholars have argued that autism and the ability to process information differently could become an advantage (Little, 2014). Furthermore, the evolution of the various iterations of the *Diagnostic and Statistical Manual of Mental Disorders* (5th ed.; DSM-5) tell a story about what behaviors and ways of being are socially constructed as normal versus problematic. The larger point is that disability is a common and normal part of the human experience that takes on meaning based on evolving societal discourse (see Box 9.4).

The epistemological knowledge base of rehabilitation counseling practice, including rehabilitation research and policy development, is an area where critical analysis should occur. Although practitioners typically do not conduct research, there is a need to understand fundamental concerns regarding the construction of rehabilitation knowledge. Specifically, there is concern that traditional rehabilitation knowledge was constructed from a medical model approach to disability (Bricher, 2000). From a Disability Rights perspective, most of this research has been conducted *on* rather than *with* people with disabilities (Barnes, 1996; Oliver, 1992; Shakespeare, 1996). Research influences healthcare policies and practices, and the Disability Rights community is wary of research on disability conducted without input from people with disabilities (Barnes; Oliver; Shakespeare). As noted by Charlton (1998), without input from individuals with disabilities, research on disability violates the notion of "Nothing About Us, Without Us" (p. 3). Rehabilitation researchers have responded to this concern, and participatory action research is growing in importance.

The goal of **participatory action research** is to enhance the relevance of research to the lives of people with disabilities by including people with disabilities in all aspects of the process, beginning with the generation of research questions (Bruyère, 1993; Walker, 1993; White, 2002). Participatory action research is likely to lead to more collaboration; however, there will always be conflict between proponents of the medical model and the social model. As a result, RCs without disabilities may find it "difficult to find a rightful place in relation to research with disabled people and the social model" and struggle to find a comfortable role in discussing traditional rehabilitation knowledge and research with individuals with disabilities (Bricher, 2000, p. 782). It is most important for RCs to recognize disabilities as a social and emotional experience, not a medical issue that has to be solved or prevented. Critically examining how knowledge is constructed is a part of developing a climate of respect and reciprocity with the Disability Rights community.

As frontline service providers, RCs work directly with people with disabilities, and these interactions can have a major impact on how agency policies and practices are implemented. RCs need to be aware that rehabilitation policies and practices have been compared to a caste system, in which individuals with disabilities are forced to show deficits before being eligible for services (Szymanksi & Trueba, 1994). For instance, a common eligibility requirement for VR services is proof that an individual cannot maintain work, which usually means remaining unemployed for a certain period (Szymanksi & Trueba, 1994). For instance, Golfus, a filmmaker, made the documentary *When Billy Broke His Head* and chronicled his experiences after a traumatic brain injury. Sometimes shown in master's-level rehabilitation counseling courses, RCs who watch the film often express frustration with how Golfus portrays the rehabilitation system as ineffectual and removed from the lived experience of disability because it perpetuates a caste-like system. For instance, clients who are successful in the VR system make average incomes that are barely over the poverty line (Lustig & Strauser, 2007). While rehabilitation policies and practices have good intentions, if biological and cultural determinism and the social stigma of disability are not addressed, people with disabilities will continue to experience poverty (Yeo & Moore, 2003). Thus, rehabilitation policies and practices cannot be separated from the larger social context. RCs need to consider the policies and practices that unintentionally limit the lives of people with disabilities (Hartley & Tarvydas, 2013).

Without considering the economic realities associated with disability and social class, RCs may unintentionally recommend treatment options that an individual client cannot afford. They may fail to address material concerns such as housing, transportation, food, and clothing. Thus, RCs need to consider the policies and practices that unintentionally limit the lives of people with disabilities (Gill, 1995; Pledger, 2003). Rehabilitation services that are not flexible enough to address the holistic needs of individuals are not likely to make positive differences in their lives and may cause harm to families by using up already scarce resources. Without considering the social realities associated with disability, RCs may fail to address the social discrimination inherent in limited access to housing and transportation (see Box 9.5). As an extension of

BOX 9.5 LEARNING ACTIVITY: TED TALKS

The Teacher Leaders for Inclusion Project (https://www.lead4inclusion.com) has compiled an extensive list of TED Talks on Disability and Difference (https://www.lead4inclusion.com/ted-talks). Each TED Talk discusses disability and diversity including the need to be wary of "single stories." Choose one or more TED Talks to watch. After watching each TED Talk, write down the main message in a single sentence. Reflect on how this message can better prepare you and other RCs to situate disability within sociopolitical contexts and thus be more empathetic and respectful of people with disabilities?

this approach, RCs can serve as an important link between not-for-profit organizations and the Disability Rights community, bridging the gap between the medical and social model perspectives. Many groups, such as United Cerebral Palsy and National Alliance on Mental Illness (NAMI) originated from a medical model of disability perspective that looked to eradicate disability by finding a cure. These organizations are shifting toward the social model of disability perspective when people with disabilities assume leadership roles (Varela, 2001).

CONCLUSION

This chapter overviewed the Disability Rights community. Rehabilitation counseling is an important mechanism for offsetting the economic and social disadvantage associated with disability, and thus, RCs can partner with the Disability Rights community to promote a more inclusive society by increasing opportunities and services for people with disabilities. The three models of disability (biomedical model, functional limitations model, social model) are the best places for dialogue between disability studies and the rehabilitation counseling communities. Rather than forming opinions from a single model of disability, RCs need to actively engage with the Disability Rights community around distributive justice issues that directly impact the lives of individuals with disabilities. Perhaps most important, RCs need to be responsive to the lived experience of disability by continuing to evolve rehabilitation policies and practices.

CONTENT REVIEW QUESTIONS

1. With respect to the disability rights movement, what is meant by the phrase coined by Charlton (1998): "Nothing About Us, Without Us?"
2. What are the principles of the independent living movement?
3. What are three important domains for the critique of the dominant perspectives of disability?
4. What is the significance of disability culture?
5. What are the benefits of understanding the Disability Rights community prior to working as an RC?
6. What are important considerations for respectful communication between rehabilitation counseling professionals and Disability Rights community members?

REFERENCES

Americans with Disabilities Act. (1990). 42 U.S.C. § 12101. *Et Seq.*

Armstrong, M. J., & Fitzgerald, M. H. (1996). Culture and disability studies: An anthropological perspective. *Rehabilitation Education, 10,* 247–304.

Baker, D. L. (2009). Bridging the deficiency divide: Expressions of non-deficiency models of disability in health care. *Disability Studies Quarterly, 29*(2), 6–12. https://doi.org/10.18061/dsq.v29i2.919

Barnartt, S., & Scotch, R. (2001). *Disability protests.* Gallaudet Press.

Barnes, C. (1996). Disability and the myth of the independent researcher. *Disability & Society, 11*(1), 107–112. https://doi.org/10.1080/09687599650023362

Barnartt, S. N. (1996). Disability culture or disability consciousness? *Journal of Disability Policy Studies, 7*(2), 1–19. https://doi.org/10.1177/104420739600700201

Barnes, C., & Mercer, G. (2001). Disability culture. In G. Albrecht, K.. Seelman, & M. Bury (Eds.), *Handbook of disability studies* (pp. 515–534). Sage.

Barnes, C., Oliver, M., & Barton, L. (2002). *Disability studies today.* Blackwell.

Baynton, D. C. (1996). *Forbidden signs.* University of Chicago Press. https://doi.org/10.7208/chicago/9780226039688.001.0001

Baynton, D. (2013). Disability and the justification of inequality in American history. In L. Davis (Ed.), *The disability studies reader* (4th ed., pp. 17–33). Routledge.

Beers, C. W. (1908). *A mind that found itself*. Doubleday. https://doi.org/10.1037/10534-000

Berne, P., Morales, A. L., Langstaff, D., & Invalid, S. (2018). Ten principles of disability justice. *WSQ, 46*(1–2), 227–230. https://doi.org/10.1353/wsq.2018.0003

Bernstein, R. (2001). *Disintegrating systems: The state of state's public mental health system*. Bazelon Center for Mental Health Law.

Block, P., Balcazar, F., & Keys, C. (2001). From pathology to power: Rethinking race, poverty, and disability. *Journal of Disability Policy Studies, 12*, 18–39.

Bolton, B., & Brookings, J. (1998). Development of a multifaceted definition of empowerment. *Rehabilitation Counseling Bulletin, 19*, 12–18.

Brandt, D. (2009). Writing over reading: New directions in mass literacy. In M. Baynham & M. Prinsloo (Eds.), *The future of literacy studies* (pp. 54–74). Palgrave Macmillan.

Bricher, G. (2000). Disabled people, health professionals and the social model of disability: Can there be a research relationship? *Disability & Society, 15*(5), 781–793. https://doi.org/10.1080/713662004

Brockley, J. A. (2001). Martyred mothers and merciful fathers: Exploring disability and motherhood in the lives of Jerome Greenfield and Raymond Repouille. In P. Longmore & L. Umansky (Eds.), *The new disability history: American perspectives* (pp. 268–292). New York University Press.

Brown, S. E. (2001). Editorial: What is disability culture? *Independent Living Institute Newsletter 2001–12*. Retrieved June 25, 2010, from. http:www.independentliving.org/newsletter/12–01.html

Bruyère, S. M. (1993). Participatory action research. *Journal of Vocational Rehabilitation, 3*(2), 62–68. https://doi.org/10.3233/JVR-1993-3213

Bruyère, S. M. (2000). Civil rights and employment issues of disability policy. *Journal of Disability Policy Studies, 11*(1), 18–28. https://doi.org/10.1177/104420730001100108

Byrom, B. (2001). A pupil and a patient. In P. Longmore & L. Umansky (Eds.), *The new disability history* (pp. 133–156). New York University Press.

Carluccio, L. W., & Patterson, J. (2001). Promoting independent living in the rehabilitation curriculum. *Rehabilitation Education, 15*, 409–419.

Chamberlin, J. (1977). *On our own: Patient-controlled alternatives to the mental health system*. National Empowerment Center.

Charlton, J. I. (1998). *Nothing about us without us*. University of California Press. https://doi.org/10.1525/9780520925441

Chen, A. (2016). *How YouTube videos help people cope with mental illness*. National Public Radio. https://news.wfsu.org/2016-06-13/how-youtube-videos-help-people-cope-with-mental-illness

Chubon, R. A. (1992). Defining rehabilitation from a systems perspective: Critical implications. *Journal of Applied Rehabilitation Counseling, 23*(1), 27–32. https://doi.org/10.1891/0047-2220.23.1.27

Cole, J. A. (2001). Developing new self-images and interdependence. In N. M. Crewe & I. K. Zola (Eds.), *Independent living for physically disabled people* (pp. 187–204). People with Disabilities Press.

Conyers, L. M. (2003). Disability culture. *Rehabilitation Education, 3*, 139–154.

Corker, M. (2001). Sensing disability. *Hypatia, 16*(4), 34–52. https://doi.org/10.1111/j.1527-2001.2001.tb00752.x

Corrigan, P. W. (2016). *Principles and practice of psychiatric rehabilitation: An empirical approach* (2nd ed.). Guilford Press.

CRCC. (2016). *Rehabilitation counseling*. http://www.crccertification.com/pages/rehabilitation_counseling/30.php

Crenshaw, K. (1989). *Demarginalizing the intersection of race and sex* (pp. 139–167). University of Chicago Legal Forum.

Crewe, N. M., & Zola, I. K. (Eds.). (2001). *Independent living for physically disabled people*. People with Disabilities Press.

Cushing, P., & Smith, T. (2009). Multinational review of english language disability studies degrees and courses. *Disability Studies Quarterly, 29*(3), 11–22. https://doi.org/10.18061/dsq.v29i3.940

Davidson, L., Rowe, M., Tondora, J., O'Connell, M. J., & Lawless, M. S. (2009). *A practical guide to recovery-oriented practice*. Oxford University Press. https://doi.org/10.1093/oso/9780195304770.001.0001

Davis, L. J. (Ed.). (2021). *The disability studies reader* (5th ed.). Routledge.

DeJong, G. (1979). Independent living: from social movement to analytic paradigm. *Archives of Physical Medicine and Rehabilitation, 60*(10), 435–446.

Dobransky, K., & Hargittai, E. (2021). Piercing the Pandemic Social Bubble: Disability and Social Media Use About COVID-19. *American Behavioral Scientist, 65*(12), 1698–1720. https://doi.org/10.1177/00027642211003146

Donoghue, C. (2003). Challenging the authority of the medical definition of disability: An analysis of the resistance to the social constructionist paradigm. *Disability & Society, 18*(2), 199–208. https://doi.org/10.1080/0968759032000052833

Dunn, D. S., & Andrews, E. E. (2015). Person-first and identity-first language: Developing psychologists' cultural competence using disability language. *The American Psychologist, 70*(3), 255–264. https://doi.org/10.1037/a0038636

Farber, S. (1993). *Madness, heresy, and the rumor of angels.* Open Court.

Frain, M., Tschopp, M. K., & Bishop, M. (2009). Empowerment variables as predictors of outcomes in rehabilitation. *Journal of Rehabilitation, 75*(1), 27–35.

Frieden, L. (2001). Understanding alternative program models. In N. M. Crewe & I. K. Zola (Eds.), *Independent living for physically disabled people* (pp. 62–72). People with Disabilities Press.

Gill, C. J. (1995). A psychological view of disability culture. *Disability Studies Quarterly, 15*, 16–19.

Grob, G. (1994). *The mad among us: A history of the care of America's mentally ill.* Harvard University Press.

Hahn, H. (1988). The politics of physical differences: Disability and discrimination. *Journal of Social Issues, 44*(1), 39–47. https://doi.org/10.1111/j.1540-4560.1988.tb02047.x

Haller, B. (2010). *Representing disability in an ableist world.* Avocado Press.

Hartley, M. T., Johnson, S. P., & Tarvydas, V. M. (2015). The ethics and practice of social media advocacy in rehabilitation counseling. *Journal of Rehabilitation, 81*(1), 43–52.

Hartley, M. T., Mapes, A. C., Taylor, A., & Bourgeois, P. (2016). Digital media technology and advocacy: Addressing attitudes toward disability on college campuses. *Journal of Postsecondary Education and Disability, 29*(3), 239–247.

Hartley, M. T., & Tarvydas, V. M. (2013). Rehabilitation issues, social class and counseling. In W. Liu (Ed.), *Oxford handbook of social class in counseling psychology* (pp. 218–228). Oxford Press.

Hershenson, D. B. (1998). Systematic, ecological model for rehabilitation counseling. *Rehabilitation Counseling Bulletin, 42*, 40–50.

Illich, I., Zola, I. K., McKnight, J., Caplan, J., & Shaiken, H. (2005). *Disabling professions.* Marion Boyers.

Jenkins, W., Patterson, J. B., & Szymanski, E. M. (1992). Philosophical, historic, and legislative aspects of the rehabilitation counseling profession. In R. M. Parker & E. M. Szymanski (Eds.), *Rehabilitation counseling: Basics and beyond* (2nd ed., pp. 1–41). Pro-Ed.

Johnson, M. (2003). *Make them go away.* The Avocado Press.

Kilbury, R. F., Benshoff, J. J., & Rubin, S. E. (1992). The interaction of legislation, public attitudes, and access to opportunities for persons with disabilities. *Journal of Rehabilitation, 58*(4), 6–9.

Koestler, F. A. (1975). *The unseen minority.* American Foundation of the Blind.

Kosciulek, J. F. (1993). Advances in trait-and-factor theory: A person x environment fit approach to rehabilitation counseling. *Journal of Applied Rehabilitation Counseling, 24*(2), 11–14. https://doi.org/10.1891/0047-2220.24.2.11

Kosciulek, J. F. (1999). The consumer directed theory of empowerment. *Rehabilitation Counseling Bulletin, 42*, 196–213.

Kosciulek, J. F. (2000). Implications of consumer direction for disability policy development and rehabilitation service delivery. *Journal of Disability Policy Studies, 11*(2), 82–89. https://doi.org/10.1177/104420730001100204

Kosciulek, J. F. (2005). Structural equation model of the consumer-directed theory of empowerment in a vocational rehabilitation. *Rehabilitation Counseling Bulletin, 49*(1), 40–49. https://doi.org/10.1177/00343552050490010501

Ladau, E. (2021). *Demystifying disability.* Ten Speed Press.

Lane, H. (1984). *When the mind hears.* Random House.

Lewis, B. (2013). A mad fight: Psychiatry and disability activism. In L. J. Davis (Ed.), *The disability studies reader* (4th ed., pp. 100–114). Routledge.

Linton, S. (1998). *Claiming disability, knowledge and identity.* New York University Press.

Little, M. (2014). *Introduction to bioethics: Bioethics & the human body.* https://www.youtube.com/watch?v=-h0qnGKYjPY

Longmore, P. K. (1995). The second phase: From disability rights to disability culture. *Disability Rag* (September/October), 4–11.

Longmore, P. K. (2003). *Why I burned my book and other essays on disability*. Temple University Press.

Longmore, P. K., & Goldberger, E. (2003). The league of physically handicapped and the great depression. In P. Longmore (Ed.), *Why I burned my book and other essays on disability* (pp. 53–101). Temple University Press.

Longmore, P. K., & Umansky, L. (Eds.). (2001). *The new disability history*. New York University Press.

Lustig, D. C., & Strauser, D. R. (2007). Causal relationships between poverty and disability. *Rehabilitation Counseling Bulletin, 50*(4), 194–202. https://doi.org/10.1177/00343552070500040101

Lustig, D. C., Strauser, D. R., Dewaine Rice, N., & Rucker, T. F. (2002). The relationship between working alliance and rehabilitation outcomes. *Rehabilitation Counseling Bulletin, 46*(1), 24–32. https://doi.org/10.1177/00343552020460010201

Marini, I., Glover-Graf, N. M., & Millington, M. J. (2018). *Psychosocial aspects of disability: Insider perspectives and counseling strategies* (2nd ed.). Springer. https://doi.org/10.1891/9780826180636

Marrs, R. W. (1995). A meta-analysis of bibliotherapy studies. *American Journal of Community Psychology, 23*(6), 843–870. https://doi.org/10.1007/BF02507018

Matson, F. (1990). *Walking alone and marching together*. National Federation of the Blind.

McCarthy, H. (2003). The disability rights movement. *Rehabilitation Counseling Bulletin, 46*(4), 209–223. https://doi.org/10.1177/003435520304600402

Middleton, R. A., Rollins, C. W., & Harley, D. A. (1999). The historical and political context of the civil rights of persons with disabilities: A multicultural perspective for counselors. *Journal of Multicultural Counseling and Development, 27*(2), 105–120. https://doi.org/10.1002/j.2161-1912.1999.tb00218.x

Murugami, M. W. (2009). Disability and identity. *Disability Studies Quarterly, 29*(4). https://doi.org/10.18061/dsq.v29i4.979

Noll, S., & Trent, J. (Eds.). (2004). *Mental retardation in America: A historical reader*. New York University Press.

Nosek, M. A., Zhu, Y., & Howland, C. (1992). The evolution of independent living programs. *Rehabilitation Counseling Bulletin, 35*, 174–179.

Oakes, D. (2002). *From patients to passion (Plenary address alternatives 2002 Convention)*. http://www.mindfreedom.org

Oliver, M. (1990). *The politics of disablement*. Macmillan Press. https://doi.org/10.1007/978-1-349-20895-1

Oliver, M. (1992). Changing the social relations of research production? *Disability, Handicap & Society, 7*(2), 101–114. https://doi.org/10.1080/02674649266780141

Packard, E. (1868). *The prisoner's hidden life, or insane asylums unveiled: As demonstrated by the report of the investigating committee of the legislature of Illinois*.

Peters, S. (2000). Is there a disability culture? a syncretisation of three possible world views. *Disability & Society, 15*(4), 583–601. https://doi.org/10.1080/09687590050058198

Piepzna-Samarasinha, L. L. (2018). *Care work*. Arsenal Pulp.

Pledger, C. (2003). Discourse on disability and rehabilitation issues. *American Psychologist, 58*, 279–284. 10.1037/0003-066X.58.4.279

Porter, R. (1989). *A social history of madness*. Dutton.

Pratt, M. L. (1991). Arts of the contact zone. *Profession, 91*, 33–40.

Price, M. (2013). Defining mental illness. In L. J. Davis (Ed.), *The disability studies reader* (4th ed., pp. 298–307). Routledge.

Richards, L., & Smith, Q. (n.d.). *An orientation to independent living centers. ILRU field work: A national technical assistance project for independent living (pp. 1–6). Developed as part of the National Technical Assistance Project for Independent Living. ILRU Research & Training Center on Independent Living at TIRR*. http://www.ilru.org

Sales, A. (2007). *Rehabilitation counseling: An empowerment perspective*. Pro-Ed.

Satel, S. (2000). *Review of P.C., M.D.: How political correctness is corrupting medicine*. Basic Books.

Saxton, M. (2001). Peer counseling. In N. M. Crewe & I. K. Zola (Eds.), *Independent living for physically disabled people* (pp. 171–186). People with Disabilities Press.

Schwab, L. (2001). Developing programs in rural areas. In N. M. Crewe & I. K. Zola (Eds.), *Independent living for physically disabled people* (pp. 73–87). People with Disabilities Press.

Schweik, S. M. (2008). *The ugly laws.* New York University Press.

Scotch, R. K. (1988). Disability as the basis for a social movement: Advocacy and the politics of definition. *Journal of Social Issues, 44*(1), 159–172. https://doi.org/10.1111/j.1540-4560.1988.tb02055.x

Shakespeare, T. (1996). Rules of engagement: Doing disability research. *Disability & Society, 11*(1), 115–121. https://doi.org/10.1080/09687599650023380

Shakespeare, T. (2013). The social model of disability. In L. J. Davis (Ed.), *The disability studies reader* (4th ed., pp. 214–221). Routledge.

Shakespeare, T., & Watson, N. (1997). Defending the social model. *Disability & Society, 12*(2), 293–300. https://doi.org/10.1080/09687599727380

Shapiro, J. P. (1993). *No pity.* Three Rivers Press.

Shreve, M. (1991). Peer counseling in independent living centers. *ILRU Program,* 1–29. www.ilru.org

Smart, J. (2015). *Disability, society, and the individual* (3rd ed.). Aspen Press.

Smith, S. K., Rayer, S., & Smith, E. A. (2008). Aging and disability: Implications for the housing industry and housing policy in the United States. *Journal of the American Planning Association, 74*(3), 289–306. https://doi.org/10.1080/01944360802197132

Stein, M. (2017, June 22). "No cuts to Medicaid!": protesters in wheelchairs arrested after release of health care bill. https://www.vox.com/policy-and-politics/2017/6/22/15855424/disability -protest-medicaid-mcconnell

Stuntzner, S., & Hartley, M. T. (2014). Disability and the counseling relationship: What counselors need to know. In *In Ideas and research you can use: VISTAS 2014.* Retrieved from www.counseling.org

Switzer, J. V. (2003). *Disability rights.* Georgetown University Press.

Szymanksi, E. M. & Trueba, H. T. (1994). Castification of people with disabilities. *Journal of Rehabilitation, 60,* 12–21.

Tarvydas, V., Hartley, M., Jang, Y. J., Johnston, S., Moore-Grant, N., Walker, Q., O'Hanlon, C., & Whalen, J. (2012). Collaborating with the disability rights community: Co-writing a code of ethics as a vehicle for ethics education. *Rehabilitation Research, Policy, and Education, 26*(3), 241–254. https://doi.org/10.1891/2168-6653.26.3.241

Trent, J. W. (1994). *Inventing the feeble mind.* University of California Press.

Umucu, E., Tansey, T. N., Brooks, J., & Lee, B. (2021). The protective role of character strengths in COVID-19 stress and well-being in individuals with chronic conditions and disabilities: An exploratory study. *Rehabilitation Counseling Bulletin, 64*(2), 67–74. https://doi.org/10.1177/0034355220967093

Varela, R. A. (2001). Changing social attitudes and legislation regarding disability. In N. M. Crewe & I. K. Zola (Eds.), *Independent living for physically disabled people* (pp. 28–48). People with Disabilities Press.

Walker, M. L. (1993). Participatory action research. *Rehabilitation Counseling Bulletin, 37,* 2–5.

White, G. W. (2002). Consumer participation in disability research: The golden rule as a guide for ethical practice. *Rehabilitation Psychology, 47*(4), 438–446. https://doi.org/10.1037/0090-5550.47.4.438

Wong, J., Kudla, A., Pham, T., Ezeife, N., Crown, D., Capraro, P., Trierweiler, R., Tomazin, S., & Heinemann, A. W. (2021). Lessons learned by rehabilitation counselors and physicians in services to COVID-19 long-haulers: A Qualitative Study. *Rehabilitation Counseling Bulletin,* 003435522110600. https://doi.org/10.1177/00343552211060014

Yeo, R., & Moore, K. (2003). Including disabled people in poverty reduction work. *World Development, 31,* 571–590.

Zola, I. K. (2001). Developing new self-images and interdependence. In N. M. Crewe & I. K. Zola (Eds.), *Independent living for physically disabled people* (pp. 49–59). People with Disabilities Press.

CHAPTER 10

Disability Issues in a Global Context

LISA LÓPEZ LEVERS AND CONNIE SUNG

LEARNING OBJECTIVES

After reading this chapter, you should be able to:

- *Compare and contrast global disability issues in high-resource and low-resource countries.*
- *Recognize the scope of rehabilitation counseling in an international context.*
- *Identify some of the global epidemiological implications for disability, including the COVID-19 pandemic.*
- *Identify some of the concerns regarding the lack of data related to global disability issues.*
- *Give examples of current global contextual factors and other issues affecting disability, such as culture, poverty, trauma, crisis, large-scale disaster, anthropogenic climate change, HIV and AIDS, and psychosocial issues across the life span.*
- *Develop an awareness of the intersections among disability, race, gender, and gender-identity issues.*
- *Create an attitude of antiracism to assist clients with related issues.*
- *Identify additional resources for promoting better understandings of disability and rehabilitation in an international context.*

CACREP STANDARDS

CACREP 2016 CORE: 2F1.c, 2F1.e., 2F2.a, 2F2.d., 2F2.h, 2F3.h, 2F3f, 2F3.g, 2F4.g, 2F5.k, 2F8.a

CACREP 2016 Specialties:

   Clinical Rehabilitation Counseling: 5D1.b, 5D2.g, 5D2.h, 5D2.i., 5D2.j, 5D2.n, 5D2.o, 5D2.p, 5D2.q, 5D2.r, 5D2.v, 5D3.b

   Rehabilitation Counseling: 5H1.b, 5H1.e, 5H2.a, 5H2.b, 5H2.c, 5H2.d, 5H2.e, 5H2.g, 5H2.h, 5H2.n, 5H2.o, 5H3.e, 5H3.h, 5H3.k, 5H3.l

INTRODUCTION

The world is changing rapidly and so are the multiple environments in which we all live. Social influences such as globalization, migration, and urbanization affect us all, as do environmental and health influences like anthropogenic climate change and pandemics. This is the current context in which disability issues and the expanding role of rehabilitation counselors (RCs) are explored in this chapter. Even in the 21st century, accordance about what constitutes disability is not a settled matter (e.g., Officer & Groce, 2009; World Health Organization [WHO], 2011a). The most recent World Health Organization's *World Report on Disabilities* (WHO, 2011a) has noted that, "there is no agreement on definitions and little internationally comparable information on the incidence, distribution and trends of disability" (p. xxi). Indeed, Wass and Jones described disability as a "complex, multi-faceted and evolving concept" (2020, p. 1) with the WHO (2020a) asserting that "disability is extremely diverse" ("Disability—a public health issue," para. 2). One common matter that emerges as salient, however, is that people living with disabilities, internationally, often lack accessibility to and equity of opportunity in many areas, including employment, education, community living, built environments, and healthcare services (WHO, 2011a, WHO, 2020b). In fact, the WHO (2020a) has identified the following barriers that may be encountered by people with disabilities when attempting to gain access to healthcare: "Prohibitive costs, limited availability of services, physical barriers, and inadequate skills and knowledge of health workers" ("Barriers to healthcare," para. 2–5).

The purpose of this chapter is to parse out contemporary issues related to disability and to discuss and illuminate the expanding role of RCs within an international context. In order to do this, it is imperative to understand relevant worldwide issues and trends concerning disability, disability policy, and disability classification systems, especially as the needs in developing contexts compare and contrast with disability-related needs in North America and other developed countries. In this chapter, the reader is introduced to relevant disability demographics, constructs, and resources that relate to global perspectives of disability issues and the expanding role of RCs.

DISABILITY GLOBALLY

According to Human Rights Watch (2014) and the WHO (2020a), more than 1 billion people are living with some form of disability globally; this figure accounts for approximately 15% of the population, making people with disability the "world's largest minority group" (Lancet Global Health Editorial, 2021, p. e1028). The World Bank (2021, para. 1) has reported that "one-fifth of the estimated global total, or between 110 million and 190 million people, experience significant disabilities." The WHO indicated that the "number of people living with disability is increasing, in part due to ageing [sic] populations and an increase in chronic health conditions" (WHO, 2020a, "Disability—a public health issue," para. 1).

Data have indicated that about 80% of all people with disabilities reside in low-resource countries (Lancet Global Health Editorial, 2021; WHO, 2011a). According to WHO (2011a), "disability disproportionately affects vulnerable populations. . . . People who have a low income, are out of work, or have low educational qualifications are at an increased risk of disability" (p. 8). There is a relationship between disability and poverty, with disability considered both a cause and a consequence of poverty (Banks et al., 2018; Mitra et al., 2011; WHO, 2011a). According to a "Disability: Beyond the medical model" (2009), the majority of the world's people with disabilities who live in low-income countries have "little or no access to basic health services, including rehabilitation facilities" (p. 1793). It becomes essential to focus not only on Western and developed countries but also on non-Western and developing systems of rehabilitation to understand international disability (Mpofu et al., 2018; UNDP, 2016, 2018; WHO, 2020a).

Well-established social safety mechanisms for people with disabilities exist in many high-resource countries; for example, Sweden, England, and Canada arguably have some of the strongest disability-related systems in the world (Levers et al., 2010). Although popular thought would suggest that the United States has a comparable disability-related system, recent evidence has called this into question. In particular, the United States has struggled with the quality versus the cost of medical care (e.g., AHRQ, 2019;

Commonwealth Fund, 2020; Nunn et al., 2020), health inequities (e.g., AHRQ, 2019), and negative perceptions about people with disabilities (e.g., Babik & Gardner, 2021). Although the United States is not at the forefront of health and QOL when compared to other developed countries, rehabilitation services typically are delivered by relatively well-trained personnel. This is often the case in higher resource countries with embedded social safety nets (SSNs) for people with disabilities. SSNs often are not present in middle- and low-resource countries.

Throughout the world, many people with disabilities live in poverty without the advantage of government-sponsored assistance. In many countries with low resources, service provision by a master's-level RC simply is not feasible. This is not to say that services are completely unavailable or that no one assumes the functions of rehabilitation counseling; however, the rehabilitation delivery systems look much different in lower resource societies. This chapter focuses on the relevant discrepancies between high- and low-resource rehabilitation systems, as these relate to the experience of disability across a global context. As a starting point, we define *disability* and *rehabilitation counseling* in an international context.

DISABILITY AND SCOPE OF PRACTICE IN AN INTERNATIONAL CONTEXT

In the United States, the Rehabilitation Act of 1973, the Rehabilitation Act Amendments of 1998, and the Americans with Disabilities Act (ADA) of 1990 represent hallmark legislation that has defined disability and rehabilitation services. Internationally, a number of documents offer parallel benchmark definitions of globally relevant rights-based frameworks: the UN Convention on the Rights of Persons with Disabilities (CRPD; UN, 2006); the WHO's *International Statistical Classification of Diseases and Related Health Problems, 11th Revision* (ICD-11; WHO, 2018); the WHO's *International Classification of Functioning, Disability and Health* (ICF; WHO, 2001); and the WHO's *Children and Youth Version of the International Classification of Functioning, Disability and Health* (2007a). While disability has been addressed internationally, it is important to note that the UN Millennium Declaration, commonly referred to as the *Millennium Development Goals* (MDGs; United Nations [UN], 200), was criticized largely for originally ignoring the health needs of people with disabilities (e.g., "Disability: Beyond the medical model, 2009"; Levers, 2017; Levers et al., 2010; UN, 2011). Subsequently, the more recent UN (2015) *Millennium Development Goals Report* addressed disability issues and antipoverty progress in greater detail.

The governments of many countries have demonstrated the political will to improve the lives of people with disabilities by taking action and signing important conventions such as the CRPD; however, the fiduciary power to follow through has not always been available. This gap in power includes the availability of human as well as material resources. In addition, the struggle for human rights has been trying for people with disabilities when the security nets do not materialize to meet concrete needs. For example, in an evaluation of the effects of poverty on people with disabilities in a southern African country, consumers of services indicated that "rights do not provide the immediate solution to problems of poverty such as lack of food . . . [arguing] that 'we do not eat rights'" (Levers et al., 2010, p. 119). Despite obvious challenges, emerging trends and strategic plans have provided frameworks for setting goals that can contribute to legislative and policy change, eventually having a real impact on the quality of living for people with disabilities worldwide (see data table available in Ritchie & Roser, 2018). According to the (UN, 2006, Overview section, para. 12), comparative examinations of disability policies and laws have indicated that "only 45 countries have anti-discrimination and other disability-specific laws," thereby highlighting the urgent need to advocate for disability-friendly policies worldwide. These important issues relate directly to (a) theoretical perspectives on disability, (b) definitions of disability, and (c) the role of RCs, all of which are discussed more fully in the following subsections.

Theoretical Perspectives on Disability

As mirrored by developments in North America, the international perspective on disability has shifted from a purely medical model to one with a greater social systems emphasis, and more recently, to a biopsychosocial or ecological model (Mpofu et al., 2018; Petasis, 2019). This shift is accepted so widely that a special issue of the British-based *Lancet (2009),* one of the world's leading medical journals, had a special issue dedicated to the topic of disability "beyond the medical model" (p. 1793). A shift away from a purely medical understanding of disability has opened the door to social model perspectives of disability, including cultural meaning.

Many international organizations have begun to reevaluate definitions of *disability.* One example is the WHO's *International Classification of Impairments, Disabilities and Handicaps (ICIDH;* WHO, 1980). Early WHO classification systems were more or less restrictive and reductionistic biomedical or disease-model perspectives. However, the need eventually emerged for a more contextual understanding of disability focused on the community-based inclusion of people with disabilities. Later versions of the *ICF* by the WHO (2001) reflected a biopsychosocial or ecological model. In a review of the literature that was conducted 3 years after the publication of the *ICF,* Bruyère et al. (2005) summarized discussions that reflect both support for and reservations about the *ICF's* most recent conceptualization of disability. However, the *ICF* is considered by most as offering a contextual and holistic approach to disability, one that is applicable to diverse disability issues focused on quality of life (e.g., Fox et al., 2015; Mpofu et al., 2018; Pollard et al., 2009; WHO, 2013).

Legal frameworks to protect the rights of individuals with disability policies remain relatively underdeveloped around the world (Durocher et al., 2012). This situation is unfortunate, because how disability is defined in governmental policies determines eligibility for people with disabilities to access social protection programs. For example, impairment-oriented definitions, largely used in developing countries, tend to underreport the prevalence of disability and inadvertently exclude people with disabilities from eligibility for social protection services (Levers et al., 2008; Mpofu et al., 2018). Conversely, more inclusive definitions of disability based on activity and participation limitations result in a higher census of people eligible for social protection programs (Centers for Disease Control and Prevention [CDC], 2020; Mitra et al., 2011). Most contemporary models of rehabilitation service delivery already tend to be humanitarian in nature. So by definition, ecologically oriented models have allowed for greater incorporation of mechanisms that encourage empowerment, self-determination, and self-efficacy, concepts that are central to the practice of rehabilitation counseling (Ackerman, 2021). Empowerment and self-efficacy are instrumental to advancing the rights of people with disabilities throughout the world through universal health care.

Defining Disability

The CRPD (UN, 2006, Article 1—Purpose, para. 2) has defined disability as including people "who have long-term physical, mental, intellectual or sensory impairments which in interaction with various barriers may hinder their full and effective participation in society on an equal basis with others." The *ICF* also has provided an ecological definition of disability, offering a common language and framework for considering health and health-related issues (WHO, 2002). Therefore, this ecological definition is essential as a disability-related tool in an international context. The ICF defines **disability** as "an umbrella term for impairments, activity limitations and participation restrictions," further stating that "[f]unctional limitations occur as a result of the interaction between an individual (with a health condition) and that individual's contextual factors (environmental and personal factors)" (WHO, 2001, p. 10). The *ICF* does not focus on the etiology of dysfunction or underlying pathology; rather, these are focal points of its companion classification, the *ICD-11* (WHO, 2018).

The presence of impairments does not necessarily imply the presence of disorder or disease; rather, according to the WHO (2001, p. 12), they "represent a deviation from certain generally accepted population standards" of functioning. Determinations of impairment are made by "those qualified to judge physical and mental functioning according to these standards" (WHO, 2001, p. 12). Disability, then, refers to "the outcome or result of a complex relationship between an individual's health condition and personal factors, and of the external factors that represent the circumstances in which the individual lives" (WHO, 2001, p. 17). In this international and ecological context, the meaning of disability is intended to imply a focus on the comprehensive individual, societal, and body-related aspects of impairments, along with activity limitations and other participation restrictions in the environment. Also in this international and ecological context, its determination may be made by various professionals or paraprofessionals, who may or may not resemble RCs in a Euro-American context.

In September 2007, the WHO published the *ICF-CY* to better address disability among children and youth. A number of ambitious objectives have been associated with the *ICF-CY*. Much like the *ICF*, the *ICF-CY* has aimed to shift views regarding disability issues from a more medically oriented model to one that accounts for contextual and environmental factors. As an extension of a more contemporary focus on child and youth issues in the disability arena, recent literature has emphasized the importance of assessing and involving families (e.g., Mpofu et al., 2015, 2021).

The **ecological model of functioning** is operationally advanced in both the *ICF* and the *ICF-CY* and suggests dynamic and reciprocal relationships among various health-related conditions; these relationships occur within the context of multiple personal and environmental influences. Functioning and disability are then conceptualized within dynamic interactions between health conditions and contextual factors, including culture. The components and interactions that can be used to describe the relationship between disability and functioning are illustrated in Figure 10.1.

According to the *ICF* model, disability is defined by activity and participation limitations due to health conditions, particularly as these are linked to environments in which people live with disabilities. In concert with the underlying theory of the bioecological model of human development, social protection policies primarily are intended to mitigate or prevent activity restrictions and participation limitations. For example, poverty is a determinant that can affect environmental context, and disability is associated with poverty in most countries. This association suggests a complex situation that is not necessarily determined by a clear cause-and-effect relationship. It ultimately may lead to the socioeconomic exclusion of people with disabilities, which then influences other dimensions of living. Some performance-based benchmarks even indicate that the extent to which a country provides social protection programs may have a connection with international expenditure norms, thus emphasizing complex interactions between disability and economics (Grech, 2016; Wass & Jones, 2020; WHO, 2011a).

Regardless of socioeconomic status, activity restrictions, participation limitations, or environmental barriers, the *ICF* model recognizes that people can have disabilities and still be healthy (CDC, 2020; Stein et al., 2009; WHO, 2001). Health or well-being is mediated by cognitive and bodily functions and structures that enable activity and participation (Murray et al., 2015). **Activity** is based on what a person is capable of doing to meet daily living needs, and **participation** arises from the roles that a person is able to fulfill. Both the environment and personal factors influence the conditions and pathways for activity and participation by people with disabilities. For example, people in chronic poverty may have significant health challenges and risk factors (Banks et al., 2018; Mpofu

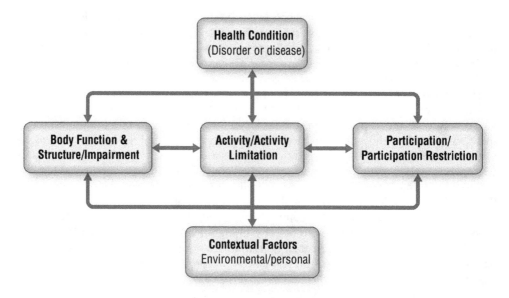

FIGURE 10.1 Interactions among the components of *ICF*.

Source: Pollard, B., Dixon, D., Dieppe, P., & Johnston, M. (2009). Measuring the ICF components of impairment, activity limitation and participation restriction: An item analysis using classical test theory and item response theory. *Health and Quality of Life Outcomes, 7.* https://doi.org/10.1186/1477-7525-7-41

et al., 2018) that could be relieved by social protection programs. When living in poverty, people with disabilities may perform less optimally in engaging the full range of activities and roles that are necessary for successful daily living. Personal factors such as self-attitudes can differentiate social outcomes for people who may have the same health conditions: While some individuals may perceive a need to adapt and take control of their situations, others may not. Given the same objective environment and similar health conditions, people with disabilities may differ in their motivation to acquire the social protection services for which they are eligible. Based on all of these assumptions and derived from an ecological perspective of disability, a useful operational definition of **disability**, suggested by Levers et al. (2008, p. 22) in their evaluation of one African nation's disability system, is "any physical, sensory, cognitive, or psychiatric impairment that, when combined with environmental and societal barriers, limits the person's functional ability to perform major life activities."

Defining the Role of Rehabilitation Counselors

The Commission on Rehabilitation Counselor Certification (CRCC, 2021) website states that "Rehabilitation counselors are the only professional counselors educated and trained at the graduate level to specifically serve individuals with disabilities" (para. 1). In the United States and worldwide, the Bureau of Labor Statistics (USBLS, 2022, What rehabilitation counselors do, para. 1), defined the scope of practice for RCs as "helping people with physical, mental, developmental, and emotional disabilities live independently." Over time, RCs have served an increasingly broad population of individuals, including those injured in industrial accidents and through war (Moering et al., 2022). Furthermore, the practice of rehabilitation counseling shifted from the RC providing services *for* rather than *with* the client, shifting away from paternalism and toward empowerment. Unfortunately, there continue to be distributive justice concerns with the availability of rehabilitation services. For example, rehabilitation services tend to be located in more centralized urban areas, and many people with disabilities live in rural regions. This is especially true in developing countries with the lack of accessible transportation, long distances, and prohibitive costs interfering with services (Mpofu et al., 2018; WHO, 2011a). Additionally, the focus on individualism is a core component of Western-allied healthcare. It has limited the development of social structures that are more collectivist in nature, such as accessible transportation in rural areas.

Although professionals who work as RCs in the United States typically possess a master's degree in rehabilitation counseling, this situation is not necessarily the case in other parts of the world. First, regardless of specialty area, counseling is not viewed as a distinct profession in some countries. Psychology and social work are recognized more universally as allied health professions. Until recently, preparing graduate students to become professional counselors largely was an American endeavor. In recent years, there are indications that this situation is changing, with students being trained in the United States who return to their non-Western countries to provide counseling (e.g., Duenyas et al., 2020), including rehabilitation counseling (Alsaman, 2014). Additionally, there has been an international growth of counselor education programs (e.g., Astramovich & Pehrsson, 2009; Garcia, 2012), global counseling identity and credentials (e.g., Mariotti et al., 2019), and a greater focus on integrating modern counseling techniques with Indigenous forms of counseling (e.g., Levers, 2006; Levers et al., 2019; Radomsky & Levers, 2012). However, in low-resource countries, there continues to be a large treatment gap for individuals with psychiatric disabilities (Levers et al., 2019; Mukamana et al., 2019). For people who experience psychiatric disabilities, human services are not always available, and when they are, they are usually not provided by a master's-level practitioner. Putting all this together, it is plausible that although the scope of practice for those fulfilling the role of RC is similar throughout the world, practitioners vary considerably in training and access to resources. With this understanding in mind, it is important to identify some of the relevant issues of concern that have global implications for those working in the disability and rehabilitation arena. This summary focuses on international trends that have been identified in the relevant professional literatures, and they are discussed in the next section.

INTERNATIONAL DISABILITY AND REHABILITATION LITERATURES

The presentation of a thorough and complete examination of global disability and rehabilitation issues is beyond the scope of this chapter. However, several salient trends emerge from the literature and inform the discourse on disability issues and rehabilitation counseling in a global context. There is a plethora of transnational literature that relates to disability and rehabilitation issues—for example, comparisons of disability statistics between two or among several specific countries. However, there is little literature that integrates and synthesizes international information in a meaningful way. Beyond the documents of global relevance that were identified earlier in this chapter, our review of the international literature has revealed two major currents of thought: (a) A huge gap still exists in terms of any thorough examination of global disability issues (e.g., Lancet Global Health Editorial, 2021), and (b) there are a number of identifiable trends or concerns having an impact on the delivery of rehabilitation services globally. These two currents of thought are discussed next.

Lacunae in the Disability and Rehabilitation Literature

Lacunae (gaps) exist in the international literature concerning the understandings of the epidemiological and evidentiary implications of, and the contextual factors associated with, disability and rehabilitation. Cross-national studies remain an emerging area of research in public health and disability (Lee et al., 2018; Leroi et al., 2021; Opoku et al.,

2021). In recent years, more cross-national comparisons can be found in the relevant literature than ever before (e.g., Erickson et al., 2021; Jesus et al., 2020; Leroi et al., 2021; Opoku et al., 2021; Pettinicchio & Maroto, 2021). Even so, some of the earlier comparisons remain germane to this discussion (e.g., Murray et al., 2015; Soerjomataram et al., 2012). Some of the earlier studies compared risks and disease burden across as many as 188 countries (e.g., Murray et al., 2015) and as many as 12 regions of the world (e.g., Soerjomataram et al., 2012). This emerging literature has begun to shed light on disability and rehabilitation as a complex and multifaceted issue in the global context, beginning with epidemiological implications.

Epidemiological Implications

The collection of valid health-related statistics is vital to ascertain disease and injury levels across the world. Various compilations of data regarding mortality, morbidity, and epidemiological trends exist at national and regional levels that have offered "comparable regional and global estimates and projections of disease and injury burden based on a common set of methods and denominated in a common metric" (Murray & Lopez, 1996, p. xxvii). *The Global Burden of Disease: A Comprehensive Assessment of Mortality and Disability from Diseases, Injuries, and Risk Factors in 1990 and Projected to 2020* (Murray & Lopez, 1996) is considered a landmark publication for its singularity in this arena. It has offered a mechanism for beginning to gather and analyze international disease- and disability-related data in a comprehensive and aligned fashion, as well as for using historical trends to project the mortality and disease burden forward to 2020.

The Murray and Lopez (1996) study has provided consistent estimates of disease and injury rates. More importantly, for the purposes of this chapter, it has "attempted to provide a comparative index of the burden of each disease or injury, namely the number of **Disability-Adjusted Life Years (DALYs)** lost as a result of either premature death or years lived with disability" (Henderson, 1996, p. xiii). The design of this common metric is unique in its inclusion of both physical and mental illnesses, as psychiatric disability has been a low priority in the international disability discourse (WHO, 2010a; Levers et al., 2019). This landmark study has offered a foundation for comparative and aggregate transnational research efforts.

Beginning with Murray and Lopez (1996), the emerging literature has presented a fuller and more comprehensive picture of globally significant epidemiological disability and rehabilitation issues. More recent analyses have focused on assessment of disease and injury risks (Erickson et al., 2021; Jesus et al., 2020; Lee et al., 2018; Leroi et al., 2021; Murray et al., 2015; Pettinicchio & Maroto, 2021; Soerjomataram et al., 2012) as well as behavioral, intellectual, environmental, occupational, and metabolic risks (Opoku et al., 2021). Additionally, Murray et al. (2015) built upon international studies that have explored the relationship between QOL and self-determination and quantified what they have termed an epidemiological transition. They analyzed data for global, regional, and national DALYs for 306 diseases and injuries, including healthy life expectancy for 188 countries. Prüss-Üstün and colleagues (2016) assessment of global disease illuminated ways for improving the environment, and thus for promoting health and well-being.

Evidentiary Concerns

The WHO and the World Bank published a pioneering text, the WHO (2011a), responding to the reality that there had been "no global document that compiles and analyses [*sic*] the way countries have developed policies and the responses to address the needs of people with disabilities" (WHO, n.d.; I. Background and justification magnitude, para. 3). The conception for the project was an outcome of the World Health Assembly's Resolution 58.23, of May 2005, regarding the provision *Disability, including prevention, management and rehabilitation* to "produce a World report on disability based on the best available scientific evidence" (WHO, n.d., I. Background and justification magnitude, para. 3). For the first time, a report became available to the public that comprehensively outlined the evidence-based information regarding disability issues from an international perspective.

WHO (2011a) was organized to convey the following key messages: (a) Full and effective participation and inclusion of persons with disabilities in society is essential and within reach; (b) disability is a human rights issue; (c) poverty is a cause and effect of disability; (d) disability affects entire families; (e) disability is an economic development issue (particularly in low-resource countries); (f) disability is likely to affect most people at some time in their lives; (g) disability is a continuum of experience that varies across the life span; (h) disability is difficult to define, as it is varied, multidimensional, cross-cutting, and complex; (i) primary prevention must be balanced with respect for the integrity of people with disabilities; (j) (re)habilitation is important; and (k) evidence on what works is presented, it must be used, and much remains to be done (WHO, 2007, Box 10.1: Key messages). The report was made available to the public at an official launch on June 9, 2011 (WHO, 2011b).

Contextual Factors

Gross inequalities in health care exist among the nations of the world (Banks et al., 2018; Marmot et al., 2012; Mpofu et al., 2018). The reality of so many people with disabilities living in poverty throughout the world underscores the numerous avoidable health inequities. The notion of *social determinants of health* is an internationally accepted public health concept (Marmot et al., 2012). The WHO's Commission on Social Determinants of Health (CSDH) has identified many contextual factors as social determinants of health. The CSDH has advanced the following three overarching recommendations and aligned principles of action:

(1) improving the conditions of daily life; (2) addressing inequity; and (3) using a relevant monitoring and evaluation framework (CSDH, 2008, p. 2). The work of the CSDH has informed the discourse on social determinants of health and health inequities, advocating for less focus on individual behavioral change and greater emphasis on nurturing the conditions for health and well-being (Baum & Fisher, 2010; Levers et al., 2007).

Culture

Nurturing the social conditions that promote health and well-being has everything to do with culture. As noted by Mpofu and Harley (2002), "conceptions of disability vary widely across societies, and are influenced by the unique sociopolitical and cultural histories of those societies" (p, 26). Yet the biomedical model of disability and rehabilitation historically has ignored the relevance of local culture in general, and on an international scale, the importance of indigenous knowledge in particular. In terms of cultural understanding, rehabilitation counselor education programs have begun to address this through a greater emphasis on including multicultural and diversity issues in the curriculum. In terms of the importance of acknowledging Indigenous knowledge, researchers and scholars have begun to examine disability issues within their relevant cultural frameworks (e.g., Levers, 2006; Levers & Maki, 1994, 1995; Levers et al., 2019; Mpofu & Harley, 2002; Radomsky & Levers, 2012).

Indigenous Knowledge and Ethnorehabilitation

In their inquiry into African traditional healing and Indigenous knowledge, Levers and Maki (1994) proposed the consideration for advancing the concept of

ethnorehabilitation and advocated for its further examination by defining it as an "eco-systemic, praxeological construct which acknowledges the comprehensive nature of persons with disabilities through functional relationship to their respective cultures . . . [in] interaction with their environments" (p. 86). The study illuminated this view as one that "simultaneously permits a holistic and ecologic perspective which is vertically attentive to the spiritual dimensions of the person and horizontally reflective of the environmental dialectic" (Levers & Maki, 1994, p. 86). Levers and Maki also indicated that it is only when ethical respect is paid to the person that this perspective can be measured, and the result is a philosophy of empowerment. Most people with disabilities live in low-resource areas of the world, thereby necessitating reliance on Indigenous knowledge systems and traditional healing practices, an issue largely ignored by the Western, biomedically oriented community (Levers, 2006; Levers et al., 2009, 2019; Radomsky & Levers, 2012).

Emerging Trends in the International Literature

A number of global trends have emerged in the disability and rehabilitation literature. The most salient are highlighted and discussed in the following subsections: (a) poverty; (b) trauma, crisis, and disaster; (c) HIV and AIDS; (d) COVID-19; (e) psychosocial issues across the life span; and (f) international economic development.

Poverty

Social protection systems differ greatly in high-resource (developed) versus low-resource (developing) countries. This has led to numerous avoidable health and other life inequities. The association between poverty and disability is complex (Grech, 2016; Handicap International, 2014; Levers et al., 2007, 2008, 2010; Mpofu et al., 2018; WHO, 2011a), as are the data that are linked to this intricate situation (Banks et al., 2018).

Approximately 15% of the world's population has some form of disability, and the vast majority of all people with disabilities live in low- or middle-income countries (Banks et al., 2018; UN, 2011; WHO, 2011a; WHO, 2016). At least 20% (1 in 5) of the very poorest people, who are living in developing countries, have a disability (WHO, 2011a). According to the World Bank (as cited in Laurin-Bowie, 2005), about 43% of the people globally, who are living on less than $1.00 per day, have a disability. The UN review of disability and MDGs has emphasized that, worldwide, the most pertinent matter facing people living with disabilities is not the disability itself, "but rather their lack of equitable access to resources such as education, employment, health care and the social and legal support systems, resulting in persons with disabilities having disproportionately high rates of poverty" (UN, 2011, p. vii).

Social systems often overlook people with disabilities, and yet current thinking suggests that it is preferable, more efficient, more cost-effective, and less stigmatizing to include people with disabilities in mainstream programs from the onset (Banks et al., 2018; UN, 2011). In addition, social and economic exclusion typically does not affect the individual alone; rather, it results in high economic dependency on family members and relatives. People living with disabilities face enormous barriers to obtaining equitable services and opportunities. This phenomenon is due primarily to a combination of stigma, ignorance, discrimination, exclusion, and inaccessible environments. The ways in which poverty and disability interface with and reinforce one another not only negate the rights of people with disabilities, but they also perpetuate vulnerability and advance the vicious cycle of poverty (Banks et al., 2018; Handicap International, 2014).

Trauma, Crisis, and Disaster

Although global and regional statistics regarding injury-specific causes of disability are not available, by extrapolating data from various countries, the WHO (2016) suggested that up to 25% of disabilities are the result of injuries and violence. A UNICEF (n.d) fact sheet states that "persons with disabilities are more likely to be victims of violence or rape, according to a 2004 British study, and less likely to obtain police intervention, legal protection or preventive care" (Violence, para. 3). Traumatic experiences can affect individuals and communities, in profound ways, across the life span (Levers, 2020, Levers, 2022), including people with disabilities (Johnson & Tarvydas, 2022; Mpofu et al., 2022). A few ways that such trauma may manifest, and constitute some of the emerging issues in the disability literature, are war, anthropogenic climate change, and migration.

War

In warfare, three children are injured and permanently disabled for every one child killed (UNICEF, n.d.). Research further indicates that the annual rate of violence against children with disabilities is at least 1.7 times greater than for their peers who are not disabled (UNICEF, n.d.). Mpofu et al. (2022) have emphasized the lack of inclusion concerning people with disabilities and disability issues in trauma-response efforts, particularly situations of armed conflict, disasters, and other emergencies. They also have pointed to the fact that local DPOs are seldom included in the planning and coordination of crisis or disaster responses. This is echoed by Tarvydas et al. (2017, 2018), and Teahen et al. (2017). Johnson and Tarvydas (2022) further have suggested best ethical practices related to people with disabilities in trauma, crisis, and disaster situations.

Anthropogenic Climate Change

Human-caused changes in the Earth's climate are having an impact on the entire planet, causing both human-made and natural disasters. In this sense, people with disabilities may be particularly vulnerable to both physiological risks and psychosocial challenges (e.g., Boikanyo & Levers, 2017; Levers & Drozda, 2018, 2022; Prüss-Ustün et al., 2016) associated with climate change. Teahen et al. (2017) have identified disability-related disaster and climate-change issues regarding public health demands and the need for building social-ecological resilience.

Migration

Both war and climate change have effected an increase in global migration. Refugees are arriving at new locations daily, many sustaining injury during dangerous treks in an attempt to leave war, poverty, famine, and drought behind. The literature points to the urgency of addressing immigrant and refugee health issues (e.g., Levers et al., 2015; Levers & Drozda, 2018, 2022). The children of undocumented immigrant parents also constitute a vulnerable population, with the potential for experiencing both traumatizing and disabling conditions (Levers & Mancilla, 2013).

HIV and AIDS

The United Nations Programme on HIV/AIDS (UNAIDS, 2021) reported that approximately 37.7 million people worldwide were living with HIV and AIDS in 2020. The AIDS pandemic has strained fragile healthcare systems throughout the world. Although there are resources available to respond to the AIDS pandemic, they have been woefully inadequate to meet public health needs. Data from the UNDP (2010) have indicated that healthcare delivery has improved in many nations; in fact, (UNAIDS, 2021, AIDS-related deaths, para. 1) reported that "AIDS-related deaths have been reduced by 64% since the peak in 2004 and by 47% since 2010." However, various sources have detailed the disabling effects of HIV and AIDS on the lives of people who contract the virus (e.g., Avert, 2020; UNAIDS, 2021). Researchers at Yale University and the World Bank (Groce, 2004) conducted a Global Disability Survey to assess the impact further. The most salient issue to report here regards the risk of HIV infection for people with disabilities and the reality that they largely have been ignored by prevention and care services (Levers et al., 2010). In addition, individuals with HIV and AIDS are at greater risk of developing more severe illnesses and comorbidities if exposed to COVID-19 (UNAIDS), which certainly has disability-related implications.

The prevalence of HIV and AIDS among people with disabilities is equal to or higher than that among the rest of the population, yet they are largely excluded from HIV and AIDS services (Avert, 2020; WHO, 2011a). Groce (2004) has captured the essence of the problem by noting that while research has identified disabling aspects of HIV and AIDS, little has been gleaned regarding the risk of HIV and AIDS for people with disabilities. It appears that people with disabilities generally have not been included in outreach efforts due to the stereotype that they are not sexually active, and therefore not at risk (Avert, 2020; Groce, 2004). This fact has obvious and dire implications, and Handicap International, 2014 has strongly advocated the inclusion of disability in HIV policy and programming on the international stage. Finally, children and youth with disabilities, who also are affected by HIV and AIDS, may face additional challenges (Maundeni et al., 2017).

COVID-19

The WHO declared the outbreak of COVID-19 a pandemic in March 2020, due to the overwhelming number of new cases reported worldwide (WHO, 2020b). As of February 2022, over 410 million cases were confirmed across six continents and nearly 6 million deaths had been reported worldwide (WHO, 2022). COVID-19 has caused acute respiratory disease and serious health complications among individuals worldwide and has rattled healthcare systems, education, businesses, and individuals globally. In addition to those who were directly impacted by this infectious disease, billions of people were indirectly affected due to disruption to daily life, social isolation, financial challenges, loss of employment, economic recession, and health and safety concerns, leading to heightened stressors and worsening well-being (Achdut & Refaeli, 2020; Huang et al., 2020; Wang et al., 2020). Furthermore, social-distancing and stay-at-home orders led to devastating economic impacts around the world, resulting in large numbers of businesses closing or declaring bankruptcy and high rates of furlough and unemployment (Fernandes, 2020).

While COVID-19 has affected everyone, its impacts on individuals with disabilities have been particularly harsh. Individuals with disabilities face the same issues experienced by the public—social isolation, health concerns, and heightened stressors—but are also at greater risk of experiencing economic inequities and job loss due to the restrictions in place to slow the spread of the virus (Berger et al., 2020; Perera et al., 2020). Along with the economic threats to persons with disabilities during pandemics of infectious diseases like COVID-19, the financial toll of the pandemic on rehabilitation agencies and state budgets further reduces the likelihood that individuals with disabilities will have access to already insufficient resources, specialized employment, healthcare services, and other specialized supports (Navas et al., 2020; Sakellariou et al., 2020). For instance, a lack of internet access and technology literacy are significant barriers to telehealth support services and remote work prospects for individuals with disabilities (Gleason et al., 2020; Schur et al., 2020).

Psychosocial Trends Across the Life Span

Psychosocial issues, both related and not related to disability, have an impact across the life span. These are discussed briefly, from a global perspective, in the following subsections.

Gender

In many developing countries, females report higher incidences of disability than males (UNICEF, n.d.). In addition, females with disabilities typically experience stigmatization on multiple levels; that is, exclusion due to both gender and disability. Women and girls are particularly vulnerable to maltreatment and abuse. According to the UNICEF fact sheet, a 2004 survey in India "found that virtually all of the women and girls with disabilities were beaten at home, 25% of women with intellectual disabilities had been raped and 6% of disabled women had been forcibly sterilized" (UNICEF, n.d, Overview, para. 9). These findings have been consistent with assessments carried out in other developing countries (e.g., Levers et al., 2008, 2010; Mukamana et al., 2019). Office on Women's Health (2015) cited research suggesting that "women with disabilities are more likely to suffer domestic violence and sexual assault than women without disabilities. And women with disabilities report abuse that lasts longer and is more intense than women without disabilities" (para. 1). Gender-related rites of passage across the life span, such as dating, courtship, marriage, and childbirth, may pose additional challenges for both male and female people with disabilities. Additionally, people with disabilities coming out as gay or transitioning genders may face added layers of gender bias.

Race and Ethnicity

Data from the 2019 American Community Survey found that within racial and ethnic groups, African Americans and non-Hispanic Whites have some of the highest percentages of people with disabilities (each group at 14%), followed by Latinos (9%) and Asian Americans (7%; U.S. Census Bureau, 2019). Different cultural, religious and underrepresented groups may attribute different causes and meanings to disability and emphasize different coping strategies. The **intersectionality** of poverty, disability, and multiple minoritized identities (e.g., race, ethnicity) is well documented (McAlpine & Alang, 2021). The different cultures among various racial and ethnic groups may influence the ways in which groups seek help as well as the help-seeking behaviors of individuals with disabilities. Belgrave et al. (2019) offered an excellent discussion of the intersections of culture, race, and disability with clear implications for psychological practice. Although they may not apply to every individual, attributions of blame for disability may be generally relevant in some cultures but not others, and an emphasis on beliefs also may impact coping strategies (e.g., religion among Blacks; family among Hispanics; Belgrave et al.). Similarly, disability-related concepts such as independent living may vary or not apply to different groups (Bryan, 2007). When societal preconceptions, beliefs, and emotional reactions toward persons with disabilities are carefully examined, an awareness emerges of existing implicit biases that contribute to negative views of people with disabilities. In turn, such biases also may be compounded by potential intersections of poverty, disabilities, and multiple minoritized identities (Rynders, 2019).

In relation to the COVID-19 pandemic, ethnic minorities, as well as individuals with disabilities, were overly represented in the lives lost due to COVID-19. For instance, building on the National Disability Institute (NDI) report, *Financial Inequality: Disability, Race and Poverty in America* (Goodman et al., 2017), updated research on the financial conditions of individuals, grouped by disability status and racial/ethnic identity, reflects that individuals who live at this intersection of race and disability experience disproportionate levels of financial distress. In addition, the poverty rate for White Americans without a disability, based on 2021 U.S. Census data, is 9%, while the poverty rate for White Americans with a disability is 24%, and for Black Americans with a disability, 36% (Erickson et al., 2021). For most individuals, discrimination based on race and disability significantly affects their lives. Thus, BIPOC (Black, Indigenous, People of Color) Americans with disabilities face unique systemic challenges as a result of intersecting identities.

Children and Youth

Although comparative studies of childhood disabilities exist (e.g., Gottlieb et al., 2009; WHO, CDC, ICBDSR, 2014), they tend to focus on a cluster of countries, a region, or a single nation (e.g., Christoffersen, 2019), thus offering little comparative information, of a comprehensive nature, regarding childhood disability issues. The importance of early screening of children for disabilities cannot be overstated. Congenital anomalies, or birth defects, have a wide range of causes globally. WHO, CDC, ICBDSR (2014) have called for prevention approaches related to sexually transmitted infections, vaccinations, legislation management involving toxic chemicals, and fortification of staple foods.

ProChild (2020) asserted that children living with disabilities are more likely to experience violence, thereby necessitating greater focus on developing legal and policy frameworks, at national and international levels, to prevent such abuse of human rights. According to the United Kingdom's Department for International Development, "mortality for children with disabilities may be as high as 80% in countries where under-five mortality as a whole has decreased below 20% . . . [and] in some cases it seems as if children are being 'weeded out'" (cited in UNICEF, n.d., Overview, para. 11). Such apprehension begs the question of disability-related infanticide. Although a full discussion of this complex issue is beyond the scope of this chapter, in a UNICEF-sponsored report on violence against children with disabilities, Groce and Paeglow (2005) have asserted that infanticide (done immediately or soon after birth) and "mercy killings" (done at a later time after birth, sometimes years later) continue to be global manifestations of violence against children with disabilities. As with information regarding other childhood disability issues, there is little comprehensive data concerning infanticide on an international level. UNICEF has taken on a key role in promoting the rights of children with disabilities on an international scale.

Education

In a report funded by the Global Partnership for Education and the World Bank, Male and Wodon (2017) note that, "Children with disabilities are especially at a disadvantage in terms of school enrollment, educational attainment, and learning" (Background, para. 2). According to UNESCO, about 98% of children living with disabilities in developing countries do not attend school (cited in ILO, 2007, 2021), and approximately 30% of street youths are disabled (UNICEF, n.d.). In a more recent global monitoring report, the United Nations Educational, Scientific and Cultural Organization (UNESCO, 2020) states that fewer than 10% of all countries, globally, ensure full inclusion in education through national legal or policy frameworks. A UNICEF fact sheet reports that in some developing countries, disability rates are significantly higher among groups with lower educational levels, and that, "on average, 19% of less educated people have disabilities, compared to 11% among the better educated" (UNICEF, n.d., Overview, para. 5). Based on a 1998 UNDP study (cited in UNICEF, n.d., Education, para. 2), UNICEF reported that "the global literacy rate for adults with disabilities is as low as 3%, and 1% for women with disabilities." Assessment (Gottlieb et al., 2009), early intervention (Gottlieb et al., 2009), and access to assistive technology (Borg et al., 2009) are linked with the issue of education and disability. Studies continue to emerge regarding the inclusion of children with intellectual disabilities (e.g., Schalock et al., 2011), with an emphasis on their educational processes. Finally, a recent U.S.-based study has shown that accommodations as simple as course and test adjustments, like extension of time and modification of materials, had a significant positive influence on college students with disabilities (Kim & Lee, 2016).

Work

According to the International Labour Organization (ILO, 2021), about 80% of the world's estimated 1 billion people living with a disability are of working age, yet many are not able to achieve gainful employment. People with disabilities face higher unemployment rates and lower earnings than people without disabilities; they often are excluded and marginalized, being particularly vulnerable during times of economic crisis (ILO, 2021). Although automation is a swiftly emergent phenomenon, in a review of academic literature and popular print media, Wolbring (2016) could not identify a single article that "thematized the potential negative impact of robots on the employability situation of disabled people or the relationship of disabled people and robots as co-workers." Unemployment rates vary among the types of disabilities; the highest rates tend to exist among those people having psychiatric disabilities (ILO, 2007). Men with disabilities are nearly twice as likely as women with disabilities to have gainful employment (ILO, 2007).

If work conditions are conducive, supportive, and adaptive, people with disabilities have proved that they can contribute and produce at all levels (ILO, 2007, 2021). Yet a prevalent bias is that workers with disabilities cost employers extra money, when in reality their exclusion from the workplace "deprives societies of an estimated $1.37 to 1.94 trillion in annual loss in GDP" (ILO, 2007, para. 1). Assistive technology clearly has implications in this arena (Borg et al., 2009), and greater access is needed. Some of the international donor organizations and NGOs have begun to implement income-generation projects among people with disabilities, but real employment opportunities in the governmental and private sectors have been slow to emerge.

Aging

A number of contemporary issues face aging populations around the world, and this has implications both for older adults with disabilities and for RCs (Mpofu et al., 2022). The most recent edition (26th) of the *World Population Prospects* notes the unprecedented aging of international populations as a key finding—in fact, for the first time in history, in 2018, people aged 65 and older outnumbered children younger than 5 years of age (United Nations, Department of Economic and Social Affairs, Population Division, 2019). According to the WHO (2011a), in higher resource countries where life expectancies are over age 70, people spend an average of about 8 years, or 11.5% of the life span, living with disabilities. Regardless of the geopolitical advantages of living in a high- versus low-resource country, most people surviving to an older age are likely to experience increasing disability in their elder years (Cieza et al., 2020; Mpofu et al., 2022). Sousa et al. (2009) have noted, for example, the increase of dementia and the contribution of other chronic diseases to disability in elderly people in both low- and middle-income countries. Studies have suggested an association between the impact of metabolic syndrome on aging adults and an increase in disability (Liaw et al., 2016). The risk of death, due to the effects of COVID-19, has been greater for older adults, and for those who have survived the virus, serious disease and long-term impairments are more likely (Servick, 2020).

Economic Development

According to WHO (2011a, p. 10), "disability is a development issue, because of its bidirectional link to poverty: disability may increase the risk of poverty, and poverty may increase the risk of disability." Officer and Groce (2009, p. 1795) assert that "[d]isability is a neglected development issue," and that people with disabilities, for the most part, have not benefited from international economic development efforts. As indicated earlier in this chapter, people with disabilities disproportionately are underrepresented in the development arena, universally, and this fact has a direct relationship to their poverty levels; they also tend to be poorer than people without disabilities (Banks et al., 2018; Mpofu et al., 2018). The need continues for the advocacy of policies for greater inclusion of people with disabilities in international development efforts.

USEFUL REHABILITATION COUNSELING PRACTICES

Trends in the international disability and rehabilitation literatures have raised many important issues, concerns, and challenges. As noted previously in this chapter, existing data are not sufficient, and the need for more research related to disability and rehabilitation interventions in an international context is great; therefore, it is difficult to identify *best practices* in the sense that usually is intended in the behavioral and social sciences. However, in terms of the salient issues that have emerged from the relevant international literatures, it is possible to identify several *useful practices* that have real implications for RCs. The following useful practices are discussed: (a) rights-based approach, (b) antiracism, (c) CBR, (d) professional training, (e) web-resource access, and (f) research.

Rights-Based Approach

The rights-based approach fortunately has replaced the charity model. The CSDH has emphasized the relevance of Article 25(a) of the UN *Universal Declaration on Human Rights* (UN, 1948, cited in CSDH, 2008, p. 84), by focusing on each individual's "right to a standard of living adequate for the health and well-being of himself and of his family." The declaration further asserts that these rights include "food, clothing, housing and medical care and necessary social services, and the right to security in the event of unemployment, sickness, disability, widowhood, old age or other lack of livelihood in circumstances beyond his control" (p. 84).

The core principles of the UN's CRPD include respect for all aspects of human dignity and participation; rights related to equal access to healthcare are found in separate disability- and rehabilitation-related articles. Additional articles of the CRPD deal with the special needs of women and of children with disabilities, as well as with issues of accessibility, mobility, and the responsibilities of the professionals providing care to people with disabilities, among others. To date, some 167 nation-states have signed on to the CRPD (UN, 2016), but the work related to advocating for human rights continues.

Clearly, in the international arena, disability is viewed as an issue of human rights and social justice. Although this obviously is significant, rights alone do not provide the immediate solution to problems of poverty such as lack of food, shelter, and employment. A tension exists between *human rights* in idealist abstraction, and *human rights* in terms of the pragmatic and concrete reality of everyday needs. This tension is articulated by people with disabilities the world over. Social justice must inform the discourse, and social justice *action* must mediate the results related to fully realizing the rights-based approach. For example, although social justice advocacy for equity is essential, people with disabilities and DPOs assert that it must be followed by action that leads to ensuring that concrete needs are met, like food and shelter. As noted earlier in this chapter, some African consumers of rehabilitation services have clearly echoed this sentiment: "We do not eat rights" (Levers et al., 2010, p. 119).

Antiracism

Individuals who experience racism in addition to ableism may experience a compounded form of oppression not often considered in designing clinical practices (Nario-Redmond et al., 2019). Disparities may result from a complex interaction of socioeconomic and demographic characteristics as well as from the intersection of such compounded oppression. To work effectively with clients with disabilities, professionals should consider how a client's disability-related issues interact with other cultural and social identities and experiences as well as the potential combined effects of ableism and racism on the individual's well-being. It is important to keep in mind how these factors may intersect with each other as well as create complex relationships in understanding the individual's experience of disparities. As an extension of the earlier discussion regarding a rights-based approach and social justice, educational programs and professional associations need to take strong advocacy positions concerning the adaptation of antiracist attitudes and strategies.

People living with disabilities already deal with numerous environmental barriers. The intersectionality of multiple discriminatory factors, like disability-associated stigma and racial bias, can be overwhelming. In order to take the next step forward, it is important for the professionals to be allies with the disability community and fully engage in a process to move from words into action, in order to address the racism and bias that exists within the disability community. Strategies and approaches to take include, but are not limited to, supporting the advocacy efforts of BIPOC individuals with disabilities; increasing the active training, recruitment, hiring, promotion, and retention of diverse professionals in ways that reflect the diversity of the clients served; ensuring that diversity, equity, and inclusion policies are explicitly stated and included in organization policy, practices, and procedures; identifying and creating spaces to amplify these intersectional disability voices throughout the mainstream community; reaching out to organizations serving racial/ethnic minority communities to gather input and perspectives; and building relationships based on trust, consistency, and accountability with marginalized individuals and groups (FitzGerald & Hurst, 2017).

Lately, professional associations have spoken more about disability, race, and intersectionality than ever before. It is important for us to work actively to promote an understanding of intersectionality and to elevate the voices of BIPOC with disabilities. For instance, in 2021, the APA Council of Representatives passed the Resolution on Harnessing Psychology to Combat Racism: Adopting a Uniform Definition and Understanding, the Role of Psychology and APA in Dismantling Systemic Racism Against People of Color in the U.S., and an Apology to People of Color for APA's Role in Promoting, Perpetuating, and Failing to Challenge Racism, Racial Discrimination, and Human Hierarchy in the U.S.

Community-Based Rehabilitation

First introduced by the WHO in the late 1970s, **community-based rehabilitation** (CBR) has been influenced and strengthened by people with disabilities and DPOs as it has developed over the last several decades (Mpofu et al., 2018). According to the WHO (2010a), para. 1), CBR "has evolved to become a multi-sectoral strategy that empowers persons with disabilities to access and benefit from education, employment, health and social services." Its scope has broadened significantly over the past 30 years, with an increased readiness of CBROs to implement CBR (Mpofu et al., 2020; WHO, 2010b).

Much more than an intervention, CBR is a system of care and service delivery that has involved all relevant stakeholders in the community, including people with disabilities and their families. Regarded as a general strategy for community development of rehabilitation, CBR has positively affected social inclusion of people with disabilities as well as equalized opportunities (Mpofu, 2015). Research has shown that participation in CBR programs can have a positive impact on people with disability (Biggeri et al., 2014). The major aims of CBR have included enhancing the QOL for people with disabilities and their families and ensuring that basic needs are met in the least restrictive environment (Mpofu et al., 2015). As noted by Hartley et al. (2009), CBR's goals are to "support access to regular services and opportunities and assist people with disabilities to actively contribute to their own communities as well as encouraging communities to promote and respect their human rights" (p. 1803). Because any person living with a disability may have experienced trauma at any point across the lifespan, an essential contemporary practice issue is the incorporation of a trauma-informed perspective into all community-based services (Levers, 2020; Levers, 2022; Mpofu et al., 2020).

The WHO (2010b) has published guidelines for CBR, including a matrix that covers the five components of health, education, livelihood, social dimension, and empowerment. The information is presented in seven separate booklets, all of which are available online. The seven booklets include an introduction, examinations of the five components, and a supplementary booklet that focuses on specific issues that have been overlooked, to date, in most CBR programs (i.e., mental health, HIV and AIDS, leprosy, humanitarian crises). Hartley et al. (2009) reported that the WHO guidelines and matrix also reflect critiques of CBR and are aimed at improving the implementation and efficacy of CBR. Although more rigorous research needs to be conducted in this area, CBR shows great promise, especially as it relates to efficacy, and is associated with positive social outcomes.

Professional Training

Based on the global burden of disease, the need for rehabilitation is far greater than the services that are available (Servick, 2020). This dilemma has educational implications as well as the obvious economic dimensions. The preservice training of RCs and other rehabilitation personnel is critical to an enhanced understanding of disability and rehabilitation issues in a global context, and a number of examples can be found in the literature. Alsaman (2014) has examined the efficacy of educating international RCs and ways that university-based programs can contribute to and enhance the advocacy of disability-related training globally. Astramovich and Pehrsson (2009) have promoted the advancement of counselor education, in general, as a means for fostering international perspectives. Stein et al. (2009) have suggested that disability be included with other diversity issues in training programs. Borgen et al. (2021) have suggested that diversity and social justice competencies are imperative in training rehabilitation counselors to meet the demands of globalized understandings of disability.

Some academics have espoused the utility of international exchanges of rehabilitation scholars (e.g., Fabian & Madsen, 2007) and cross-cultural field exchanges for rehabilitation students (e.g., Luecking et al., 2007) as mechanisms for training RCs about the importance of global context. Tingey et al. (2007) have recommended a **communities-of-practice** approach to training RCs; *communities of practice* is a term that has been borrowed from social learning theory which, as used here, refers to building an evidence-based theory of shared knowledge and practice among RCs. Advancing quality preservice and in-service training for rehabilitation personnel is an essential practice and is important in enhancing service delivery for and with people with disabilities throughout the world.

Web-Resource Access

A UNICEF publication (n.d., Overview, para. 13) noted that in the United Kingdom, "75% of the companies of the FTSE 100 Index on the London Stock Exchange do not meet basic levels of web accessibility, thus missing out on more than $147 million in revenue." Web accessibility for people with disabilities has continued to be a growing concern . The W3C Web Accessibility Initiative ([W3C WAI], 2021) has offered strategies, guidelines, and resources to make the web accessible to people with disabilities, emphasizing universal access for everyone. W3C WAI provides links for numerous resources, as well as identifying success criteria.

Research

The unmet health and rehabilitation needs of people with disabilities worldwide are open for inquiry (Cieza et al., 2020). For example, Stein et al. (2009, p. 1797) suggested that more "research is required on how disability affects relative access to health care and medical outcomes." Salvador-Carulla and Saxena (2009) have identified a research gap between intellectual disability and other neuropsychiatric disorders. Although publications such as the *ICF* (WHO, 2001), *The Global Burden of Disease* (Murray & Lopez, 1996), and the *World Report on Disability* (WHO, 2011a) make the need for robust epidemiological and statistical analyses obvious, Hanley-Maxwell et al. (2007), Levers (2001), Levers and Maki (1994, 1995), and McNeil (2019) have suggested that qualitative and ethnographic understandings of the lived experiences of people with disabilities and in-depth examinations of disability-related phenomena also are essential in the global context of rehabilitation. Community-based research with indigenous populations with disabilities, such as with Native American Indians or with indigenous practitioners such as African traditional healers, can yield important information that informs the cross-cultural discourse (Levers et al., 2019). Because accurate information about the health patterns of people with disabilities is inadequate, and in light of the scarcity of resources, disability-related research should be prioritized systematically and involve relevant stakeholders. The National Disability Authority (2009) offers ethical guidance for research with people with disabilities, in accordance with the ethical principles involving any research with human subjects. Good (2020) has outlined more recent knowledge regarding the ethical conduct of research related to disability.

CONCLUSION

This chapter has introduced germane disability and rehabilitation issues in a global context. Those topics that have been emphasized include definitions of disability, the scope of rehabilitation counseling in an international context, theoretical perspectives on disability, the role of RCs, the international disability and rehabilitation literatures, and useful practices. A number of available, recently published, and soon-to-be-published resources has been identified concerning disability and rehabilitation in an international context. Several reflection activities have been suggested in Box 10.1 to assist in developing insight about the important disability-in-global-context issues that have been raised throughout this chapter.

A dearth of evidence concerning global disability and rehabilitation issues exists and only begins to intersect with the lived experiences and paramount needs of people with disabilities. There is a great deal of work yet to be done at the international level, which calls for our attention. Several pertinent recommendations can be derived from this discussion; it is hoped that RCs, educators, and researchers might take these topics under consideration for future action in reference to international disability issues.

First, the issue of advocacy merits further consideration. RCs can advocate for improvements for people with disabilities in terms of infrastructural access, access to services, and, especially in the 21st century, access to electronic resources. RCs can advocate for continual reinforcement of the rights-based approach, for poverty mitigation efforts, for antiracism, for gender equity, and for expanded global ways of applying the ecological model. RCs are positioned to advocate for greater professionalization opportunities within the field, especially related to preservice and in-service training while at the same

BOX 10.1 REFLECTION ACTIVITIES

1. The literature indicates that approximately 80% of all people with disabilities reside in low-resource countries. Identify some of the intersections between poverty and living with a disability. How does poverty affect the lives of people with disabilities? How do the poverty-related challenges of clients affect your ability to provide rehabilitation counseling services?
2. Review the importance of the WHO's (2001) *International Classification of Functioning, Disability and Health* (ICF) model. How is it relevant, in an international landscape, that the refined definitions of disability reflect a biopsychosocial or ecological model? How does the ICF model thereby engender greater personal and international utility and applicability?
3. How might the role of rehabilitation counselors, based in North America, differ from the role of parallel workers in other parts of the world? What role similarities exist?
4. Reflect on the gross inequalities in healthcare that exist across the nations of the world. What barriers do healthcare inequities present to rehabilitation counselors working in an international context, especially in low-resource countries?

time understanding that Indigenous knowledge systems may offer culturally relevant sources of information and voices of knowledge as well.

Second, the number of people with disabilities is growing worldwide, in both low- and high-resource countries. Issues such as poverty, pandemics such as COVID-19 and HIV and AIDS, conditions such as psychiatric disabilities, and life-span situations, such as aging, along with circumstances involving trauma, crises, and disasters, have a global impact on programming aimed at improving the lives of people with disabilities, and at mitigating the negative impact of barriers. RCs have the expertise to construct new ways of building capacity so that relevant rehabilitation services are available to all who need them.

Third, the importance of disability- and rehabilitation-related training beyond the industrialized West cannot be emphasized enough. A number of evaluations have reported the lack of basic training in developing countries, along with a hunger for more education among the people working in such rehabilitation settings (e.g., Levers & Maki, 1994, 1995; Levers et al., 2007, 2008, 2010). RCs in high-resource countries need to find ways to share instructional resources with and construct training opportunities for colleagues in low-resource countries (Alsaman, 2014; Borgen et al., 2021). RCs can support related endeavors through service learning, advocacy projects, community-engaged scholarship, volunteerism, and grant-seeking activities.

Finally, the paucity of research related to international disability and rehabilitation issues illuminates the need for inquiry that is pertinent to the lives of people with disabilities and the systems that serve them. RCs have a wide-open field for identifying important issues and pursuing research agendas that can contribute to the expansion of our thinking about and our increased understandings of related global issues.

In summary, little has been written about international disability issues from a comprehensive and synthesis-oriented perspective. However, we know that a number of avoidable inequities continue to have deleterious effects on the lives of children and adults living with disabilities. RCs, in all of our international and cultural permutations, have the opportunity and the responsibility to assist people with disabilities to empower themselves. We also have the opportunity and the responsibility to contribute to the international knowledge base in ways that continue to close the disability-related gaps—gaps in knowledge, practice, service delivery, social justice, and equity—in the global context.

CONTENT REVIEW QUESTIONS

1. How do culture, race, and ethnicity play roles in understanding disability issues on an international scale?
2. How does the *ICF* model of rehabilitation differ from the more traditional medical model? Why is this significant?
3. In what ways does the role of the RC enhance opportunities for people with disabilities globally, and in what ways can RCs serve in an advocacy capacity for global disability concerns? Why does this matter?
4. What roles do international organizations such as the WHO and the UN play in advancing progress, concerning disability issues, throughout the world? Why is this important?
5. In what ways does a more ecologically oriented model of rehabilitation universally support the rights-based approach and the CBR approach? How does this relate to equity, social justice, and anti-racism?
6. What kinds of training experiences can help to prepare RCs for international work?

REFERENCES

Achdut, N., & Refaeli, T. (2020). Unemployment and psychological distress among young people during the COVID-19 pandemic: Psychological resources and risk factors. *International Journal of Environmental Research and Public Health, 17*(19), 7163. https://doi.org/10.3390/ijerph17197163

Ackerman, C. E. (2021, 15 February). Self-determination theory of motivation. Positive Psychology. https://positivepsychology.com/self-determination-theory/

Agency for Healthcare Research and Quality. (2019). *2019 national healthcare quality and disparities report.* https://www.ahrq.gov/research/findings/nhqrdr/nhqdr19/index.html

Alsaman, M. A. (2014). Effectiveness of Training for International Rehabilitation Counseling Graduates. *Rehabilitation Research, Policy, and Education, 28*(2), 66–79. https://doi.org/10.1891/2168-6653.28.2.66

Astramovich, R. L., & Pehrsson, D-E. (2009). Advancing counselor education: Fostering international perspectives and open access scholarship. *Journal for International Counselor Education, 1,* 1–6. http://digitalcommons.library.unlv.edu/jice

Avert. (2020). *People with disabilities, HIV and AIDS.* https://www.avert.org/people-disabilities-hiv-and-aids

Babik, I., & Gardner, E. S. (2021). Factors affecting the perception of disability: A developmental perspective. *Frontiers in Psychology, 12,* 1–26. https://doi.org/10.3389/fpsyg.2021.702166

Banks, L. M., Kuper, H., & Polack, S. (2018). Correction: Poverty and disability in low- and middle-income countries: A systematic review. *PloS One, 13*(9), e0204881. https://doi.org/10.1371/journal.pone.0204881

Baum, F., & Fisher, M. (2010). Health equity and sustainability: extending the work of the Commission on the Social Determinants of Health. *Critical Public Health, 20*(3), 311–322. https://doi.org/10.1080/09581596.2010.503266

Belgrave, F. Z., Gary, K. W., & Johnson, K. R. (2019). Culture, race, and disability. In D. S. Dunn (Ed.), *Understanding the experience of disability: Perspectives from social and rehabilitation psychology.* (pp. 122–136). Oxford University Press.

Berger, Z. D., Evans, N. G., Phelan, A. L., & Silverman, R. D. (2020). Covid-19: control measures must be equitable and inclusive. *BMJ (Clinical Research Ed.), 368,* m1141. https://doi.org/10.1136/bmj.m1141

Biggeri, M., Deepak, S., Mauro, V., Trani, J.-F., Kumar, J., & Ramasamy, P. (2014). Do community-based rehabilitation programmes promote the participation of persons with disabilities? A case control study from Mandya District, in India. *Disability and Rehabilitation, 36*(18), 1508–1517. https://doi.org/10.3109/09638288.2013.823244

Boikanyo, M. N., & Levers, L. L. (2017). The effects of climate change on water insecurity in Botswana: Links to the criminal justice system. In G. Magill & K. Aramesh (Eds.), *The urgency of climate change: Pivotal perspectives* (pp. 434–449). Cambridge Scholars Publishing.

Borgen, W., Caverley, N., Robertson, S., & Patterson, P. (2021). Making the case for counsellor education accreditation in Canada: A cross-jurisdictional review of emerging trends in the pre-service training of counsellors and related mental health professionals. *Canadian Journal of Counselling and Psychotherapy, 55*(1), 74–95. https://doi.org/10.47634/cjcp.v55i1.70427

Borg, J., Lindström, A., & Larsson, S. (2009). Assistive technology in developing countries: national and international responsibilities to implement the Convention on the Rights of Persons with Disabilities. *Lancet, 374*(9704), 1863–1865. https://doi.org/10.1016/S0140-6736(09)61872-9

Bruyère, S. M., Van Looy, S. A., & Peterson, D. B. (2005). The International Classification of Functioning, Disability and Health: Contemporary Literature Overview. *Rehabilitation Psychology, 50*(2), 113–121. https://doi.org/10.1037/0090-5550.50.2.113

Bryan, W. V. (2007). Multicultural aspects of disabilities: A guide to understanding and assisting minorities in the rehabilitation process (2nd ed.). Charles C Thomas.

Centers for Disease Control and Prevention. (2020). *Disability inclusion. Disability and health promotion.* https://www.cdc.gov/ncbddd/disabilityandhealth/disability-inclusion.html

Christoffersen, M. N. (2019). Violent crime against children with disabilities: A nationwide prospective birth cohort-study. *Child Abuse & Neglect, 98*, 104150. https://doi.org/10.1016/j.chiabu.2019.104150

Cieza, A., Causey, K., Kamenov, K., Hanson, S. W., Chatterji, S., & Vos, T. (2020). Global estimates of the need for rehabilitation based on the Global Burden of Disease study 2019. Lancet, 396(10267), 2006–2017. https://doi.org/10.1016/S0140-6736(20)32340-0

Commission on Rehabilitation Counselor Certification. (2021). *What is a certified rehabilitation counselor?.* https://crccertification.com/crc-certification/

Commission on Social Determinants of Health. (2008). *Closing the gap in a generation: Health equity through action on the social determinants of health (Final Report of the Commission on Social Determinants of Health).* World Health Organization.

Commonwealth Fund. (2020, January). *U.S. health care from a global perspective, 2019: Higher spending, worse outcomes?.* https://www.commonwealthfund.org/publications/issue-briefs/2020/jan/us-health-care-global-perspective-2019

Disability: Beyond the medical model, [Editorial]. (2009). [Editorial]. *Lancet (London, England), 374*(9704), 1793. https://doi.org/10.1016/S0140-6736(09)62043-2

Duenyas, D. L., Akcil, S., & Osborn, C. (2020). Professional adjustment experiences of international counseling graduates. *International Journal for the Advancement of Counselling, 42*(1), 21–36. https://doi.org/10.1007/s10447-019-09386-6

Durocher, J., Lord, J., & Defranco, A. (2012). Disability and global development. *Disability and Health Journal, 5*(3), 132–135. https://doi.org/10.1016/j.dhjo.2012.04.001

Erickson, W., Lee, C., & von Schrader, S. (2021). *Disability Statistics from the 2018 American Community Survey (ACS).* Cornell University Yang-Tan Institute (YTI). https://www.disabilitystatistics.org/

Fabian, E. S., & Madsen, M. K. (2007). International Exchange in Disability and Social Inclusion: American Educators' Perspectives. *Journal of Applied Rehabilitation Counseling, 38*(3), 12–17. https://doi.org/10.1891/0047-2220.38.3.12

Fernandes, N. (2020). Economic effects of coronavirus outbreak (COVID-19) on the world economy. *SSRN Electronic Journal*, WP-1240. https://doi.org/10.2139/ssrn.3557504

FitzGerald, C., & Hurst, S. (2017). Implicit bias in healthcare professionals: A systematic review. *BMC Medical Ethics, 18*(1), 19. https://doi.org/10.1186/s12910-017-0179-8

Fox, M. H., Krahn, G. L., Sinclair, L. B., & Cahill, A. (2015). Using the international classification of functioning, disability and health to expand understanding of paralysis in the United States through improved surveillance. *Disability and Health Journal, 8*(3), 457–463. https://doi.org/10.1016/j.dhjo.2015.03.002

Garcia, J. A. S. (2012). Charting directions for counselor education in the Philippines. *Philippine Journal of Counseling Psychology, 14*(1), 119–141.

Gleason, C., Valencia, S., Kirabo, L., Wu, J., Guo, A., Carter, J. E., Bigham, P. J., Bennett, L. C., & Pavel. (2020, October). [Paper presentation]. *22nd International ACM SIGACCESS Conference on Computers and Accessibility (ASSETS'20), Virtual Event*, 26–28. Paper presentation. https://doi.org/10.1145/3373625.3417023

Good A. (2020). Disability research ethics. In R. Iphofen (Ed.) *Handbook of research ethics and scientific integrity*. Springer, Cham. https://doi.org/10.1007/978-3-030-16759-2_30

Goodman, N., Morris, M., & Boston, K. (2017). *Financial inequality: Disability, race and poverty in America*. National Disability Institute. https://www.nationaldisabilityinstitute.org/wp-content/uploads/2019/02/disability-race-poverty-in-america.pdf

Gottlieb, C. A., Maenner, M. J., Cappa, C., & Durkin, M. S. (2009). Child disability screening, nutrition, and early learning in 18 countries with low and middle incomes: data from the third round of UNICEF's Multiple Indicator Cluster Survey (2005-06). *Lancet (London, England)*, 374(9704), 1831–1839. https://doi.org/10.1016/S0140-6736(09)61871-7

Grech, S. (2016). Disability and poverty: Complex interactions and critical reframings. In S. Grech & K. Soldatic (Eds.), *Disability in the global South. International perspectives on social policy, administration, and practice* (pp. 217–235). Springer.

Groce, N. E. (2004). *HIV/AIDS and disability: Capturing hidden voices*. The World Bank/Yale University. http://siteresources.worldbank.org/DISABILITY/Resources/Health-and-Wellness/HIVAIDS.pdf

Groce, N. E., & Paeglow, C. (2005). *Summary report: Violence against disabled children* (UN Secretary General's Report on Violence against Children). Thematic Group on Violence against Disabled Children, Findings and Recommendations, Convened by UNICEF at the United Nations. http://www.unicef.org/videoaudio/PDFs/UNICEF_Violence_Against_Disabled_Children_Report_Distributed_Version.pdf

Handicap International. (2014, December). *Including disability in HIV policy and programming: Good practices drawn from country-based evidence* (LL N° 07 Brief). http://www.hiproweb.org/uploads/tx_hidrtdocs/LL07Brief.pdf

Hanley-Maxwell, C., Al Hano, I., & Skivington, M. (2007). Qualitative research in rehabilitation counseling. *Rehabilitation Counseling Bulletin*, 50(2), 99–110. https://doi.org/10.1177/00343552070500020801

Hartley, S., Finkenflugel, H., Kuipers, P., & Thomas, M. (2009). Community-based rehabilitation: Opportunity and challenge. *Lancet (London, England)*, 374(9704), 1803–1804. https://doi.org/10.1016/S0140-6736(09)62036-5

Henderson, R. H. (1996). *The global burden of disease: A comprehensive assessment of mortality and disability from diseases, injuries, and risk factors in 1990 and projected to 2020* (pp. xiii–xiv). *The Harvard School of Public Health on behalf of the World Health Organization and the World Bank, distributed by Harvard University Press*.

Huang, C., Wang, Y., Li, X., Ren, L., Zhao, J., Hu, Y., Zhang, L., Fan, G., Xu, J., Gu, X., Cheng, Z., Yu, T., Xia, J., Wei, Y., Wu, W., Xie, X., Yin, W., Li, H., Liu, M., … Cao, B. (2020). Clinical features of patients infected with 2019 novel coronavirus in Wuhan, China. *Lancet (London, England)*, 395(10223), 497–506. https://doi.org/10.1016/S0140-6736(20)30183-5

Human Rights Watch. (2014). *One billion forgotten: Protecting the human rights of persons with disabilities*. https://www.hrw.org/sites/default/files/related_material/2014%20disabilities_program_low.pdf

International Labour Organization. (2007, November). *Facts on disability in the world of work*. http://www.ilo.org/wcmsp5/groups/public/@dgreports/@dcomm/documents/publication/wcms_087707.pdf

International Labour Organization. (2021). *ILO disability and inclusion policy and strategy 2020–2023*. https://www.ilo.org/wcmsp5/groups/public/---ed_emp/---ifp_skills/documents/publication/wcms_821102.pdf

Jesus, T. S., Landry, M. D., Hoenig, H., Zeng, Y., Kamalakannan, S., Britto, R. R., Pogosova, N., Sokolova, O., Grimmer, K., & Louw, Q. A. (2020). Physical Rehabilitation Needs in the BRICS Nations from 1990 to 2017: Cross-National Analyses Using Data from the Global Burden of Disease Study. *International Journal of Environmental Research and Public Health*, 17(11), 44139. https://doi.org/10.3390/ijerph17114139

Johnson, S., & Tarvydas, V. M. (2022). Ethical perspectives on trauma work. In L. L. Levers (Ed.), *Trauma counseling: Theories and interventions for managing trauma, stress, crisis, and disaster* (2nd ed., pp. 461–478). Springer.

Kim, W. H., & Lee, J. (2016). The effect of accommodation on academic performance of college students with disabilities. *Rehabilitation Counseling Bulletin*, 60(1), 40–50. https://doi.org/10.1177/0034355215605259

Lancet Global Health Editorial. (2021). Disability: measurement matters [Editorial]. *Lancet, Global Health, 9*(8), E1028. https://doi.org/10.1016/S2214-109X(21)00312-0

Laurin-Bowie, C. (2005). Poverty, disability and social exclusion: New strategies for achieving inclusive development. *Journal for Disability and International Development, 2,* 51–56.

Lee, J., Phillips, D., Wilkens, J., Chien, S., Lin, Y.-C., Angrisani, M., & Crimmins, E. (2018). Cross-country comparisons of disability and morbidity: Evidence from the Gateway to Global Aging data. *The Journals of Gerontology. Series A, Biological Sciences and Medical Sciences, 73*(11), 1519–1524. https://doi.org/10.1093/gerona/glx224

Leroi, I., Wolski, L., Charalambous, A. P., Constantinidou, F., Renaud, D., Dawes, P., Hann, M., Himmelsbach, I., Miah, J., Payne, M., Simkin, Z., Thodi, C., Yeung, W. K., & Yohannes, A. M. (2021). Support care needs of people with hearing and vision impairment in dementia: A European cross-national perspective. *Disability and Rehabilitation,* 1–13. https://doi.org/10.1080/09638288.2021.1923071

Levers, L. L. (2001). Representations of psychiatric disability in fifty years of Hollywood film: An ethnographic content analysis. *Theory and Science, 2*(2). http://theoryandscience.icaap.org/content/vol002.002/lopezlevers.html

Levers, L. L. (2006). Traditional Healing as Indigenous Knowledge: Its Relevance to HIV/AIDS in Southern Africa and the Implications for Counselors. *Journal of Psychology in Africa, 16*(1), 87–100. https://doi.org/10.1080/14330237.2006.10820108

Levers, L. L. (2017). Disability issues in a global context. In V. M. Tarvydas & M. Hartley (Eds.), *The professional practice of rehabilitation counseling* (pp. 173–200). Springer.

Levers, L. L. (2020). Crisis, disaster, and trauma. In L. L. Levers & D. Hyatt-Burkhart (Eds.), *Clinical mental health counseling: Practicing in integrated systems of care* (pp. 91–116). Springer. https://doi.org/10.1891/9780826131089

Levers, L. L. (2022). Theoretical contexts of trauma counseling: Understanding the effects of trauma, stress, crisis, and disaster. In L. L. Levers (Ed.), *Trauma counseling: Theories and interventions for managing trauma, stress, crisis, and disaster* (2nd ed., pp. 23–43). Springer.

Levers, L. L., Amador, F. J. R., & Mashumba, L. (2019). Examining African traditional health care: The role of indigenous healers and community health workers in helping to address mental illness. In S. Okpaku (Ed.), *Innovations in global mental health* (pp. 1–18). Springer Nature. https://link.springer.com/referenceworkentry/10.1007/978-3-319-70134-9_16-1

Levers, L. L., Biggs, B-A., & Strickler, A. (2015). International implications for addressing immigrant and refugee health issues. In E. Mpofu (Ed.), *Community-oriented health services: Practices across disciplines* (pp. 271–292). Springer.

Levers, L. L., & Drozda, N. (2022). A confluence of crises: Migration, anthropogenic climate change, mass casualties, war, and civil unrest. In L. L. Levers (Ed.), *Trauma counseling: Theories and interventions for managing trauma, stress, crisis, and disaster* (2nd ed.). Springer.

Levers, L. L., & Drozda, N. A. (2018). Embracing a human ecological approach to anthropogenic climate change: The mandate for moving beyond empathy and raising levels of compassion. In G. Magill & J. Potter (Eds.), *Integral ecology: Protecting our common home* (pp. 83–131). Cambridge Scholars Publishing.

Levers, L. L., Magweva, F. I., Maundeni, T., & Mpofu, E. (2008). *A report on A comprehensive study of social safety nets for people with disabilities in Botswana* [A study sponsored by the Botswana Ministry of Health, at the request of the Botswana Office of the President). Ministry of Health].

Levers, L. L., Magweva, F. I., & Mpofu, E. (2007). *A review of district health systems in east and southern Africa: Facilitators and barriers to participation in health* (EQUINET Discussion Paper no.40). Regional Network for Equity in Health in East and Southern Africa (EQUINET). http://www.equinetafrica.org/bibl/docs/DIS40ehsLOPEZ.pdf

Levers, L. L., Magweva, F. I., & Mufema, E. (2010, March). *Poverty levels among people with disabilities: An evaluation of the need for developing a disability social protection scheme in Zimbabwe* (Final Report to the Terms of Reference Committee Regarding the Consultancy for the National Association of Societies for the Care of the Handicapped [NASCOH], the National Association of Non-Governmental Organizations [NANGO], and the Republic of Zimbabwe Ministry of Labour and Social Services [MoLSS]). National Association of Societies for the Care of the Handicapped.

Levers, L. L., & Maki, D. R. (1994). *An ethnographic analysis of traditional healing and rehabilitation services in southern Africa: Cross-cultural implications* (An International Exchange of Experts and

Information in Rehabilitation [IEEIR] Research Fellowship Monograph prepared for the World Rehabilitation Fund, National Institute on Disability and Rehabilitation Research, U.S. Dept. of Education. Oklahoma State University. National Clearing House of Rehabilitation Training Materials.

Levers, L. L., & Maki, D. R. (1995). African indigenous healing, cosmology, and existential implications: Toward a philosophy of ethnorehabilitation. *Rehabilitation Education, 9*, 127–145.

Levers, L. L., & Mancilla, R. (2013). Educating the children of undocumented immigrant parents: The impact of trauma on citizen children's development. In F. E. McCarthy, M. H. Vickers, & E. Brown (Eds.), *International advances in education: Global initiatives for equity and social justice* (Vol. 6: *Migrants and refugees: equitable education for displaced populations*, pp. 51–72). Information Age.

Levers, L. L., Radomsky, L., & Shefer, T. (2009). Voices of African Traditional Healers: Cultural Context and Implications for the Practice of Counselling in Sub-Saharan Africa. *Journal of Psychology in Africa, 19*(4), 497–502. https://doi.org/10.1080/14330237.2009.10820321

Liaw, F.-Y., Kao, T.-W., Wu, L.-W., Wang, C.-C., Yang, H.-F., Peng, T.-C., Sun, Y.-S., Chang, Y.-W., & Chen, W.-L. (2016). Components of Metabolic Syndrome and the Risk of Disability among the Elderly Population. *Scientific Reports, 6*(1), 1–9. https://doi.org/10.1038/srep22750

Luecking, R. G., Cuozzo, L., McInerney, C., Cury, S. H. M., & Lorca, M. C. B. C. (2007). Cross Cultural Field Exchange as a Rehabilitation Professional Development Experience. *Journal of Applied Rehabilitation Counseling, 38*(3), 18–24. https://doi.org/10.1891/0047-2220.38.3.18

Male, C., & Wodon, Q. (2017, December). The price of exclusion: Disability and education: Disability gaps in educational attainment and literacy. Global Partnership for Education and The World Bank. https://documents1.worldbank.org/curated/en/396291511988894028/pdf/121762-replacement-PUBLIC-WorldBank-GapsInEdAttainmentLiteracy-Brief-v6.pdf

Mariotti, D., McAuliffe, G. J., Grothaus, T., West-Olatunji, C., & Snow, K. C. (2019). Towards a new profession: Counselor professional identity in Italy. A Delphi Study. *International Journal for the Advancement of Counselling, 41*(4), 561–579. https://doi.org/10.1007/s10447-019-09376-8

Marmot, M., Allen, J., Bell, R., Bloomer, E., Goldblatt, P., & Consortium for the European Review of Social Determinants of Health and the Health Divide. (2012). WHO European review of social determinants of health and the health divide. *Lancet (London, England), 380*(9846), 1011–1029. https://doi.org/10.1016/S0140-6736(12)61228-8

Maundeni, T., Jankey, O., & Levers, L. L. (2017). Social welfare issues in childhood: The Botswana Experience. In I. Tshabangu (Ed.), *Global ideologies surrounding children's rights and social justice* (pp. 57–73). IGI Global.

McAlpine, D. D., & Alang, S. M. (2021). Employment and economic outcomes of persons with mental illness and disability: The impact of the Great Recession in the United States. *Psychiatric Rehabilitation Journal, 44*(2), 132–141. https://doi.org/10.1037/prj0000458

McNeil, J. F. (2019). *Attitudes: Exploring the lived experiences of employees with visual impairments.* Unpublished doctoral dissertation. Duquesne University.

Mitra, S., Posarac, A., & Vick, B. (2011). Disability and poverty in developing countries: A snapshot from the world health survey. SP Discussion Paper no.1109, the World Bank, Social Protection and Labor Unit, Human Development Network (HDNSP). http://siteresources.worldbank.org/SOCIALPROTECTION/Resources/SP-Discussion-papers/Disability-DP/1109.pdf

Moering, R. G., Buck, R. P., & Levers, L. L. (2022). The impact of war on military veterans. In L. L. Levers (Ed.), *Trauma counselling* (2nd ed., pp. 393–411). Springer.

Mpofu, E. (Ed.). (2015). *Community-oriented health services.* Springer.

Mpofu, E., & Harley, D. (2002). Rehabilitation in Zimbabwe: Lessons and implications for rehabilitation practice in the United States. *Journal of Rehabilitation, 68*(4), 26–33.

Mpofu, E., Levers, L. L., Makuwire, J., Mpofu, K., & Mamboleo, G. (2018). Community-based rehabilitation for human development in sub-Saharan Africa. In A. Abubakar & van de V. F. (Eds.), *Handbook of applied developmental science in sub-Saharan Africa* (pp. 335–345). Springer.

Mpofu, E., Levers, L. L., Mpofu, K., Tanui, P., & Hossain, Z. S. (2015). Family assessments in rehabilitation service provision. In M. Millington & I. Marini (Eds.), *Families in rehabilitation counseling: A community-based rehabilitation approach* (pp. 251–266). Springer.

Mpofu, E., McDaniels, B., & Watts, J. (2022). Trauma survivorship and disability. In L. L. Levers (Ed.), *Trauma counseling: Theories and interventions for managing trauma, stress, crisis, and disaster* (2nd ed.). Springer.

Mpofu, E., Nyiransekuye, H., & Levers, L. L. (2021). Identity development among African youth refugee immigrants to Australia. In S. S. Chuang, D. J. Johnson, S. Rasmi, & J. Glozman (Eds.), *Formation and identity: The intersectionality of development, culture, and immigration* (pp. 381–396). Springer.

Mpofu, E., Watts, J., Li, Q., Adaralegba, N. J-F. C., & Igbeka, P. (2020). Community-based mental health counseling, recovery models, and multidisciplinary collaboration. In L. L. Levers & D. Hyatt-Burkhart (Eds.), *Clinical mental health counseling: Practicing in integrated systems of care* (pp. 119–140). Springer.

Mukamana, D., Levers, L. L., Johns, K., Gishoma, D., Kayiteshonga, Y., & Ait Mohand, A. (2019). A Community-based mental health intervention: Promoting mental health services in Rwanda. In S. Okpaku (Ed.), *Innovations in global mental health* (pp. 1–17). Springer Nature. https://link .springer.com/referenceworkentry/10.1007%2F978-3-319-70134-9_36-1

Murray, C. J. L., Barber, R. M., Foreman, K. J., Abbasoglu Ozgoren, A., Abd-Allah, F., Abera, S. F., Aboyans, V., Abraham, J. P., Abubakar, I., Abu-Raddad, L. J., Abu-Rmeileh, N. M., Achoki, T., Ackerman, I. N., Ademi, Z., Adou, A. K., Adsuar, J. C., Afshin, A., Agardh, E. E., & Vos, T. (2015). Global, regional, and national disability-adjusted life years (DALYs) for 306 diseases and injuries and healthy life expectancy (HALE) for 188 countries, 1990-2013: Quantifying the epidemiological transition. *Lancet (London, England)*, 386(10009), 2145–2191. https://doi.org/10.1016/S0140-6736(15)61340-X

Murray, C. J. L., & Lopez, A. D. (Eds.). (1996). *The global burden of disease: A comprehensive assessment of mortality and disability from diseases, injuries, and risk factors in 1990 and projected to 2020.* Harvard University Press.

Nario-Redmond, M. R., Kemerling, A. A., & Silverman, A. (2019). Hostile, benevolent, and ambivalent ableism: Contemporary manifestations. *Journal of Social Issues*, 75(3), 726–756. https://doi .org/10.1111/josi.12337

National Disability Authority. (2009). Ethical guidance for research with people with disabilities. *Disability Series*, 13. http://nda.ie/nda-files/Ethical-Guidance-for-Research-with-People-with -Disabilities.pdf

Navas, P., Amor, A. M., Crespo, M., Wolowiec, Z., & Verdugo, M. Á. (2020). Supports for people with intellectual and developmental disabilities during the COVID-19 pandemic from their own perspective. *Research in Developmental Disabilities*, 108, 103813. https://doi.org/10.1016/j.ridd.2020 .103813

Nunn, R., Parsons, J., & Shambaugh, J. (2020, March). *A dozen facts about the economics of the U.S. health-care system.* Brookings Foundation, The Hamilton Project. https://www.brookings.edu/ wp-content/uploads/2020/03/HealthCare_Facts_WEB_FINAL.pdf

Office on Women's Health. (2015, September 4). *Violence against women with disabilities.* http://www .womenshealth.gov/violence-against-women/types-of-violence/violence-against-women-with -disabilities.html

Officer, A., & Groce, N. E. (2009). Key concepts in disability. *Lancet (London, England)*, 374(9704), 1795–1796. https://doi.org/10.1016/S0140-6736(09)61527-0

Opoku, M. P., Elhoweris, H., Jiya, A. N., Ngoh, N. A.-P., Nketsia, W., Kumi, E. O., & Torgbenu, E. L. (2021). Cross-national study of communal attitudes toward individuals with intellectual disabilities in sub-Saharan Africa: Cameroon vs. Ghana. *PloS One*, 16(9), e0257482. https://doi.org/10 .1371/journal.pone.0257482

Perera, B., Kandasamy, N., & Soldatic, K. (2020). Disability Exclusion during the Coronavirus Pandemic (COVID-19) in Sri Lanka. *University of Colombo Review*, 1(1), 47. https://doi.org/10 .4038/ucr.v1i1.28

Petasis, A. (2019). Discrepancies of the medical, social and biopsychosocial models of disability: A comprehensive theoretical framework. *The International Journal of Business Management and Technology*, 3(4). https://www.theijbmt.com/archive/0928/1686534688.pdf

Pettinicchio, D., & Maroto, M. (2021). Who Counts? Measuring Disability Cross-Nationally in Census Data. *Journal of Survey Statistics and Methodology*, 9(2), 257–284. https://doi.org/10.1093/ jssam/smaa046

Pollard, B., Dixon, D., Dieppe, P., & Johnston, M. (2009). Measuring the ICF components of impairment, activity limitation and participation restriction: an item analysis using classical test theory and item response theory. *Health and Quality of Life Outcomes*, 7, 41. https://doi.org/10.1186/1477 -7525-7-41

ProChild. (2020, December 22). *Children with disabilities are more likely to face violence.* https:// www.prochildproject.org/2020/12/22/children-with-disabilities-are-more-likely-to-face -violence/

Prüss-Ustün, A., Wolf, J., Corvalán, C., Bos, R., & Neira, M. (2016). *Preventing disease through healthy environments: A global assessment of the burden of disease from environmental risks.* http://apps.who .int/iris/bitstream/10665/204585/1/9789241565196_eng.pdf?ua=1

Radomsky, L., & Levers, L. L. (2012). Voices of the African traditional healer: Implications for cross cultural educational practices. In A. S. Yeung, C. F. K. Lee, & E. L. Brown (Eds.), *Communication and language* (of *International advances in education: Global initiatives for equity and social justice*, Vol. 7, pp. 79–100). Information Age Publishing.

Ritchie, H., & Roser, M. (2018, 20 September). *Now it is possible to take stock – did the world achieve the Millennium Development Goals?* Our World in Data. https://ourworldindata.org/millennium -development-goals

Rynders, D. (2019). Battling implicit bias in the idea to advocate for African American students with disabilities. *Touro Law Review, 35*(1), 461–480.

Sakellariou, D., Malfitano, A. P. S., & Rotarou, E. S. (2020). Disability inclusiveness of government responses to COVID-19 in South America: A framework analysis study. *International Journal for Equity in Health, 19*(1), 131. https://doi.org/10.1186/s12939-020-01244-x

Salvador-Carulla, L., & Saxena, S. (2009). Intellectual disability: between disability and clinical nosology. *Lancet (London, England), 374*(9704), 1798–1799. https://doi.org/10.1016/S0140-6736(09)62034-1

Schalock, R. L., Verdugo, M. A., & Gomez, L. E. (2011). Evidence-based practices in the field of intellectual and developmental disabilities: an international consensus approach. *Evaluation and Program Planning, 34*(3), 273–282. https://doi.org/10.1016/j.evalprogplan.2010.10.004

Schur, L. A., Ameri, M., & Kruse, D. (2020). Telework after COVID: A "silver lining" for workers with disabilities? *Journal of Occupational Rehabilitation, 30*(4), 521–536. https://doi.org/10.1007/ s10926-020-09936-5

Servick, K. (2020). For survivors of severe COVID-19, beating the virus is just the beginning. *Science.* https://doi.org/10.1126/science.abc1486

Soerjomataram, I., Lortet-Tieulent, J., Parkin, D. M., Ferlay, J., Mathers, C., Forman, D., & Bray, F. (2012). Global burden of cancer in 2008: A systematic analysis of disability-adjusted life-years in 12 world regions. *Lancet (London, England), 380*(9856), 1840–1850. https://doi.org/10.1016/S0140 -6736(12)60919-2

Sousa, R. M., Ferri, C. P., Acosta, D., Albanese, E., Guerra, M., Huang, Y., Jacob, K. S., Jotheeswaran, A. T., Rodriguez, J. J. L., Pichardo, G. R., Rodriguez, M. C., Salas, A., Sosa, A. L., Williams, J., Zuniga, T., & Prince, M. (2009). Contribution of chronic diseases to disability in elderly people in countries with low and middle incomes: A 10/66 Dementia Research Group population-based survey. *Lancet (London, England), 374*(9704), 1821–1830. https://doi.org/10.1016/S0140-6736(09) 61829-8

Stein, M. A., Stein, P. J. S., Weiss, D., & Lang, R. (2009). Health care and the UN Disability Rights Convention. *Lancet (London, England), 374*(9704), 1796–1798. https://doi.org/10.1016/S0140 -6736(09)62033-X

Tarvydas, V. M., Levers, L. L., & Teahen, P. R. (2017). Ethical guidelines for mass trauma and complex humanitarian emergencies. *Journal of Counseling & Development, 95*(3), 260–268. https://doi.org/ 10.1002/jcad.12140

Tarvydas, V., Levers, L. L., & Teahen, P. (2018). Ethics narratives from lived experiences of disaster and trauma counselors. In J. Webber & J. B. Mascari (Eds.), *Disaster mental health counseling: A guide to preparing and responding* (4th ed.). ACA.

Teahen, P., Levers, L. L., & Tarvydas, V. (2017). Disaster, climate change, and public health: Building social-ecological resilience. In G. Magill & K. Aramesh (Eds.), *The urgency of climate change: Pivotal perspectives* (pp. 133–160). Cambridge Scholars Publishing.

Tingey, K. B., Millington, M. J., & Graham, M. (2007). A communities of practice approach to train-ing and education: Building sociocognitive networks in rehabilitation counseling [White Paper]. *National Clearinghouse of Rehabilitation Training Materials.*

United Nations. (2000, September 18). *United Nations Millennium Declaration.* http://www.un.org/ millenniumgoals/bkgd.shtml

United Nations. (2006). *United Nations Convention on the Rights of Persons with Disabilities.* http://www.un.org/disabilities/convention/conventionfull.shtml

United Nations. (2011). *Disability and the Millennium Development Goals: A review of the MDG process and strategies for inclusion of disability issues in Millennium Development Goal efforts.* http://www.un.org/disabilities/documents/review_of_disability_and_the_mdgs.pdf

United Nations. (2015). *The millennium development goals report: 2015.* https://www.un.org/millenniumgoals/2015_MDG_Report/pdf/MDG%202015%20rev%20(July%201).pdf

United Nations Programme on HIV/AIDS. (2021). *Fact sheet 2021.* https://www.unaids.org/sites/default/files/media_asset/UNAIDS_FactSheet_en.pdf

United Nations. (2016, September 23). *Iceland ratifies CRPD (total: 167). Division for Social Policy and Development Disability.* https://www.un.org/development/desa/disabilities/news/dspd/iceland-ratifies-crpd-total-167.html

United Nations, Department of Economic and Social Affairs, Population Division. (2019). *World population prospects 2019: Highlights (ST/ESA/SER.A/423.* https://population.un.org/wpp/Publications/Files/WPP2019_Highlights.pdf

United Nations Development Program. (2010, November). *Human development report 2010, The real wealth of nations: Pathways to human development.* 20th anniversary edition. http://hdr.undp.org/en/media/HDR_2010_EN_Complete.pdf

United Nations Development Program. (2016). *Disability rights.* http://www.undp.org/content/undp/en/home/ourwork/povertyreduction/focus_areas/focusinclusive_development/disability-rights.html

United Nations Development Program. (2018, December). *Disability inclusive development in UNDP: Guidance and entry points.* https://www.undp.org/publications/disability-inclusive-development-undp

United Nations Educational, Scientific and Cultural Organization. (2020). *Global education monitoring report 2020: Inclusion and education: All means all.* https://unesdoc.unesco.org/ark:/48223/pf0000373718

United Nations International Children's Education Fund. (n.d.). *Voices of youth: Be in the know: Fact sheet.* http://www.unicef.org/explore_3893.html

U.S. Bureau of Labor Statistics. (2022, April 18). Rehabilitation counselors. *Occupational outlook handbook.* https://www.bls.gov/ooh/community-and-social-service/rehabilitation-counselors.htm

U.S. Census Bureau. (2019). *American Community Survey.* https://data.census.gov/cedsci/table?q=American%20Community%20Survey%202019%20disability&tid=ACSST1Y2019.S1810

Wang, S.-X., Wang, Y., Lu, Y.-B., Li, J.-Y., Song, Y.-J., Nyamgerelt, M., & Wang, X.-X. (2020). Diagnosis and treatment of novel coronavirus pneumonia based on the theory of traditional Chinese medicine. *Journal of Integrative Medicine, 18*(4), 275–283. https://doi.org/10.1016/j.joim.2020.04.001

Wass, V., & Jones, M. (2020, August). *Measuring disability and interpreting trends in disability-related disadvantage.* Disability at Work. https://www.disabilityatwork.co.uk/wp-content/uploads/2020/08/Briefing-Note-disability-measurement-.pdf

Wolbring, G. (2016). Employment, Disabled People and Robots: What Is the Narrative in the Academic Literature and Canadian Newspapers? *Societies, 6*(2), 15. https://doi.org/10.3390/soc6020015

World Bank. (2021, October 10). *Disability inclusion.* https://www.worldbank.org/en/topic/disability#1

World Health Organization, Centers for Disease Control and Prevention, & International Clearinghouse for Birth Defects Surveillance and Research. (2014). *Birth defects surveillance: a manual for programme managers.* https://www.cdc.gov/ncbddd/birthdefectscount/documents/bd-surveillance-manual.pdf

World Health Organization. (1980). *International classification of impairments, disabilities and handicaps.* Author.http://apps.who.int/iris/bitstream/10665/41003/1/9241541261_eng.pdf

World Health Organization. (2001). *International classification of functioning, disability and health* [ICF]. https://www.who.int/standards/classifications/international-classification-of-functioning-disability-and-health

World Health Organization. (2002). *Towards a common language for functioning, disability and health: ICF.* http://www.who.int/classifications/icf/training/icfbeginnersguide.pdf

World Health Organization. (2007, April). WHO world report on disability and rehabilitation update no.1. http://siteresources.worldbank.org/DISABILITY/Resources/News---Events/BBLs/20070411WHOissue1.pdf

World Health Organization. (2010a). *Community-based rehabilitation.* http://www.who.int/disabilities/cbr/en/index.html

World Health Organization. (2010b, October). *Community-based rehabilitation (CBR) guidelines.* http://www.who.int/disabilities/cbr/guidelines/en/index.html

World Health Organization. (2011a). *A world report on disability.* http://www.who.int/disabilities/world_report/2011/report.pdf

World Health Organization. (2011b, February). *The WHO Newsletter on Disability and Rehabilitation, 12.* http://www.who.int/disabilities/publications/newsletter/dar_issue12.pdf?ua=1

World Health Organization. (2013, October). *How to use the ICF: A practical manual for using the International Classification of Functioning, Disability and Health (ICF). Exposure draft for comment.* https://www.who.int/classifications/drafticfpracticalmanual.pdf

World Health Organization. (2016). *Injury-related disability and rehabilitation. Violence and injury prevention.* http://www.who.int/violence_injury_prevention/disability/en

World Health Organization. (2018). *International classification of diseases for mortality and morbidity statistics.* https://icd.who.int/browse11/l-m/en

World Health Organization. (2020a, December 1). *Disability and health [Fact sheet].* https://www.who.int/news-room/fact-sheets/detail/disability-and-health

World Health Organization. (2020b, March 11). *WHO Director-General's opening remarks at the media briefing on COVID-19.* https://www.who.int/director-general/speeches/detail/who-director-general-s-opening-remarks-at-the-media-briefing-on-covid-19---11-march-2020

World Health Organization. (2022, February 14). *WHO coronavirus disease (COVID-19) dashboard.* https://covid19.who.int

World Health Organization. (n.d.). *Concept note: World report on disability and rehabilitation.* http://www.who.int/disabilities/publications/dar_world_report_concept_note.pdf

CHAPTER 11

Assessment

NGONIDZASHE MPOFU AND ELIAS MPOFU

LEARNING OBJECTIVES

After reading this chapter, you should be able to:

- ▪ *Define the construct of person-centric assessments as it applies to rehabilitation counseling practice settings.*
- ▪ *Categorize person-centric assessments from those focused on impairment and disability.*
- ▪ *Describe the structure of the World Health Organization (WHO's)* International Classification of Functioning, Disability and Health (ICF).
- ▪ *Discuss applications of the* ICF *as a framework for the design, selection, and implementation of person-centric assessments, and use of ICF core sets.*
- ▪ *Explain prospective use of the* ICF *together with the* Diagnostic and Statistical Manual of Mental Disorders *(5th ed.; DSM-5), the* International Statistical Classification of Diseases and Related Health Problems, Tenth Revision (ICD-10), *the* ICD-11, *and the* World Health Organization Disability Assessment Schedule 2.0 *(WHODAS 2.0) for person-centric rehabilitation support assessments.*
- ▪ *Evaluate the incremental value of person-centric data for rehabilitation support interventions.*

CACREP STANDARDS

CACREP 2016 CORE: 2F7.a, 2F7.e, 2F7.h, 2F7.i, 2F7.j, 2F7.l, 2F7.m
CACREP 2016 Specialties:
　Clinical Rehabilitation Counseling: 5D1.d, 5D1.f, 5D2.f, 5D2.g, 5D2.m, 5D2.n, 5D2.q, 5D.3.a
　Rehabilitation Counseling: 5H1.d., 5H1.f, 5H1.g, 5H2.b, 5H2.d, 5H3.a, 5H3.b, 5H3.c, 5H3.l

INTRODUCTION

This chapter discusses the nature and significance of person-centric assessments to rehabilitation support interventions for people with disabilities. It defines person-centric assessments and positions them within the framework of the WHO (2001) *ICF*. The *ICF* provides a universally accepted biosocial conceptual framework for understanding health and disability. Its full implementation in rehabilitation service provisioning requires acquiring and integrating information on three health conditions (body structure and functions, activities, participation) and two contextual conditions (environmental and personal factors) to optimize personal functioning. Increasingly rehabilitation is considered a health strategy rather than just an intervention (Prodinger et al., 2016; Stucki et al., 2018). The *ICF* core sets enable the characterization or profiling of health and function by contextual conditions for the better targeting of rehabilitation intervention to disability populations.

This chapter discusses the ways in which the *ICF* can be used in conjunction with the *DSM-5* and (American Psychiatric Association [APA], 2013) other WHO classification systems to provide person-centric data for rehabilitation support interventions with people with disabilities. Finally, the chapter proposes a conceptual model for applying *ICF* framework concepts to the design, selection, and use of person-centric rehabilitation assessments for life design with disability.

A priority goal of rehabilitation counseling is to ensure that people with disabilities have access to regular community services and the same opportunities to engage in full community citizenship roles as their peers without disabilities (Skempes et al., 2015; United Nations, 2009, 2012). In the context of the day-to-day reality of people with disabilities and their support systems (family, significant others, rehabilitation and health service providers), priorities include the successful orchestration of basic resources, services, and supports for enhancing their capacity to attain a satisfactory life with full community inclusion (Mpofu et al., 2012; Thompson & DeSpain, 2016; Seger, 2018). A *satisfactory life* is defined by two complementary statuses: hedonic and eudaimonic well-being (Diener, 1984; Kahneman et al., 1999; Ryff, 2014; Ryff & Singer, 2008; Waterman, 1993). **Hedonic well-being** is associated with experiencing a sense of enjoyment, contentment, and happiness (Diener, 1984; Waterman, 1993) with pleasurable positive affect (Diener, 1984; Kahneman et al., 1999; Ryff, 2014; Ryff & Singer, 2008), and the absence of emotional pain (Ryan et al., 2008). **Eudaimonic well-being** is associated with opportunities for self-realization, personal expressiveness (Waterman, 1993), being fully functional and successful in attaining a meaningful life (Ryff & Singer, 2008), living well with disability (Mpofu, 2013), or successful participation (Thompson et al., 2015), purposeful engagement with life, the realization of personal talents and capacities, and enlightened self-knowledge across the person's lifespan (Ryff, 2014). Many people with disabilities are able to participate meaningfully in their communities with appropriate long-term rehabilitation counseling supports (Putnam & Frieden, 2014), and rehabilitation counselors can play a critical role in identifying and providing the rehabilitation supports necessary for a person with a disability to "participate in activities linked to normative human functioning" (Schalock et al., 2010, p. 105).

Working around the realities of accessing supports for a satisfying life requires interlinked and person-centric information on what is needed, how, when, by whom, and for what personal function purposes (Madden et al., 2013; Stancliffe et al., 2016). In most cases, people with disabilities are the most valuable informants on their individual needs for support—yet often they are neither listened to nor asked about their priorities (Bond et al., 2015; Mpofu, 2013). Person-centric assessment places the life choices of people with disabilities at the center of the rehabilitation counseling process, tapping into the lived experience with disability to construct solutions for meaningful community involvement (Mpofu, 2013).

Person-centric assessment involves the active participation of people with disabilities in generating the evidence on which interventions are based (Peterson & Elliott, 2008; Stancliffe et al., 2016). Assessment is critical because it involves managing complexity in types of data and data sources to inform interventions. The specific instruments for person-centric data gathering may include the use of self-report measures, information from support providers, unstructured and structured interviews, and personal portfolios, as well as standard assessments (see Mpofu & Oakland, 2010a, and Mpofu & Oakland, 2010b, for a comprehensive discussion of related procedures and instruments). With the right types of data, it is possible to construct optimal solutions for maximizing personal and community living with disability (Kellett et al., 2013). Rehabilitation support interventions are a disability right (United

Nations, 2012, 2016), , and what constitutes the data on which such supports are premised is an important consideration (Umeasiegbu et al., 2013). The person-centric approach to rehabilitation counseling interventions (Schalock et al., 2010; Thompson et al., 2009) is in recognition of the fact that with appropriate personal and environmental enablers, the impact of disability on human functioning can be minimized if not eliminated (Harley et al., 2015).

Person-centric assessment aligns well with the rehabilitation counseling emphasis on the whole person, rather than a purely medical focus on disease and disorders (Madden et al., 2013; Mpofu et al., 2016), to inform rehabilitation counseling supports and interventions (Dune & Mpofu, 2015; Mpofu et al., 2012). Person-centered care has been studied more in primary care practice settings (de Silva, 2014) than in rehabilitation counseling practice settings (Mpofu et al., 2012, Mpofu et al., 2016). With this fact in mind, there is an urgent need for the consideration of the types and nature of person-centric assessments with people with disabilities to inform the design and implementation of rehabilitation counseling supports and interventions.

PERSON-CENTRIC ASSESSMENTS

Person-centric assessments are designed to yield or provide data on supports needed by a person with a disability to attain their optimal "functioning vector" within "his or her reach" (Sen, 1985, p. 201). Data from person-centric assessments are useful in activity and participation decisions with chronic illness and disability across a number of life domains or for life design (Mpofu et al., 2016). **Life design** is a whole-person concept that is consistent with a disability rights approach to creating linkages and synergies among personal and environmental assets for successful living. From a disability rights perspective, people with disabilities are competent to lead and advise on their own health and well-being (Sepucha et al., 2008) as well as their inclusion in the community (Mpofu, 2013). From their experience living with disability, these individuals are the most knowledgeable about the supports necessary for successful living with disability. People with disabilities are continually engaged in exploring and enacting choices to optimize successful living with disability in particular environments (Mpofu & Bishop, 2006), and person-centric assessment data are essential to best configure personal and environmental qualities that optimize life design choices for living well with a disability (Mpofu et al., 2012).

Person-centric assessments can be distinguished from other types of assessments because of their focus on individualized interventions to support the self-determination of people with disabilities. In contrast, other assessment procedures focused primarily on impairment rather than life design may inadvertently contribute to the disablement process because of their exclusive focus on the impact of health conditions on the "functioning in specific body systems, generic physical and mental actions and activities of daily living," considering personal and environmental factors only to the extent they "speed or slow disablement" (Verbrugge & Jette, 1994, p. 1). Often, assessments preselected by service providers to collect data on specific aspects of disability may not address the individualized concerns of people with disabilities (Iglehart, 2011; Üstün & Kennedy, 2009). Some assessment procedures may be preordained or dictated by funding-stream policies about which aspects of disability they will record, how they will gather the information, and how they will interpret and summarize it and for what purposes (Iglehart, 2011; Kaiser Family Foundation, 2011). However, rehabilitation counselors may also collect person-centric data. Rather than being preoccupied with impairment, person-centric assessment focuses on how impairment restricts functioning in ways that are unique to the individual, which may have important implications for disability eligibility assessments that are mandated by policy (Madden et al., 2011) or to support the provision of integrated care service as medically necessary (Cloninger, 2011).

With person-centric assessments, people with disabilities and rehabilitation counselors are equal partners as to the types and sources of data that are needed to maximize living well with a disability. Person-centric data prioritize the preferences or expressed needs of people with disabilities for rehabilitation supports helpful to their activity and participation (Dijkstra et al., 2006) and community living (Mpofu, 2013; Mpofu et al., 2012). A benefit of person-centric assessment is that people with disabilities are more likely to follow through with treatment decisions that have prioritized their individual needs rather than decisions based on what are perceived to be routine, provider-oriented assessment procedures (de Silva, 2014; Olsson et al., 2013;). Consistent with the rehabilitation counseling emphasis on the person–environment fit, the WHO (2001) *ICF* provides a framework for a whole-person approach to the use of person-centric assessment for rehabilitation support interventions.

THE INTERNATIONAL CLASSIFICATION OF FUNCTIONING, DISABILITY AND HEALTH FRAMEWORK FOR PERSON-CENTRIC ASSESSMENTS

The *ICF* is not an assessment tool; rather, it is a framework for the collection of health information across various settings describing human functioning on the basis of which person-centric assessments may be selected or designed and implemented with people with disabilities (Cieza, Fayed, et al., 2019). The *ICF* has been described as an information system with the goals to "represent and process information . . . to create new knowledge" (Hollenweger, 2013, p. 1091), as would be the case with person-centric assessments for life design with disability. It provides for the systematic recording and processing of patient information for analysis, interpretation, and comparison, including across different cultures and the human life span. The design of the ICF framework allows for its combined use with the *International Classification of Diseases and Related Health Problems, 11th Revision* (ICD-11; WHO, 2019). The ICD is used to gather systematic diagnostic health data across cultures and time providing unified healthcare decision-making support in areas such as resource allocation and disability reimbursement guidelines (WHO, 2019). The ICD-11 and ICF provide internationally comparable, operationalizable health statistics (Bickenbach et al., 2020). A brief overview of the *ICF* follows to provide context for the discussion of the person-centric assessment applications.

Structure of the *International Classification of Functioning, Disability and Health*

The *ICF* considers health and disability to be defined by the interaction between body structure and function of people, and impairments they may experience; activities of people and the limitations they may experience on their ability or performance; participation or involvement in all areas of life and restrictions people may experience; and environmental and personal factors that affect physical functioning as well as the activities people can or will do and their participation in life roles (see Figure 11.1).

According to the *ICF*, disability involves dysfunction at one or more of these levels: biological impairments, activity limitations, and participation restrictions. *Biological impairment* refers to differences in anatomical structure or function, such as the ability to move one's arms or legs. In contrast, *disability* refers to the restriction or lack of ability that arises from the interaction between features of the person and features of the overall context in which the person lives. This is not to deny the fact that some aspects of disability are almost entirely internal to the person (from impairment), whereas other aspects are almost entirely external (from environmental restrictions). In other words, data on both the medical aspects (impairment-oriented) and social aspects (environment-oriented) of disability are important for successful living with disability.

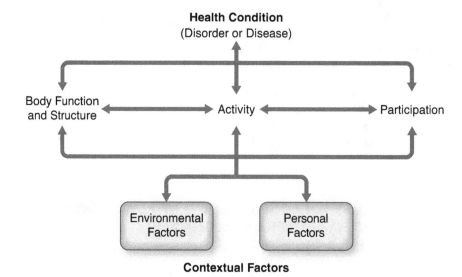

FIGURE 11.1 International Classification of Functioning, Disability and Health Structure for Understanding Health and Disability.

Source: Reproduced with permission from World Health Organization. (2001). *International classification of functioning, disability and health: ICF* (p. 18).

The *ICF* is a biopsychosocial model of disability in that it synthesizes what is true from the medical, psychological, and social models of disability without overly privileging one of the aspects or reducing the whole, complex notion of disability to one of its aspects (Loidl et al., 2016). Historically, the biopsychosocial model has remained on the periphery of disability interventions given the heavy influence of the medical and surgical domain in intervention funding decision-making (Schulz, 2009). This tendency is now changing as the increasing use the ICF framework allows for the insertion of psychology domains, including those identified by the cross-cultural *DSM-5* (APA, 2013), and the *ICD-11* (Cieza, Fayed, et al., 2019; WHO, 2019). Understanding human behavior increasingly has been recognized as a key factor in health literacy, and the development of complex health promotion and healthcare activities (Wade & Halligan, 2017).

The *ICF* model, with its emphasis on functioning, proposes a view of "health" and "disability" in which every human being can experience a decrement in health and thereby experience some level of disability. From this perspective, good health and living well with disability are both possible with the right supports or resources (Bickenbach et al., 2020; Schalock et al., 2010; Seger, 2018; Thompson et al., 2015; WHO, 2019). Box 11.1 presents the definitions of components of the *ICF* framework.

Box 11.2 and Box 11.3 present case conceptualizations utilizing the *ICF*. The *ICF* components are indications for the clinical and personal function presentations of a person with a complete spinal cord injury (Box 11.2) and with Guillain-Barré syndrome, an autoimmune disorder in which the body's immune system attacks part of the peripheral nervous system (Box 11.3).

As should be apparent from these two case conceptualizations, applying the *ICF* framework has the unique advantage of establishing a transparent language for describing health- and disability-related personal function statuses in nontechnical terms accessible to a variety of users and audiences (WHO, 2002). The next sections describe in more detail each of the components of the *ICF*. In each case, consideration is given to person-centric assessment applications associated with each of the *ICF* components (see Figure 11.2 for a summary).

BOX 11.1 *ICF* DEFINITION OF TERMS

Body functions—the physiological functions of body systems (including psychological functions).

Body structures—anatomical parts of the body such as organs, limbs, and their components.

Impairments—problems in body function or structure such as a significant deviation or loss.

Activity—the execution of a task or action by an individual.

Participation—involvement in a life situation.

Activity limitations—difficulties an individual may experience in involvement in life situations.

Participation restrictions—problems an individual may experience in involvement in life situations.

Environmental factors—make up the physical, social, and attitudinal environment in which people live and conduct their lives. These are either barriers to or facilitators of the person's functioning.

Functioning—an umbrella term encompassing all body functions, activities, and participation. It denotes the positive or neutral aspects of the interaction between a person's health condition(s) and that individual's contextual factors (environmental and personal factors).

Source: (WHO (2001), pp. 3, 8, 10).

ICF Components and Chapters

In the *ICF* manual, the core components are presented as chapters, as outlined in Table 11.1.

Body Structures and Function

As listed in Table 11.1, the *ICF* defines disability in body functions and structures as a deviation from population norms. According to the *ICF*, **structures** are anatomically based, as in the physical components of the cardiovascular and respiratory systems. **Functions** are defined as physiological correlates of such structures regarding how they support bodily

BOX 11.2 CASE CONCEPTUALIZATION UTILIZING THE *ICF*: A PERSON WITH A SPINAL CORD INJURY

Mr. Sig is a 26-year-old man with a T9 complete spinal cord injury from a motor vehicle accident. He has received care from a multidisciplinary spinal rehabilitation unit following initial care in an acute surgical ward. Mr. Sig's complete paraplegia translates into problems of lower muscle power and sensations (*body structure/function*). This impairment results in difficulty walking and moving (*activity limitation*). Mr. Sig is improving slowly with wheelchair mobility and requires ongoing assistance with bathroom transfers. He would have complete difficulty in a nonmodified home environment without the use of equipment or aids and the assistance of others. He would have difficulty returning to his usual work as a bricklayer (*participation restriction*). Mr. Sig is supported by both his long-term girlfriend and his parents (*environmental factors*). He prefers outdoor living and wilderness adventure with boyhood friends (*personal factors*).

BOX 11.3 CASE CONCEPTUALIZATION: A PERSON WITH GUILLAIN-BARRÉ SYNDROME

Ms. Blandish is a 37-year-old woman with Guillain-Barré syndrome. She has weakness in all four limbs, paresthesia, and decreased balance (*body function and structure*) as well as dysphagic and dysphonic symptoms. On admission to a rehabilitation unit, she was independent with bed mobility, mobilized with four-wheeled walker and standby assistance. Ms. Blandish needs assistance with feeding and some aspects of self-care due to upper limb weakness and reduced dexterity. She experiences fatigue during the day with resultant impaired concentration (*activity limitations*). Ms. Blandish is a self-employed chef in the family catering business. She worked a busy schedule of 50 to 60 hours per week and has had to cut down on work hours significantly because of the illness (*participation restriction*). Ms. Blandish previously was well and healthy, with no medical history (*personal factors*). She was an avid long-distance runner, nonsmoker, drank alcohol occasionally, and drove a sports car (personal factors). She lives with her father in a single-story house with two steps and no rail at the front (*environmental factor*).

activities. These correlates are biological health indicators of an individual's intrinsic, physiological capacity given the structural limitations imposed by the health condition or impairment to functioning (Stucki & Bickenbach, 2017) or the "care needed with a person is experiencing limitations in everyday functioning due to aging or a health condition" (Cieza, 2019, p. 2212). Different health conditions often imply a need for disability-specific assessments. In the last decade, *ICF*-based core sets have been proposed that list common impairments for prevalent health conditions such as stroke (Bickenbach et al., 2020; Geyh et al., 2004). The *ICF* core sets provide healthcare professionals and researchers with standardized tools tailored with information of specific health conditions for both long-term and short-term contexts (Bickenbach et al., 2020).

Similarly, modular forms of assessments have been proposed with common core indicators and different branches of indicators from differential diagnoses of disease subtypes (Leone et al., 2005). For example, with stroke the body functions likely impacted are consciousness, orientation, memory, and muscle tone and power. The impact of the stroke experience on these body structures and functions would depend on the site and severity of the lesion (Andelman et al., 2004; Keenan & Gorman, 2007), the specification

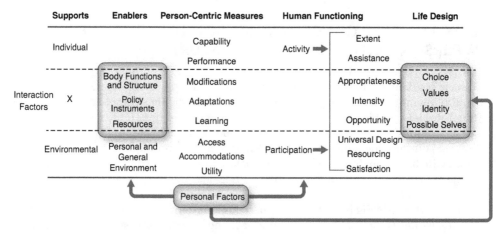

FIGURE 11.2 The Central Role of Person-centric Measures in Rehabilitation Support Interventions for Life Design.

TABLE 11.1 *International Classification of Functioning, Disability and Health* Components and Chapters

Body Functions	Activities and Participation
■ Mental functions	■ Learning and applying knowledge
■ Sensory functions and pain	■ General tasks and demands
■ Voice and speech functions	■ Communication
■ Functions of the cardiovascular, hematological, immunological, and respiratory systems	■ Mobility
	■ Self-care
	■ Domestic life
■ Functions of the digestive, metabolic, and endocrine systems	■ Interpersonal interactions and relationships
■ Genitourinary and reproductive functions	■ Major life areas
■ Neuromusculoskeletal and movement-related functions	■ Community, social, and civil life
■ Functions of the skin and related structures	

Body Structures	Environmental Factors
■ Structure of the nervous system	■ Products and technology
■ The eye, ear, and related structures	■ Natural environment and human-made changes to environment
■ Structures involved in voice and speech	
■ Structure of the cardiovascular, immunological, and respiratory systems	■ Support and relationships
	■ Attitudes
■ Structures related to the digestive, metabolic, and endocrine systems	■ Services, systems, and policies
■ Structure related to genitourinary and reproductive systems	
■ Structures related to movement	
■ Skin and related structures	

Source: Data from WHO, 2001. *International classification of functioning, disability and health: ICF* (pp. 29–30).

of which would make for better targeted rehabilitation intervention (Jacoby et al., 2013). For another example, people with epilepsy, with right-hemisphere lesions, might lack in self-awareness and report less reliably regarding existing difficulties (Keenan & Gorman, 2007). Person-centric assessments with people with right-hemisphere lesions would prioritize support tools for self-monitoring for seizure control medications and physical safety with seizure occurrence.

Nonetheless, even with the benefit of core set listings, assessment for rehabilitation supports must still be individualized, as a person's premorbid functioning and life circumstances may influence recovery and personal functioning in significant life domains.

Activity

The *ICF* defines **activity** as the execution of a task or action by an individual (WHO, 2002). A person can have activity limitations due to an impairment in bodily structure or function that might constrain participation in a preferred or normative role. Alternatively, it is possible for a person to have the ability to engage in an activity yet not be able to carry out the activity due to a lack of opportunity or support (Stancliffe et al., 2016). Nonetheless, a certain level of activity capability or potential is necessary for meaningful participation in key life areas. For instance, if a person is independent in performance of certain core activities, such as mobility, body transfers, and personal activities of daily living (ADLs), they likely would also have an enhanced capacity to participate in life domains that presume such competencies. The *ICF* can provide a list of the activities a person may still able to perform without difficulty due to a condition or impairment. The limitations of those activities communicate the capacity that the individual has for certain ADLs or those routine tasks that are essential for independent living, including getting in and out of bed, eating, showering, and dressing oneself (Edemekong et al., 2019; Maritz et al., 2021; Rovner, 2009).

There is a certain degree of overlap between "activity" and "participation" in Table 11.1. For practical purposes, the first five aspects listed under "Activities and Participation" (learning and applying knowledge, general tasks and demands, communication, mobility, self-care) fall under activities, whereas the last four aspects (domestic life, interpersonal interactions and relationships, major life areas, and community, social, civil life) fall under participation.

ICF qualifiers are utilized to frame and collect person-centric data for rehabilitation support interventions for identified activities and participation roles. When using *ICF* qualifiers, a numerical code is used to record the impact of a problem on the individual across the domains of impairment, activity limitation, participation restrictions, and environmental factors. The numeric qualifiers are on a scale from 0 (*no problem*) to 4 (*complete problem*). (There are two additional qualifiers: 8, *not specified*, and 9, *not applicable*.) For example, Australian health and community services data standards for functioning and disability are based on the *ICF* and are person-centric in their emphasis on person-reported difficulties with activities (applying the *ICF* generic qualifier, noted previously) and perceived need for assistance (0 = *no assistance*; 4 = *high assistance*; Madden, 2010).

Participation

The *ICF* framework considers **participation** to be "involvement in life situations" (WHO, 2001, p. 10). For instance, participation in work, family, recreation and leisure, and education is primary to a satisfying life. Successful participation is defined by "engagement in all aspects of an activity as judged against contemporary . . . community standards and resulting in maximal involvement of the person in the activity" (Thompson et al., 2015, p. 13). Person-centric data on participation are those related to the individual autonomy and independence of people with disabilities, including their freedom to make their own choices regarding priority life areas to invest in, and opportunities to be actively involved in decision-making processes about policies and programs concerning them. The selection or use of person-centric assessments for participation should prioritize those that yield data usable for the design and implementation of rehabilitation supports for meaningful involvement in life situations. Sample person-centric participation-oriented questions might include *What would you like for yourself?* and *How would you like to get that?* For the participation in life domains, the generic *ICF* extent of participation qualifier would be used (0 = *full participation*; 4 = *complete restriction*).

Generic qualifiers to record the extent of functioning or disability in a life domain or category are interpreted so that "0" means *no problem*, "2" means mild problem, "3" means *severe problem*, and "4" is indicative of *complete problem*. For example, a record of *mild problem* means participation restrictions in a life domain that are present less than 25% of the time and with an intensity a person can tolerate, with relatively rare problem instances over the last 30 days. A record of *complete problem* means participation restrictions are pervasive and present more than 95% of the time, with an intensity that totally disrupts the person's day-to-day life and problems experienced every day over the last 30 days.

Standards for person-centric measures of participation are evolving (Madden, 2010), and thus far only Australian standards apply the degree of satisfaction with participation (0 = *high satisfaction*; 5 = *complete restriction and dissatisfaction*; Madden, 2010). Regardless of practice jurisdiction, person-centric measures of participation should be collected on at least three areas of life that the person with a disability identifies as important to start with, and with a focus on (a) *where they are very pleased with their participation/involvement* and (b) *where they want to see change*. Ancillary questions should ask about things and people around the person in the everyday environment that help their participation in priority life domains. This inquiry should include questions about the equipment used (or needed), building design, people, attitudes, and services.

Environment

The *ICF* defines **environmental factors** as those that constitute the physical, social, and attitudinal environment in which individuals live and conduct their lives. In rehabilitation service provisioning, a key consideration is to surmount and not circumvent the participation restrictions on the individual (Thompson et al., 2015). Environmental factors are essential to understanding the interaction between the health condition or impairment and its impact on activity limitations, participation restrictions, and the individual's personal factors (Loidl et al., 2016). The physical, social, and attitudinal environments in which people live or conduct their lives are important for the supports they would require for a satisfying life. These include their use of products and technology as well as social networks for health and well-being, including at home, in the workplace, and when shifting community attitudes toward to a more positive orientation toward severe disabilities.

The impact of environmental barriers is determined by the assessed level of difficulty in activity capacity and personal access to physical and social resources (Loidl et al., 2016). With physical disability or cognitive impairment, an assessment for accessibility of environments and attention to modifiable falls risk factors are important to participation support considerations. For example, this would be the case in home environment assessments to provide supports needed for safety from injuries (Lockwood et al., 2015). However, the definition of physical environment is much broader than just the home setting and includes the built environment for which health impact assessments may be needed as a part of comprehensive rehabilitation (Dannenberg et al., 2008; Dannenberg, 2016;). Social and attitudinal barriers consist of elements that often are outside the individual's control, although they also modifiable through supportive pro-disability policy implementation. Within the disability and health policy frameworks, practices cognizant of *ICF* environmental social–attitudinal barriers to living with a disability include eligibility criteria to access disability support funding and enforcing accessibility requirements for transport or for public spaces.

The environmental factors domain attributes are scored on two qualifiers. The first qualifier addresses access/barriers issues with reverse scoring, so that a higher value denotes less access or more barriers: 0 (*no barrier*) to 4 (*complete barrier*). The second qualifier addresses the activity or participation facilitation that would be needed, with a higher value denoting greater need for support: 0 (*no facilitator*) to 4 (*complete facilitator*).

Person-centric assessments consider possible environmental influences on goal attainment and value realization. They seek to address solution-focused questions about the environment of participation, such as (a) How might the environmental context (actual or perceived) affect the scope and nature of personal goals in rehabilitation? (b) What aspects of the environment can be changed? and (c) What perceptions of the environment can be changed?

Personal Factors

Personal factors refer to "the particular background of an individual's life and living, including features of the individual that are not part of a health condition or health states, and which can impact functioning positively or negatively" (Grotkamp et al., 2012, Grotkamp et al., 2020). They include individual differences such as gender, age, ethnicity, learning orientation, educational level, personality traits, "coping styles, social background, education, profession, past and current experience, overall behaviour pattern, character and other factors that influence how disability is experienced by the individual. Their assessment is left to the user, if needed" (Grotkamp et al., 2020; WHO, 2001, p. 19).

Some personal factors, such as age, gender, and ethnicity, are not modifiable even though they may carry risk factors for disability. For example, the risk factor for colorectal cancer increases with age (Danaei et al., 2005) and the risk of Tay–Sachs disease is higher with Ashkenazi Jewish ancestry (Bach et al., 2001). Some personal factors are modifiable such as the health-related risk factors associated with preventable, diet and smoking disease-specific mortality associated with personal lifestyle choices (Danaei et al., 2011). Other factors are changeable or modifiable, and important for rehabilitation goal setting, intervention design, implementation, and evaluation (Mpofu & Oakland, 2010a). These include personal psychological assets such as learning or applying knowledge, coping and resilient living, and so forth. Grotkamp et al. (2012) classified personal factors into 72 categories, arranged in chapters as follows: general factors normally unchangeable; a person's inherent physical and mental constitution; more modifiable factors such as attitudes, basic skills, and behaviour patterns; life situation and socioeconomic/sociocultural factors; and other health factors (premorbid functioning, preexisting health conditions, prior interventions).

Person-centric assessments for personal factors tap into the priority value preferences of the person with a disability for types of activities and participation across life domains (Mpofu et al., 2010). For each area of life, person-centric assessments should address (a) how *important* this area of life is to the person, (b) whether they have good *opportunities* to participate and the *choice* about participating, (c) whether they feel able to *control* his or her involvement in this area of life, (d) whether they spend enough *time* on activities in this area (and frequently enough), and (e) whether they feel fully *involved* and pleased with the way he or she is able to participate. Person-centric assessment of personal factors presumes adherence to ethical aspects of nonmaleficence as characterized by respect for privacy issues, personal autonomy and choices, and the use of the data in nonstigmatizing ways (Grotkamp et al., 2012; Peterson, 2009; Peterson & Threats, 2005).

INTERNATIONAL CLASSIFICATION OF FUNCTIONING, DISABILITY AND HEALTH CORE SETS

ICF core sets are the "minimal standards for the assessment, communication and reporting of functioning and health for clinical studies, clinical encounters and multi-professional comprehensive assessment and management" (Grill et al., 2005, p. 361). They are narrowed selections of *ICF* categories for specific health conditions for guiding rehabilitation interventions (Grill et al., 2005). The *ICF* core sets are developed mostly by expert consensus-building surveys of health professionals from various fields accustomed to work regarding that health condition and are informed by the extant literature (Cieza et al., 2010; Selb et al., 2005; Stier-Jarmer et al., 2005). The *ICF* brief core sets are abbreviated categories describing disability and functioning in specific populations for expedited decision-making in research, planning for treatment, and patient support (Cieza et al., 2010; Selb et al., 2005). While *ICF* core sets exist for health conditions, such as, spinal cord injury and neurological conditions, more continue to be developed using the research evidence and expert survey consensus process (Cieza et al., 2010; Ewert et al., 2005).

THE INTERNATIONAL CLASSIFICATION OF FUNCTIONING, DISABILITY AND HEALTH AND OTHER NOSOLOGIES OF DISABILITY, FUNCTIONING, AND HEALTH

The *ICF* classifies functioning and disability associated with health conditions. It can be used to complement other medical-oriented systems, such as the *DSM-5* (APA, 2013), the

WHODAS 2.0 (WHO, 2012), and the *ICD-10* (WHO, 2011, 2014). The *DSM-5* is a diagnostic tool for mental disorders, whereas the *ICD-10* gives users an etiological framework for classification by diagnosis of diseases, disorders, and other health conditions. The **WHODAS 2.0** is a measure of general functioning with mental disorder and is used together with the *DSM-5*. The **ICD-10** belongs to the WHO family of international classifications, including the *ICF* and the *WHODAS 2.0* (WHO, 2012).

The *Diagnostic and Statistical Manual of Mental Disorders, Fifth Edition* and the *International Statistical Classification of Diseases and Related Health Problems, 10th Edition*

The *DSM-5* and *ICD-10* enable comprehensive assessment of the anatomical or physiological, structural, and mental health aspects of disability to inform interventions framed on the *ICF*. This assessment includes the impact that the specific health condition may have on activity restrictions and participation limitations for which rehabilitation support interventions would be needed (Mpofu et al., 2016; Peterson, 2011; WHO, 2013). Moreover, data on disease or disorders (from the *DSM-5, ICD-10*) may have implications for policies on health and functioning at the population level, as in disability support funding-stream eligibility. For person-centric assessments, information on incidence and prevalence of disease, disorders, and health conditions (provided by *DSM-5, ICD-10*), and information about health and health-related functioning (provided by *ICF, WHODAS 2.0*) can be combined to inform person-oriented health and well-being support systems. Using these health and disability systems together in a person-centric way would enable the appropriate targeting of supports for living well with disability.

Physical and psychological functioning (as framed in the *ICF*) do not necessarily overlap with the severity or clinical significance of a diagnosis (as diagnosed per the *DSM-5*). This is because personal functioning is realized in interaction with one's environment, which includes the available supports for enacting specific life roles. Thus, a person with a severe psychiatric disorder and with supports for work participation (e.g., flexible hours, digital task prompting, coworker/supervisor task sharing) may be successful in a competitive work environment. This vocational outcome of would be contraindicated by a reliance on a *DSM-5* (or *ICD-10*) diagnosis alone. This clinical reality calls for psychiatric diagnosis (per *DSM-5*) to be considered separate and apart from personal functioning with psychiatric disability (per the *ICF* framework; see also WHO, 2001).

The *World Health Organization Disability Assessment Schedule 2.0*

The *WHODAS 2.0* is a self-administered questionnaire developed for adults that is used to measure the disability-related difficulties a person may have due to a long- or short-term physical or mental health conditions (Andrews et al., 2009; WHO, 2012; Kimber et al., 2015). Based on the *ICF*, it is used to measure global health and disability levels as they relate to a person's health-related quality of life (Carlozzi et al., 2015; Üstün et al., 2010).

The *International Society of Physical and Rehabilitation Medicine's Universal Clinical Functioning Information Tool*

Based on the ICF framework, the *International Society of Physical and Rehabilitation Medicine's Universal Clinical Functioning Information Tool* (*ClinFIT*) "captures individual [levels of] functioning across the continuum of care and over the lifespan" (Frontera et al., 2019, p. 19). This tool assesses for the essential rehabilitation service needs and

BOX 11.4 CASE CONCEPTUALIZATION UTILIZING THE *ICF* AND *DSM-5:* A PERSON WITH A SOMATIC SYMPTOM DISORDER

Ms. Chandler had a lower right below-the-knee amputation following a car accident. She has recovered successfully from the physical treatment with a healthy amputation stump and uses a prosthesis. She reports that she experiences ongoing pain from "the leg" (i.e., the prosthesis). Her physician treatment team cannot find probable cause for the pain. Ms. Chandler has been taking pain medications for suspected stump neuromas (sensitive nerve endings that may form under an amputation stump). The pain did not improve on opioids and she experienced side effects, including severe constipation. Ongoing monitoring of analgesia and side effects of pain relief medication has been a critical part of the medical treatment plan, as pain was a central problem for Ms. Chandler. Nonetheless, she reports significant distress and anxiety from the pain around the amputation stump, despite a seemingly well-fitting prosthetic device. She states that she experiences significant restrictions to mobility in her house, with pain that escalates when climbing stairs or transferring onto the driver's seat of her high-ride-height sport utility vehicle. Ms. Chandler uses adaptive seating in her workplace, including a flexi-desk that allows her to work while standing, which improves her back and leg muscle tone. However, she reports restrictions to her leisure activities, such as shopping. Rehabilitation support interventions for Ms. Chandler to enhance her mobility included gait retraining, balance training, strengthening exercises, and fall prevention education. Other rehabilitation supports included weight control with dietician support, an assessment of ADLs, and home modifications with an occupational therapist.

types for different patient populations, across age groups and cultural contexts reporting patient functioning (ISPRM, 2020). With the ability to be tailored throughout all phases of a health condition and corresponding changes to health condition treatment over time, *ClinFIT* is a long-term assessment tool useful for clinical practice, rehabilitation care quality management, and health-related research (Frontera et al., 2019).

Successful living with a health condition often requires attention to influences on personal functioning beyond those predicated on the clinical diagnosis per se. Moreover, physical health conditions may influence mental health functioning, necessitating treatment for the mental health condition as part of a comprehensive health management plan. Consider the case described in Box 11.4 of a woman who sustained a below-the-knee amputation from a motor vehicle accident, and the extent to which the *ICF* framework can be used together with *DSM-5* for a comprehensive treatment plan. Ms. Chandler would be diagnosed, using the *DSM-5*, with somatic symptom disorder. Clearly, comprehensive treatment would have to consider both her *DSM-5* diagnosis and her personal functioning have framed per the *ICF*.

INTERNATIONAL CLASSIFICATION OF FUNCTIONING, DISABILITY AND HEALTH FRAMEWORK APPLICATIONS TO LIFE DESIGN WITH DISABILITY

The *ICF* is a highly adaptable framework for the provision of rehabilitation counseling services (Hollenweger, 2013). Thus far, these applications have tended to address rehabilitation support needs in the context of physical medicine and rehabilitation with priority goals to restore, maintain, and augment functioning with disability. This focus will remain an important goal of rehabilitation services. However, life design with disability goes beyond the interventions aimed at restoring, maintaining, and augmenting functioning to reach toward enhancing participation in life domains of significance to the person with a disability in the context of his or her environment (Mpofu et al., 2019). The *ICF* framework concepts are adaptable for the design, selection, and use of person-centric assessments in the context of a rehabilitation counseling approach to support the maximum self-determination and inclusion of individuals with disabilities.

A figure (Figure 11.2) presented earlier depicts the central role of person-centric measures in rehabilitation support interventions for life design. The model presents person-centric assessments that are at the core of support interventions for life design with disability. According to Figure 11.2, rehabilitation supports are required at the individual and environmental levels with requisite enablers. Data from person-centric assessments are needed to inform the supports for human functioning in regard to activities and participation to enable life design with disability. Personal factors or the attributes of the individual (as stated earlier) underlie individualized rehabilitation support interventions for life design with disability. Ongoing life design choices and outcomes influence the types of evidence needed for their sustenance through the agency of personal factors, making for a cyclic or mutually reinforcing system for human functioning with disability. The components of the rehabilitation supports model based on person-centric assessments are explained next.

Individual and Environmental Supports

Individual supports have been defined as the "resources and strategies that aim to promote the development, education, interests and personal well-being of a person and enhance individual functioning" (Schalock et al., 2010, p. 224). Examples of individual supports include information and education on living well with disability, technology to enable the person to function optimally, and other supports for successful transactions with the environment. The individual and environmental support needs are interactive, in that supports to enhance a person's capabilities also enable their participation in the environment as much as environmental support enhances the person's functioning.

Environmental supports are those aimed at bridging the gap between a person's capabilities and the demands for successful living with disability. The specific nature and function of environmental supports will depend on the level of environment for personal functioning. Two levels of the environment are relevant to human functioning: personal and typical or general. The typical or general environment is one in which everyone participates. Examples include community venues and amenities, such as shopping, recreation, work setting, health, and public transportation systems. This typical or normative environment is what the *ICF* framework describes regarding participation needs when a person has a health condition for which support may be indicated. It is objective and verifiable as to its characteristics and often policy instruments for its regulation exist.

By contrast, the **personal environment** is defined by the individual's lived experiences. The personal environment is mostly subjective. For example, workplace social climate may be different for a person with a disability, in how he or she perceives being treated by peers and supervisors. If a workplace social climate is discriminatory, an inequitable work participation situation exists for people with disabilities, suggesting needs for evidence on the employing organization's implementation of disability-inclusive work practices. The extent to which the personal environment overlaps the typical environment as interpreted by the individual largely determines the levels of environmental supports needed. The larger the overlap between the personal and normative environments, the lower the need for individualized environmental supports. General environments with universal design features (those with wide scope to accommodate diversity in human performance attributes) have person-centric qualities (Mpofu & Oakland, 2010a, 2010b). Person-centric rehabilitation support interventions may be aimed at bridging the gap between the personal and typical environments.

Enablers

Enablers are the supports needed for engagement in activities and environments of choice. In the *ICF* framework, body structure and function are enablers in that the type and severity of disability from impairment affect personal functioning. In other words, some level of physical functioning would enable participation (with personal and environmental supports). Disability support policy instruments and their implementation mechanisms are enablers to living with disability if appropriately targeted to the needs of the person with a disability (Putnam & Frieden, 2014). However, some policy-determined disability supports may not address the needs for meaningful community living with disability, and evidence is needed as to which aspects of policy-determined tools are enablers or barriers to successful community living with disability (Wallace, 2011). Finally, the resources available to the individual (material, financial, social) are significant enablers of rehabilitation supports for life design with disability. For instance, health needs that may arise from living with disability may be materially and financially costly (Iglehart, 2011, Iglehart, 2016; Kaiser Family Foundation, 2011; National Council on Disability, 2009), requiring innovative management solutions for successful living with disability. Assessments that provide data on disability supports enablers are critical to provision of person-centric rehabilitation care service.

Person-Centric Assessments

As previously discussed, person-centric assessments for individual supports are those that yield data on the person's capabilities (what a person can do) and performance (what a person does). Assessments for environmental supports will provide data on environmental access for and accommodations of disability. In addition, person-centric assessments would also provide data on the utility of specific environmental supports for disability, including on environmental modifications and adaptations to bridge the gap between the person's abilities (capacities and performance) and the personal learning required for successful living with disability.

Human Functioning

Human functioning is defined primarily as engagement or participation in the major life areas (WHO, 2001). Types of person-centric assessment indicators for activity (i.e., need for assistance) and participation (i.e., satisfaction with participation) with disability were previously considered in some detail following the *ICF* framework guidelines. As previously noted, activity and participation overlap only partially, in that a person capable of specific activities may not necessarily participate in life domains in which those activity abilities would be required. The gap between activity and participation involvement may be explained variously, including the perceived (in)appropriateness (Mpofu & Oakland, 2006), the intensity of support demands (Stancliffe et al., 2016; Thompson et al., 2015), or a lack of opportunity (Mpofu & Wilson, 2004; Stancliffe et al., 2016). Person-centric assessments for rehabilitation supports provide data on the appropriateness, intensity demands, and opportunity affordances for a satisfying life with disability.

Life Design

Previous sections considered the significance of a life design approach to rehabilitation supports with disability. Appropriate person-centric outcome measures for life design would include those regarding prioritized choices (autonomy), personal values and salient identities (relational worth, possible selves; Mpofu & Conyers, 2004), and aspirations for present and future living (competencies; Dune & Mpofu, 2015; Mpofu, 2013) and satisfaction with life (e.g., Diener et al., 1985; Waterman et al., 2010).

Autonomy refers to the need to feel that one is free to regulate one's own behavior rather than being controlled by external sources (Deci & Ryan, 2000); it indicates a sense of personal choice, free will, and ownership of one's behavior (Haivas et al., 2014). *Competence* refers to the need to interact effectively with one's environment to take opportunities to engage in activities within one's ability (Deci & Ryan, 2000; Haivas et al., 2014). *Relatedness* refers to being connected to others, in meaningful reciprocal relationships in which the individual is supported by and cared for by others (Deci & Ryan, 2000; Haivas et al., 2014; Mpofu, 2013). As people with disabilities are supported in achieving their choices in the context of meaningful relationships with their allies and the community in general, they realize the wide array of possible selves they can aspire to be in their life settings.

CONCLUSION

Person-centric assessments have the unique strength of adopting a whole-person perspective premised on capabilities and potential, rather than being overly focused on disability and participation restrictions. Assessments for treating impairment alone, though important, may lack person-centric qualities and undervalue the individualized needs of people with disabilities from a life design perspective. Person-centric assessment is premised on personal choices, values, and attainment of a satisfying life with disability, and uses appropriate data for understanding how people with disabilities construct meaning in activities and participation. Person-centric interventions are aligned with disability rights-based approaches in rehabilitation counseling that value the views of people with disabilities regarding their self-determination and full community inclusion. The WHO *ICF* provides a framework for a whole-person approach to assessment in which biological impairments are considered in the context of personal functioning, while also taking into account the environmental factors. Using *ICF* qualifiers personalizes assessment data to be responsive to specific ompetencies, offering the potential for assessments to be supported with customized rehabilitation counseling interventions. The *ICF* can be used to complement the *DSM-5*, *WHODAS 2.0*, and *ICD-10/ICD-11* approaches to gather data usable in person-centric ways to optimize the effectiveness of rehabilitation counseling interventions.

CONTENT REVIEW QUESTIONS

1. How does prioritizing person-centric data in rehabilitation assessments enable the identification of competencies and resources for effective life design with disability?
2. How does the construct of person-centric assessment apply to rehabilitation counseling practice settings?
3. What differentiates person-centric assessments from those focused on impairment and disability?
4. How does the *ICF* framework apply to the design, selection, and implementation of person-centric assessments?
5. Describe the structure of the WHO *ICF*.
6. How does using the *ICF* together with the *DSM-5* and *ICD-10/ICD-11* give incremental value to person-centric data for rehabilitation support interventions?

REFERENCES

American Psychiatric Association. (2013). *Diagnostic and statistical manual of mental disorders* (5th ed.). American Psychiatric Publishing. https://doi.org/10.1176/appi.books.9780890425596

Andelman, F., Zuckerman-Feldhay, E., Hoffien, D., Fried, I., & Neufeld, M. Y. (2004). Lateralization of deficit in self-awareness of memory in patients with intractable epilepsy. *Epilepsia, 45*(7), 826–833. https://doi.org/10.1111/j.0013-9580.2004.51703.x

Andrews, G., Kemp, A., Sunderland, M., Von Korff, M., & Ustun, T. B. (2009). Normative data for the 12 item WHO Disability Assessment Schedule 2.0. *PloS One, 4*(12), Article e8343. https://doi.org/10.1371/journal.pone.0008343

Bach, G., Tomczak, J., Risch, N., & Ekstein, J. (2001). Tay-Sachs screening in the Jewish Ashkenazi population: DNA testing is the preferred procedure. *American Journal of Medical Genetics, 99*(1), 70–75. https://doi.org/10.1002/1096-8628(20010215)99:1<70::aid-ajmg1120>3.0.co;2-0

Bickenbach, J. E., Cieza, A., Selb, M., & Stucki, G. (2020). *ICF core sets: Manual for clinical practice* (2nd ed.). Hogrefe Publishing. https://doi.org/10.1027/00572-000

Bond, K. S., Mpofu, E., & Millington, M. (2015). Treating women with genito-pelvic pain/penetration disorder: Influences of patient agendas on help-seeking. *Journal of Family Medicine, 2*(4), 1033–1041.

Carlozzi, N. E., Kratz, A. L., Downing, N. R., Goodnight, S., Miner, J. A., Migliore, N., & Paulsen, J. S. (2015). Validity of the 12-item World Health Organization Disability Assessment Schedule 2.0 (WHODAS 2.0) in individuals with Huntington disease (HD). *Quality of Life Research, 24*(8), 1963–1971. https://doi.org/10.1007/s11136-015-0930-x

Cieza, A. (2019). Rehabilitation the health strategy of the 21st century, really? *Archives of Physical Medicine and Rehabilitation, 100*(11), 2212–2214. https://doi.org/10.1016/j.apmr.2019.05.019

Cieza, A., Fayed, N., Bickenbach, J., & Prodinger, B. (2019). Refinements of the ICF Linking Rules to strengthen their potential for establishing comparability of health information. *Disability and Rehabilitation, 41*(5), 574–583. https://doi.org/10.3109/09638288.2016.1145258

Cieza, A., Kirchberger, I., Biering-Sørensen, F., Baumberger, M., Charlifue, S., Post, M. W., Campbell, R., Kovindha, A., Ring, H., Sinnott, A., Kostanjsek, N., & Stucki, G. (2010). ICF Core Sets for individuals with spinal cord injury in the long-term context. *Spinal Cord, 48*(4), 305–312. https://doi.org/10.1038/sc.2009.183

Cloninger, C. R. (2011). Person-centred integrative care. *Journal of Evaluation in Clinical Practice, 17*(2), 371–372. https://doi.org/10.1111/j.1365-2753.2010.01583.x

Danaei, G., Ding, E. L., Mozaffarian, D., Taylor, B., Rehm, J., Murray, C. J. L., & Ezzati, M. (2011). The preventable causes of death in the United States: comparative risk assessment of dietary, lifestyle, and metabolic risk factors. *PLoS Medicine, 6*(4), e1000058. https://doi.org/10.1371/journal.pmed.1000058

Danaei, G., Vander Hoorn, S., Lopez, A. D., Murray, C. J. L., Ezzati, M., & Comparative Risk Assessment collaborating group (Cancers). (2005). Causes of cancer in the world: Comparative risk assessment of nine behavioural and environmental risk factors. *Lancet (London, England), 366*(9499), 1784–1793. https://doi.org/10.1016/S0140-6736(05)67725-2

Dannenberg, A. L. (2016). Effectiveness of health impact assessments: A synthesis of data from five impact evaluation reports. *Preventing Chronic Disease, 13*, E84. https://doi.org/10.5888/pcd13.150559

Dannenberg, A. L., Bhatia, R., Cole, B. L., Heaton, S. K., Feldman, J. D., & Rutt, C. D. (2008). Use of health impact assessment in the U.S.: 27 case studies, 1999-2007. *American Journal of Preventive Medicine, 34*(3), 241–256. https://doi.org/10.1016/j.amepre.2007.11.015

de Silva, D. (2014). *Helping measure person-centred care*. The Health Foundation.

Deci, E. L., & Ryan, R. M. (2000). The "what" and "why" of goal pursuits: Human needs and the self-determination of behaviour. *Psychological Inquiry, 11*(4), 227–268. https://doi.org/10.1207/S15327965PLI1104_01

Diener, E. (1984). Subjective well-being. *Psychological Bulletin, 95*(3), 542–575. https://doi.org/10.1037/0033-2909.95.3.542

Diener, E., Emmons, R. A., Larsen, R. J., & Griffin, S. (1985). The Satisfaction With Life Scale. *Journal of Personality Assessment, 49*(1), 71–75. https://doi.org/10.1207/s15327752jpa4901_13

Dijkstra, R. F., Niessen, L. W., Braspenning, J. C. C., Adang, E., & Grol, R. T. P. M. (2006). Patient-centred and professional-directed implementation strategies for diabetes guidelines: a cluster-randomized trial-based cost-effectiveness analysis. *Diabetic Medicine*, 23(2), 164–170. https://doi.org/10.1111/j.1464-5491.2005.01751.x

Dune, T., & Mpofu, E. (2015). Evaluating Person-Oriented Measures to Understand Sexuality with Cerebral Palsy: Procedures and Applications. *International Journal of Social Science Studies*, 3(4), 144–155. https://doi.org/10.11114/ijsss.v3i4.903

Edemekong, P. F., Bomgaars, D. L., Sukumaran, S., & Levy, S. B. (2019). Activities of daily living. In *StatPearls*. StatPearls Publishing. https://doi.org/10.4135/9781452240121

Ewert, T., Grill, E., Bartholomeyczik, S., Finger, M., Mokrusch, T., Kostanjsek, N., & Stucki, G. (2005). ICF Core Set for patients with neurological conditions in the acute hospital. *Disability and Rehabilitation*, 27(7–8), 367–373. https://doi.org/10.1080/09638280400014014

Frontera, W., Gimigliano, F., Melvin, J., Li, J., Li, L., Lains, J., & Stucki, G. (2019). ClinFIT: ISPRM's Universal Functioning Information Tool based on the WHO's ICF. *The Journal of the International Society of Physical and Rehabilitation Medicine*, 2(1), 19. https://doi.org/10.4103/jisprm.jisprm_36_19

Geyh, S., Cieza, A., Schouten, J., Dickson, H., Frommelt, P., Omar, Z., Kostanjsek, N., Ring, H., & Stucki, G. (2004). ICF Core Sets for stroke. *Journal of Rehabilitation Medicine*, (44 Suppl), 135–141. https://doi.org/10.1080/16501960410016776

Grill, E., Ewert, T., Chatterji, S., Kostanjsek, N., & Stucki, G. (2005). ICF Core Sets development for the acute hospital and early post-acute rehabilitation facilities. *Disability and Rehabilitation*, 27(7–8), 361–366. https://doi.org/10.1080/09638280400013974

Grotkamp, S., Cibis, W., Brüggemann, S., Coenen, M., Gmünder, H. P., Keller, K., Nüchtern, E., Schwegler, U., Seger, W., Staubli, S., von Raison, B., Weißmann, R., Bahemann, A., Fuchs, H., Rink, M., Schian, M., & Schmitt, K. (2020). Personal factors classification revisited: A proposal in the light of the biopsychosocial model of the World Health Organization (WHO). *The Australian Journal of Rehabilitation Counselling*, 26(2), 73–91. https://doi.org/10.1017/jrc.2020.14

Grotkamp, S. L., Cibis, W. M., Nüchtern, E. A. M., von Mittelstaedt, G., & Seger, W. K. F. (2012). Personal factors in the International Classification of Functioning, Disability and Health: Prospective evidence. *The Australian Journal of Rehabilitation Counselling*, 18(1), 1–24. https://doi.org/10.1017/jrc.2012.4

Haivas, S., Hofmans, J., & Pepermans, R. (2014). "What Motivates You Doesn't Motivate Me": Individual Differences in the Needs Satisfaction-Motivation Relationship of Romanian Volunteers. *Applied Psychology*, 63(2), 326–343. https://doi.org/10.1111/j.1464-0597.2012.00525.x

Harley, D., Mpofu, E., Scanlan, J., Umeasiegbu, V., & Mpofu, N. (2015). Disability social inclusion and community health. In E. Mpofu (Ed.), *Community-oriented health services: Practices across disciplines* (pp. 207–222). Springer Publishing. https://doi.org/10.1891/9780826198181

Hollenweger, J. (2013). Developing applications of the ICF in education systems: addressing issues of knowledge creation, management and transfer. *Disability and Rehabilitation*, 35(13), 1087–1091. https://doi.org/10.3109/09638288.2012.740135

Iglehart, J. K. (2011). Desperately seeking savings: states shift more Medicaid enrollees to managed care. *Health Affairs (Project Hope)*, 30(9), 1627–1629. https://doi.org/10.1377/hlthaff.2011.0836

Iglehart, J. K. (2016). Future of Long-Term Care and the Expanding Role of Medicaid Managed Care. *The New England Journal of Medicine*, 374(2), 182–187. https://doi.org/10.1056/NEJMhpr1510026

International Society of Physical and Rehabilitation Medicine. (2020). *Survey: Proposal ClinFIT Covid-19*. https://www.isprm.org/survey-proposal-clinfit-covid-19

Jacoby, A., Baker, G. A., Crossley, J., & Schachter, S. (2013). Tools for assessing quality of life in epilepsy patients. *Expert Review of Neurotherapeutics*, 13(12), 1355–1369. https://doi.org/10.1586/14737175.2013.850032

Kahneman, D., Diener, E., & Schwarz, N. (1999). *Well-being: The foundations of hedonic psychology*. Russell Sage.

Kaiser Family Foundation. (2011). *Managing costs and improving care: Team-based care of the chronically ill*. http://kff.org/health-costs/event/managing-costs-and-improving-care-team-based

Keenan, J. P., & Gorman, J. (2007). The causal role of the right hemisphere in self-awareness: It is the brain that is selective. *Cortex; a Journal Devoted to the Study of the Nervous System and Behavior, 43*(8), 1074–1082. https://doi.org/10.1016/S0010-9452(08)70705-6

Kellett, D., Mpofu, E., & Madden, R. (2013). Reflective action assessment with a prospective clinical problem solving tool in the context of rehabilitation medicine: an illustrative case study. *Disability and Rehabilitation, 35*(13), 1048–1054. https://doi.org/10.3109/09638288.2012.720348

Kimber, M., Rehm, J., & Ferro, M. A. (2015). Measurement invariance of the WHODAS 2.0 in a population-based sample of uouth. *PloS One, 10*(11), e0142385. https://doi.org/10.1371/journal.pone.0142385

Leone, M. A., Beghi, E., Righini, C., Apolone, G., & Mosconi, P. (2005). Epilepsy and quality of life in adults: A review of instruments. *Epilepsy Research, 66*(1–3), 23–44. https://doi.org/10.1016/j.eplepsyres.2005.02.009

Lockwood, K. J., Taylor, N. F., & Harding, K. E. (2015). Pre-discharge home assessment visits in assisting patients' return to community living: A systematic review and meta-analysis. *Journal of Rehabilitation Medicine, 47*(4), 289–299. https://doi.org/10.2340/16501977-1942

Loidl, V., Oberhauser, C., Ballert, C., Coenen, M., Cieza, A., & Sabariego, C. (2016). Which environmental factors have the highest impact on the performance of people experiencing difficulties in capacity? *International Journal of Environmental Research and Public Health, 13*(4), 416. https://doi.org/10.3390/ijerph13040416

Madden, R. H. (2010). *Self-reporting on participation and environment: Can we make more use of Australia's national data standards.* Australian ICF Disability and Rehabilitation Research Program. Australian Institute of Health and Welfare.

Madden, R. H., Fortune, N., Cheeseman, D., Mpofu, E., & Bundy, A. (2013). Fundamental questions before recording or measuring functioning and disability. *Disability and Rehabilitation, 35*(13), 1092–1096. https://doi.org/10.3109/09638288.2012.720350

Madden, R. H., Glozier, N., Mpofu, E., & Llewellyn, G. (2011). Eligibility, the ICF and the UN Convention: Australian perspectives. *BMC Public Health, 11*(Suppl 4), S6. https://doi.org/10.1186/1471-2458-11-S4-S6

Maritz, A., Eager, B., & De Klerk, S. (2021). Entrepreneurship and self-employment for mature-aged people. *Australian Journal of Career Development, 30*(1), 3–14. https://doi.org/10.1177/1038416220978971

Mpofu, E. (2013). Qualities of life design measures with chronic illness or disability. *Disability and Rehabilitation, 35*(13), 1055–1058. https://doi.org/10.3109/09638288.2012.720352

Mpofu, E., & Bishop, M. (2006). Value change and adjustment to disability: Implications for rehabilitation education, practice, and research. *Rehabilitation Education, 20*(3), 147–161. https://doi.org/10.1891/088970106805074412

Mpofu, E., Bishop, M., & Hirschi, A. (2010). Assessment of values. In E. Mpofu & T. Oakland (Eds.), *Rehabilitation and health assessment: Applying ICF guidelines* (pp. 381–407). Springer Publishing.

Mpofu, E., & Conyers, L. M. (2004). A representational theory perspective of minority status and people with disabilities: Implications for rehabilitation education and practice. *Rehabilitation Counseling Bulletin, 47*(3), 142–151. https://doi.org/10.1177/00343552040470030301

Mpofu, E., Madden, R., Athanasou, J. A., Manga, R. Z., Gitchel, W. D., Peterson, D. B., & Chou, C. (2012). Person-centered assessment in rehabilitation and health. In P. J. Toriello, M. Bishop, & P. D. Rumrill (Eds.), *New directions in rehabilitation counseling: Creative responses to professional, clinical, and educational challenges* (pp. 209–235). Aspen Professional Services.

Mpofu, E., Madden, R., Madden, R., Kellett, D., Peterson, D. B., Gitchel, W. D., & Lee, E. J. (2016). Advances in rehabilitation and health assessments. In F. T. L. Leong, D. Bartram, F. M. Cheung, K. F. Geisinger, & D. Iliescu (Eds.), *The ITC international handbook of testing and assessment* (pp. 244–255). Oxford University Press.

Mpofu, E., & Oakland, T. (2006). Assessment of value change in adults with acquired disabilities. In M. Hersen (Ed.), *Clinician's handbook of adult behavioral assessment* (pp. 601–630). Elsevier.

Mpofu, E., & Oakland, T. (Eds.). (2010a). *Rehabilitation and health assessment: Applying ICF guidelines.* Springer Publishing.

Mpofu, E., & Oakland, T. (Eds.). (2010b). *Assessment in rehabilitation and health.* Merrill/Pearson.

Mpofu, E., Tansey, T., Mpofu, N., Tu, W., & Li, Q. (2019). Employment practices with people with autism spectrum disorder in the digital age. In I. L. Potgieter, N. Ferreira, & M. Coetzee (Eds.),

Theory, research and dynamics of career wellbeing (pp. 309–326). Springer Cham. https://doi.org/10 .1007/978-3-030-28180-9

Mpofu, E., & Wilson, K. B. (2004). Opportunity structure and transition practices with students with disabilities: The role of family, culture, and community. *Journal of Applied Rehabilitation Counseling, 35*(2), 9–16. https://doi.org/10.1891/0047-2220.35.2.9

National Council on Disability. (2009). *The current state of health care for people with disabilities.* http:// www.ncd.gov/rawmedia_repository/0d7c848f_3d97_43b3_bea5_36e1d97f973d.pdf

Olsson, L. E., Jakobsson Ung, E., Swedberg, K., & Ekman, I. (2013). Efficacy of person-centred care as an intervention in controlled trials - A systematic review. *Journal of Clinical Nursing, 22*(3–4), 456–465. https://doi.org/10.1111/jocn.12039

Peterson, D. B. (2009). The international classification of functioning, disability, and health (ICF): Applications for professional counseling. In I. Marini & M. A. Stebnicki (Eds.), *The professional counselor's desk reference* (pp. 529–542). Springer Publishing Company.

Peterson, D. B. (2011). *Psychological aspects of functioning, disability and health.* Springer Publishing.

Peterson, D. B., & Elliott, T. R. (2008). Advances in conceptualizing and studying disability. In S. Brown & R. Lent (Eds.), *Handbook of counseling psychology* (4th ed., pp. 212–230). Wiley.

Peterson, D. B., & Threats, T. T. (2005). Ethical and clinical implications of the International Classification of Functioning, Disability and Health (ICF) in rehabilitation education. *Rehabilitation Education, 19*(2/3), 129–138.

Prodinger, B., Cieza, A., Oberhauser, C., Bickenbach, J., Üstün, T. B., Chatterji, S., & Stucki, G. (2016). Toward the international classification of functioning, disability and health (ICF) rehabilitation set: A minimal generic set of domains for rehabilitation as a health strategy. *Archives of Physical Medicine and Rehabilitation, 97*(6), 875–884. https://doi.org/10.1016/j.apmr.2015.12.030

Putnam, M., & Frieden, L. (2014). Sharpening the Aim of Long-Term Services and Supports Policy. *Public Policy & Aging Report, 24*(2), 60–64. https://doi.org/10.1093/ppar/pru013

Rovner, J. (2009). Activities of daily living (ADLs). *In Health Care Policy and Politics A to Z, 1*, 14–14. https://www.doi.org/10.4135/9781452240121.n8

Ryan, R. M., Huta, V., & Deci, E. L. (2008). Living well: A self-determination theory perspective on eudaimonia. *Journal of Happiness Studies, 9*(1), 139–170. https://doi.org/10.1007/s10902-006 -9023-4

Ryff, C. D. (2014). Psychological well-being revisited: advances in the science and practice of eudaimonia. *Psychotherapy and Psychosomatics, 83*(1), 10–28. https://doi.org/10.1159/000353263

Ryff, C. D., & Singer, B. H. (2008). Know Thyself and Become What You Are: A Eudaimonic Approach to Psychological Well-Being. *Journal of Happiness Studies, 9*(1), 13–39. https://doi.org/10.1007/ s10902-006-9019-0

Schalock, R., Borthwick-Duffy, S., Bradley, V., Buntinx, W., Coulter, D., Craig, E., Gomez, S. C., Lachapelle, Y., Luckasson, R., Reeve, A., Shogren, K. A., Snell, M. E., Spreat, S., Tasse, M. J., Thompson, J. R., Verdugo-Alonso, M. A., Wehmeyer, M. L., & Yeager, M. H. (2010). *Intellectual disability: Definition, classification, and systems of support* (11th ed.). American Association on Intellectual and Developmental Disabilities.

Schulz, S. L. (2009). Psychological Theories of Disability and Sexuality: A Literature Review. *Journal of Human Behavior in the Social Environment, 19*(1), 58–69. https://doi.org/10.1080/ 10911350802631578

Seger, W. (2018). The rediscovery of the social side of medicine: Philosophy and value of the international classification of functioning, disability and health (ICF). *Electronic Physician, 10*(3), 6426–6429. https://doi.org/10.19082/6426

Selb, M., Escorpizo, R., Kostanjsek, N., Üstün, B., & Cieza, A. (2005). A guide to how to develop an international classification of functioning, disability and health core set. *European Journal of Physical and Rehabilitation Medicine, 51*(1), 105–117.

Sen, A. (1985). Well-being, agency and freedom: The Dewey Lectures 1984. *The Journal of Philosophy, 82*(4), 169. https://doi.org/10.2307/2026184

Sepucha, K. R., Levin, C. A., Uzogara, E. E., Barry, M. J., O'Connor, A. M., & Mulley, A. G. (2008). Developing instruments to measure the quality of decisions: early results for a set of symptom-driven decisions. *Patient Education and Counseling, 73*(3), 504–510. https://doi.org/10.1016/j.pec .2008.07.009

Skempes, D., Stucki, G., & Bickenbach, J. (2015). Health-related rehabilitation and human rights: Analyzing states' obligations under the United Nations convention on the rights of persons with disabilities. *Archives of Physical Medicine and Rehabilitation, 96*(1), 163–173. https://doi.org/10.1016/j.apmr.2014.07.410

Stancliffe, R. J., Arnold, S. R. C., & Riches, V. C. (2016). The supports paradigm. In R. L. Schalock & K. D. Keith (Eds.), *Cross-cultural quality of life: Enhancing the lives of persons with intellectual disability* (2nd ed., pp. 133–142). American Association on Mental Retardation.

Stier-Jarmer, M., Grill, E., Ewert, T., Bartholomeyczik, S., Finger, M., Mokrusch, T., Kostanjsek, N., & Stucki, G. (2005). ICF Core Set for patients with neurological conditions in early post-acute rehabilitation facilities. *Disability and Rehabilitation, 27*(7–8), 389–395. https://doi.org/10.1080/09638280400014022

Stucki, G., & Bickenbach, J. (2017). Functioning: the third health indicator in the health system and the key indicator for rehabilitation. *European Journal of Physical and Rehabilitation Medicine, 53*(1), 134–138. https://doi.org/10.23736/S1973-9087.17.04565-8

Stucki, G., Bickenbach, J., Gutenbrunner, C., & Melvin, J. (2018). Rehabilitation: The health strategy of the 21st century. *Journal of Rehabilitation Medicine, 50*(4), 309–316. https://doi.org/10.2340/16501977-2200

Thompson, J. R., Bradley, V. J., Buntinx, W. H. E., Schalock, R. L., Shogren, K. A., Snell, M. E., Wehmeyer, M. L., Borthwick-Duffy, S., Coulter, D. L., Craig, E. P. M., Gomez, S. C., Lachapelle, Y., Luckasson, R. A., Reeve, A., Spreat, S., Tassé, M. J., Verdugo, M. A., & Yeager, M. H. (2009). Conceptualizing supports and the support needs of people with intellectual disability. *Intellectual and Developmental Disabilities, 47*(2), 135–146. https://doi.org/10.1352/1934-9556-47.2.135

Thompson, J. R., Bryant, B., Schalock, R. L., Shogren, K. A., Tassé, M. J., Wehmeyer, M. L., Campbell, E. M., Craig, E. M., Hughes, C., & Rotholz, D. A. (2015). Supports Intensity Scale—Adult Version: A user's manual. American Association on Intellectual and Developmental Disabilities.

Thompson, J. R., & DeSpain, S. N. (2016). Community support needs. In N. N. Singh (Ed.), *Handbook of evidence-based practices in intellectual and developmental disabilities* (pp. 137–168). Springer.

Umeasiegbu, V. I., Bishop, M., & Mpofu, E. (2013). The conventional and unconventional about disability conventions: A reflective analysis of United Nations Convention on the Rights of Persons With Disabilities. *Rehabilitation Research, Policy, and Education, 27*(1), 58–72. https://doi.org/10.1891/2168-6653.27.1.58

United Nations. (2009). *Rights and dignity of persons with disabilities.* http://www.un.org/disabilities

United Nations. (2012). *Convention on the rights of persons with disabilities: Latest development.* http://www.un.org/disabilities

United Nations. (2016). *Convention of the rights of persons with disabilities.* https://www.un.org/development/desa/disabilities/convention-on-the-rights-of-persons-with-disabilities.html

Ustün, B., & Kennedy, C. (2009). What is "functional impairment"? Disentangling disability from clinical significance. *World Psychiatry : Official Journal of the World Psychiatric Association (WPA), 8*(2), 82–85. https://doi.org/10.1002/j.2051-5545.2009.tb00219.x

Üstün, T. B., Kostanjsek, N., Chatterji, S., & Rehm, J. (2010). *Measuring health and disability: Manual for WHO disability assessment schedule.* World Health Organization. WHO Press.

Verbrugge, L. M., & Jette, A. M. (1994). The disablement process. *Social Science & Medicine (1982), 38*(1), 1–14. https://doi.org/10.1016/0277-9536(94)90294-1

Wade, D. T., & Halligan, P. W. (2017). The biopsychosocial model of illness: a model whose time has come. *Clinical Rehabilitation, 31*(8), 995–1004. https://doi.org/10.1177/0269215517709890

Wallace, J. (2011). Assistive technology funding in the United States. *NeuroRehabilitation, 28*(3), 295–302. https://doi.org/10.3233/NRE-2011-0657

Waterman, A. S. (1993). Two conceptions of happiness: Contrasts of personal expressiveness (eudaimonia) and hedonic enjoyment. *Journal of Personality and Social Psychology, 64*(4), 678–691. https://doi.org/10.1037/0022-3514.64.4.678

Waterman, A. S., Schwartz, S. J., Zamboanga, B. L., Ravert, R. D., Williams, M. K., Agocha, V. B., Kim, S. Y., & Donnellan, M. B. (2010). The Questionnaire for Eudaimonic Well-Being: Psychometric properties, demographic comparisons, and evidence of validity. *The Journal of Positive Psychology, 5*(1), 41–61. https://doi.org/10.1080/17439760903435208

World Health Organization. (2001). *International classification of functioning, disability and health: ICF.* https://apps.who.int/iris/handle/10665/42407

World Health Organization. (2002). *Towards a common language for functioning disability and health: ICF*. Author.

World Health Organization. (2011). *International statistical classification of diseases and related health problems, tenth revision.*

World Health Organization. (2012). *Measuring health and disability: Manual for WHO Disability Assessment Schedule WHODAS 2.0.*

World Health Organization. (2013). *How to use the ICF: A practical manual for using the International Classification of Functioning, Disability and Health*. http://apps.who.int/classifications/network/en

World Health Organization. (2014). *ICD-11*. http://www.who.int/classifications/icd/revision/en

World Health Organization. (2019). *International statistical classification of diseases and related health problems (ICD)*. https://www.who.int/classifications/classification-of-diseases

CHAPTER 12

Counseling and Mental Health

MICHAEL GERALD

LEARNING OBJECTIVES

After reviewing this chapter, you should be able to:

- *Identify the significance of mental health and its impact on persons with disabilities.*
- *Analyze the role of mental health counseling as a component of the rehabilitation counseling process.*
- *Identify and describe major components of the counseling process, such as therapeutic relationship, assessment and diagnosis, case conceptualization, treatment planning, and evidence-based practice.*
- *Distinguish different forms of counseling within the rehabilitation counseling process, such as crisis counseling, disaster mental health counseling, and trauma-informed counseling.*
- *Discover specific counseling techniques and theories for providing affective counseling for persons with disabilities.*

CACREP STANDARDS

CACREP 2016 CORE: 2F1.c, 2F1.i, 2F3.g, 2F5.a, 2F5.f, 2F5.h, 2F5.j, 2F5.l, 2F5.m, 2F5.n
CACREP 2016 Specialties:
   Clinical Rehabilitation Counseling: 5D1.b, 5D2.a, 5D3.h
   Rehabilitation Counseling: 5H1.b, 5H2.a, 5H2.b, 5H2.c, 5H2.d, 5H2.e, 5H2.f, 5H2.g, 5H2.i, 5H2.q, 5H2.r

INTRODUCTION

Rehabilitation counseling has evolved as a result of advances in rehabilitation science, greater understanding of the experiences of persons with disabilities, and persons with disabilities advocating for a more holistic approach to counseling and rehabilitation services. In this way, rehabilitation counseling has aimed to address mental health as an essential aspect of wellness and well-being, including the long-term treatment of mental disorders and rehabilitation needs of people with mental illnesses and disabilities. Today, there are two different CACREP accreditations that guide the training and education of rehabilitation counselors (RCs). The first is Rehabilitation Counseling, which emphasizes traditional vocational and rehabilitation counseling practices. The second is Clinical Rehabilitation Counseling, which emphasizes psychotherapy and services to persons with primary or co-occurring mental health disorders. Clinical Rehabilitation Counseling overlaps considerably with the CACREP accreditation in Clinical Mental Health Counseling. Depending on their training, not all RCs diagnose and treat mental health disorders. However, the holistic nature of rehabilitation counseling means that all RCs are involved in the promotion of mental health as a critical dimension of global health and functioning.

RCs have long understood the value and necessity of the counseling relationship in promoting successful rehabilitation and mental health outcomes. In order to develop the counseling relationship with clients, RCs must intentionally apply their counseling skills. This is especially true when working with persons with chronic illness and disability (CID), who are at a greater likelihood to experience trauma, abuse, and distress than persons without disabilities. Of all the counseling specialties, RCs have always worked with clients who have experienced the most significant trauma and distress, which often are barriers to successful rehabilitation and mental health outcomes. Therefore, it is important that RCs serve persons with CID in a holistic manner, promoting their mental health alongside their physical health. The intent of this chapter is to focus on critical concepts underlying effective counseling to promote mental health, such as working alliance and therapeutic relationship, as well as key elements, such as empathy, congruence, and positive regard. Viewing counseling as a nontransferable job function within the professional practice of rehabilitation counseling, this chapter discusses mental health counseling as practiced by RCs.

MENTAL HEALTH IN THE UNITED STATES

Presently the United States is experiencing a mental health crisis. **Mental health** is composed of one's emotional, psychological, and social well-being (Hays, 2017). Furthermore, the Centers for Disease Control and Prevention (CDC) describes mental health as affecting how we think, feel, act, respond to stressors, relate to others, and make everyday choices and decisions (CDC, 2021). Mental health is neither positive or negative and instead simply refers to the culmination of a person's emotional, psychological, and social functioning.

Recent data underscored this crisis as the number of persons in the United States experiencing mental health distress, suicidal ideation and attempts, and limited access to healthcare has continued to grow (Substance Abuse and Mental Health Services Administration [SAMHSA], 2020). Results from the 2019 NSDU administered revealed the following troubling trends:

- 51 million adults (20.6% of the population) reported **any mental illness** (**AMI**), which could be a mental, behavioral, or emotional disorder with mild to severe functional impairment in the past year. This was a 3% increase from 2008.
- 13.1 million adults (5.2% of the population) reported a **serious mental illness** (**SMI**), which could be a mental, behavioral, or emotional disorder with serious functional impairment and/or disability. This was a 1.5% increase from 2008.
- 12 million adults (4.8% of the population) reported suicidal ideation and 3.5 million adults (1.4% of the population) reported a plan for suicide, which represented an increase of 1% and 0.4%, respectively, from 2002.
- 3.8 million adolescents (15.7% of the population) reported experiencing an MDE in the past year, with 2.7 million adolescents (11.1% of the population) reporting severe impairment from the MDE, which represented an increase of 6% and 5%, respectively, from 2004 and 2006.
- 4.1 million adolescents (16.7% of the population) and 40.2 million adults (16.1% of the population) utilized mental health services, which represented an increase of 5% and 3%, respectively, from 2002.

Unfortunately, while more adults and adolescents accessed mental health services than ever before, the SAMHSA (2020) reported that 26% of adults with AMI and 47.7% of adults with SMI reported unmet need for mental health services. In other words, although more people are accessing mental health services than in years prior, the increasing rates of psychological distress among the population is outpacing the rate of service provision and availability of mental health services (SAMHSA, 2020).

In response to the growing need for mental health services, any mental health treatment is defined by SAMHSA (2020) as including outpatient/inpatient mental health treatment and prescription medication. Unfortunately, a report published by Mental Health America (MHA; Reinert et al., 2021) identified significant barriers to accessing mental health treatments such as (a) insurance with limited coverages for mental health treatment, (b) an undersized mental health workforce, (c) lack of available specialized treatment (e.g., inpatient, individual therapy), (d) disconnect between primary care and behavioral health systems, and (e) financial barriers such as inability to pay copays, deductibles, or private pay when providers do not accept insurance. The most striking finding from the MHA report was that the majority (54%) of those with AMI who had insurance still did not receive mental health services. These results document that even those who have access to private health insurance still experience barriers in access to mental health services due to the lack of providers and specific treatment options as well as limited insurance coverages and inability to pay copays or deductibles (Reinert et al., 2021).

Sadly, these numbers are even worse for youth experiencing depression with as many as 60% not receiving mental health services (Reinert et al., 2021). Even for adolescents with private insurance, 8% were covered by health insurance plans that did not offer behavioral health coverage (Reiner et al., 2021). The lack of access to mental health care for youth is particularly problematic given that approximately one in six adolescents (16%) has experienced a mental health disorder (Whitney & Peterson, 2019). The rate of mental health disorders among persons aged 18 to 25 (29%) is greater than other adult age groups included in the SAMHSA (2020) report. In fact, suicide represented the *second-leading cause of death* among individuals aged 10 to 34 and the 10th-leading cause of death among the entire U.S. population (National Institute of Mental Health [NIMH], 2021). Rates of suicide among the general population had been increasing every year between 1999 and 2018, with a current rate of 10.5 out of 100,000 people representing a 32.3% increase from 1999 to 2021 (NIMH, 2021).

Structural inequities means that racial and ethnic minorities are particularly at risk of not being able to access mental health care. Reinert et al. (2021) found that youth of color with major depression were particularly less likely to receive mental health treatment than their hite peers. For instance, 22.0% of White youth reported seeing a health professional in the past year for depression, compared to 8.3% of Asian youth, 9.4% of Black youth, 9.5% of Hispanic youth, and 15.2% of Native American youth (Reinert et al., 2021). Among adults with SMI, 34.5% did not receive *any mental health services* in the last year (SAMHSA, 2020). There are more than 61 million persons with disabilities in the United States (Okoro et al., 2018), with 32.9% reporting experiencing frequent mental distress (Cree et al., 2020). Cree et al. (2020) analyzed CDC data and found that the prevalence of frequent mental distress, defined as 14 or more self-reported mentally unhealthy days in the past 30 days among persons with disabilities was 4.6 times greater for persons with disabilities as compared to those without disabilities. Part of the reason for the more frequent mental distress is that persons with disabilities are more likely than persons without disabilities to live in poverty, be unemployed, and report less access to healthcare (Cree et al., 2020). In other words, persons with disabilities experience both barriers to mental health care as well as socioeconomic conditions that exacerbate mental distress (Cree et al., 2020). For example, 29% of adults with cognitive disabilities were unable to access medical care due to costs (Reinert et al., 2021). In sum, individuals with disabilities are more likely to experience mental distress as well as significant barriers to accessing mental health treatment

Mental health needs are far outpacing the supply of mental health providers nationally, despite the fact that the number of mental health providers has grown relative to previous years (Reinert et al., 2021). Reinert et al. analyzed the availability of mental health providers across states in the United States, defining *mental health providers* as "psychiatrists, psychologists, licensed clinical social workers, counselors, marriage and family therapists, and advanced practice nurses specializing in mental health care" (p. 39). In calculating the availability of mental health providers, a ratio is created based on the number of mental health providers in a given state relative to that state's population. Reinert et al. found that a wide range in ratios from 150:1 (Massachusetts) to 920:1 (Alabama). Stated another way, in Alabama, there is one mental health provider for every 920 persons. According to the Health Resources and Services Administration (HRSA), the shortage of mental health providers far exceeds that of medical and dental providers (HRSA, 2021). In Health Professional Shortage Areas (HPSAs), which are geographic areas, populations, and facilities that have a shortage of health professionals, only 27% of mental health needs are being met (HRSA, 2021). According to the HRSA (2021) data, over 133 million people live in HRSA-designated locations and more than 61700 mental health practitioners would be required to meet the mental health needs of more than 5,900 HPSAs.

In summary, the strains experienced by the mental health system and workforce are having a particularly negative impact on persons with disabilities who report greater levels of psychological distress than persons without disabilities. RCs are both needed and well positioned to address the high rates of mental distress among persons with disabilities. RCs have an opportunity and responsibility to provide mental health counseling support to address the mental distress experienced by persons with disabilities as part of a holistic approach to the rehabilitation process. While the mental health needs of persons with disabilities continues to grow, counseling has always been a nontransferable job function of the professional practice of rehabilitation counseling.

COUNSELING AS PART OF THE REHABILITATION COUNSELING PROCESS

Rehabilitation counseling is a professional process and practice that involves the counselor who "works collaboratively with the client to understand existing problems, barriers, and potentials in order to facilitate the effective use of personal and environmental resources for career, personal, social, and community adjustment following disability" (Tarvydas & Hartley, 2018, p. 16). Rehabilitation counselors primarily serve persons with disabilities, including mental, developmental, cognitive, and emotional disabilities, in working toward their personal, career, and independent living goals in the most integrated setting possible (CRCC, 2021) According to the CRCC Scope of Practice statement, the techniques and modalities utilized within the rehabilitation counseling process include, but are not limited to, assessment and appraisal, diagnosis and treatment planning, career (vocational) counseling, *individual and group counseling focused on adjustment to disability*, case management, program evaluation and research, psychosocial interventions and advocacy, consultation, and job analysis and job placement. This statement means counseling is identified by the CRCC as an *essential* job function of RCs (McCarthy, 2014). More specifically, counseling and psychological interventions utilized within the professional practice of rehabilitation counseling (Tarvydas & Hartley, 2018) include those highlighted in Box 12.1.

While these types of counseling skills are practiced in many settings, some RCs have reported that time intensive counseling is not always possible. Particularly in the state–federal VR system, RCs have reported they cannot provide more time intensive counseling due to agency demands for large numbers of case closures (i.e., clients obtaining gainful employment) and extensive documentation demands (Rubin & Roessler, 2008). According to Rubin and Roessler, "the preference to do more counseling expressed by

BOX 12.1 LEARNING ACTIVITY

Select Counseling and Psychological Interventions in Rehabilitation Counseling
Counseling is a diverse job function performed by RCs that may take some of the
forms that follow. Reflect on the different forms. Which forms are you most comfortable with providing? What about least comfortable? Why?

- Counseling techniques to promote client self-exploration
- Therapeutic relationship facilitative of client growth
- Identification of internal barriers to rehabilitation goals
- Helping clients identify and employ personal strengths and resources
- Identifying and mitigating emotional reactions to disability
- Assessing psychological problems necessitating referral
- Confronting client incongruence
- Helping clients develop skills for resolving adjustment problems
- Counseling regarding sexuality and disability
- Working with client families to promote familial coping
- Utilizing behavioral techniques to develop skills and promote emotional and
  behavioral self-regulation.

rehabilitation counselors may stem more from idealization of that function encountered
in their graduate training than from a valid picture of the requirements of the jobs performed by many rehabilitation counselors" (2008, p. 274). Roessler and Rubin concluded
that the job function of counseling likely is not going to become a key part of the role of
the RC in more traditional vocational rehabilitation settings due to paperwork demands
and other various roles and functions (e.g. job placement, eligibility determination, vocational evaluation). This conclusion is supported by Leahy et al. (2009), who found that
case management along with medical, functional, and environmental aspects of disabilities were the most important knowledge and job functions of more traditional RCs. While
individual counseling was rated as only moderately important despite being used weekly
or almost weekly. For counselors who work in the VR system, counseling is better thought
of as *one* component of the rehabilitation counseling process rather than the central component. In contrast, RCs who work in other settings, such as private practice or behavioral
health, may experience counseling as the core job function.

What Is the Role of Counseling in the Rehabilitation Counseling Process?

Counseling takes many forms within the professional practice of rehabilitation counseling. Historically, vocational or career counseling involved vocational assessment, assessing work preferences on the part of the client, linking of work interests and client strengths
and abilities, and identifying potential vocational opportunities in collaboration with
the client (Tarvydas & Hartley, 2018). While more traditional rehabilitation counseling
focused more on vocational and career counseling, RCs with the necessary training and
credentials can also practice psychotherapy. Counseling, broadly, can be thought of as a
spectrum of practices that lie on a series of continua based on their emphasis, approach,
and goals. For instance, **psychotherapy** represents one form of counseling and is interpersonal in nature, based on psychological principles, and involving a therapist who is
trained in psychotherapy. Wampold (2010) described the process of psychotherapy as
involving "a client who has a mental disorder, problem, or complaint," and its intention
is to be "remedial for the client disorder, problem, or complaint, and is adapted or individualized for the particular client and his or her disorder, problem, or complaint" (p. 8).

Considering the continuum of counseling practices, traditional counseling can be differentiated from psychotherapy by the depth of the client's problems and the amount of time needed to resolve them in therapy, with psychotherapy being more in-depth and intensive (Howatt, 2000). Counseling is more likely to provide guidance and support for clients on more short-term problems. With that said, both psychotherapy and counseling are an intensive, and personal process and through the process of listening to the client and understanding their life experiences, counselors help facilitate strategies for personal growth (Ivey et al., 2018).

Counseling that is not directly related to vocation or career issues is often referred to as **affective counseling** or emotional and behavioral adjustment. Affective counseling that takes place between the RC and client is often directed toward the "reintegration of self-image and reformulation of personal goals to enhance the person's work adjustment and motivation" (Rubin & Roessler, 2008, p. 283). This distinction means that affective counseling is utilized as an ancillary skill or technique when clients experience problems related to adjustment or acute stress. For RCs who work with high caseloads in traditional settings like VR, they may need to refer clients to RCs who work in other settings for affective counseling, who can offer more long-term, targeted mental health support (Rubin & Roessler, 2008). As an example, a potential referral may be to another RC who practices in behavioral health from the perspective of areas of psychiatric rehabilitation, clinical rehabilitation, or mental health counseling.

While RCs who work in traditional settings like VR may not have time for affective counseling, that does not mean it would not improve client outcomes. Research demonstrates that career counseling and vocational adjustment are closely associated with psychosocial and mental health. Unresolved mental distress can be a barrier to clients achieving their vocational and rehabilitation goals (Chan et al., 2015). Counseling within the rehabilitation counseling process is thus critical to reduce client anxiety and depression regarding problems they may face. In this way, RCs who are able to provide counseling within more traditional VR settings may assist clients to emotionally adjust and cope with disability, develop greater emotional and behavioral self-regulation, and improve their relationships (Rubin & Roessler, 2008). It is thus not surprising that RCs have indicated a need for additional training and preparation as counselors due to the increasing complexity of the needs of their clients as well as the increasing rates of mental health problems encountered by persons with disabilities (Barros-Bailey et al., 2009). Prior research has demonstrated that rehabilitation counseling clients also want counselors who employ counseling skills effectively (McCarthy, 2014). This research suggests that RCs trained robustly as professional counselors may be more effective in traditional settings like the VR system.

McCarthy (2014) evaluated whether RCs' self-assessment of their ability to utilize counseling skills was related to client outcomes. While McCarthy did not find a linear relationship between RCs self-efficacy to implement counseling skills and the number of successful client outcomes, post hoc analysis did find a correlation between successful client outcomes and RC self-efficacy for executing microskills and supporting the needs of clients with the most complex needs (McCarthy, 2014). Similarly, Torres et al. (2019) utilized an experimental design to determine the effect of **motivational interviewing (MI)** training for RCs on client outcomes. MI is a "client-centered, directive, yet nonconfrontational counseling approach to enhancing motivation for change by exploring and resolving ambivalence" (Torres et al., 2019, p. 329). Torres et al. (2019) demonstrated a large effect on the counselor-client working alliance and client engagement in the rehabilitation counseling process. MI thus has the potential to enhance client motivation and engagement in the rehabilitation counseling process, as well as the therapeutic alliance between counselor and client, which are both indicators of successful client outcomes (Torres et al., 2019).

In sum, it is difficult to draw a direct line between the use of counseling skills in the rehabilitation counseling process and client outcomes due to the dynamic process of rehabilitation counseling. What prior research has demonstrated is that the use of counseling skills by RCs is likely to increase client engagement and enhance the therapeutic alliance. Both of these factors are related to successful client outcomes. This link suggests that counseling is a component of the rehabilitation counseling process with counseling skills serving as an important conduit for achieving vocational and rehabilitation goals.

MAJOR COMPONENTS OF THE COUNSELING PROCESS

Counseling is a dynamic, evidence-based process that involves multiple roles and functions on the part of the counselor in facilitating growth and change among their clients (Chan et al., 2015). As a result, counseling is best thought of in terms of an evolving relational process, rather than a series of singular interventions. This view means that counseling is aimed at helping clients grow, develop, and resolve internal barriers to adjustment. It is a multifaceted approach that requires the development and maintenance of a counseling relationship, consistent demonstration of microcounseling skills, the incorporation of applicable theories for treatment and case conceptualization, assessment and diagnosis, treatment planning, and documentation, among other practices. RCs wishing to employ counseling skills in their practice should focus on a holistic, coherent approach to counseling rather than the deployment of disparate skills that may be preferred or accessible in a particular setting. Counseling is a process that progresses from the establishing the a working alliance to the termination of services. In the ensuing section, major components of the counseling process are described as well as their overall place in the rehabilitation counseling process.

Working Alliance and Evidence-Based Practice

Researchers have long sought to answer the question: Do counseling and psychotherapy work? Among the first empirical evaluations, Eysenck (1952) determined psychotherapy was largely ineffective and potentially harmful if not planned properly. Eysenck's study primarily focused on psychodynamic and eclectic therapies rather than behavioral theories, of which Eysenck was more in favor. Despite obvious limitations of his study, it was 20 years before meta-analytic research compared treatment to no-treatment control groups. This research demonstrated that psychotherapy was not only effective but was also dramatically more effective than no treatment, with effect sizes around .80 (Duncan et al., 2010). Although research has demonstrated that therapy is more effective than no therapy at all, research has not demonstrated the superiority of one theory over another. In evaluating the overall effectiveness of counseling, comparisons have been made among different theories to determine if certain theories are more effective than others. Research has demonstrated consistently that different counseling treatments have similar effects on client outcomes (Duncan et al., 2010). Saul Rosenzweig famously declared, "All have won, and all must have prizes," in reference to the famous statement of the dodo bird from Alice in Wonderland. This declaration came to be known as the dodo-bird verdict and laid the foundation for what came to be known as the common factors approach to counseling.

The **common factors model** emphasized all treatments will be effective, regardless of what theory or techniques are employed, if the client and counselor are equally motivated and engaged in treatment and certain specific ingredients are present (Duncan et al., 2010). These specific elements undergird all forms of counseling and psychotherapy to a certain degree. Early models of the common factors, or ingredients, pointed to the following factors as influencing treatment success: (a) the working alliance, (b) client acceptance of the rationale for treatment and expectations for change (*hope*), and (c) agreement between counselor and client on the necessary goals and tasks for change. More recent research, however, has demonstrated that there continue to be questions regarding *how* psychotherapy works (Cuijpers et al., 2019). For instance, an early iteration of the common factors came from Lambert (1992): (a) 40% of therapy change comes from the client or factors outside of therapy, (b) 30% from the counseling relationship, (c) 15% from hope, and (d) 15% to specific factors related to theories and techniques (Cuijpers et al., 2019). However, that breakdown was not supported by empirical evidence, in part because these factors do not operate in a vacuum, but rather interact with one another. Cuijpers et al. (2019) offered a simpler, sequential breakdown of the common ingredients of therapeutic effectiveness: support, learning, and action. For instance, if a client feels supported, they are more like to experience corrective emotional experiences, gain insight, and change their behavior.

Foundational to counseling practice is the relationship between the client and counselor. In fact, research has found that clients often attribute the effectiveness of treatment to the relationship with their counselor (Duncan et al., 2010). In other words, clients often perceive the relationship they have with their counselor to be more important than the theory or techniques employed by the counselor. The counseling relationship can be thought of as comprised of two components: the therapeutic relationship and the working alliance (Duncan et al., 2010; Gelso, 2011). The **therapeutic relationship** is defined as "the feelings and attitudes that therapist and client have toward one another and the manner in which these are expressed" (Gelso, 2011, p. 5). Essentially, how much do the client and counselor like and respect one another and how is this expressed in the context of counseling. The **working alliance** is defined as "the bond between the therapist and client as well as the agreement about the tasks and goals of therapy" (Duncan et al., 2010, p. 68). The working alliance itself is comprised of the therapeutic bond between client and counselor, agreement on therapy goals, and agreement on therapy tasks (Cuijpers et al., 2019). However, not all counselors are equal with respect to forming an alliance with their clients. Furthermore, some clients naturally embody traits that make them much more likely to form relationships with others. Therefore, the types of alliances formed with clients who already are better able to relate to others, including their counselors, may not in and of themselves be related to therapeutic outcomes. Instead, the traits needed to forge relationships with others may allow for clients to engage in therapy more readily, while their continued therapeutic interactions with counselors may be the more important ingredient with respect to behavioral and personality change (Cuijpers et al., 2019). The bottom line is that clients need to be engaged in therapy through the forging of a therapeutic relationship with their counselor.

In rehabilitation counseling, the overarching goal is to "empower individuals with disabilities" (Lustig et al., 2002, p. 24). A collaborative working relationship between a rehabilitation counselor and their client is imperative and foundational for rehabilitation outcomes (Rubin & Roessler, 2008). Within RC practice, the working alliance has been discussed as the agreement between the RC and client with respect to the **goals,** referring to the targeted outcomes of interventions, and **tasks,** referring to the specific techniques and activities involved in the interventions (Lustig et al., 2002). Finally, the **bond** refers to the counseling relationship itself and the degree of mutual respect and trust between the counselor and client. The bond can be strengthened by the RC demonstrating empathy, warmth, respect for, and interest in their clients.

Lustig et al. (2002) evaluated the role of the working alliance on employment outcomes and expectations for more than 2,700 persons with disabilities who had participated in vocational rehabilitation services. Lustig et al. found clients who were employed reported a stronger working alliance with their counselor. Additionally, a strong working alliance was correlated with a more positive outlook on future employment. Importantly, these findings were true even among clients who were currently unemployed, suggesting that a strong working alliance led to a more positive employment outlook even among those unemployed (Lustig et al., 2002). This study suggests that RCs should strive to forge a strong working alliance with their clients. Furthermore, a strong working alliance is critical early in the rehabilitation counseling process, due to the relatively brief nature of counseling within the rehabilitation counseling process. Additionally, RCs should be explicit in discussing the goals and tasks with clients early on in the process in order to form a strong bond with the client.

Counseling Theory

While the effectiveness of counseling extends beyond any specific theory, it is important to understand the role a counseling theory plays as an explanation or explanatory system to describe how and why a phenomenon operates in the manner that it does (Johnson & Christensen, 2012). In this way, a **counseling theory** is "an organized set of assumptions that provides a framework for (a) generating hypotheses about what change processes will support therapeutic goals, (b) formulating specific tasks to facilitate desired change processes, and (c) evaluating progress toward the goals of therapy" (Truscott, 2015, p. 7). Counseling theories provide a helpful tool for counselors because they are a framework for organizing information to identify client problems and potential interventions. Consistently practicing through a specific theoretical lens is an organizational aid to more accurately identify appropriate counseling interventions. It is important to distinguish between adopting a single theory and preferring a certain type of intervention. Adopting a theory helps clinicians identify and conceptualize client problems and issues in terms of a specific theoretical framework (Truscott, 2015). For instance, through a cognitive theory lens, a client experiencing depression may demonstrate maladaptive or unhelpful automatic thoughts. In response, the goal of cognitive therapy is to then help clients develop more adaptive thinking, which can be accomplished using a wide range of interventions. Although it is recommended counselors adopt and develop competence in a single theory of counseling, their ability to utilize multiple different intervention strategies is critical because it can promote greater clinical flexibility and efficacy (Truscott, 2015).

Counseling theories are more readily distinguished based on which school of thought they belong. According to Halbur and Halbur (2019), there are six prominent schools of thought in counseling and psychotherapy: psychodynamic, behavioral, humanistic, pragmatic (cognitive), constructivist, and family approaches. The psychodynamic school of thought believes human beings basically are driven by psychic energy and are molded by early experiences. Counseling theories in the psychodynamic school of thought include, but are not limited to, psychoanalytic, individual psychology, and psychodynamic. The behavioral school of thought believes humans are shaped and determined by sociocultural and environmental conditioning. Counseling theories in the behavioral tradition include behaviorism (e.g., Watson, Pavlov) and radical behaviorism (e.g., Skinner). The humanistic school of thought believes humans have a basic inclination to become fully functioning, or to grow and develop psychologically. Counseling theories consistent with the humanistic tradition include but are not limited to person-centered, existential, and gestalt. The pragmatic (cognitive) school of thought believes that what people think and want is at the root of their emotional and behavioral lives. Counseling theories within the pragmatic, or cognitive, school of thought include cognitive behavioral therapy (CBT), rational emotive behavioral therapy, and reality therapy. Constructivist approaches to counseling theory are focused heavily on phenomenology, human uniqueness, multicultural concerns, and client empowerment. Counseling theories that are foundationally constructivist include multicultural approaches, feminist theory, narrative therapy, and solution-focused brief therapy. Family approaches such as Bowen family therapy and strategic family therapy focus on the family as a systemic unit and change of one family member will cause the rest of the system and its members to change (Halbur & Halbur, 2019).

In adopting a theory of counseling, Halbur and Halbur (2019) recommended counselors select and adopt a theory of counseling in an intentional manner, meaning that counselors should adopt a theory of counseling that fits their style, personality, values, theory of problem, and theory of change. Counselors should first consider their personal values and beliefs about counseling: What causes client problems? and How people change? Considering the nature of client "problems," or barriers they may encounter in their life, a counselor might say, "It's a client's attitudes that impact their functioning," or "Clients experience difficulties in life due to skill deficits." In considering how people change, a counselor might say, "People just need to do things that make them happy" or "People need to experience close, supportive relationships." Both answers are equally valid and point to different potential theories with which a counselor may be more personally aligned. In this way, counselors should review the various schools of thought, or a family of theories, and find a school of thought that fits best with them. Do you think it is a client's personal thoughts that lead to distress? Do I think it is a client's family system that leads to distress or impairment? Finally, once a counselor has identified a school of thought that best fits their values, personality, style, and personal theory of counseling, they can begin to sort through the specific theories within a school of thought to find one that fits best. It is recommended counselors become proficient in one theory before branching out to other theories of counseling and techniques.

A Brief Note on Eclecticism. Not all counselors believe in choosing a single theory for practice and believe they can better serve their clients by flexibly utilizing many different techniques from different theories depending on their client's needs (Halbur & Halbur, 2019). For instance, if a client is having trouble quitting smoking, then MI may be most effective. During another session, the same client shares how they are struggling with anxiety, so maybe CBT is used. **Eclecticism,** which research suggests is the *most common theoretical approach* identified by practitioners, involves "an atheoretical approach in which interventions are selected from any system of psychotherapy" (Truscott, 2015, p. 8). The appeal of eclecticism is the feeling that practitioners can utilize "what works" with clients in a flexible manner. However, research has demonstrated that eclectic practitioners are not fully versed in all theories they apply but rather apply interventions they feel comfortable with in a relatively random manner rather than based on a sound theoretical foundations. Additionally, being eclectic requires a great deal of knowledge regarding theories, their techniques, and *when* to apply those techniques. Clinicians who identify as eclectic may be conflating theory and technique, as they borrow techniques during the intervention stage, without identifying how a given theory might explain client behavior (Halbur & Halbur, 2019).

There is an important distinction between theoretical eclecticism and technical eclecticism. **Technical eclecticism** can be thought of as applying a variety of counseling techniques while still remaining grounded in a single theory (Halbur & Halbur, 2019). Lazarus and Beutler (1993) caution that **theoretical integration**, as the process of combining concepts from different theoretical approaches, can be more challenging because many constructs from disparate theories are irreconcilable. This should seem intuitive, as the history of theory development in counseling is one in which theories arose in response to, or often in dissatisfaction with prior theories. CBT arouse out of dissatisfaction with psychoanalysis, while ACT emerged as a new conceptualization of cognitive theory and approaches. Thus, attempting to blend these theories conceptually or in practice means one runs the risk of blending incongruent theoretical constructs.

Lazarus and Beutler (1993) provided a systematic framework for eclectic work that begins with a *multimodal assessment* summarized by the acronym BASIC ID. BASIC ID stands for Behavior, Affect Sensation, Imagery, Cognition, Interpersonal, and Drugs/Biology. Based on the results of this assessment a *technical eclecticist* might borrow proven procedures from different theories to meet client needs in these domains, without necessarily adopting the theory supporting each intervention. Rather, they continue to work with their preferred theory. As an example, a cognitive behavioral therapist might believe that a client's thoughts, such as "I'm a terrible person," are leading to distress. But, upon attempting to challenge and dispute the client's way of thinking, they find the client becoming further entrenched in their unhelpful thinking patterns. The therapist may then adopt an acceptance-based technique, such as one from ACT, in order to help the client develop more adaptive thinking styles, without switching their theory or conceptualization altogether.

Microcounseling Skills and the Basic Listening Sequence

Microskills, also referred to as **microcounseling skills** represent "the behavioral foundations of intentional counseling and psychotherapy" (Ivey et al., 2018). Microskills are the specific communication skills that comprise counseling interactions in counseling relationships and serve as the "how" when it comes to incorporating theory into practice (Martin, 1999). The basic empathic listening skills are: questioning, observation, encouraging, paraphrasing, summarizing, and reflecting feelings. **Questions** are a verbal or nonverbal prompts intended to elicit information from a client, set the foundation for communication with a client, or promote greater understanding or insight for the client. **Observation** involves observing the client's verbal and nonverbal behavior and pointing that out in the moment. **Encouraging** includes verbal and nonverbal expressions the therapist can use to prompt clients to continue talking. **Paraphrasing** involves reflection or rephrasing of the content of the what the client said. **Summarizing** and summaries are brief, overall reviews of multiple topics covered during a session. Finally, **reflecting feelings** involves a restatement or rephrasing of clearly stated or demonstrated emotion or deeper meaning.

Ivey et al. (2018) identified a *basic listening sequence (BLS)* that entails: Questioning → Encouraging → Paraphrasing → Reflecting Feelings or Meaning → Summarizing. Meaning, a counselor may start a conversation with a client with an open question ("What brings you to counseling today?") and follow that with nonverbal and verbal encouragers ("I see, tell me more."). As the client continues to disclose, the counselor will paraphrase, "So you thought it meant more." Encouragers and paraphrases demonstrate to the client that the counselor is engaged and promote further disclosures. In order to deepen the session, the counselor will then want to reflect feelings or meaning. For example, "Well it makes sense to me, as you stand to lose a lot if the relationship ends." Eventually, the clinician will want to summarize the various topics covered in the session as a means to organize the topics discussed to this point coherently and check for understanding of the primary issues and themes presented by the client. For example, "I want to pause us here for a second and make sure I am understanding . . ." Ivey et al. (2018) also proposed a five-stage model for a therapy session: Empathic Relationship → Story and Strengths → Goals → Restory → Action. Empathic relationship involves initiating the session, developing rapport, and structuring the session in an effort to build the therapeutic relationship. Story and strengths involves using BLS to draw out client stories, concerns, problems, or issues, in order to clarify and discover the impetus for counseling on the part of the client. Goals are the next stage and refer to using the BLS to collaboratively identify and define potential goals for counseling. Following goal setting, restory involves exploring alternatives, confronting client incongruities, and identifying conflict. Finally, a counselor would move a client into the action phase of the session where the client and counselor collaboratively generate a plan or ideas for generalizing skills learned in session to other settings (Ivey et al., 2018). Microskills and the basic listening sequence serve as the foundational communication skills employed by counselors in relating to and understanding their clients and their problems. The five-stage model for a session can help counselors structure their sessions in such a way as to efficiently manage time in session in an effort to maximize client learning and growth.

Assessment and Diagnosis

Assessment and diagnosis are critical aspects of the treatment process as they can provide a guiding framework, while also identifying potential barriers to treatment implementation or success. is an umbrella term for the evaluation methods counselors use to better understand characteristics of people, places, and things (Hays, 2017). Assessment in counseling can be used to evaluate areas of psychological interest such as intelligence, ability, career interests and readiness, personality, and general mental health functioning. A **mental health diagnosis**, on the other hand, refers to a clinically important syndrome characterized by a collection of behavioral and psychological symptoms that cause a person distress or impairment social, personal, or occupational functioning (Hays, 2017).

Assessment in counseling helps set the foundation for counseling services through the processes of concern or issue orientation, concern or issue identification, generation of alternatives, decision-making, and verification. *A concern or issue orientation* refers to the utility of assessment as a means to stimulate clients and counselors to consider a diverse array of problems (e.g. needs assessment), which can help the client accept and recognize the problems they may be currently experiencing. *Concern or issue identification* refers to the function of assessment as a means to clarify the nature, or etiology, or a client's presenting problem or issue (e.g. personality inventory). *Generation of alternatives* refers to assessment as a means to help clients and counselors generate multiple potential solutions for problems (e.g. strengths-based assessment). *Decision-making* refers to determination of an appropriate course of treatment for clients based on assessment (e.g., values clarification). *Verification* involves the evaluation of treatment success or the outcomes of recommended solutions through assessment (e.g., How will we know when the problem is solved?).

Assessment and diagnosis can be conducted through psychological testing (e.g., intelligence testing) and clinical interviewing. A full psychological evaluations often involve a combination of the two. *Clinical interviewing*, which is both a process and a set of techniques, is defined by Sommers-Flanagan and Sommers-Flanagan (2013) as a professional relationship between a client and a counselor, collaboration on goals regarding assessment and treatment, both verbal and nonverbal interactions in which the counselor utilizes active listening to evaluate, understand, and facilitate progress toward client goals, and clinician awareness of the influences of client culture, personality, setting, and attitudes.

The goals of clinical interviewing are to conduct a clinical evaluation in order to identify client needs, problems, and potential sources of problems, as well as to initiate counseling or therapy (Sommers-Flanagan & Sommers-Flanagan). Clinical interviewing can often initiate treatment and is a means to gather more in-depth disclosures. Therefore, it is imperative that counselors conducting clinical interviews also work to initiate the development of the counseling relationship with the client being evaluated. One potential outcome of clinical interviewing is mental health diagnosis. Diagnosis of mental health conditions involves **differential diagnosis**, or the process by which counselors determine a client's diagnosis based on a client's presenting symptoms (First, 2014). Differential diagnosis using the *DSM-5* involves six steps: (a) rule out malingering and factitious disorder, (b) ruling out a substance etiology, (c) ruling out an etiological medical condition, (d) determining the specific primary disorder(s), (e) differentiating adjustment disorder from the residual Other Specified and Unspecified conditions, and (f) establishing the boundary with no mental disorder. The *DSM-5* establishes the diagnostic and classification criteria for mental health disorders (American Psychiatric Association, 2013). Treatment often is most effective when it is directed toward client diagnosis. This fact further establishes the importance of identifying mental health diagnoses in clients served in rehabilitation counseling. For instance, a client who reports anxiety might benefit from coping skills aimed at reducing anxious distress and improving vocational adjustment. However, if that client feels anxious due to a fear of being abandoned or rejected, and upon assessment is revealed to have a personality disorder, then simply providing coping skills for anxiety will likely be insufficient and unsuccessful.

> ## BOX 12.2 CASE CONCEPTUALIZATION
>
> If a counselor were to utilize CBT as a means to case conceptualize a client's issues. CBT represents a blend of second-wave cognitive therapy (e.g. Aaron Beck) and behavior therapy (e.g. Joseph Wolpe, B.F. Skinner) and views the client's distressing emotions and maladaptive behaviors as being the result of maladaptive cognitive evaluations of their experiences (Truscott, 2015). The counselor would consider the following:
>
> Gathering information from the client on the *presenting concern or issue*. If a client reported their marriage was in trouble and they were looking for solutions to improve their relational functioning, the counselor would first gather some additional detail regarding the state of the marriage and potential sources of relational strain.
>
> Of greatest import, from a CBT perspective determining *how the client is cognitively interpreting the situation* and *whether those cognitions are leading to client distress*. The counselor might observe the client saying things like, "I just wish I was a better partner for my spouse, and if I was a better spouse, we wouldn't be in this position." The counselor might make a *clinical inference* that the client has a core belief of "I'm not good enough" and an intermediate belief of "If I am good enough, people will not leave me."
>
> These inferences then provide the clinician with valuable data that they can utilize in identifying treatment targets and a plan for treatment.

Case Conceptualization

Case conceptualization is "a method and clinical strategy for obtaining and organizing information about a client, understanding and explaining the client's situation and maladaptive patterns, guiding and focusing treatment, anticipating challenges and roadblocks, and preparing for successful termination" (Sperry & Sperry, 2020, p. 4). Case conceptualizations provide practitioners with a more cohesive means of planning and focusing treatment interventions, thus increasing the likelihood of successful outcomes. Case conceptualizations help counselors understand and explain a client's concerns through the lens of a counseling theory as a means to guide the treatment process and serve as a bridge between assessment and treatment. Sperry and Sperry proposed five functions for case conceptualizations: (a) obtaining and organizing—gathering information from the client and making initial hypotheses regarding patterns and problems; (b) explaining—as the counselor reviews diagnostic, clinical, and cultural information gathered from the client potential explanations of client problems and a rationale for treatment emerge; (c) guiding and focusing treatment—based on the hypothesized explanations for client problems, the counselor begins to formulate treatment targets and treatment strategies; (d) anticipating obstacles and challenges—case conceptualizations can provide counselors with preliminary information regarding the likelihood that a client will adhere to treatment, engage in treatment, relapse, and how the therapeutic alliance might develop; and (e) preparing for termination—case conceptualization helps counselors identify when the goals of treatment have been accomplished and when to begin the process of termination of services (Sperry & Sperry). See Box 12.2 for a brief example of a few factors in case conceptualization.

Treatment Planning

In counseling, **treatment** essentially refers to what will be done in order to help clients address, mitigate, and adapt to current problems (Woo & Keatinge, 2016). The standard of care in counseling practice currently is the application of **evidence-based practice (EBP)**, which is defined as "the integration of the best available research with clinical expertise in the context of patient characteristics, culture, and preferences" (Berghuis et al., 2014, p. 2). EBP not only includes the application of specific treatment techniques, but also the therapeutic relationship, working alliance, the individual counselor, and the client themselves (Berghuis et al.). In assisting clients in their rehabilitative and/or recovery goals, the fundamental elements and guiding principles of treatment planning are self-direction, individualization and person-centered, empowerment, holistic, nonlinear, strengths-based, peer support, respect, responsibility, and hope. Structurally, treatment plans comprised the following components: diagnosis, problem selection, problem definition, goals, objectives, and interventions.

Treatment planning always begins with assessment and diagnosis, as **diagnosis** can help identify pathological symptoms and other problem areas of the client's functioning, while providing the foundation for clinical decision-making (Reichenberg & Seligman, 2016). Diagnosis involves the determination of a clinical syndrome that best encapsulates the client's symptoms as well as the behavioral, cognitive, emotional, and interpersonal symptoms that contribute to client impairment. *Concern or issue selection* involves the identification of the most significant problems the client is experiencing and those that will be the focus of treatment (Berghuis et al., 2014). *Concern or issue definition* involves the provision of a definition of the problem that is specific to how a given client exhibits, demonstrates, or manifests the problem selected for treatment intervention. *Goal development* refers to setting broad goals that are global and long term, and do not necessarily need to be measurable. For instance, a client exhibiting symptoms of depression might develop a goal: Client will reduce symptoms of depression and improve functioning. The next common component of treatment plans, *objective construction*, involves the development of behaviorally, objectively measurable short-term steps that will demonstrate work toward and accomplishment of broad overarching goals. For example, a client exhibiting symptoms of depression with an overall goal of reducing symptoms and improving functioning might have a short-term objective : Complete a psychiatric evaluation and follow through with recommendations for medication management. Objectives should be written in a manner that makes their completion clear and functionally and incrementally related to accomplishing an overarching treatment goal. Many objectives may be necessary to complete before accomplishment of an overall goal. Finally, *interventions*, or the actions and behaviors that take place in the process of counseling, are selected that will lead to the accomplishment of objectives. For instance, a counselor might refer a client for potential medication management for their symptoms, and utilize warmth, empathy, and unconditional positive regard to develop a therapeutic bond with their client.

There are multiple models available for constructing treatment plans for mental health counseling, but three in particular come from: Berghuis et al. (2014), Reichenberg and Seligman (2016), and Woo and Keatinge (2016). Berghuis et al. offered a model that includes: Diagnosis → Concern or issue Selection → Concern or issue Definition → Goal Development → Objective Construction → and Intervention. Reichenberg and Seligman proposed the DO A CLIENT MAP model, which includes: Diagnosis → Objectives (treatment goals) → Assessment (e.g. interview, testing) → Clinician (Who will provide treatment?) → Location (e.g. residential, outpatient) → Interventions (e.g. CBT) → Emphasis (e.g. directive, exploratory) → Numbers (e.g. individual, group, family) → Timing (e.g. frequency of sessions) → Medication → Adjunct Services (what other services might be involved?) → and Prognosis. Woo and Keatinge provided the following framework for treatment planning: Preparation and Planning (assessment and diagnosis) → Establishing and Building the Therapeutic Relationship (e.g., building rapport) → Crisis Intervention and the Decision to Treat (identification of barriers to and resources for treatment) → Case Conceptualization → Selecting Interventions and Writing the Treatment Plan → Assessing Treatment Effectiveness and Outcome → and Termination. It should be noted that these models of treatment planning for mental health care are very similar to the four-phase vocational rehabilitation treatment model proposed by Rubin and Roessler (2008), which involves Evaluation Phase (assessment and diagnosis) → Planning Phase (treatment and intervention planning) → Treatment Phase → and Termination Phase. Treatment planning is critical to the success of mental health, vocational rehabilitation counseling, and clinical rehabilitation counseling as it provides a coherent roadmap for clients and counselors that links assessment to the mitigation of client problems.

Clinical Documentation

Clinical documentation and record keeping involve the physical recording of all elements of the counseling process, from intake information to informal contact with clients, such as phone calls (Levers & Hyatt-Burkhart, 2019). Record keeping and documentation are not only an ethical and legal requirement for counselors, but they also contribute to effective counseling services by providing counselors with a record of client problems, treatment goals, assessment results, client strengths and internal resources, and client progress in treatment. Documentation as a record of counseling allows clinicians to provide treatment without needing to remember and recall all details of a client's history or progress in treatment. Documentation is also often a requirement of third-party payors or governing agencies for remuneration and accountability of counseling services. From a liability standpoint, documentation protects counselors in instances of ethical or legal complaints (Levers & Hyatt-Burkhart, 2019). For instance, a counselor who encounters a client with suicidal ideation and a plan for suicide needs to document not only what the client stated but also what they provided as an intervention and the ethical decision-making process that supports their decision-making. In the tragic event of a client suicide, counselors can demonstrate their thought process and actions in the context of risk assessment and crisis intervention that may protect them from legal liability.

In counseling and psychotherapy, documentation usually includes records of informed consent, the intake assessment, any assessment or testing information, treatment plans, session notes, discharge summaries, and other client data (such as records received from other providers about this client; Levers & Hyatt-Burkhart, 2019). Although there are multiple types of progress and session note formats, two of the more common formats are the DAP notes and SOAP note formats. In a DAP note, the data section refers to session data or what was discussed, the assessment sections includes the clinical assessment on the part of the counselor, and the plans section involves future plans or directions for sessions. The SOAP note format includes subjective data, or data presented to the counselor by the client (such as what the client said); objective data, or data from the session that is concrete and observable (such as what interventions were employed); assessment data, or the counselor's clinical assessment of the client; and plans, such as what directions the counselor intends to take with the client going forward. Documentation should be legible and clearly written; broad yet specific, including only the information pertinent to treatment goals and progress without relying heavily on specific details; empirical and logical; prompt; and in chronological order (Levers & Hyatt-Burkhart, 2019). Third-partypayors often have specific requirements for their documentation, such as information that is required for reimbursement. This usually involves the identification of treatment goals and documentation that clearly identifies interventions targeted towards goals and objectives, as well as indicators of client progress toward goals. Clinical documentation may not be a preferred activity of counselors. Nonetheless, it should be thought of as an integral component of a client's treatment, not simply as a task to be completed.

Managed Care

In counseling and psychotherapy, providers typically rely on third-party payors in order to receive reimbursement for services provided. Third-party payors, often insurance companies, cover services under a system of managed care. Managed care plans date back to the 1970s and were initially devised as a means to control healthcare costs. **Managed care plans** are defined as a

> type of health insurance. They have contracts with healthcare providers and medical facilities to provide care for members at reduced costs. These providers make up the plan's network, how much . . . care the plan will pay for depends on the network's rules. (Levers & Hyatt-Burkhart, 2019, p. 244)

As a system managed care sets forth the guidelines for determining which treatments are needed and therefore will be covered (Levers & Hyatt-Burkhart, 2019). This guideline means that even if a counseling or mental health provider is **paneled** or contracted with a given insurance company, that insurance company can still determine what services they will or will not cover. There are different models of healthcare coverage plans, such as **Health Maintenance Organizations (HMO)**, **Preferred Provider Organization (PPO)**, and **Point of Service (POS)**. Clients utilizing an HMO can choose a provider from within their insurance plan's network, and they then rely on that provider to make referrals to other in-network providers. If clients choose a provider that is out of network, services may or may not be covered by their insurance. In a PPO plan, clients are not required to choose a provider within their network, but if they choose an out-of-network provider they may be required to pay higher copays or deductibles. POS plans reimburse a certain percentage of costs, regardless of who the provider is. Medicaid and Medicare are government-funded healthcare plans for seniors and persons with disabilities (among others). Presently, licensed professional counselors are not able to be paneled with Medicare, but can be paneled and bill under Medicaid (Levers & Hyatt-Burkhart, 2019).

Essentially, managed care billing in mental health care requires that clients have some form of insurance, specifically one that has provisions for behavioral health, which not all plans include. For some plans, clients require a **preauthorization**, or verification with an insurance company that a health service is medically necessary, and therefore likely to be covered. In many plans if clients select in-network providers, or those who take their insurance, counseling can start once their benefits have been verified and a preauthorization may not be required. After a session is completed, counselors utilize *electronic medical record* (EMR) systems to complete a session note on which they indicate a diagnosis and a billing code (such as a 90791 for an evaluation/intake session) and submit the note to an insurance provider. It should be noted that although providers are welcome to charge a rate for service that they think is commensurate with their efforts, training, and expertise, insurance companies may have a maximum that they reimburse, regardless of the provider's qualifications. If the session note content meets the requirements of an insurance provider and the diagnosis is one that is covered, then the insurance company will pay for the session. This process does raise the ethical question of ethical diagnosis, meaning that counselors should refrain from providing diagnoses simply because they know it will be reimbursed by insurance providers. Such practices can be unethical and can constitute insurance fraud. Managed care as a system is one that has attempted to keep down costs for those with insurance, and it can serve as a vehicle for receiving the care they need at a cost they can afford. However, for those without insurance, or those with insurance plans that only provide minimal coverage for mental health services, the situation is quite different. Managed care systems can provide significant barriers to mental healthcare and clients may be forced to make health-related decisions based on finances.

Risk Assessment and Crisis Counseling

As noted previously suicidal ideation and deaths by suicide are continuing to increase in the United States. The prominence of suicidal behavior among clinical populations in particular makes it so **risk assessment**, or the assessment and evaluation of suicidality, an imperative component of counseling practice. It is the primary ethical imperative for counselors is to preserve the welfare of their clients (Sommers-Flanagan & Sommers-Flanagan, 2013). Understanding the terms utilized in suicide risk assessment is important (Hays, 2017). **Suicide** is a self-inflicted act resulting in death, and suicidal intent can vary. **Attempted suicide** is a self-injurious behavior with varying degrees of suicidal intent and lethality. **Suicidal ideation** includes thoughts of self-injurious behavior with variable suicidal intent and limited lethality. **Self-harm** refers to deliberate, nonfatal self-injury with limited suicidal intent, which differentiates it from suicide attempts. Typically, counselors evaluate a client's suicidality, or their suicidal intent and lethality. *Suicidal intent* is the wish to die, while *lethality* represents the physical threat to life presented by a person's risk, plan, and access to means for suicide (Hays, 2017). Research has demonstrated higher rates of suicidality among persons with disabilities due to higher rates of depression and anxiety, social disconnection, lower rates of employment and higher rates of poverty, and distress caused by disability (Lund et al., 2017).

Conducting a risk assessment for suicide includes assessing the presence or absence of risk factors for suicide, or a "measurable demographic, trait, behavior, or situation that has a positive correlation with suicide attempts and/or death by suicide" (Sommers-Flanagan & Sommers-Flanagan, 2013). One model for suicide risk assessment involves the acronym, *IS PATH WARM?* (Reichenberg & Seligman, 2016). This acronym covers known risk factors for suicide in a helpful mnemonic and stands for Ideation; Substance abuse or intoxication; Purposelessness, such as loss of meaning and purpose; Anxiety, or manic states and agitation; Trapped, feeling as though there is no way out of the situation; Hopelessness, or lack of belief that situations will improve; Withdrawal, such as from family, friends, and preferred activities; Anger, such as hostility and vindictiveness; Recklessness, or impulsive behavior; and Mood, such as sudden and dramatic mood changes (Reichenberg & Seligman, 2016). Utilizing these risk factors, as well as an empathic, understanding, and accepting disposition can help counselors determine a client's present level of risk for suicide, which is usually characterized as low, moderate, or high risk of death by suicide. It should be noted that suicide risk assessment never results in a characterization of *no risk*, and instead risk assessment is a predictive assessment of what is *most likely* to occur based on balancing of the risk and protective factors against suicide.

When a client presents in a **crisis**, or a risk of harm to themselves or others, counselors essentially are left with three options dependent on the results of their risk assessment: immediate hospitalization and/or involvement of emergency services, referral to a partial hospitalization or residential program, and outpatient therapy and medication management (Reichenberg & Seligman, 2016). It should be noted that outpatient therapy may be beneficial for those experiencing suicidal ideation, but *are not* at risk of imminent harm to themselves or others. **Crisis counseling** involves intervening when clients are experiencing acute crises as a means to provide stabilization and safety (Duffey & Haberstroh, 2020). Foundational to crisis intervention with persons who are demonstrating a risk of harm to themselves is relationship building. Relationships with caring others who are warm, accepting, and demonstrating unconditional positive regard are necessary components of crisis intervention. This basic step is followed by assessing a person's current level of risk, while providing social, informational, and physical support. As the person experiences support and feels heard, the counselor can begin to explore alternatives to suicide, such as reaching out to friends and family or presenting to an inpatient program. The counselor and client in crisis then develop an action plan in order to keep the person safe in the moment and the near future. This is followed by the provision of resources, referrals, and follow-up by the counselor (Duffey & Haberstroh, 2020). It is important for counselors to understand that risk assessment and crisis counseling and intervention are ethical and legal mandates and should be thought of as ongoing processes, rather than a singular event.

Disaster Mental Health Counseling

A **disaster** is defined as "a serious disruption of the functioning of a community or society causing widespread human, material, economic or environmental losses which exceed the ability of the affected community or society to cope using its own resources" (Levers & Hyatt-Burkhart, 2019, p. 95). People, communities, and nations can experience both natural and human-made disasters, which can often be hard to distinguish. For instance, the effects of climate change can cause severe weather, political and social upheaval, and resource scarcity, and climate change is considered to be influenced by human behavior. As disasters can affect entire communities as well as the individuals within them, mobilizing supports can include mental health care and support for those affected by disasters (Levers & Hyatt-Burkhart, 2019). Responding to humanitarian crises requires responding counselors to tailor their interventions to the specific needs of the community and to provide brief mental health interventions that help people adapt to and persist in the face of their current circumstances (Levers & Hyatt-Burkhart, 2019). Counselors can help communities prepare for disasters by advocating for systemic networks of support, preparedness and prevention of the consequences of disasters, and by building resilient and supportive communities.

One approach to disaster mental health counseling is **psychological first aid** (PFA; Levers & Hyatt-Burkhart, 2019). PFA is a useful mental health counseling strategy in the immediate aftermath of a traumatic event (Duffey & Haberstroh, 2020). PFA provides a structured intervention to help people curb the emotional bleeding and promotes adaptive coping in the face of a traumatic event. PFA involves eight core actions: Contact and Engagement, Safety and Comfort, Stabilization, Information Gathering, Practical Assistance, Connection with Social Supports, Imparting Information on Coping Strategies, and Linkage with Collaborative Services. PFA is not meant to be an ongoing counseling intervention and instead is intended to help people cope in the immediate aftermath of a traumatic event. This coping is meant to help people adjust and adapt in an acute manner so as to be able to access resources that can help them persist in the face of an imminent crisis. Duffey and Haberstroh (2020) stressed the relational nature of crisis and trauma support and counselors are advised in their work with clients experiencing crisis, trauma, and disaster to emphasize personal connection and the development of supportive relationships, as these are crucial in adaptation to traumatic events.

COUNSELING PERSONS WITH DISABILITIES

Persons with disabilities represent a significant portion of the U.S. population and experience greater frequency of psychological distress than persons with disabilities (Cree et al., 2020). Persons with CID may experience stress, trauma, and other difficulties adjusting to their disabilities. These emotional experiences may be exacerbated by experiencing societal barriers such as limited employment opportunities, higher rates of poverty and disenfranchisement, and medical providers who may ignore emotional distress while focusing solely on physical aspects of illness or disability. For many persons with disabilities, counseling may involve interventions that help provide persons with CID tools for coping with the consequences of disability or trauma related to disability experience (Chan et al., 2015). General counseling theories also can apply to persons with CID, but it is important to note that the experiences of persons with CID are unique and varied. Counselors need to be aware of the psychological, social, and behavioral aspects of adjustment to disability as they seek to apply therapy techniques with persons with CID.

Chan et al. (2015) summarized two counseling interventions intended to promote coping responses in persons with CID: **coping effectiveness training (CET)** and **cognitive coping therapy (CCT)**. CET involves "teaching a framework for choosing among coping strategies and fitting the coping strategy to the changeability of an event, in order to promote adaptive coping and reduce distress" (Chan et al., 2015, p. 388). CET focuses on teaching individuals about stress and coping, techniques for problem-solving, the differences between adaptive and maladaptive coping, and how to enlist the support of helpful others. CET helps individuals evaluate their current coping methods and determine a strategy for coping that matches their current stressor.

CCT teaches clients to view thoughts as hypotheses to be tested for validity, rather than as facts. CCT focuses on skills a person may employ to adapt to stressful situations as a means to identify internal resources. Furthermore, CCT helps people utilize imagery, role models, anchoring, value clarification, acceptance, emotional self-regulation, limit setting, and the blending of past and present identities as techniques for promoting coping in persons with CID (Chan et al., 2015). In discussing coping among persons with CID, it is important to identify the potential for posttraumatic growth concurrent with posttraumatic distress among persons with CID. **Posttraumatic growth** occurs as individuals experience distress and attempt to cope with CID and involves discovering new sources of strength, gaining a greater appreciation for relationships, and a more intentional approach to living life (Chan et al., 2015). This potential is important to consider for counselors as trauma experienced relative to CID may also provide persons with CID with a source of growth and strength, rather than simply a wound that needs to be healed.

Psychology of Disability

The **psychology of disability** is defined as "the study of how human organisms respond to a set of stimulus conditions associated with disability" (Vash & Crewe, 2004, p. xi). The psychological impact of disability varies depending on a number of factors. For one, the nature of the disability has a unique impact on an individual (Vash & Crewe, 2004). Variables such as the time of onset, type of onset, functions impaired, levels of pain, stability of disability, visibility, and severity all impact the manner in which a chronic illness or disability can impact the psychological functioning of a person with a disability. As an example, a person with an invisible autoimmune condition who experiences pain and fatigue may experience difficulty coping due to others not believing in the severity or validity of their symptoms. In contrast, a person with a mobility impairment that is more visible may engender pity. Persons who acquire disabilities later in life may experience different stressors than those who are born with a disability. Obviously, these variables interact with one another in a dynamic manner as disabilities typically touch each of these categories and can change over time (Vash & Crewe, 2004). The psychosocial environment of the individual also influences the psychological effect as does a person's gender, interests, values, goals, temperament, and spirituality.

RCs also must understand the different coping styles persons with disabilities might employ as a means of dealing with the consequences of their disability or the negative impacts of stigma and exclusion. Falvo and Holland (2018) provided a list of five coping strategies for persons with health conditions: (a) denial, (b) regression, (c) compensation, (d) rationalization, and (e) diversion of feelings. *Denial* may involve a person with a disability denying the existence or severity of their condition, which may in turn lead to less maintenance of their health condition. In defense of denial, however, initially denial can serve an important protective function in that it may prevent people from shutting down or giving up in the face of extraordinary circumstances. *Regression* refers to individuals subconsciously reverting to an earlier stage of development, which may entail their becoming more passive, more dependent, or more emotionally dysregulated. *Compensation* describes any number of behaviors a person with a disability may engage in that are designed to enhance functioning in areas unaffected by disability as a means to cope with functional loss. *Rationalization* refers to individuals seeking out socially acceptable reasons for their behavior or to excuse themselves for failing to achieve goals or complete necessary tasks. Finally, *diversion of feelings* refers to a person diverting negative emotional states or ideas into more socially acceptable ones. An example includes an athlete viewing the chance of a comeback as a motivator to engage in rehabilitation from their injury. It should be noted that the term **coping** simply represents a constellation of behaviors that are intended to help an individual manage, tolerate, or reduce stress associated with major life events. Coping can be adaptive, in that it helps reduce stress while also enhancing well-being and functioning. It also can be maladaptive, or reducing stress while inhibiting long-term growth potential or directly contributing to declines in health or functioning (Falvo & Holland, 2018).

Part of the psychological milieu associated with the psychological impact of disability on individuals has to do with the threat that disability poses to a person's life (Smart, 2009). CID can threaten: life and health; body integrity and comfort; independence, privacy, autonomy; self-concept; life goals; relationships; economic well-being; and home and place. Depending on the nature of the CID there is the potential that the CID can threaten someone's life and long-term health. CID also can threaten someone's body integrity, or how much they trust their body, and overall physical comfort. Disability can also threaten independence, autonomy, and privacy, through invasive procedures and questions from doctors, as well as the potential need for assistance in times of vulnerability (e.g., assistance with bathing and grooming). CID can also threaten a person's self-concept, or their overall idea of themselves, in such a way as to be left feeling damaged, broken, or inferior. Disability can threaten life goals and people can feel like the life they had envisioned for themselves is now unattainable or cannot happen in the way it was envisioned initially. It can threaten relationships, as people may choose not to continue their relationships with persons with CID. People may relate to them differently, perhaps seeing them as fragile. Disability and its management can be costly, and CID can threaten one's economic well-being through medical costs as well as fewer or less desirable job opportunities. Finally, disability can threaten one's living situation as people may not be able to afford to live somewhere due to the costs of disability or may need a more accessible living situation than they once had (Smart, 2009). The degree to which CID can psychologically affect a person depends on environmental and personal variables, the manner in which a person copes, and how a health condition may threaten different aspects of their life. Persons with CID can benefit from counseling as a means to reframe their perceptions of their disability and its impact on their life and personhood to promote more adaptive functioning.

Psychosocial Adaptation to Chronic Illness and Disability

Psychosocial adaptation to CID, sometimes referred to as **response to disability**, refers to the process and end result of coping with a disability and successfully integrating the disability into the individual's life and identity (Smart, 2009). The process of responding to CID "includes a search for meaning in the experience and an attempt to regain control and self-determination over the vents that affect one's life" (Falvo & Holland, 2018, p. 28). Although many individuals who experience CID may feel some degree of loss, the manner in which they respond and adapt varies depending upon the circumstances surrounding the CID itself. A prominent model of psychosocial adaptation to CID has been developed and updated by Livneh (2001, 2021) and contains three overarching components: Antecedents, Processes, and Outcomes. The concept of *antecedents* refers to "conditions and events that prevailed during the time of onset of CID" and includes the triggering events of CID, such as genetics, injury, disease or illness, and contextual status, such as an individual's environment, sociocultural status, and psychological state (Livneh, 2021, p. 3). The *process* refers to a person's medical and psychological status, their psychological responses to CID, and their perceptions of CID impact as well as coping strategies they employ. Finally, the *outcomes* of psychosocial adaptation can be thought of in three domains: the intrapersonal domain, the interpersonal functional domain, and the extra-personal (community) functional domain. The intrapersonal domain refers to health and psychological status, the interpersonal domain refers to relationship status, and the extra-personal domain refers to living situations, work, education, and leisure activities. It should be noted that Livneh (2021) model does not prescribe a method for adaptation and instead provides a framework with which counselors can evaluate the current status and understand the process of adaptation in their clients with CID.

Another model of adjustment to disability is the *stage model of adjustment to disability*. The stage model of adjustment to disability parallels the grief model first proposed by Elisabeth Kubler-Ross and progresses through the following stages: shock, denial, depression/mourning, questioning/anger, and adaptation, change, and integration (Smart, 2009). *Shock* refers to the initial emotion typically experienced at the onset of disability and a person may feel disorganized, overwhelmed, or confused. *Denial*, sometimes referred to as defensive retreat, refers to the denial of the presence, implications, or permanence of disability, which can help an individual temporarily preserve their identity. *Depression* and mourning may follow denial as a person with CID begins to confront and lament an uncertain future and uncertain sense of self. Depression may be followed by *personal questioning and anger*, when a person may question "why" this happened to them and feel the presence of a CID is unfair. Finally, a person with CID may move to *adaptation, change*, and *integration*, where they begin to understand and accept the reality of disability, establish new values and goals, and explore residual strengths and abilities (Smart, 2009). There is a hypothesized final stage of adjustment known as *transcendence*. Transcendence of disability involves finding meaning and purpose in disability, reevaluating goals and identities, discovering personal strengths, finding positive aspects of CID, taking pride in mastery of CID, seeking out new challenges and experience, and helping other persons with disabilities. Transcendence, like self-actualization in humanistic psychology, is likely never completed. Instead, it is a stage individuals remain in as they continue to adapt and cope with new experiences related to their CID. It should be noted that there is considerable fluidity in the stages, as a person may move from adaptation and change back to depression and mourning should their condition worsen, or they receive a novel diagnosis. Similarly, people can move through the stages at varying rates depending upon the factors listed previously regarding coping styles, personal resources, environmental conditions, and threats posed by disability. Being able to identify the stage of adjustment that a person with CID is in can help a counselor determine appropriate interventions and foci for their counseling sessions as they seek to support persons with CID in their adjustment to disability.

Disability-Related Counseling Competencies

In 2018, the ARCA board of directors approved the *Disability-Related Counseling Competencies*. These competencies were designed "to serve as a resource and provide aspirational guidelines to help shape best practices in counseling by expanding meaningful understanding and support of [Persons with Disabilities] in contemporary American society" (Chapin et al., 2018, p. 1). It should be noted the competencies are not a requirement for counselors, but instead are considered to be aspirational. As such, counselors are encouraged to work toward implementation of the competencies as a means to better support and assist persons with CID. The competencies are divided into five sections: Section A—Understanding and Accommodating the Disability Experience; Section B—Advocacy for Persons with CID and Support of their Self-Advocacy; Section C—The Counseling Process and Relationship; Section D—Testing and Assessment; and Section E—Working with or Supervising Persons with CID in School, Employment, Community, or Clinical Settings (Chapin et al., 2018). A full review of the competencies is beyond the scope of the present chapter, but a copy of the competencies can be downloaded for free at https://www.counseling.org/docs/default-source/competencies/arca-disability-related-counseling-competencies-final-version-5-15-19.pdf?sfvrsn=c376562c_6.

Trauma-Informed Care

The connection between trauma and disability has long been understood as persons with disabilities are at greater risk of experiencing trauma in their lives (O'Sullivan et al., 2019). Persons with disabilities may experience trauma at the onset of disability (e.g., traumatic injury or life-threatening illness), trauma due to abuse or exploitation, or trauma due to maltreatment or abuse because of their disability status. **Trauma** is "defined as a highly distressing or life-threatening event which can encompass a single, acute event (such as a sexual assault, automobile accident, or natural disaster), or can be chronic (living with a domestically violent partner or parent, or living in a combat zone)" (O'Sullivan et al., 2019, p. 300). **Child maltreatment** refers to violence, neglect, or exploitation that involves a child and their caretaker. **Adverse childhood experiences (ACEs)** includes maltreatment as well as other stressful experiences such as witnessing domestic violence, parental mental illness, parental substance abuse, losing a parent through divorce or incarceration, or bullying from peers. Persons who have experienced multiple ACEs are at a higher likelihood for long-term physical and mental health consequences (O'Sullivan et al., 2019). **Trauma-informed care (TIC)** is a model used by counselors and agencies that places the assessment, treatment, and recovery from trauma as a primary goal for counseling (Duffey & Haberstroh, 2020). Trauma-informed providers understand that persons who have experienced trauma may not be aware of the impact that trauma has had in their lives and that people cope with trauma in diverse ways. People who experience trauma can experience a disconnection from others, from their mind and body, and from spirituality as a result of being in a constant state of threat. Due to the high likelihood that persons with CID have experienced trauma, child maltreatment, or adversity (O'Sullivan et al., 2019), as well as their continued risk for traumatic and adverse experiences, counselors must take steps to ensure they approach clients holistically in an effort to validate, understand, and help clients make sense of their traumatic experiences.

CONCLUSION

In conclusion, counseling plays a pivotal role in the rehabilitation counseling process. Counseling skills can help clients develop relationships with their rehabilitation counselor that promotes engagement in the counseling process, helps increase client self-understanding, develops problem solving skills, and empower clients to address barriers in their lives while pursuing goals. Persons seeking rehabilitation counseling services are demonstrating increasing levels of mental health needs and rehabilitation counselors must be responsive to these needs as they can serve as barriers to rehabilitation goals. Although counseling represents part of the rehabilitation counseling process and is not the sole purpose, research continues to demonstrate the positive impact of the working alliance on rehabilitation outcomes, and counseling skills are the primary means for developing the working alliance with clients. When seeking to understand and intervene with respect to client mental health distress, it is important to understand skills consistent with clinical mental health counseling such as the working alliance, counseling skills, assessment and diagnosis, case conceptualization, treatment planning, application of counseling theory, the psychological impact of disability, models of response to disability, and TIC. Despite the fact that counseling is not the sole or primary role of some rehabilitation counselors, it is a vital component of adaptation to CID, and therefore, counselors would be well served to continue developing, refining, and applying their counseling skills while demonstrating intentionality in their application of counseling skills as a means to support clients with CID who are also experiencing mental health distress.

CONTENT REVIEW QUESTIONS

1. How is psychotherapy defined? How are psychotherapy and counseling related as part of the continuum of counseling services?
2. What is the definition of *therapeutic relationship*?
3. What is the common factors model? What are the three common factors indicated in the chapter?
4. What are the steps in mental health counseling treatment planning? How are these similar to the treatment planning steps in rehabilitation counseling?
5. What is response to disability?
6. What are the five coping strategies indicated as responses to disability?

REFERENCES

American Psychiatric Association. (2013). *Diagnostic and statistical manual of mental disorders: DSM-5*. https://doi.org/10.1176/appi.books.9780890425596

Barros-Bailey, M., Benshoff, J. J., & Fischer, J. (2009). Rehabilitation counseling in the year 2011: Perceptions of Certified Rehabilitation Counselors. *Journal of Applied Rehabilitation Counseling, 39*(4), 39–45. https://doi.org/10.1891/0047-2220.39.4.39

Berghuis, D. J., Peterson, M. L., & Bruce, T. J. (2014). *The complete adult psychotherapy treatment planner* (5th ed., Ser. Practice Planners.). John Wiley and Sons, Inc.

Centers for Disease Control and Prevention. (2021, June 28). *About mental health*. https://www.cdc.gov/mentalhealth/learn/index.htm

Chan, F., Berven, N. L., & Thomas, K. R. (Eds.). (2015). *Counseling theories and techniques for rehabilitation and mental health professionals* (2nd ed.). Springer Publishing Company.

Chapin, M., McCarthy, H., Shaw, L., Bradham-Cousar, M., Chapman, R., Nosek, M., Peterson, S., Yilmaz, Z., & Ysasi, N. (2018). *Disability-related counseling competencies*. American Rehabilitation Counseling Association, a division of ACA.

Commission on Rehabilitation Counselor Certification. (2021, March 1). *Scope of practice statement*. https://crccertification.com/scope-of-practice

Cree, R. A., Okoro, C. A., Zack, M. M., & Carbone, E. (2020). Frequent Mental Distress Among Adults, by Disability Status, Disability Type, and Selected Characteristics - United States, 2018. *MMWR. Morbidity and Mortality Weekly Report, 69*(36), 1238–1243. https://doi.org/10.15585/mmwr.mm6936a2

Cuijpers, P., Reijnders, M., & Huibers, M. J. H. (2019). The Role of Common Factors in Psychotherapy Outcomes. *Annual Review of Clinical Psychology, 15*, 207–231. https://doi.org/10.1146/annurev-clinpsy-050718-095424

Duffey, T., & Haberstroh, S. (2020). *Introduction to crisis and trauma counseling*. American Counseling Association.

Duncan, B. L., Miller, S. D., Wampold, B. E., & Hubble, M. A. (2010). *The heart and soul of change: Delivering what works in therapy* (2nd ed.). American Psychological Association. https://doi.org/10.1037/12075-000

Eysenck, H. J. (1952). The effects of psychotherapy: an evaluation. *Journal of Consulting Psychology, 16*(5), 319–324. https://doi.org/10.1037/h0063633

Falvo, D. R., & Holland, B. E. (2018). *Medical and psychosocial aspects of chronic illness and disability* (6th ed.). Jones & Bartlett Learning.

First, M. B. (2014). *DSM-5 Handbook of Differential Diagnosis*. CBS Publishers and Distributors.

Gelso, C. J. (2011). *The real relationship in psychotherapy: The hidden foundation of change*. American Psychological Association. https://doi.org/10.1037/12349-000

Halbur, D., & Halbur, K. V. (2019). *Developing your theoretical orientation in counseling and psychotherapy*. Pearson.

Hays, D. G. (2017). *Assessment in counseling: Procedures and practices* (6th ed.). American Counseling Association.

Health Resources & Services Administration. (2021). *Health professional shortage areas*. Shortage areas. https://data.hrsa.gov/topics/health-workforce/shortage-areas

Howatt, W. A. (2000). *The human services counseling toolbox: Theory, development, technique, and resources.* Wadsworth/ Thomson Learning Company.

Ivey, A. E., Ivey, M. B., & Zalaquett, C. P. (2018). *Intentional interviewing and counseling: Facilitating client development in a multicultural society* (9th ed.). Cengage learning.

Johnson, R. B., & Christensen, L. B. (2012). *Educational research: Quantitative, qualitative, and mixed approaches* (4th ed.). SAGE.

Lambert, M. J. (1992). Psychotherapy outcome research: Implications for integrative and eclectical therapists. In J. C. Norcross & M. R. Goldfried (Eds.), *Handbook of psychotherapy integration* (pp. 94–129). Basic Books.

Lazarus, A. A., & Beutler, L. E. (1993). On Technical Eclecticism. *Journal of Counseling & Development, 71*(4), 381–385. https://doi.org/10.1002/j.1556-6676.1993.tb02652.x

Leahy, M. J., Muenzen, P., Saunders, J. L., & Strauser, D. (2009). Essential Knowledge Domains Underlying Effective Rehabilitation Counseling Practice. *Rehabilitation Counseling Bulletin, 52*(2), 95–106. https://doi.org/10.1177/0034355208323646

Levers, L. L., & Hyatt-Burkhart, D. (2019). *Clinical mental health counseling: Practicing in integrated systems of care.* Springer Publishing Company. https://doi.org/10.1891/9780826131089

Livneh, H. (2001). Psychosocial Adaptation to Chronic Illness and Disability. *Rehabilitation Counseling Bulletin, 44*(3), 151–160. https://doi.org/10.1177/003435520104400305

Livneh, H. (2021). Psychosocial adaptation to chronic illness and disability: An updated and expanded conceptual framework. *Rehabilitation Counseling Bulletin, 65*(3), 171–184. https://doi.org/10.1177/00343552211034819

Lund, E. M., Schultz, J. C., Nadorff, M. R., Galbraith, K., & Thomas, K. B. (2017). Experience, knowledge, and perceived comfort and clinical competency in working with suicidal clients among vocational rehabilitation counselors. *Rehabilitation Counseling Bulletin, 61*(1), 54–63. https://doi.org/10.1177/0034355217695776

Lustig, D. C., Strauser, D. R., Dewaine Rice, N., & Rucker, T. F. (2002). The relationship between working alliance and rehabilitation outcomes. *Rehabilitation Counseling Bulletin, 46*(1), 24–32. https://doi.org/10.1177/00343552020460010201

Martin, D. G. (1999). *Counseling & therapy skills* (2nd ed.). Waveland Press, Inc.

McCarthy, A. K. (2014). Relationship between rehabilitation counselor efficacy for counseling skills and client outcomes. *Journal of Rehabilitation, 80*(2), 3–11.

National Institute of Mental Health. (2021). *Suicide.* U.S. Department of Health and Human Services. https://www.nimh.nih.gov/health/statistics/suicide

Okoro, C. A., Hollis, N. D., Cyrus, A. C., & Griffin-Blake, S. (2018). Prevalence of disabilities and health care access by disability status and type among adults - United States, 2016. *MMWR. Morbidity and Mortality Weekly Report, 67*(32), 882–887. https://doi.org/10.15585/mmwr.mm6732a3

O'Sullivan, D., Watts, J. R., & Strauser, D. R. (2019). Trauma-sensitive rehabilitation counseling: Paradigms and principles. *Journal of Vocational Rehabilitation, 51*(3), 299–312. https://doi.org/10.3233/JVR-191047

Reichenberg, L. W., & Seligman, L. (2016). *Selecting effective treatments: A comprehensive systematic guide to treating mental disorders* (5th ed.). John Wiley & Sons, Inc.

Reinert, M, Fritze, D. & Nguyen, T. (October, 2021). "The State of Mental Health in America 2022" Mental Health America.

Rubin, S. E., & Roessler, R. (2008). *Foundations of the vocational rehabilitation process* (6th ed.). PRO-ED.

Smart, J. (2009). *Disability, society, and the individual* (2nd ed.). PRO-ED.

Sommers-Flanagan, J., & Sommers-Flanagan, R. (2013). *Clinical interviewing* (5th ed.). John Wiley & Sons.

Sperry, L., & Sperry, J. J. (2020). *Case conceptualization: Mastering this competency with ease and confidence* (2nd ed.). Routledge. https://doi.org/10.4324/9780429288968

Substance Abuse and Mental Health Services Administration. (2020). *Key substance use and mental health indicators in the United States: Results from the 2019 National Survey on Drug Use and Health (HHS Publication no.PEP20-07-01-001, NSDUH Series H-55).* https://www.samhsa.gov/data

Tarvydas, V. M., & Hartley, M. T. (2018). *The Professional Practice of Rehabilitation Counseling* (2nd ed.). Springer Publishing Company. https://doi.org/10.1891/9780826138934

Torres, A., Frain, M., & Tansey, T. N. (2019). The impact of motivational interviewing training on rehabilitation counselors: Assessing working alliance and client engagement. A randomized controlled trial. *Rehabilitation Psychology, 64*(3), 328–338. https://doi.org/10.1037/rep0000267

Truscott, D. (2015). *Becoming an effective psychotherapist: Adopting a theory of psychotherapy that's right for you and your client.* American Psychological Association.

Vash, C. L., & Crewe, N. M. (2004). *Psychology of disability* (2nd ed.). Springer Publishing Company.

Wampold, B. E. (2010). *The basics of psychotherapy: An introduction to theory and practice.* American Psychological Association.

Whitney, D. G., & Peterson, M. D. (2019). US national and state-level prevalence of mental health disorders and disparities of mental health care use in children. *JAMA Pediatrics, 173*(4), 389–391. https://doi.org/10.1001/jamapediatrics.2018.5399

Woo, S. M., & Keatinge, C. (2016). *Diagnosis and treatment of mental disorders across the lifespan* (2nd ed.). John Wiley & Sons.

CHAPTER 13

Clinical Case Management and Coordination

VANESSA M. PERRY AND MARTHA H. CHAPIN

LEARNING OBJECTIVES

After reading this chapter, you should be able to:

- *Define case management and caseload management.*
- *Describe the role of a case manager in the rehabilitation process.*
- *Recognize the purpose of medical, psychological, and vocational case management.*
- *Explain how your client would benefit from medical, psychological, and vocational case management.*
- *Explain how Lewy body dementia (LBD) can affect a client's rehabilitation.*

CACREP STANDARDS

CACREP 2016: 2F2.e, 2F5.b, 2F5.g, 2F5.h.
CACREP 2016 Specialties:
   Clinical Rehabilitation Counseling: 5D1.f, 5D2.a, 5D2.b, 5D2.c, 5D2.m, 5D3.c
   Rehabilitation Counseling: 5H1.b, 5H1.c, 5H1.g, 5H2.b, 5H2.c, 5H2.e, 5H3.a, 5H3.b, 5H3.g, 5H3.l

INTRODUCTION

Case management is a critical professional function underlying contemporary rehabilitation counseling practice. As rehabilitation counselors (RCs), we are trained to research, problem-solve, and coordinate the diverse services necessary for our clients to "achieve their personal, career, and independent living goals" (Commission on Rehabilitation Counselor Certification [CRCC], 2017). With an arsenal of services and tools at our disposal, RCs possess extensive knowledge of medical, psychological, and vocational resources. Furthermore, we apply our counseling and interpersonal skills as well as administrative expertise to communicate with not only our clients but also other healthcare professionals. Case management is the complex process of coordinating an array of services to help our clients achieve their desired goals.

In this chapter, we introduce key concepts and describe the value of case management within the professional practice of rehabilitation counseling. We then present a detailed case study and walk the reader through the case management process that includes medical, psychological, and vocational case management from initial referral to case closure. Because a client's needs may change across the life span, we then review these same processes for each decade of the client's life.

VALUE OF CASE MANAGEMENT

Case management consistently has been identified as one of the most important activities or job functions of the RC (Leahy et al., 2009, 2013). Case management is defined as "a collaborative process of assessment, planning, facilitation, care coordination, evaluation and advocacy for options and services to meet an individual's and family's comprehensive health needs through communication and [the use of] available resources to promote patient safety, quality of care, and cost-effective outcomes" (Case Management Society of America [CMSA], 2016, p. 11). The unique complexities of case management practice also has led to advanced practice certifications offered to RCs and other professionals by the CMSA, and that may be held in addition to other professional credentials. Case management is consistent with a **holistic approach** to rehabilitation counseling that addresses client concerns related to not only medical, but also vocational, recreational, social, and spiritual domains, to name a few.

It is important to note that the CMSA (2016) definition of case management includes the family because family members or family caregivers are part of the client's support system and play an integral role in the client's life. Clients are much more than medical patients receiving medical services. Rather, clients may also have roles such as being parents, children, siblings, friends, neighbors, or coworkers. RCs must be aware of family dynamics from the perspective of an individual client. They also must be aware that in order to serve the needs of their clients, they must move away from outdated notions of a nuclear family, meaning two heterosexual parents and their biological children. Depending on the RC's role and the client's request, the RC may assess the needs of the client and the family and, through collaboration with the client and family, create a case management plan that will serve the client effectively. This plan includes educating the client and family about available resources, linking them to these resources, discussing financial responsibility, and facilitating the client's access to these resources (CMSA, 2016). The value of case management is reflected in its individualized and holistic approach to understanding and supporting all aspects of clients' lives.

The job function of case management is ubiquitous and multi-faceted. Shaw et al. (2005) described case management as the "disciplined application of skills, tools, and techniques" that "assesses, plans, implements, coordinates, monitors, and evaluates options and services" to meet an individual client's needs (p. 4). It is not surprising that RCs use case management skills in a variety of work settings, including public rehabilitation, private for-profit rehabilitation, behavioral health treatment programs, community-based rehabilitation, private not-for-profit rehabilitation programs, and managed care (CMSA, 2016; Shaw et al., 2005). Case management also is used in hospitals and integrated care delivery systems; ambulatory care clinics and community-based organizations; corporations; schools; public health insurance and benefit programs; private health insurance programs; government-sponsored programs; geriatric services; long-term care; end-of-life, hospice, palliative, and respite care programs; physician and medical groups; and LCP, as well as health, wellness, prevention, and disease management programs (CMSA, 2016, p. 14). The number of work sites using case management demonstrates how RCs might use these same skills throughout their own life span to help themselves and their families traverse life's challenges.

RC work with clients who have a variety of medical conditions throughout their life span. For example, youth and adults with intellectual and developmental disabilities that may affect students' ability to succeed in school and transition to employment. School- and working-age clients who have orthopedic, traumatic brain and spinal cord injuries and need help with hospital discharge planning to move them home or into short term or long-term care facilities and return to work. Workers' compensation clients who have carpal tunnel syndrome, tenosynovitis, amputations, and knee or back injuries and need help with medical treatment and return to work are assisted by RCs. Clients with mental health or substance use disorders may need assistance transferring to or from inpatient, outpatient, or partial hospitalizations and aftercare. These are only a few examples of the services RCs might provide clients with various disabilities.

Knowledge of case management can be demonstrated through credentialing in this specialized area of expertise. There are three primary certifications for RCs who provide case management services. These certifications include becoming a certified rehabilitation counselor (Commission on Rehabilitation Counselor Certification [CRCC], 2021), a certified disability management specialist (Certification of Disability Management Specialist [CDMS], 2021a), or a certified case manager (Commission for Case Management Certification [CCMC], 2021; Shaw et al., 2005).The certified rehabilitation counselor credential is designated specifically for RCs (CRCC, 2021) and is recommended for graduates of rehabilitation counseling programs. RCs also may obtain certification as disability management specialists when they practice in insurance-based rehabilitation (CDMS, 2021b) and as case managers when their primary job duty is case management (CCMC, 2021). Furthermore, some RCs working in behavioral health may provide case management services to individuals with psychiatric disabilities.

Caseload management is defined as "how to work with more than one case at a time, how to select which case to work with, how to move from one case to another, how to establish a system to ensure movement of all cases" (Henke et al., 1975, as cited in Greenwood & Roessler, 2018, pp. 241–242). Caseload management refers to the management of a total caseload, rather than coordinating services for an individual client. For RCs who work in the public VR system, caseload sizes range from 60 to 183 cases, with an average caseload size of approximately 100 cases (Eischens, 2016; Jackson, 2019). In contrast, other employment settings may have smaller caseloads, such as disability management specialists who tend to have caseload sizes ranging from 26 to 50 cases (Rosenthal et al., 2007). In a review of effective case management of mental health services, Rapp and Goscha (2004) noted that caseload size should be small enough to allow for a relatively high frequency of contact between the case manager and client. With that said, the amount of contact between case managers and clients often varies by employment setting as well as the individual needs of a client.

The amount of contact with clients on the RC's caseload also may differ depending on the different phases of the rehabilitation process. In order for the RC to meet quotas for successful case closure, caseload management requires that RCs effectively plan, manage, and evaluate each client's case to help clients accomplish their goals in a timely manner. The RC also needs to manage their own time effectively and prioritize which cases to service first (Roessler et al., 2018). This planning includes allowing time for unexpected caseload needs to arise as well as anticipating that some caseload management tasks will take longer than projected. One way to manage the amount of contact with clients effectively is for the RC to "touch" each case on their caseload monthly. This approach would require the RC to divide all the cases by the number of days available in the month and each day check the status of the clients on that day's schedule and provide these clients with the needed services. Through the course of the month, the RC would have "touched" each case (Emmerton, 2016). While this processing of "touching" each case may or may not result in direct contact with the client, such a process will ensure that the RC is assessing what is going on with the case and what needs to occur to move things forward.

One key aspect of caseload management is case documentation. **Case documentation** is the process of maintaining a record of the case management process, often including the justification of interventions and expenditures, as well as the RC's interactions with the client and other service providers (CRCC, 2017). Typically, the case management process begins with the RC conducting an initial interview with the client to gather

BOX 13.1 REFERRAL LETTER AND LETTER TO REQUEST INFORMATION

- Return address
- Date
- Mailing address
- Regarding line
- Describe your role working with this client —why are you helping this client?
- Purpose of the letter—reason for referral, current issue(s) to be resolved
- Appointment date if already scheduled
- Biopsychosocial history relevant to the diagnosis (Ask yourself, does the person to whom I am making the referral need to know this information about my client to facilitate effective treatment?)
- Desired outcome—diagnosis, prognosis, current treatment plans, report with recommendations, specific questions you need answered
- If you are making a referral for physical therapy, occupational therapy, or work hardening, include the prescription from the physician for treatment
- Statement related to the release of information, if attached
- Signature line
- Enclosures, if applicable—list information enclosed

Letters requesting information

- Return address
- Date
- Mailing address
- Regarding line
- Describe your role working with this client Introduction of you and your relationship to the client—why are you helping this client?
- Purpose of the letter—reason for referral, current issue to be resolved
- Desired outcome—diagnosis, prognosis, current treatment plans, specific questions you need answered
- Statement related to the release of information, if attached
- Signature line
- Enclosures, if applicable—list information enclosed
- Remember to write the letters clearly and succinctly.

medical, psychological, vocational, and financial information. Following this meeting, the RC writes an initial assessment report and establishes recommendations or treatment goals. These recommendations may include contacting the client's medical and psychological providers to gather information to document the existence of a disability, which may be required for the client to be eligible for services. Letters to request information and to refer the client for services may be needed also. Progress reports or case notes are written to document the activities completed based on the recommendations. Additional recommendations will be made to move the client toward medical or psychological stability, return to work, and a more independent lifestyle. The frequency of these reports depends upon agency guidelines, but likely occurs every 30, 60, or 90 days. If the RC is working for a fee-for- service agency, a bill documenting the time spent by the RC providing these case services will be included with the initial assessment or progress reports. Today electronic health records are used more often than paper case files. Box 13.1 summarizes information to be included in a referral letter or a letter requesting information about a client.

PROCESS OF CASE MANAGEMENT

The case management process is cyclical rather than linear, and recurrent rather than unidirectional (CMSA, 2016). Even though the case management process is not linear, it can be helpful to think of the following components in a logical sequence of:

- Client identification, selection, and engagement
- Assessment and opportunity identification
- Case management plan of care:
  - Development of the plan
  - Implementation and coordination
  - Monitoring and evaluation
- Case closure (CMSA, 2016)

To implement these steps, the RC usually receives a referral either directly from the client or from another agency. Once the referral is received, the RC reviews the client's case file, meets with the client to complete an initial assessment, and then explores the client's medical, psychological, and vocational case management needs (Chapin, 2005a, 2005b; Roessler & Rubin, 2006; Rubin & Roessler, 2008). If the client is eligible for services, the RC develops a treatment plan and decides which steps are needed to help the client achieve their goals. Throughout the case management process, the RC monitors and evaluates the services the client is receiving and modifies the treatment plan as needed. Additional details on each stage of the case management process are described in the following sections.

File Receipt and Review

When receiving referrals for new clients, RCs likely will receive some basic background information about them, such as their name, age, gender, type of disability, and reason for referral. In order to comprehend clients' stories, RCs should review each of the documents found in clients' files. RCs can expect to review educational records, medical records, psychological evaluations, vocational evaluations, and so forth. In reviewing what documents are present in case files, RCs also will be able to observe what information is notably absent (Roessler & Rubin, 2006; Rubin & Roessler, 2008).

Conferring with previous service providers may help RCs gain insight into the history of clients' presenting condition(s), supports clients have utilized in the past, and clients' prognoses. In order for RCs to request records from other service providers, clients must complete a written release of information. Releases of information should be prepared by RCs and should include the client's name and the nature of documents requested (e.g., vocational evaluation report, counseling diagnosis and clinical impressions, medical history). RCs should take care to interpret documents within their scope of practice and consult with experts when interpreting documents beyond their scope. This is true for the medical, psychological, and vocational case management areas described next.

Medical Case Management

Each step in the rehabilitation process has multiple facets and includes an interdisciplinary team approach. For example, medical case management can encompass discharge planning and assist a client in the client's transfer home, or to custodial care (i.e., personal or supervisor care, assisted living, group and foster homes), intermediate care, skilled nursing, or, long-term care. Hospice care may also be needed by a client (Powell & Tahan, 2019), but most RCs will not coordinate transfer to hospice care even though the same process and skills would be helpful. A client who transfers home may need the RC's assistance in finding and compensating home health aides, coordinating environmental modifications, hiring a personal care attendant, and ensuring that home healthcare services are provided. Home healthcare services and outpatient treatment may require coordination with an interdisciplinary team that may include nurses, occupational and physical therapists, speech and language pathologists, audiologists, prosthetists, and orthotists, to name just a few areas of medical case management. Follow-up with a client's treating physician or referral to a new physician also may be necessary (Chapin, 2005a, 2005b; Roessler & Rubin, 2006). In conjunction with medical case management, psychological issues may have to be addressed.

Psychological Case Management

Psychological case management may require assisting the client in referral to a mental health professional. The mental health professional may treat the client's mental health or addiction concerns, assist in adjustment to disability, address issues of domestic violence, or help the client cope with surviving a crisis or disaster, as well as deal with issues of sexuality that occur as a result of the client's disabling condition. Pain management treatment may also be required (Chapin, 2005b). For clients with substance use or mental health concerns, referral to a day treatment program or halfway house may be required. A psychological or neurological evaluation may be completed if additional information regarding the client's cognitive and emotional functioning is required (Roessler et al., 2018). Although medical and psychological case management is being pursued, discussions regarding return to work may also occur.

For clients with profound, recurring mental health concerns, RCs may engage with or refer clients to assertive community treatment (ACT) teams, or provide vocational rehabilitation as part of an ACT team or some other type of psychiatric rehabilitation program. Psychiatric rehabilitation is described in a later chapter of this text. ACT is a service appropriate for clients who experience persistent, severe mental health symptoms that cause a serious, negative psychosocial impact on clients' lives. In the ACT model, team-based services are provided to clients in the clients' environment when needed, 24 hours per day, 7 days per week. ACT teams work together to provide collaborative treatment tailored to the individual client, including services like medication management, substance use disorder treatment, housing assistance, financial management, and vocational rehabilitation (Phillips et al., 2001; Thorning & Dixon, 2020). RCs wishing to learn more about the ACT model may delve into the existing body of literature on effective replication of the model by adhering to forensic assertive community treatment fidelity scales (Lamberti & Weisman, 2021).

Vocational Case Management

Vocational case management requires that RCs have knowledge of their clients' educational backgrounds and prior work and volunteer experiences. This information, in conjunction with medical and psychological knowledge, facilitates decisions regarding the client's ability to return to work. The return-to-work process includes exploring return to work with the same or a different employer in the same job or in a new job with or without job modifications. If employment is not possible, then coordinating short-term retraining to facilitate return to work with the same or a new employer, or self-employment, may be pursued (Matkin, 1981; Welch, 1979). To facilitate return to work, the RC will contact the employer, if one exists at the time of injury or illness, and discuss the client's ability to return to work. If returning to work with the former employer is possible, the RC may obtain a functional capacity evaluation from the treating physician or another healthcare-professional (Chapin, 2005a, 2005b). The RC may also complete a functional job analysis that is reviewed with the treating physician to ensure placement into a physically appropriate job (Roessler et al., 2018).

If returning to work with the same employer in the same or a similar job is not possible, the RC may need to look at developing a new job goal and alternate job placement. Techniques the RC may use to help determine a new job goal within the client's physical capabilities include a transferable skills analysis and labor-market survey. The RC may also use an on-the-job evaluation to determine if a new job or short-term retraining is appropriate or if on-the-job training is needed to transition a client into a new job. If a new job is pursued, the client may also need assistance with developing a résumé and cover letter and learning job-seeking skills. A functional capacity evaluation may be needed and a job analysis may be completed and reviewed with the treating physician in order for the RC to obtain a release to return to work (Chapin, 2005a, 2005b).

If the aforementioned techniques are not beneficial in helping the client return to work, the client may benefit from the RC providing interest and aptitude testing to help the client develop a job goal. If more in-depth testing is required to help a client develop a job goal, the RC may refer the client for a vocational evaluation or psychological assessment (Roessler et al., 2018). Some of these techniques are discussed in the case study of Carla. The reader should note how medical, psychological, and vocational aspects of the case management process overlap in the following case study.

Life Care Planning

Life care planning (LCP) is a "systematic methodology for identifying and quantifying the multidimensional, disability-related needs of an individual" (Reid et al., 2005, p. 229). Some RCs are qualified to become certified LCP practitioners, whereas others may refer clients to LCP providers. In either situation, case management skills are essential for LCP. RCs working with LCPs may need to forward vocational assessments/evaluations, particularly for a client who "has no clear vocational goal, has no work history or a series of short, sporadic jobs, [and] who has not been determined ineligible for vocational opportunities" (Berens & Weed, 2009, p. 44). While practicing, LCPs may need to negotiate cost services over a life span for a client. RCs can view LCP as a "problem-solving approach that promotes continuity and consistency of care" (Reid et al., 2005, p. 228).

CASE STUDY

Case Narrative

Carla is a 45-year-old woman with major depressive disorder who was diagnosed recently with early onset Lewy body dementia (LBD) with hallucinations. Carla has scheduled an appointment with a RC at her public vocational rehabilitation (VR) services office. The RC reviews the initial assessment and researches LBD in preparation for Carla's visit.

LBD is a brain disorder that affects more than 1 million Americans. Often compared to Alzheimer's disease, LBD is characterized by abnormal protein deposits in the brain. Consequently, thought, movement, behavior, and mood are negatively affected. Because LBD affects many parts of the brain, clients may have both physical and psychological manifestations. Physical manifestations may include problems with motor functioning, including difficulty walking or rigidity (parkinsonism), rapid eye movement (REM) sleep behavior disorders, and difficulty recognizing smells (USDHHS, 2021). From a physical perspective, clients may also experience syncope (fainting) and frequent falls. Dementia with Lewy bodies and Parkinson's disease dementia are two LBD diagnoses (USDHHS, 2021).

People affected by LBD may have difficulty performing activities of daily living or managing personal finances, and may experience hallucinations (LBDA, n.d.). LBD is progressive in nature and diagnosed most commonly at age 50 or later. Individuals with LBD often live with the disease for 5 to 8 years (from diagnosis to death), but the disease may also span 2 to 20 years. At onset, symptoms may be mild but as the disease progresses individuals with LBD may express symptoms of dementia, unpredictable changes in ability to concentrate, and depressed mood. Up to 80% of people with LBD experience visual hallucinations. As LBD becomes terminal, people with LBD may rely almost entirely on others for care. The etiology of LBD remains unknown (USDHHS, 2021).

Initial Assessment

When the initial referral was received, the RC would likely have received records such as a neurological assessment and medical report. Carla's RC should consult with a medical expert when interpreting her neurological assessment. Medical records would provide information about Carla's diagnosis of having LBD. The RC has gathered the following information about Carla.

Carla, in her mid-40s, has been experiencing difficulty at work and will be terminated from her position as a nursing assistant at the end of the month due to her lack of interpersonal skills and causing dissension among coworkers. Carla has worked with an RC in the past and believes she will need assistance in finding new employment as she now has the responsibility of maintaining medical insurance for herself and her husband (who is not working due to illness). Carla is extremely anxious because her husband physically abuses her, and she knows that a loss of employment and a new diagnosis will trigger his abuse.

Carla explained that she feels as if she gets along with her coworkers; however, she believes that they plotted against her and that is the reason she was terminated. She states that her employer never gave her a warning and just informed her that she would lose her job. Carla reports that she uncovered that her employer was a prostitute and that is why she was fired by her employer.

Carla explains to the RC that there is no cure for her LBD and that the doctors have given her clozapine for her hallucinations (LBDA, 2021a). Carla does not believe she has hallucinations and does not want to take the medication, but has agreed to take it to see how it makes her feel. Carla states that she has to make regular appointments with her physician to have her blood drawn, so she does not acquire a rare blood disease due to the clozapine. Blood tests are needed because "clozapine can decrease the number of neutrophils, a type of white blood cell, that function in the body to fight off infections" (U.S. Food and Drug Administration, 2021, para. 2). Carla believes this blood work may impede her work schedule.

Medical Case Management

One of the recommendations from the initial assessment is to obtain medical documentation of Carla's LBD. Physicians who treat LBD include neurologists, geriatric psychiatrists, and neuropsychologists (LBDA, 2021b). Since a neurologist is treating Carla, medical records will be requested from the neurologist to gain a better understanding of Carla's diagnosis and how LBD is affecting Carla. Medical testing that might be received from the neurologist includes results from magnetic resonance imaging, electroencephalography reports, and a cerebrospinal fluid analysis (Mollenhauer et al., 2010). Because Carla will soon be terminated from her job as a nursing assistant, the RC will ask the physician about Carla's functional capabilities for work. Contact with Carla's neurologist reveals that she is experiencing cognitive rather than physical limitations from her LBD.

Psychological Case Management

Overall, Carla could benefit from counseling support to help her navigate the many obstacles she is facing in her life, such as loss of employment, adjustment to disability, domestic violence, poor interpersonal communication, and symptoms of depression. If Carla's RC works at an agency that does not allow RCs to provide mental health counseling and Carla is not receiving counseling services currently, the RC should refer Carla to a clinical rehabilitation or mental health counselor so that she may receive additional support as she navigates life with LBD.

Counseling also could help Carla explore and improve her interpersonal skills, given that they are the reason for dismissal from her previous employer. In counseling, Carla may also have the opportunity to explore what losing her job has meant to her and what effect it might have had on her self-concept. As LBD progresses, counseling may also help Carla process what having a disability is like and teach her positive coping strategies. Counseling could also provide an opportunity for Carla to discuss her marriage, the cycle of abuse, and the supports available to her as a woman in a domestic violence situation.

Carla reports a diagnosis of major depressive disorder. This diagnosis indicates that Carla's mental health has been treated in the past. Requesting her mental health records will help the RC understand her diagnosis and how it affects Carla. Since Carla already has been diagnosed with LBD, the RC should request a neuropsychological assessment, which will provide medical documentation so Carla will be eligible for services from state VR.

Vocational Case Management

After the RC has acknowledged and discussed the impact of Carla's medical, psychological, and familial issues with Carla, vocational exploration can begin. Reviewing the functional capacity evaluation completed by an occupational therapist prior to creating Carla's vocational plan will prove advantageous due to Carla's comorbidity (having both depression and LBD). Depending on the results of that evaluation, maintaining employment as a nursing assistant may or may not be a viable vocational option for Carla. If working as a nursing assistant is determined to be an option, identification of workplace accommodations should be explored for medication management and interpersonal issues (e.g., use of a support person or supervisor when behavior becomes unprofessional; Job Accommodation Network, n.d.).

In the event Carla is unable to pursue employment as a nursing assistant, vocational exploration will be necessary. Vocational exploration may include activities such as vocational evaluations/assessments, which assess work preferences, skills, and capacity to work in a variety of roles (Roessler et al., 2018). Equally important is an assessment of the prospective work environments Carla is interested in pursuing. Conducting a job analysis will help Carla and the RC identify the physical and mental demands of jobs, environmental stressors, hazards, and characteristics of the work environment (Roessler et al., 2018). While the aforementioned services cater to the client directly, RCs may wish to engage with potential employers to secure employment for Carla. Demand side engagement is focused on assisting employers by prioritizing the needs or demands for qualified, prescreened potential employees. Demand side engagement also provides RCs the opportunity to dispel any myths or address any concerns employers might have about workers with disabilities (Chan et al., 2010). In engaging with potential employers, the RC may be able to identify an employer and job for which Carla is a mutually beneficial match.

RCs have an ethical obligation to maintain case files in an appropriate manner (American Counseling Association (ACA, 2014) *Code of Ethics*; CRCC *Code of Professional Ethics for Rehabilitation Counselors* (CRCC, 2017); National Board for Certified Counselors *Code of Ethics* (NBCC, 2016). In the case of Carla, case file management is imperative. Carla's history of ruptured relationships may recur in a disruption of the counselor–client dynamic. Maintaining appropriate and consistent case files will assist in documenting conflicts and monitoring Carla's progress in her vocational endeavors.

CASE MANAGEMENT THROUGH THE LIFE SPAN

Viewing Carla's case management needs throughout her life span demonstrates the cyclical and recurrent nature of case management (CMSA, 2016).

Carla in Her Mid-50s

Carla has found herself back at Vocational Rehabilitation Services because she was just released from a mental health facility. Carla reports that her relationship with her only son is strained because he had Carla committed. Carla believes the reason for her committal was that she uncovered that her daughter-in-law was laundering money from her place of employment. Since the last time working with the RC, Carla that reports her LBD has been the same and that she does not need to continue the use of medication.

Carla's husband has since passed away and she is living in their house, which is about 45 minutes away from her son. Carla would like to pursue a nursing assistant position, as that is the only type of work she enjoys; however, Carla is trying to pass the certified nursing assistant examination (American Red Cross, 2021) without much success.

Medical Case Management

Although there are no physical issues for the RC to address at this time, the RC should request updated medical information from Carla's neurologist to stay abreast of Carla's medical status.

Psychological Case Management

Upon release from mental health inpatient care, clients usually have follow-up mental health services coordinated by a discharge planner. The RC should seek permission from Carla to follow up with aftercare providers to ensure streamlined services for Carla. Her son's involvement in her involuntary commitment likely would have damaged their relationship and put a strain on their family as a whole. The RC should ask Carla about family members' relationships with one another and see if additional support is needed. A referral to a marriage and family therapist could help Carla's family address conflict and concerns about Carla. The RC may want to address possible unresolved grief and bereavement from the passing of Carla's husband and how the family as a whole is handling his loss. Additionally, Carla should continue to receive medication management.

Vocational Case Management

Collaborating with providers is an essential function of case management for RCs (Roessler et al., 2018). Carla's RC should gather as much information as possible concerning the committal from Carla and the appropriate medical professionals. Obtaining current medical information can assist in identifying whether Carla has a release to return to work from her treating provider and factors that may impact her vocational plan (i.e., noncompliance with medication). In addition, updating the functional capacity evaluation is necessary to develop appropriate vocational goals.

Carla's difficulty in passing the certified nursing assistant examination may cause frustration and conflict within the counselor–client alliance. Carla may express resistance to pursuing employment that is out of her comfort zone. Revisiting vocational assessments and evaluations will aid Carla in identifying additional employment opportunities she enjoys and has the skills to pursue. RCs can further support clients in new positions by providing on-the-job training. On-the-job training allows clients to have one-on-one training, which should acclimate them to their work responsibilities and the work environment.

Carla in Her Mid-60s

Carla is about to lose a job she obtained through a neighbor. She reports that she recently was diagnosed with breast cancer, but doesn't believe the diagnosis and has refused treatment. Carla states that she feels just fine and really needs to work. She has changed treating physicians and is no longer taking her medication for LBD. Carla does not want to receive financial help from her son and is resistant to applying for social security disability insurance (SSDI) due to the lengthy application process and the fact that none of the people she knows was ever able to receive the benefit.

Carla is now living in a low-income independent living community because maintaining her home was too much for her. She enjoys the people in the community, but needs work to maintain her living expenses. Carla is determined to be as independent as possible and plans to work hard until the end of her life.

Medical Case Management

With Carla's permission, the RC would request medical information regarding the breast cancer diagnosis from Carla's treating physician. If further medical treatment is recommended, the RC will discuss treatment options with Carla. However, if Carla refuses treatment, the RC must honor Carla's decision and would document in Carla's case file her decision to refuse treatment.

Psychological Case Management

Carla recently has received another serious diagnosis: breast cancer. Denying the veracity of her diagnosis is a significant barrier to Carla's treatment. The RC should review medical documentation of the diagnosis with Carla and explore her denial of the diagnosis and general feelings about cancer. Particularly, what previous experience with cancer does Carla have? What are her thoughts about loved ones' cancer treatments? Carla has had difficulty maintaining employment throughout the years. The RC should explore how Carla's self-concept related to employment has evolved throughout the years and offer support as she faces dismissal from a job. Carla's perspective about the role employment may take in her life will evolve as she ages and considers whether she would like to be a member of the workforce. Carla's psychiatrist should continue to monitor hallucinations and provide medication management.

Vocational Case Management

Assessing Carla's functional capacity to work is central to moving forward with a vocational plan. Understanding how Carla's new diagnosis of breast cancer will impact her overall health, medications, treatments, and psychological health is imperative to identifying her capacity to carry out job functions. Case management is grounded in the premises of client choice and minimizing the imposition of provider values at all costs (Leahy & Kline, 2014). Some RCs may struggle with Carla's choice to continue to work given her previous work history and her medical conditions. As long as Carla is cleared medically to work with supports, she should be afforded the opportunity to seek vocational opportunities.

As Carla's medical issues have increased, she may require a comprehensive employment accommodation evaluation. Consequently, reviewing a job analysis with her medical provider would be helpful to identify the most appropriate vocational environment. As Carla's interpersonal issues continue to persist, a behavioral plan may have to be developed to monitor relationships with employees and employers. Carla can be successful with attention to medical, physical, psychological, and vocational needs.

Carla in Her Mid-70s

Carla did not show up for work, and the employer contacted the RC on file. Because the RC had a release of information on file to talk with Carla's personal care attendant, the RC called the attendant and asked the personal care attendant to check on Carla. The attendant found Carla passed out at her home. Carla was taken to a local hospital where doctors informed Carla and her family that she had 6 months to 1 year to live. The doctor recommended locating hospice care for Carla.

Medical Case Management

Because Carla was hospitalized, the RC would gather current medical information regarding the recent hospitalization and the recommendation for hospice care. If the RC works at an agency whose purpose is to assist Carla with employment, then the RC will be required to refer Carla to another agency to coordinate her hospice care. The RC or new case manager may attend the treatment team meeting and work directly with the discharge planner at the hospital to coordinate hospice care. Carla and her son, in conjunction with Carla's physician, will decide whether Carla will receive home hospice care or inpatient care. Because a personal care attendant has assisted Carla in her home, Carla's home already may be equipped with a temporary ramp to allow easy entrance and exit. Carla might also benefit from home healthcare services, including a nurse to draw her blood because she is still on clozapine.

As Carla's condition deteriorates, she may benefit from physical therapy to decrease the rapid decline of physical functioning and mobility and from occupational therapy to assist her in activities of daily living, particularly self-care needs (LBDA, n.d.). Grab bars, a raised toilet seat, and a tub transfer chair for the bathroom may be required to assist Carla in her activities of daily living. If Carla has difficulty ambulating, a walker, and then a wheelchair, would assist her with mobility. Carla previously had been using the services of a personal care attendant, and the need for the attendant will increase as her health declines. Furthermore, Carla's dementia will affect her thinking, remembering, and reasoning skills. At some point, the cost of inpatient care, possibly in an Alzheimer's unit, at a nursing home or assisted living facility may be less than the cost of a personal care attendant. Also, as Carla's health declines, she may need inpatient hospice care (LBDA, n.d.). Since Carla is in her 70s, she would be eligible for Medicare. Medicare should cover Carla's hospice care expenses, but Carla would still be required to pay her monthly premiums, deductibles, and coinsurance for treatment unrelated to her terminal illness (Medicare.gov, n.d.). Support for the family will be essential during Carla's life transitions.

Psychological Case Management

Carla has faced serious deterioration of her physical health. Because LBD has impacted her cognitive skills negatively, the RC should follow up with Carla's neurologist for more detailed information on her cognitive functioning. Carla's ability to live independently has decreased and will continue to decrease over time. She would need to discuss what relying on others means to her and ways she might age with dignity. Watching Carla's slow decline may also have a negative impact on Carla's family, who likely would benefit from caregiver and family supports. Support groups and group counseling are two of many resources available to loved ones of people with dementia that the RC could coordinate for Carla's family.

Vocational Case Management

There would be no further need for vocational case management, as Carla will not be returning to work.

CONCLUSION

In this chapter, we have provided a brief overview of case management, defined *case management* and *caseload management*, discussed the value of case management, and reviewed the steps in the case management process. The case study of Carla was examined to show the application of case management skills. Since the case management and caseload management procedures may differ across different service delivery systems and client populations, RCs often learn these job functions within particular agencies (Chan et al., 2018). With that said, the professional function of case management is one that requires considerable knowledge as well as counseling and interpersonal skills to communicate with clients as well as other healthcare professionals. To be sure, the effectiveness of case management is often dependent on the ability of the RC to navigate complex human service systems. For additional information on case management and the case management process, the reader is directed to *Case Management and Rehabilitation Counseling* (Roessler et al., 2018), *Case Management for the Health, Human, and Vocational Rehabilitation Services* (Wilson et al., 2018), and *The Case Manager's Handbook* (Mullahy, 2017).

CONTENT REVIEW QUESTIONS

1. How might case management in VR differ from other professions?
2. What are some ways that RCs can invite clients' family members to be partners in the case management process?
3. What are some settings in which RCs use case management?
4. Examine the pros and cons of an injured or ill client returning to a previous job or finding a new job.
5. How can RCs avoid impeding a client's autonomy while providing case management?

REFERENCES

American Counseling Association. (2014). *Code of ethics.* https://www.counseling.org/resources/aca-code-of-ethics.pdf

American Red Cross. (2021). *Nurse Assistant/CNA Testing.* https://www.redcross.org/take-a-class/cna-testing

Berens, D. E., & Weed, R. O. (2009). The role of the vocational rehabilitation counselor in life care planning. In R. O. Weed & D. E. Berens (Eds.), *Life care planning and case management handbook* (3rd ed., pp. 41–61). Taylor & Francis.

Case Management Society of America. (2016). *Standards of practice for case management.* https://www.abqaurp.org/DOCS/2016%20CM%20standards%20of%20practice.pdf

Certification of Disability Management Specialist. (2021a). *About CDMS.* https://cdms.org/about-cdms

Certification of Disability Management Specialist. (2021b). *Scope of practice.* https://www.cdms.org/about-cdms/scope-practice

Chan, F., Bishop, M., Chronister, J., Lee, E. J., & Chiu, C. (2018). *Certified Rehabilitation Counselor examination preparation* (2nd ed.). Springer.

Chan, F., Strauser, D., Gervey, R., & Lee, E. J. (2010). Introduction to demand-side factors related to employment of people with disabilities. *Journal of Occupational Rehabilitation, 20*(4), 407–411. https://doi.org/10.1007/s10926-010-9243-7

Chapin, M. H. (2005a). Case management in private sector rehabilitation. In F. Chan, M. J. Leahy, & J. L. Saunders (Eds.), *Case management for rehabilitation health professionals* (2nd ed., Vol. 1, pp. 304–329). Aspen Professional Services.

Chapin, M. H. (2005b). Community resources. In F. Chan, M. J. Leahy, & J. L. Saunders (Eds.), *Case management for rehabilitation health professionals* (2nd ed., Vol. 1, pp. 176–196). Aspen Professional Services.

Commission for Case Management Certification. (2021). *About CCMC.* https://ccmcertification.org/about-ccmc

Commission on Rehabilitation Counselor Certification. (2017). *Code of professional ethics for rehabilitation counselors.* https://crccertification.com/wp-content/uploads/2021/03/CRC_CodeEthics_Eff2017-FinaLnewdiesign.pdf

Commission on Rehabilitation Counselor Certification. (2021). *What is a Certified Rehabilitation Counselor?.* https://crccertification.com/crc-certification

Eischens, P. (2016). Vocational counselor credentials and case closures for consumers with co-occurring substance use disorders. *Culminating Projects in Community Psychology, Counseling and Family Therapy. 17.* https://repository.stcloudstate.edu/cpcf_etds/17

Emmerton, B. (2016, October 26). *Re: Case Management.* Online forum comment. http://engage.crccertification.com/communities/community-home/digestviewer/viewthread?MID=2246&GroupId=19&tab=digestviewer&UserKey=48b27495-dc4a-4d5b-9153-12ad42667a21&sKey=ab002621bc4e45cf942f#bm2

Greenwood, R., & Roessler, R. T. (2018). Systematic caseload management. In R. T. Roessler & S. E. Rubin (Eds.), *Case management and rehabilitation counseling* (4th ed., pp. 233–246). Pro-Ed.

Jackson, M. E. (2019). *Factors contributing to burnout levels among public sector rehabilitation counselors* [Doctoral dissertation]. Walden University]. ProQuest Dissertations and Theses Global.

Job Accommodation Network. (n.d.). *Support person.* https://askjan.org/solutions/Support-Person.cfm

Lamberti, J. S., & Weisman, R. L. (2021). Essential elements of forensic assertive community treatment. *Harvard Review of Psychiatry, 29*(4), 278–297. https://doi.org/10.1097/HRP.0000000000000299

Leahy, M. J., Chan, F., Sung, C., & Kim, M. (2013). Empirically Derived Test Specifications for the Certified Rehabilitation Counselor Examination. *Rehabilitation Counseling Bulletin, 56*(4), 199–214. https://doi.org/10.1177/0034355212469839

Leahy, M. J., & Kline, K. M. (2014). Case management practices in rehabilitation and human services. In J. D. Andrew & C. W. Faubion (Eds.), *Rehabilitation services: An introduction for the human services professional* (3rd ed., pp. 326–341). Aspen Professional Services.

Leahy, M. J., Muenzen, P., Saunders, J. L., & Strauser, D. (2009). Essential knowledge domains underlying effective rehabilitation counseling practice. *Rehabilitation Counseling Bulletin, 52*(2), 95–106. https://doi.org/10.1177/0034355208323646

Lewy Body Dementia Association. (n.d.). *Diagnosing and managing Lewy body dementia: A comprehensive guide or healthcare professionals.* https://www.lbda.org/wp-content/uploads/2011/02/3737-lbda-physicians-book-22dec17.pdf

Lewy Body Dementia Association. (2021a). *Treatment options.* https://www.lbda.org/treatment-options

Lewy Body Dementia Association. (2021b). *Those living with LBD: Diagnosis and prognosis: What kind of healthcare professional diagnoses LBD?.* https://www.lbda.org/diagnosis-and-prognosis

Matkin, R. E. (1981). Program evaluation: Searching for accountability in private rehabilitation. *Journal of Rehabilitation, 47*(1), 65–68.

Medicare.gov. (n.d.). *Hospice care.* https://www.medicare.gov/coverage/hospice-care

Mollenhauer, B., Förstl, H., Deuschl, G., Storch, A., Oertel, W., & Trenkwalder, C. (2010). Lewy body and Parkinsonian dementia: Common, but often misdiagnosed conditions. *Deutsches Arzteblatt International, 107*(39), 684–691. https://doi.org/10.3238/arztebl.2010.0684

Mullahy, C. M. (2017). *The case manager's handbook* (6th ed.). Jones & Bartlett Learning.

National Board for Certified Counselors. (2016). *National Board for Certified Counselors code of ethics.* https://www.nbcc.org/Assets/Ethics/NBCCCodeofEthics.pdf

Phillips, S. D., Burns, B. J., Edgar, E. R., Mueser, K. T., Linkins, K. W., Rosenheck, R. A., Drake, R. E., & McDonel Herr, E. C. (2001). Moving assertive community treatment into standard practice. *Psychiatric Services (Washington, D.C.)*, *52*(6), 771–779. https://doi.org/10.1176/appi.ps.52.6.771

Powell, S. K., & Tahan, H. A. (2019). *Case management: A practical guide for education and practice* (4th ed.). Wolters Kluwer.

Rapp, C. A., & Goscha, R. J. (2004). The principles of effective case management of mental health services. *Psychiatric Rehabilitation Journal*, *27*(4), 319–333. https://doi.org/10.2975/27.2004.319.333

Reid, C., Deutsch, P., & Kitchen, J. (2005). Life care planning. In F. Chan, M. Leahy, & J. Saunders (Eds.), *Case management for rehabilitation health professionals* (2nd ed., Vol. 1, pp. 228–263). Aspen Professional Services.

Roessler, R. T., & Rubin, S. E. (2006). *Case management and rehabilitation counseling* (4th ed.). Pro-Ed.

Roessler, R. T., Rubin, S. E., & Rumrill, P. D. (2018). *Case management and rehabilitation counseling* (5th ed.). Pro-Ed.

Rosenthal, D. A., Hursh, N., Lui, J., Isom, R., & Sasson, J. (2007). A survey of current disability management practice: Emerging trends and implications for certification. *Rehabilitation Counseling Bulletin*, *50*, 76–86. https://doi.org/10.1177/00343552070500020601

Rubin, S. E., & Roessler, R. T. (2008). Utilizing rehabilitation facilities and support services. In S. E. Rubin & R. T. Roessler (Eds.), *Foundations of the vocational rehabilitation process* (6th ed., pp. 365–397). Pro-Ed.

Shaw, L. R., Leahy, M. J., & Chan, F. (2005). Case management: Historical foundations and current trends. In F. Chan, M. J. Leahy, & J. L. Saunders (Eds.), *Case management for rehabilitation health professionals* (2nd ed., Vol. 1, pp. 3–27). Aspen Professional Services.

Thorning, H., & Dixon, L. (2020). Forty-five years later: The challenge of optimizing assertive community treatment. *Current Opinion in Psychiatry*, *33*(4), 397–406. https://doi.org/10.1097/YCO.0000000000000615

U. S. Department of Health & Human Services, National Institutes of Health, National Institute of Aging. (2021, July 29). *What is Lewy body dementia? Causes, symptoms, and treatments*. https://www.nia.nih.gov/health/what-lewy-body-dementia-causes-symptoms-and-treatments

U.S. Food and Drug Administration. (2021, July 29). *Information on clozapine*. https://www.fda.gov/drugs/postmarket-drug-safety-information-patients-and-providers/information-clozapine

Welch, G. T. (1979). The relationship of rehabilitation in industry. *Journal of Rehabilitation*, *45*(3), 24–25.

Wilson, K. B., Acklin, C. L., & Chao, S.-I. (2018). *Case management for the health, human, and vocational rehabilitation services*. Aspen Professional Services.

CHAPTER 14

Advocacy

WILLIAM MING LIU, REBECCA L. TOPOREK, AND MICHAEL T. HARTLEY

LEARNING OBJECTIVES

After reading this chapter, you should be able to:

- *Describe the relationship between advocacy, empowerment, and social justice.*
- *Explain advocacy in connection to multicultural competencies and rehabilitation.*
- *Apply the advocacy competencies within the broader professional roles of counseling, consultation, and coordination.*

CACREP STANDARDS

CACREP 2016 Core: 2F1.e, 2F2.a, 2F2.b, 2F2.c, 2F2.e
CACREP 2016 Specialties:
   Clinical Rehabilitation Counseling: 5D2.a, 5D2.k, 5D.2.p, 5D3.c
   Rehabilitation Counseling: 5H2.a, 5H2.e, 5H2.f, 5H2.n, 5H3.f, 5H3.j, 5H2.p, 5H3.j

INTRODUCTION

Advocacy in rehabilitation counseling is not new. In fact, "advocacy is embedded in the very nature of the rehabilitation counseling field" (Middleton et al., 2010, p. 175). In many professional practices, rehabilitation counselors (RCs) find themselves at the forefront of helping clients in multiple ways to create optimal environments for growth and development (Maki & Riggar, 1997; Toporek, Blando, et al., 2009). Yet there have been some challenges to advancing the practice of advocacy within rehabilitation counseling. We propose that a multicultural counseling framework serves as a valuable resource to meet this challenge. Two issues are illuminated when considered through the lens of multiculturalism. First, the intersections of identity and oppression operate across all specializations in counseling, including rehabilitation counseling. For example, Middleton et al. (2010) asserted that advocacy in rehabilitation counseling has tended to focus on facilitating access to services and has been somewhat slower to address advocacy with individuals who are marginalized within the rehabilitation system based on other aspects of identity such as race and ethnicity. As with other areas of human services, there also has been research pointing to differential access and referral to rehabilitation services related to racial identity of the client (e.g., Perrin et al., 2019; Reed et al., 2005; Wilson, 2002; Yin et al., 2021). Second, a deficit approach is present when the medical model of disability is used. This parallels historic conceptualizations and treatment used by counseling and psychology regarding individuals from other identity communities that have faced oppression (e.g., race or ethnicity, sexual orientation). Advocacy has been one way for counseling professionals to begin to address problematic circumstances within the profession, whether it be neglect, bias, or mistreatment based on racism, sexism, and other forms of oppression. Furthermore, a broad approach to advocacy can be useful, as described in the ACA Advocacy Competencies model (J. A. Lewis et al., 2002; Toporek & Daniels, 2018) including individual, organizational, and societal levels.

Multicultural counseling literature has critiqued traditional counseling practices, research, and education for cultural bias toward individualism, middle-classness, and certainly ability (Olkin, 1999, 2002; Prilleltensky, 1997; Sue et al., 2019). The combination of an individualism bias and the social class or ability bias can create a situation in which anyone outside those norms is viewed as having a deficit. This focus centers attention on the individual and results in a neglect of the role of systemic barriers. Treatment focuses on "fixing" the individual or community experiencing difficulties rather than addressing problems within the system. Parallel issues can arise in rehabilitation services when the medical model implicitly, or explicitly, shapes the way an individual's presenting issues are viewed. Within the framework of the medical model, the problem and pathology are located within the individual (Jun, 2010). When rehabilitation practice operates through a medical model, it focuses on the disability and the characteristics of the individual with the intent of minimizing pathology and treating symptoms rather than addressing problems in the environment (Middleton et al., 2010). Alternatively, the disability rights movement consistently has advocated for a social model that identifies the environment as problematic, rather than the individual with the disability. In this model, dominant power systems shape the environment in ways that cater to the majority population and those with privilege, rather than to all individuals, hence creating barriers for those with disability. In reality, there are a range of practice settings, each with constraints, policies, and practices shaped by sources of funding. When eligibility for services is dependent on a diagnosis, the medical model may be the entree to services—yet it is to be hoped that the actual services themselves will shift to focusing on the environment to reduce barriers rather than working to "fix" the individual. This blend may be considered closer to a biopsychosocial model. At its best, rehabilitation counseling integrates, or even prioritizes, advocacy with the individual or community to effect change in the system.

Within the counseling profession broadly, an individual focus often is perpetuated when traditional counseling theories are the basis of practice. The denial of power systems that perpetuate the marginalization of "minority" peoples has been identified as a problematic theme reflected in many theoretical orientations (Caldwell & Vera, 2010; Liu & Hernandez, 2010; Pieterse et al., 2009; Singh et al., 2020; Toporek & Liu, 2001; Toporek & Vaughn, 2010). When these models shape practice, a client's "failure" to be "self-actualized" and be "productive" often is considered to be the fault of the client rather than context, history, or access to resources. This type of bias also has been found within rehabilitation counseling, when bias based on identity dimensions such as ethnic minority race and ethnicity is present along with disability (Perrin et al., 2019). To correct these issues and more fully integrate context into professional practice, many in the counseling profession have taken upon themselves the responsibility to work beyond the confines of the counseling space and to engage directly in social action and advocacy (Toporek & Ahluwalia, 2019). Within rehabilitation counseling, advocacy with and for individuals with disabilities continues in its strong tradition.

The focus of this chapter is to describe advocacy in rehabilitation counseling by attending to the contribution of multicultural counseling perspectives. To meet this goal, we first discuss the relevance of incorporating multicultural competency and advocacy in rehabilitation counseling. Second, we discuss the role of advocacy in professional practice and describe various models and definitions of advocacy. Finally, we discuss education and practice implications, with particular attention to the professional responsibilities of RCs and the challenges they face as they attempt to advocate for their clientele.

MULTICULTURAL COUNSELING COMPETENCIES

By now, most counselors understand the necessity of multicultural competencies. The best-known framework for **multicultural competence** was articulated by D. W. Sue et al. (1992). They stated that counselors need to have knowledge, awareness, and skills in three areas of understanding: their biases, their clients' worldviews, and culturally congruent interventions. Newer scholarship complements the competency framework by focusing on multiculturally oriented counselors (Owen, 2013). **Multicultural orientation** is focused on the counselor's humility or "other-oriented stance which is marked by openness, curiosity, lack of arrogance, and genuine desire to understand clients' cultural identities" (Owen et al., 2016, p. 31). Although advanced cultural competence may be aspirational (to be worked on and improved continually), a basic multicultural orientation suggests a form of cultural humility as a critical counselor characteristic. Hook et al. (2013) defined **cultural humility** as "the ability to maintain an interpersonal stance that is other-oriented (or open to the other) in relation to aspects of cultural identity that are most important to the client" (p. 354). The concept of cultural humility is central to models of cultural competencies, such as the American Counseling Association (ACA) Multicultural and Social Justice Counseling Competencies (MSJCC; Ratts et al., 2016) that have attempted to integrate the original multicultural competencies (D. W. Sue et al., 1992) with the ACA Advocacy Competencies (J. A. Lewis et al., 2002; Toporek & Daniels, 2018). The MSJCC sought to expand on previous models to centralize the role of the counselor and client experiences of oppression and privilege and assert that those are brought into the counseling relationship.

Early in the multicultural counseling movement, the argument for the integration of multiculturalism (both competency and orientation) into counseling rested on the changing racial and ethnic demographics of the United States (Ridley & Kleiner, 2003; Smith & Trimble, 2016). Over time, other existing aspects of diversity (e.g., sexual orientation, gender, and ability) have been integrated and acknowledged as essential components of culture and an inclusive definition of multiculturalism has been used (Stone, 1997). There are several works that support this broader definition and thus can effectively contribute to the relevance of multicultural competencies to rehabilitation counseling. Arredondo et al. (1996) discussed an inclusive perspective of multiculturalism and elaborated the competencies within the framework of personal dimensions of identity. They suggested that counselors must consider the multiple ways that individuals define themselves as well as the multiple communities of importance to clients. Arredondo et al. asserted that counselors must strive for competence in these different realms.

An important lens for understanding the relationships between identity, power, and privilege is the concept of intersectionality. Crenshaw's (1989) theory of **intersectionality** shifted away from a one-dimensional understanding of discrimination to mapping the ways in which multiple systems of oppression intersect rather than being mutually exclusive. Terms like *twice disadvantaged, twice penalized*, and *double jeopardy* describe how women and minority groups with disabilities often experience multiple forms of discrimination in society (Alston & Bell, 1996; O'Hara, 2004; McMahon et al., 2008). In addition to understanding and dismantling oppressive systems of power, Singh et al. (2020) noted that intersectionality theory is a way for counselors to be attuned to daily interactions and inequities. In particular, counselors need to be aware of **privilege**, defined as a special right, benefit, or advantage afforded to more powerful social groups within systems of oppression (Case et al., 2012; McIntosh, 2015). Informed by constructions of who is expected to participate in society (Kahneman & Miller, 1986), privilege comes from situations and environments where particular social identities are considered normative. Hampton et al. (2017) asserted that cultural humility could be integrated into rehabilitation counseling as a way to address power differentials and multicultural counseling.

In keeping with the expansive definition of multiculturalism, it is easy to understand how advocacy, multiculturalism, and rehabilitation counseling may form a strong partnership. A number of authors have supported the need to attend to the intersection of identity when working with ethnic minority clients with disabilities (e.g., Hennessey et al., 2008; Wilson, 2002). There has been some consideration of multicultural counseling competence when working with clients with disabilities (e.g., Artman & Daniels, 2010; Hampton et al., 2017; Olkin, 2002, 2007), yet attention to the intersections of identity beyond disability has been inconsistent. Middleton et al. (2000) recognized these limitations and advocated for the adoption of multicultural rehabilitation competencies. These competencies articulate the importance of cultural competence including awareness, knowledge, and skills. Middleton and her colleagues endorsed and provided practical guidance regarding the implementation of these competencies. This move reinforced the connection between rehabilitation counseling and multicultural competence. Later, Middleton et al. (2010) noted that, although the multicultural rehabilitation competencies had been developed, the field was still slow to advocate for underrepresented groups.

It is important to note that there has been significant growth in the literature attending to the need for integration of the multiplicity of identities in working with individuals with disabilities (e.g., Chronister & Johnson, 2009; Cordes et al., 2016; Hampton et al., 2017; Middleton et al., 2010; Mpofu & Harley, 2015). One example is advocacy around the inclusion of specific attention to ethical practice in rehabilitation counseling when working with culturally diverse individuals (Cartwright & Fleming, 2010). Cartwright et al. (2012) built on this work and provided a discussion and application of models for RCs to use for working with multiple dimensions of identity that might be presented by clients. This orientation is critical because the social experience of disability often differs for men and women, middle-class White and nondominant minority communities, and heterosexual and lesbian, gay, bisexual, and transgender people. For instance, a study by Shaw et al. (2012) found that "generally speaking, various combinations of specific characteristics, that is, being female, being older, having a behavioral disability, racial minority status . . . place individuals at higher risk of experiencing disability harassment" (p. 88). It is thus critical that RCs account for and address intersecting social locations and identities.

Analogous to the ways in which race, gender, and class are socially constructed, the social prejudice of **ableism** is the false belief that disability in and of itself makes lesser one in some way (Slesaransky-Poe & García, 2014). Ableism has created an oppressive system in which people without disabilities have power over people with disabilities, often in the form of unearned privileges (Devlin & Pothier, 2006). Rather than separating ableism from other forms of discrimination such as racism and sexism, it is important to recognize that ableism is explicitly linked with other oppression systems such as anti-Blackness, eugenics, misogyny, colonialism, imperialism and capitalism (T. L. Lewis, 2022). Unless the intersections of these oppression systems are recognized and addressed, group-based inequalities will perpetuate a caste-like status whereby people with disabilities and other groups continue to have less power and privilege in the dominant culture (Pratto & Stewart, 2012), referred to as *"dis-citizenship"* (Rioux & Valentine, 2006, p. 2).

A foundational component of multicultural and social justice counseling is awareness of how construction of power and privilege impact daily interactions, sometimes unknowingly. **Microaggressions** refer to "brief and commonplace daily verbal or behavioral indignities, whether intentional or unintentional, that communicate hostile, derogatory, or negative racial slights and insults that potentially have [a] harmful or unpleasant psychological impact on the target person or group" (D. W. Sue et al., 2007, p. 72). Cartwright et al. (2018) provided examples of microaggressions such as asking a Latino American person, "Where are you from?" with the implication that the person was not born in the United States or saying, "I don't see color," to deny a person of color their racial/ethnic experiences (D. W. Sue & Sue, 2013). Similar to denying skin color, microaggressions toward disability may include statements about not "seeing disability" and avoiding the term disability, which may be perceived as ignoring an important aspect of being human, which can be disempowering, patronizing, and even hurtful (Ladau, 2021). The difference between microaggressions and overt discrimination or macroaggressions is that people who commit microaggressions might not even be aware of them.

It is heartening that there has been increased recognition of historical and current bias within rehabilitation services, as with other areas of mental health and counseling, and movement toward better service. The history of advocacy generally within rehabilitation counseling and the recent increased attention to multicultural perspectives points to the potential for integrating multicultural competence and advocacy. To facilitate further development of this integration, reflecting on how the broader multicultural movement has expanded to integrate these two frameworks can be helpful. Toporek and Reza (2000) used the base of multicultural counseling competencies provided by D. W. Sue et al. (1992) to assert that multicultural competencies should include attention to institutional dimensions as well as professional and personal realms. They described institutional cultural competence as actions that counselors may need to take in addressing institutional issues that impact the well-being of clients. Counselors may do this work through administrative roles, coordinator roles, as members of an organization, or in a variety of other functions. This attention to institutional competence directly suggests that advocacy may be critical in working in culturally competent ways—beyond one-on-one work with clients.

Focusing on rehabilitation counseling specifically, Middleton et al. (2010) asserted that advocacy is inherent in the multicultural counseling competencies (D. W. Sue et al., 1992) and the multicultural rehabilitation counseling competencies. Acknowledging the importance of advocacy within rehabilitation, Middleton and her colleagues also noted that access to institutional power varies based on a number of identity variables, such as race, gender, sexual orientation, and disability status. Consequently, advocacy may be needed from others who have greater access to institutional power: namely, counselors. Middleton and her colleagues charged that there are two major gaps in the rehabilitation counseling profession: the lack of endorsement of multicultural competencies and the absence of common language, definitions, and competencies for advocacy.

In general, multiculturalism encourages institutions and individuals to seek out a transformation of systems rather than to settle for additive changes or superficial reorganizing (Liu & Pope-Davis, 2003). As such, advocacy becomes an implicit activity of those who identify themselves as multiculturally competent and oriented counselors. In a similar manner, RCs may find themselves in situations in which they must facilitate client self-advocacy or advocate for client welfare—with or on behalf of the client—to make environmental accommodations and facilitate change with and for the client. This advocacy activity is congruent with the aims of multiculturalism because environments that are not adaptive or accommodating may be construed as marginalizing and oppressive milieus for clients. As a function of their role, RCs acting as advocates in promoting changes in a client's environment are engaging in multiculturally competent work for the betterment of their clients.

Although it may appear that there is a dichotomy between counseling and advocacy, Lerner (1972) believed that this perception results in a false dichotomy between social action and counseling. For some counselors, the idea of advocacy is perceived as a confluence between the personal and the private world of counseling versus the public and the political world of social action (Pope-Davis et al., 2001). Consequently, reluctance toward advocacy may be construed as a fear of politicizing counseling (Pope-Davis et al., 2001). This fear, of course, assumes that counseling is a nonpolitical activity (Liu & Pope-Davis, 2003). But if counselors understood the realm of political and politics" as a venue or situation in which a person's values, beliefs, and worldviews are used to facilitate another person's movement toward some intrapersonal and interpersonal change, then counselors would see that politics is inflected in every personal and professional activity.

Advocacy in counseling, especially rehabilitation counseling, challenges many of the values inherent in traditional counseling and psychotherapy (Toporek & Liu, 2001). Among these conflicts are the value of individualism, insight as a cure, and ableism (Olkin, 2002). It also challenges the notion of time-limited or brief therapy, psychological distance between the client and the counselor, and dual relationships. Advocacy and being an advocate confront the notion that clients are, by themselves, responsible for their situations (i.e., it is their distorted perceptions that are creating the problem) and that only they can change their environment. Often, many of these values are implicit in the way clients are treated (i.e., diagnosed) in counseling (Follette & Houts, 1996). Moving away from this dualistic worldview, rehabilitation counseling recognizes that the environment significantly impacts their clients. However, the controversy in rehabilitation counseling is often the extent to which counselors use their own power and privilege for the benefit of their client (Liu et al., 2007). Advocacy actions risk and threaten the status quo on which the counselor may depend. That is, RCs may be at risk of losing their jobs if their advocacy actions challenge the system in which they exist. Kivel (2009) presented a particularly provoking argument along this vein. He charged that helping professionals and the systems within which they work intentionally and actively, albeit unconsciously, function to maintain oppressive power structures.

One of the principles in multicultural counseling is the idea of collaboration with clients. Rather than wallow in the ambiguity between what we do "with" or "for" a client (Lerner, 1972), the focus always should be on what we can do "along" with clients in order to better their environment, situation, or condition (e.g., Freire, 1989). In traditional psychotherapy, clients tend to be disempowered and may feel a lack of agency due to the assumptions many counselors may hold about clients. These assumptions may be that the counselor knows what is best for the client, does not include clients in decisions, and stigmatizes individuals through deficit-oriented labels (e.g., disabled client versus a client with a disability; Prilleltensky, 1997). Based on the disability rights mantra "nothing about us without us" (Charlton, 1998, p. 3), the necessity of collaborating with clients is central to applying the ACA Advocacy Competencies ethically (J. A. Lewis et al., 2002; Toporek & Daniels, 2018). It is particularly important in rehabilitation counseling to work with clients collaboratively to identify the part of the problem that is internal (intrapsychic) and the part that is external (systemic), as well as actions that the client may take to change the systemic issues.

An example of multicultural collaboration with a client may be reflected in understanding how the client's culture constructs a person's illness via **culturally adapted psychotherapy (CAP;** Benish et al., 2011; Griner & Smith, 2006). In CAP, the focus is on exploring the ways in which illness is explained in the client's particular culture (illness myth). Understanding how the client conceptualized illness also allows the counselor to adapt current psychotherapy interventions to help with the client. Mental illness and interventions for recovery are both culturally constructed. That is, the manifestations may be similar (e.g., depressive symptoms), but often the explanations may vary as well as what may be considered to be healing interventions. As a part of a culturally adapted therapy, the counselor works with the client to explore what the client believes is causing the illness. This practice involves "asking explicit questions about what the client believed caused the problems, symptoms experienced, consequences of the illness, and treatments that were acceptable to the client" (Benish et al., p. 287).

In addition, there are times when it is appropriate for counselors to recognize their responsibility in addressing systemic issues. Thus, when the help-giving organization is one that is perpetuating barriers, not only is it important for clients to voice their concerns, but it is also a responsibility of the counselor—as a member of the organization— to actively facilitate change within the organization (Hopps & Liu, 2006). If counselors do not take such action, they are in danger of colluding with the problematic system. The client may sense the counselor's implicit collusion and may interpret counselor–client discourse in counseling as a double-bind message of "I'll help you only if I don't risk anything on my part." Consequently, the counselor's trustworthiness, credibility, and ability to conduct counseling may be jeopardized (S. Sue & Zane, 1987). In fact, the American Counseling Association (ACA) *Code of Ethics* stipulates that if policies or practices of the organization are "potentially disruptive or damaging to clients or may limit the effectiveness of services provided and change cannot be affected, counselors take appropriate further action" (ACA, 2014).

It is important to see counseling as an interactional process in which the client and counselor are conceived as collaborators. The counselor is open to change as much as the client, and they both must envision potential changes within their environment. It is important to construe the "client" or "consumer" as a participant in their own change. We would like to posit that the consumer language often used in rehabilitation counseling be challenged for not fully incorporating the notion of client agency in the environment. The consumer label for clientele is popular because it puts the potential "power" within the consumer and not necessarily with the service provider. However, the marketplace metaphor still resonates with an adversarial theme. If the consumer is unhappy with a particular service, then the service provider is to change and meet the new demands. Yet implicit in this notion of the consumer and the market is also a "bottom line." Based on cost–benefit calculations, some agencies may not change at all, and eventually clients may find themselves without adequate services altogether. The notion of collaboration or equality is not inherent in an economic model of service provision (e.g., Eriksen, 1997, 1999). Consequently, we will use the language of collaboration to denote the role of the client and counselor rather than using the common language of the consumer in this chapter.

Before continuing, it is necessary to understand the role advocacy has in counseling and in the counseling profession. In addition, we discuss the various models from which advocacy can be operationalized. The following section is a brief overview of these two facets of advocacy in counseling.

ADVOCACY IN COUNSELING

Historical Perspective

The issue of advocacy is partly a professional identity issue and not solely a practical concern. Actions that benefit clients by eliminating or diminishing institutional and cultural barriers may have a secondary effect of empowering clients and encouraging future social action by clients and counselors. Many sentiments toward institutional and cultural change were elements of advocacy and community organizing in the 1970s when changing structural inequities was considered an appropriate professional role (J. A. Lewis & Lewis, 1983). Yet through the 1980s and 1990s, the advocacy perspective seemingly lost its prominence (McClure & Russo, 1996; Toporek & Liu, 2001). McClure and Russo (1996) speculated that a focus by the counseling profession toward credibility and individualism contributed to the decreasing emphasis on advocacy as a legitimate professional role.

With the increasing emphasis on multiculturalism and multicultural competencies, the pendulum swung back toward advocacy and social justice with increasing literature and research supporting the relevance of the advocacy role. With the advent of multiculturalism and feminist orientations, traditional notions of psychotherapy and counseling were challenged to become relevant for historically marginalized groups (Toporek & Liu, 2001; Singh et al., 2020). Because multiculturalism is concerned with social justice, especially for disenfranchised and marginalized groups, and because advocacy also is typically aligned with combating marginalization (Chesler et al., 1976), advocacy has become an important professional concern. Recognizing that counseling has been effective differentially and sometimes biased against minority individuals, there have been increasing challenges to the profession to explore the individual, cultural, and institutional barriers that perpetuate oppression (Hopps & Liu, 2006; Middleton et al., 2010; Ridley, 1995; Sutton & Kessler, 1986). Recognizing the ways in which multiple systems of oppression intersect, the **Disability Justice** movement has emerged to account for unique and complex understandings of disability that also account for other cultural identities such as race, gender, and sexuality (Berne et al., 2018; Piepzna-Samarasinha, 2018). Although some of these systems of oppression can be acted on in dyadic interactions, some can only be targeted through advocacy (Atkinson et al., 1993; Middleton et al., 2010). For instance, a negative sense of self related to internalizing negative stereotypes of their racial group (i.e., internalized racialism; Cokley, 2002) can be a pertinent dyadic issue in individual counseling. But if a client reports that they cannot gain access to a building due to wheelchair restrictions to doorways and steps, the "in-session" (individual-focused) counseling is likely to be unsuccessful in ameliorating client distress, anger, and frustration. Only through appropriate advocacy and "out-of-session" actions will clients start to build a sense of efficacy and empowerment (McWhirter, 1994). Gruber and Trickett (1987) posit that advocacy operationalizes the privileges and power of the advocate, which are the intimate knowledge of rules, norms, and systems and are the resources that counselors can use to work with clients in a concerted and effective way for change. In the latter case, the counselor is the most effective agent to start the change process to make the agency more accessible. Within rehabilitation counseling, the role of counselor as advocate has been accepted relatively widely regarding issues related to disabilities. This perspective has not necessarily carried over to issues related to other ways in which clients or communities may experience marginalization or oppression.

Definitions and Models

Although we focus specifically on advocacy in this chapter, one of the confusions that can occur is between definitions of advocacy, empowerment, and social action. Sometimes, all three labels can be used synonymously to describe a particular activity, and we would draw some distinctions that may not be apparent. For us, **advocacy** is "the action a mental health professional, counselor, or psychologist takes in assisting clients and client groups to achieve therapy goals through participating in clients' environments" (Toporek & Liu, 2001).

Historically, authors have sought to refine the overall idea of advocacy to include a variety of activities. J. A. Lewis and Lewis (1983) differentiated between *case advocacy*, which is advocacy on behalf of a client, and *class advocacy*, which is advocacy on a systemic level. They also describe three types of advocacy as *here and now advocacy* or responding to a situation, *preventive advocacy* or actions to create a just environment, and *citizen advocacy* or action encouraging others to challenge social issues. Chan et al. (1981) elaborated further on the concept of advocacy and suggested three types of advocacy that may be used. First, **representative advocacy** is when a counselor takes on the issues of their client because the client is unable to express or act on their needs. This concept is similar to the counselor–advocate model of Atkinson et al. (1993), in which the counselor "speaks on behalf of the client, often confronting the institutional sources of oppression that are contributing to the client's problem" (p. 301). Second, **group advocacy** is when a "group seeks to intervene in a problem situation in order to achieve a goal consistent with the interest of the members of the group or others" (Chan et al., p. 195). Finally, there is **self-advocacy** when the individual is taught agentic knowledge, actions, and behaviors. In this last case, Chan et al. illustrated their "self-advocacy" by presenting cases wherein clients are faced with a problematic situation. Counselors, working in this model, help clients define the problem and develop a list of possible actions from which the client chooses alternatives. Importantly, while self-advocacy means that the RC will not act on behalf of the client, a collaborative interaction between the counselor and the client is critical to ensure that the client is ready to take on the responsibilities necessary to learn to assert control over the social justice problem (Chan et al., 1981).

In considering advocacy in counseling, we have found it useful to describe advocacy as a continuum of activity on which empowerment and social action reside (Toporek & Liu, 2001). For us, empowerment is considered to be on one end of the agentic continuum. In this model, **empowerment** implies that the counselor and client work to develop efficacy within the client's and counselor's sociopolitical world (McWhirter, 1994, 1997; Toporek & Liu, 2001). Thus, empowerment encompasses a specific action and behavior with a specific client. As a result of empowerment, clients are able to cope with specific situational problems and concerns, and have a sense of self-efficacy to contend with similar problems in the future. **Social action**, in contrast, means that the counselor is working constantly on removing institutional and cultural barriers for a community or population. Social action implies advocacy on a societal level on issues such as legislation or public policy that affect all clients. Thus, social action implies broad-based action and not specific activities focused on the issues of just one individual. Social action also means that counselors are working toward a socially just world: one in which benefits, rights, privileges, and resources are equally distributed as well as social costs and vulnerabilities (i.e., everyone shares equally in the good and bad in society; B. L. Lewis, 2010). Within this model, there are a range of behaviors in which counselors may engage to remove barriers and address injustice. We assert that all these activities may be considered under the umbrella of advocacy and that each of these behaviors may be appropriate at various times in work with clients.

In recognition of the fact that many counselors across specializations may need to utilize advocacy in their work but may not have the training to do so effectively, the ACA adopted a set of **advocacy competencies** (J.A. Lewis et al., 2002). Updated by Toporek and Daniels (2018), these advocacy competencies are a resource to facilitate the ethical implementation of advocacy and assist counselors in identifying advocacy actions that would be appropriate at individual, community or school, and public or societal levels (Toporek, Lewis, et al., 2009). Furthermore, the advocacy competencies acknowledged that some types of advocacy may be collaborative actions in which the client and the counselor work together and other types where the counselor may take action on behalf of the client. This framework resulted in six domains, including empowerment and client advocacy (individual level), community collaboration and systems advocacy (community or school level), and public information or social/political action (societal). Middleton et al. (2010) examined the advocacy competencies and integrated the Multicultural Rehabilitation Counseling Competencies providing guidelines for appropriate advocacy within rehabilitation counseling. Furthermore, they illustrate concrete examples of advocacy for a number of common situations that RCs may encounter.

A common thread through advocacy, empowerment, and social action is that any action along all these dimensions may be positive for clients and counselors alike. In all these cases, changing environments for the optimal growth and development of the client is the goal. Although these actions are necessary and important in the professional lives of RCs, the challenge is to ensure that counselors learn and train to be effective advocates for their clients. Building upon the work of countless advocates, a unique set of the DRCC were developed recently by the ARCA and endorsed by the ACA Governing Council in 2019. Aligned with the ACA Advocacy Competencies and the ACA Multicultural and Social Justice Competencies, the DRCC are aspirational guidelines to assist all counselors to promote "disability as a part of personal identity and cultural diversity" and in affirmation of the counseling profession's commitment to social justice (Chapin et al., 2018, p. 1). With a focus on the need to address the effects of ableism and multiple forms of oppression in counseling and rehabilitation, the DRCC are a resource for the application of advocacy within rehabilitation counseling practice.

PRACTICE

Advocacy in practice may take many forms, as suggested by the continuum model we described earlier. Hershenson (1990) **C-C-C model of rehabilitation counseling** may be used as a framework for considering how advocacy is an integral part of the role of the

RC. In this model, the RC's role includes three primary functions: coordinating, counseling, and consulting. Within each aspect of this role, the counselor may find that some form of advocacy is an appropriate intervention. Example standards from the Disability-Related Counseling Competencies (DRCC; Chapin et al., 2018) are used to reinforce the need for RCs to apply advocacy competencies across each role to address sociopolitical factors impacting the lives of people with disabilities (PWDs). Furthermore, ethical standards from the Commission on Rehabilitation Counselor Certification (CRCC, 2017) Code of Ethics also are included to reinforce the need for RCs to have the knowledge, competency, and orientation necessary to be ethical advocates.

Counseling. The counseling function of rehabilitation counseling lends itself to advocacy in relation to individual issues. A multicultural and advocacy mindset requires RCs to recognize the potential impact of discrimination on mental health. They must specifically address how internalized marginalization can be a source of pain for so many people (Comstock et al., 2008), engendering feelings such as "alienation, learned helplessness, and internalized hatred" (Roysircar, 2009, p. 288). According to the DRCC, RCs understand how individuals with disabilities "may be negatively impacted by their own internationalization of oppression" (A.7., p. 3) They must work to "validate and collaboratively problem-solve client concerns about their experiences of oppression and ableism" (A.6., p. 3). Teaching and empowering clients to advocate for themselves is an avenue to reclaim a sense of power and control over their environments (Vash, 1991). Chan et al. (1981) provided some excellent examples of self-advocacy and a model for working with individual clients to facilitate their knowledge and agency in addressing barriers.

Since assisting individuals to self-advocate can be a complex process, RCs are expected to "identify resources that promote self-determination and self-advocacy by PWDs, and work to reduce factors that act as barriers to PWDs through collaboration with these individuals, groups, or organizations" (DRCC, B.12, p. 5). Advocacy is a skill that is learned (Roysircar, 2009), and thus clients may benefit from referrals to advocacy-related organizations such as Centers of Independent Living (CILs). By "providing opportunities to problem-solve and role-play or by providing referrals to advocacy resources," RCs can "support the efforts of PWD to self-advocate at school, work, and in the community (DRCC, B.11, p, 4). Today, social media advocacy is an important place to learn to advocate (Haller, 2010, 2022). RCs who are competent in technology and advocacy can support their clients to engage in social media advocacy (Hartley et al., 2015).

Although promoting client self-advocacy is certainly an important rehabilitation counseling goal, RCs also need to consider situations in which it is appropriate to intervene directly in organizations or systems, even those in which they work. RCs are expected to "identify resources to improve their organization's culture or services, when the needs of PWDs are not being appropriately met" (DRCC, B.13, p. 5). The RC taking the primary role as advocate may be most appropriate in a situation in which the power and privilege of the RC's role lend something that is not attainable by the client. This type of advocacy is supported by the CRCC (2017) *Code of Ethics,* mandating RCs to address "attitudinal barriers that inhibit the growth and development of their clients, including stereotyping and discrimination" (CRCC, C.1.a, p. 14). With this type of behavior, it is critical that the RC and client collaboratively decide on what action the RC might take, including goals and strategy for the action. For this reason, RCs are expected to "remain aware of actions taken by their own and cooperating organizations on behalf of clients. When possible, to ensure effective service delivery, rehabilitation counselors act as advocates for clients who cannot advocate for themselves" (CRCC, C.1.c., p. 14). Advocating for clients in their presence can serve as a model of agentic behavior for clients as well as serving as a visible demonstration of the RC's commitment to advocacy and social justice.

Since advocacy may take many forms, it is perhaps most important to consider the ethics of collaboration and consent. According to the CRCC (2017) *Code of Ethics,* "rehabilitation counselors work to help clients, parents, or legal guardians understand their rights and responsibilities, speak for themselves, and make informed decisions. When appropriate and with the consent of a client, parent, or legal guardian, rehabilitation counselors act as advocates on behalf of that client at the local, regional, and/or national levels" (CRCC, C.1.b., p. 14). Regarding informed consent, RCs must "obtain client consent prior to engaging in advocacy efforts on behalf of an identifiable client to improve the provision of services and to work toward removal of systemic barriers or obstacles that inhibit client access, growth, and development" (CRCC, C.1.d., p. 14). Thus, while RCs have an ethical obligation to advocate, they also must negotiate the tensions related to the principles of social justice and the needs and desires of the individual client, especially within the counseling role. Specifically, they also are obligated to honor the client's right to confidentiality (CRCC, Standard C.1.e).

Coordinating. The coordinating function of rehabilitation counseling also lends itself to advocacy. Advocacy at this level may address individual or group concerns. Within the coordination function, counselors may be participants in decision- and policy-making bodies such as clinical and administrative management teams and have access at a level different from that available to the client or client groups. With this complexity in mind, RCs should "understand that various forms of ignorance about or prejudice against disability tend to influence authorities and others to make discriminatory decisions, either conscious or unconscious, that limit opportunities for PWDs within the social, familial, vocational, housing, and healthcare environments" (DRCC, A.5., p. 2). Within their own organizations, RCs are expected to become familiar with their "organization's disability-related, equal opportunity policies and practices (e.g., non-discriminatory job requirements or criteria for admission to educational institutions) and disseminate this information to others as appropriate" (DRCC, B.7, p. 4). More than just awareness, a multicultural and social justice orientation recognizes the ways in which "prejudice and fear of disability are a part of the history and ingrained culture of many institutions and social practices and, therefore, continue to contribute to higher rates of disenfranchisement, abuse, and neglect" (DRCC, A.8., p. 3). As part of their coordinating role, RCs need to address unequitable policies and practices that may be impacting their clients negatively within organizations and institutions.

Advocacy models often use laws and legislation as the highest authority, recommending that RCs become familiar with legislative acts and court interpretations of the law (Chan et al., 1981). At the same time, it is important to recognize that laws and legislation often reflect societal bias. As an example, Corrigan et al. (2004) noted that approximately one third of the 50 states at that time restricted the rights of "an individual with mental illness to hold elective office, participate in juries, and vote" (p. 482). Reflecting myths that individuals with psychiatric disabilities are "unstable" and "volatile," such laws are an example of the ways in which the rights of certain groups of individuals with disabilities may not be met by institutional or governmental policies. In such cases, RCs can advocate to craft new policies, funding, and institutional support that may meet the needs of a specific population. For RCs who work for government entities like the state–federal Vocational Rehabilitation system, advocacy in the coordinating role thus may involve a critique and examination of such elements as eligibility requirements, order of selection, and other institutional policies that may perpetuate social inequities.

Consultation. The consultation role provides a noteworthy avenue for advocacy. As with coordination, advocacy in this role may serve individuals or groups. One example of advocacy at this level would be to engage legislators as consultees around issues that represent barriers to clients from marginalized groups. By serving as consultants who advocate for the social inclusion of individuals with disabilities, RCs can promote more welcoming environments for individuals with disabilities in all aspects of education and employment (DRCC, E.5.). In their role as consultants, RCs are expected to "recognize and constructively confront misinformation and biases about PWDs when interacting with other professionals, students, supervisees, consumers, and the public" (DRCC, B.5., p. 4). This activity is consistent with the ethical obligation of RCs to consider whether organizations and environments are "appropriately accessible and that do not condone

BOX 14.1 LEARNING ACTIVITY

Review the Disability-related Counseling Competencies at https://www.counseling.org/docs/default-source/competencies/arca-disability-related-counseling-competencies-final-version-5-15-19.pdf?sfvrsn=c376562c_6. As you review the competencies, pay attention to the verbs such as "understand," "advocate," and "take action." In thinking about the DRCC on a continuum of awareness to action, in what ways could you translate individual standards practices into actions in your current and future practice across the roles of coordinating, counseling, and consulting? More broadly, how can you use the DRCC to better understand and demonstrate allyship and sensitivity to the lived experience of disability?

or engage in the prejudicial treatment of an individual or group based on their actual or perceived membership in a particular group, class, or category" (CRCC, C.2.b., p. 15). Advocacy within the consultation role often is focused on environmental change to make environments more welcoming to people with disabilities.

Other examples of advocacy in the consultation role might include providing training around multicultural competence, prejudice and discrimination, or consulting with faculty to ensure that new curriculum includes issues-related disabilities and other issues. This focus fits with the expectation that RCs "make efforts to provide and/or take advantage of periodic staff training and ongoing resources on best practices for PWDs" (DRCC, E.6., p. 8). The expertise of people with disabilities could be honored by ensuring that there is representation either by client groups or community groups in these efforts. It is important that RCs "promote inclusion of PWDs in organizational advisory boards and other governing or policy-making bodies" (DRCC, E.7., p. 8). An example of this work would be lobbying the institution to include a permanent disability advocate on planning committees for access issues in remodeling or construction. Informed by the Community Collaboration or Public Information domain of advocacy from the ACA Advocacy Competencies (Lewis et al., 2002; Toporek & Daniels, 2018), the DRCC provide guidance for partnering in advocacy with communities and clients (see Box 14.1).

There are a multitude of avenues for RCs to engage in advocacy. While the examples provided focused explicitly on disability, a core tenet of the DRCC is an emphasis on intersectionality and the need to understand and address discrimination and prejudice especially in instances where "multiple minority statuses of a PWD intersect" (DRCC, A.5., p. 3). Furthermore, the examples are only a starting point for RCs to apply the DRCCs in ways that are consistent with the CRCC (2017) Code of Ethics.

Training

Advocacy training may be one of the most challenging issues in counselor education. Along with coursework, counselor education centralizes the need for face-to-face work with clients as well as competent supervision. But how does one go about receiving competent supervision for advocacy work? One possible answer may come from the advocacy literature as well as training strategies described within multicultural competencies.

First, a distinction must be made between advocacy self-efficacy and specific competent behaviors (B. L. Lewis, 2010). For example, multicultural competency can be perceived as the sense of self-efficacy that counselors may have about working with diverse peoples and groups, and multicultural competencies may be the specific proficiencies counselors have in working with diverse peoples (Pieterse et al., 2009). Although counselors sometimes have a high sense of self-efficacy (competency), they may not have the exact proficiencies that allow them to work effectively with diverse peoples and groups

(Ridley & Kleiner, 2003). For instance, it is possible that counselors who perceive themselves as highly multiculturally competent may not be experienced as such by their clients (Pope-Davis et al., 2002). This issue also is pertinent to advocacy in rehabilitation counseling because counselors may have a sense of competency in being an advocate for their clients, but may find themselves at a loss when it comes to the real behavior and action of advocacy. Thus, training and supervision become integral aspects of rehabilitation counseling advocacy.

Another training issue for RCs is that the very environment that they are challenging for their client may be the one that employs them. Hence, as RCs seek to engage and transform environments for their clients, they may become acutely aware that their jobs may be threatened. Power differentials in supervision and in the field are considerable forces for trainees (Toporek & Vaughn, 2010). For many trainees, there is a delicate balance between maintaining openness to a new system while also recognizing systemic barriers that may require advocacy. This balance is difficult and trainees often need guidance regarding the timing and appropriateness of challenging the systems in which they are often some of the least powerful players. At the same time, trainees may have a tendency to observe injustice and feel angry with the system without a full understanding of the larger context. Training regarding ways of identifying and resolving these dilemmas would be useful.

One model that may provide a good guide is that of a portfolio approach to advocacy training. Coleman and Hau (2003) provided a model of using portfolio assessment to evaluate and support students' development around multicultural issues. A similar model may be applied for advocacy in rehabilitation counselor education. Using this type of model, students would develop a portfolio of training and practice activities related to advocacy work they have completed throughout the program. The portfolio may include examples of specific cases within practicum, papers they have written, workshops they have attended, and so forth. This process would provide the student with the opportunity to do a comprehensive self-review and the program faculty with more data on which to evaluate the students' progress.

Currently, a major challenge in rehabilitation counseling is that training on the issue of being an advocate for clients may not be well integrated into curriculum or internship (Collison et al., 1998; Ebener, 2007; Eriksen, 1997, 1999). Effective training could be enhanced with exercises such as developing skills in identifying problem situations and determining which type of advocacy might be appropriate. The ACA Advocacy Competencies (J. A. Lewis et al., 2002; Toporek & Daniels, 2018) and the Disability-related Counseling Competencies (Chapin et al., 2018) may be helpful with that. In addition, it would be important for counselors to be able to identify the consequences of advocacy actions for both clients and themselves, for example, living with a changed system or, less optimistically, the ramifications of challenging a hostile system. Although advocacy issues are not new for rehabilitation counseling, there is a need for more attention to coursework, curriculum, and supervision necessary to be an effective rehabilitation counseling advocate.

OPPORTUNITIES AND CHALLENGES IN IMPLEMENTING ADVOCACY

The movement toward advocacy within the counseling professions is not without its detractors. Some argued that counselors cannot be involved in clients' environments and that advocacy is an unrealistic expectation (Weinrach & Thomas, 1998), or that it is a dangerous ideology (Ramm, 1998). This attitude assumes that the counseling profession is value-neutral and that we are not constantly practicing our politics in session (Pope-Davis et al., 2001). In fact, counselors are constantly negotiating their values in session and practicing their worldviews out of session.

Others have noted the need for intentionality and awareness in advocacy so as not to create unrealistic dependencies (Pinderhughes, 1983) or disempower clients (McWhirter, 1994). It is important to emphasize that dependency building does not represent the type of advocacy about which we are speaking. Rather, actions that promote dependency building are problematic and represent values and worldviews imposed by the counselor on the client in a noncollaborative relationship, wherein the counselor retains their position as "healer" and the client's position as that of the "sick person." Both are examples of nonadvocacy relationships and are more likely traditional counseling relationships masquerading as advocacy.

There are some promising developments in rehabilitation counseling practice and training. For example, models for CBR have placed collaboration with clients and consumers as guiding practice (Millington, 2016). In this approach, the counselor collaborates with the client's family and community, their social network, to facilitate empowerment, and inclusion and ensure a safety net of care. The goals of this approach, according to Millington (2016), go further than individual care, and he stated that "its communitarian aims include: reducing poverty, promoting local ownership of programs and the health issues they address; building capacity in support networks; engaging disability advocacy groups in CBR programming; and pursuing evidence-based practice" (p. 111). Models such as this provide ways of reconceptualizing the role of counselor as partner in advocacy and social change.

CONCLUSION

Rehabilitation counseling provides a natural forum for integrating advocacy into practice and education, and there is an increasing body of literature and models to facilitate with implementation. In order for the field to advance, there are some philosophical and ethical issues as well as skills training that must be included in order for counselors and education programs to effectively use this approach with clients. Some of these issues include concerns about creating dependency, balancing client agency with counselors' responsibilities to address systemic barriers, dilemmas regarding conflict of interest between counselors and their home institution, and many others. In addition, research is needed regarding the nuances of process and client outcomes using advocacy in rehabilitation practice. Training will be critical in providing RCs an avenue for developing appropriate skills in resolving these issues and identifying appropriate times and strategies for advocacy. Multicultural counseling and disability-related counseling competencies can provide useful guidance in terms of training models and the establishment of competency standards that recognize issues faced by clients who are marginalized and impeded by systemic barriers. It is hoped that this chapter provided a useful framework as well as tools that may help RCs and educators to integrate advocacy thoughtfully and effectively.

CONTENT REVIEW QUESTIONS

1. How are the definitions of advocacy and empowerment similar and divergent?
2. What is the C-C-C model?
3. What are the professional and ethical issues related to advocacy?
4. What is a double-bind message in advocacy?
5. What are the definitions of *social justice* and *social action*?
6. What is the relationship between the multicultural counseling competencies,the Multicultural Rehabilitation Counseling Competencies and the Disability-related Counseling Competencies?
7. What are some of the recent advances in the field of rehabilitation counseling that address issues of intersectionality and multicultural identities beyond disability?

REFERENCES

Alston, R., & Bell, T. (1996). Cultural mistrust and the rehabilitation enigma for African Americans. *Journal of Rehabilitation, 62*(2), 16–20.

American Counseling Association. (2014). *Code of ethics.* https://www.counseling.org/resources/aca-code-of-ethics.pdf

Arredondo, P., Toporek, R., Brown, S. P., Jones, J., Locke, D. C., Sanchez, J., & Stadler, H. (1996). Operationalization of the multicultural counseling competencies. *Journal of Multicultural Counseling and Development, 24*(1), 42–78. https://doi.org/10.1002/j.2161-1912.1996.tb00288.x

Artman, L. K., & Daniels, J. A. (2010). Disability and psychotherapy practice: Cultural competence and practical tips. *Professional Psychology, 41*(5), 442–448. https://doi.org/10.1037/a0020864

Atkinson, D. R., Morten, G., & Sue, D. W. (1993). *Counseling American minorities: A cross-cultural perspective* (4th ed.). William C. Brown.

Benish, S. G., Quintana, S., & Wampold, B. E. (2011). Culturally adapted psychotherapy and the legitimacy of myth: A direct-comparison meta-analysis. *Journal of Counseling Psychology, 58*(3), 279–289. https://doi.org/10.1037/a0023626

Berne, P., Morales, A. L., Langstaff, D., & Invalid, S. (2018). Ten principles of disability justice. *WSQ, 46*(1–2), 227–230. https://doi.org/10.1353/wsq.2018.0003

Caldwell, J. C., & Vera, E. M. (2010). Critical incidents in counseling psychology professionals' and trainees' social justice orientation development. *Training and Education in Professional Psychology, 4*(3), 163–176. https://doi.org/10.1037/a0019093

Cartwright, B. Y., & Fleming, C. L. (2010). Multicultural and diversity considerations in the new code of professional ethics for rehabilitation counselors. *Journal of Applied Rehabilitation Counseling, 41*(2), 20–24. https://doi.org/10.1891/0047-2220.41.2.20

Cartwright, B. Y., Harley, D. A., & Burris, J. L. (2012). Cultural competence. In D. R. Maki & V. M. Tarvydas (Eds.), *The professional practice of rehabilitation counseling* (pp. 371–389). Springer Publishing.

Cartwright, B. Y., Harley, D. A., & Burris, J. L. (2018). Cultural competence and social justice. In V. M. Tarvydas & M. T. Hartley (Eds.), *The professional practice of rehabilitation counseling* (2nd ed., pp. 343–358). Springer Publishing.

Case, K. A., Iuzzini, J., & Hopkins, M. (2012). Systems of privilege. *Journal of Social Issues, 68*(1), 1–10.

Chan, A., Brophy, M. C., & Fisher, J. C. (1981). Advocate counseling and institutional racism. In *National Institutes of Mental Health, institutional racism and community competence.* U.S. Department of Health and Human Services.

Chapin, M., McCarthy, H., Shaw, L., Bradham-Cousar, M., Chapman, R., Nosek, M., Peterson, S., Yilmaz, Z., & Ysasi, N. (2018). *Disability-related counseling competencies.* https://www.counseling.org/docs/default-source/competencies/arca-disability-related-counseling-competencies-final-version-5-15-19.pdf?sfvrsn=c376562c_6

Charlton, J. I. (1998). *Nothing about us without us: Disability oppression and empowerment.* University of California Press.

Chesler, M. A., Bryant, B. I., & Crowfoot, J. E. (1976). Consultation in schools: Inevitable conflict, partisanship, and advocacy. *Professional Psychology, 7*(4), 637–645. https://doi.org/10.1037/h0078615

Chronister, J., & Johnson, E. (2009). Multiculturalism and adjustment to disability. In F. Chan, E. Da Silva Cardoso, & J. A. Chronister (Eds.), *Understanding psychosocial adjustment to chronic illness and disability: A handbook for evidence-based practitioners in rehabilitation* (pp. 479–518). Springer Publishing.

Cokley, K. O. (2002). Testing Cross's revised racial identity model: An examination of the relationship between racial identity and internalized racialism. *Journal of Counseling Psychology, 49*(4), 476–483. https://doi.org/10.1037/0022-0167.49.4.476

Coleman, H. L. K., & Hau, J. M. (2003). Multicultural counseling competency and portfolios. In D. B. Pope-Davis, H. L. K. Coleman, W. M. Liu, & R. L. Toporek (Eds.), *Handbook of multicultural counseling competencies in counseling and psychology* (pp. 168–182). Sage.

Collison, B. B., Osborne, J. L., Gray, L. A., House, R. M., Firth, J., & Lou, M. (1998). Preparing counselors for social action. In C. C. Lee & G. R. Walz (Eds.), *Social action: A mandate for counselors* (pp. 263–278). American Counseling Association.

Commission on Rehabilitation Counselor Certification. (2017). *Code of professional ethics for rehabilitation counselors*. Author.

Comstock, D. L., Hammer, T. R., Strentzsch, J., Cannon, K., Parsons, J., & Ii, G. S. (2008). Relational-cultural theory: A framework for bridging relational, multicultural, and social justice competencies. *Journal of Counseling & Development, 86*(3), 279–287. https://doi.org/10.1002/j.1556-6678.2008.tb00510.x

Cordes, C. C., Cameron, R. P., Mona, L. R., Syme, M. L., & Coble-Temple, A. (2016). Perspectives on disability within integrated health care. In J. M. Casas, L. A. Suzuki, C. M. Alexander, & M. A. Jackson (Eds.), *Handbook of multicultural counseling* (4th ed., pp. 401–410). Sage.

Corrigan, P. W., Markowitz, F. E., & Watson, A. C. (2004). Structural levels of mental illness stigma and discrimination. *Schizophrenia Bulletin, 30*(3), 481–491. https://doi.org/10.1093/oxfordjournals.schbul.a007096

Crenshaw, K. (1989). Demarginalizing the intersection of race and sex. *University of Chicago Legal Forum,* 139–167.

Devlin, R., & Pothier, D. (2006). Introduction. In D. Porthier & R. Devlin (Eds.), *Critical disability theory: Essays in philosophy, politics, policy, and law* (pp. 1–22). UBC Press.

Ebener, D. J. (2007). Skill emphases in rehabilitation counselor education curricula. *Rehabilitation Education, 21*(3), 195–203. https://doi.org/10.1891/088970107805059652

Eriksen, K. (1997). *Making an impact: A handbook on counseling advocacy.* Taylor & Francis/Accelerated Development.

Eriksen, K. (1999). Counseling advocacy: A qualitative analysis of leaders' perceptions, organizational activities, and advocacy documents. *Journal of Mental Health Counseling 21*(1), 33–49.

Follette, W. C., & Houts, A. C. (1996). Models of scientific progress and the role of theory in taxonomy development: A case study of the DSM. *Journal of Consulting and Clinical Psychology, 64*(6), 1120–1132. https://doi.org/10.1037//0022-006x.64.6.1120

Freire, P. (1989). *Pedagogy of the oppressed.* Continuum.

Griner, D., & Smith, T. B. (2006). Culturally adapted mental health intervention: A meta-analytic review. *Psychotherapy, 43*(4), 531–548. https://doi.org/10.1037/0033-3204.43.4.531

Gruber, J., & Trickett, E. J. (1987). Can we empower others? The paradox of empowerment in the governing of an alternative public school. *American Journal of Community Psychology, 15*(3), 353–371. https://doi.org/10.1007/BF00922703

Haller, B. A. (2010). *Representing disability in an ableist world.* Avocado Press.

Haller, B. A. (2022). *Disability advocacy through media training course.* http://disabilitymediaadvocacy.wordpress.com/unit-7

Hampton, N. Z., Guillermo, M. S., Tucker, M., & Nichols, T. (2017). Broadening rehabilitation education and research through cultural humility: A conceptual framework for rehabilitation counseling. *Rehabilitation Research, Policy, and Education, 31*(2), 70–88. https://doi.org/10.1891/2168-6653.31.2.70

Hartley, M. T., Johnson, S. P., & Tarvydas, V. M. (2015). The ethics and practice of social media advocacy in rehabilitation counseling. *Journal of Rehabilitation, 81*(1), 43–52.

Hennessey, M. L., Rumrill, P. D., Fitzgerald, S., & Roessler, R. (2008). Disadvantagement-related correlates of career optimism among college and university students with disabilities. *Work (Reading, Mass.), 30*(4), 483–492.

Hershenson, D. (1990). A theoretical model for rehabilitation counseling. *Rehabilitation Counseling Bulletin 33* 268–278.

Hook, J. N., Davis, D. E., Owen, J., Worthington, E. L., & Utsey, S. O. (2013). Cultural humility: Measuring openness to culturally diverse clients. *Journal of Counseling Psychology, 60*(3), 353–366. https://doi.org/10.1037/a0032595

Hopps, J., & Liu, W. M. (2006). Working for social justice from within the health care system: The role of social class in psychology. In R. L. Toporek, L. H. Gerstein, N. A. Fouad, G. Roysircar, & T. Israel (Eds.), *Handbook for social justice in counseling psychology: Leadership, vision, and action* (pp. 318–337). Sage.

Jun, H. (2010). *Social justice, multicultural counseling and practice: Beyond a conventional approach.* Sage.

Kahneman, D., & Miller, D. T. (1986). Norm theory. *Psychological Review, 93,* 136–153.

Kivel, P. (2009). Social service or social change? In INCITE: Women of Color Against Violence (Ed.), *The revolution will not be funded: Beyond the non-profit industrial complex* (pp. 129–149). South End Press.

Ladau, E. (2021). *Demystifying disability.* Ten Speed Press.

Lerner, B. (1972). *Therapy in the ghetto: Political impotence and personal disintegration.* Johns Hopkins University.

Lewis, B. L. (2010). Social justice in practicum training: Competencies and developmental implications. *Training and Education in Professional Psychology, 4*(3), 145–152. https://doi.org/10.1037/a0017383

Lewis, T. L. (2022, January 1). *Update: Working definition of ableism.* https://www.talilalewis.com/blog/january-2021-working-definition-of-ableism

Lewis, J. A., Arnold, M. S., House, R., & Toporek, R. L. (2002). *ACA advocacy competencies.* http://www.counseling.org/Publications

Lewis, J. A., & Lewis, M. D. (1983). *Community counseling: A human services approach.* Wiley.

Liu, W. M., & Hernandez, N. (2010). Counseling those in poverty. In M. J. Ratts, J. A. Lewis, & R. L. Toporek (Eds.), *American Counseling Association Advocacy Competencies: An advocacy framework for counselors* (pp. 43–54). American Counseling Association.

Liu, W. M., Pickett, T., & Ivey, A. E. (2007). White middle-class privilege: Social class bias and implications for training and practice. *Journal of Multicultural Counseling and Development, 35*(4), 194–206. https://doi.org/10.1002/j.2161-1912.2007.tb00060.x

Liu, W. M., & Pope-Davis, D. B. (2003). Moving from diversity to multiculturalism: Exploring power and the implications for psychology. In D. B. Pope-Davis, H. L. K. Coleman, W. M. Liu, & R. L. Toporek (Eds.), *The handbook of multicultural competencies* (pp. 90–102). Sage.

Maki, D. R., & Riggar, T. F. (1997). Rehabilitation counseling: Concepts and paradigms. In D. R. Maki & T. F. Riggar (Eds.), *Rehabilitation counseling: Profession and practice* (pp. 3–31). Springer Publishing.

McClure, B. A., & Russo, T. R. (1996). The politics of counseling: looking back and forward. *Counseling and Values, 40*(3), 162–174. https://doi.org/10.1002/j.2161-007X.1996.tb00849.x

McIntosh, P. (2015). Extending the knapsack. *Women & Therapy, 38*(3–4), 232–245.

McMahon, B. T., Roessler, R., Rumrill, P. D., Hurley, J. E., West, S. L., Chan, F., & Carlson, L. (2008). Hiring discrimination against people with disabilities under the ADA: characteristics of charging parties. *Journal of Occupational Rehabilitation, 18*(2), 122–132. https://doi.org/10.1007/s10926-008-9133-4

McWhirter, E. H. (1994). *Counseling for empowerment.* American Counseling Association.

McWhirter, E. H. (1997). Empowerment, social activism, and counseling. *Counseling and Human Development 29*(8), 1–14.

Middleton, R. A., Robinson, M. C., & Mu'min, A. S. (2010). Rehabilitation counseling: A continued imperative for multiculturalism and advocacy competence. In M. J. Ratts, R. L. Toporek, & J. A. Lewis (Eds.), *ACA Advocacy Competencies: A social justice framework for counselors* (pp. 173–183). American Counseling Association.

Middleton, R. A., Rollins, C. W., Sanderson, P. L., Leung, P., Harley, D. A., Ebener, D., & Leal-Idrogo, A. (2000). Endorsement of professional multicultural rehabilitation competencies and standards: A call to action. *Rehabilitation Counseling Bulletin, 48*, 233–244. https://doi.org/10.1177/003435520004300407

Millington, M. J. (2016). Community-based rehabilitation: Context for counseling. In I. Marini, & M. A. Stebnicki (Eds.), *The professional counselor's desk reference* (2nd ed., pp. 111–116). Springer Publishing.

Mpofu, E., & Harley, D. A. (2015). Multicultural rehabilitation counseling: Optimizing success with diversity. In F. Chan, N. L. Berven, & K. R. Thomas (Eds.), *Counseling theories and techniques for rehabilitation and mental health professionals* (2nd ed., pp. 417–441). Springer Publishing.

O'Hara, B. (2004). Twice penalized: Employment discrimination against women with disabilities. *Journal of Disability Policy Studies, 15*(1), 27–34.

Olkin, R. (1999). *What psychotherapists should know about disability.* Guilford Press.

Olkin, R. (2002). Could you hold the door for me? Including disability in diversity. *Cultural Diversity & Ethnic Minority Psychology, 8*(2), 130–137. https://doi.org/10.1037/1099-9809.8.2.130

Olkin, R. (2007). Disability affirmative therapy and case formulation: A template for understanding disability in clinical context. *Counseling and Human Development 39*(8), 1–20.

Owen, J. (2013). Early career perspectives on psychotherapy research and practice: psychotherapist effects, multicultural orientation, and couple interventions. *Psychotherapy, 50*(4), 496–502. https://doi.org/10.1037/a0034617

Owen, J., Tao, K. W., Drinane, J. M., Hook, J., Davis, D. E., & Kune, N. F. (2016). Client perceptions of therapists' multicultural orientation: Cultural (missed) opportunities and cultural humility. *Professional Psychology, 47*(1), 30–37. https://doi.org/10.1037/pro0000046

Perrin, P. B., Goldberg, L. D., & Pierce, B. S. (2019). Multicultural issues and international perspectives on disability. In L. A. Brenner, S. A. Reid-Arndt, T. R. Elliott, R. G. Frank, & B. Caplan (Eds.), *Handbook of rehabilitation psychology*, (3rd ed., pp. 157–169). American Psychological Association. https://doi-org.jpllnet.sfsu.edu/10.1037/0000129-011

Piepzna-Samarasinha, L. L. (2018). *Care work*. Arsenal Pulp.

Pieterse, A. L., Evans, S. A., Risner-Butner, A., Collins, N. M., & Mason, L. B. (2009). Multicultural competence and social justice training in counseling psychology and counselor education: A review and analysis of sample multicultural course syllabi. *The Counseling Psychologist 37* 93–115.

Pinderhughes, E. B. (1983). Empowerment for our clients and for ourselves. *Social Casework, 64*(6), 331–338. https://doi.org/10.1177/104438948306400602

Pope-Davis, D. B., Liu, W. M., Toporek, R., & Brittan, C. (2001). How do we identify cultural competence in counseling: Review, introspection, and recommendations for future research. *Cultural Diversity and Ethnic Minority Psychology 7* 121–138.

Pope-Davis, D. B., Toporek, R. L., Ortega-Villalobos, L., Ligiéro, D. P., Brittan-Powell, C. S., Liu, W. M., Bashshur, M. R., Codrington, J. N., & Liang, C. T. H. (2002). A qualitative study of clients' perspectives of multicultural counseling competence. *The Counseling Psychologist, 30*(3), 355–393. https://doi.org/10.1177/0011000002303001

Pratto, F., & Stewart, A. L. (2012). Group dominance and the half-blindness of privilege. *Journal of Social Issues, 68*(1), 28–45. https://doi.org/10.1111/j.1540-4560.2011.01734.x

Prilleltensky, I. (1997). Values, assumptions, and practices: Assessing the moral implications of psychological discourse and action. *The American Psychologist, 52*(5), 517–535. https://doi.org/10.1037//0003-066x.52.5.517

Ramm, D. R. (1998). Consider the scientific study of morality. *American Psychologist, 53*(3), 323–324. https://doi.org/10.1037/0003-066X.53.3.323

Ratts, M. J., Singh, A. A., Nassar-McMillan, S., Butler, S. K., & McCullough, J. R. (2016). Multicultural and social justice counseling competencies: Guidelines for the counseling profession. *Journal of Multicultural Counseling and Development, 44*(1), 28–48. https://doi.org/10.1002/jmcd.12035

Reed, J. M., Holloway, L. L., Leung, P., & Menz, F. E. (2005). Barriers to the participation of hispanic/latino individuals in community rehabilitation programs. *Journal of Applied Rehabilitation Counseling, 36*(2), 33–41. https://doi.org/10.1891/0047-2220.36.2.33

Ridley, C. R. (1995). *Overcoming unintentional racism in counseling and therapy*. Sage.

Ridley, C. R., & Kleiner, A. J. (2003). Multicultural counseling competence: History, themes, and issues. In D. B. Pope-Davis, H. L. K. Coleman, W. M. Liu, & R. L. Toporek (Eds.), *The handbook of multicultural competencies* (pp. 3–20). Sage.

Rioux, M. H., & Valentine, F. (2006). Does theory matter? In D. Porthier & R. Devlin (Eds.), *Critical disability theory* (pp. 47–69). UBC Press.

Roysircar, G. (2009). The big picture of advocacy: Counselor, heal society and thyself. *Journal of Counseling & Development, 87*(3), 288–294. https://doi.org/10.1002/j.1556-6678.2009.tb00109.x

Shaw, L. R., Chan, F., & McMahon, B. T. (2012). Intersectionality and disability harassment: The interactive effects of disability, race, age, and gender. *Rehabilitation Counseling Bulletin, 55*(2), 82–91.

Singh, A. A., Appling, B., & Trepal, H. (2020). Using the multicultural and social justice counseling competencies to decolonize counseling practice: The important roles of theory, power, and action. *Journal of Counseling & Development, 98*(3), 261–271. https://doi.org/10.1002/jcad.12321

Slesaransky-Poe, G., & García, A. (2014). Social construction of difference. In D. Lawrence-Brown & M. Sapon-Shevin (Eds.), *Condition critical* (pp. 66–85). Teachers College Press.

Smith, T. B., & Trimble, J. E. (2016). *Foundations of multicultural psychology: Research to inform effective practice*. American Psychological Association.

Stone, G. L. (1997). Multiculturalism as a context for supervision: Perspectives, limitations, and implications. In D. B. Pope-Davis & H. L. K. Coleman (Eds.), *Multicultural counseling competencies: Assessment, education and training, and supervision* (pp. 263–289). Sage.

Sue, D. W., Arredondo, P., & McDavis, R. J. (1992). Multicultural counseling competencies and standards: A call to the profession. *Journal of Counseling & Development, 70*(4), 477–486. https://doi.org/10.1002/j.1556-6676.1992.tb01642.x

Sue, D. W., Bucceri, J., Lin, A. I., Nadal, K. L., & Torino, G. C. (2007). Racial microaggressions and the Asian American experience. *Cultural Diversity & Ethnic Minority Psychology, 13*(1), 72–81. https://doi.org/10.1037/1099-9809.13.1.72

Sue, D. W., & Sue, D. (2013). *Counseling the culturally diverse: Theory and practice* (6th ed.). Wiley.

Sue, D. W., Sue, D., Neville, H. A., & Smith, L. (2019). *Counseling the culturally diverse: Theory and practice* (8th ed.). Wiley.

Sue, S., & Zane, N. (1987). The role of culture and cultural techniques in psychotherapy. A critique and reformulation. *The American Psychologist, 42*(1), 37–45. https://doi.org/10.1037//0003-066x.42.1.37

Sutton, R. G., & Kessler, M. (1986). National study of the effects of clients' socioeconomic status on clinical psychologists' professional judgments. *Journal of Consulting and Clinical Psychology, 54*(2), 275–276. https://doi.org/10.1037//0022-006x.54.2.275

Toporek, R. L., & Ahluwalia, M. K. (2019). *Helping counselors and psychologists: Strength, solidarity, strategy and sustainability* [Video]. Alexander Street Press.

Toporek, R. L., Blando, J. A., Chronister, J., Kwan, K.-L. K., Liao, H.-Y., & VanVelsor, P. (2009). Counselor to the core: Serving the whole client through creative blending of counselor roles. *Counseling and Human Development, 41*(5), 1–16.

Toporek, R. L., & Daniels, J. (2018). *2018 update and expansion of the 2003 ACA Advocacy Competencies: Honoring the work of the past and contextualizing the present.* www.counseling.org

Toporek, R. L., Lewis, J., & Crethar, H. C. (2009). Promoting systemic change through the advocacy competencies: Special section on ACA advocacy competencies. *Journal of Counseling and Development, 87*, 260–268.

Toporek, R. L., & Liu, W. M. (2001). Advocacy in counseling: Addressing race, class, and gender oppression. In D. B. Pope-Davis & H. L. K. Coleman (Eds.), *The intersection of race, class, and gender in multicultural counseling* (pp. 385–416). Sage Publishing.

Toporek, R. L., & Reza, J. V. (2000). Context as a critical dimension of multicultural counseling: Articulating personal, professional, and institutional competence. *Journal of Multicultural Counseling and Development, 29*(1), 13–30. https://doi.org/10.1002/j.2161-1912.2001.tb00500.x

Toporek, R. L., & Vaughn, S. R. (2010). Social justice in the training of professional psychologists: Moving forward. *Training and Education in Professional Psychology, 4*(3), 177–182. https://doi.org/10.1037/a0019874

Vash, C. (1991). More thoughts on empowerment. *Journal of Rehabilitation 57*(4), 13–16.

Weinrach, S. G., & Thomas, K. R. (1998). Diversity-sensitive counseling today: A postmodern clash of values. *Journal of Counseling & Development, 76*(2), 115–122. https://doi.org/10.1002/j.1556-6676.1998.tb02384.x

Wilson, K. (2002). Exploration of VR acceptance and ethnicity: A national investigation. *Rehabilitation Counseling Bulletin 45*, 168–176.

Yin, M., Pathak, A., Lin, D., & Dizdari, N. (2021). Identifying racial differences in vocational rehabilitation services. *Rehabilitation Counseling Bulletin, 0*, 003435522110482. https://doi.org/10.1177/00343552211048218

CHAPTER 15

Career Development and Employment of People With Disabilities

DAVID R. STRAUSER, STEPHEN M. KWIATEK, NICOLE L. BIRRI, D. GEORGE STRAUSER, AND CHELSEA E. GRECO

LEARNING OBJECTIVES

After reading this chapter, you should be able to:

- *Recognize the relationship between work, human needs, and development.*
- *Identify how good work can contribute to increased well-being.*
- *Evaluate the Illinois Work and Well-Being Model and how rehabilitation counselors (RCs) can apply the model to guide career and vocational counseling services and interventions for people with disabilities.*
- *Identify the basic tenets of seven important career development theories.*
- *Employ rehabilitation counseling interventions using theory in conjunction with the Work and Well-Being Model.*

CACREP STANDARDS

CACREP 2016: 2F2.a, 2F2.b, 2F2.c, 2F2.d, 2F2.e, 2F2.f, 2F2.g, 2F2.h, 2F2i, 2F2.j
CACREP 2016 Specialities:
    Clinical Rehabilitation Counseling: 5D1.b, 5D2.n, 5D2.t, 5D3.b
    Rehabilitation Counseling: 5H1.b, 5H1.f, 5H2.d, 5H2.e, 5H2.f, 5H2.k, 5H3.b, 5H3.h, 5H3.m

INTRODUCTION

Historically, the field of rehabilitation counseling has been concerned with the career development, employment, and vocational behavior of individuals with disabilities (Patterson et al., 2005; Wright, 1980). Underlying the vocational focus of rehabilitation counseling is the philosophy that work is a fundamental and central component of people's lives and is the primary means by which individuals define themselves in society (Blustein, 2008; Gottfredson, 2002; Super, 1969; Szymanski & Hershenson, 2005). Rehabilitation counselors (RCs) who provide career and vocational services to individuals with disabilities must understand the complex interaction among work, society, and the individual to facilitate and maximize an individual's career development, employment, and overall work adjustment. This chapter introduces the constructs, theories, and strategies that are relevant for practicing RCs to assist individuals with addressing contextual domains (i.e., personal factors, functioning, environmental factors) to develop career development (i.e., individual awareness, education/employment acquisition, education/employment maintenance) and participate in home, society, community, and work, ultimately leading to increased well-being.

In addition to the core value that work is central to people's lives, this chapter is based on several assumptions the authors believe are relevant and fundamental to the field and practice of rehabilitation counseling. First, the practice of rehabilitation counseling is focused on positive behavior change through the development of new skills or the enhancement of existing skills. Even when rehabilitation counseling focuses on job maintenance, we believe this is a focus on positive behavior change, because the individual would not need rehabilitation counseling services if they had the necessary skills to achieve this goal independently. Second, the focus of rehabilitation counseling is to maximize the individual's ability to function independently in the environment of their choice. Third, we believe career counseling is important because we are bringing about a change, based about on an individual's personal choices.

CENTRALITY OF WORK

Work is central to all human societies and provides individuals with opportunities to advance, obtain social support, and develop self-expression and self-determination—all necessary components of psychological health (Blustein, 2008; Neff, 1985). To fully understand the importance of work in people's lives and its impact on individuals' overall health and well-being, it is important to understand what constitutes "good" work and how it differs from "bad" work.

Good Work

According the International Labour Organization (2017), **good work** provides a fair and livable wage, a safe and secure workplace, and the freedom to express themselves in and out of work.

Good work includes job security, the provision of benefits, a fair wage, respect for the individual, and the individual's participation in the work environment (Marmot, 2015). A significant and growing body of research provides support that individuals who participate in a healthy work environment, derive physical and mental health benefits and experience an increased level of well-being. For individuals with disabilities, engaging in productive work addresses issues related to social isolation, stigma, and financial burdens (Blustein, 2008; Strauser et al., 2010). Individuals with disabilities often become isolated and experience decreased self-esteem related to their diagnosis, disability, or chronic health condition. The work environment can offset this experience by providing opportunities for income, social interaction, support, health, and retirement benefits. According to Neff (1985), most work provides social environments that require a person to interact with others, perform meaningful rituals and customs, and provide growth opportunities. These activities sustain physical and mental health (Blustein, 2006, 2008).

Poor Work

Poor work environments can have negative effects on an individual's physical and mental health and overall well-being. Physical exposure to repetitive work, toxins, chemicals, and noise are examples of physical hazards, and low wages and the lack of benefits are examples of financial factors that contribute to poor work and impact health and well-being negatively. An often-overlooked way work can cause harm is psychosocially. Work that has high demands and low control negatively impacts an individual's health and well-being due to an imbalance among effort and reward, social isolation, and a real or job insecurity ; (Marmot, 2015; Moscone et al., 2016). Often poor/bad work environments are made worse when there is an incongruent fit between a person and an environment. An incongruent fit is most often defined as an environment where a person's needs are not met by the environment, and/or the environment's needs are not met by the person. This lack of congruence leads to negative health outcomes such as higher levels of depression, anxiety, and stress (Neff, 1985; O'Sullivan & Strauser, 2010). Reasons for an incongruent fit often relate to an individual's personal work style, personality, and value system (Hershenson, 1981; Holland, 1985; Neff, 1985). Service-sector positions, common employment sites for individuals, often constitute poor work environments because they are noisy and dirty, require long hours, and often involve extreme weather conditions that lead to increased stress levels (Szymanski & Parker, 2010). Other factors that impact health include job role ambiguity, a lack of control or input, lack of support in high-responsibility jobs, and low pay (Marmot, 2015; Neff, 1985; Strauser et al., 2010). These factors may lead to negative work stress, which has been a topic of considerable concern for both psychology and business and has a significant negative impact on the overall work environment (Baron & Greenberg, 1990; Kahn & Byosiere, 1990; Quick et al., 1997; Szymanski & Parker, 2010). For an individual with disabilities, the relationship between the job and work stresses is more complex, with the presence of a disability or chronic health condition further complicating the individual's ability to manage stress in the workplace. Managing work stress for individuals is an important factor for RCs to consider in the career development and job-placement process.

Environmental Factors

A seminal study of urban Chicago (Wilson, 1996) found loss of employment empirically connected to a lower quality of life, including increased drug use, violence, and crime. According to Wilson (1996), employment status is more important than poverty for predicting family discord, violence in neighborhoods, and low-performing school systems. Wilson found that families who function in communities with high employment and who are poor experience fewer problems than families who function in communities with high unemployment and high poverty. In contrast, the loss of employment from an individual perspective is linked to higher rates of anxiety, depression, and substance abuse (Blustein, 2008) and has been linked to decreased levels of well-being and health status. It is of great concern that even when reemployment occurs, the negative impact of unemployment remains. (Blustein, 2008; Blustein, Kenna, et al., 2008). The term **scarring** points to the lasting negative physical and psychological impacts experienced by those who experience unemployment, even after employment has been regained (Thompson & Dahling, 2019). Specifically, psychological research related to scarring has found that job loss and underemployment contribute to lower levels of job and life satisfaction and higher mortality rates (Marmot, 2015; Verbruggen et al., 2015).

In addition, unemployment can have a ripple effect on the family and children of those unemployed. The term **vicarious unemployment** describes the negative effect of unemployment on the family, including children, and has been found to contribute to increased financial strain and instability, increased rates of abuse, and divorce (Thompson et al., 2013). Children whose primary caregiver experiences unemployment are more likely to experience anger, confusion, insecurity, embarrassment, loneliness, depression, anxiety, stress, decreased social support, and increased suicidal ideation (Thompson et al., 2017). A lack of parental employment can also be related to decreased school performance, increased rates of expulsion, dropout rates, lowered likelihood of attending college, increased disillusion-ment regarding future employment, increased worry about future career prospects, and lower earning as adults (Oreopoulos et al., 2008; Thompson et al., 2013).

To contextualize the negative impact on individual well-being derived from being dis-connected from the labor market, it is important that RCs have clear definitions of import-ant terms related to employment. **Poverty** can be defined as financial circumstances that preclude an individual from achieving an acceptable standard of living and negatively impact an individual's ability to exercise personal agency to pursue opportunities includ-ing employment (Sen, 1999). Engaging in appropriate career development activities focused on obtaining and supporting employment can help individuals gain access to jobs that provide necessary income needed to avoid or escape poverty. However, not all work provides sufficient financial resources to avoid poverty, and as a result, employ-ment does not guarantee an individual moves out of, or escapes, poverty (Smith, 2015; Thompson & Dahling, 2019). **Underemployment** is a state of employment in which the individual occupies or holds a position that is inadequate to meet their needs and desires (McKee-Ryan & Harvey, 2011). In contrast, **unemployment** is a state where the individ-ual presently is unable to utilize their current skills and abilities to obtain or maintain employment. **Nonemployment** is a state where unemployment has persisted for so long that an individual has chosen to exit the workforce entirely (Thompson & Dahling, 2019).

Across disability categories, employment rates are much lower for people with dis-abilities compared to the national average. A U.S. Bureau of Labor Statistics (BLS) employment situation report for 2020 estimated the employment rate of individuals with disabilities to be 17.9% compared to 61.8.% for people without disabilities (BLS, 2020). For workers with disabilities, the unemployment rate of 12.6.% was significantly higher than the 7.9% rate for workers without disabilities (BLS, 2020). Disability employment statis-tics also indicate a large percentage of people with disabilities were no longer looking for employment. In 2020, approximately 80% of adults with a disability were not in the labor force, compared to 30% of people with no disability (BLS, 2020). Between 1970 and 2009, the number of people receiving Social Security Disability Insurance (SSDI) benefits more than tripled, from 2.7 million to 9.7 million. Less than 1% of individuals on the rolls of the Disability Insurance (DI) and Supplemental Security Income (SSI) programs ever resume employment (Lui et al., 2010). As a result of the low employment and underemployment rates, individuals with disabilities are at increased risk for experiencing decreased levels of physical and psychological health, further complicating future career development and employment. Without a doubt, a lack of employment opportunities excludes people with disabilities and chronic health conditions from full community participation, significantly affecting the quality of their lives.

WORK AND HUMAN NEEDS

Due to the centrality of work and its positive effect on individuals' physical and psycholog-ical health, work has been identified as a foundation for meeting human needs. According to Blustein (2006, 2008) and Blustein, et al. (2008), work provides a means by which indi-viduals can fulfill the following three basic human needs: (a) survival and power, (b) social connection, and (c) self-determination and well-being. In providing vocational and career services, it is important for RCs to understand from the perspective of the individ-ual with disability how their educational experiences, conceptualization of work, work experience, familial and cultural background, and disability-related factors impact these three basic human needs. Understanding the impact of work on these three fundamental human needs also highlights the complex way in which working functions in the human experience and the need for multidimensional outcomes in measuring the effectiveness of rehabilitation counseling interventions. Specifically, the traditional dichotomous outcome of employed versus unemployed does not cover the multidimensional impact of work in the lives of individuals with disabilities. Refer to Table 15.1 for an overview of these three sets of human needs.

ILLINOIS WORK AND WELL-BEING MODEL

As rehabilitation practitioners, researchers, and administrators work to maximize the career development and employment of individuals, it is important to have a conceptual model to guide services, assist with the allocation of limited resources, and guide the measurement of effective VR outcomes. The Illinois Work and Well-Being Model (Figure 15.1) provides a foundation for conceptualizing and addressing important domains and factors related to the career development of individuals. Derived from the *International Classification of Functioning, Disability, and Health (ICF)*, the model is designed to be parsimonious in nature, facilitate broad application, and promote in-depth research related to each of the domains and factors comprising the model. In short, the model highlights important factors to address (i.e., the interaction of contextual, career/employment development, participation domains) in explaining how personal, environmental, treatment, educational, career/employment development, and potential interventions serve as facilitators or barriers to overall societal participation and well-being.

Conceptual Model Domains

The Illinois Wellness and Well-Being Model consists of Contextual, Career/Employment Development, and Participation domains that interact to provide a structure for understanding the career and employment development of individuals (Figure 15.1). The interventions component is purposefully situated between the Contextual and Career/Employment Development domains, implying interventions directly and indirectly influence both domains (i.e., Contextual, Career/Employment Development) and have an indirect effect on the Participation domain. Each domain is composed of factors, allowing analysis at both the individual domain and factor levels. As a result, domains and factors can be conceptualized as both independent and interdependent. All arrows between domains and factors are bidirectional, indicating a reciprocal effect between the model components. Relationships between domains, factors, and interventions can be positive, negative, or neutral, indicating the value of the directional impact is determined by the situation-specific activities, expressions, and reactions to specific and broad stimuli. In the following section, each domain is described with an emphasis on structure and the reciprocal interaction between major domains.

Contextual Domain

The **Contextual domain** of the Illinois Wellness and Well-Being Model applies the *ICF* model as a guide to operationalize how personal and environmental factors interact with medical and treatment-related functioning and restrictions. Therefore, the specific domain factors of personal, environmental, and functioning should be conceptualized according to the guidelines offered by the *ICF*. The bidirectional arrows between the domain factors indicate a reciprocal relationship, implying that growth or change in one factor can directly or indirectly impact growth or change in other factors. The factors that make up the Contextual domain collectively or individually impact the individual's participation in home, society, community, and work. Likewise, any Participation domain areas can impact the Contextual domain or specific factors individually or collectively. This property implies the interaction of personal, environmental, medical, or treatment-related factors impacts participation independent of any career development activities or processes. By default, the Career/Employment Development domain is a cognitive, affective, and

TABLE 15.1 *Work and Human Needs*

Concept	Context	Considerations	Pros	Cons
Survival and Power	Survival can be equated with the individual being able to meet his or her basic needs, which can be addressed through work.	■ Globalization and changing labor markets make it more difficult for individuals to escape poverty (Szymanski & Parker, 2010); therefore, many individuals are unable to meet their needs.	■ The human need for the acquisition of psychological, economic, and social power is tied closely to meeting basic needs (Blustein, 2006). ■ Work can provide purpose and relevance within the broader environment.	■ Structural and cultural barriers impact individuals' access to high-status employment, ultimately relegating them to disempowered and low-status occupational and social roles and perpetuating dependence on others (Szymanski & Parker, 2010).
Social Connection (See Box 15.1)	Participation in work-related activities provides individuals an opportunity to connect with others and learn their broader social and cultural environments (Blustein, 2008).	■ Working provides a mechanism for individuals to develop a sense of connection with their broader social world by contributing to larger economic structures of society (Blustein, 2006). ■ Earning a paycheck and contributing to society's well-being by paying taxes is a valued social role.	■ Ideally, through work, individuals develop positive relationships that supply the support needed to manage work-related stress and foster identity development (Schein, 1990; Blustein, 1994).	■ If individuals experience a negative work environment, where the individual feels isolated, disconnected, and under stress, the individual's job performance and work adjustment will most likely be negatively affected.
Self-Determination	Self-determination comprises multiple components and skills (e.g., self-awareness, self-advocacy, self-realization). These skills and components are critical for improving the likelihood for postschool employment success (McConnell et al., 2012).	■ Instruction is self-advocacy, a component of self-determination, is one of five required pre-employment transition services.	■ Maximizes individual voice and choice throughout the process of obtaining and maintaining employment. ■ There is a large evidence base for the importance of teaching self-determination skills (Algozzine et al., 2001; Rowe et al., 2021).	■ Like other skills, individuals must be taught self-determination skills (Algozzine et al., 2001).

BOX 15.1 LEARNING ACTIVITY

Survival and Power

Alexia is a young woman with comorbid disabilities (i.e., autism spectrum disorder, intellectual disability, orthopedic impairment). Due to her multiple disabilities, she uses a wheelchair and communication device. Alexia would like to live independently of her parents in the community. Currently, she is employed at a nationally known box store and makes several dollars an hour above minimum wage at $12.00/hour. In addition, she has health insurance benefits and an employer-sponsored retirement plan. Alexia used to have a few coworkers with whom she would directly interact daily; however, due to budget cuts, Alexia is now the only employee in her position. Even earning above minimum wage, she only works 10 hours per week. Based on her current income, she is currently unable to achieve her goals of independence in the community. Thinking about your own experiences, to what extent has employment been able to provide the basic need of survival and power? Were there times when you stayed with employment when those basic needs were not addressed, and, if so, what did you do to meet your need for survival and power? To what extent has employment contributed to your need for social connectedness?

behavioral process serving as a moderator that facilitates or creates barriers between the contextual factors and participation in life's major Participation domain factors.

Career/Employment Development Domain

The **Career/Employment Development domain** of the Illinois Wellness and Well-Being Model is based on career and employment research related to individuals with chronic health conditions and disabilities. The domain consists of three factors: Individual

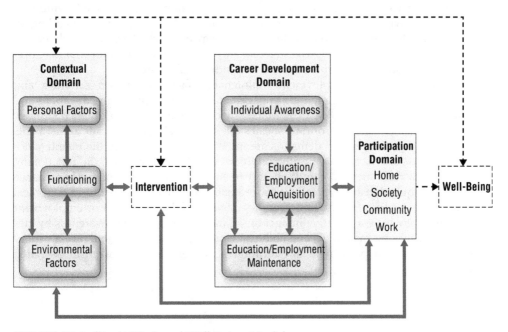

FIGURE 15.1 Illinois Work and Well-Being Model.

BOX 15.2 LEARNING ACTIVITY

Self-Awareness: Career Development Factors
As suggested in the Illinois Work and Well-Being Framework, the bidirectional arrow from the Contextual and Career Employment Domain demonstrates a mutual relationship across domains. Thinking about your career development experience, what factors in terms of Personal, Environmental, and Functioning influenced your varying career development factors? What aspects within the contextual domain were affected both positively and negatively within your career development?

Awareness, Educational and Employment Acquisition, and Educational and Employment Maintenance. The **Individual Awareness factor** addresses an individual's levels of personal awareness regarding how their skills, abilities, interests, values, needs, personality, assets, functioning, and preferences relate to broader societal and work-related activities and participation. Specifically, awareness is developmentally mediated, with the individual becoming aware of how they relate to the world and what activities in which they may choose to participate. Ideally, this developmental process should be based on self-exploration that facilitates the expression of personal choice. The Individual Awareness factor theoretically provides the foundation for the acquisition and maintenance factors; all factors have a reciprocal impact influencing the continual development of each factor (Box 15.2).

The **Education and Employment Acquisition factor** addresses the process in which individuals acquire access to educational and employment-related activities. From an educational perspective, acquisition includes, but is not limited to, the process and activities associated with applying for appropriate education-related activities (e.g., 2-year and 4-year training programs). Education-related acquisition can occur at multiple points of educational transition and may occur multiple times over one's life course. Employment-related acquisition primarily focuses on activities related to job development, placement, and job-seeking activities. Like educational acquisition, employment-related acquisition in all likelihood will occur multiple times throughout the life course and, depending on the developmental stage, may have different requirements to meet acquisition demands. The *Employment and Educational Acquisition* factor provides foundation for Maintenance-related activities and has a reciprocal impact on individual awareness.

The Educational and Employment Maintenance factor addresses activities and behaviors associated with maintaining engagement and participation in education- and occupation-related activities (Box 15.3). Managing educational and work-related stresses, employing functional and appropriate social skills, and making appropriate adjustments to personal and environmental demands are important components of the maintenance factor. Individuals with chronic health conditions also have to manage the functioning associated with their medical condition and related treatment. Although Maintenance occurs after Acquisition and typically is conceptualized as an outcome, it has a reciprocal effect on the preceding factors. For example, unsuccessful educational or employment maintenance may have a negative impact on an individual's level of awareness by creating doubt regarding their skills and abilities, which could affect the individual's motivation to pursue and participate in educational- and employment-acquisition-related activities.

Participation Domain

The *Participation* **domain** of the Illinois Wellness and Well-Being Model utilizes the *ICF* model as a guide to identify meaningful and broad-based participation in major life areas,

BOX 15.3 LEARNING ACTIVITY

Within the Illinois Work and Well-Being Model, the Educational and Employment Maintenance factor encompasses behaviors and activities correlated to maintaining educational and occupational engagement and participation. Reflect on your own educational and employment setting maintenance-related activities. What impact might personal and environmental factors have on engagement in those activities? Why is it important to examine environmental and personal factors when working with an individual with a chronic health condition, and how might those factors affect one's perceptions of their functioning?

which is conceptualized as contributing to one's overall level of well-being. In this model, the life areas of home, society, community, and work can serve as outcomes of interest. The *work* area may seem an obvious focal area for those working to improve career development and employment outcomes for individuals with chronic health conditions. However, the model stresses the interconnectivity of all participation areas. In practical terms, this perspective means participation in one area directly and indirectly impacts participation in the other three remaining areas. The concept of participation area interconnectivity is important because it reinforces the understanding that work has a broad impact on the individual's (a) employment outcomes and individual functioning in their homes, (b) participation in broader societal activities, and (c) engagement in community activities that provide social, recreational, and leisure opportunities. A fundamental tenet embedded in the model is that increased positive participation in the areas identified in the *Participation* domain will lead to an overall increase an individual's well-being and quality of life.

Interventions

According to the Illinois Wellness and Well-Being Model, the **Intervention domain** is situated between the Contextual and Career/Employment Development domains. This placement suggests the primary goal of career, educational, and employment interventions is to facilitate and maximize direct interaction between the Contextual and Career/Employment domains, which will indirectly impact the Participation domain. Historically, career and employment interventions have been conceptualized as existing within the career/employment development domain, excluding or minimizing the impact of the contextual factors identified in this model. By pulling the Intervention component outside of the Career/Employment Development domain and placing it between the Contextual and Career/Employment Development domains, the model implies that interventions should focus on the correspondence between the two respective domains. Effective interventions should focus on maximizing the personal, environmental, and functioning to impact the Career/Employment Development domain and specific career/employment development domain factors. For example, the model implies that for an intervention addressing a deficiency in job-seeking skills (Acquisition factor) to be effective, the intervention should consider how an individual's age, education, gender (personal factors); labor market, culture, familial factors (environmental factors); and depreciated executive processing, fatigue, and limited mobility (functioning) affect the efficacy, adequacy, and acceptability of the intervention. Finally, the dashed bidirectional arrow between the Intervention component and the Participation domain implies that interventions can have an impact independent of the Career/Employment Development domain on an individual's participation.

THEORIES OF VOCATIONAL BEHAVIOR AND CAREER DEVELOPMENT

Theories provide language and explanation for given phenomena. Before a practitioner can implement a treatment plan effectively, the problem and possible range of solutions must be understood. Science provides a process to test ideas about which solutions work for different populations. Over time, consistency in research findings from these tests generated theories that help explain what is observable. Practices guided by research findings are known as **evidence-based practices**. Counselors who do not understand and use research findings and theory are not practicing from an evidence base. In this chapter, vocational behavior and career development are the phenomena of interest. The population of interest is people with disabilities. Here, we outline the key principles of major theories, so rehabilitation professionals can use these theoretical principles when conceptualizing individuals and their career and vocational needs. Models and conceptual models help practitioners use theories in practical ways. As we outline each theory, we explain how the key points from each can be used to guide practice and interventions with individuals. Keeping in mind that all theories have limits, and that a comprehensive discussion of each theory is beyond the scope of this chapter, we provide a summary of major theories applicable to those with disabilities in vocational and career contexts. The additional lens of the Illinois Work and Well-Being Model can help the practitioner fill in the gaps of any given theory and personalize practice to each individual.

When reading the rest of the chapter, keep in mind key points derived from the culmination of career and vocational theories: (a) there are likely *multiple vocational options* for which a person is qualified and well suited, (b) success at work most likely occurs when the *person fits the environment*, and (c) people and environments change over time, so vocational and career decision-making must be considered a *developmental process*.

THEORIES OF CAREER DEVELOPMENT

Career development is a concept that describes the complex, multifaceted, lifelong process of an individual's career experience. It encompasses structural and long-term changes of career behavior (Herr, 1992). Thus, career development theories seek to explain the complicated components that make up an individual's career experience. Donald Super and John Holland were some of the first scholars to tease apart the complexity of career development. The many elements that influence the complex experience of career development are outlined in their theories and will be described in detail. Their relevance has been sustained over time because of their current utility to rehabilitation practitioners in providing research-driven assessments and intervention practices for individual clients. Also, Holland and Super remain pertinent because they have been precursors to the construction of later theories of career development and work adjustment. After detailing Super's and Holland's theories, we discuss social cognitive career theory, cognitive information processing theory, and career construction theory, which were built on the foundations of Super and Holland. Understanding the following theories of career development will set the stage for work adjustment theories that are described later in this chapter.

Super's Career Theory

Donald E. Super's career theory expresses work primarily from a developmental perspective. Nonetheless, the person–environment approach to the career experience is also part of Super's career theory. The fundamental feature of Super's theory is the assertion that career choice develops over time (Tang, 2019). This feature explores the change in vocational choice and ability as an individual matures through life stages. This experience is identified by Super as the life span. Super's theory also explores influencing roles individuals gain and maintain in a variety of environments (Super, 1980). From this approach, Super's career theory has some person–environment components. The developmental and person–environment approaches to Super's career theory will be examined further to illustrate its complexity.

The person–environment interaction that occurs in the life space of Super's theory has two important terms: life roles and theaters. The nine identified **life roles** include child, student, leisurite, citizen, worker, spouse, homemaker, parent, and pensioner. These roles are not all-encompassing, nor will everyone experience every role. Similar to Super's life roles, Super identified four **theaters** (i.e., environments) including the home, community, school, and workplace. Roles are cultivated within one or more environments (Super, 1980). For instance, the role of the student can emerge in the theater of school as well as the home. Theaters and roles are meaningful because of their impact throughout the life span. Roles will vary in significance depending on an individual's goals, self-awareness, and emotional involvement, along with the temporal importance the role has in a specific situation (Super, 1980). Furthermore, the number of roles occupied by an individual is determined by the specific stage of development the individual is in within the life span. Earlier and later stages typically occupy fewer roles than the middle stages.

For Super, the developmental life span is described across five stages of development. Coping within each of these stages is determined on a cognitive and affective level. To manage the demands of the environments within each stage, an individual acquires career maturity. Essentially, **career maturity** is the psychological, physical, and social readiness an individual possesses to cope with the demands of the environments presented within a specific stage in the life span (Super, 1990). The five **stages of the life span** include growth, exploratory, establishment, maintenance, and decline. The growth stage is from birth to 14 years (Salomone, 1996). The demands of this stage manifest through the child and student roles as well as the home, neighborhood, and school theaters. Occupational preferences reflect emotional needs as opposed to ability and interest during this stage. The exploratory stage is from age 15 to 24 years (Salomone, 1996). This period is when an individual explores an array of activities, roles, and environments. Exploration may not be goal oriented at first, but with time it becomes more focused on specific interests and abilities (Super, 1980). The establishment stage is from age 25 to 44 years (Salomone, 1996). During this stage, an individual establishes their roles, including work-related roles. It is not uncommon for the average person typically to change jobs several times while still in the establishment stage (Super, 1990). The maintenance stage is from age 45 to 64 years (Salomone, 1996). During this time, an individual is maintaining their position at a particular job. Technology and the emergence of younger career seekers are competing forces during this stage. The primary demand during the maintenance stage is maintaining control over an individual's career (Super, 1990). The last stage is the decline stage that is from age 65 years onward (Salomone, 1996). At this stage in life, an individual is disengaging in several activities in life. The number of roles an individual possesses begins to decrease at this point in time, including work (Super, 1980). While each stage is described with ages and demands, they are flexible and approximate to each individual.

Super's career theory also is represented by understanding the terms maxi-cycle, mini-cycle, and re-cycle. The maxi-cycle, mini-cycle, and re-cycle are constructs to Super's theory that describe the adaptability and flexibility his theory has to each unique individual. The previously described five stages of development are the **maxi-cycle**. In contrast, the **mini-cycle** occurs at each transition of the maxi-cycle. For each transition of the maxi-cycle, all the stages take place but in a much shorter period. For instance, when an individual transitions from the exploratory stage to the establishment stage, they will mini-cycle through each of the stages beginning with growth and concluding with the decline stage before continuing on to establishment. Therefore, shifting to the establishment stage of a career requires its own individual cycle of cognitive and affective demands to transition an individual's abilities, interests, and commitments to the establishment of a career. Finally, **re-cycling** takes place after the occurrence of a major life event. A major life event may cause an individual to return to an earlier stage of development of the maxi-cycle (Leung, 2008) For example, an individual obtaining a disability while in the maintenance stage may require resuming to the exploratory stage to readjust to their abilities, interests, and overall self-concept. Re-cycling, the maxi-cycle, and the mini-cycle each exhibit Super's theory as being malleable to describe each individual's life experiences.

Super's career theory certainly addresses the complicated experience of an individual's career throughout time. Super emphasized the developmental aspect of a career while also considering the holistic experience of competing roles, environments, personal determinants, and situation determinants. There is a strong developmental, as well as a person–environment, approach to the theory. Critics have stated that Super's career theory lacks cultural and contextual variables such as the role of socioeconomic status and the cultural economic structure within which we operate (Krumboltz, 1994). Despite these critiques, Super's theory remains an important historical career development theory that has influenced the way rehabilitation practitioners approach career interventions.

Holland's Theory

Holland's theory has many characteristics of a person–environment theory while simultaneously having some developmental aspects. The foundation of Holland's theory is the idea that individuals and work environments can be characterized by their resemblance to the following six personality types and environmental models: realistic, investigative, artistic, social, enterprising, and conventional. Knowing the type of personality and environment characteristics that a person and an environment possess helps predict vocational and educational outcomes. The interaction between the individual's personality and the environment is what determines the outcome of their relationship. Furthermore, there are moderators that assist with outcome prediction (Holland, 1997). Each of the six personality types is described, followed by a description of the moderators that Holland emphasizes in his theory.

According to Holland, each personality type and environment possess unique characteristics that can be examined within our culture (see Table 15.2). To begin with, the **realistic** type refers to activities that include practical problems and solutions. A realistic person is often uninsightful, hardheaded, conforming, and inflexible. Occupations such as an automobile mechanic, a farmer, or an electrician are those that function within the realistic environmental model. The **investigative** type refers to work activities that have to do with ideas, thinking, and gathering information, rather than with physical activity. An investigative person values scientific or scholarly achievements and is more inclined to be analytical, intellectual, pessimistic, and independent. An investigative-type individual likes jobs such as a biologist, a geologist, and an anthropologist. The **artistic** type refers to work activities that deal with the artistic side of things, such as forms, designs, and patterns. An artistic individual is often disorderly, emotional, open, and intuitive. Favorable occupations may include a musician, a sculptor, a writer, and an actor/actress. The **social** type refers to activities that assist others and promote learning and personal development. A social person prefers to communicate with other people more than they like working with objects, machines, or data. Occupations compatible with a social-type individual might include a counselor, teacher, and speech therapist. The **enterprising** type refers to work activities that have to do with starting up and carrying out projects, especially business ventures. An enterprising person persuades and leads people. These people prefer action rather than thinking and are often adventurous, excitement-seeking, extroverted, and self-confident. A few examples of jobs an enterprising personality type enjoys are a television producer, salesperson, and business executive. The **conventional** type refers to work activities that follow set procedures and routines. A conventional person prefers to work with data and detail rather than with ideas. Conventional jobs include

TABLE 15.2 Holland's Personality Types

Personality Type	Vocational Preferences	Values	Beliefs	Problem-Solving Style
Realistic	Prefers realistic occupations such as an electrician or mechanic	Values ambition, self-control, and practical-minded characteristics	Believes self as having mechanical, technical, and athletic abilities. Enjoys working with hands, tools, and machines	Prefers concrete, practical, and structured solutions
Investigative	Prefers investigative occupations such as a biologist or medical technologist	Values scientific or scholarly activities as well as self-determination and personal traits such as being a logical, intellectual, and ambitious person	Believes self as being analytical, curious, and scholarly, and having broad interests	Prefers challenging problems that rely on thinking, gathering information, careful analyses, objective data, and related scholarly practices
Artistic	Prefers artistic occupations such as a writer or interior decorator	Values self-expression, equality for all, and personal characteristics such as being imaginative and courageous	Believes self as being expressive, open, original, intuitive, liberal, nonconforming, introspective, and independent	Prefers to use artistic talents and personal traits (e.g., intuition, expressiveness, originality) to solve problems
Social	Prefers social occupations such as a teacher or counselor	Values being helpful and forgiving as well as serving others in a medical, institutional, or reciprocal way	Believes self as understanding others, having teaching ability, social skills, and lacking mechanical and scientific ability	Prefers to use social competencies and traits (e.g., seeking mutual interactions and help from others) to solve problems
Enterprising	Prefers enterprising occupations such as a salesperson or a manager	Values controlling others, the opportunity to be free of control, and ambition	Believes self as being aggressive, popular, self-confident, sociable, and possessing leadership and speaking skills	Prefers to use competencies and values (e.g., control of others, traditional beliefs) to dominate the problem-solving process
Conventional	Prefers conventional occupations such as a bookkeeper or banker	Values ambition, obedience, politeness, and business and economic achievement	Believes self as being conforming, orderly, and having clerical and numerical ability	Prefers to use rules, practices and procedures (e.g., advice from authority) to solve problems

Source: Adapted from Holland (1997). *Making vocational choices: A theory of vocational personalities and work environments.* Psychological Assessment Resources.

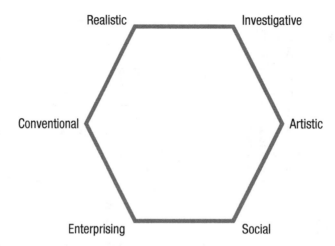

FIGURE 15.2 The Holland Hexagon.

Source: Adapted from Holland, J. L. (1997). *Making vocational choices: A theory of vocational personalities and work environments.* Psychological Assessment Resources.

those of financial analyst, tax expert, and banker (Holland, 1997). Each personality type is matched explicitly to a complementary environment by recognizing the defining characteristics that correspond to one another. This focus on the congruence of a person–environmental fit between the basic individual personalities and environmental characteristics is at the core of the Holland theory (Holland). This matching system is a classic approach to understanding career development for the purposes of career counseling.

Five important secondary concepts that moderate the personality types and environmental models previously described include consistency, differentiation, identity, congruence, and calculus. **Consistency** refers to the relatedness between the environment models and personality types. For instance, a personality type that is artistic is most likely to have similarities to investigative and social personality types. Furthermore, a person who conforms to the personality type of conventional–enterprising should be easier to predict than social–realistic. The next moderator **differentiation** refers to the extent to which a person or environment is defined by one as opposed to many types. For instance, a person who displays a stronger investigative–realistic personality type will be more predictive than a person who displays personality characteristics in four different personality types evenly. **Identity** refers to the clarity and stability of the person's personality type or the environment's model. Clear goals, interests, tasks, and skills all contribute to identity for the person and the environment. **Congruence** refers to the degree to which personality types fit a particular environment. For instance, incongruence occurs when a person with an artistic personality type finds themselves in a conventional environment. An artistic person's interests and skills are unlikely to fit with this environment. Finally, **calculus** refers to the hexagonal model that displays the proportional relationship between the different personality types and environmental models. Through this geometrical model, the relationships of the theory are represented visually including the direct and inverse relationships (Holland, 1997; Figure 15.2).

While Holland's model has so far been portrayed as a person–environment model, there are developmental aspects to the model. Holland explained that personality types develop by means of specific environmental experiences throughout human development. Environments can be perpetuated by parents as well as the choices children have within the limits of parental demands. For instance, parents or guardians who are social tend to engage their children in social environmental models. Similarly, preferences with which an individual identifies at an earlier age can also influence what behaviors remain consistent at a later age. For example, preferences in activities, interests, competencies, and values from earlier in life may support a tendency toward certain personality types that develop later in life (Holland, 1997). For instance, a child displaying characteristics of a certain personality type may indeed perpetuate that personality type as time continues and new experiences are achieved. However, new opportunities and experiences may instead lead personality development in a different direction because of the feedback from these experiences (e.g., a previously social child realizing that they dislike speaking in front of groups of people). Clearly, the environmental experiences of an individual play a part in the development of a personality type throughout the life span. This phenomenon confirms that Holland's theory possesses a developmental approach to career development.

Like other theories, Holland's theory does not exist without opposition. The theory has been criticized for being simplistic and sexist. These criticisms have been challenged by both theory and evidence supported by research (Holland, 1997; Weinrach & Srebalus, 1990). As a whole, Holland's theory is a tool that can be used by practitioners to better understand the way in which an individual can achieve work-environmental integration and congruence.

Social Cognitive Career Theory

The development of the social cognitive career theory was based on Bandura's general social cognitive theory (Bandura, 1986). This theory emphasizes the complex ways in which individuals' personal attributes, external environmental factors, and overt behaviors operate as interlocking mechanisms that mutually influence one another and the individuals' learning experiences (Lent, 2005; Lent et al., 1996, 2002). Following the basic tenets of social cognitive theory, social cognitive career theory highlights the interplay of three variables that enable the exercise of personal agency in career development, namely, self-efficacy (i.e., judgments of one's own capabilities to attain specific tasks), outcome expectations (i.e., beliefs about the anticipated results of performing particular behaviors), and personal motivations (i.e., intention to carry out a particular activity or to produce a particular outcome). The theory acknowledges that people are capable of directing their own vocational behavior (human agency) and even negotiating personal (e.g., predispositions, race, ethnicity, gender, disability, health status) and contextual variables (e.g., sociostructural barriers, support, culture) to prevail in career development. Social cognitive career theory provides a potentially unifying model to explain how people develop vocational interests, make career choices, and achieve varying levels of career success and stability (Lent, 2005; Lent et al., 1996, 2002).

Social cognitive career theory shares certain goals and features with trait factor (or person–environment fit) and developmental career theories. It has been useful in guiding practice and research on career counseling and vocational interventions for people with disabilities (Strauser et al., 2002) and minorities (Lent et al., 2002). In particular, this theory offers a unifying model to guide RCs as they assist clients in examining and overcoming barriers engendered by personal functioning, environmental factors, and/or learning experiences. In addition, this theory also provides a blueprint for guiding rehabilitation counseling research and practice of facilitating career choice making, promoting career aspirations, expanding vocational alternatives, improving self-efficacy, and promoting work satisfaction among people with disabilities.

Cognitive Information Processing Theory

Cognitive information processing (CIP) theory provides a framework to understand and intervene on the career decision-making process. CIP focuses primarily on the way in which career decisions are made and seeks to develop awareness and skills to enhance career decision making. The reduction in the gap between the actual decision-making process and the ideal is a key component of CIP. To achieve this goal, CIP breaks the career decision-making process into two distinct categories: what you need to know and what you need to do. To help inform the career decision-making process, CIP also focuses on the importance of understanding the cognitive and emotional strengths of an individual and then applying those strengths in the career decision-making process (Kleiman et al., 2004).

There are some key assumptions made in CIP: career decision-making is a cognitive process; the capacity to make appropriate career decisions is dependent on the cognitive operations and knowledge of a person; career development involves continual growth and change in knowledge structures; the goal of career counseling is to enhance career decision making capacities through the facilitating the growth of information processing skills. The Career Thoughts Inventory is a key aspect of the CIP counseling. It allows RCs to gain insights into a client's career decision-making process and to develop appropriate interventions to help reduce the gap in the actual/ideal career decision making. CIP is conceptualized in three ways: the Readiness Model, the Pyramid of Information Processing, and CASVE Cycle.

Readiness Model

The readiness model is a key part of the career decision-making process because it seeks to understand the capability and complexity of an individual. The capability and complexities of an individual are assessed on a scale of high to low, related to their cognitive and emotional capacity. **Capability** is defined as the internal factors that may impact career decision-making. The term **complexities** refers to external factors that may impact career decision-making. RCs assess both the emotional and cognitive capacities of an individual in those settings, and rate them on a high-to-low scale. These ratings provide information that informs the RC about the challenges of the case. They also will help identify the level of support needed and any career thought distortions that may impact career decision-making process. The Career Thoughts Inventory is an assessment that commonly is used to assess an individual's level of career readiness.

Pyramid of Information Processing

CIP views the knowledge acquisition in relation to a Pyramid of Information Processing. In this pyramid, there are three components that help inform career decision-making. The base of the pyramid is focused on the basic levels of knowledge, including knowledge of oneself and knowledge of career options. The second level is focused on career decision-making, and that process is often referred to as the CASVE cycle. The top of the period is defined through executive processing or metacognition. People at this level of the pyramid are able to have awareness of their self-talk, self-awareness, monitoring, and control. RCs may utilize this pyramid to help identify ways to support a client, and research suggests there is evidence of CIP's effectiveness in reducing negative career thoughts and that process can be particularly helpful for individuals (Sampson et al., 2004).

CASVE and the Pyramid of Information Processing

The CASVE cycle is utilized to help work through the career decision making of an individual. The CASVE cycle is an acronym that for Communication, Analysis, Synthesis, Valuing, and Execution. Each stage relates to a specific behavior and set of expectations. Communication is used to help talk through a specific challenge and takes into consideration both internal and external factors that may influence career decisions. Analysis examines what an individual knows about their specific problem highlighted earlier.

Synthesis is a solution-focused stage in which the RC and individual may seek to identify action steps. Valuing prioritizes the solutions based on an individual's interests, values, needs, and wants. Execution is the implementation of the plan. After the execution, the person may revert to the communication stage to assess the execution of their plan (Tang, 2019).

Career Construction Theory

Super's and Holland's theories established key theoretical frameworks essential in cementing a foundation for career counseling. Each theory was developed against the backdrop of an economy that differed drastically from our present economy. Globalism and the information age engendered a shift in the labor force. These influences brought about the advent of insecure work, which has become so prevalent that terms like *gig economy* have entered the vernacular. Insecure work differs greatly from the previous employment norms through which individuals climbed the proverbial career ladder at one company over the course of their entire professional lifecycle. Savickas described this approach as the company owning the individual's career. New age work has transferred ownership from the company to the individual, requiring a worker to exercise more vocational choice and to experience more career transitions (Savickas, 2020). In short, this evolution necessitates the construction of a vocational narrative aligned with a person's vocational identity. Self-awareness and an ability to convey skills and experiences acquired in a variety of work and nonwork settings into transferrable vocational skills and experiences are essential in this type of identity development. This process led to the formation of Career Construction Theory (CCT). To meet this need, counselors must encourage a process of self-inventorying skills and experiences in multiple arenas of their lives and helping themselves self-actualize vocational meaning, direction, and identity. In essence, CCT attempts to provide an internal and explanatory process in which a person can become more aware of themselves to better direct their career aspirations.

CCT can be described as a metatheory designed to renovate career counseling. This theory recognizes the limitations of established vocational theories in the "gig economy" and looks to meet the needs of this more fluid economy. The primary goal of CCT is to help an individual develop and understand their own identity. To do this, the person goes through a process to cultivate their own internal meaning with the goal of having them confidently express and pursue their own career narrative. The counselor in the CCT context is an expert on process, guiding an individual through their own journey of self-discovery. Hopefully as one better understands themselves, they will understand how their vocational interests and skills that can be transferred into careers. This process often requires a deconstruction and reconstruction of that identity and pulls experiences and skills from multiple aspects of one's life (Savickas, 2020). The process of deconstruction and reconstruction often is buoyed by multiple features of other career theories, notably Super's and Holland's theories. Incorporating central themes of those theories, including trait and factor and developmental and social cognitive learning perspectives, can be useful for individuals to better understand themselves and help them determine what vocational skills and identity they may seek to self-actualize.

The framework of the CCT is centered on three perspectives of self: self as the actor, self as the agent and self as the author. According to Savickas (2013), these perspectives may be developed across the lifespan starting at an early age and developing into adolescence and adulthood. They mark gradual changes in one's self-awareness, self-efficacy and self-advocacy. This trifold model was influenced by the personality theory of McAdams (1995), which described the three layers of self as an object, subject, and project. Individuals begin the process of self-construction as an actor, often found in early childhood, where they simply act out behaviors; evolve into agents able to direct actions, often found in adolescence; and then evolve to authors able to explain the action.

To better understand this framework, it is helpful to assess how these concepts interact with each other. The self as an actor perspective resonates strongly with the self-as-object perspective. This understanding matches person–environment fit and is influenced heavily by the 20th-century career developmental theories. It is through this outlook which Holland (1997) RIASEC model of vocational choice and work environments becomes particularly helpful. This prescriptive model often matches a worker to specific employment. In short, a person completes an assigned work behavior. The evolution from actor to agent often relates to one achieving some vocational meaning. In developing meaning, one also is able to develop self-discovery goals. Setting vocational goals, achieving those goals, and enjoying predictable career advancement demonstrate there is more control in a person's vocational plan. A person is not just going through vocational behaviors and instead is providing direction to those behaviors. Self as project is a relatively novel concept that materialized as a response to the more fluid employment structure of our current labor market. Employment requires individuals to shift frequently and manage their careers in a way makes them responsive to the ever-evolving needs of employers. In order to meet these evolving needs, a person needs to be the author of their own career narrative, controlling the story and actions in a way that allows them to borrow identity traits from innumerable settings and amend them in a way that best suits their current needs (Savickas, 2013).

Other valuable insights fundamental to CCT are formulated during the CCI. This formulaic first step allows the counselor to gain insights into the vocational identity of the client. Insights of particular value are early role models and the reputation of an individual. The internalization of role models at an early age can provide a springboard into self-assessment. Understanding what an individual values in the role model (i.e., work ethic, compassion) can provide a lexicon that can aid in defining vocational traits the individual possesses and values. Assessing other arenas of one's life can also be beneficial during a CCI. Understanding one's reputation in a social setting can help gain understanding of what an individual's personality may be like and can be implemented concurrently with Holland's RAISEC to assess a person-environment fit (Savickas, 2020). For example, if a person reports they enjoy having family and friends over and hosting them in social setting, they may be suited for a profession in hospitality. CCI requires a more concentrated discussion, but what is important is the understanding that the CCI is key in CCT. The CCI provides a holistic evaluation of a person and can lead one to better understand and/or develop a person's vocational identity which is the central goal of CCT.

THEORIES OF WORK ADJUSTMENT

Frank Parsons's 1909 work on career choice commonly is referred to as the first career development theory. In Parsons's theory, he highlights the process of career choice. The **career choice process**, according to Parsons, is a result of learning about the person, learning about the world of work, and then using what was learned to match a person with their environment. In Parsons's writings, career choice was considered a onetime event (Parsons; Szymanski & Parker, 2003). This emphasis on career choice has since misguided career professionals to preconceive career development as a process that distinctly begins with the cognitive decision or career choice. Work adjustment theories recognize that career choice is not necessarily a cognitive step that is imperative to experiencing a career or interacting with the work environment. In other words, most individuals spend more time working rather than choosing a career (Hershenson, 1996a). As opposed to the traditional career choice approach Parsons proposed, work adjustment theories focus less on choice and more on the experience of a career or work as it is occurring. The MTWA and Hershenson's model of work adjustment have been described by Salomone (1993) as two important theories of work adjustment because of their utility in assisting individuals to adapt to new environments.

Theories of work adjustment are meaningful to rehabilitation professionals partly because individuals with disabilities typically experience restrictions on career choice because of the disability in and of itself (Conte, 1983; Hershenson, 1996). Therefore, for individuals with disabilities, work adjustment is foreseeably vital. Work adjustment may be more important than the experience of career choice. As the work adjustment theories are described in the next section, it will become apparent how they deviate from the career development theories since they focus on career adjustment rather than the occurrence of career choice.

Minnesota Theory of Work Adjustment

The MTWA takes a person–environment fit approach to an individual's career experience (Dawis, 1994; Szymanski & Parker, 2003). This theory of work adjustment begins with the assumption that a person has needs that can be met through the work environment. Similarly, the environment also has needs or skill requirements that can be met through a person. For example, these needs could be biological (i.e., needs that are necessary for survival, e.g., food). Similarly, these needs could be psychological (i.e., needs that are necessary for psychological health, e.g., self-esteem). To meet an individual's needs, the person can utilize their skills in exchange for work reinforcements. Work reinforcements can come in the form of pay, prestige, or direct satisfaction of a need. According to this theory, the needs and skills of a person are used to describe the person's work personality. The work personality defines how a person behaves while interacting with the work environment to meet their needs. When a person's work performance meets the needs of the work environment, and the needs of the person are fulfilled, job satisfaction or satisfactoriness is achieved (Dawis, 2005).

Job satisfaction or satisfactoriness is important in this theory to understand where change will take place. Satisfaction is a state variable and is characterized as an emotional response to a cognitive assessment of the person–environment fit (Dawis, 2005). Some of the environment's needs can be met by a person in the same way that some of a person's needs can be met by the environment. In this way, the person and environment are complementary. For example, when the reinforcements of the environment meet the values and needs of the person, satisfaction is achieved. **Values** are an important construct to the MTWA. Unlike previous theories, the MTWA focuses on values rather than interests. The MTWA describes values as "reference dimensions underlying needs" (Dawis, 2005, p. 6).

To understand the difference between satisfaction for the person and satisfaction for the environment, the MTWA labels the environment's satisfaction with the person as **satisfactoriness**, and then the person's satisfaction with the environment simply as **satisfaction**. As a result, there are four possible satisfaction circumstances a person can experience with their environment: satisfied and satisfactory, satisfied but unsatisfactory, dissatisfied but satisfactory, or dissatisfied and unsatisfactory (Dawis, 2005). In this theory, satisfaction plays a central motivational role in work adjustment. When the person and the environment fit well, they are experiencing a satisfied and satisfactory state and, therefore, display maintenance behavior. If there is dissatisfaction, as represented in the last three circumstances, adjustment behavior will take place to establish a higher fit between the person and the work environment (Dawis, 1994). Thus, the satisfaction and satisfactoriness of the person–environment experience in essence help predict the **tenure** or rather the length a person remains in their job.

The interaction of work adjustment and maintenance can be cyclical in nature. For instance, the person and environment may begin with adjustment and then transition into maintenance. Later, changes that impact the person–environment fit may require the individual to transition back into work adjustment. Both the environment and the person may be completing work adjustment and maintenance behavior at the same time, or one may be in maintenance and the other in adjustment (Dawis, 2005). The work environment and the person do not have to be in the same state of work adjustment.

There are four concepts that help predict the satisfactoriness of the person in the environment and make up the personality style of the person, as well as the environment style (Dawis, 1994, 2005). These concepts are celerity, pace, rhythm, and endurance: **Celerity** is the quickness of interaction or response between the person and the environment, **pace** is the intensity of the interaction; **rhythm** is the pattern of the response (whether it is stable, cyclical, or erratic), and **endurance** is the persistence (length of time) of the interaction (Dawis, 2005). Variation in any of these areas may lead to a satisfactory or unsatisfactory outcome. If there is unsatisfaction or unsatisfactoriness, then adjustment will take place. Adjustment could be in the form of changing specific behaviors, or they can take the form of termination of employment within a particular environment to seek a more complementary fit.

There are four additional concepts that are useful in understanding the TWA. These concepts explain when adjustment begins and ends. In combination, these four concepts encompass the adjustment style of the person–environment interaction (Dawis, 2005). These concepts are flexibility, activeness, reactiveness, and perseverance: **Flexibility** is the degree of discorrespondence tolerated before becoming dissatisfied enough to engage in adjustment behavior, **activeness** is acting on the environment to reduce discorrespondence, **reactiveness** is acting on the person to reduce discorrespondence, and **perseverance** refers to the duration of the person's attempts to adjust before quitting. One or all of these may explain when adjustment begins and ends. As time continues, a person's adjustment style may become more stable. If this occurs, these concepts may be described as traits or behavior tendencies. The more evident each of these traits becomes, the more significant they are for practitioners within the field of vocational rehabilitation. Each of these concepts can be imperative to achieving a fit between the person and the work environment.

The TWA has application in many areas of career development and employment. For instance, by using the TWA, educators can focus on the skills and needs of a child or adolescent to assist with guidance of career adjustment. Adults or young adults similarly can climb the career ladder by focusing on skill attainment and becoming cognizant of the skills the work environments need. Within the field of rehabilitation, the TWA can also assist an individual in rationally thinking through work dissatisfaction and solving problems. By focusing in on what will allow an individual to meet the needs of the work environment, rational decisions are easier to achieve. On the other hand, there are critics of the TWA. Critics have stated that job satisfaction or satisfactoriness may rely on a person's perception rather than the reality of the person–environment fit. Others argue that a person's perception is important and cannot be neglected when examining the person–environment fit. In all, understanding the TWA can lead to greater job satisfaction and satisfactoriness as well as overall work integration.

Hershenson's Theory of Work Adjustment

Like other theories, Hershenson's theory has elements of a person–environment theory as well as prominent developmental characteristics. Hershenson's theory has three sequential domains that make up an individual. The first domain developed is the **work personality**, which is composed of the person's self-concept and work motivation. This domain is developed in the preschool years and mostly is influenced by the family. Next, during the school years, the second domain emerges: **work competency**. Work competency is composed of work habits, physical and mental skills, and interpersonal skills in the work setting (Strauser et al., 2002; Szymanski & Hershenson, 2005). The last domain develops while an individual transitions from school to work. This final domain is **work**

goals. Work goals are the goals an individual has that by this age have become clear and stable. Each of the three domains can only develop to a level that it is supported by its predecessor. In contrast, each domain can influence the domains that came before it. For instance, an individual's navigation through school may influence their work personality. If an individual fails unexpectedly within a particular curricular area, then their self-concept may change (i.e., work personality) and, therefore, this experience will influence their eventual work goals. Similarly, work goals may require adjustment as the life course takes place as well. For example, a person who experiences a significant disability during this time of life may be forced to reevaluate work goals. This process in turn might call into question the appropriateness of existing work competencies and work personality (Szymanski & Parker, 2003). While these three domains emerge sequentially, they can nonetheless be influenced throughout the life course.

The work environment also influences the work adjustment process. Hershenson's theory describes three components of the work environment that mediate work adjustment. The first component is the **behavioral expectations**. This component is made up of the expectations of the work environment (e.g., employers). Examples of behavioral expectations may include timeliness and appropriate communication with customers. The second component is **skill requirements**. Skill requirements include the tasks a particular work environment needs. These skills vary from job to job. For instance, a job in an office setting may require specific computer skills, while a job in a factory setting may require specific machine operating skills. Finally, the last component Hershenson describes for the work environment is **rewards and opportunities**. Rewards and opportunities may come in the form of money, benefits, social networking, or power. Impacting the individual and work setting are formative and intervening influences. The formative influences include an individual's family, school, peer group, and wider culture. Each of these influences impacts the formation of a person's work personality, work competencies, and work goals. The intervening influences include the experiences of living, learning, socializing, and culture. All intervening influences impact how the individual and work setting fit together (Hershenson, 1981).

According to Hershenson's theory, the product of the interaction between the person and work environment is called **work adjustment** (Hershenson, 1981, 1996b; Hershenson & Szymanski, 1992). Work adjustment has three components: work role behavior, task performance, and work satisfaction. **Work role behavior** refers to displaying appropriate behaviors in the work setting, which is primarily related to the work personality of the person and the behavioral expectations of the work setting. **Task performance** refers to the quality and quantity of one's work output, which is related primarily to work competencies in the person and the skill requirements of the work setting. **Work satisfaction** refers to one's degree of gratification resulting from work, which is related primarily to the work goals of the person and the rewards and opportunities in the work setting (Hershenson, 1981).

Hershenson's theory was designed particularly to be applicable to people with disabilities. Theoretically, individuals must address two major environmental transitions in facilitating work adjustment: the transition from home to school and the transition from school to work. However, for individuals who experience an impediment in their career track, there may be a third or fourth environmental transition (e.g., the individual may participate in vocational rehabilitation). Success in the current transition will depend on the individual's experience during previous transitions (Szymanski, et al., 2010; Szymanski & Hershenson, 2005). Research has found that individuals who had higher levels of desirable work personality traits have higher levels of job readiness, self-efficacy, and more internalized work locus of control (Strauser et al., 2002).

The Hershenson model of work adjustment contributes a language for understanding the elements of work adjustment for both the employee and the employer. Work personality, work competency, and work goals interact with the work environment to form the essential framework of worker satisfaction. Hershenson's model differs from other

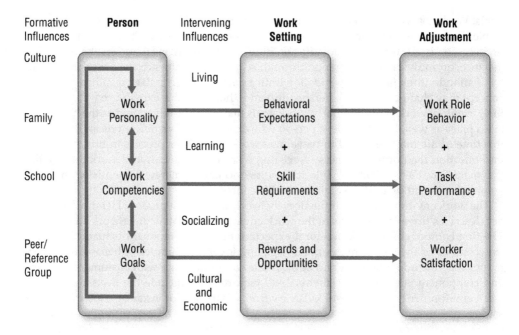

FIGURE 15.3 The Hershenson Model of Work Adjustment.

Source: Reproduced with permission from Hershenson, D. B. (1996). Work adjustment: A neglected area in career counseling. *Journal of Counseling and Development, 74,* 442–448. doi:10.1002/j.1556-6676.1996.tb01890.x

models in the degree of emphasis placed on the post-placement role that RC interventions play in work adjustment. Simply finding a job to match a skill set is insufficient. By accurately identifying areas of deficiency and directing interventions directly to those areas, Hershenson theorized that worker adjustment can be maximized (Figure 15.3).

The seven career development and work adjustment theories discussed in the previous section have their strengths and utility but also have limitations that may affect their complete application to the career and vocational counseling of individuals (Conte, 1983; Szymanski & Hershenson, 2005). Research regarding the career development and employment of individuals with disabilities has identified the following three factors that limit the application of existing career and vocational theories: (a) limitations in career exploratory experiences, (b) limited opportunities to develop decision-making abilities, and (c) a negative self-concept resulting from negative societal attitudes toward individuals (Curnow, 1989). Because of the various limitations of the seven theories discussed, RCs need to be aware of how these limitations potentially impact the prediction, planning, and implementation of career development and employment interventions for individuals with disabilities.

Over the past 15 years, several attempts have been made to address the limitations noted and develop a comprehensive model that would address these issues (Hershenson & Szymanski, 1992; Szymanski & Hershenson, 1998; Szymanski et al., 1996). As introduced earlier in this chapter, the Illinois Work and Well-Being model can be applied to individuals regardless of specific disability, life factors, or career goals. The career and context domains provide a framework for RCs to conceptualize the link between domains and factors and examine the direct, indirect, and tertiary impact on the career development and vocational outcomes of individuals with disabilities. Overall, the model facilitates a comprehensive conceptualization of diverse individuals, with the ultimate goal being the selection of appropriate interventions using tenets of career and vocational theory in combination with prioritization of health and contextual factors that are impacting work (Table 15.3) .

TABLE 15.3 Summary of Major Vocational and Career Theories

Theory	Key Concepts
Super's Life-Span, Life-Space Theory	Career rainbow
	Life roles
	Life stages
	Career maturity
Holland's Theory	RIASEC hexagon
	Congruence
	Personal identity
	Environmental identity
Cognitive Information Processing	CASVE
Career Construction Theory	Pyramid of Information Processing
	Career Thoughts Inventory
	Vocational Narrative
	Vocational Identity
	Vocational Self-Awareness
Theories of Work Adjustment	Person–Environment Fit
Minnesota Theory of Work Adjustment	Satisfaction
	Satisfactoriness
	Reinforcers
	Skill requirements
Hershenson's Theory of Work Adjustment	Work personality
	Work competencies
	Work goals/values
Bandura's Social Cognitive Career Theory	Self-efficacy
	Outcome expectations
	Motivations

Note: PWD, people with disabilities.

REHABILITATION COUNSELING INTERVENTIONS

RCs provide a full array of career and vocational services across multiple contexts to facilitate the career development and employment of people with disabilities. The largest provider of vocational rehabilitation services is the state/federal Vocational Rehabilitation (VR) system. Within the system, services are categorized by areas of emphasis (e.g., eligibility, guidance and counseling, training). Table 15.4 profiles VR services offered within the VR system across the domains of the Illinois Work and Well-Being Model.

The Workforce Investment Act of 1998 was reauthorized on July 22, 2014, and is now the Workforce Innovation and Opportunity Act (WIOA) of 2014. The WIOA was federally mandated to improve employment outcomes of transition-aged youth with disabilities. The WIOA funding is required to be provided by state/federal VR system to require state vocational rehabilitation agencies (e.g., Illinois Department of Human Services), in collaboration with local schools, to implement pre-employment transition services (pre-ETS) for students with disabilities qualifying, or potentially qualifying, for vocational rehabilitation services. WIOA also requires that both teachers and vocational rehabilitation counselors implement the five required pre-ETS: (a) job exploration counseling, (b) work-based learning experiences, (c) counseling on opportunities for enrollment in comprehensive transition or postsecondary educational programs, (d) workplace readiness training to develop social skills and independent living, and (e) instruction in self-advocacy (Strauser et al., 2019; WIOA, 2014).

In addition to organizing and describing career and vocational services by system and legislation, we offer a brief overview of traditional and commonly used career and vocational counseling interventions used across rehabilitation counseling settings.

TABLE 15.4 Service and Description Aligned With the Illinois Work and Well-Being Model

Type of Service and Description	Contextual Domain		Career Domain			
	Personal	Environmental	Functioning	Awareness	Acquisition	Maintenance
Preemployment Transition Services						
Job Exploration Counseling—*Participating in various activities that will assist youth with disabilities in identifying their vocational interests, work values, and provide opportunities to explore various careers* (Flum & Blustein, 2000).	✓	✓	✓	✓		
Work-Based Learning Experiences—*Experiencing real work by youth with disabilities to learn job skills within the natural environment, which facilitates the connection between what students are taught in the classroom, so those skills can be applied in the workplace* (WINTAC, 2016). *There are several types of WBLEs: career exploration, job shadowing, service learning, internships, work sampling, apprenticeships, and paid employment* (Luecking, 2020).	✓	✓	✓	✓	✓	✓
Counseling on Opportunities for Enrollment in Comprehensive Transition or Postsecondary Educational Programs—*Supporting youth with disabilities and caregivers in the transition from school to postsecondary education process.*	✓	✓	✓	✓		

Workplace Readiness—*Teaching youth with disabilities skills that can be transferred across various jobs and work situations. These skills, also known as soft skills, focus on personal qualities, social/interpersonal skills, professional competencies, and independent living skills that are necessary for gaining and maintaining employment.*	✓	✓	✓	✓	✓
Instruction in Self-Advocacy—*Teaching youth with disabilities self-advocacy skills, which are developed across four main areas: (a) knowledge of self, (b) knowledge of rights, (c) communication, and (d) leadership (Test et al., 2005).*	✓	✓	✓	✓	✓
Eligibility					
Assessment—Services provided and activities performed to determine an individual's eligibility for VR services, to assign an individual priority category of a state VR agency that operates under an order of selection, and/or to determine the nature and scope of VR services to be included in the IPE	✓	✓	✓		
Diagnosis of Treatment of Impairments—Surgery, prosthetics and orthotics, nursing services, dentistry, occupational therapy, physical therapy, speech therapy, and drugs and supplies; also diagnosis and treatment of mental and emotional disorders	✓	✓			

(continued)

TABLE 15.4 Service and Description Aligned With the Illinois Work and Well-Being Model (*continued*)

Type of Service and Description	Contextual Domain		Career Domain			
	Personal	Environmental	Functioning	Awareness	Acquisition	Maintenance
Counseling and Guidance						
Vocational Rehabilitation Counseling and Guidance—Discrete therapeutic counseling and guidance services necessary for an individual to achieve an employment outcome, including personal adjustment counseling; counseling that addresses medical, family, or social issues; vocational counseling; and any other form of counseling and guidance necessary for an individual with a disability to achieve an employment outcome; this service is distinct from the general counseling and guidance relationship that exists from between the counselor and the individual during the entire rehabilitation process.	✓	✓		✓		
Training						
College or University Training—Full-time or part-time academic training above the high school level that leads to a degree (associate, baccalaureate, graduate, or professional), a certificate, or other recognized educational credential; such training may be provided by a 4-year college or university, community college, junior college, or technical college.			✓	✓	✓	

Occupational/Vocational Training— Occupational, vocational, or job skill training provided by a community college and/or a business, vocational/trade, or technical school to prepare students for gainful employment in a recognized occupation; this training does not lead to an academic degree or certification.

On-the-job training— Training in specific job skills by prospective employer; generally the individual is paid during this training and will remain in the same or a similar job upon successful completion; this category also includes apprenticeship training programs conducted or sponsored by an employer, a group of employers, or a joint apprenticeship committee representing both employers and a union.

Basic Academic Remedial or Literacy Training—Literacy training or training provided to remediate basic academic skills needed to function on the job in the competitive labor market.

Job Readiness Training—Training to prepare an individual for the world of work (e.g., appropriate work behaviors, methods for getting to work on time, appropriate dress and grooming, methods for increasing productivity).

(continued)

TABLE 15.4 Service and Description Aligned With the Illinois Work and Well-Being Model (*continued*)

Type of Service and Description	Contextual Domain			Career Domain		
	Personal	Environmental	Functioning	Awareness	Acquisition	Maintenance
Disability-Related, Augmentative Skills Training—Service includes, but is not limited to, orientation and mobility, rehabilitation teaching, training in the use of low-vision aids, braille, speech reading, sign language, and cognitive training/retraining.	✓	✓	✓	✓	✓	✓
Miscellaneous Training—Any training not recorded in one of the other categories listed, including GED or high school training leading to a diploma.			✓	✓	✓	✓
Job Placement						
Job Search Assistance—Job search activities that support and assist a consumer in searching for an appropriate job; may include help in preparing resumes, identifying appropriate job opportunities, and developing interview skills, and may include making contacts with companies on behalf of the consumer.	✓		✓	✓	✓	
Job Placement Assistance—A referral to a specific job resulting in an interview, whether or not the individual obtained the job.		✓			✓	
Supportive Modalities						

On-the-Job Supports—Support services to an individual who has been placed in employment in order to stabilize the placement and enhance job retention; such services include job coaching, follow-up and follow-along, and job retention services.

Transportation Services—Travel and related expenses necessary to enable an applicant or eligible individual to participate in VR service; includes adequate training in the use of public transportation vehicles and systems.

Rehabilitation Technology—The systematic application of technologies, engineering methodologies, or scientific principles to meet needs of, and address the barriers confronted by individuals with disabilities in areas that include education, rehabilitation, employment, transportation, independent living, and recreation; includes rehabilitation engineering services, assistive technology devices, and assistive technology services.

(continued)

TABLE 15.4 Service and Description Aligned With the Illinois Work and Well-Being Model (*continued*)

Type of Service and Description	Contextual Domain			Career Domain		
	Personal	Environmental	Functioning	Awareness	Acquisition	Maintenance
Reader Services—Services for individuals who cannot read print because of blindness or other disability; includes reading aloud and transcribing printed information into Braille or sound recordings if requested by the individual; generally are offered to individuals who are blind or deaf-blind but may also be offered to individuals unable to read because of serious neurological disorders, specific learning disabilities, or other physical or mental impairments.	✓		✓			
Interpreter Services—Sign language or oral interpretation services performed by specifically trained persons for individuals who are deaf or hard of hearing, and tactile interpretation services for individuals who are deaf-blind; includes real-time captioning services; does not include language interpretation.	✓	✓	✓		✓	✓
Personal Attendant Services—Those personal services that an attendant performs for an individual with a disability such as bathing, feeding, dressing, providing mobility and transportation, and so on.	✓	✓	✓		✓	✓

Technical Assistance Services—Technical assistance and other consultation services provided to conduct market analyses, to develop business plans, and to provide resources to individuals in the pursuit of self-employment, telecommuting, and small business operation outcomes.	✓	✓		✓	✓
Information and Referral Services—Services provided to individuals who need assistance from other agencies (through cooperative agreements) not available through the VR program.	✓	✓	✓	✓	✓
Other Services—All other VR services that cannot be recorded elsewhere; included here are occupational licenses, tools and equipment, initial stocks and supplies, and medical care for acute conditions arising during rehabilitation and constituting a barrier to the achievement of an employment outcome.	✓	✓	✓	✓	✓

Note. Information on service categories extracted from the RSA-911 code book.

Individual and Group Career Counseling

Individual career counseling is a largely verbal process in which the counselor and client engage in a dynamic interaction where the counselor employs a repertoire of diverse behaviors. These behaviors are used to help bring about self-understanding and action in the form of "good" decision-making on the part of the individual who has responsibility for their own actions (Herr & Cramer, 1996). Recent research regarding the vocational behavior of individuals receiving VR services has indicated that core elements of the working alliance are especially powerful facilitators of change when providing individual career counseling services (Strauser et al., 2004). The working alliance is a transtheoretical process that consists of the following three elements: (a) bonds, (b) goals, and (c) tasks (Strauser et al., 2004). Individuals who reported higher levels of working alliance with their VR counselor reported more satisfaction with their rehabilitation services and increased vocational outcomes (Lustig et al., 2003). Research also has suggested that individuals receiving vocational services reported they would have liked to receive more vocational counseling and desired a strong working relationship with their RC (Lustig et al.). Group counseling is beneficial when counseling for career exploration, using visual imagery, developing locally relevant occupational information, teaching career decision-making, and teaching job-interviewing skills (Pope, 1999).

Vocational Evaluation

Vocational evaluation is a comprehensive and systematic process in which RCs and clients work together to assess and identify the client's vocational interests, abilities, aptitudes, work values, functional limitations, and barriers to employment. The main function of vocational evaluation services provided by RCs is to identify the client's strengths and weaknesses relative to the rehabilitation goal and employment outcome.

Situational Assessment

Situational assessment is a valuable tool for RCs when assisting clients to make choices about the types of jobs and work environments that would be of interest. A **situational assessment** is an assessment that commonly involves actual employment and community settings but can also be developed within the private sector for people with disabilities to explore their interests, assess current skill level, and provide training (Fraser & Johnson, 2010). It allows information to be generated quickly concerning employment options that are worth pursuing further and avoids wasting time on inappropriate job searches. In addition, many situational assessments can provide a transition to actual paid employment. Situational assessments can assist RCs and individuals in determining potential accommodations that will be necessary for successful competitive employment.

Job Site Accommodation

The Americans with Disabilities Act (ADA) of 1990 instituted the policy that employers must make reasonable accommodations to the known physical and mental functioning of a qualified applicant or employee with a disability. RCs involved in the accommodation process can work with other rehabilitation professionals to determine what type of workplace accommodation may be needed or beneficial to facilitate competitive employment.

Job Development and Placement

Job development and placement interventions help clients with disabilities connect with the jobs that match their knowledge, skills, and abilities. RCs can assist with revising a resume, preparing the individual for a job interview, finding job leads, assisting with the submission of a job application, and setting up and attending interviews. They can also provide assistance and support needed to help the individual attain their desired employment outcome.

Supported Employment

According to the Rehabilitation Act Amendments of 1998, supported employment is a program to assist people with the most significant disabilities to become and remain successfully and competitively employed in integrated workplace settings. It is targeted at individuals with the most significant disabilities for whom competitive employment has not occurred traditionally, or for whom competitive employment has been interrupted or has been intermittent because of a disability. Extensive research has found that supported employment is a robust and effective intervention to increase the employment of people with disabilities (Wehman & Avellone, 2021). Supported employment usually provides assistance such as job coaches, transportation, assistive technology, specialized job training, and individually tailored supervision. Typically, supported employment is a way to move people from dependency on a traditional service delivery system to independence via competitive employment (Wehman, 1996). There are several features of supported employment programs that differ from traditional job-placement service approaches. First, supported employment programs seek to identify jobs that provide wages above minimum wage, fringe benefits, and positions with career trajectories. Second, supported employment programs focus on providing the ongoing support required to get and keep a job rather than on getting a person ready for future employment. Third, supported employment programs emphasize creating opportunities to work rather than simply providing services to develop job skills for people with disabilities. Fourth, supported employment programs encourage full participation. Thus, all people—regardless of the degree of their disability—have the capacity to undertake supported employment if appropriate support services can be provided. Fifth, supported employment programs promote social integration in which people with disabilities are encouraged to interact with coworkers, supervisors, and others at work during lunch times or breaks and during nonwork hours as a result of wages earned. Finally, supported employment programs promote flexibility in which people with disabilities are provided with various work options consistent with the wide range of job opportunities available in the community.

Customized employment is closely related to supported employment. The key differences between them occur during the job acquisition phase. In customized employment an environment is modified to meet the specific skills of the individual. Often this means an RC works closely with an employer to identify specific needs within the environment that can be satisfied by the client. For this reason, customized employment often requires the development of new jobs. Customized employment is included with supported employment because many of the more extensive supports synonymous with supported employment often are provided to the individual after the initial job acquisition.

Benefits Counseling

Obtaining and maintaining competitive employment may have a significant impact on the benefits that individuals with disabilities receive. The provision of benefits counseling focuses on reviewing, with the individual and RC, what can be earned through work without jeopardizing or losing existing benefits if this is a concern for the individual. The goal of benefits counseling would be to develop a plan for achieving self-sufficiency or a work-related expense plan, so the individual can maximize workplace participation and retain important benefits (Fraser & Johnson, 2010).

Assistive Technology

Assistive technology is a class of interventions in which people with disabilities use technology to facilitate the performance of functional tasks (Kirsch & Scherer, 2010). Assistive technology not only includes mobility devices such as walkers and wheelchairs; it also includes computerized devices, software, and peripherals that assist people with disabilities in accessing and using computers or other information technologies. Various service delivery models regarding the application of assistive technology for people with disabilities have been developed in state rehabilitation agencies. Some of these services are provided by a vendor who is an RC who has special responsibility for providing assistive technology services; others are offered by pertinent healthcare providers, such as an occupational therapist or an assistive technologist. Evidence also showed that assistive technology can be used to enhance the employment opportunities for people with disabilities (Noll et al., 2006). Thus, it is important that RCs are knowledgeable and competent in assistive technology services. RCs should identify the need for assistive technology services or devices for people with disabilities, provide information regarding assistive technology to people with disabilities, and coordinate assistive technology services.

CONCLUSION

Career development, vocational behavior, and employment of individuals are complex and dynamic processes that are developmental in nature, involve the person interacting with the environment, and are moderated by social cognitive factors. In this chapter, we provided an overview of information that is important in understanding career and vocational behavior to enhance the career and employment outcomes of individuals with disabilities. In discussing the centrality of work and how work is critical in meeting human needs, RCs gain an understanding that work plays an important role in the individual's level of mental health and social integration. Theories of career development were reviewed briefly in an effort to provide RCs with a model to understand the complex nature of vocational behavior. The Illinois Work and Well-Being Model was introduced as a framework that RCs can use in conceptualizing and strategizing the delivery of rehabilitation services. Finally, we briefly described various interventions that can be used by RCs in facilitating vocational behavior change.

Much work is still needed to gain a better understanding of work and disability. There is a very significant need to conduct studies that evaluate the impact of career counseling and vocational interventions for individuals with disabilities. To date, most of the research in this area has focused on supported employment and related interventions. These types of interventions appear to be very robust for those with severe disabilities. However, little research has been done to examine the development and efficacy of interventions directed at those without severe disabilities. Expanding research beyond those with severe disabilities is a needed priority over the next 10 to 15 years.

CONTENT REVIEW QUESTIONS

1. Describe why work is important and how it can contribute to increased well-being.
2. Explain the difference between good and bad work and discuss how bad work can negatively impact individuals.

3. Identify and describe the three domains that make up the Illinois Work and Well-Being Model and how RCs can apply the model to guide career and vocational counseling services and interventions for people with disabilities.
4. Identify and describe the basic tenets of the seven career development theories.
5. Explain how RCs can implement traditional vocational evaluation and counseling interventions with the Work and Well-Being Model.

REFERENCES

Algozzine, B., Browder, D., Karvonen, M., Test, D. W., & Wood, W. M. (2001). Effects of interventions to promote self-determination for individuals with disabilities. *Review of Educational Research, 71*(2), 219–277. https://doi.org/10.3102/00346543071002219

Bandura, A. (1986). *Social foundations of thought and action: A social-cognitive theory*. Prentice Hall.

Baron, R. A., & Greenberg, J. (1990). *Behavior in organizations: Understanding and managing the human side of work*. Allyn & Bacon.

Blustein, D. L. (1994). "Who am I?": The question of self and identity in career development. In M. L. Savickas & R. W. Lent (Eds.), *Convergence in career development theories: Implications for science and practice* (pp. 139–154). Consulting Psychologists Press.

Blustein, D. L. (2006). *The psychology of working: A new perspective for career development, counseling, and public policy*. Lawrence Erlbaum.

Blustein, D. L. (2008). The role of work in psychological health and well-being. *American Psychologist, 63*(4), 228–240. https://doi.org/10.1037/0003-66X.63.4.228

Blustein, D. L., Kenna, A. C., Gill, N., & DeVoy, J. E. (2008). The psychology of working: A new framework for counseling practice and public policy. *The Career Development Quarterly, 56*(4), 294–308. https://doi.org/10.1002/j.2161-0045.2008.tb00095.x

Bureau of Labor Statistics. (2020). *Persons with disabilities: Labor force characteristics*. https://www.bls.gov/news.release/pdf/disabl.pdf

Conte, L. (1983). Vocational development theories and the disabled person: Oversight or deliberate omission. *Rehabilitation Counseling Bulletin, 26*, 316–328.

Curnow, T. C. (1989). Vocational development of persons with disability. *The Career Development Quarterly, 37*(3), 269–278. https://doi.org/10.1002/j.2161-0045.1989.tb00831.x

Dawis, R. (1994). The theory of work adjustment as convergent theory. In M. L. Savikas & R. W. Lent (Eds.), *Convergence in career development theories: Implications for science and practice* (pp. 33–43). CPP Books.

Dawis, R. V. (2005). The Minnesota theory of work adjustment. In S. D. Brown & R. W. Lent (Eds.), *Career development and counseling: Putting theory and research to work* (pp. 3–23). Wiley.

Flum, H., & Blustein, D. L. (2000). Reinvigorating the study of vocational exploration: A framework for research. *Journal of Vocational Behavior, 56*(3), 380–404. https://doi.org/10.1006/jvbe.2000.1721

Fraser, R. T., & Johnson, K. (2010). Vocational rehabilitation. In R. G. Frank, M. Rosenthal, & B. Caplan (Eds.), *Handbook of rehabilitation psychology* (pp. 357–363). American Psychological Association.

Gottfredson, L. (2002). Gottfredson's theory of circumscription, compromise, and self-creation. In D. Brown & Associates (Ed.), *Career choice and development* (pp. 85–148). Jossey-Bass.

Hagner, D., & Salomone, P. R. (1989). Issues in career decision making for workers with developmental disabilities. *The Career Development Quarterly, 38*(2), 148–159. https://doi.org/10.1002/j.2161-0045.1989.tb00417.x

Herr, E. L. (1992). Emerging trends in carrer counselling. *International Journal for the Advancement of Counselling, 15*(4), 255–288. https://doi.org/10.1007/BF02449904

Herr, E. L., & Cramer, S. H. (1996). *Career guidance and counseling through the lifespan: Systematic approaches*. HarperCollins College.

Hershenson, D. B. (1981). Work adjustment, disability, and the three Rs of vocational rehabilitation: A conceptual model. *Rehabilitation Counseling Bulletin, 25*, 91–97.

Hershenson, D. B. (1996a). A systems reformulation of a developmental model of work adjustment. *Rehabilitation Counseling Bulletin, 40*, 2–10.

Hershenson, D. B. (1996b). Work adjustment: A neglected area in career counseling. *Journal of Counseling & Development, 74*(5), 442–446. https://doi.org/10.1002/j.1556-6676.1996.tb01890.x

Hershenson, D. B., & Szymanski, E. M. (1992). Career development of people with disabilities. In R. M. Parker & E. M. Szymanski (Eds.), *Rehabilitation counseling: Basics and beyond* (pp. 273–303). Pro-Ed.

Holland, J. L. (1985). *The self-directed search professional manual.* Psychological Assessment Resources.

Holland, J. L. (1997). *Making vocational choices: A theory of vocational personalities and work environments.* Psychological Assessment Resources.

International Labour Organization. (2017). *Decent work.* https://www.ilo.org/global/topics/decent-work/lang--en/index.htm

Kahn, R. L., & Byosiere, P. (1990). Stress in organizations. In M. Dunnette (Ed.), *Handbook of industrial and organizational psychology* (2nd ed., Vol. 3, pp. 571–650). Rand-McNally.

Kirsch, N. L., & Scherer, M. J. (2010). Assistive technology for cognition and behavior. In R. G. Frank, M. Rosenthal, & B. Caplan (Eds.), *Handbook of rehabilitation psychology* (pp. 273–284). American Psychological Association.

Kleiman, T., Gati, I., Peterson, G., Sampson, J., Reardon, R., & Lenz, J. (2004). Dysfunctional thinking and difficulties in career decision making. *Journal of Career Assessment, 12*(3), 312–331. https://doi.org/10.1177/1069072704266673

Krumboltz, J. D. (1994). The career beliefs inventory. *Journal of Counseling & Development, 72*(4), 424–428. https://doi.org/10.1002/j.1556-6676.1994.tb00962.x

Lent, R. W. (2005). A social cognitive view of career development and counseling. In S. D. Brown & R. W. Lent (Eds.), *Career development and counseling: Putting theory and research to work* (pp. 101–127). Wiley.

Lent, R. W., Brown, S. D., & Hackett, G. (1996). Career development from a social cognitive perspective. In D. Brown & L. Brooks (Eds.), *Career choice and development* (pp. 373–421). Jossey-Bass.

Lent, R. W., Brown, S. D., & Hackett, G. (2002). Contextual supports and barriers to career choice: A social cognitive analysis. *Journal of Counseling Psychology, 47*(1), 36–49. https://doi.org/10.1037/0022-0167.47.1.36

Leung, S. A. (2008). The big five career theories. In J. A. Athanasou & R. V. Esbroeck (Eds.), *International handbook of career guidance* (pp. 115–132). Springer.

Luecking, R. G. (2020). *The way to work* (2nd ed.). Paul H. Brooks Publishing Co.

Lui, J. W., Chan, F., Fried, J. H., Lin, C.-P., Anderson, C. A., & Peterson, M. (2010). Roles and functions of benefits counseling specialists: A multi-trait analysis. *Journal of Vocational Rehabilitation, 32*(3), 163–173. https://doi.org/10.3233/JVR-2010-0507

Lustig, D. C., Strauser, D. R., Weems, G. H., Donnell, C. M., & Smith, L. D. (2003). Traumatic brain injury and rehabilitation outcomes: Does working alliance make a difference? *Journal of Applied Rehabilitation Counseling, 34*(4), 30–37. https://doi.org/10.1891/0047-2220.34.4.30

Marmot, M. (2015). *The health gap: The challenge of an unequal world.* Bloomsbury Publishing.

McAdams, D. P. (1995). What do we know when we know a person? *Journal of Personality, 63*(3), 365–396. https://doi.org/10.1111/j.1467-6494.1995.tb00500.x

McConnell, A. E., Martin, J. E., Juan, C. Y., Hennessey, M. N., Terry, R. A., el-Kazimi, N. A., Pannells, T. C., & Willis, D. M. (2012). Identifying nonacademic behaviors associated with post-school employment and education. *Career Development and Transition for Exceptional Individuals, 36*(3), 174–187. https://doi.org/10.1177/2165143412468147

McKee-Ryan, F. M., & Harvey, J. (2011). "I Have A Job, But...": A review of underemployment. *Journal of Management, 37*(4), 962–996. https://doi.org/10.1177/0149206311398134

Moscone, F., Tosetti, E., & Vittadini, G. (2016). The impact of precarious employment on mental health: The case of Italy. *Social Science & Medicine, 158*, 86–95. https://doi.org/10.1016/j.socscimed.2016.03.008

Neff, W. S. (1985). *Work and human behavior.* Aldine.

Noll, A., Owens, L., Smith, R. O., & Schwanke, T. (2006). Survey of state vocational rehabilitation counselor roles and competencies in assistive technology. *Work: A Journal of Prevention, Assessment and Rehabilitation, 27*(4), 413–419.

Oreopoulos, P., Page, M., & Stevens, A. H. (2008). The intergenerational effects of worker displacement. *Journal of Labor Economics, 26*(3), 455–483. https://doi.org/10.1086/588493

O'Sullivan, D., & Strauser, D. (2010). Validation of the developmental work personality model and scale. *Rehabilitation Counseling Bulletin, 54*(1), 46–56. https://doi.org/10.1177/0034355210378045

Patterson, J. B., Szymanski, E. M., & Parker, R. M. (2005). Rehabilitation counseling: The profession. In R. M. Parker, E. M. Szymanski, & J. B. Patterson (Eds.), *Rehabilitation counseling: Basics and beyond* (pp. 1–25). Pro-Ed.

Pope, M. (1999). Applications of group career counseling techniques in Asian cultures. *Journal of Multicultural Counseling and Development, 27*(1), 18–30. https://doi.org/10.1002/j.2161-1912.1999.tb00209.x

Quick, J. C., Quick, J. D., Nelson, D. L., & Hurrell, J. J. (1997). *Preventative stress management in organizations.* American Psychological Association. https://doi.org/10.1037/10238-000

Rowe, D. A., Mazzotti, V. L., Fowler, C. H., Test, D. W., Mitchell, V. J., Clark, K. A., Holzberg, D., Owens, T. L., Rusher, D., Seaman-Tullis, R. L., Gushanas, C. M., Castle, H., Chang, W.-H., Voggt, A., Kwiatek, S., & Dean, C. (2021). Updating the secondary transition research base: Evidence- and research-based practices in functional skills. *Career Development and Transition for Exceptional Individuals, 44*(1), 28–46. https://doi.org/10.1177/2165143420958674

Salomone, P. R. (1993). Annual review: Practice and research in career counseling and development, 1993. *The Career Development Quarterly, 42*(2), 99–128. https://doi.org/10.1002/j.2161-0045.1993.tb00423.x

Salomone, P. R. (1996). Tracing Super's theory of vocational development: A 40-year retrospective. *Journal of Career Development, 22*(3), 167–184. https://doi.org/10.1177/089484539602200301

Sampson, J. P., Reardon, R. C., Peterson, G. W., & Lenz, J. G. (2004). *Career counseling and services: A cognitive information processing approach.* Thomson/Brooks/Cole.

Savickas, M. L. (2013). Career construction theory and practice. *Career Development and Counseling: Putting Theory and Research to Work, 2*, 144–180.

Savickas, M. L. (2020). Career construction theory and counseling model. *Career Development and Counseling: Putting Theory and Research to Work, 3*, 165–200.

Schein, E. H. (1990). Organizational culture. *American Psychologist, 45*(2), 109–119. https://doi.org/10.1037/0003-066X.45.2.109

Sen, A. (1999). *Commodities and capabilities.* OUP Catalogue.

Smith, L. (2015). *Psychology, poverty, and the end of social exclusion: Putting our practice to work.* Teachers College Press.

Strauser, D. R., Ketz, K., & Keim, J. (2002). The relationship between self-efficacy, locus of control and work personality. *Journal of Rehabilitation, 68*(1), 20–26.

Strauser, D. R., Lustig, D. C., & Donnell, C. (2004). The impact of the working alliance on therapeutic outcomes for individuals with mental retardation. *Rehabilitation Counseling Bulletin, 47*, 215–223.

Strauser, D. R., O'Sullivan, D., & Wong, A. W. K. (2010). The relationship between contextual work behaviours self-efficacy and work personality: an exploratory analysis. *Disability and Rehabilitation, 32*(24), 1999–2008. https://doi.org/10.3109/09638281003797380

Strauser, D. R., Rumrill, P. D., & Greco, C. (2019). Applying the Illinois Work and Well-Being Model to increase labor force participation among people with multiple sclerosis. *Journal of Vocational Rehabilitation, 51*(1), 11–20. https://doi.org/10.3233/JVR-191021

Super, D. E. (1969). The development of vocational potential. In D. Malikin & H. Rusalem (Eds.), *Vocational rehabilitation of the disabled: An overview* (pp. 75–90). New York University Press.

Super, D. E. (1980). A life-span, life-space approach to career development. *Journal of Vocational Behavior, 16*(3), 282–298. https://doi.org/10.1016/0001-8791(80)90056-1

Super, D. E. (1990). A life-span, life-space approach to career development. In D. Brown & L. Brooks (Eds.), *Career choices and development: Applying contemporary theories to practice* (pp. 197–261). Jossey-Bass.

Szymanski, E. M., Enright, M. S., Hershenson, D. B., & Ettinger, J. M. (2010). Career development theories and constructs: Implications for people with disabilities. In E. M. Szymanski & R. M. Parker (Eds.), *Work and disability: Contexts, issues, and strategies for enhancing employment outcomes for people with disabilities* (pp. 87–131). Pro-Ed.

Szymanski, E. M., & Hershenson, D. B. (2005). An ecological approach to vocational behavior and career development of people with disabilities. In R. M. Parker, E. M. Szymanski, & J. B. Patterson (Eds.), *Rehabilitation counseling: Basics and beyond* (pp. 225–280). Pro-Ed.

Szymanski, E. M., & Hershenson, D. B. (1998). Career development of people with disabilities: An ecological model. In R. M. Parker & E. M. Szymanski (Eds.), *Rehabilitation counseling: Basics and beyond* (pp. 327–378). Pro-Ed.

Szymanski, E. M., Hershenson, D. B., Enright, M. S., & Ettinger, J. M. (1996). Career development theories, constructs, and research: Implications for people with disabilities. In E. M. Szymanski & R. M. Parker (Eds.), *Work and disability: Issues and strategies in career development and job placement* (pp. 79–126). Pro-Ed.

Szymanski, E. M., & Parker, R. M. (2010). Work and disability: Basic concepts. In E. M. Szymanski & R. M. Parker (Eds.), *Work and disability: Contexts, issues, and strategies for enhancing employment outcomes for people with disabilities* (pp. 1–15). Pro-Ed.

Szymanski, E. M., & Parker, R. M. (2003). *Work and disability: Issues and strategies in career development and job placement*. Pro-ed.

Tang, M. (2019). *Career development and counseling: Theory and practice in a multicultural world*. Sage Books.

Test, D. W., Fowler, C. H., Wood, W. M., Brewer, D. M., & Eddy, S. (2005). A conceptual framework of self-advocacy for students with disabilities. *Remedial and Special Education, 26*(1), 43–54. https://doi.org/10.1177/07419325050260010601

Thompson, M. N., & Dahling, J. J. (2019). Employment and poverty: Why work matters in understanding poverty. *The American Psychologist, 74*(6), 673–684. https://doi.org/10.1037/amp0000468

Thompson, M. N., Nitzarim, R. S., Her, P., & Dahling, J. J. (2013). A grounded theory exploration of undergraduate experiences of vicarious unemployment. *Journal of Counseling Psychology, 60*(3), 421–431. https://doi.org/10.1037/a0033075

Thompson, M. N., Nitzarim, R. S., Her, P., Sampe, M., & Diestelmann, J. (2017). Financial Stress and Work Hope Beliefs Among Adolescents. *Journal of Career Assessment, 25*(2), 254–267. https://doi.org/10.1177/1069072715621517

Verbruggen, M., van Emmerik, H., Van Gils, A., Meng, C., & de Grip, A. (2015). Does early-career underemployment impact future career success? A path dependency perspective. *Journal of Vocational Behavior, 90*, 101–110. https://doi.org/10.1016/j.jvb.2015.08.002

Wehman, P. (1996). Supported employment: Inclusion for all in the workplace. In W. Stainback & S. Stainback (Eds.), *Controversial issues confronting special education: Divergent perspectives* (pp. 293–304). Allyn & Bacon.

Wehman, P., & Avellone, L. (2021). Supported employment and customized employment. In D. R. Strauser (Ed.), *Career Development, Employment, and Disability in Rehabiltation* (2nd ed., pp. 261–272). Springer Publishing Company.

Weinrach, S. G., & Srebalus, D. J. (1990). Holland's theory of careers. *Personality & Individual Differences, 15*(5), 555–562.

Wilson, W. J. (1996). When work disappears. *Political Science Quarterly, 111*(4), 567. https://doi.org/10.2307/2152085

Workforce Innovation and Opportunity Act. (2014). *Pub. L. no.113–128 Sat.1425*. https://www.gov-info.gov/content/pkg/PLAW-113publ128/pdf/PLAW-113publ128.pdf

Workforce Innovation and Technical Assistance Center. (2016). *Work-based learning activities*. http://www.wintac.org/topic-areas/preemployment-transition-services/overview/workbased-learning-experiences

Wright, G. N. (1980). *Total rehabilitation*. Little, Brown.

CHAPTER 16

Forensic and Indirect Services

MARY BARROS-BAILEY

LEARNING OBJECTIVES

After reading this chapter, you should be able to:

- *Identify the purpose and origins of forensic rehabilitation counseling and indirect service provision practice.*
- *Contrast forensic rehabilitation and indirect service provision.*
- *Distinguish the settings within which forensic rehabilitation and indirect services are used.*
- *Identify the main methods and techniques applied in forensic and indirect service provision.*
- *Recognize the use of teams in forensic and indirect rehabilitation practice.*
- *Describe the main ethical issues for the forensic rehabilitation and indirect service practitioner.*

CACREP STANDARDS

CACREP 2016 Specialties:
  Rehabilitation Counseling: 5H1.a, 5H1.c, 5H2.a, 5H2.i, 5H2.l, 5H2.q, 5H2.r., 5H3.b, 5H3.h, 5H3.i, 5H3.m
  Clinical Rehabilitation Counseling: 5D1.a, 5D2.a, 5D2.c, 5D2.t, 5D2.u, 5D2.w, 5D3.b

INTRODUCTION

Two decades after *CSI*, the popular American police drama television series that started in 2000, made its debut, the effect on pop culture's understanding of forensic disciplines is evident. When forensic rehabilitation counselors (FRCs) mention they are in forensic practice, they are often met with questions about their experiences in criminal cases as the common perception is of them in a lab coat examining DNA samples or evidence from a crime scene. The inquirer's interest is nonetheless piqued, and it affords the FRC an opportunity not only to explain forensic practice from the rehabilitation perspective but also to introduce the discipline of rehabilitation counseling itself.

Forensic and indirect service practice is a fast-growing specialty of rehabilitation counseling, and is the best paid. The specialty has much to contribute to general counseling. Scant literature exists regarding forensic practice in other counseling specialties (e.g., mental health, marriage and family, school, career, and so forth). The vast majority of the literature in general counseling uses the term *forensic* as a synonym in corrections or criminal justice practice settings in which mental health, addictions, or other counseling practitioners may assess or treat a client (Cherner et al., 2013; Cianciulli, 1993; Dickens et al.,

2007; Gardner-Elahi & Zamiri, 2015; Glassmire et al., 2007; Jasper et al., 1998; Larson et al., 2013; Livingston et al., 2013; Pinter, 1999; Ryan, 1999, 2003; Suarez et al., 1978; Thurman et al., 2011; Travis & Sturmey, 2013) or the training of counselors working in corrections (DiCataldo et al., 2021). Even the National Association of Forensic Counselors (2022) stated that its purpose is to "enhance delivery of safe and effective treatment of offenders in both civil and criminal cases" (para. 5). In this chapter, as within rehabilitation counseling, **forensics** describes those counselors performing evaluations and giving recommendations that inform the trier of fact about liability/damages in civil and—rarely—in criminal cases. Different specialties within the counseling profession have existing with untapped opportunities to contribute to the forensic and indirect service practice in civil and criminal legal systems within their respective scopes of practice.

To clarify the role of an FRC, the Commission on Rehabilitation Counselor Certification (CRCC, 2017) defined **forensic** practice as "conducting evaluations and/or reviews of records and . . . research for the purpose of providing unbiased and objective expert opinions via case consultations and testimony" (p. 37). The American Counseling Association (ACA, 2014) further defined one of the tasks performed by practitioners in this practice setting, describing the **forensic evaluation** as "the process of forming professional opinions for court or other legal proceedings, based on professional knowledge and expertise, and supported by appropriate data" (p. 20).

Although the CRCC (2010) did not provide a glossary definition for **indirect service practice**, it described the practice as when "rehabilitation counselors [are] . . . employed by third parties as case consultants [and] . . . when there is no intent to provide rehabilitation counseling services directly to clients or evaluees" (p. 15). This reference was completely removed from the 2017 CRCC *Code of Professional Ethics for Certified Rehabilitation Counselors*. What is important about forensic and indirect practice is that "file review, second-opinion services, and other indirect services are not considered an ongoing professional relationship" (CRCC, 2017, p. 11). Indeed, in forensic or indirect service practice, there is no client–counselor relationship, but the person for whom the services are being provided is called an **evaluee** (Barros-Bailey et al., 2008).

Forensic and indirect service provision in rehabilitation counseling started long before the modern generation of RCs may believe, and the need for those with RC training in these practice settings continues to grow. In its first practice-wide salary survey of rehabilitation counseling, the CRCC (2008) documented that FRCs are paid at a higher rate than any other RC specialty. The average salary for an RC in any setting was $50,000 annually; for those in forensic practice, the average annual salary was $93,000; for those RCs employed in settings such as workers' compensation agencies, private/proprietary rehabilitation, or private practice, average earnings ranged from $58,000 to $74,000 annually (2008). Early data analysis from the 2021 CRCC compensation survey suggested that this wage differential between the average salary for rehabilitation counselors and those in forensics or private practice continues (P. Shlemon, personal communication, February 3, 2022). This chapter identifies the origins of forensic and indirect service provision at the very start of the rehabilitation counseling profession over a century ago, and traces its growth and trajectory to its continued spread and growth today. The settings, methods, techniques, resources, and ethics of FRC practice also are identified.

HISTORY OF FORENSIC AND INDIRECT SERVICES

The history of forensic rehabilitation and indirect service provision in rehabilitation counseling has often been assumed to be a modern phenomenon emerging with the current or immediately prior generation of practitioners. This impression is incorrect. In fact, the need for practitioners to answer the kinds of questions and provide the kinds of services typically addressed today by forensic practitioners can be traced back as far as the mid- to late 1800s. At that time, issues of just compensation for loss of the ability to work due to personal injuries were being addressed by juries in cases involving workers and injuries in railroad transportation during the Industrial Revolution (Barros-Bailey, 2014).

By the first decade of the 1900s when the first known counselor, Frank Parsons (1909), was writing *Choosing a Vocation*, states began enacting legislation for no-fault coverage of injuries at work, called **workers' compensation laws**. These laws produced questions that could not be determined just by the administrative rules enacted by such legislation but were argued in hearings before administrative law bodies and appealed into higher courts by the interested parties. The trier of fact attempted to establish a precedent of how the law should be applied in practice. For example, in 1919 the Supreme Court of Illinois ruled on fair compensation for an injured worker in *The Peabody Coal Company v. The Industrial Commission et al.* (Peabody, 1919) case, appealed from lower courts. This is also the first case in which an expert witness is found to testify on identical issues addressed by FRCs today. Specifically, the case stated that "the employer contended that the testimony of the employee's expert witnesses that his partial disability permanently impaired his earning capacity 25 percent was inadmissible because it was an ultimate issue of fact before the arbitrator and the Commission" (Sec. Case Summary, para. 2). From references in case law, it appears that early expert witnesses providing testimony in these kinds of compensation cases were physicians.

The Illinois Supreme Court ruled on the *Peabody* case the year before the Smith-Fess Act (1920) was enacted that provided counseling, training, prosthetic appliances, and job placement for people with physical disabilities from work injuries. In the Smith–Fess Act, the initial definition of who qualified for services was expanded. Thus, that act subsequently created the need and structure for what would become the federal–state rehabilitation program of today. In this process, Tracy Copp and William Faulkes from the Wisconsin industrial rehabilitation system brought their expertise of working in the rehabilitation of injured workers to the national capital to spread the philosophy and practice of rehabilitation to all people with disabilities across the nation. Workers' compensation legislation in the civilian sector was concurrent with similar legislation for World War I veterans from 1914 through 1918 (War Risk Insurance Act, 1914); Smith-Hughes Act (1917); and the Smith-Sears Act (1918).

These developments created the need for a new kind of professional. This new practitioner would understand function resulting from physical, mental, and cognitive conditions within the context of the major functions of living (e.g., employment) and develop interventions (e.g., training, aids for independent functioning) to help bridge and maximize opportunities for that individual with a disability. RCs were uniquely qualified not only to work in the delivery of services across silos of other disciplines, such as medicine and psychology, but also to apply that knowledge base to questions addressed in the courts by physicians.

The intermarriage between the industrial rehabilitation system and the public rehabilitation system and the application to forensic practice is evident in historical records documenting such relationships beginning in the late 1920s (Barros-Bailey, 2014). Indeed, by the mid-1930s, RCs from the federal–state rehabilitation system were being used as expert witnesses on lump-sum settlement decisions involving injured workers (Dawson, 1936).

Although the inception of RCs used as expert witnesses is documented in the literature and cases from the late 1920s, such use expanded slowly for 30 years. The boom in the practice of forensic rehabilitation started in the early 1960s as a result of two acts by Congress a half decade earlier. The first legislation enacted was the Vocational Rehabilitation Act of 1954, which professionalized rehabilitation counseling through graduate education and research. The second was the U.S. Social Security Act Amendments of 1956, which integrated disability into its covered benefits. In 1960, the Second Circuit Court of Appeals decided, in *Kerner v. Fleming*, that the U.S. Social Security Administration (SSA) had the burden of proof as to a claimant's disability (Kerner, 1960). The source for such expert witness testimony was readily found in a well-educated and prepared professional: the RC. By 1962, the *Kerner* criteria swelled the need for vocational expert testimony to 10,000 instances per month and the U.S. Social Security Administration established a formal program for using vocational expert witness testimony in the disability adjudication process.

Attorneys representing clients attempting to qualify for U.S. Social Security disability benefits suddenly were exposed to RCs in a forensic arena in substantial numbers. The legal representatives recognized the usefulness of the FRC's skill set for cases in other jurisdictions. This recognition began the expansion of FRC retention outside the historical workers' compensation and U.S. Social Security social insurance settings, to a larger continuum of cases: bankruptcy law; civil injury; employment law (e.g., Age Discrimination in Employment Act, the ADA and its amendments, the Federal and Medical Leave Act, the Individuals with Disabilities Education Act), insurance (credit disability, life, liability, no-fault automobile, short/long-term disability), marital dissolution, pension funds, student loan default, tort (the Jones Act, the Longshore Act, the Railroad Retirement Board/Federal Employees Liability Act), trust fund management, and more (Barros-Bailey, 2014).

Those vocational experts filling the needs of the U.S. SSA and other sources came primarily from rehabilitation counseling. However, the vast demand for the number of experts outstripped the number of RCs available to provide services. As a result, other professionals were recruited to provide vocational expert witness testimony, such as psychologists (particularly from vocational and rehabilitation specialties), counselors (e.g., career), nurses (e.g., rehabilitation), occupational therapists, and other adjunct professions. Some of these professionals were already in private practice in clinical specialties. Others were practicing in government or industry and were drawn to a different application of their skill set.

As the forensic rehabilitation and indirect service sector expanded in the 1970s and 1980s, FRCs sought opportunities to connect and discuss issues particular to the growing practice setting. New organizations were formed such as the American Board of Vocational Experts and the National Association of Rehabilitation Professionals in the Private Sector (now called the International Association of Rehabilitation Professionals [IARP]), or sections of existing organizations were formed (e.g., National Association of Service Providers in Private Rehabilitation with the National Rehabilitation Association). These groups created a platform where FRCs could connect not only about the business mechanics of practice, such as marketing, insurance, and paraprofessional staffing, but also on advocacy, training, and self-regulation (e.g., ethics, standards of practice).

THE LEGAL AND SYSTEMIC CONTEXT

A detailed review of the legal and systemic context in which an FCR or indirect service provider may practice is beyond the scope of this chapter. The reader is directed to the "Introduction to the American Legal System and Rules of Civil Procedure: A Primer for Vocational Experts" by Patrick Dunn (2014) or any contemporary survey of the legal context of practice within the jurisdiction(s) in which the RC practices. Generally, an understanding of how the courts are structured and the jurisdiction is delineated at various local, regional, or national levels; the venue; procedural rules; and the FRC's place with the structure, jurisdiction, or system are recommended (Dunn, 2014).

In any case, the FRC can be asked to be a testifying expert, where the FRC's involvement is disclosed as an **expert retained for litigation** to offer opinions; or as an **expert not retained for litigation**, such as an RC who provides direct service, but who will not be providing expert opinions but testifying about factual knowledge.

The FRC could be asked to serve as a **consulting expert**; in this instance their involvement in the case is never divulged to anyone outside of the retaining party. As a consulting expert, the FRC provides indirect services that may involve a review of the data and evidence in the case to assist the retaining party to prepare or deliver a strategy. In some circumstances, the FRC could be hired for indirect services that are not related specifically to forensic issues or do not involve direct contact with the evaluee. Examples are performing a labor market analysis after a chef acquired a mild traumatic brain injury in an automobile accident resulting in anosmia (loss of smell), providing second opinions as to rates of disability or interventions for someone who injured their back on the job as a concrete finisher, assisting the retaining party to identify the merits of a case based on a review of the evidence of a student who is defaulting on a student loan after sustaining a spinal cord injury, or any other related service that may be within the FRC's general or individual scope of practice.

Vocational Expert Testimony

RCs in forensic and indirect service practice typically are hired to provide opinions as to the vocational losses, capacities, or potential interventions for an individual given an acquired condition anywhere along the life span from birth (e.g., wrongful birth cases) to natural or traumatic death (e.g., wrongful death cases). For example, the RC may evaluate the earning capacity of a kindergartener with mixed-type cerebral palsy in a claim against the obstetrician for a family in which the parents come from multiple generations of construction painters and the next day evaluate an 80-year-old woman who continued to work as a paralegal because she loved what she did and then sustained an amputation of her dominant hand fingers from a freak accident while she was shredding documents at work. Each system or jurisdiction where FRCs work has separate rules. Knowing the rules in each system is important so FRCs are not using standards or criteria for the development of an opinion that do not correspond to the system in which they are providing services. For example, because someone is found to be qualified for disability benefits under the criteria of the SSDI program does not mean that, given the same exact facts, the individual would likewise be considered equally qualified as disabled under a state's workers' compensation program or by a jury in a personal injury case, because the decision-making criteria for each jurisdiction is different. In U.S. Social Security disability adjudication, the vocational expert generally cannot take into consideration issues of accommodation, training capacity or current engagement, or another intervention plan. However, these interventions can be part of the opinions provided by FRCs in other systems and may even be expected if the plaintiff has a duty to mitigate damages. Knowing the difference between systems is imperative if the FRC is to provide the appropriate services to the evaluee. A few of the most prominent jurisdictions employing FRCs are covered in this chapter.

Civil Injury Litigation

Civil injury litigation is based on a concept that citizens have basic rights as proclaimed through guiding societal documents such as the Bill of Rights or the Massachusetts Body of Liberties (Robinson & Drew, 2014a). The basic principles of civil injury litigation come from these fundamental principles of common law to protect individuals from unjustified harm (Robinson & Drew, 2014a).

The practice areas in civil injury litigation include personal injury, product liability, and professional malpractice. The common vocational issues to be addressed by the FRC include loss of earning capacity, interventions (rehabilitation plan covering services and products to restore the evaluee to maximum vocational capacity based on their residual functional capacities), and damage mitigation efforts (Robinson & Drew, 2014a). Where preexisting or other confounding factors exist in a case, the FRC may be asked to apportion an opinion as to capacity of losses or costs of interventions between incident-specific and non-incident factors—the proverbial splitting of hairs in forensic practice. Let's say that someone who sustained a low-level complete paraplegia is not adequately secured onto a gurney while at an imaging service getting a chest x-ray and falls, thereby sustaining a higher level legion at the cervical spine resulting tetraplegia and the inability to independently transfer, catheterize, drive, and so on. The FRC must consider what vocational and other needs the individual had as a paraplegic before becoming a tetraplegic, not what needs the evaluee had before the first spinal cord injury occurred.

FRCs practicing in civil injury law have very little probability of going to trial. The American Bar Association estimated in 1962 that 11.5% of cases made it to trial (Refo, 2004). Currently, the literature is inconclusive regarding what number of cases actually get to trial. What is clear is that the number has declined significantly in the last six decades. About 95% cases resolve by settlement (Eisenberg & Lanvers, 2009), while others are dismissed. One estimate has the number of cases going to trial dropping to 1.8% (Refo, 2004). In some states, such as Florida, by 2010–2011, fewer than 0.2% of cases went to trial (Williams, 2013).

Employment Law

Over the last century, employment law legislation has followed a trajectory starting with the rise of labor regulation, wage and hour laws, antidiscrimination laws, protected leave and whistleblower protection at the state and national levels (Heitzman et al., 2014). The role of the FRC in this type of case is to "evaluate mitigation of damages and issues such as reasonableness of job search, duration of unemployment, existence of career damage, impact on earning capacity, and job accommodations" (Heitzman et al., p. 377).

In this setting, it is likely that the FRC may be asked to testify on both liability and damages sides of a case. **Liability issues** in a case involve *what happened* that was purportedly negligent, or often what is referred to as the incident that resulted in assumed injuries. **Damages issues** in a case do not consider the cause of the incident, but attempt to measure the *impact* of the losses created by the assumed incident. An example is a FRC who is retained as an expert witness to opine in an ADA case on the kinds of accommodations someone who is deaf or hard of hearing could have received on the job to perform the essential functions of a position from which they were discharged. For the same evaluee, the FRC may evaluate whether there was any earning capacity lost from the alleged wrongful dismissal. The first set of opinions are in the causation side of a case whereas the second set of opinions are in the damages side. Most often, however, FRCs are hired to give opinions about damages and should stay away from the liability issues of a case unless qualified to provide such opinions such as in this ADA example.

Marital Dissolution

When a couple agrees to legally separate their lives and their assets, sometimes issues of compensation or support of a spouse arise and must be evaluated. Even after they have been divorced for a while, job or labor-market changes may change what someone earns and how much they could pay in child or spousal support. Kohlenberg (2014) outlined the essential services in the marital dissolution analysis performed by an FRC as involving (a) an earning capacity evaluation, (b) labor-market research, and (c) vocational planning, which would be this system's version of the intervention or rehabilitation plan. The four areas of further consideration by an FRC as outlined by Kohlenberg are reentry problems, such as when the spouse has not worked in years and does not know what they could or want to do; disability concerns that affect vocational functioning and choice; motivation questions that may be inconsistent with the evaluee's capacities; and possessing unrealistic expectations of support through prolonged training. Kohlenberg also identified other factors that could affect the evaluation, such as someone's ability to participate in the labor market and self-employment tax returns that suggest actual profits lower than someone's earning capacity. Special evaluation issues in marital dissolution cases may involve health, accommodations, location, language/culture, age, and childcare or related costs (Kohlenberg). Example of cases may be a couple who met in college and married immediately upon graduation of their mechanical engineering degrees. One spouse decides to go to medical school to become a neurosurgeon and the other spouse becomes the stay-at-home parent and never works as a mechanical engineer. As their twin children graduate from high school, the couple finds they are no longer compatible and file for divorce. The RC receives a referral to evaluate what the spouse who has not worked in almost two decades can earn with or without additional training as well as develop a plan to return to work. Many of the cases in family law do not involve the evaluation of someone with a disability. However, others do and may require an FRC with additional training as a life care planner to determine the amount of care someone with a disability may need after a divorce to assist in determining the separation of assets.

U.S. Social Security Disability

Vercillo (2014) outlined the factors the FRC considers when presented with hypothetical questions at a disability adjudication hearing. Under U.S. Social Security disability law, the vocational factors considered in decisions regarding someone's capacity to work include age, education, and work experience as well as the claimant's level of skill within the context of strength or exertional levels and non-exertional physical and mental requirements (Vercillo).

These factors are adjudicated within the **Five-Step Sequential Evaluation Process**. The first three steps of the process include whether the claimant (a) is working or engaged in substantial gainful activity, (b) has a severe medically determinable impairment, and (c) the impairment meets or equals a medical listing (U.S. Social Security Administration, 2012,). The FRC's input is relevant at the last two steps of that process, which are whether the individual can do their past work as they performed and as it is generally performed in the labor market (Step 4), or whether the individual could perform other work in the labor market (Step 5). Sometimes, these last two steps in the process are also evident in short- and long-term disability systems and are referred to as the **own occ** (own occupation) or **any occ** (any occupation) decision. For example, an SSA vocational expert may need to determine whether a nurse's aide who sustained bilateral shoulder injuries when lifting a patient and now has a 20-pound lifting restriction can do their past relevant work as an aide (Step 4), or any unskilled or semiskilled job in the competitive labor market (Step 5).

Workers' Compensation

Workers' compensation cases are the first cases found in the literature in which FRC involvement became evident. However, because workers' compensation laws are different in each state, territory, or country, the variability between the jurisdictional requirements is the most difficult to generalize.

Broadly, the process of returning someone to work falls into an **order and priority model**. This model has been associated with two conditions that anchor a range. One end of the range contains the shortest and most effective means to return to work using the most accessible resources, skills, and conditions, and assumes the lowest risk and cost. On the other end of the range are the least accessible or newest resources, skills, and conditions that contain the highest risk and costs. Although the origins of the following model have been lost to history and the detail and depth of the model may change between systems or countries, the general components of a workers' compensation return-to-work model include the following:

- Same job, same employer (with or without accommodation)
- Different job, same employer (transferability of skill and/or with or without accommodation)

- Different job, different employer (transferability of skill, with or without accommodation, and/or new skill acquisition)
- Retraining (new shortor long-term skill acquisition)
- Self-employment (transferability of skill, with or without accommodation, with or without short- or long-term skill acquisition, often require financial and consultative or other supports)

In some jurisdictions, participation in vocational rehabilitation services is mandatory (e.g., federal Office of Workers' Compensation Programs). In most systems, however, participation is voluntary, or perhaps is not offered at all. In some jurisdictions, there is little room for forensic expert services, but great demand for direct or indirect service provisions. For example, the private-sector RC might receive a referral to perform a job analysis of the work an injured janitor did or a labor-market survey for specific occupations the janitor could do given a foot amputation resulting from the industrial injury. In many workers' compensation system, these may be some of the many services provided to the janitor, while others could be vocational psychometric testing, adjustment counseling, vocational exploration, developing a return-to-work plan along the order and priority model, and monitoring after the evaluee has resumed work activity. In other systems, the greatest demand may be for forensic and indirect services, such as determining if someone has the capacity to work at all based on the rules of that jurisdiction. It is important to understand the idiosyncrasies of any jurisdiction where an FRC practices. What is standard across all workers' compensation systems internationally, however, is that the evaluee has an acquired physical, mental, and/or cognitive condition based in part or in total due to their engagement in work covered by the workers' compensation laws of that jurisdiction.

Life Care Planning

A subspecialty in forensic rehabilitation counseling is life care planning, which merits mention in any discussion of forensic rehabilitation practice. **Life care planning** is best described as an extension of the intervention or care plan commonly mainly found in traditional rehabilitation counseling and nursing. In this case the case plan is expanded to cover probable future needs in the areas of evaluation, therapies, diagnostics, medications, mobility, equipment, supplies, nutrition, transportation, attendant services, adapted recreation, invasive procedures, architectural retrofitting, or other areas of need. Deutsch and Sawyer (2005) often are credited with creating and formalizing the method and practice of modern-day life care planning. Along with colleagues in the nursing profession (Riddick-Grisham, 2011), they have professionalized the subspecialty and developed it to its contemporary form that includes a multitude of professionals from other allied health specialties, such as nursing, occupational therapy, orthotics and prosthetics, physiatry, physical therapy, physician assistants, psychology, recreation, speech and language pathology, and many others. Postsecondary or graduate certificate programs have existed in this subspecialty since the mid-1990s. These programs provide further training, mentoring, and supervision to develop this individual scope of practice (Box 16.1).

COMPONENTS OF FORENSIC OR INDIRECT SERVICE PRACTICE METHODS

Beyond the history and context of forensic and indirect service practice and the role of the FRC within that practice, the process of how the FRC performs these services merits discussion.

> ### BOX 16.1 CASE CONCEPTUALIZATION
>
> An example of a medical malpractice case involving an RC life care planner could be of a 40-year-old parent of four working as an electronics technician who sustained quadrilateral amputations as a result of a misdiagnosis and delayed treatment of a staph infection. The life care planner could collaborate with members of the treatment of damages team to develop a plan of care for the various areas of medical, vocational, and avocational needs sufficient to function and return as much as possible to the personal and family lifestyle enjoyed at the time of the incident.

Evidence-Based Practice

Elaborating on a typology of evidence in case study research introduced by Yin (2017), Barros-Bailey (2018) refined the evidence model as it applies to clinical or forensic practice in any setting in which a single individual ($N = 1$) is the subject of service provision or an evaluation. The model has two main components falling into **primary data** (collected by the FRC) and **secondary data** (collected by someone other than the FRC) categories. Each domain has three subdomains:

- Primary
  - *Interviews* (structured, semistructured, unstructured, informal, focus)
  - *Observation* (experimentation, psychometric assessment (Robinson & Drew, 2014b)
  - *Participant observation* (FRC as part of the observation, such as performing the tasks of a job while collecting data for a job analysis; Paquette & Heitzman, 2014)
- Secondary
  - *Documents* (medical, psychological, school, employment, legal, peer-reviewed articles, standards of care or practice, and so forth)
  - *Archival* (raw data not interpreted by any source, such as databases from government agencies)
  - *Physical artifacts* (e.g., durable medical equipment, artwork, or other work product)

Thomas (2011) explained that **data** are individual units of information, whereas **evidence** is the use of the data in support of a proposition, a position, or an opinion. Through content analysis using the Yin model of evidence types, evidence was found to include any data source used in an individualized assessment in clinical or forensic practice (Barros-Bailey, 2018, 2022). The evidence model may be useful for any FRC, indirect service, or clinical practitioner to consider when determining the depth or breadth of evidence contained or needed for an assessment. With some aspects of document and archival evidence, understanding and interpreting rehabilitation research is a pivotal part of evidence-based practice (Reid, 2014). An RC or FRC might use the model to demonstrate how the information collected through meetings with the client, family, or providers (primary data) is consistent or inconsistent with data collected by other individuals and provided in medical records, peer-reviewed articles, and so on (secondary data) and combines to provide internal consistency to the individualized assessment. One of the predominant questions that an FRC or indirect service provider is asked to answer revolves around vocational capacity along some timeline spanning birth to death. Robinson (2014) documented the 20 models published since the early 1980s that provide structural frameworks to help guide such an analysis. A review of the models (Barros-Bailey, 2022) suggested that they fall into three categories. **Content models** indicate what constructs or elements should be contained in the analysis, such as social, vocational, and educational histories, and physical, mental, or cognitive abilities and function. **Process models** may imply the content but never directly note or reference it, instead focusing on the processes of the evaluation, such as performing a transferable skills analysis (Field & Dunn, 2014), including occupational information (Barros-Bailey & Karman, 2014; Barros-Bailey & Robinson, 2012), or performing labor-market research (Barros-Bailey & Heitzman, 2014). However, most are **hybrid models** that include both content and process elements.

In clinical analysis, such as for clinical RCs, it is important to understand and articulate a personal counseling approach. In forensic and indirect service provision, it is also important to review the different models of analysis, determine the model that fits the jurisdiction or system or approach by the FRC, and consciously study and adopt the use of such a model. At some point in an FRC's career, they may have their testimony challenged as inadmissible (called a **motion in limine**); therefore, careful research, selection, and application of the model are recommended. Variations from any published model based on either systemic or specific case needs should be carefully thought out and justified.

Residual Functional Capacity and the Forensic Analysis

A diagnosis does not necessarily result in a prescribed functional outcome, but may be associated with a series of outcomes that may or may not apply to a specific evaluee. Therefore, understanding medical evidence and residual functional capacity is an essential component of a forensic analysis (Paquette & Lacerte, 2014). For example, someone with a traumatic brain injury could have single or multiple functional outcomes that are physical (e.g., loss of vision or olfactory senses), mental (e.g., adjustment issues, disinhibition), or cognitive (e.g., attention, distraction, memory, executive functioning, social cognition). The FRC may rely on those professionals who are trained to measure and opine on specific functions to provide the foundation on which the FRC depends for their projective vocational or disability opinion. Diagnoses alone likely are insufficient information to obtain from the qualified professionals, such as therapists, neuropsychologists, or physicians, if those diagnoses also do not describe the functional outcomes in terms of limitations or restrictions. The difference between **limitations** and **restrictions** is not always understood. For example, let us assume that I wear prism glasses for double vision (diplopia). Although my ophthalmologist may not restrict my vision, I have an obvious limitation in that function. Therefore, someone may have a limitation in a function although no medical, psychological, or other specialist provides a specific restriction to engage in the activity.

How these functional outcomes relate to a forensic or indirect service analysis rests upon the conceptual principles and standards that underlie such an analysis. Many of these principles relate to concepts, measures, or proxies of vocational functioning adopted by the U.S. DOL (*Dictionary of Occupational Titles*; 1991a; and *Revised Handbook for Analyzing Jobs*; 1991b) and the U.S. Social Security Administration, with the following as the core concepts:

- **Cognitive ability**: Aptitudes to perform work activity have often been used as a proxy for cognitive function or in types of intelligence (U.S. DOL, 1991a, 1991b).
- **Reasoning development:** Levels of mathematical, language, and reasoning development based on academic curricula (U.S. DOL, 1991a, 1991b).
- **Skill:** How long it takes for an individual to acquire the skill through training, experience, or other means to perform a work activity; this is often referred to as Specific Vocational Preparation (U.S. DOL, 1991a, 1991b) and is clustered into descriptors called unskilled, semiskilled, and skilled work activity (U.S. Social Security Administration, 1978).

A host of other factors may be relevant, depending on the individual analysis, such as dexterity, values, personality, or interests.

Temporal aspects of the analysis are often a consideration. These typically are tied to timelines of when (frequency and duration estimates) someone is engaged in the labor market over their life, called **work-life expectancy** (Barrett et al., 2014) and levels of tenure. Someone who may have had an average level of labor-market participation pre-incident may have functional or treatment issues resulting in altered rates of participation post-incident, leading to a reduced ability to participate in the labor market with more turnover in jobs and more periods of unemployment between jobs.

Clinical Judgment

Clinical judgment in forensics is not a subjective distal inference, guess, or opinion. Faust and Nurcombe (1989) stated that clinical judgment is not specific to the decision-making process, but rather to a method of judgment. Clinical judgment is not a belief that is devoid of evidence that can be skewed by biases and errors (Barros-Bailey & Beveridge, 2015). Rather, it starts with a knowledge base of qualitative and quantitative data (Barros-Bailey & Neulicht, 2005). It evaluates the relevance of such data, determines if it is a factor for the individual, and whether it provides evidence leading to a conclusion and opinion. There is no preconception of the outcome; rather, the clinical judgment process involves data integration using inherent validity and reliability criteria (e.g., data saturation, member checking) to arrive at findings, conclusions, opinions, and/or recommendations (Barros-Bailey & Neulicht, 2005; Choppa et al., 2004, 2014; Field et al., 2009; Strohmer & Leierer, 2000).

TEAMS IN FORENSIC AND INDIRECT SERVICES

Much like FRCs in clinical and primary care practice are accustomed to working as members of a team, so, too, do FRCs belong to a team in forensic and indirect services. Who is included on the team revolves around the system or jurisdiction and the scopes of practice of those retained by the referral source. The FRC's ultimate conclusions are projective based on assumptions of physical, mental, and cognitive function in vocational and related areas of capacity. Therefore, unless the FRC has an individual scope of practice that allows them to give opinions about function (e.g., holds dual credentials as physical therapist and an RC, a neuropsychologist and an RC), a qualified professional providing those underlying functional opinions is an important addition to the team. In some systems, such as in civil injury litigation, a **forensic economist** may be a team member. This professional takes the FRC's opinions and applies growth and discount rates to arrive at present-value calculations of projected losses (Brookshire, 2014). Other members of the team are often physiatrists for physical conditions or neuropsychologists for cognitive or mental conditions.

ETHICS IN FORENSICS

A discussion regarding forensic and indirect services in rehabilitation counseling would be incomplete without addressing the ethical issues inherent in the practice. The first known reference included in rehabilitation counseling codes of ethics specific to forensics was in the 1981 IARP *Standards and Ethics* (Barros-Bailey & Carlisle, 2014). This mention called for FRCs to remain within their scopes of practice and set standards for the permissibility of providing opinions on individuals who have been examined in person or hypothetically. This initial reference evolved in the mid-1980s to an expectation that FRCs will provide objective opinions regardless of who retains the FRC's services and avoid conflicts of interest that may introduce bias, such as accepting a case on a contingency basis (Barros-Bailey, 2014).

In 2010, the CRCC created a stand-alone section to its code of ethics for forensic and indirect services (Section F). The section was modified slightly in the recently revised code but remains an early and innovative addition to the understanding of the ethical obligations of all counselors working in forensic areas. Forensic ethics standards in the 2017 code are classified in the following categories:

- *Client and evaluee rights* (primary obligations, informed consent, role changes, consultation)
- *Forensic competency and conduct* (objectivity, qualification to provide expert testimony, avoiding potentially harmful relationships, conflict of interest, validity of resources consulted, foundation of knowledge, duty to confirm information, and review/critique of opposing work product)
- *Forensic practices* (case acceptance and independent opinion, and termination of assignment transfer)
- *Forensic business practices* (payments and outcome, and fee disputes)

The first significant change in the current revision includes the removal of the term **indirect services** and the inclusion of a standard on consultation. The similarity between indirect services and FRC practice is that in either instance there exists no client–counselor relationship. However, indirect services are not necessarily performed in a forensic setting. When an FRC is hired to perform services on a forensic case, but the FRC's presence will not be disclosed, and there is no expectation of the FRC providing testimony, the practice is considered **forensic consultation**.

The second significant change to Section F in the 2017 code is the removal of the confidentiality standard. Privilege exists between the client and the attorney, but not between the FRC and the evaluee. However, the CRCC's action is not to be construed that confidentiality does not exist in forensic practice. Counselors just need to understand the limits of confidentiality, as they would in any other practice setting, and be able to explain such limits through disclosure and informed consent. Indeed, the Section of Litigation of the American Bar Association (2011) cleared any doubts on the issue of confidentiality with expert witnesses with the *Standards of Conduct for Experts Retained by Lawyers*. This document indicated that only as required by law or by consent of a client or advisement by a retaining attorney would the expert be able to break confidentiality.

In their review of CRCC complaints, Hartley and Cartwright (2015) noted that 10.4% of these between 2006 and 2013 were related to forensic and indirect services. The violations reported by the authors involved primary obligations; unbiased opinions; objective opinions; assessment instrument selection and interpretation; critique of the opposing FRC's work product; conflicts of interest; and failure to disclose role and role limitations. Additional research performed by Hartley and Cartwright (2016) among CRCs found that 9.1% of identified dilemmas fell into forensics and evaluation, which is fairly consistent with the rate of actual complaints over the previous decade. Given the continued expansion of forensics and indirect service provision and the adversarial nature of many systems in which FRCs practice, continued attention to and training in ethics for current and emerging professionals are advised.

The CRCC's treatment of forensic and indirect service ethics is the most comprehensive in any counseling specialty. By comparison, the ACA's *Code of Ethics* (2014) has five standards where forensic practice is mentioned, four of these within the "Forensic Evaluation: Evaluation for Legal Proceedings" section. The section covers primary obligations, consent for evaluation, evaluation prohibited with current or former clients or their partners or family members, and avoiding potentially harmful relationships. The fifth standard involves the purpose of information gathering in assessment.

CONCLUSION

Forensic and indirect service delivery in rehabilitation counseling has existed for nearly a century and uses traditional vocational rehabilitation counseling principles. The practice started in workers' compensation adjudication and expanded within social insurance to the U.S. Social Security disability system in 1960. Since the 1960s, forensic rehabilitation has spread further to a variety of other jurisdictions and systems, such as civil injury litigation, employment law, marital dissolution, and life care planning.

Because FRCs provide expertise based on their specialized knowledge in rehabilitation and disability in legal settings, their services are expected to involve evidence-based procedures through collected primary and reviewed secondary data. These specialists discern and use case conceptualization models appropriate to the analysis and integrate qualitative and quantitative data through clinical judgment processes to arrive at opinions and/or offer recommendations. Forensic rehabilitation professionals may work in teams with other forensic disciplines and are expected to have strong analytical and research skills. Forensic ethics expectations involve evaluee rights, strong competencies, disclosed conflicts, and appropriate business practices and can be a challenge for those working in what are often adversarial systems.

CONTENT REVIEW QUESTIONS

1. How can the century of experiences in forensic rehabilitation contribute to other counseling specialties' development of respective forensic applications within their scopes of practice?
2. What would be some decision-making criteria that an FRC could use when deciding what earning capacity model to adopt in a civil litigation matter? In a workers' compensation matter? If the existing models do not fit the needed application precisely, how should the FRC proceed?
3. An FRC begins work on a case as a consulting expert not retained for litigation and is not disclosed to the opposing parties. After some initial work on the case, the opposing party contacts the FRC to retain them as a testifying expert on the same case. How should the FRC handle the situation?
4. As a newcomer to the rehabilitation counseling specialty, what resources might you explore to enter forensic or indirect service practice settings?
5. What do you anticipate might be the greatest challenges or opportunities for those working in forensic rehabilitation and indirect service provision in the future?

REFERENCES

American Bar Association, Section of Litigation. (2011). *Standards of conduct for experts retained by lawyers.* Author.

American Counseling Association. (2014). *Code of ethics.* https://www.counseling.org/resources/aca-code-of-ethics.pdf

Barrett, G., Jayne, K. A., & Robinson, R. H. (2014). Worklife expectancy models and concepts. In R. Robinson (Ed.), *Foundations of forensic vocational rehabilitation* (pp. 401–428). Springer Publishing.

Barros-Bailey, M. (2014). History of forensic vocational consulting. In R. Robinson (Ed.), *Foundations of forensic vocational rehabilitation* (pp. 13–31). Springer Publishing.

Barros-Bailey, M. (2018). An evidence source model for clinical and forensic practice. *The Rehabilitation Professional, 26*(3), 117–128.

Barros-Bailey, M. (2022). *A content analysis of the Federal Rules of Evidence using A case study research evidence typology.* Manuscript submitted for publication.

Barros-Bailey, M., & Beveridge, S. (2015). What is and is not clinical judgment in forensics? In *IARP Annual Conference on Unmask Your Potential: Connect. Grow, Learn—an Opportunity Jambalaya.*

Barros-Bailey, M., & Carlisle, J. (2014). Professional identity, standards, and ethical issues. In R. Robinson (Ed.), *Foundations of forensic vocational rehabilitation* (pp. 443–466). Springer Publishing.

Barros-Bailey, M., Carlisle, J., Graham, M., Neulicht, A. T., Taylor, R., & Wallace, A. (2008). Who is the client in forensics? [White paper]. Published in. *Published in: Estimating Earning Capacity, 1(2)*, 132–138; *Journal of Forensic Vocational Analysis, 12(1)*, 31–33; *Journal of Life Care Planning, 7(3)*, 125–132; *Journal of Rehabilitation Administration, 33(1)*, 59–64; *Rehabilitation Professional, 16(4)*, 253–256; *Rehabilitation Counselors and Educators Journal, 2(2)*, 2–6; and *Vocational Evaluation and Career Assessment Professionals Journal, 5(1)*, 8–14.

Barros-Bailey, M., & Heitzman, A. M. (2014). Labor market survey. In R. Robinson (Ed.), *Foundations of forensic vocational rehabilitation* (pp. 167–202). Springer Publishing.

Barros-Bailey, M., & Karman, S. (2014). Occupational and labor market information. In R. Robinson (Ed.), *Foundations of forensic vocational rehabilitation* (pp. 13–31). Springer Publishing.

Barros-Bailey, M., & Neulicht, A. (2005). Opinion validity: An integration of quantitative and qualitative data. *Rehabilitation Professional, 13(2)*, 32–41.

Barros-Bailey, M., & Robinson, R. (2012). 30 years of rehabilitation forensics: Inclusion of occupational and labor market information competencies in earning capacity models. *Rehabilitation Professional, 20(3)*, 157–166.

Brookshire, M. (2014). Issues in the handoff to a forensic economist. In R. Robinson (Ed.), *Foundations of forensic vocational rehabilitation* (pp. 429–442). Springer Publishing.

Cherner, R., Nandlal, J., Ecker, J., Aubry, T., & Pettey, D. (2013). Findings of a formative evaluation of a transitional housing program for forensic patients discharged into the community. *Journal of Offender Rehabilitation, 52(3)*, 157–180. https://doi.org/10.1080/10509674.2012.754826

Choppa, A., Johnson, C. B., Fountaine, J., Shafer, K., Jayne, K., Grimes, J. W., & Field, T. F. (2004). The efficacy of professional clinical judgment: Developing expert testimony in cases involving vocational rehabilitation and care planning issues. *Journal of Life Care Planning, 3(3)*, 131–150.

Choppa, A., Johnson, C. B., & Neulicht, A. T. (2014). Case conceptualization: Achieving opinion validity through the lens of clinical judgment. In R. Robinson (Ed.), *Foundations of forensic vocational rehabilitation* (pp. 261–278). Springer Publishing.

Cianciulli, J. M. (1993). The outpatient forensic substance abuse profile. *International Journal of Offender Therapy and Comparative Criminology, 37(3)*, 231–237. https://doi.org/10.1177/0306624X9303700304

Commission on Rehabilitation Counselor Certification. (2008). *2008 salary report: An update on salaries in the rehabilitation counseling profession.* https://www.crccertification.com/filebin/pdf/career-center/CRCcareers_SalaryReport.pdf

Commission on Rehabilitation Counselor Certification. (2010). *Code of professional ethics for rehabilitation counselors.* https://www.usf.edu/cbcs/cfs/documents/crc-code-of-ethics.pdf

Commission on Rehabilitation Counselor Certification. (2017). *Code of professional ethics for rehabilitation counselors.* https://crccertification.com/wp-content/uploads/2021/03/CRC_CodeEthics_Eff2017-FinaLnewdiesign.pdf

Dawson, M. (1936). Cooperation of workmen's compensation administrators with rehabilitation agencies. *Monthly Labor Review, 42*, 300–312.

Deutsch, P. M., & Sawyer, H. W. (2005). *Guide to rehabilitation.* AHAB Press.

DiCataldo, F., DeJesus, B., & Whitworth, D. (2021). Training needs of counseling trainees in corrections: A survey of clinical directors. *The Journal of Counselor Preparation and Supervision, 14(1)*. https://repository.wcsu.edu/jcps/vol14/iss1/2

Dickens, G., Sugarman, P., & Walker, L. (2007). HoNOS-secure: A reliable outcome measure for users of secure and forensic mental health services. *Journal of Forensic Psychiatry & Psychology, 18(4)*, 507–514. https://doi.org/10.1080/14789940701492279

Dunn, P. (2014). Introduction to the American legal system and rules of civil procedure: A primer for vocational experts. In R. Robinson (Ed.), *Foundations of forensic vocational rehabilitation* (pp. 239–260). Springer Publishing.

Eisenberg, T., & Lanvers, C. (2009). What is the settlement rate and why should we care? [Paper 203]. *Journal of Empirical Legal Studies, 6(1)*, 111–146. Cornell Law Faculty Publications. https://doi.org/10.1111/j.1740-1461.2009.01139.x

Faust, D., & Nurcombe, B. (1989). Improving the accuracy of clinical judgment. *Psychiatry, 52(2)*, 197–208. https://doi.org/10.1080/00332747.1989.11024443

Field, T. F., Choppa, A. J., & Weed, R. O. (2009). Clinical judgment: A working definition for the rehabilitation professional. *Rehabilitation Professional, 17(4)*, 185–194.

Field, T. F., & Dunn, P. L. (2014). Transferability of skills: Historical foundations and development. In R. Robinson (Ed.), *Foundations of forensic vocational rehabilitation* (pp. 133–144). Springer Publishing.

Gardner-Elahi, C., & Zamiri, S. (2015). Collective narrative practice in forensic mental health. *Journal of Forensic Practice, 17*(3), 204–218. https://doi.org/10.1108/JFP-10-2014-0034

Glassmire, D. M., Welsh, R. K., & Clevenger, J. K. (2007). The development of a substance abuse treatment program for forensic patients with cognitive impairment. *Journal of Addictions & Offender Counseling, 27*(2), 66–81. https://doi.org/10.1002/j.2161-1874.2007.tb00022.x

Hartley, M. T., & Cartwright, B. Y. (2015). Analysis of the reported ethical complaints and violations to the Commission on Rehabilitation Counselor Certification, 2006–2013. *Rehabilitation Counseling Bulletin, 58*(3), 154–164. https://doi.org/10.1177/0034355214543565

Hartley, M. T., & Cartwright, B. Y. (2016). A survey of current and projected ethical dilemmas of rehabilitation counselors. *Rehabilitation Research, Policy, and Education, 30*(1), 32–47. https://doi.org/10.1891/2168-6653.30.1.32

Heitzman, A. M., Amundsen, C., Gann, C., & Christensen, D. R. (2014). Consultation in employment law. In R. Robinson (Ed.), *Foundations of forensic vocational rehabilitation* (pp. 363–378). Springer Publishing.

Jasper, A., Smith, C., & Bailey, S. (1998). One hundred girls in care referred to an adolescent forensic mental health service. *Journal of Adolescence, 21*(5), 555–568. https://doi.org/10.1006/jado.1998.0177

Kerner, V. (1960). Fleming, 283 F.2d 916. https://doi.org/10.1136/bmj.2.5203.916

Kohlenberg, B. (2014). Consultation in marital dissolution and family law. In R. Robinson (Ed.), *Foundations of forensic vocational rehabilitation* (pp. 341–361). Springer Publishing.

Larson, K., DiCataldo, F., & Kinscherff, R. (2013). Miller v. Alabama: Implications for forensic mental health assessment at the intersection of social science and the law. *Criminal and Civil Confinement, 39*, 319–345.

Livingston, J. D., Nijdam-Jones, A., & Team, P. E. E. R. (2013). Perceptions of treatment planning in A forensic mental health hospital: A qualitative participatory action research study. *International Journal of Forensic Mental Health, 12*(1), 42–52. https://doi.org/10.1080/14999013.2013.763390

National Association of Forensic Counselors. (2022). *The origination of the forensic counselor and criminal justice specialist.* Retrieved October 4, 2016 from. http://www.forensiccounselor.org/?Home__About_NAFC_and_the_Origination_of_the_Forensic_Counselor

Paquette, S., & Heitzman, A. M. (2014). Job analysis. In R. Robinson (Ed.), *Foundations of forensic vocational rehabilitation* (pp. 145–166). Springer Publishing.

Paquette, S., & Lacerte, M. (2014). Medical evidence and residual functional capacity. In R. Robinson (Ed.), *Foundations of forensic vocational rehabilitation* (pp. 63–87). Springer Publishing.

Parsons, F. (1909). *Choosing a vocation.* Houghton Mifflin.

Peabody Coal Co. v the Industrial Commission et al. (1919). 289 Ill. 353, 124 N.E. 552.

Pinter, D. (1999). Forensic counseling: Collection of data and effective counseling. *Forensic Examiner, 5–6*, 39.

Refo, P. L. (2004). Opening statement: The vanishing trial. *Litigation, 30*(2), 2–4. https://www.americanbar.org/publications/litigation_journal/2016-17/winter.html

Reid, C. (2014). Interpreting rehabilitation research. In R. Robinson (Ed.), *Foundations of forensic vocational rehabilitation* (pp. 279–296). Springer Publishing.

Riddick-Grisham, S. (2011). *Pediatric life care planning and case management* (2nd ed.). Routledge. https://doi.org/10.1201/b10844

Robinson, R. H. (2014). Forensic rehabilitation and vocational earning capacity models. In R. Robinson (Ed.), *Foundations of forensic vocational rehabilitation* (pp. 33–62). Springer Publishing.

Robinson, R. H., & Drew, J. L. (2014a). Consultation in civil injury litigation. In R. Robinson (Ed.), *Foundations of forensic vocational rehabilitation* (pp. 325–339). Springer Publishing.

Robinson, R. H., & Drew, J. L. (2014b). Psychometric assessment in forensic vocational rehabilitation. In R. Robinson (Ed.), *Foundations of forensic vocational rehabilitation* (pp. 87–132). Springer Publishing.

Ryan, E. S. (1999). Forensic counseling: To be or not to be. *Forensic Examiner, 8*(11–12), 34.

Ryan, E. S. (2003). Forensic counseling: A new approach to school crime. *Education, 124*(2), 219–222.

Smith-Fess Act. (1920). Pub. L. no.66–236.

Smith-Hughes Act. (1917). Pub. L. no.64–347.

Smith-Sears Act. (1918). Pub. L. No. 65–178.

Strohmer, D. C., & Leierer, S. J. (2000). Modeling rehabilitation counselor clinical judgment. *Rehabilitation Counseling Bulletin, 44*(1), 3–9. https://doi.org/10.1177/003435520004400102

Suarez, J. M., Weston, N. L., & Hartstein, N. B. (1978). Mental health interventions in divorce proceedings. *The American Journal of Orthopsychiatry, 48*(2), 273–283. https://doi.org/10.1111/j.1939-0025.1978.tb01315.x

Thomas, G. (2011). *How to do your case study: A guide for students and researchers.* Sage.

Thurman, M. T., Wortzel, H. S., & Martinez, R. (2011). Mental health evaluation/counseling as a special condition of supervised release. *Journal of the American Academy of Psychiatry and the Law, 39*(3), 432–434.

Travis, R. W., & Sturmey, P. (2013). Using behavioural skills training to treat aggression in adults with mild intellectual disability in a forensic setting. *Journal of Applied Research in Intellectual Disabilities, 26*(5), 481–488. https://doi.org/10.1111/jar.12033

U.S. Department of Labor, Employment and Training Administration. (1991a). *Dictionary of occupational titles.* https://www.dol.gov/agencies/oalj/topics/libraries/LIBDOT

U.S. Department of Labor, Employment and Training Administration. (1991b). *Revised handbook for analyzing jobs.* https://wdr.doleta.gov/opr/fulltext/document.cfm?docn=87

U.S. Social Security Administration. (1978). *SSR 83–10: Titles II and XVI: Determining capability to do other work—the medical-vocational rules of Appendix 2.* https://www.ssa.gov/OP_Home/rulings/di/02/SSR83-10-di-02.html

U.S. Social Security Administration. (2012). SSR 86–8: Titles II and XVI: The sequential evaluation process effective August 20, 1980. https://www.socialsecurity.gov/OP_Home/rulings/di/01/SSR86-08-di-01.html

Vercillo, A. E. (2014). Consultation in Social Security disability law. In R. Robinson (Ed.), *Foundations of forensic vocational rehabilitation* (pp. 311–323). Springer Publishing.

War Risk Insurance Act. (1914). Pub. L. No.65–90.

Williams, J. M. (2013). *What are the odds a case is going to trial?.* https://legalteamusa.net/civillaw/2013/01/03/what-are-the-odds-a-case-is-going-to-trial

Yin, R. K. (2017). *Case study research: Design and methods* (6th ed.). Sage.

CHAPTER 17

Ethics and Ethical Decision-Making

SARA P. JOHNSTON AND VILIA M. TARVYDAS

LEARNING OBJECTIVES

After reading this chapter, you should be able to:

- *Summarize the major characteristics of the three components of professional standards.*
- *Discuss the elements and processes of ethics governance.*
- *Explain the decision-making process as a value-laden, but rational, process.*
- *Provide examples of multicultural considerations in ethical decision-making.*
- *Summarize and apply an integrative model of ethical decision-making.*

CACREP STANDARDS

The following CACREP Standards are addressed in this chapter:
CACREP 2016: 2F1.b, 2F1.c, 2F1.e, 2F1.g, 2F1.i, 2F2.a, 2F2.c, 2F2.d, 2F.2.e, 2F.2.f, 2F.2.g, 2F.2.h
CACREP 2016 Specialties
   Clinical Rehabilitation Counseling: 5D2.k, 5D2.o, 5D2.p, 5D2.r, 5D2.s, 5D2.w, 5D3.c
   Rehabilitation Counseling: 5H2.e, 5H2.f, 5H2.n, 5H2.q, 5H3.f, 5H3.j

INTRODUCTION

Increased quality of life for clients with disabilities depends on professional counselors heeding the caution embodied in the words of Samuel Johnson (n.d.): "Integrity without knowledge is weak and useless, and knowledge without integrity is dangerous and dreadful." The development of a strong professional identity rests on clear professional standards of practice. Clients need solution-focused, respectful, nonexploitative, and empowering—and, therefore, ethical—relationships with their counselors.

Clearly, clients require the services of professionals who are grounded firmly in the awareness of their value-laden mission and who are willing and able to assist people through appropriate knowledge and competencies (Gatens-Robinson & Rubin, 1995). The unusually strong tradition of explicit philosophical foundations is critical to the field of rehabilitation and led to an early recognition of the value-based nature of rehabilitation counseling (Wright, 1983). This treasured legacy provides a strong basis for understanding the ethical principles at the heart of the ethical decision-making skills needed within the practice of rehabilitation counseling.

COMPONENTS OF PROFESSIONAL STANDARDS

The practice of counseling is both an art and a science, requiring the practitioner to make both value-laden and rational decisions. Rather than being incompatible stances, both facts and values must be considered in juxtaposition to one another to arrive at rational decisions (Gatens-Robinson & Rubin, 1995). Within ethical deliberation, the practitioner blends such elements as personal moral sensitivities and philosophies of practice with clinical behavioral objectivity and the quest for efficient care of clients.

The nature and complexity of standards of practice for all professions have changed and grown over the last several decades. The term *professional standards* no longer simply means specifically the ethical standards of the profession. This term is a general term meaning professional criteria indicating acceptable professional performance (Powell & Wekell, 1996) and may encompass ethical and/or clinical care standards. There are three types of standards relevant to describing professional practice: (a) the **internal standards** of the profession, (b) **clinical standards** for the individual practitioners within a profession, and (c) **external regulatory standards**. Taken together, these professional standards increase the status of the profession and its ability for self-governance, as well as enhancing the external representation of and accountability for the profession's competence with clients, the public, employers, other professionals, external regulators, and payors (Rinas & Clyne-Jackson, 1988). These types of standards, their major characteristics, and their principal components are depicted in Figure 17.1.

Internal Standards

First, the internal standards of the profession form the underpinnings of the appropriate role and functions of the profession. Internal standards are characterized by being focused on advancing the professionalism of the group in question, having the intent of setting a profession-wide standard of practice, and assisting individual practitioners through defining their professional identity and obligations. Prominent examples of mechanisms in this category are the profession's code of ethics and any guidelines for specialty practice relevant to the discipline.

Clinical Standards

The clinical standards for professional practitioners are close to the internal standards, as both are directly relevant to services delivered to the individual client or patient. Additional characteristics of clinical standards include focusing on single professional or interprofessional standards of clinical care. These standards may be specific to a particular setting or client population: They evaluate the competency of individual professionals based on the specific care rendered, and they have a client or patient care outcome measurement focus. Peer-review processes and standards, as well as clinical care pathways, are examples of these standards.

Standards of External Regulatory Bodies

The last component of the professional standards is the standards of external regulatory bodies. These standards are focused on regulatory- or institutional-level concerns. They usually involve legal or risk management questions and deal with funding or institutional fiduciary perspectives. There is a judicial type of component in which legal or quasi-legal

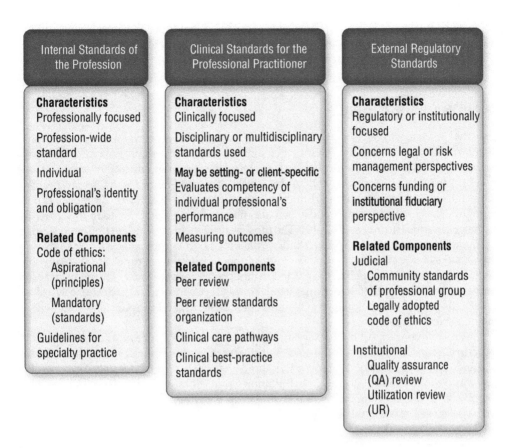

FIGURE 17.1 The structure of professional standards.

processes are at play, for example, community standards of a professional group being used in a malpractice suit or a code of ethics adopted by a licensure board to discipline licensees. General social values typically underlie both law and the values of the profession, making them generally compatible. The society would not long tolerate a profession that is routinely operated in a manner significantly at variance with its core value structure. Corey et al. (2019) noted that law and ethics are similar, because they both constitute guidelines for practice and, in some sense, are regulatory in nature. However, law can be seen as representing the minimum standards that society will tolerate, and ethics involves the ideal standards set by the profession itself. The law also informs the counselor of what is likely to happen if a professional is caught committing a prohibited act, such as sanctions or restrictions to a professional license to practice as a counselor. The other component of external regulatory standards involves institutional standards used to judge the effectiveness and efficiency of an entire agency or institutional unit, as is typically done in quality assurance or utilization review. Such strategies have been common in medical settings and are becoming increasingly common in counseling—as the influence of managed care on the profession accelerates—through increasing demands for outcome-based treatment planning. An emphasis on evidence-based practices (such as those discussed in a later chapter) increasingly is reflected in such standards of care.

This chapter is concerned with the ethical standards of rehabilitation counseling, but it is important to note the synergistic relationship among these three types of professional standards. **Ethics** are the moral principles that are adopted by a group to provide rules for right conduct (Corey et al., 2019). The **code of ethics** for a professional organization is a specific document formally adopted by the organization, which is an attempt to capture the profession's current consensus regarding what types of professional conduct are appropriate or inappropriate. However, they are normative statements, rather than absolute dictates of situational guidance.

ETHICS GOVERNANCE

Effective processes to govern ethics practice are necessary to give meaning to professional standards of practice and to enhance the societal stature of the profession. These governance processes guide the profession's practitioners through education and socialization into the professional role, and subsequently discipline them if they do not practice within the standards established. Ethical components of the standards of practice can be thought of as being either mandatory or aspirational in the level of direction they provide to the practitioner (Corey et al., 2019). The most basic level of ethical functioning is guided by mandatory ethics. At this level, individuals focus on compliance with the law and the dictates of the professional codes of ethics that apply to their practice. They are concerned with remaining safe from legal action and professional censure. The more ethically sophisticated level is the aspirational level. At this level, individuals additionally reflect on the effects of the situation on the welfare of their clients, and the effects of their actions on the profession as a whole.

These same concepts of mandatory and aspirational ethics can be applied to the overall structure of governance for a profession's ethical standards of practice as a whole. Codes of ethics are binding only on people who hold that particular credential (e.g., certification through the Commission on Rehabilitation Counselor Certification [CRCC]), or have membership in that organization (e.g., member of the American Counseling Association [ACA]). Those professionals so governed must adhere to this ethical guidance, and sanctions may be applied based on the specific ethical codes and disciplinary process of this specific professional entity. The disciplinary process of the CRCC is an example of such a process applicable to rehabilitation counseling practice. If a credential holder or member of a particular professional entity violates its code of ethics, the entity has the responsibility to provide a disciplinary procedure to enforce its standards. After due process, the entity applies an appropriate sanction to the violator. In the case of a professional organization, the ultimate sanction would typically be removal from membership, with possible referral of the findings to other professional or legal jurisdictions. For a credentialing entity such as the CRCC or a counselor licensure board, the violator could face the more serious option of certificate or license revocation, thus possibly removing an individual's ability to practice. Less serious levels of sanction, such as reprimand or probation, are also available. Often these statuses are coupled with significant educational or rehabilitative conditions, such as taking an ethics course or treatment of an addiction and supervised practice, to assist practitioners in regaining appropriate ethical standards of practice, while protecting their clients. A letter of instruction may be used when no ethical violation is found, but the disciplinary body determines that information could be provided to the practitioner about the best ethical practices that might improve the future provision of services to clients. Once the individual is adjudicated as being in violation of the code of ethics, the assessment of the level of seriousness of the ethical violation will affect the actual choice of sanction. Factors often considered include intentionality, degree of risk or actual harm to the client, motivation or ability of the violator to change, and recidivism of the violator (Koocher & Keith-Spiegel, 2007).

Responsible practitioners supplement this basic mandatory level of practitioner ethics with advanced knowledge of clinical wisdom and scholarly literature on best practices in ethics. In addition, they will gain guidance from other codes of ethics and specialty guidelines for ethical practice that are relevant to their practices. These sources should be sought to supplement the required mandatory ethical standards with the more aspirational principles and ethical concepts to which the more sophisticated practitioner should

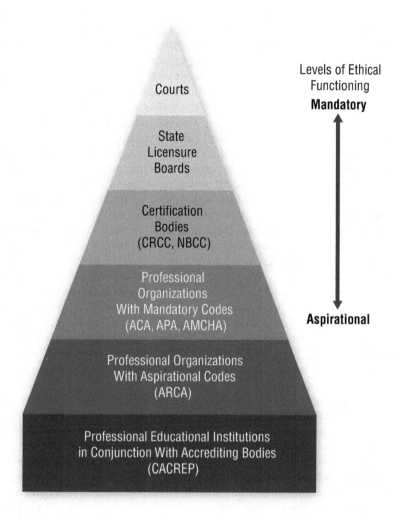

FIGURE 17.2 Model of ethics governance for rehabilitation counselors.

Notes. ACA, American Counseling Association; AMCHA, American Mental Health Counselors Association; APA, American Psychological Association; ARCA, American Rehabilitation Counseling Association; CACREP, Council for Accreditation of Counseling and Related Educational Programs; CRCC, Commission on Rehabilitation Counselor Certification; NBCC, National Board for Certified Counselors.

aspire. In fact, for certain situations, the course of action suggested by the aspirational ethics perspective may contradict that required by the dictates of mandatory ethics. Such a situation leaves the practitioner in the stressful position of needing to responsibly reconcile the two directions.

The contemporary structure of ethics governance for counselors is presented in Figure 17.2. This representation depicts types of professional organizational entities in counseling—organized hierarchically in the shape of a pyramid. The levels of ethical governance are represented by the vertical arrow to the side of the pyramid, depicting the entities as existing roughly on a continuum from a primarily aspirational to a primarily mandatory level of function.

Colleges and universities provide professional education and research services, doing so under the review of credentialing bodies such as the Council for Accreditation of Counseling and Related Educational Programs (CACREP). As such, they are entities that have the broadest function to provide aspirational education and guidance in ethics, and that represent the foundation of the structure of ethics governance. In addition, they build the theoretical and research base for understanding ethical issues, decision-making processes, and ethics educational methods. These aspects of the aspirational knowledge base are needed to support the ethical development of the profession. Colleges and universities also ensure that proper preservice education and professional socialization occur to inculcate future practitioners and educators with a proper ethics base from which to conduct their future practice of counseling. This obligation includes active role modeling and supporting ethical analysis and ethical behavior in teaching, supervision, and actual clinical practice. Educational institutions also serve as a resource to other professional organizations and regulatory bodies to provide teaching, research, and service, supporting aspirational and mandatory ethical practice in the community.

At the next level sit the professional organizations with aspirational codes of ethics, but with no internal mandatory enforcement mechanisms for them. For example, the Association for Specialists in Group Work and the American Rehabilitation Counseling Association (ARCA), as divisions of ACA, occupy this position. For such organizations, the primary task is to encourage aspirational ethical levels of function in their members. Mandatory enforcement tasks are not undertaken by such professional organizations because of such factors as a lack of appropriate consumer access and protection in the disciplinary process; appropriate remedies for serious infractions, and the substantial financial, staff, and professional resources necessary for responsible enforcement. In some cases, the mandatory enforcement function of the organization is referred to a parent organization (e.g., to the ACA, in the case of ARCA members who are ACA members), or the complainant is referred to another appropriate jurisdiction to initiate a disciplinary process.

Nonetheless, professional organizations with aspirational codes perform several significant functions within the ethics governance structure. They may provide supplemental, complementary codes of ethics for their members, which extend and explicate other more general codes of ethics. Such a document provides guidelines for ethical practice for special issues frequently encountered or of particular concern to these professionals. For rehabilitation counselors, examples of such issues might include assessment of people with functional limitations caused by disability, interprofessional team practice relationship issues, managed care practice, and the responsibility of advocacy for people with disabilities. A supplementary code may take the form of specialty guidelines for practice, which address specialty setting or function-specific issues. One example of this type of guideline is the American Psychological Association (2009) Revised Guidelines for Child Custody Evaluations in Family Law Proceedings.

In addition to maintaining supplementary, specialty ethical standards for practice, some professional organizations, with an aspirational ethical level of function, collect information regarding ethical trends and needs for revision of either the specialty or the generalist ethics codes. Their leaderships should also participate in the code revision and writing processes for both types of codes. These organizations should identify and supply qualified professionals to serve on the various mandatory enforcement bodies. They provide educational programs to further knowledge and the quality of ethical practice by performing significant educational and socialization functions. An innovative role—yet one that is potentially most meaningful—is the provision of mechanisms and expertise to offer remediation or rehabilitation programs for impaired professionals who have been found in violation (or are at risk of violation) of ethical standards.

At the third level of ethical governance are professional organizations that maintain and enforce a mandatory code of ethics, such as the ACA and the International Association of Rehabilitation Professionals. These organizations provide an entry-level mandatory code of ethics and enforcement process for their members, and, in the case of the ACA, the enforcement for referred complaints of its specialty memberships. This level of organization consults with certification and licensing bodies and the specialty professional organizations to ensure active participation of all parties in the ethics enforcement process and attempts to incorporate specialty viewpoints into a compatible and continually revised code of ethics. They provide referrals to other jurisdictions for complaints against accused parties, as appropriate. They may provide important educational programs to increase practitioner expertise in ethical practice and may issue advisory opinions to members who inquire to assist in proactively guiding ethical practice.

At the next two levels of ethics governance are professional regulatory bodies that either certify or license professionals which constitute the preeminent enforcers of the mandatory code. National certification bodies, such as the CRCC and the National Board for Certified Counselors, as well as the state counselor licensure boards, operate at this level. They perform a pivotal role in the promulgation and enforcement of ethical standards. However, they draw their specific codes of ethical standards from the professional organizations because they do not constitute the profession but rather regulate it, based on the profession's own internal standards. They may provide information and consultation to professional organizations in revising and maintaining the current codes of ethics. Beyond the ethical regulatory function, the regulatory bodies encourage ethical proficiency of their licensees and certificants by requiring preservice education and continuing education in ethics.

As a practical matter, many states that license professional counselors adopt the ACA *Code of Ethics and Standards of Practice* (2014), and a counselor licensed in a state that has adopted the ACA code would be governed by that code or one very closely related to it. In addition, the 2017 CRCC *Code of Professional Ethics for Rehabilitation Counselors* is very similar to the ACA *Code of Ethics* (Tarvydas & Cottone, 2000). In essence, this consistency provides rehabilitation counselors with a unified code of ethics within the profession, which is highly compatible with ethical standards of the ACA and most counseling licensure boards.

At the pinnacle of the ethics governance hierarchy are civil and criminal courts and other legal jurisdictions that impact the ethical practice of counselors. For example, engaging in sexual intimacy with a client is a criminal offense in many states, and may even result in arrest and incarceration if a practitioner is found guilty of this offense (Corey et al., 2019). However, one of the primary mechanisms of legal governance of ethics is through malpractice suits filed in civil courts. In malpractice actions, one of the central points is to establish a violation of duty, which requires determining the standard of what constitutes "good professional practice" as applied to the matter being litigated. The issue of "good professional practice" may be difficult to determine because it is often ill defined and nuanced. It is not unusual for various expert witnesses to be called to testify regarding such practices. In addition, there might be an attempt to establish that a blatant violation of the general rules of the profession occurred by reference to the profession's ethical standards (Thompson, 1990).

Another standard of practice that might be applied would be consideration of whether the action or service in question was both within the scope of practice of the profession and within the individual's personal scope of practice (see Appendix B of this book for the CRCC Scope of Practice). The specialty of rehabilitation counseling has established its scope of practice, with which practitioners must be familiar, to appropriately and ethically establish their personal scopes of practice. In addition, state-licensed professional counselors are governed by the scope of practice described for counselors within their state's licensure regulatory language and may be required to declare their personal scopes of practice at the time they are licensed and to revise them as appropriate. Practitioners are ethically bound to limit their own scopes of practice to areas within the profession and specialty's scope, in which they are personally competent to practice, by virtue of appropriate types and levels of education, supervision, and professional experience.

Through these six levels, the various professional governance entities interact to provide a network of mandatory and aspirational ethics functions. Concern for the protection of clients is very strong among these professional governance structures, and they have cooperated to share information about the most serious ethical infractions that are adjudicated within their organizations. In their totality, they are an interactive system of research, educational, and enforcement services that shape and regulate the ethical practice of counselors. Taken together, these systems of knowledge, traditions, rules, and laws form the regulatory content, but they do not provide the practitioner with possibly the most crucial tool for ethical practice: knowledge and experience in the application of a decision-making process that can be applied to specific situations in clinical practice.

ETHICAL DECISION-MAKING PROCESSES

The intent of a code of ethics is to provide rehabilitation counselors with guidance for specific situations they experience in their practices. However, authorities have long recognized that codes of ethics must be written in general enough terms that they apply across a wide range of practice settings. They also are reactive in nature; that is, they address situations that have already been part of the profession's experience (Kitchener, 1984; Mabe & Rollin, 1986). As a result, even with knowledge of the profession's code of ethics, rehabilitation counselors may find that they do not have sufficient guidance to resolve the dilemma in question. They may find that the situation with which they are faced is not addressed in their code; that their practice is governed by more than one code, providing conflicting direction in the situation; or that conflicting provisions within any one code appear to apply to the situation. For that reason, rehabilitation counselors must be prepared to exercise professional judgment in ethics responsibly. This type of occurrence is not so much a failure of ethical codes but rather a natural and appropriate juncture recognizing the importance and role of professional judgment. In other words, it is an affirmation that one is involved in the practice of a profession rather than doing a job, however skilled. To exercise professional judgment, the rehabilitation counselor must be prepared to recognize underlying ethical principles or conflicts between competing interests and apply appropriate ethical decision-making skills to resolve the dilemma and act in an ethical manner (Cottone & Tarvydas, 2007; Francoeur, 1983; Kitchener, 1984). In fact, expanding on the expectation stated in the 2014 ACA Code of Ethics for use of an ethical decision-making model, CRCC's Code of Professional Ethics charges counselors with the responsibility to "be familiar with and apply a credible model of decision making that can bear public scrutiny of its application" (CRCC, 2017) by including an ethical standard for applying it. In addition, counselors must be able to "recognize underlying ethical principles and conflicts among competing interests" (p. 35). This trend is in keeping with the growing recognition that counselors must be prepared to go well beyond the simple knowledge of codes of ethics to know how to reason about complex and sometimes seemingly conflicting types of information through application of a formal ethical decision-making model (Cottone, 2012). Fortunately, professionals are assisted in this task by examination and refinement of their ordinary moral sense, as well as by the availability of thoughtful models for the ethical decision-making process. Many components of ethical decision-making involve teachable, learnable skills to supplement the professional's developing intuitive professional judgment.

Several types of models exist, which seek to explain and structure the process of ethical decision-making (Cottone, 2012; Cottone & Claus, 2000). Some prominent examples view the ethical decision-making process as professional self-exploration (Corey et al., 2019); a moral reasoning discourse (Kitchener, 1984); the result of a moral developmental process (Van Hoose & Kottler, 1985); a multidimensional, integrative psychological process (Rest, 1984); and involving a hierarchy of four contextual levels that affect the process of decision making (Tarvydas & Cottone, 1991). Generally, ethical decision-making models can be thought of as having the characteristics of either principle or virtue ethics (Corey et al., 2019). Principle ethics focus on the objective, rational, cognitive aspects of the process. Practitioners who adhere to this perspective tend to view the application of universal, impartial ethical principles, rules, codes, and laws as being the core elements of ethics. Virtue ethics consider the characteristics of the counselors themselves as the critical element for responsible practice. Thus, proponents of virtue ethics approaches would tend to concern themselves more with counselors reflecting on and clarifying their moral and value positions. In addition, they would examine other personal issues that might impact their ethical practice, such as unresolved emotional needs, which might negatively affect their work with their clients. Preferred approaches to ethical decision-making should include both aspects (Corey et al., 2019; Meara et al., 1996). Among other positive contributions of such a synergistic approach, Vasquez (1996) has speculated that the addition of virtue ethical perspectives may improve ethical conduct in multicultural and diverse interactions and settings. Cottone (2012) has identified multicultural sensitivity as a major theme in the evolution of ethical decision-making models, and Garcia et al. (2003) have addressed it through infusing multicultural and transcultural elements into the Tarvydas integrative decision-making model of ethical behavior discussed in the following section.

THE TARVYDAS INTEGRATIVE DECISION-MAKING MODEL OF ETHICAL BEHAVIOR

The Tarvydas integrative decision-making model of ethical behavior builds on several well-known decision-making models widely used by professionals in the mental health and counseling communities. It incorporates the most prominent principle and virtue aspects of several decision-making approaches and introduces some contextual considerations into the process. The Tarvydas integrative model emphasizes the constant process of interaction between the principle and the virtue elements and places a reflective attitude at the heart of the process. The model also focuses on the actual production of ethical behavior within a specified context rather than prematurely terminating analysis by merely selecting the best ethical course of action. This approach considers the importance of setting and environmental factors, which are crucial in counseling. In reviewing the various approaches to ethical decision-making, Garcia et al. (2003) observed that the Tarvydas integrative model uses virtue ethics and behavioral strategies that are consistent with a multicultural approach to counseling and ethical decision-making and proposed an integrative transcultural ethical decision-making model that is based primarily on the Tarvydas integrative model. Nearly 20 years later, the approach outlined by Garcia and colleagues in 2003 is even more salient to ethical practice and decision-making. The Black Lives Matter movement and the COVID-19 pandemic increased societal awareness about the depth and breadth of structural inequities faced by clients who are members of marginalized groups (Levine & Breshears, 2019). A transcultural approach to ethical decision-making includes the voices and perspectives of clients and other stakeholders, which is in keeping with both the concept and practice of client empowerment in rehabilitation counseling, and with the philosophy of "Nothing about us without us" of the Disability Rights movement (Charlton, 2000). Box 17.1 displays the model updated to include transcultural and intersectionality considerations and approaches (Garcia et al., 2003).

Themes and Attitudes

In addition to the four stages of the Tarvydas integrative model, there are four underlying themes or attitudes that are necessary for the professional counselor to enact: reflection, balance, context, and collaboration (see Box 17.1).

Under a social justice model of counseling practice, counselor–client collaboration is encouraged throughout the counseling relationship to encourage client self-advocacy and empowerment (Ratts et al., 2010). However, traditionally, ethics and ethical decision-making have been the "sole province of the counselor" (Tarvydas et al., 2015, p. 230). Prilleltensky et al. (1996) termed this counselor-focused approach to ethical

BOX 17.1 TARVYDAS INTEGRATIVE MODEL FOR ETHICAL BEHAVIOR INFUSED WITH TRANSCULTURAL BEST PRACTICES (GARCIA, ET AL., 2003)

Themes or Attitudes in the Integrative Model

Maintain an attitude of *reflection*.

Address *balance* between issues and parties to the ethical dilemma.

Pay close attention to the *context(s)* of the situation.

Utilize a process of *collaboration* with all rightful parties to the situation.

Stage I. Interpreting the Situation

Component 1. Enhance *sensitivity* and awareness,

Transcultural Best Practice: in a manner that considers counselor and client culture and worldview.

Component 2. Determine the major stakeholders, their ethical claims in the situation,

Transcultural Best Practice: and the potential impact of stakeholder cultural history, traditions, and values on the situation.

Component 3. Engage in the *fact-finding* process,

Transcultural Best Practice: including culturally relevant information, such as history, traditions, values, and family and community relationships.

Stage II. Formulating an Ethical Decision

Component 1. *Review* the problem or dilemma,

Transcultural Best Practice: ensuring that any culturally relevant information is included and considered.

Component 2. Determine what *ethical codes, laws, ethical principles*, and *institutional policies and procedures* exist that apply to the dilemma,

Transcultural Best Practice: being mindful of the potential discriminatory, exclusionary, or inequitable impacts of codes, laws, ethical principles, policies and procedures on the client or stakeholders.

Component 3. Generate possible and probable courses of action and consider potential positive and negative *consequences* for each course of action,

Transcultural Best Practice: as well as how client and counselor worldviews may influence both the choice of and potential consequences of the action.

Component 4. *Consult* with supervisors and other knowledgeable professionals,

Transcultural Best Practice: including those who have culturally relevant experience.

Component 5. Select the best ethical course of action

Transcultural Best Practice: that considers client and stakeholder cultural history, traditions, values, and family and community relationships.

Stage III. Selecting an Action by Weighing Competing, Nonmoral Values

Component 1. Engage in reflective recognition and analysis of *competing nonmoral values, personal blind spots*, or *prejudices*,

Transcultural Best Practice: considering how differing counselor-client cultural experiences may influence values, blind spots, or prejudices.

Component 2. Consider *contextual influences* on values selection at the counselor–client, interprofessional team, institutional, societal,

Transcultural Best Practice: and cultural levels.

Component 3. Select *preferred course* of action.

Stage IV. Planning and Executing the Selected Course of Action

Component 1. Figure out a reasonable *sequence of concrete actions* to be taken

Transcultural Best Practice: and ensure that any culturally relevant information and resources needed to facilitate the action are provided.

(continued)

BOX 17.1 TARVYDAS INTEGRATIVE MODEL FOR ETHICAL BEHAVIOR INFUSED WITH TRANSCULTURAL BEST PRACTICES (GARCIA, ET AL., 2003) (*CONTINUED*)

Component 2. Anticipate and work out *personal and contextual barriers* to effective execution of the plan of action, and effective *countermeasures* for them,

    Transcultural Best Practice: including culture-specific barriers, such as bias, discrimination, prejudice, and lack of access to resources.

Component 3. Carry out, document, and *evaluate* the course of action as planned,

    Transcultural Best Practice: ensuring that data collected and analyzed include culturally relevant information.

Note. Infusions adapted from Table 17.2 in Garcia, J., Cartwright, B., Winston, S. M., & Borzuchowska, B. (2003). A transcultural integrative ethical decision-making model in counseling (p. 273). *Journal of Counseling and Development, 81,* 268–277.

decision-making the restrictive orientation. Under the restrictive orientation, the counselor does not consult or collaborate with the client in the ethical decision-making process, which stands in stark contrast to the recommendation for more client involvement in other stages of the counseling relationship. To address the lack of client involvement in the ethical decision-making process, Tarvydas et al. (2015) suggested that counselors use a participatory orientation, which infuses the client into the ethical decision-making process. By including the client in ethical decisions that affect the client's therapeutic goals, well-being, and quality of life, counselors can strengthen the counselor–client working alliance and facilitate client empowerment—all of which inform and improve the decision-making process. The participatory orientation is the basis for the Applied Participatory Ethics Model, which places the counselor's ethical decision-making knowledge and skills on a continuum from profession-centered (exclusive) to client-centered (inclusive; Tarvydas et al., 2015).

By adopting these background attitudes of reflection, balance, context, and collaboration; using a transcultural approach; and working toward a participatory orientation in ethical decision-making, counselors engage in a more thorough process that will help preserve the integrity and dignity of all parties involved. This will be the case even when outcomes are not considered equally positive for all participants in the process, as is often true in a serious dilemma when such attitudes can be particularly meaningful. Indeed, Betan and Stanton (1999) studied students' responses to ethical dilemmas, analyzing how emotions and concerns influence willingness to implement ethical knowledge. They concluded that "subjectivity and emotional involvement are essential tools for determining ethical action, but they must be integrated with rational analysis" (Betan & Stanton, 1999, p. 295).

Reflection is the overriding attitude of importance throughout the enactment of the specific elements of stages and components that constitute the steps of the Tarvydas integrative model. Many complex decision-making processes easily become overwhelming, either in their innate complexity or in the real-life pressure of the speed or intensity of events. In the current approach, the counselor is urged always to "Stop and think!" at each point in the process. The order of operations is not critical or absolute, nor is it more important than being reflective and invested in a calm, dignified, respectful, and thorough analysis of the situation. Not until we recognize that we are involved in the process and appreciate its critical aspects can we call forth other resources to assist the process and the people within it. Such an attitude of reflection will serve the counselor well at all stages of this process.

Elements

The specific elements that constitute the operations within the Tarvydas integrative model have four main stages with several components, including the steps to be taken within each stage. The concepts summarized are drawn, in the main, from the work of Kitchener (1984), Rest (1984), and Tarvydas and Cottone (1991).

Stage I: Interpreting the Situation Through Awareness and Fact-Finding

At this stage, the primary task of counselors is to be sensitive to and aware of the needs and welfare of the people around them, and of the ethical implications of these situations. This level of awareness allows counselors to imagine and investigate the effects of the situation on the parties involved and the possible effects of various actions and conditions. The sense of this state is somewhat like the idea of "situational awareness" as used in military parlance, through which the agents scan the circumstances for potential threats and resources that are relevant to addressing the conflict at hand. This research and awareness must also include emotional as well as cognitive and fact-based considerations. Three components constitute the counselor's operations in this stage.

Component 1 involves enhancing one's sensitivity and awareness. In Component 2, the counselor takes an inventory of the people who are major stakeholders in the outcome of the situation. It is important to reflect on any parties who will be affected and who play a major role in the client's life, as well as considering what their exact relationship is—ethically and legally—to the person at the center of the issue, which is the client. Imagine dropping a rock into a pond: the point of impact is where the central figure, the client, is situated; however, the client is surrounded by people at varying levels of closeness, such as parents, foster parents, intimate partners, spouse, children, employer, friends, and neighbors, all radiating out from the client in decreasing levels of intimacy and responsibility to the client.

Figure 17.3 depicts how the spheres of influence of these stakeholders in the client's life, as well as the stakeholders at each of the four levels in the professional world of the counselor, may be seen as intersecting. This way of thinking about the relationships among the different stakeholders in the situation allows for a fuller appreciation of the specific people and contexts of the counselor's practice and the client's situation.

A number of people and levels of the professional service hierarchy will (or should) play a part in any ethical decision. These social forces will create both positive and negative influences on the ethical situation and should be taken into account in the ethical analysis. The ethical claims of these parties on the counselor's level of duty are not uniform. Almost all codes of ethics in counseling make it clear that the client is the person to whom the first duty is owed, but there are others to whom the counselor has lesser, but important, levels of duty. It is always important to determine whether any surrogate decision makers for the client exist, such as a foster parent, guardian, or person with power of attorney, so that they may be brought into the central circle of duty early in the process. Sensitivity, cultural awareness, and proactivity are useful in working through situations in which the legal relationships involved do not coincide with the social and emotional bonds between the client and other people involved in the dilemma.

The final element in Stage I is Component 3, in which the counselor undertakes an extensive fact-finding investigation, with a scope appropriate to the situation. The nature of the fact-finding process should be carefully considered and is not intended to be a formal investigative or quasi-legal process. The intent is that the counselor should carefully review and understand the information at hand and then seek out new information. Only information that is appropriately available to a counselor should be involved. The scope and depth of information that would be rightfully available to the counselor are

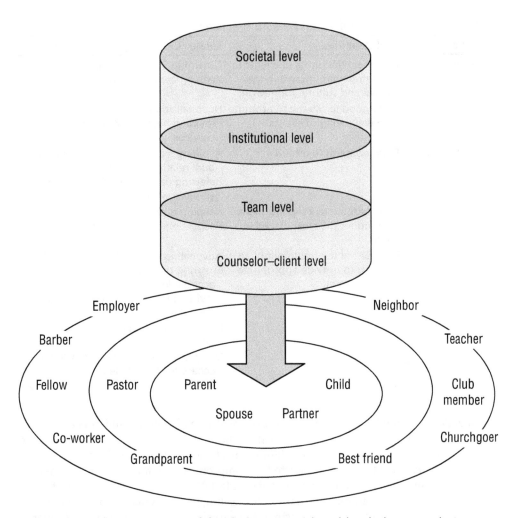

FIGURE 17.3 The intersection of the client's personal world with the counselor's professional hierarchical contexts.

surprising, but it is often not fully utilized. For example, information might be gained from such sources as further discussion with the client, contacts with family (with appropriate permission of the client), case records, expert consultation and reports, legal resources, or agency policy and procedures.

Stage II: Formulating an Ethical Decision

This aspect of the process is most by professionals, and many may erroneously think it is the end of the process. The central task in this stage is to identify which of the possible ethical courses of action appears to come closest to the moral ideal in the situation under consideration (Rest, 1984). Many decision-making models in other areas of counseling can be applied as a template at this stage, but the following components are drawn from the work of Van Hoose and Kottler (1985).

Component 1 suggests that the counselor review the problem or dilemma to be sure that it is clearly understood considering any new information obtained in Stage I. In *Component 2*, the counselor researches the standards of law and practice applicable to the situation. This component includes Kitchener (1984) attention to ethical codes, laws, and ethical principles, and Tarvydas and Cottone (1991) concern for the team and

TABLE 17.1 Ethical Principles and Related Practices

Principle	Brief Definition	Related Counseling Practice
Autonomy	To respect the rights of clients to be self-governing within their social and cultural framework	Obtaining informed consent Keeping confidentiality
Beneficence	To do good to others; to promote the well-being of clients	Hospitalizing a suicidal client Providing high-quality counseling services
Nonmaleficence	To do no harm to others	Avoiding a potentially detrimental dual relationship with a client Referring or not providing counseling services when not fully qualified
Fidelity	To be faithful; to keep promises and honor the trust placed in one	Keeping promises to clients Respecting clients' privacy
Justice	To be fair in the treatment of all clients; to provide appropriate services to all	Advocating on behalf of clients Ensuring that services are fully accessible to all Providing fair access to services to all, even difficult clients
Veracity	To be honest	Providing detailed professional disclosure Describing completely who will have access to clients' files

organizational context in the examination of institutional policies and procedures, to make mention of other useful areas for consideration. The counselor would also analyze which of the six core ethical principles (autonomy, beneficence, nonmaleficence, justice, fidelity, veracity) may be either supported or compromised by the types of actions that are being contemplated in the situation (see Table 17.1 for a brief description of these ethical principles and examples of common counseling practices that are based on them). This operation is formally known as **principle analysis** and is one of the most challenging, yet critical, aspects of the ethical analysis of a dilemma. The core, or main, principle analysis concerns the ethical obligations owed to the client, rather than to other parties to the situation.

Component 3 initiates the process of formally envisioning and generating possible and probable courses of action. As with all decision-making processes, it is important not to truncate this exploratory process by prematurely censoring the possibilities, or succumbing to a sense of being too overwhelmed, or too limited, in options. After the list of possible and probable courses of action is generated, positive and negative consequences are identified and assessed in relation to risks, as well as to material and personal resources available. In *Component 4*, the counselor is reminded to consult with supervisors and trusted and knowledgeable colleagues for guidance if this has not been done before this point. Professional standards of practice emphasize the importance of appropriate collegial consultation to resolve difficult clinical and ethical dilemmas. Research has also demonstrated that such consultations can have a significant influence on those seeking such consultation (Butterfield et al., 2000; Cottone et al., 1994). There is value in reviewing the reasoning employed in working through the ethical dilemma to this point, and the solutions and consequences envisioned to be sure that all potentially useful and appropriate considerations have been taken into account. Finally, the best ethical course of action is determined and articulated in Component 5. The ethical decision at this stage of the model should be contrasted with the decision about what the counselor actually decided to do, which is the product of Stage III.

Stage III: Selecting an Action by Weighing Competing, Nonmoral Values, Personal Blind Spots, and Prejudices

Many people would think that the ethical decision-making process is concluded at the end of Stage II. This impression is limited in its realization of the many additional forces that may affect the counselor and result in the counselor not actually executing the selected ethical course of action. Component 1 of Stage III interjects a period of reflection and active processing of what the counselor intends to do, in view of competing, nonmoral values (Rest, 1984). At this point, the counselor considers any personal factors that might intervene to pull him or her away from choosing the ethical action or cause that action to be substantially modified. Nonmoral values involve anything that the counselor may prize or desire, which is not in and of itself a moral value, such as justice. Such values may include such things as valuing social harmony, spending time with friends or working on one's hobby, desiring control or power, or having personal wealth. In this component, counselors are also called upon to examine themselves to determine if they have some personal blind spots or prejudices that might affect their judgment or resolve to do the ethical thing, such as a fear of HIV infection, or the conviction that gay men are also likely to molest children. This portion of the model provides an excellent opportunity for counselors to carefully evaluate whether they have adequately incorporated multicultural considerations and competencies in their work on this ethical dilemma and to be sure that they are not operating from a culturally encapsulated frame of reference.

Counselors must allow themselves to become aware of the strength and attractiveness of other values they hold, which may influence whether they will discharge their ethical obligations. If they are self-aware, they may more effectively and honestly compensate for their conflicted impulses at this point. Counselors may have strong needs for acceptance by peers or supervisors, for prestige and influence, to avoid controversy, or to be financially successful. These value orientations may come into conflict with the course of action necessary to proceed ethically and must be reconciled with ethical requirements if the client is to be ethically served. In contrast, counselors may place a high value on being moral or ethical and on being accepted as respected professionals with high ethical standards, or they may value the esteem of colleagues who place a high value on ethical professional behavior. Those forces should enhance the tendency to select ethical behavioral options (the influence of the ethical climate on the ethical behavior of the counselor is more fully explored in Tarvydas et al., 2007). Therefore, the importance of selecting and maintaining ethically sensitized and positive professional and personal cultures should be recognized as critical to full professional functioning, as the next component would suggest.

In *Component 2*, counselors systematically inventory the contextual influences on their choices at the counselor–client, team, institutional, and societal levels. This is not a simple process of weighing influences, but it should serve as an inventory of influences, which may be either dysfunctional or constructive, for selecting the ethical course over other types of values present in these other interactions. Counselors may also use this type of information to think strategically about the influences they will need to overcome to provide ethical service in the situation. Beyond the immediate situation, counselors should control their exposure to contexts that consistently reinforce values that run counter to the dictates of good ethical practices. For example, rehabilitation counselors working in private practices where their employers consistently pressure them to favor the attorneys that hire them in their forensic evaluations run the risk of eventually succumbing to these pressures.

Component 3 is the final aspect of Stage III, in which the counselor selects the preferred course of action or the behavior that he or she plans to undertake.

This decision may be a reaffirmation of the intention to take the ethical course of action, as determined at the conclusion of Stage II, but augmented to deal with some contextual barriers discovered in Stage III. However, it may be some other course of action that may even not be ethical, or a modified version of the ethical course of action selected in Stage

II. Whatever the choice, the counselor has selected it after this more extensive reflection on their own competing values and personal blind spots, as well as the contextual influences in the situation in question.

Stage IV: Planning and Executing the Selected Course of Action

Rest (1984) described the essential tasks of this stage as planning to implement and executing what one plans to do. This operation includes *Component 1*, in which the counselor figures out a reasonable sequence of concrete actions to be taken. In *Component 2*, the task is to anticipate and work out all personal and contextual barriers to effectively executing the plan. Preparing countermeasures for barriers that may arise is useful. Here, the earlier attention to other stakeholders and their concerns may suggest problems or allies to the process. In addition, earlier consideration of the contextual influences in Stage III assists the counselor in this type of strategic planning. *Component 3* is the final step of this model, in that it provides for the execution, documentation, and evaluation of the course of action as planned. Rest noted that the actual behavioral execution of ethics is often not a simple task, frequently drawing heavily on the personal, emotional qualities and professional and interpersonal skills of the counselor. He mentions such qualities as firmness of resolve, ego strength, and social assertiveness. To this list could be added countless skills, such as persistence, tact, time management, assertiveness skills, team collaboration, and conflict resolution skills. Considerations are limited only by the characteristics and requirements of the counselor and the specific situation involved. Clear and thorough documentation of the entire plan and the rationale behind it, and ethical decision-making steps taken in responding to the ethical dilemma as the process unfolds, are critical to protecting the interests of both the counselor and the client. The information gained in this documentation process will prove critical in evaluating the effectiveness of the entire ethical decision-making process.

Practicing the Tarvydas Integrative Model

Just like the basic counseling microskills, the skills of ethical decision-making as described do not come automatically, or even easily, after merely reading about the concepts in a book. Practice in solving mock ethical dilemmas—working to address actual ethical dilemmas under the supervision of an ethically knowledgeable instructor, clinical supervisor, master counselor, or mentor—and incorporating ethical analysis into clinical training process are all essential to gradual progression in gaining practical skills and sensitive, accurate ethical knowledge. A complex ethical scenario, with a full ethical analysis using the Tarvydas integrative model and all its stages and components, is presented in the following case study. This enables readers to begin an exploration of how to use this rich approach to ethical decision-making.

The following analysis does not represent the only answer to this dilemma. Sometimes, information discovered, or concerns raised by other reasonable people, can lead to important shifts in the elements of a case. Also, because reasonable professionals can judge and weigh even the same ideas or risks differently, there may be other valid conclusions to the same case. This process is not so much about getting the hidden, correct answer but rather is about going through the process of decision-making thoroughly and carefully and exercising due care and good, reasonable professional judgment throughout. If this is done, in the end, the counselor is more likely to have arrived at an explicable judgment that minimizes risk to the client, the counselor, and others. Counselors will also benefit from increased confidence and peace of mind, assured that they have done the best in the situation, having used a thorough, thoughtful approach to solving a dilemma that may not have a solution that is satisfying to the parties involved.

CASE STUDY: THE TARVYDAS INTEGRATIVE DECISION-MAKING MODEL OF ETHICAL BEHAVIOR

Case Narrative

John is a 43-year-old Black male who is meeting with a counselor at the Department of Correctional Services (DCS). He recently has been released from prison on parole and is meeting with a counselor voluntarily to deal with some issues of depression. He is currently on medication for depression and has made previous suicide attempts. He was married to a woman for 9 years, and they had two children together, now 7 and 5 years old. She also had two children from a previous relationship, now 12 and 9 years old, whom John also considers to be his children. John recently began a new job as a food-service worker at a local nursing home and has been making child support payments. He is very proud of the fact that his new job will allow him to support his children. He mentions that he has concerns about how long he can keep this job, because he will be required to be vaccinated for influenza and COVID-19. He states, "People in my community do not trust vaccines." He and his wife are recently divorced. Before their divorce, John and his former wife met with a family therapist for several sessions; their children continue to meet with the therapist. At first, his ex-wife would not allow the children to visit their dad, but just recently John says they have been talking again, and his ex-wife has started to trust him again and let the children visit whenever they wanted. Just recently, his youngest girl confided in him that their mom and her new friends are still using drugs and are also selling them from the house. She had found a syringe at the home, which her mom had thought was hidden. John is very adamant that he does not want to contact the Department of Human Services (DHS) or any other similar agency about this. He had contacted DHS for a similar situation a few years ago and had a bad experience. The caseworker he met with initially was helpful; however, in the end, DHS had "done nothing," and his ex-wife had found out that he had made the report. She did not let him see the kids for a long time after the incident. He feels that, at this point, he can do the most good by keeping a close relationship with his children and a civil relationship with his ex-wife. He is living a clean and drug-free life and feels that he is his ex-wife's best hope right now to straighten out. He says that if a report is made, the only thing he is sure of is that his ex-wife would not let him see the children, and he does not know if he could live without being part of his children's lives. He states he is also anxious about the possibility of losing his job due to the vaccination requirements because he fears his ex-wife may use his inability to keep up with his child support payments as another reason to keep him for seeing the children. In this case, the client has his reasons for not wanting to contact DHS, and client autonomy must be respected. The client also raises the issue that maybe contacting the authorities really is not in the best interest of the children. He also made some statements regarding not being able to live without being a part of his children's lives, which must be taken seriously given the client's suicidal history and current state of depression. However, young children are involved in a dangerous situation. There is no report of physical or sexual abuse occurring, yet drug use in the home and young children coming across needles is dangerous and could be considered abuse. At this point, the counselor feels there may be a potential dilemma that should be explored further.

Stage I: Interpreting the Situation Through Awareness and Fact-Finding

The primary task of counselors in Stage I is to be sensitive to and aware of the needs and welfare of the people around them, and of the ethical implications of these situations. This level of awareness allows counselors to imagine and investigate the effects of the situation on the parties involved and the possible effects of various actions and conditions. This research and awareness must also include emotional, as well as cognitive and fact-based, considerations. At this stage, the counselor considers the benefits of including the client in the ethical decision-making process by using a participatory ethics approach.

Component 1: Sensitivity and Awareness

At this point, the counselor talks to John and gets his impression of who will be affected by this situation, and how they will be affected. John clearly cares about his children, but firmly believes that the best chance they have is if he continues to be a part of their lives. He has no guarantee for what would happen if he did contact DHS, and he does not want to take that risk. Given what happened the last time he called, John is very distrustful of the system. He worries about losing his job, which may also limit his access to the children. He also expressed some concerns for his ex-wife and, even though they parted on unfriendly terms, he still seems to care about her and wants what is best for her. He says that they are just starting to talk again, and he feels that he may be the only one who truly understands what she is going through with the drugs and might be able to help her kick the habit. Although he admits that he worries about what kind of environment his children are living in, John feels that this is the best chance they have.

The counselor also notes that there are four children of varying ages in the house. An 18-year-old might understand how dangerous finding a needle in the house really is, but a 5-year-old most likely would not. Even aside from needles being in the house, there is also the potential for danger with what kind of people are around the children. If their mother is dealing drugs from the home, many of those she sells to are probably in the house also, and around the children.

The client says he understands all of this, but still feels that he is making progress with his ex-wife, and that he is the best chance for his children. John acknowledges that he is taking on a lot of responsibility but says that he would do anything for his children and truly believes that he is doing the best for them in the long run.

Component 2: Major Stakeholders and Their Ethical Claims

The counselor identifies the parties who will be affected and what their exact relationship is—ethically and legally—to the person at the center of the issue. There are often others to whom the counselor has lesser, but important, levels of duty, such as parents, intimate partners, spouse, children, employer, friends, neighbors, guardian, or persons with power of attorney. It is critical for the counselor to consider any cultural considerations that may influence who is included as a stakeholder, for example, religious or community leaders or elders. All important parties with an ethical or legal claim in this case are listed in Table 17.2.

Component 3: Fact-Finding Process

The counselor undertakes an extensive fact-finding investigation, of a scope appropriate to the situation, by reviewing and understanding current information and seeking out new information. This investigation involves gathering information appropriately available to the counselor, either through professional records and channels (with appropriately obtained releases of information) or through part of public domain information. Sources might include further discussion with the client, contacts with family or other professionals working with the family (with the client's permission), current and old client records in one's own or another agency, expert consultation and reports, legal resources, or agency policy and procedures. There are all the facts or factual questions the counselor should reasonably be able to research or answer.

TABLE 17.2 Analysis of Ethical Claims

Parties	Ethical Claim
The client, John	He does not want to contact any authorities.
The children	They may be in danger, may not know all of their options or how they could get help.
Department of Correctional Services	They are responsible for their counselors and could be held liable for mistakes made by their employees.
The counselor	May be held liable for any harm that befalls the children or the client.
The ex-wife	She could face an abuse investigation and the subsequent consequences.
Grandparents	If Department of Human Services (DHS) did find abuse, they would most likely get custody of the children.
The family therapist	The therapist may have information about conditions in the home, which she is required to report to the authorities.
DHS	DHS is responsible for its employees and could be held liable for mistakes made by those employees.
John's employer	John's employer may terminate John's position if he violates company policies related to vaccine requirements or illegal drug use. The employer feels great responsibility for the vulnerable residents of the nursing home. The employer does not understand why African Americans, including John, have any more reason to be concerned about vaccines than employees who are members of other racial/ethnic groups. As a parolee, John is putting himself at risk for relapse and/or legal action related to his wife's drug use.

A call was made to the DHS confidential hotline to find out if the situation in general fell under the guidelines for mandatory reporting, which it did not. DHS stated that it did not fall under mandatory guidelines because it was third-party information.

The counselor talked to the supervisor and found out DCS has an unwritten rule or policy. This policy is to convince the client to call authorities and report the situation.

John stated that if DHS was contacted, an investigation was conducted, and action was taken to remove the children from their mother, her parents would probably receive custody. The client stated that he has a good relationship with his ex-wife's parents. He thought that they would allow him to see the children if they did get custody of the children.

The counselor was informed by a supervisor that one reason DHS may not have done anything the last time John reported was that there may have been some type of drug investigation going on. If there is a current investigation into drug trafficking or selling, they can postpone going into the house for a child abuse charge because the house is under supervision as part of a larger investigation.

The counselor should also consider the multicultural and legal implications related to John's employment. John has reported that his job is very important to him because it allows him to pay child support to provide for his children. However, John's job security may be threatened both by his reluctance to follow his company's vaccine requirements and his ex-wife's suspected illegal drug use. Together, the counselor and John reviewed John's employer's policies to gather information about vaccine requirements and illegal drug use. During the process of gathering information about his employer's policies, John expressed concerns about "being a guinea pig" for the vaccine. When the counselor asked John to explain, John stated that in his community, people talk about friends and family who weren't told the truth about their health conditions or weren't asked for their permission before being given treatments or weren't believed when they reported the treatment didn't work. He said that he's heard that the COVID-19 vaccine can "cause problems," and he doesn't know whom to trust. The counselor concurred with John about the historical mistreatment of Black Americans by the medical profession and asserted that research supports what John has heard in the community. For example, a recent report stated that the majority of Blacks don't trust the medical system and believe they are treated unfairly by medical professionals and that, compared to Whites, Blacks are more likely to be undermedicated for pain (Hostetter & Klein, 2021). The counselor asked John if he knows that Blacks have a higher risk of becoming seriously ill and dying from COVID-19 than do Whites, yet despite the increased risks to their health, Black Americans are less likely than Whites to be vaccinated against COVID-19 (Hostetter & Klein, 2021; Willems et al., 2022). John replied he doesn't know about the numbers, but from his perspective, it seems almost every family in his community has lost someone due to COVID-19. John reported that two of his cousins died recently from COVID-19. The counselor expressed sympathy on the loss of John's cousins. The counselor then stated that the report provides information about addressing Black Americans' concerns about healthcare, including vaccines, and asked John if he'd like a copy of the report. John stated that he'd be interested in looking at the report. The counselor then asked if John would like to work together to educate his employer about Black employees' concerns about vaccines to ensure that John and his coworkers have the information they need to feel more comfortable about receiving required vaccinations. John stated that the loss of his cousins has been hard on his family and that he would consider taking a more active role to improve his health and the health of his family and community. John and the counselor finished the fact-finding process with a discussion about the potential risks that his ex-wife's drug use poses to his job and to his children's safety, and some actions John can take to reduce or eliminate those risks.

Stage II: Formulating an Ethical Decision

The counselor's task in this stage is to identify which of the possible ethical courses of action appears to come closest to the ethical ideal in the situation under consideration. If the counselor is following a participatory ethics orientation, the client would be included in the process of formulating an ethical decision. The counselor should also ensure that any multicultural considerations are addressed and included in the decision-making process.

Component 1: Review Problem or Dilemma

Review the problem or dilemma to be sure that it is clearly understood in relation to any new information.

Because this situation does not fall into the category of mandatory reporting, the counselor is not legally bound to break the client's confidence. However, we now know that the unwritten policy of the institution (DCS) is to try to convince or coerce the client to call DHS on his own. Thus, the counselor must decide whether to respect the client's wishes not to call DHS or to try to coerce the client to call, in accordance with the institution's unwritten policy. If the counselor is following a participatory ethics orientation, the client may be informed of the informal policy and his input sought on how to proceed in light of the informal policy.

Component 2: Determine Ethical Codes, Laws, Principles, and Institutional Policies and Procedures

The counselor must determine and research the standards of law (in any and all applicable local jurisdictions) and professional practices applicable to the situation. The latter material includes ethical codes and related standards of care, laws, ethical principles, and institutional policies and procedures.

Ethical Codes

List any rules or canons from applicable code(s) of ethics and provide a summary of their dictates. For counselors, the ACA *Code of Ethics* and any applicable specialty standards, such as the CRCC *Code of Professional Ethics for Rehabilitation Counselors,* are recommended. If the counselor is licensed or holds national certification, the codes of ethics that apply to that credential must also be consulted. Although there may be differences among codes of ethics depending on professional practice standards, it is important to understand that all professional codes of ethics for the health care professions, including the counseling profession, include a set of agreed-on ethical principles, as well as aspirational and mandatory standards for ethical practice. The following sections of the CRCC *Code of Professional Ethics for Rehabilitation Counselors* (2017) apply to the case scenario. Excerpted listings of the sections of the code that are relevant are provided here, in addition to citations of the Code Standards that are most applicable. The reader is encouraged to locate and read the important details provided in these Section standards.

CRCC Code of Ethics

Section A. The Counseling Relationship. Introduction. Rehabilitation counselors work in cooperation with their clients to promote client welfare and support them in developing and progressing toward their goals. Rehabilitation counselors understand that trust is the cornerstone of the counseling relationship, and they have the responsibility to respect and safeguard the client's right to privacy and confidentiality. Rehabilitation counselors respect the rights of clients to make their own decisions about matters that affect their own lives. Rehabilitation counselors make reasonable efforts to ensure clients are able to make informed choices about every aspect of the rehabilitation counseling process. Rehabilitation counselors actively attempt to understand the diverse cultural backgrounds of the clients they serve and do not discriminate in their provision of rehabilitation counseling services. Rehabilitation counselors also explore their own cultural identities and how these affect their values and beliefs.

A.e. Autonomy.

A.2. Respecting Diversity

A.2.a. Respecting Culture.

A.2.b. Nondiscrimination.

A.3. Client Rights.

A.3.e. Support Network Involvement.

A.4. Avoiding Value Imposition.

Section B. Confidentiality, Privileged Communication, and Privacy. Rehabilitation counselors recognize that trust is the cornerstone of the counseling relationship. Rehabilitation counselors aspire to earn the trust of current and prospective clients by creating an ongoing partnership, establishing and upholding appropriate boundaries, and maintaining confidentiality. Rehabilitation counselors communicate the legal and ethical parameters of confidentiality to their clients in a culturally competent manner.

B.1. Respecting Client Rights.

B.1.d. Cultural Diversity Considerations.

Section C: Advocacy and Accessibility. Introduction. Rehabilitation counselors are aware of and sensitive to the needs of individuals with disabilities. Rehabilitation counselors advocate at individual, group, institutional, and societal levels to: (1) promote opportunity and access; (2) improve the quality of life for individuals with disabilities; and (3) remove potential barriers to the provision of or access to services. Rehabilitation counselors recognize that disability often occurs in tandem with other social justice issues (e.g., poverty, homelessness, trauma).

C.1.a. Attitudinal Barriers.

C.1.b. Empowerment.

C.1.c. Organizational Advocacy.

C.1.f. Areas of Knowledge and Competency.

Section D: Professional Responsibility. Rehabilitation counselors aspire to open, honest, and accurate communication in dealing with other professionals and the public. Rehabilitation counselors facilitate access to rehabilitation counseling services, practice in a nondiscriminatory manner within the boundaries of professional and personal competence, and have a responsibility to abide by the Code.

D.1. Professional Competence

D.2a. Cultural Competency.

D.2.b. Interventions.

D.2.c. Nondiscrimination.

Section E. Relationships with Other Professionals and Employers: Introduction. Rehabilitation counselors recognize the quality of interactions with colleagues can influence the quality of services provided to clients. They work to become knowledgeable about the role of other professionals within and outside the profession. Rehabilitation counselors are respectful of approaches to counseling services that differ from their own and of traditions and practices of other professional groups with which they work. Rehabilitation counselors develop positive working relationships and systems of communication with colleagues to enhance services to clients. Rehabilitation counselors are committed to the equal treatment of all individuals. Rehabilitation counselors secure employment in settings that support and uphold the ethical standards outlined in the Code. They attempt to reach agreement with employers as to acceptable standards of client care and professional conduct that allow for changes in employer policies conducive to the growth and development of clients.

E.1.b. Negative Employment Conditions.

Section L. Resolving Ethical Issues. Introduction. Rehabilitation counselors behave in an ethical and legal manner. They are aware that client welfare and trust in the profession depend on a high level of professional conduct. They hold other rehabilitation counselors to the same standards and are willing to make reasonable efforts to ensure that standards are upheld. Rehabilitation counselors strive to resolve ethical dilemmas with direct and open communication among all parties involved and seek consultation with colleagues and supervisors when necessary. Rehabilitation counselors incorporate ethical practice into their daily professional work and engage in ongoing professional development on current topics in ethical and legal issues in counseling. Rehabilitation counselors become familiar with the CRCC Guidelines and Procedures for Processing Complaints and use it as a reference for assisting in the enforcement of the Code.

L.1.a. Knowledge of the Code.

L.1.b. Knowledge of Related Codes of Ethics.

L.1.c. Conflicts between Ethics and Laws

LAWS/LEGAL CONSIDERATIONS

List any laws or legal considerations that may apply. Research those relevant to your own jurisdiction. The example provided is based on Iowa law, circa 2009. This example is not to be considered a legal opinion, only an example. For further information, consult legal counsel and resources in your own area.

TABLE 17.3 Example of Principle Analysis

Action A. Pressuring the Client	
Principles Upheld	*Principles Compromised*
Beneficence (to children)	Beneficence (to client)
	Nonmaleficence (to client)
	Autonomy (of client)
	Fidelity (to client)
	Veracity (to client)
Resultant Obligations: Work with client?[a]	
Action B. Not Pressuring the Client	
Principles Upheld	*Principles Compromised*
Beneficence (to client)	Beneficence (to children)
Nonmaleficence (to client)	Nonmaleficence (to children)
	Autonomy (of client)
	Fidelity (to client)
	Veracity (to client)
Resultant Obligations: Work with client?[a]	

[a]In principle analysis, the obligations owed to the client normally outweigh those to others. Therefore, frequently they are the only ones considered; if obligations to others are considered, those owed to the client generally supersede them, because the counselor incurs these primary obligations by virtue of entering into a professional relationship with the client. The exception to this case would involve obligations to vulnerable others (e.g., small children), and/or those situations in which there a high degree of serious danger or risk. This reasoning is why this case presents a particularly troublesome dilemma.

Iowa Code

Section 232.69 Mandatory and permissive reporters—training required. [A counselor is considered to be a mandatory reporter] "1.b . . . who, in the scope of professional practice or in their employment responsibilities, examines, counsels, or treats a child and reasonably believes a child has suffered abuse". [Note: This section includes a list of professionals, e.g., (7) An employee of a department of human services institution listed in section 218.1; and (12) A counselor or mental health professional.]

Section 232.68(2)(a)(6) [Included in the definitions of child abuse] An illegal drug is present in a child's body as a direct and foreseeable consequence of the acts or omissions of the person responsible for the care of the child.

Ethical Principles

List all ethical principles that describe relevant obligations. Describe the courses of action, the principles upheld, the principles compromised, and the obligations. Sometimes, this process is referred to as **principle analysis,** a process wherein ethical principles are specified and subjected to balancing considerations (Table 17.3).

Each of the two courses of action can be supported by one or more ethical principles. Contacting authorities could fall under the category of beneficence toward the children. Keeping John's confidence could fall under the category of autonomy, for honoring the right to individual decisions. There is also the possibility that both scenarios could fit into the category of nonmaleficence. Not telling anyone could lead to harm for the children, in some way. Also, by telling, it is possible that John's fears could materialize and the ex-wife could keep the children away from him. In this way, it may be harmful to the client and for the children if they are not allowed to see their father.

The ethical principles supporting the other course of action will be compromised. If the authorities are told, the counselor is not respecting the client's autonomy. If authorities are not told, the counselor may be compromising the principles of nonmaleficence toward the children and the concept of beneficence, in the same way.

This situation is an ethical dilemma, not just an ethical issue. An ethical issue has a fairly identifiable course of action that is appropriate, even if taking that action is not necessarily easy in practice (i.e., as in the case of involuntarily committing a seriously suicidal individual).

Institutional/Agency Rules or Policies

List any institutional/agency rules or policies that may apply.

In the experience of the counselor, the unwritten policy of the DCS is to try to coerce the client into reporting the possible child abuse to the DHS. Despite the unwritten policy, other counselors at the DCS may know of situations where this unwritten policy was not followed, and why the policy was not followed. Alternatively, if the counselor is following a participatory ethics orientation, the client may be informed of the informal policy and his input sought on how to proceed in light of the informal policy.

Component 3: Courses of Action and Positive and Negative Consequences

List all possible and probable courses of action (Table 17.4). If you can boil this selection down to two opposing options, this strategy is recommended.

Action A: Attempt to coerce the client into reporting.

Action B: Do not try to coerce the client into reporting.

Action B could be expanded to include a variety of actions under a participatory ethics approach.

Consider potential positive and negative consequences for each course of action, in light of the risks.

TABLE 17.4 Example of Weighing Consequences of Courses of Action

Action A: Pressure the Client	
Positive Consequences	*Negative Consequences*
May protect the children from abuse	Does not respect the client's autonomy or
Follows unwritten DCS policy	confidentiality
DCS would not step in to coerce the client	Hurts the client's trust of counselor
Protects DCS from liability	Ex-wife may cut off child visitation
Protects client's employment	Negative relationship with ex-wife
	May evoke suicidal thoughts
	Less time for other pressing issues of the client

Action B: Do Not Pressure the Client	
Positive Consequences	*Negative Consequences*
Respects the client's autonomy and	Does not protect children from possible abuse
confidentiality	Counselor is defying employer (DCS)
Time for the other client issues	DCS might step in and coerce the client anyway
Does not evoke suicidal thoughts	DCS might be liable (if the child is harmed)
Child visitation is preserved	Employer may terminate client's employment
Positive relationship with ex-wife	if client relapses and/or if client faces legal
	consequences related to ex-wife's illegal drug
	use

DCS, Department of Correctional Services.

TABLE 17.5 Example of Consultations

Individual	Type of Consultation
1. ACA Ethics Committee	Review situation, obtain
2. Counselors from other corrections professional organizations	suggestions and opinion
3. Other colleagues at DCS, and other professionals involved in the case (e.g., the family therapist)	
4. DHS confidential hotline again; DHS caseworker that the client believed was helpful	
5. Attorney	

DCS, Department of Correctional Services; DHS, Department of Human Services.

Component 4: Consult With Others

Consult with supervisors and other knowledgeable professionals (Table 17.5). Review the reasoning employed so far in working through the ethical dilemma in consulting with others.

Component 5: Determine Best Ethical Action

Select the best ethical course of action.

The best ethical course of action would be not to pressure the client to report to DHS, for the following reasons:

1. More ethical principles support this course of action, especially for the client.
2. More positive than negative consequences are likely to result.
3. The Iowa Code does not consider this a situation of mandatory child abuse reporting, because the counselor is not working directly with the children, and the only information is "hearsay."

Stage III: Selecting an Action by Weighing Competing, Nonmoral Values, Personal Blind Spots, or Prejudices

The counselor, in this stage, must realize the many additional forces that may affect the counselor and tempt the counselor to not actually execute the selected ethical course of action.

Component 1: Competing Values or Concerns

The counselor engages in a period of reflection and active processing of personal competing values (e.g., need to be liked by coworkers or the supervisor, or a desire to be seen as a team player, to be promoted by the supervisor), personal blind spots, or prejudices that may influence whether or not the counselor will discharge their ethical obligations. These value orientations may either come into conflict with the course of action necessary to proceed ethically or enhance the tendency to select ethical professional behavior. At this point in the decision-making process, the counselor should also consider any differences in culture or worldview that may influence the counselor's decision-making (Table 17.6) .

Component 2: Contextual Influences

Counselors systematically inventory the contextual influences on their choices at the collegial, team, institutional, and societal levels. These influences might be either dysfunctional

TABLE 17.6 Example of Analysis of Competing Values

Conflicting Concern	Potential Effects
1. Fear of a negative evaluation by DCS, if unwritten policy is not followed	Loss of job, license, respect, financial consequences
2. Feel the need to protect the children at all costs, no matter what the situation	Loss of reputation and seen as a confidentiality risk
3. Fear of legal repercussions if abuse situation is not reported to DHS	Children are harmed Loss of license and/or job
4. Fear of harm to DCS	Personal mental health Financial impact on agency/self
5. Fear of losing respect of colleagues	Personal mental health Future relationships
6. Feeling that the client should not be pressured and have autonomy in the decision	Harm to children Increased client confidence
7. Feeling that counseling session should be used to work on the client's problems (e.g., depression), rather than using all of the time trying to convince the client to call DHS	DHS not contacted and children are harmed Clients benefit from counseling
8. Feelings of disgust and anger related to possible drug abuse on the part of a mother of young children	Loss of professional judgment Harm to the client

DCS, Department of Correctional Services; DHS, Department of Human Services.

or constructive for selecting the ethical course over other types of values. John's counselor analyzes the contextual influences on John:

Level 1: Clinical (Counselor–Client)

1. Counselor's professors/supervisors have recommended advocating for clients' autonomy in the past.

Level 2: Team

1. A few coworkers note that DHS said that the counselor is not required to report the situation to DHS, because it is third-party information.
2. Other professionals are involved in this case, and may be operating under different policies and procedures, and different codes of ethics.

Level 3: Institutional/Agency

1. DCS has an unwritten policy of convincing clients to report abuse on their own.
2. Counselor's supervisor and most colleagues support the institution's policy and feel that all counselors at DCS should adhere to both written and unwritten policies.

Level 4: Social Policy/General Cultural

1. Society values children and children's welfare.
2. Society has little tolerance for drug abuse or the selling of drugs, especially when children are involved.
3. There is a fear of transmitted diseases in society, especially HIV and AIDS, which can be passed through intravenous drug use.
4. Society has a prejudiced attitude toward ex-cons on parole and makes little distinction between those who are successfully recovering and those who are not.
5. Society benefits when individuals are vaccinated against a transmissible and potentially fatal disease.

Component 3: Select Preferred Action

The counselor selects the preferred course of action.

This course of action is to attempt to convince the client to call DHS anonymously. Yet, the counselor still respects the client's autonomy and will not coerce John to report the situation to DHS.

Stage IV: Planning and Executing the Selected Course of Action

The counselor in this stage plans to implement and execute the selected course of action.

Component 1: Possible Sequences of Actions

The counselor figures out a reasonable, practical sequence of concrete actions to be taken. Following is the list of action steps to be taken.

1. Talk with the client about the consequences of his reporting versus not reporting the situation (using the "hotline" at least) to DHS. (This action is consistent with a participatory ethics orientation.)
2. Attempt to convince the client to call DHS anonymously for information about what would happen if the situation were reported.
3. If the client does not call, do not continue to try to convince him any further.
4. If the client does call and receives the information, give support for what he decides to do next.

Component 2: Contextual Barriers and Countermeasures

The counselor will need to anticipate and work out all personal and contextual barriers to an effective execution of the plan. It is useful to prepare countermeasures for any contextual barriers that may arise. Where possible, the counselor should be aware of systemic barriers, including stigma and discrimination, that may affect the situation, and engage in advocacy efforts to address the barriers (Table 17.7).

Component 3: Carry Out, Document, and Evaluate

This step provides for the execution, documentation, and evaluation of the course of action as planned. Describe here the planned goal(s) and potential types of measurements of plan effectiveness and sources of information.

The counselor would carry out the plan by talking to the client about the consequences of reporting versus not reporting the abusive situation to DHS and attempt to get the client to call for information. Or, alternatively, under a participatory ethics orientation, discuss with the client the pros and cons of contacting the DHS in a way that empowers the client to make the final decision about whether to call. If the client decides to call, the counselor would support his next step. The counselor would document the ethical decision-making steps taken. Finally, the counselor would evaluate the effectiveness of the plan of action and the entire ethical decision-making process, taking care to ensure that any multicultural considerations are addressed and included in the plan (Table 17.8). *Note:* This case study was developed by Vilia Tarvydas, PhD, CRC, revised by Sara Johnston, PhD, CRC, and uses the Tarvydas Integrative Decision-Making Model of Ethical Behavior.

TABLE 17.7 Systemic Barriers

1. The client does not wish to call.	Document the attempts to get him to call and do not press the issue any further.
2. Supervisor may want the counselor to continue to coerce the client to call.	Counselor could let the supervisor know what they are not comfortable doing and apprise someone in authority above the supervisor of the situation.
3. DCS may assign the case to someone else.	No countermeasure unless the client insists upon seeing the current counselor.
4. John's ex-wife may refuse to let him see the children, if he reports the situation to DHS.	Counselor could encourage the client to speak with an attorney about his rights with the children.
5. John's refusal to be vaccinated for influenza and COVID-19 may result in him losing his job and his ability to pay child support.	Counselor could advocate for the client by referring the client to culturally appropriate information and resources about the benefits of vaccination from trusted community members who understand the barriers to vaccination in the Black American community. Counselor can advocate for the client and/ or encourage client to self-advocate with employer, to improve employer knowledge about Black American employees' distrust of the medical profession, including vaccine resistance.

TABLE 17.8 Evaluating the Plan

1. Review consequences of reporting or not reporting and attempt to get the client to call DHS for information.	Weigh benefits and costs of the client's decision; assess the client's level of comfort with either decision.
2. Support the client if he decides to call.	Assess what the client needs from the counselor.
3. Prevent harm to children and help mother.	Follow up with treatment referrals for mother and on the children's welfare.

CONCLUSION

Rehabilitation counseling continues to grow in stature and visibility, as a specialty practice within the counseling profession. As a result, contemporary rehabilitation counselors should anticipate the need to demonstrate high levels of competency in the ethical aspects of their practices. The professional practice as a whole has provided substantial tools to inform this process, including the revised 2017 Ethical Standards of Practice provided by CRCC, mechanisms to educate and govern the practice of these ethical standards, and knowledge and wisdom for individual counselors, embodied within models of ethical decision-making and behavior. With responsible utilization of these sizable assets for ethical practice, rehabilitation counseling should continue its leadership in the counseling professionalization movement.

CONTENT REVIEW QUESTIONS

1. What are the three components of professional standards? Provide examples of each and describe how they contribute to the quality of care in the profession.
2. What are the major levels of ethics governance, and what role does each play in the enforcement of ethical standards? What bodies represent counseling and rehabilitation counseling at each level?
3. What is the difference between mandatory and aspirational ethics? Provide an illustration of a set of ethical standards that represents each type of ethical standard and discuss why, as well as how they serve complementary roles.

4. What themes or attitudes must one consider when using the Tarvydas Integrative Decision-Making Model of Ethical Behavior? Why do you think these are important in the process?
5. What are the major stages of the Tarvydas Integrative Decision-Making Model of Ethical Behavior? What main processes and goals are characteristic of each one?
6. Describe the concepts of participatory and restrictive ethics that may affect the ethical decision-making process. Provide an example of a situation in which a client may benefit from a participatory ethics approach.
7. Describe how multicultural considerations should be incorporated into the counselor's ethical decision-making process.
8. Compare the ACA *Code of Ethics* with the CRCC *Code of Professional Ethics* and discuss the similarities and differences between the two codes.

REFERENCES

American Counseling Association. (2014). *Code of ethics.* https://www.counseling.org/resources/aca-code-of-ethics.pdf

American Psychological Association. (2009). Revised guidelines for child custody evaluations in family law proceedings.

Betan, E. J., & Stanton, A. L. (1999). Fostering ethical willingness: integrating emotional and contextual awareness with rational analysis. *Professional Psychology, Research and Practice, 30*(3), 295–301. https://doi.org/10.1037/0735-7028.30.3.295

Butterfield, K. D., Trevin, L. K., & Weaver, G. R. (2000). Moral awareness in business organizations: Influences of issue-related and social context factors. *Human Relations, 53*(7), 981–1018. https://doi.org/10.1177/0018726700537004

Charlton, J. I. (2000). *Nothing about us without us: Disability oppression and empowerment.* University of California Press.

Commission on Rehabilitation Counselor Certification. (2017). *Code of professional ethics for rehabilitation counselors.* https://crccertification.com/code-of-ethics-4/

Corey, G., Corey, M. S., & Corey, C. (2019). *Issues and ethics in the helping professions* (10th ed.). Cengage Learning.

Cottone, R. R. (2012). Ethical decision making in mental health contexts: Representative-models and an organizational framework. In S. Knapp (Ed.), *The handbook on ethics in psychology* (pp. 99–121). American Psychological Association.

Cottone, R. R., & Claus, R. E. (2000). Ethical decision-making models: A review of the literature. *Journal of Counseling and Development, 78*(3), 275–283. https://doi.org/10.1002/j.1556-6676.2000.tb01908.x

Cottone, R. R., & Tarvydas, V. M. (2007). *Counseling ethics and decision making* (3rd ed.). Merrill/Prentice Hall.

Cottone, R. R., Tarvydas, V., & House, G. (1994). The effect of number and type of consulted relationships on the ethical decision making of graduate students in counseling. *Counseling and Values, 39*(1), 56–68. https://doi.org/10.1002/j.2161-007X.1994.tb01007.x

Francoeur, R. T. (1983). Teaching decision-making skills in biomedical ethics for the allied health student. *Journal of Allied Health, 12*(3), 202–209.

Garcia, J. G., Cartwright, B., Winston, S. M., & Borzuchowska, B. (2003). A transcultural integrative model for ethical decision making in counseling. *Journal of Counseling & Development, 81*(3), 268–277. https://doi.org/10.1002/j.1556-6678.2003.tb00253.x

Gatens-Robinson, E., & Rubin, S. E. (1995). Societal values and ethical commitments that influence rehabilitation service delivery behavior. In S. E. Rubin & R. T. Roessler (Eds.), *Foundations of the vocational rehabilitation process* (pp. 157–174). Pro-Ed.

Hostetter, M., & Klein, S. (2021, January 14). *Understanding and ameliorating medical mistrust among Black Americans. The Commonwealth Fund.* https://www.commonwealthfund.org/publications/newsletter-article/2021/jan/medical-mistrust-among-black-americans#:~:text=Medical%20Mistrust%20and%20Its%20Impacts&text=In%20an%20October%202020%20poll,prevent%20people%20from%20getting%20care

Johnson, S. (n.d.). *Samuel Johnson quotes.* http://quotes.yourdictionary.com/author/samule-johnson/168000

Kitchener, K. S. (1984). Intuition, critical evaluation and ethical principles: The foundation for ethical decisions in counseling psychology. *The Counseling Psychologist, 12*(3), 43–55. https://doi.org/10.1177/0011000084123005

Koocher, G. P., & Keith-Spiegel, P. (2007). *Ethics in psychology and the mental health professions: Standards and cases* (2nd ed.). Oxford University Press.

Levine, A., & Breshears, B. (2019). Discrimination at every turn: An intersectional ecological lens for rehabilitation. *Rehabilitation Psychology, 64*(2), 146–153. https://doi.org/10.1037/rep0000266

Mabe, A. R., & Rollin, S. A. (1986). The role of a code of ethical standards in counseling. *Journal of Counseling & Development, 64*(5), 294–297. https://doi.org/10.1002/j.1556-6676.1986.tb01113.x

Meara, N. M., Schmidt, L. D., & Day, J. D. (1996). Principles and virtue: A foundation for ethical decisions, policies, and character. *The Counseling Psychologist, 24*(1), 4–77.

Powell, S. K., & Wekell, P. M. (1996). *Nursing case management.* Lippincott.

Prilleltensky, I., Rossiter, A., & Walsh-Bowers, R. (1996). Preventing harm and promoting ethical discourse in the helping professions: conceptual, research, analytical, and action frameworks. *Ethics & Behavior, 6*(4), 287–306. https://doi.org/10.1207/s15327019eb0604_1

Ratts, M. J., Toporek, R. L., & Lewis, J. A. (2010). *ACA Advocacy Competencies. A social justice framework for counselors.* American Counseling Association.

Rest, J. R. (1984). Research on moral development: Implications for training counseling psychologists. *The Counseling Psychologist, 12*(3), 19–29. https://doi.org/10.1177/0011000084123003

Rinas, J., & Clyne-Jackson, S. (1988). *Professional conduct and legal concerns in mental health practice.* Appleton & Lange.

Tarvydas, V. M., & Cottone, R. R. (2000). The code of ethics for professional rehabilitation counselors: What we have and what we need. *Rehabilitation Counseling Bulletin, 43*(4), 188–196. https://doi.org/10.1177/003435520004300402

Tarvydas, V. M., & Cottone, R. R. (1991). Ethical responses to legislative, organizational, and economic dynamics: A four level model of ethical practice. *Journal of Applied Rehabilitation Counseling, 22*(4), 11–18. https://doi.org/10.1891/0047-2220.22.4.11

Tarvydas, V. M., O'Rourke, B. J., & Urish C. (2007). Ethical climate. In R. R. Cottone & V. M. Tarvydas (Eds.), *Counseling ethics and decision making* (3rd ed., pp. 116–137). Merrill/Prentice Hall.

Tarvydas, V. M., Vazquez-Ramos, R., & Estrada-Hernandez, N. (2015). Applied participatory ethics: Bridging the social justice chasm between counselor and client. *Counseling and Values, 60*(2), 218–233. https://doi.org/10.1002/cvj.12015

Thompson, A. (1990). *Guide to ethical practice in psychotherapy.* Wiley.

Van Hoose, W. H., & Kottler, J. A. (1985). *Ethical and legal issues in counseling and psychotherapy.* Jossey-Bass.

Vasquez, M. J. T. (1996). Will virtue ethics improve ethical conduct in multicultural settings and interactions? *The Counseling Psychologist, 24*(1), 98–104. https://doi.org/10.1177/0011000096241006

Willems, S. J., Castells, M. C. D., & Baptist, A. P. (2022). The magnification of health disparities during the COVID-19 pandemic. *The Journal of Allergy and Clinical Immunology, 10*(4), 903–908. https://doi.org/10.1016/j.jaip.2022.01.032

Wright, B. A. (1983). *Physical disability—A psychosocial approach.* Harper & Row.

CHAPTER 18

Cultural Competence and Social Justice

TERRILYN BATTLE, GLACIA ETHRIDGE, AND DAVID STATEN

LEARNING OBJECTIVES:

After reading this chapter, you should be able to:

- *Describe the multicultural counseling competencies across the American Counseling Association (ACA) standards relevant to social justice and cultural competence.*
- *Review relevant CACREP Standards pertaining to cultural competence and social justice.*
- *Analyze societal laws and policies that impact marginalized groups*
- *Apply newly acquired knowledge of terms and standards by analyzing case scenarios and responding to discussion questions.*

CACREP STANDARDS

CACREP 2016: 2F1.e, 2F2.a, 2F2.b, 2F2.c, 2F2.d, 2F2.e, 2F2.f, 2F2.g, 2F2.h, 2F3.g, 2F3.i, 2F4.g, 2F4.i, 2F5.d, 2F5.k, 2F6.g, 2F7.m, 2F8.j
CACREP 2016 Specialties:
   Clinical Rehabilitation: 5D1.g, 5D2.k, 5D2.p, 5D2.s, 5D2.t, 5D3.c
   Rehabilitation Counseling: 5H1.e, 5H2.e, 5H2.f, 5H2.n, 5H3.f, 5H3.j, 5H3.k

INTRODUCTION

Rehabilitation counselors (RCs) work in an array of sectors, including state vocational rehabilitation, private practice, community rehabilitation providers, and the Veterans Administration. Regardless of sector, RCs' caseloads are composed of individuals from various cultural and other backgrounds, such as race/ethnicity, disability type, the severity of disability, and environments. Each client's background may present with unique assets and challenges. It is important that RCs thus understand the importance of culture as it pertains to their clients to ensure that quality services are provided. As part of this commitment, RCs need to know key concepts such as social justice, cultural competence, broaching, and cultural humility including their applicability to the professional practice of rehabilitation counseling.

Ratts (2009) indicated that **social justice** is the fifth force in counseling. Although newly operationalized, the author noted that social justice is something that has always been a part of the counseling profession. Social justice is defined as an approach to counseling in which practitioners strive to recognize and address the fact that not all people have the same economic, political, and social rights and opportunities (Crethar et al., 2008; Rawls, 1971). The counseling profession was born out of humanitarian concerns, and thus social justice advocacy for clients has long been one of the many roles and functions of the counselor. While social justice is a broad term related to human rights, **advocacy** is a more "behavioral and action orientated, and is an activity that often involves actions to correct some social injustice" (Marini, 2012). The historical foundation of rehabilitation counseling is grounded in acts of social justice advocacy as it pertains to the rights of individuals with disabilities. Advocacy in areas such as education, housing, transportation, employability, and access to healthcare are just a few areas in which efforts towards assisting individuals with disabilities have been made. The advocacy efforts of RCs are rooted in a genuine desire to address the societal barriers restricting the lives of individuals with disabilities. RCs work with diverse clients, regardless of the setting. **Diversity** can be defined as "the existence of variety in human expression, especially the multiplicity of mores and customs that are manifested in social and cultural life" (McAuliffe, 2020).

This chapter defines *cultural competence* and explores current societal events through the lens of social justice. In this chapter, the terms *cultural competence* and *multicultural competence* are used interchangeable to describe the ability of RCs to negotiate cultural difference in a respectful and responsive manner. Easier said than done, this chapter highlights the larger competencies necessary for providing services to diverse client populations. Specifically, the chapter content synthesizes several sets of ACA-endorsed cultural competency and social justice standards including the (a) Multicultural and Social Justice Counseling Competencies, (b) Multicultural Career Counseling Competencies, (c) Competencies for Counseling Multiracial Population, (d) Competencies for Counseling Transgender Clients, and (e) Disability-Related Counseling Competencies. Concepts such as broaching and cultural humility are discussed, including societal trends reflect in political laws and actions that affect groups who have been historically marginalized by societal barriers.

Intersection Between Cultural Competence and Social Justice

Important multicultural counseling standards will be explored in detail later in the chapter. They govern the counseling profession and emphasize the importance of being aware of the needs of diverse clients. **Cultural competence** is defined as having an appreciation and understanding of cultures that are similar and different from that of the counselor. Components of cultural competence are often broken down into (a) attitudes and beliefs, (b) knowledge, (c) skills, and (d) action. According to Ratts et al. (2015), counselors should possess attitudes and beliefs, knowledge, skills, and action "to implement multicultural and social justice competencies into counseling theories, practices, and research" (Ratts et al., 2015, p. 3). Social justice intersects with cultural competence in that counselors need to move beyond acknowledging the cultural background of the client within the counseling space, to ensure that all clients have access to quality and equitable services. Cultural competence thus requires a commitment to social justice to ensure that all clients receive equal treatment and services (Box 18.1).

As part of providing culturally competent services, Day-Vines et al. (2007) defined **broaching** as "the counselor's ability to consider how sociopolitical factors such as race influence the client's counseling concerns" (p. 401). Broaching is critical because research has found that individuals with disabilities who are Black, Indigenous, and people of color (BIPOC) often do not have the same employment outcomes as their white counterparts. Given this, RCs need to hear the concerns of their BIPOC clients with respect to their employment experiences as well as their concerns about the service delivery system itself. Day-Vines and colleagues described broaching behavior on a continuum that invites the client to explore issues of diversity beginning with general conversations

BOX 18.1 DISCUSSION QUESTIONS

1. Provide your own definitions for social justice and cultural competence. For each definition, provide an example of how you can practice social justice and cultural competence when working with clients.
2. How might a lack of cultural competence impact the counselor–client relationship? What can rehabilitation counseling as a field do to improve the cultural competence of its practitioners?

such as the counselor saying: "We're both from different ethnic backgrounds. I'm wondering how you feel about working with a White European American woman on your concerns?" (2007, p. 402). However, the concept of broaching is much more than a single question or conversation. Rather, it is about the RC intentionally introducing culture and diversity with an emphasis on their openness to the client's cultural identities and experiences. Broaching is essential to opening the door to cultural conversations that may not otherwise happen within the counseling relationship.

More than just initiating cultural conversations, RCs need to strive for cultural humility. Hook et al. (2013) defined **cultural humility** as "the ability to maintain an interpersonal stance that is other-oriented (or open to the other) in relation to aspects of cultural identity that are most important to the client" (p. 354). The concept of cultural humility reflects the notion of the helping professional's ability to "express respect and a lack of superiority even when cultural differences threaten to weaken the therapy alliance" (Hook et al., 2013, p. 354). It is important to note that when exploring the context of cultural humility, counselors rarely assume an all-or-nothing approach to cultural competence (Hook et al., 2013). Rather than a false dichotomy of fully competent to incompetent, cultural competence exists along a continuum of constant improvement, yet with minimum standards of competence defined by professional standards. Instead, cultural humility encourages the professional's capacity to self-reflect and self-critique throughout the duration of their career as lifelong learners. The concept of cultural humility aids in our understanding of multicultural counseling competence as a journey, rather than destination.

Intersectionality, a termed coined by Kimberlé Crenshaw in 1989, is the notion that people are comprised of multiple identities (Crenshaw, 1989). Specifically, Crenshaw examined the intersection of race and gender. Race and gender in her seminal work was geared towards African American women and how feminism and antiracist politics oftentimes overlook or dismiss the concerns, needs, and rights of Africa American women. Intersectionality has evolved beyond that of race and gender to include the many facets of individual, such as ability, socioeconomic status, educational level, and so on.

Council for Accreditation of Counseling and Related Educational Program Standards on Cultural Competence and Social Justice

The Council for Accreditation of Counseling and Related Educational Program (CACREP) is the accreditation body for all counseling education programs. The CACREP (2016) standards are separated by sections. All counseling programs that are pursuing and/or renewing their accreditation must adhere to the standards in the first four sections (i.e., The Learning Environment, Professional Counseling Identity, Professional Practice, and Evaluation in the Program). The remaining sections are separated by program specialty areas, two of which are relevant to this chapter: (a) Clinical Rehabilitation Counseling and (b) Rehabilitation Counseling. These two specialty areas have additional disability-related cultural and social justice content beyond what is covered in the common core for all counselors.

It is important to note that the CACREP has adopted numerous specific standards associated with cultural competence and social justice that have been infused across the education of all counselors. This coverage reinforces the importance of working with individuals from diverse backgrounds and ensuring that these individuals are able to access services and receive fair treatment. Additionally, the CACREP (2016) standards make note of the impact of systemic barriers. Consistent with social justice work, all counselors must recognize the systemic barriers that can make it challenging for individuals marginalized by systemic barriers to participation in society.

The CACREP competencies strive to push a multiculturally sound narrative as part of the education of professional counselors. Within the counseling curriculum, the CACREP (2022) has adopted clear standards regarding the importance of social and cultural diversity as it pertains to the professional counseling identity of all counselors (Section 2). Specifically, the foundational CACREP (2016) standards "reflect current knowledge and projected needs concerning counseling practice in a multicultural and pluralistic society" as well as "input from all persons involved in the conduct of the program" (CACREP, 2022, para. 1). To meet this standard, many counselor education programs engage in ongoing cultural and social justice considerations, including diversity surveys of students, faculty, staff, and cooperating agencies as well as continuing education workshops for faculty and staff.

Additionally, all counseling students are expected to demonstrate competency regarding the educational standards across eight common core areas that represent the foundational knowledge for all entry-level counselors-in-training. Specific to Section 2.2 of the CACREP standards related to social and cultural diversity:

a. Multicultural and pluralistic characteristics within and among diverse groups nationally and internationally
b. Theories and models of multicultural counseling, cultural identity development, and social justice and advocacy
c. Multicultural counseling competencies
d. The impact of heritage, attitudes, beliefs, understandings, and acculturative experiences on an individual's views of others
e. The effects of power and privilege for counselors and clients
f. Help-seeking behaviors of diverse clients
g. The impact of spiritual beliefs on clients' and counselors' worldviews
h. Strategies for identifying and eliminating barriers, prejudices, and processes of intentional and unintentional oppression and discrimination (CACREP, 2022, para. 3)

These educational standards are often taught within a graduate course specific to social and cultural diversity as well as infused across the curriculum of other courses. For example, many RC programs will have a course titled, *Multicultural Counseling*, in the curriculum. However, multicultural counseling concepts and knowledge should also be infused in other courses, such as introduction to rehabilitation counseling, medical and psychosocial aspects of disability, career counseling, vocational assessment, just to name a few. Disability, which is a type of culture, is the basis for many courses in rehabilitation counseling; however, when working with clients with disabilities, RCs must consider other aspects of the cultural background of the client when providing services. Background information may consist of the intersection of disability factors such as severity and type, along with socioeconomic status, educational level, armed services, and gender, to name a few.

It is well known that rehabilitation counseling is grounded in advocacy to support the rights of persons with disabilities, especially in the area of employment. Other social justice action areas have been focused on housing, education, and healthcare, which directly impact the societal inclusion of people with disabilities. The training of RCs is thus integral to ensuring that RCs are equipped with the knowledge and skills to work with individuals with disabilities. For this reason, students in rehabilitation counseling programs must meet the core standards for social and cultural diversity as well as standards specific to disability found in the specialty standards of Clinical Rehabilitation Counseling and Rehabilitation Counseling.

While the CACREP standards are a starting place to consider what it means to demonstrate cultural competence, the CACREP standards alone are not enough. Specifically, there is a need for more detailed guidance on considerations for working with specific populations. Additionally, there is a need for more guidance on how as practicing clinicians, RCs can be intentional as multiculturally competent change agents.

AMERICAN COUNSELORS ASSOCIATION–ENDORSED STANDARDS RELATED TO CULTURE AND SOCIAL JUSTICE

Within the realm of their role as counselors, RCs are expected to effectively demonstrate their knowledge, skill, and proficiency with an emphasis on cultural competence. These competencies are reflected in following ACA-endorsed documents: the MSJCC (Ratts et al., 2015), the Multicultural Career Counseling Competencies (NCDA, 2009), the Competencies for Counseling Multiracial Populations (Kenney et al., 2015), the Competencies for Counseling Transgender Clients (Burnes et al., 2009), and the Disability-Related Counseling Competencies (Chapin et al., 2018). For the purposes of this chapter, these competencies are used to reflect cultural proficiencies that promote social justice.

As we explore and observe the competencies under inquiry, it is important to acknowledge that these competencies are grounded within the paradigm of the ACA. Furthermore, it is important to note that these multicultural competencies may not hold the same credence among other professional associations for RCs. RCs may hold national certification issued by the Commission on Rehabilitation Counselor Certification (CRCC) and not seek state licensure for clinical practice as a licensed professional counselor. Due to this, there may be limited exposure to multicultural competencies held by professional associations such as ACA that are more specific regarding multicultural competency than only what is covered in the CRCC code of ethics. With that said, we hope that readers will embrace this list of cultural competencies as not an exhaustive list but rather as starting place for understanding cultural competence.

Multicultural and Social Justice Counseling Competencies

The Multicultural and Social Justice Counseling Competencies (MSJCC) offer "counselors a framework to implement multicultural and social justice competencies into counseling theories, practices, and research" (Ratts et al., 2015, p. 3). The MSJCC are structured around counselor self-awareness, client worldview, the counseling relationship, and interventions to promote diversity inclusion and change within the field. Domains such as (a) counselor self-awareness, (b) client worldview, (c) the counseling relationship, and (d) counseling and advocacy interventions are noted as components that influence multicultural and social justice competence for practitioners and counselor educators (Ratts et al., 2015). Among the first three domains, the following are aspirational competencies to be developed: attitudes (and beliefs), knowledge, skills, and action (Ratts et al., 2015). It is important to highlight that the MSJCC is explicit about the "intersection of identities and the dynamics of power, privilege, and oppression that influence the counseling relationship" (Ratts et al., 2015, p. 3). Exploring the notions of privileged counselor, marginalized counselor, privileged client, and marginalized client, the MSJCC are an important resource for culturally competent counseling.

Within counseling practice, Ratts et al. (2015) urged the importance of three areas; (a) understanding the attitudes and beliefs with which the client may present, (b) gaining knowledge of the understanding of the underlying cultural assumptions, and (c) employing skills of reflective and critical thinking to gain a better perspective of the client's worldview. From this cultural lens, the RC can more effectively work to advocate and support the clients they serve, regardless of characteristics individuals may present within the counseling space. In turn, this perspective supports the model of social justice and multiculturalism.

Multicultural Career Counseling and Development Competencies

In 2009, the National Career Development Association (NCDA) approved the Multicultural Career Counseling and Development Competencies. These competencies replaced the 1997 Career Counseling Competencies which identified the Minimum Competencies for cultural competence (NCDA, 2009). The purpose of the new competencies was to "ensure that all individuals practicing in, or training for practice in, the career counseling and development field are aware of the expectation that we . . . practice in ways that promote the career development and functioning of individuals of all backgrounds (NCDA, 2009, para. 1). A critical element of promoting the career development and functioning of all individuals is consideration for clients' cultural backgrounds and identities. With this in mind, it is critical that counselors work toward the "promotion and advocacy of career development for individuals is ensured regardless of age, culture, mental/physical ability, ethnicity, race, nationality, religion/spirituality, gender, gender identity, sexual orientation, marital/partnership status, military or civilian status, language preference, socioeconomic status" or "any other characteristics not specifically relevant to job performance, in accordance with NCDA and ACA policy" (NCDA, 2009, para. 1).

To demonstrate professional engagement within career counseling, NCDA (2009) identified 11 designated areas in which the career professional must acknowledge multicultural competency: career development theory; individual and group counseling skills; individual/group assessment; information, resources, and technology; program promotion, management, and implementation; coaching, consultation, and performance improvement; supervision; ethical/legal issues, research/evaluation. Distinct from other sets of ACA-endorsed competencies, the focus is on cultural competence and social justice within the practice and delivery of employment and career counseling.

Competencies for Counseling Multiracial Population

Another important set of competencies were created by the Multiracial/Ethnic Counseling Concerns (MRECC) Interest Network of the ACA to "competently and effectively attend to the diverse needs of the multiple heritage population" (Kenney et al., 2015, p. 2). Specifically, the Competencies for Counseling Multiracial Population can be used by practitioners and other helping professionals who may educate, train, and/or supervise current and future practitioners and/or researcher who may provide support to members of the multiracial population. Furthermore, the utilization of these standards is intended to advocate for individuals who identify as members of multiracial populations. This group includes "interracial couples, multiracial families, and multiracial individuals, and transracial adoptees and families" (Kenney et al., 2015, p. 2).

The MRECC has been "working to raise awareness about interracial couples, multiracial families, and multiracial individuals, and transracial adoptees and families in the counseling and other helping professions since the mid-1990s" (Kenney et al., 2015, p. 2). The MRECC also Additional reflects the lesbian, gay, bisexual, and transgender (LGBT) population, as well as the lesbian, gay, bisexual, queer, questioning, intersex, and ally (LGBQQIA) population. When noting LGBT, this set of competencies reflects "the experiences of interracial couples and families" of the lesbian, gay, bisexual, and transgender identities. In the context of LGBQQIA, the MRECC reflects the acknowledgment of "multiracial individuals through the lens of other possible identities" (Kenney et al., 2015, p. 3).

There are several important terms highlighted within this set of competencies. **Transracial adoption (TRA)** is an emphasis on international (transnational or transcultural) adoptions. Additionally, the authors posited a common term utilized to identify adoption stakeholders is the **adoption triad**, "which refers to adoptees, adoptive parents, and birth parents" (Kenney et al., 2015, p. 3). However, they utilize a "more inclusive term, **Transracial Adoption Kinship Network** (TrAKN), to include extended family within adoptions and foster families and to include those impacted by transracial and international adoption" (Kenney et al., 2015, p. 3). It is important to note this competency's intention was to raise "the awareness, knowledge, and skill levels of members of the counseling and other helping professions as they work with and advocate for increasing numbers of multiracial couples, individuals and families" (Kenney et al., 2015, p. 4–5).

Section II of the competencies is focused on the multiracial population that includes considerations for working with interracial couples, multiracial families and individuals. Furthermore, Section III of the competencies is intended to aid the "the population that includes transracial adoptees and families" (Kenney et al., 2015, p. 5). Both Sections II and III explore "(a) the contextual framework used to inform and construct the competencies specific to the population; (b) the language and definitions specific to the population; (c) current issues and stances; and (d) the competencies specific to the population" (Kenney et al., 2015, p. 5). While Section II reflects competencies for working with interracial couples and multiracial families and competencies for working with multicultural individuals, Section III follows with the "competencies for working with transracial adoptees and the transracial adoption kinship network" (p. 5). These competencies were created to align with the structure of the CACREP standards.

Competencies for Counseling Transgender Clients

In 2009, the ACA Governing Council approved the Competencies for Counseling with Transgender Clients developed by the Association for Lesbian, Gay, Bisexual, and Transgender Issues in Counseling (ALGBTIC). These competencies are focused on assisting "professionally trained counselors who work with transgender individuals, families, groups, or communities" (Burnes et al., 2009). In particular, the focus of this set of competencies is to enhance the domains of wellness, resilience, and strength-based approaches for working with transgender consumers (Burnes et al., 2009).

In its conceptualization, the ALGBTIC Competencies were constructed from a theoretical framework in which multicultural contexts (Sue & Sue, 2008), social justice (Goodman et al., 2004), and feminist perspectives (Worell & Remer, 2002) were employed. At the center of the competencies is "the influence of privilege, power and oppression on clients' lives" (Burnes et al., 2009).

It is important to note that within the ALGBTIC competencies, the authors explore transgender-affirmative language. Highlighting this notion in more clarity, the authors stated that "although specific terms are used throughout the document, it is important to recognize the continuous evolution of language is to be expected with regard to working with transgender clients as there are many terms that are used" (Burnes et al., 2009). Furthermore, the authors noted the importance that "language in transgender (and any cultural) communities varies and that these competencies would not dictate 'accurate' or 'correct' language" (Burnes et al., 2009). In addition to this observation, the authors endorsed the importance of recognizing that the correct utilization of "self-identified, gender affirming pronouns for transgender clients are also important" (Burnes et al., 2009). The context of language is important and should not be dismissed when providing support to this population. This clause is supported by the authors' position that "counselors should also be aware that some transgender individuals do not identify with gender-neutral pronouns and identify with traditional gender pronouns" (Burnes et al.,

2009). The way in which a client identifies gender and affirms themselves through their transition process should be taken into consideration to aid multicultural competence.

An important context for affirmative language is within the client's family. Burnes et al. (2009) stated that "due to the heterosexism, transprejudice, transphobia, and transnegativity many transgender individuals experience, it is not uncommon [for] transgender people to be rejected from their family of origin; and, therefore, there may be conflict and/or separation from nuclear and extended families" (p. 4). Therefore, transgender individuals may define family by acknowledging those who hold roles of family, regardless of "biological or legal adoption within a family unit" (Burnes et al., 2009).

Association for Lesbian, Gay, Bisexual, and Transgender Issues in Counseling Competencies for Counseling Lesbian, Gay, Bisexual, Queer, Questionining, Intersex, and Ally Individuals

Competencies for Counseling with Lesbian, Gay, Bisexual, Queer, Questioning, Intersex and Ally Individuals were also developed by the ALGBTIC. These competencies were developed with the intention to "provide counseling and related professionals with competencies for working with Lesbian, Gay, Bisexual, Queer, Intersex, and Questioning and Ally (LGBQIQA) individuals, groups, and communities" (Harper et al., 2012, p. 2). The intent of these competencies is to constitute a safe, supportive, and caring relationship with individuals, groups, and communities that identify with LGBQIQA populations and "foster self-acceptance and personal, social, emotional, and relational development" (Harper et al., 2012, p. 2). It is important to note that this set of competencies does not address the context of individuals who identify as transgender, which is the reason for the Competencies for Counseling with Transgender Clients was developed.

The ALGBTIC Competencies for Counseling LGBQQIA Individuals is focused on "working with adult individuals, groups, and communities" and "is applicable to children" (Harper et al., 2012, p. 2). Additionally, this set of competencies suggests counseling professionals and related professionals should take into consideration the developmental needs of their work with individuals across the lifespan (Harper et al., 2012, p. 2). At its core, these competencies are the application of multicultural competencies of "knowledge, skills, and awareness for counselors" (Harper et al., 2012, p. 2) to evoke advocacy for LGBQIQA individuals, groups, and communities to promote empowerment and a "socially-just society" (2012, p. 2).

The benefit of a specific set of competencies is that it details the current issues and stances affecting LGBQIQA clients. Specifically, it highlights that counseling professionals should educate themselves about the current issues potential clients may experience. These competencies reflect an overall organizational structure of six main sections: Introduction, Competencies for working with Lesbian, Gay, Bisexual, Queer and Questioning Individuals, Competencies for working with Allies, Competencies for working with Intersex Individuals, References and Resources, and an Appendix.

Within the first section (introduction), and the second section on competencies, important considerations for working with this population are mapped onto the 2009 CACREP Standards:

A. Human Growth and Development
B. Social and Cultural Foundations
C. Helping Relationships
D. Group Work
E. Professional Orientation and Ethical Practice
F. Career and Lifestyle Development
G. Assessment
H. Research and Program Evaluation (Harper et al., 2012, p. 6)

The third section on Allyship section is focused on competencies for counseling individuals who identify as Allies, while the fourth section presents competencies related to counseling individuals who identify as Intersex. Some counselors may not be as familiar with individuals who identify as Intersex, they may be with LGBTQIQA populations. The References and Resource section reflects a list of resources to further develop and increase competence. Finally, Appendix A reflects a list of definitions and important concepts within the document.

Disability-Related Counseling Competencies

The Disability-related Counseling Competencies (DRCC) reflect the work of the American Rehabilitation Counseling Association Task Force on Competencies for Counseling Persons with Disabilities (Chapin et al., 2018). These competencies were developed to assist counselors of all backgrounds to provide support to persons with disabilities (PWDs). Specifically, the document containing these competencies has the goal to "encourage counselors to pursue the competencies identified below to better understand and assist PWDs and is not intended as a mandatory list of standards that must be met in order to provide effective counseling to PWDs" (Chapin et al., 2018, p. 1). The competencies identified within this document are organized into the following sections: (a) understanding and accommodating the disability experience, (b) advocacy for PWDs and support of their self-advocacy, (c) the counseling process and relationship, (d) testing and assessment, (e) and working with or supervising PWDs in school, employment, community, and clinical settings.

Section A of this competency reflects the notion of understanding and accommodating the Disability Experience in which it aims to provide context for working with individuals that identify as PWDs and the understanding that they, too, can live full and productive lives. Furthermore, this section informs PWDs "deserve to have encouragement and opportunities to develop and express themselves as they progress through every stage of the lifespan" (Chapin et al., 2018, p. 12), understanding "the process and timing of adapting to the onset of a disability, the way individuals develop a disability identity, and the ways in which that identity is expressed as it varies from person to person" (Chapin et al., 2018, p. 2). Collectively, this section further details advocacy and steps to ensure support from an inclusive, holistic, and strengths-based perspective.

Section B reflects perspectives of advocacy for PWDs and support of their self-advocacy by exploring the development of knowledge, skills, and commitment to social justice. From this lens, this section promotes decisions and actions to make mental health, medical, and wellness support applicable and accessible to individuals with disabilities within their communities.

Section C explores the counseling process and relationship and encourages accommodations such as alternative formats for client communication when needed. Additionally, Section C explores the utilization of accessibility of technology and consideration of interpretations of a client's experiences and worldview.

Section D reflects testing and assessment in which professionals are encouraged to demonstrate sensitivity in how some tests and assessments reflect an ableist culture and may reinforce stereotypes or disability-negative perceptions about one's abilities and capabilities. This section urges the understanding that PWDs reflect a greater risk of trauma and/or abuse and the need to screen these concepts during the initial intake assessment.

Section E observes "working with or supervising PWDs in school, employment, community, and clinical settings" (Chapin et al., 2018, p. 28). Specifically, this section examines existing practices and materials "for language, assumptions and concepts that may be inappropriate or disparaging toward PWDs" (Chapin et al., 2018, p. 8). Furthermore, this section promotes access to physical sites, equipment, and the utilization of multiple media sources to reach individuals with disabilities when publicizing employment opportunities.

The DRCC are rooted in a cultural understanding of disability intended to counter **ableism** as the "belief that disability in and of itself makes one in some way lesser—less deserving of respect, a good education, membership in the community, equal treatment . . . and opportunities to have inclusive, self-fulfilling, and productive lives" (Slesaransky-Poe & García, 2014, p. 76). As an example, the DRCC direct RCs to "validate and collaboratively problem-solve client concerns about their experiences of oppression and ableism" (Chapin et al., 2018, A.6, p. 3). As another example, the DRCC standard A.9. requires that RCs "examine their beliefs and assumptions about disability to reveal unintended, indirect, or subtle ways in which biases may influence counselor behavior and interpretations (e.g., immediately assuming that the disability is the presenting problem or the cause of it)" (Chapin et al., 2018, A.6. p. 3). The significance of the DRCC is to direct all counselors to that fact that disability may be an important part of the clients' personal identity and cultural diversity.

Synthesis of American Counselors Association–Endorsed Competencies

In review of the competency standards identified within this chapter, there is a common theme in which many of the competencies overlap with one another by identifying characteristics the client may present within the counseling setting (i.e., sexual orientation, mental/physical ability, race, gender, gender identity, marital/partnership status). Each standard urges its utilization to aid multicultural competency of the helping professional and ensuring their openness to the client's worldview. Such competencies further aid the understanding of the obligation to advocate for populations that these standards aim to support.

The emergence of multiple sets of competencies is a reflection of how multicultural concerns have been elevated to the limelight of professional controversy in the field of rehabilitation (Bellini, 2002). Multicultural competence is an important and vital context for practicing clinicians to provide competent support to their clients. Specifically, each set of competencies offers guidelines intended to promote counselors establishing an effective therapeutic alliance with their clients. Bellini (2002) posited "multicultural concerns in rehabilitation have become increasingly relevant for a number of reasons" (p. 66). Supporting the importance of multicultural competency within the realm of rehabilitation counseling, Kim et al. (2018) expounded on the position, highlighting that RCs need to know how to respond effectively to clients who identify as having multiple social identities. This urge is reinforced as the minority population continues to expand drastically.

Standards for competencies are beneficial in directing the systems within which the RC should aim to be multiculturally competent. However, as is the case with many professions, the counseling profession does have limitations with respect to teaching and regulating cultural competence. Without doubt, it is thus beneficial to have a set of standards that can guide counselors in governing their clinical practices. However, many of these competencies are not sufficiently identified and/or explored within the training and education of RCs. This is problematic because practicing RCs should be using these sets of competencies, instead of "leaving it to chance" when providing services to their population of interest. It would be beneficial to have all competencies reflect a more intentional approach to helping RCs apply these competencies in practice, especially for counselors in training and entry-level clinicians.

While all the competencies have some limitations, some like the disability-related counseling competencies do reflect ways in which clinical professionals can apply best practices. Furthermore, the Competencies for Counseling with Transgender Clients specifically list some of their limitations, such as lack of "in-depth application to counseling transgender youth, the elderly, or working with the family and loved ones of transgender individuals" (Burnes et al., 2009). Additionally, experiences of individuals who identify as male-to-female or female-to-male and individuals who may identify with other descriptions of gender (i.e., genderqueer) were not sufficiently addressed. Burnes et al. noted that "it is important for counselors to be aware of the pressure all individuals experience related to fitting into the narrow gender binary and the additional challenges one might face if clients step out of these confines" (2009, p. 5). It is safe to say that this challenge is true for how an individual may identify themselves even beyond the notion of gender identity. As practicing clinicians, it is imperative that counselors are aware of the pressures all clients may present as they navigate the confines of their lives.

This section has highlighted selected competencies. Of note, there are other related competencies within the counseling profession that can be found on the ACA website (https://www.counseling.org/knowledge-center/competencies) that RCs should review and use in their professional practice.

CRCC STANDARDS RELATED TO CULTURAL AND SOCIAL JUSTICE

The ACA-endorsed competencies discussed in the previous section are critical to RCs providing ethical and effective support to individuals who have cognitive, physical, developmental, mental, and/or emotional disabilities (CRCC, 2021). While cultural competence is an ethical part of the professional practice of rehabilitation counseling as detailed by the CRCC Code of Ethics, it is important to note that cultural competencies are not identified clearly in separate set of competencies like the ACA. In other words, guidelines for cultural competence are not addressed in a "stand alone" document by CRCC but rather only addressed through the Code of Ethics. This is different from the ACA, which has a Code of Ethics as well as multiple sets of ACA endorsed competencies. Unlike the ACA-endorsed competencies which are aspirational in nature, the cultural competence standards of the CRCC Code of Ethics are mandatory for all counselors who hold the Certified Rehabilitation Counselor (CRC) credential. With that said, the aspirational aspects of the ACA endorsed sets of competencies can assist RCs to meet their ethical guidelines related to diverse worldviews and cultures of their clients.

Within the Code of Professional Ethics for Rehabilitation Counselors, the CRCC has required CRCs to "develop and maintain knowledge, personal awareness, sensitivity, and skills and demonstrate a disposition reflective of a culturally competent rehabilitation counselor working with diverse client populations" (CRCC, 2017). Furthermore, there are specific ethical standards related to cultural competence. Specifically, standard D.2.b. has mandated RCs to "develop and adapt interventions and services to incorporate consideration of cultural perspectives of clients and recognition of barriers external to clients that may interfere with achieving effective rehabilitation outcomes" (CRCC, p. 14). Additionally, in standard D.2.c, it is stated clearly that "rehabilitation counselors do not condone or engage in the prejudicial treatment of an individual or group based on their actual or perceived membership in a particular group, class, or category" (CRCC, p. 14). While these standards are more general than the ACA endorsed sets of competencies, CRCs who are found to violate these standards could have their CRC credential revoked. It is thus important that RCs understand both the mandatory aspects of the CRCC Code of Ethics as well as the aspirational aspects of the ACA sets of multicultural and social justice competencies.

BOX 18.2 CASE CONCEPTUALIZATION

Lennox is a 21-year-old junior who identifies as male. Lennox, who is the youngest of his five siblings, grew up in a loving home and had always felt supported by his immediate and extended family alike. He comes to see you to seek rehabilitation counseling support and identify his career path beyond college. He expresses that he sees himself working within a field in which it is not bound to societal norms. Specifically, Lennox discloses to you that he grew up playing with dolls and living as "most females do throughout their childhood and adolescent years." Lennox states he knows the odds are against him since he identifies as a multiracial individual who is a part of the Lesbian, Gay, Bisexual, Transgender, Queer and/or Questioning, Intersex, Asexual and/or Agender community. Additionally, although Lennox has done well throughout his studies thus far, he struggles from time to time with focusing on his schoolwork and completing assignments on time. He informed you he had an Individualized Education Plan in high school, and he utilized accommodations for attention deficit hyperactivity disorder. He also states he stopped taking medication as a freshman in hopes that he could navigate his college years depending only on his hard work and studying. However, he is starting to see that this approach may impact his last year as a senior negatively and could potentially impact his career in the future because he has a hard time staying focused on the task at hand. As his counselor, what competencies would you consult to ensure you provide effective support to Lennox? Furthermore, how will you employ the principles in which you acknowledge your bias, become aware of your client's worldview, and employ the skills you have acquired from your newfound knowledge of multicultural competency?

LAWS AND CONTEMPORARY ACTIONS IMPACTING MARGINALIZED GROUPS

Rehabilitation counseling services do not happen in a vacuum. Rather, services are provided within the context of an evolving society. In the last half century, the rights of people with disabilities have joined the civil rights efforts of Black, feminist, and gay liberation movements to promote a more equitable, accessible, and inclusive society. With this in mind, it is important to recognize the importance of legislative and advocacy efforts for individuals of marginalized groups (Box 18.2). Such groups include but not limited to persons with disabilities, BIPOC, LGBTQ+ individuals, and women. Individuals with disabilities often identify with more than one cultural group, and thus it is critical that RCs are aware of civil rights issues and protections for diverse populations.

Persons With Disabilities

There are many laws impacting individuals with disabilities. Perhaps most importantly, the ADA of 1990 (P.L. 110–325) is a seminal legislative mandate that protects individuals with disabilities from employment discrimination. It is well documented that individuals with disabilities are employed at lower rates than individuals without disabilities. Employment barriers may be linked to lack of education, fear of losing benefits, employment history, and a host of factors. The ADA definition of **disability** is a physical or mental impairment that substantially limits one or more major life activities, a person who has a history or record of such an impairment, or a person who is perceived by others as having such an impairment. This definition is important because it views disability as much more than just a medical condition, but rather, considers major life activities and environmental factors, including social perceptions of disability.

BOX 18.3 REFLECTION ACTIVITY

1. Provide an overview of the ADA and the WIOA.
2. As a future rehabilitation counselor, how might you explain the ADA and the WIOA to clients with disabilities seeking employment?
3. What are the strengths and limitations, if any, of the ADA and the WIOA?

The Rehabilitation Counseling Act of 1973 (PL 93–112) afforded states the opportunity for grant funding for vocational rehabilitation counseling services (U.S. Equal Employment Opportunity Commission, n.d.). The act further emphasized the needs of individuals with severe disabilities to have priority to access to vocational rehabilitation services, expound federal research and training to address the needs of persons with disabilities, and provide coordination of services for persons with disabilities and their educational, health, welfare, and other-related services (U.S. Equal Employment Opportunity Commission, n.d.). There are specific areas in this act that prohibit the discrimination toward individuals with disabilities in the areas of employment in federal agencies (Section 501), federal government contractors (Section 503), education (Section 504), and accessible technology (Section 508; U.S. Equal Employment Opportunity Commission, n.d.).

The Workforce Innovative and Opportunity Act (WIOA; 20 CFR § 685.140) was enacted to further strengthen the employability of adults and youth with disabilities. This act was signed into law in 2014. Specifically, the purpose of the WIOA is to increase the accessibility of persons with disabilities in the areas of education, employment, training, and other employment-related services (U.S. Department of Labor, n.d.). In addition to assisting persons with disabilities in their vocational pursuits, the WIOA also attempts to address the needs of employers by matching them with qualified workers to fulfill employment vacancies (U.S. Department of Labor, n.d.)(Box 18.3).

Laws Impacting Black, Indigenous, and People of Color

There are many laws impacting BIPOC individuals. A few examples of important laws are addressed in this section: Civil Rights Act of 1964 (P.L. 88–352), Executive order on advancing racial equity support for underserved communities through the federal government, January 20, 2021, White House Initiative on Advancing Educational Equity, Excellence, and Economic Opportunity for Black Americans (H.R. 4981); Executive Order on Improving Public Safety and Criminal Justice for Native Americans and Addressing the Crisis of Missing or Murdered Indigenous People (E.O. 14053).

- The Civil Rights Act of 1964: This act ended public segregation, prohibited employment discrimination based upon race, gender, religion, and national origin, as well as strengthened voting rights (U.S. Department of Labor, n.d.). To prohibit employment discrimination, the Equal Employment Opportunity Commission was created (U.S. Department of Labor, n.d).
- White House Initiative on Advancing Educational Equity, Excellence, and Economic Opportunity for Black Americans: The purpose of this initiative is to address systemic racism, invest in African American communities, and enhance the safety towards African Americans. The American Rescue Plan was signed into law for the accessibility of wealth for African Americans to build small businesses (Briefing Room, 2021b).
- Executive Order on Improving Public Safety and Criminal Justice for Native Americans and Addressing the Crisis of Missing or Murdered Indigenous People: This executive order was signed into law to protect the safety and health of tribal communities in addition to providing support, prevention, and intervention (Briefing Room, 2021a).

> ## BOX 18.4 DISCUSSION QUESTIONS
>
> 1. What are the similarities and differences in the executive orders addressed in this section?
> 2. As noted in the beginning of this section, the laws highlighted in this section are just a few impacting BIPOC individuals. In a group of two to three peers, research executive orders impacting BIPOC individuals. Consider researching executive orders at the state and national levels.

The takeaway of these executive orders is that despite the progress that has been made to address the needs and protection of BIPOC individuals since the (U.S. Department of Labor, n.d.) there still exists inequality for this group in many aspects of daily living (Box 18.4).

Laws Impacting the LGBTQ+ Community

There are many laws impacting the LGBTQ+ community. In recent years, there has been instances regarding the safety and rights of this community. Oftentimes, individuals may not associate this community to persons with disabilities; however, sexuality and gender identity are identities in which individuals with disabilities may associate. The rights of the LGBTQ+ community are under attack in some states, such as the problematic "Don't Say Gay or Trans" bill (HB1557; Bibi, 2022). For this reason, it is critical that RCs understand policies and law that protect the rights of the LGBTQ+ community such as the Memorandum on Advancing the Human Rights of Lesbian, Gay, Bisexual, Transgender, Queer, and Intersex Persons Around the World, the establishment of the Gender Policy Council, Transgender Day of Visibility. These laws were enacted during the Biden-Harris administration. A summarization follows:

- Memorandum on Advancing the Human Rights of Lesbian, Gay, Bisexual, Transgender, Queer, and Intersex Persons Around the World (86 FR 11843): The purpose of this legislation is to protect the rights of LBTQI+ individuals (Yap et al., 2021).
- The Establishment of the Gender Policy Council (E.O. 14020): The purpose of this council is to protect the rights of individuals from traditionally underrepresented groups, such as LGBTQI+ and BIPOC individuals (Yap et al., 2021). The Biden–Harris administration's focus is building a just society (2021).
- Transgender Day of Visibility: This proclamation was to honor and celebrate LGBTQI individuals and communities' resiliency and accomplishments (Yap et al., 2021). The proclamation was enacted on March 31, 2021.

The takeaway of these laws is that the rights of all citizens should be protected (Box 18.5, Box 18.6).

Laws Impacting the Lives of Women

There are many laws impacting the lives and rights of women. Selected laws will be described in this section. The following laws affecting women will be addressed in this section: Paid Maternity Leave, Hair Discrimination Ban, and *Roe v. Wade*. A summarization of each law follows:

BOX 18.5 REFLECTION ACTIVITY

The laws covered in this section are just a few impacting LGBTQ+ individuals and communities. Other laws focusing on this community pertain to school sports. Search online and review Arkansas' Gender Integrity Reinforcement Legislation for Sports (GIRLS) Act found in the Yap et al. (2021) article and reflect on the following:

1. Should school sports have separate men's and women's teams? What are the advantages and disadvantages to assigning sports designations as male, female, or coed?

- Women Paid Maternity Leave: This law **only** applies to federal employees (Snider, 2020). Persons who are employed at the federal level can receive 12 weeks of paid parental leave (Snider, 2020). For workers who are not employed at the federal level, they may be able take paid leave 6 to 8 weeks after delivery; this is assuming that there are no complications after birth for the mother and/or the child (Snider, 2020). Dependent on the employer, after a certain number of weeks, no paid leave will be provided. Not having time to not only bond with their infant but also heal from the pregnancy effects can be both emotionally and physically taxing for a new mother. Stress, as known, can exacerbate symptoms and prolong recovery (Box 18.7).
- Hair Discrimination Ban (SB 188; The Crown Act): The first state to have this ban is California in 2020 (Snider, 2020). The purpose of this ban is to prevent hair discrimination of students and employees in the public school system (Snider, 2020). Examples of hair discrimination includes, but is not limited to, braids, dreadlocks, cornrows, and the like. States such as New York and New Jersey have passed similar legislative acts (Snider, 2020). This concern has been a topic and unfortunate reality for many BIPOC individuals, primarily among African American men, women, and children. For those individuals entering and/or currently in the workforce, hair discrimination may have impacted job opportunities and job promotions. For African American children, wearing a hairstyle that does not align with a White-Eurocentric perspective often has led to being dismissed from the classroom. This form of mistreatment and discrimination can have adverse impacts on African American children. Such impacts may impact the child's self-esteem, self-confidence, school performance, and racial/ethnic identity development. Although this act is placed in this section pertaining to women, it should be noted that this act does impact both women and men regarding their ability to wear hairstyles. On March 18, 2022, the U.S. House of Representatives passed the Crown Act. The act will need to be based of the U.S. Senate next.
- *Roe vs. Wade:* This piece of legislation has sparked controversy since its enactment in 1973. Roe vs. Wade established the legalization of abortion (Snider, 2020). On June 24, 2022, the United States Supreme Court overturned this decision and voted that abortion rights under the constitution no longer exists (Totenberg & McCammon, 2022). The new ruling will impact many states across this country, resulting in states overturning abortion rights and any limitations for abortions (e.g., medical exceptions, number of weeks before termination, etc.; Totenberg & McCammon, 2022).

BOX 18.6 LEARNING ACTIVITY

The Memorandum on Advancing the Human Rights of Lesbian, Gay, Bisexual, Transgender, Queer, and Intersex Persons Around the World legislation protects the LGBTQ+ individual's rights. Research and review five sources that discuss rights violation for this group.

BOX 18.7 REFLECTION ACTIVITY

1. How might you work with a client who believes that she was discriminated against for an employment opportunity because she wears dreadlocks?
2. In this section, the law pertaining to Women Paid Maternity was briefly described. Do you believe that this law should be extended to all workers, regardless of sector and gender? Support your stance with 2 to 3 citations?

BOX 18.8 LEARNING ACTIVITY

Divide students into two groups to debate the pros and cons of the Jury Duty Exemption for Breast Feeding legislation.

The takeaway message is that the rights of women have continued to be at the forefront of many laws (Box 18.8).

CONCLUSION

This chapter introduced the readers to the notion of cultural competence and social justice among rehabilitation counselors and practicing professionals. When broaching the concept of cultural competence and social justice, there is a need for understanding the many cultures that practicing clinicians encounter and the many diverse populations they support. Cultural competence, broaching, and cultural humility were defined to explore the notion of intersectionality within the field, along with the CACREP standards and their relation to cultural competence and social justice. Furthermore, standards reflecting culture and social justice were identified and explored as endorsed by the ACA. Laws and contemporary actions impacting marginalize groups were identified to explore laws impacting PWDs, BIPOC, LGBTQ+ communities, and the lives and rights of women. A case study was presented to illustrate and explore the context of cultural competency and social justice strategies that should be considered when working within the field of rehabilitation counseling.

CONTENT REVIEW QUESTIONS

1. How can intersectionality, cultural competence, and broaching impact the counselor–client relationship? Why is it important for rehabilitation counselors to consider these factors when engaging with and providing services to diverse clients?
2. How can rehabilitation professionals utilize the ACA-endorsed standards related to culture and social justice to deepen their own understanding of the contextual influences they bring to the counselor–consumer/client alliance (relationship)?
3. What actions can you take as a counselor when you become aware of the need to further engage in social justice and advocacy efforts for clients and to the rehabilitation counseling profession?

REFERENCES

Bellini, J. (2002). Correlates of multicultural counseling competencies of vocational rehabilitation counselors. *Rehabilitation Counseling Bulletin*, 45(2), 66–75. https://doi.org/10.1177/003435520204500201

Bibi, E. (2022, March 8). *Florida senate passes "don't say gay or trans" bill, legislation heads to DeSantis's desk for signature or veto.* Human Rights Campaign. https://www.hrc.org/news/florida-senate-passes-dont-say-gay-or-trans-bill-legislation-heads-to-desantis-desk-for-signature-or-veto

Briefing Room. (2021a). *Executive order on improving public safety and criminal justice for Native Americans and addressing the crisis of missing or murdered Indigenous people.* https://www.whitehouse.gov/briefingroom/statements-releases/2021/10/19

Briefing Room. (2021b). *Fact sheet: The Biden-Harris administration advances equity and opportunity for Black people and communities across the country.* https://www.whitehouse.gov/briefingroom/statements-releases/2021/10/19

Burnes, T. R., Singh, A. A., Harper, A., Pickering, D. L., Moundas, S., Scotfield, T., Maxon, W., Harper, B., Roan, A., & Hosea, J. (2009). *Association for Lesbian, Gay, Bisexual, and Transgender issues in counseling (ALGBTIC) competencies for counseling with transgender clients.* https://www.counseling.org/resources/competencies/algbtic_competencies.pdf

Chapin, M., McCarthy, H., Shaw, L., Bradham-Cousar, M., Chapman, R., Nosek, M., Peterson, S., Yilmaz, Z., & Ysasi, N. (2018). *Disablity-related counseling competencies.* https://www.counseling.org/docs/default-source/competencies/arca-disability-related-counseling-competencies-final-version-5-15-19.pdf?sfvrsn=c376562c_6

Commission on Rehabilitation Counselor Certification. (2017). *Code of professional ethics for rehabilitation counselors.* https://crccertification.com/wp-content/uploads/2020/12/CRCC-Code-Eff-20170101-FINAL.pdf

Commission on Rehabilitation Counselor Certification. (2021). *Rehabilitation counselor scope of practice.* https://crccertification.com/scope-of-practice/

Council for Accreditation of Counseling and Related Educational Program. (2016). *2016 CACREP standards.* https://www.cacrep.org/for-programs/2016-cacrep-standards/

Council for Accreditation of Counseling and Related Educational Programs. (2022). *Section 2: Professional counseling identity.* https://www.cacrep.org/section-2-professional-counseling-identity

Crenshaw, K. (1989). Demarginalization the intersection of race and sex: A Black feminist critique of antidiscrimination doctrine, feminist theory and antiracist politics. *University of Chicago Legal Forum, 1*, Article 8. http://chicagounbound.uchicago.edu/uclf/vol1989/iss1/8

Crethar, H. C., Rivera, E. T., & Nash, S. (2008). In search of common threads: Linking multicultural, feminist, and social justice counseling paradigms. *Journal of Counseling & Development, 86*(3), 269–278. https://doi.org/10.1002/j.1556-6678.2008.tb00509.x

Day-Vines, N. L., Wood, S. M., Grothaus, T., Craigen, L., Holman, A., Dotson-Blake, K., & Douglass, M. J. (2007). Broaching the subjects of race, ethnicity, and culture, during the counseling process. *Journal of Counseling & Development, 85*(4), 401–409. https://doi.org/10.1002/j.1556-6678.2007.tb00608.x

Goodman, L. A., Liang, B., Helms, J. E., Latta, R. E., Sparks, E., & Weintraub, S. R. (2004). Training counseling psychologists as social change agents: Feminist and multicultural principles in action. *The Counseling Psychologist, 32*, 793–837.

Harper, A., Finnerty, P., Martinez, M., Brace, A., Crethar, H., Loos, B., Harper, B., Graham, S., Singh, A., Kocet, M., Travis, L., & Lambert, S. (2012). *Association for Lesbian, Gay, Bisexual, and Transgender Issues in Counseling (ALGBTIC) Competencies for counseling with lesbian, gay, bisexual, queer, questioning, intersex and ally individuals.* https://www.counseling.org/docs/ethics/algbtic-2012-07

Hook, J. N., Davis, D. E., Owen, J., Worthington, E. L., & Utsey, S. O. (2013). Cultural humility: Measuring openness to culturally diverse clients. *Journal of Counseling Psychology, 60*(3), 353–366. https://doi.org/10.1037/a0032595

Kenney, R. K., Kenney, M. E., Alvarado, S. B., Baden, A. L., Brew, L., Chen-Hayes, S., Crippen, C. L., Harris, H. L., Henriksen, R. C., Malott, K. M., Paladino, D. A., Pope, M. L., Salazar, C. F., & Singh, A. A. (2015). *Competencies for counseling the multiracial population: Multi-racial/ethnic Counseling Concerns (MRECC) interest network for the American Counseling Association Taskforce.* https://www.counseling.org/docs/default-source/competencies/competencies-for-counseling-the-multiracial-population-2-2-15-final.pdf?sfvrsn=14

Kim, J. H., Barbir, L. A., Elder, E. M., Vo, A. K., McMahon, B. T., Taylor, T., & Johnson, K. (2018). Community service coordination for minority clients with disabilities: 10-step guidelines. *Work, 59*(1), 85–91. https://doi.org/10.3233/WOR-172662

Marini, I. (2012). What we counsel, teach, and research regarding the needs of persons with disabilities: What have we been missing? In I. Marini, N. M. Glover-Graff, & M. Millington (Eds.), *Psychosocial aspects of disability* (pp. 481–494). Springer.

McAuliffe, G. J., & Associates. (2020). *Culturally alert counseling*. Sage.

National Career Development Association. (2009, August). *Minimum competencies for multicultural career counseling and development*. https://www.counseling.org/docs/default-source/competencies/multi-cultural-career-counseling-competencies-august-2009.pdf?sfvrsn=727f422c_6

Ratts, M. J. (2009). Social justice counseling: Toward the development of a fifth force among counseling paradigms. *The Journal of Humanistic Counseling, Education and Development*, *48*(2), 160–172. https://doi.org/10.1002/j.2161-1939.2009.tb00076.x

Ratts, M. J., Singh, A. A., Nassar-McMillan, S., Butler, S. K., & McCullough, J. R. (2015). *Multicultural and social justice counseling competencies*. https://www.counseling.org/docs/default-source/competencies/multicultural-and-social-justice-counseling-competencies.pdf?sfvrsn=8573422c_22

Rawls, J. (1971). *A theory of justice*. Harvard University Press. 10.4159/9780674042605

Slesaransky-Poe, G., & García, A. (2014). Social construction of difference. In D. Lawrence-Brown & M. Sapon-Shevin (Eds.), *Condition critical* (pp. 66–85). Teachers College Press.

Snider, A. C. (2020). *Every woman should know these laws in 2020*. https:/www.refinary29.com/en-us/2020/01/9285371/important-laws-for-women-2020

Sue, D. W., & Sue, D. (2008). *Counseling the culturally different: Theory and practice* (5th ed.). https://endahfebrianto.files.wordpress.com/2015/06/derald_wing_sue_david_sue_counseling_the_culturbookzz-org.pdf

Totenberg, N., & McCammon, S. (2022). *Supreme Court overturns Roe v. Wade, ending right to abortion upheld for decades*. NPR. https://www.npr.org/2022/06/24/1102305878/supreme-court-abortion-roe-v-wade-decision-overturn

U.S. Department of Labor. (n.d.). *Workforce Innovation and Opportunity Act*. https://www.dol.gov/agencies/eta/wioa

U.S. Department of Labor. (n.d.). *Legal highlight: The civil rights act of 1964*. https://www.dol.gov/agencies/oasam/civil-rights-center/statutes/civil-rights-act-of-1964

U.S. Equal Employment Opportunity Commission. (n.d.). *Rehabilitation Act of 1973 (Original Text)*. https://www.eeoc.gov/rehabilitation-act-1973-original-text

Worell, J., & Remer, P. (2002). *Feminist perspectives in therapy: Empowering diverse women*. Wiley.

Yap, E., Augustin, R., & Mullins, N. (2021). Recent federal and state government impact on the LGBTQ+ Community. *The National Law Review*, *9*(165), 1–6. https://www.natlawreview.com/article/recent-federal-and-state-government-impact-lgbtq-community

CHAPTER 19

Evidence-Based Practice and Research Utilization

KANAKO IWANAGA, JIA RUNG WU, FONG CHAN, EMRE UMUCU, XIANGLI CHEN, RANA YAGHMAIAN, AND KEVIN BENGTSON

LEARNING OBJECTIVES

After reading this chapter, you should be able to:

- *Recognize how the transformation of the health healthcare system in the United States has impacted service delivery of health healthcare disciplines including rehabilitation counseling in providing the most effective clinical services.*
- *Recognize how research has provided an evidence-based foundation for the discipline in relation to role, function, and knowledge requirements.*
- *Evaluate how rehabilitation professionals can become more effective evidence-based practitioners through enhancing their knowledge in evidence-based methodologies, research utilization, and effective vocational rehabilitation (VR) service delivery practices.*
- *Identify the concepts of systematic reviews, meta-analysis, effect size, and knowledge translation.*
- *Evaluate how the mechanisms of theory development, empirical evidence, and clinical application inform practice in VR service delivery, improving evidence-based practice to enhance outcomes and quality of life of people with disabilities.*
- *Recognize the value of continually assessing the way clinical services are provided to increase the effectiveness of intervention strategies.*

CACREP STANDARDS

CACREP 2016 CORE: 2F8.a, 2F8.b, 2F8., 2F8.d, 2F8.e, 2F8.f, 2F8.g, 2F8.h, 2F8.i, 2F8.j
CACREP 2016 Specialties:
  Clinical Rehabilitation Counseling: 5D2.c, 5D2.d
  Rehabilitation Counseling: 5H1.b, 5H3.a, 5H3.d

INTRODUCTION

According to the World Health Organization (WHO, 2017), one of the underlying causes of human suffering in this world is poverty. It is well documented that lack of access to healthcare, poor nutrition, and other stressors associated with poverty frequently lead to deteriorating health and high mortality over time (Dutta et al., 2008; Krause et al., 2008; Murali & Oyebode, 2014). Poverty and income inequality also negatively impact the social and mental well-being of individuals with and without disabilities (Diette et al., 2012; Murali & Oyebode, 2014; Ngamaba et al., 2018). Unfortunately, the labor-force participation rate for people with chronic health conditions and disabilities in the United States is alarmingly low, at 37.5%, compared to 76.4% of people without disabilities (Kessler Foundation, 2022). Because of unemployment and underemployment, people with chronic health conditions and disabilities constitute a disproportionate number of the poor (Atkins & Giusti, 2005), with a poverty rate of 25.9% compared to the rate of 11.4% for people without disabilities (Annual Disability Statistics Compendium, 2020). A lack of employment opportunities prevents many people with chronic health conditions and disabilities from achieving community inclusion and participation, delays upward mobility, and greatly affects their physical health, mental health, and subjective well-being. As such, participation in competitive integrated employment and other meaningful work activities is considered crucial to the health-related quality of life (QOL) and subjective well-being of people with chronic health conditions and disabilities (Chan et al., 2020; Dutta et al., 2008).

Rehabilitation counselors (RCs) play a vital role in assisting people with chronic health conditions and disabilities to achieve their independent living and employment goals, leading to better health and QOL (Dean et al., 2014; Dutta et al., 2008; Leahy, Chan, & Lui, 2014, Leahy, Chan, Lui, Rosenthal, et al., 2014; Martin et al., 2010; U.S. Government Accountability Office, 2005). The employment rates for individuals with chronic health conditions and disabilities receiving employment services from state VR agencies have been consistently reported in the 55% to 60% range (Dutta et al., 2008; Kaye, 1998; Rehabilitation Services Administration, 2016). There is still substantial room to improve the effectiveness of VR services, which will lead to better employment outcomes and employment quality for people with chronic health conditions and disabilities. The most pressing challenge currently is the novel coronavirus disease 2019 (COVID-19) pandemic, which is placing enormous budget pressure on state and local governments to transform their business models. In particular, VR and businesses are adopting organizational innovations to harness advances in information and communication technologies to deliver outcomes expected by people with chronic health conditions and disabilities, communities, and the society at large (Leadership for a Networked World, 2010; Leahy, Chan, & Lui, 2014, Leahy, Chan, Lui, Rosenthal, et al., 2014; U.S. Government Accountability Office, 2021). The coronavirus outbreak has changed the way Americans work and provide services drastically (Pew Research Center, 2020). Similarly, RCs must provide the most effective virtual, blended, and in-person health promotions, psychosocial, and vocational interventions possible. These interventions must integrate scientific evidence with clinical expertise and client perspectives to help people with chronic health conditions and disabilities to find and maintain competitive integrated employment (Chan et al., 2021). The development of theory-driven or model-driven research to inform best practices in rehabilitation counseling will undoubtedly be important as RCs strive to improve the effectiveness of VR service delivery practices, especially for VR consumers from racial-ethnic minority backgrounds with the poorest employment outcomes (Chan et al., 2021; Leahy, Chan, & Lui, 2014, Leahy, Chan, Lui, Rosenthal, et al., 2014; Leahy et al., 2017; U.S. Department of Education, 2014).

The **evidence-based practice (EBP)** movement has had a significant influence on the professional practice of rehabilitation counseling (Chan et al., 2016; Leahy, Chan, & Lui, 2014, Leahy, Chan, Lui, Rosenthal, et al., 2014). EBP is a framework for RCs to deliver the best possible services to people with chronic health conditions and disabilities (Chan, Keegan, et al., 2009; Chan, Tarvydas, et al., 2009; Chan et al., 2016). As a result, the RSA has begun to encourage state VR agencies to integrate scientific evidence with clinical expertise and client perspectives (Chan et al., 2008). The RSA recently has funded the Vocational Rehabilitation Technical Assistance Center for Quality Employment (VRTAC-QE; https://tacqe.com) to help RCs in state VR agencies provide empirically supported interventions for consumers with disabilities. Furthermore, the National Institute on Disability, Independent Living and Rehabilitation Research (NIDILRR) has sponsored research studies to meet standards for inclusion in systematic reviews and meta-analysis (Schlosser, 2006), and emphasized the importance of knowledge translation to facilitate research utilization in clinical rehabilitation counseling practices. The agency also funded a research and training center on EBP in VR and several knowledge translation centers. Finally, the U.S. Department of Education's Institute of Educational Sciences (IES) has created a What Works Clearinghouse to provide information on scientific evidence on what works in education, including secondary transition, and postsecondary education interventions for youth with disabilities.

Vocational rehabilitation agency administrators and RCs increasingly are being asked to use empirically supported interventions to improve the effectiveness of rehabilitation service delivery practices (Chan et al., 2016; Leahy, Chan, & Lui, 2014, Leahy, Chan, Lui, Rosenthal, et al., 2014; Rubin et al., 2003). According to Chan, Keegan, et al. (2009); Chan, Tarvydas, et al. (2009) the use of high-quality research evidence to guide clinical rehabilitation counseling practices helps RCs fulfill their ethical obligations to consumers by protecting consumers from harm (nonmaleficence), improving efficiency in utilization of scarce resources (justice), and empowering consumers to exercise self-determination and informed choice (autonomy). Not surprisingly, several quantitative and qualitative studies found that RCs generally hold positive attitudes toward the use of EBPs to improve their service and counseling outcomes (Fitzgerald et al., 2017; Graham et al., 2006; Pfaller et al., 2016; Tansey et al., 2014; Yaeda et al., 2015). However, these studies also identified several major barriers to employing EBPs, including a lack of knowledge, academic preparation, organizational support, and empirically validated psychosocial and VR interventions.

To be an effective evidence-based practitioner in clinical rehabilitation counseling, knowledge of basic concepts of rehabilitation research methods acquired from a traditional master's level course is insufficient. Rehabilitation counseling professionals must become more knowledgeable about EBPs, knowledge translation, and research utilization. The purpose of this chapter is to provide a review of key evidence-based practices, knowledge translation, and research utilization concepts. The chapter further discusses how EBP can be utilized to improve the professional practice of clinical rehabilitation counseling.

CONCEPTS RELATED TO EVIDENCE-BASED PRACTICE

Sackett et al. (2000) defined **evidence-based medicine** as the integration of best research evidence with clinical expertise and patient values; this definition is easily translated into rehabilitation counseling practice. DePalma (2002) provided a comprehensive description of EBP, describing it as a process beginning with knowing what clinical questions to ask, how to find the best practice, and how to appraise the evidence for validity and applicability to the particular care situation critically. The best evidence must be applied by a clinician with expertise in considering the patient's unique values and needs. The final aspect of the process is the evaluation of the effectiveness of care and the continual improvement of the process (Chan, Chronister, et al., 2009; DePalma, 2002). Consistent with the philosophy of rehabilitation counseling practice, the definition of EBP includes the importance of considering the unique needs and values of people with chronic health conditions and disabilities (Chan, Tarvydas, et al., 2009).

Steps for Evidence-Based Practice

Formulating a clear clinical question from a client's presenting problem is the first step in effective EBP. The ability to ask appropriate background and foreground questions is crucial in this step of the clinical decision-making process. Specifically, background questions (or general questions) ask about a setting or context, whereas foreground questions ask about a specific case within that context (Walker et al., 2006). Examples of typical background questions include the following:

- What are the most effective treatments for presenting problem A?
- Is treatment X an effective treatment for presenting problem A?
- Are there any significant risks associated with treatment X?

Foreground questions should be asked using **PICO**: patient group (P), intervention (I), comparison group (C), and outcome measures (O) format. The following is an example of a foreground PICO question: For an African American woman with schizophrenia (patient group), is there any evidence that the *Individual Placement and Support (IPS) model* of supported employment (intervention) is superior to job-placement services, assertive community treatment, and the clubhouse approach (comparison groups), in improving her employment outcome and the quality of her employment (outcome)? A set of well-built background and foreground questions provide direction for determining what evidence to look for and where to search for the best scientific evidence.

To search for strong research evidence, an evidence-based practitioner in rehabilitation counseling must be knowledgeable about specific methods and resources for locating research evidence to guide the selection and implementation of empirically supported intervention as the treatment of choice for the client's presenting problem. The most reliable and scholarly approach to searching for scientific research papers and systematic reviews documents is through academic databases such as ABI/INFORM Complete, Academic Search Premier, CINAHL, Cochrane Library, Campbell Library, EBSCO, EconLit, MEDLINE, PsycINFO, PubMed, and Web of Science.

After formulating well-defined, answerable clinical questions and seeking the best evidence available to answer these questions, RCs must appraise the scientific evidence critically. Chambless and Hollon (1998) indicated that best evidence for psychosocial treatments should be evaluated in terms of **efficacy** (statistical and clinical significance), **effectiveness** (clinical utility), and **efficiency** (cost-effectiveness). In evidence-based medicine, the gold standard for best evidence is **randomized clinical trials (RCTs)**. A five-level hierarchical framework emphasizing the importance of RCTs offers RCs a format for determining the strength of the evidence-based on methodological rigor (Holm, 2000; Nathan & Gorman, 1998). This **hierarchy of levels of evidence** includes the following:

1. **Level 1** evidence is defined as strong evidence from at least one systematic review of multiple well-designed randomized controlled trials.
2. **Level 2** evidence is defined as strong evidence from at least one or more properly designed randomized controlled trials of appropriate size.
3. **Level 3** evidence is defined as evidence from well-designed trials without randomization, single-group pre–post, cohort, time-series, or matched case-controlled studies.
4. **Level 4** evidence is defined as evidence from well-designed non-experimental studies from more than one center or research group.
5. **Level 5** evidence is defined as opinions of respected authorities based on clinical evidence, descriptive studies, or reports of expert committees.

Although RCTs are useful in medicine, the emphasis on experimental studies may be too restrictive for the behavioral and social sciences. This judgment is because RCTs do not always take into account the full complexity of human behavior and clinical condition (Wampold, 2001; Wampold & Imel, 2015). The complex nature of VR makes it impossible to rely solely on experimental research to determine the effectiveness of treatment contributing to successful outcomes. Tucker and Reed (2008) suggested that evidentiary pluralism, including qualitative research and mixed-methods research designs, should be considered as valid strategies for EBP research in rehabilitation. In addition, although RCTs are vital for establishing treatment efficacy, other multivariate approaches used to test mediator and moderator effects (e.g., hierarchical regression analysis and mediation and moderation analysis), person–environment interactions (e.g., multilevel analysis), and complex theoretical models (e.g., structural equation modeling) in the natural environment can provide invaluable information about contextual, psychological, social, and treatment determinants of functioning, disability, positive person–environmen contextual factors, community participation, employment status, and quality of life in persons with disabilities (Chwalisz & Chan, 2008; Tucker & Reed, 2008). More recently, Chan and colleagues have been advocating for the use of propensity-score-matched case-controlled study design to evaluate the effectiveness of specific VR interventions (e.g., Chan et al., 2020; Iwanaga et al., 2021; O'Neill et al., 2015; Wehman et al., 2014). Chwalisz, Shah, et al. (2008) also articulated that rigorous qualitative research methods contribute to theoretical and applied knowledge in rehabilitation. When considered together with experimental studies, nonexperimental quantitative and qualitative studies can expand the scope and impact of rehabilitation counseling research focusing on interventions intended to improve the employment status and health and well-being of persons with chronic health conditions and disabilities.

After finding, evaluating, and integrating the research evidence, the next step is to select empirically supported interventions by taking into account the significance of the evidence, the professional expertise and judgment of the counselor, and the characteristics, values, needs, and context of the individual client. The American Psychological Associaion (APA) defines the **best evidence** as "evidence-based on systematic reviews, reasonable effect sizes, statistical and clinical significance, and a body of supporting evidence" (APA, 2005). Professional judgment is used to identify each client's unique disability and health status and to integrate the best evidence with the rehabilitation context. Client characteristics, values, and context are the preferences, values, character strengths, weaknesses, personality factors, sociocultural, and environmental factors, and expectations that a client brings to the rehabilitation counseling process. Consistent with the expectations of the Rehabilitation Act of 1973 (U.S. Department of Education, 2014), in evidence-based practice, decisions should be collaborative in nature, with both client and counselor as active members of the counseling process.

The use of current best evidence to guide clinical decision-making and the provision of interventions has the potential to improve the effectiveness of psychosocial and VR intervention outcomes for people with chronic health conditions and disabilities. Although research utilization in rehabilitation counseling is important, there are many individual and organizational barriers to the use of research in professional practice. Bezyak et al. (2010) identified a lack of knowledge and insufficient academic preparation in EBP as significant barriers to research utilization. Other challenges can be attributed to negative perceptions about rehabilitation research. RCs may perceive rehabilitation research to have a weak theoretical foundation and to lack practical relevance for practitioners and clients. Furthermore, there exists a dearth of well-designed experimental design studies aimed at validating the efficacy of rehabilitation counseling interventions, and qualitative and mixed-methods research methodologies have been underutilized in rehabilitation counseling research (Berkowitz et al., 1975, 1976; Chan et al., 2003, Chan et al., 2016; Chan, Keegan, et al., 2009; Parker & Hensen, 1981; Rubin & Rice, 1986). To train master's-level rehabilitation counseling students and professional counselors to be intelligent consumers of research, it is essential, although not sufficient, to teach students the basic concepts of research designs and statistical methods. They also need to be knowledgeable about EBP methodologies and concepts, including research databases, systematic reviews/meta-analyses, knowledge translation, and implementation science. Finally, they need to be able to appreciate the extent to which research evidence and utilization can be a practical and integral part of their professional practice. A brief review of systematic reviews, scoping reviews, meta-analyses, and related databases is presented next.

SYSTEMATIC REVIEW AND META-ANALYSIS

Systematic Reviews

The Cochrane Collaboration defines **systematic review** as a transparent and systematic process used to define a research question, search for studies, assess their quality, and synthesize findings qualitatively or quantitatively (Armstrong et al., 2011). The Campbell Collaboration (2019) indicated that the purpose of systematic review is to summarize the best available scientific evidence on a specific clinical question using transparent procedures to locate, evaluate, and integrate the findings of relevant research. Hence, a systematic review answers a specific clinical question by using predetermined rules for capturing the evidence, appraising it, and synthesizing it in a manner that is easily accessible to clinicians. Systematic reviews are conducted by scholars with expertise in a substantive area who review and critique the available data in the field using the following steps: (a) asking an answerable clinical question, (b) identifying one or more databases to search, (c) developing an explicit search strategy, (d) selecting titles, abstracts, and manuscripts based on explicit inclusion and exclusion criteria, and (e) abstracting data in a standardized format (Schlosser, 2006). As mentioned, strong evidence from at least one systematic review of multiple well-designed randomized clinical trials is considered the highest level of best evidence (Level 1) and is frequently labeled a meta-analytic review. Meta-analysis is a particular type of systematic review that uses quantitative methods to determine the effect of a treatment by combining the results from a number of studies.

Scoping Reviews

In recent years, the term **scoping review** also has emerged in the literature (Dijkers, 2015). Mays et al. (2001) contend that scoping reviews can be used to map the key concepts for a research area and the types of evidence available. Scoping reviews can be undertaken as stand-alone projects in their own right, especially where an area is complex or has not been reviewed comprehensively before. While a systematic review might typically focus on a well-defined question where appropriate study designs can be identified in advance, a scoping review study tends to address broader topics where many different study designs might be applicable (Arksey & O'Malley, 2005). Unlike systematic reviews, a scoping study is less concerned about addressing specific research questions or assessing the quality of the primary studies. A scoping review usually involves several steps: (a) identify the research questions (i.e., the domain needs to be explored); (b) find the relevant studies through electronic databases, reference lists (ancestor searching), websites of organizations, and conference proceedings; (c) select the studies that are relevant to the question(s); (d) chart the data; and (e) collate, summarize and report the results (Arksey & O'Malley). As an option, scoping review researchers may also consult stakeholders (e.g., RCs, policymakers, consumers, families) to obtain more references and gain insight on information the literature fails to highlight.

Meta-Analysis

The goal of science is the production of cumulative knowledge. However, the small-sample studies and overreliance on statistical tests in social and behavioral science research can produce seemingly conflicting results (Borenstein et al., 2009; Schmidt & Hunter, 2003).

Meta-analytic studies review the results of a collection of empirical studies in a specific research domain through statistical integration and analysis and synthesize the results to reveal simpler patterns of relationships, providing a basis for theory- development and clinical decision-making (Durlak, 1995; Schmidt & Hunter, 2003; Wampold & Imel, 2015). Importantly, meta-analyses can correct for the distorting effects of sampling error, measurement error, and other artifacts that produce the false impression of contradicting findings. Similar to an individual experiment, a meta-analysis contains both independent and dependent variables, with the independent variables being such characteristics as participants, interventions, and outcome measures, and the dependent variable being the effect size, or the outcome of the results of each study selected for review, transformed into a common metric across studies.

In systematic reviews, the focus of meta-analysis is on treatment effectiveness (e.g., "Is cognitive-behavioral therapy more effective than psychodynamic therapy in treating depression?") The advantages of a meta-analysis are its ability to (a) synthesize the results from many studies succinctly and intuitively to nonscientific communities, (b) illustrate the amount and relative impact of different programs on different criteria for policy decision-making purposes, and (c) identify the most effective programs and highlight gaps or limitations in the literature to suggest directions for future research (Durlak, 1995). A meta-analysis is conducted by following six major steps, which include (a) formulating research questions, (b) identifying relevant studies through a comprehensive review of the literature (computer searches, manual searches, examination of the reference lists of each identified study), (c) coding the studies (e.g., participants, research designs, therapist qualifications, control group, treatment type, presenting problem, number of sessions, method of administration), (d) computing the index of effect, (e) conducting the statistical analysis of effects, and (f) offering conclusions and interpretations (Durlak, 1995).

A common index representing the size of the effect produced by each experimental study is Cohen's d, which is the standardized difference the between sample mean of the treatment group and the sample mean of the control group (Borenstein et al., 2009). It should be noted that the population estimator δ for describing the size of effects for statistical power analysis is also sometimes called d, creating some confusion in the literature. Borenstein et al. (2009) recommend the use of the symbol δ to represent the effect size parameter and d for the sample estimate of the parameter. However, d tends to overestimate the absolute value of δ in small samples. This bias can be corrected using Hedges' g (Hedges & Olkin, 1985). As a result, both d and g can be considered unbiased effect size indexes. In general, Hedges's g provides a better estimate for studies with small sample sizes (Grissom & Kim, 2005).

A positive score indicates that the treatment group outperformed the control group, and a negative score has the reverse meaning. A typical way to interpret the size of an effect is to compare the d or g index with the standards set by Cohen (1988), with small, medium, and large effects represented by 0.20, 0.50, and 0.80, respectively. To examine the overlap of the control and treatment distributions, the effect size index (d or g) is converted to the value of the standard normal cumulative distribution. For example, if $d = 0.85$, and compared to the normal distribution curve, a z-score of 0.85 covers 80% of the normal curve; this would indicate that the average client receiving treatment will be better off than 80% of untreated clients. Other related mean difference effect size indexes include the proportion of variability (PV) and eta-squared (η^2). For PV, PV of 0.01 refers to a small effect, PV of 0.09 refers to a medium effect, and PV of 0.25 refers to a large effect. For η^2, $\eta^2 = 0.01$ indicates a small effect; $\eta^2 = 0.06$ indicates a medium effect; $\eta^2 = 0.14$ indicates a large effect. For correlational studies, the effect size is reported as r; for multiple regression analysis, the effect size is f^2; and for a Pearson chi-square test, the effect size is reported as w. A typical way to interpret effect size is to use the standards established by Cohen, as presented in Table 19.1.

Several factors can influence the effect size, including sample size, the sensitivity of measurement instruments, design characteristics, and clinical significance. Of particular

TABLE 19.1 Effect Size Measures

Effect Size	PV	r	d/g	η2	ω	f2
Small effects	.01	.10	.20	.01	.10	.02
Medium effects	.10	.30	.50	.06	.30	.15
Large effects	.25	.50	.80	.14	.50	.35

importance for meta-analytic studies are issues of homogeneity and power. The power of a statistical test is the probability that it will yield statistically significant results. Kosciulek and Szymanski (1993) analyzed empirical articles from five rehabilitation counseling–related journals and concluded that due to low statistical power, rehabilitation counseling researchers had little chance of finding small but significant relationships that exist in the population of interest. In terms of homogeneity, it is possible that studies included in a meta-analysis may have an array of different independent or dependent variables and may not have a common population parameter. Hedges and Olkin (1985) developed the Q statistics as a statistical test of homogeneity, and if the null hypothesis of homogeneity is rejected (i.e., Q statistic is significant), the studies should be partitioned based on meaningful categories. Specifically, a meta-analysis may include studies that differ in categorically predictable ways. For example, a well-designed study would produce a larger effect than a poorly designed study; therefore, to control for this difference, the independent variable "quality of research design" can be used to partition studies into two groups (well-designed studies and poorly designed studies). The between-group differences can then be tested using QB, a goodness-of-fit statistic developed by Hedges and Olkin (1985). If a significant difference between groups (QB) and no difference within groups (Q) is determined, then $d+$ can be computed to estimate the effect size for each group of studies. If there is a significant difference within groups, then the groups should be further partitioned.

Systematic Reviews Databases

To critically evaluate research evidence from a single properly designed RCT requires a relatively strong background in research methods and a working knowledge of concepts related to internal and external validity (Schlosser, 2006). Given the potential for a vast number of research articles with contradictory findings, the most efficient way for master's-level students and practicing RCs to learn how to find the best evidence may be to use databases and/or specific evidence-based intervention websites to search for high-quality systematic reviews and scoping reviews. The most useful websites for systematic reviews related to evidence-based medical, rehabilitation, and behavioral science intervention information include the Cochrane Collaboration (http://www.cochrane.org), the Campbell Collaboration (http://www.campbellcollaboration.org), the Agency for Healthcare Research and Quality (http://www.ahrq.gov/research/findings/evidence-based-reports/index.html), the American Congress of Rehabilitation Medicine (https://acrm.org/resources/evidence-and-practice), the U.S. Department of Education, Institute of Educational Sciences' What Works Clearinghouse (https://ies.ed.gov/ncee/wwc/FWW), and the Substance Abuse Health and Services Administration's National Registry of Evidence-based Programs and Practices (http://www.samhsa.gov/nrepp). In addition, the VRTAC-QE (https://tacqe.com) is a useful resource for evidence-based VR practices. The National Technical Assistance Center on Transition (https://transitionta.org) provides information on EBP related to secondary transition and postsecondary education interventions. Rehabilitation counseling professionals and students also can search for systematic reviews, scoping reviews, and meta-analytic studies through Academic Search Elite, CINAHL Plus with Full Text, MEDLINE, PsycINFO, EBSCO, and EconLit databases.

EMPIRICALLY SUPPORTED INTERVENTIONS IN CLINICAL REHABILITATION AND MENTAL HEALTH COUNSELING

Ample research evidence suggests that the provision of rehabilitation counseling and related services can produce significant positive outcomes in the lives of people with chronic health conditions and disabilities. Several frequently used empirically supported rehabilitation counseling interventions are described next.

Counseling and Psychotherapy

Counseling and psychotherapy represent some of the strongest EBPs in healthcare (Norcross & Lambert, 2011). It is also one of the most important job functions and knowledge areas for the professional practice of rehabilitation counseling (Leahy et al., 2013). The efficacy of counseling/psychotherapy is well documented (Wampold, 2001; Wampold & Imel, 2015). Specifically, Wampold (2001) analyzed several major meta-analytic reviews and concluded that a reasonable and defensible point estimate for the efficacy of counseling/ psychotherapy is $d = 0.79$ (a large effect size), meaning that the average treated person does better than 78.5% of the average untreated persons. Wampold and Imel (2015) provided an update on the importance of **common factors** (e.g., alliance, empathy, expectations, cultural adaptation of evidence-based treatments, therapist effects) in counseling/psychotherapy based on several meta-analytic studies. He reported robust effects between common factors and counseling/psychotherapy outcome: therapist empathy ($d = 0.63$), positive regard/affirmation ($d = 0.56$), and positive regard/affirmation ($d = 0.56$), and congruence/genuineness ($d = 0.49$). Thus, to help people with chronic health conditions and disabilities achieve positive behavioral change for optimal psychosocial adaptation and vocational adjustment, RCs must be competent in providing psychological and vocational counseling interventions for persons with chronic health conditions and disabilities.

Working Alliance

An effective therapeutic relationship is essential in helping people with chronic health conditions and disabilities actively engage in VR services. **Working alliance** can be defined as (a) the client's affective relationship with the therapist, (b) the client's motivation and ability to accomplish work collaboratively with the therapist, (c) the therapist's empathic response to and involvement with the client, and (d) client and therapist agreement about the goals and tasks of therapy (Horvath & Symonds, 1991). Wampold (2001) indicated that the common factors are what affect counseling/psychotherapy outcomes the most, not the techniques associated with specific theoretical orientations. He indicated that up to 70% of the benefits of psychotherapy were due to common factors, 8% were due to specific factors (i.e., different theoretical orientations and techniques), and the remaining 22% were partially attributed to individual client differences. Horvath et al. (2011) analyzed 190 studies representing more than 14,000 clients and found a relatively robust relationship between working alliance and positive counseling outcomes ($r = .27$), which is equivalent to a Cohen's d of 0.57, surpassing the threshold for a medium effect size. Working alliance is especially conducive to promoting active participation between clients and counselors in the rehabilitation process (Chan et al., 1997; McMahon et al., 2004; Shaw et al., 2004; Strauser et al., 2010). Lustig et al. (2002) examined survey data of 2,732 VR clients during the fiscal year 2000 and found that (a) employed clients had a stronger working alliance than unemployed clients ($d = 0.73$; large effect), (b) a stronger working alliance was related to more positive client perception of future employment prospects ($r = .51$; large effect), and (c) a stronger working alliance was related to employed rehabilitation clients' satisfaction with their current jobs ($r = .15$; small effect). Tansey et al.

(2017) reported a robust relationship between working alliance and outcome expectancy, VR engagement, and readiness for employment in a sample of VR consumers. Iwanaga et al. (2019) also reported a strong relationship between working alliance and stages of change for employment. This relationship was mediated by several constructs of the self-determination theory including autonomous motivation, outcome expectancy, and VR engagement.

Motivational Interviewing

Clients' self-determined motivation to work can have a positive influence on VR treatment engagement and compliance (Wagner & McMahon, 2004). Therefore, enhancing client motivation is an important factor to consider in counseling people with chronic health conditions and disabilities (Chan et al., 1997; Cook, 2004; Manthey et al., 2015). Wagner and McMahon (2004) identified several rehabilitation contexts where motivational interviewing might be appropriate, including: managing medical issues and adjusting to physical disability, adjusting to cognitive impairment, improving psychosocial functioning, and returning to work. **Motivational interviewing** is an empirically supported, client-centered, and directive counseling approach designed to promote client motivation and reduce motivational conflicts and barriers to change (Manthey et al., 2015). Most important, motivational interviewing plays an essential role in changing counselors' attitudes and beliefs about a client's change processes. Rather than negatively attributing poor rehabilitation outcomes to the low motivation levels of their clients, the use of motivational interviewing helps counselors to focus on the processes that help keep clients motivated and engaged in rehabilitation services. This approach will improve counselors' perceptions of their clients, enhance working alliance, and contribute to positive psychosocial and employment outcomes (Manthey et al., 2015).

Lundahl et al. (2010) conducted a meta-analysis based on 25 years of motivational interviewing empirical studies with substance use (tobacco, alcohol, drugs, marijuana), health-related behaviors (diet, exercise, safe sex), engagement in treatment, and gambling addiction as targeted outcomes. They found a small overall effect size of $g = 0.22$ (95% CI [0.17, 0.27]). Although motivational interviewing did not perform better than other strong substance abuse treatments such as cognitive behavior therapy and 12-step, motivational interviewing interventions, on average, require significantly less time (over 100 fewer minutes) to produce equal effects. Motivational interviewing is effective for increasing clients' engagement in treatment and their intention to change. It works relatively well for individuals with a range of distress levels and the effect of motivational interviewing was found to be durable at the 2-year mark and beyond. Recently, Maslowski et al. (2021) conducted a systematic review and meta-analysis to quantify the effectiveness of teaching students motivational interviewing. They included 15 randomized and nonrandomized studies and 8 dependent variables in their study. They reported a large and significant overall Hedges's g of 0.90 (large effect size) indicating motivational interviewing training is effective in increasing students' knowledge, empathy, and counseling outcomes.

Skills Training

Promoting self-efficacy through **skills training** in the areas of social skills, coping skills, general life skills, and specific job skills is an important intervention focus on rehabilitation counseling. **Self-efficacy** is defined as people's belief in their ability to succeed in specific situations or accomplish a task (Bandura, 1982). Dilk and Bond (1996) conducted a meta-analysis of 68 studies, including 59 between-group studies and nine within-group studies (i.e., one-group, pretest–posttest), to determine the effectiveness of skills training for individuals with serious mental illness and the influence of such factors as methodological rigor, choice of outcome measures, and service settings. For between-group studies, the overall effect size was medium at posttest ($d = 0.40$) and at follow-up ($d = 0.56$). For the within-group studies, the overall effect size was also medium at posttest ($d = 0.48$), but small at follow-up ($d = 0.30$). Dilk and Bond concluded that behavioral skills training for persons with serious mental illness can be effective for teaching inpatients interpersonal and assertiveness skills, as indicated by measures of skill acquisition and symptom reduction. Kurtz and Mueser (2008) conducted a meta-analysis to examine the efficacy of social skills training interventions for people with schizophrenia. A total of 22 studies were included, and they reported a moderate mean weighted effect size for performance-based measures of social and daily living skills ($d = 0.52$) and moderate mean weighted effect sizes for community functioning ($d = 0.52$) and negative symptoms ($d = 0.40$). Bolton and Akridge (1995) conducted a meta-analysis of skills training interventions for VR consumers and they report a large effect size of $d = 0.82$, suggesting that skills training substantially benefits the typical VR participant (Bolton & Akridge, 1995).

Postsecondary Education

It is well documented that college graduates have higher incomes and lower unemployment rates than those with only a high school diploma or less than a diploma (U.S. Department of Labor, 2014). In addition, studies have demonstrated that educational attainment is associated with employment for people with disabilities than for people without disabilities more strongly, confirming that education can be used as a means to improve employability and income (Carnevale et al., 2011; Flannery et al., 2008; Jones et al., 2006; Kidd et al., 2000; O'Neill et al., 2015; Smith et al., 2012; Yamamoto et al., 2014). As a result, postsecondary education has gained attention as a VR intervention for people with chronic health conditions and disabilities (Gilmore & Bose, 2005). Postsecondary education is also emphasized in the Workforce Innovation and Opportunity Act, and the Amendments to the Rehabilitation Act of 1973 as a way to help people with disabilities develop meaningful careers to facilitate entry to the middle class (U.S. Department of Education, 2014).

O'Neill et al. (2015) conducted a case-control study to examine the effect of postsecondary education on earnings for people with chronic health conditions and disabilities, using data extracted from the Rehabilitation Services Administration Case Service Report (RSA-911) database. Their study included 178,290 individuals with chronic health conditions and disabilities whose cases were closed as "successfully rehabilitated" by the state–federal VR program during fiscal year 2011. Propensity scores to receive college or university training were estimated based on demographic variables using the classification and regression tree (CART) method. The CART analysis yielded six homogeneous subgroups, ranging from a high propensity to receive college or university training as a VR intervention to a low propensity to receive such a service. Individuals who received college/university training had higher weekly earnings than those who did not (O'Neill et al., 2015), and postsecondary education had the greatest benefit for young adults, White Americans, Asian Americans, and Native American women with physical impairments and people with mental impairments (O'Neill et al., 2015). The effect of postsecondary education training on weekly earnings was reported to have a medium effect size (O'Neill et al., 2015). Similarly, Migliore et al. (2012) indicated that the receipt of college/university training through VR was the strongest predictor of higher earnings for youth with autism. Most recently, Chan et al. (2020) conducted a propensity-score-matched case-controlled study to examine the effect of postsecondary education on employment outcome of young adults with traumatic brain injury (TBI). They found that young adults with TBI who received postsecondary education (treatment group) as a VR service had higher employment outcome (60.4%) than those who did not postsecondary education as a VR service (42.4%).

Supported Employment

Supported employment is identified as one of the strongest EBP in VR and mental health services (Drake et al., 2005; Leahy, Chan, & Lui, 2014; Leahy, Chan, Lui, Rosenthal, et al., 2014; Wehman et al., 2014). Supported employment is defined as competitive employment in an integrated setting with ongoing support services for individuals with the most severe disabilities (Wehman et al., 2014). Specifically, Wehman et al. (2014) conducted a case-control study using propensity score matching to examine the effect of supported employment intervention on the employment outcomes of transition-age youth with intellectual and developmental disabilities. They found a moderate effect size on employment outcomes for people who received special education in high school and for individuals with intellectual and developmental disabilities, particularly those who were Social Security beneficiaries. Similarly, Campbell et al. (2011) conducted a meta-analysis to compare the effect of the IPS model of supported employment with traditional vocational interventions for people with severe mental illness. They found large effect sizes favoring the use of IPS in job acquisition ($d = 0.90$), total weeks worked ($d = 0.79$), and job tenure ($d = 0.74$).

Work Incentives Benefits Counseling

Work incentives benefits counseling is a VR service that helps individuals with disabilities and their families understand how employment and other life decisions will impact their disability-related benefits, including SSI, SSDI, Medicaid, and Medicare. It allays the fears and concerns many individuals with disabilities and their families have about a reduction in benefits if they start to work. Research has indicated that Social Security beneficiaries who received work incentives benefits counseling had significantly greater improvements in employment (Delin et al., 2010; Livermore & Prenovitz, 2010; Peikes et al., 2008) and earnings (Peikes et al., 2008; Tremblay et al., 2006), higher utilization of work incentives (Livermore & Prenovitz, 2010), and higher rate of transitioning off benefits rolls including SSI/SSDI (Livemore & Prenovitz; Livermore et al., 2011). Schlegelmilch et al. (2019) analyzed data from the Wisconsin Promoting the Readiness of Minors in Supplemental Security Income (Wisconsin PROMISE) project and found that transition-age youth who received work incentives benefits counseling were more than twice as likely to secure employment than those who had not, and more than four times as likely to have earnings over the monthly substantial gainful activity threshold set by the Social Security Administration than the control group. Importantly, Iwanaga et al. (2021) conducted a propensity-score-matched case-control study using the RSA-911 data. They evaluated the effect of work incentives benefits counseling as a VR intervention to promote job-search motivation, improve employment outcomes, and increase average work hours per week of transition-age youth and young adults with intellectual disabilities (ID) who are SSI recipients. Results indicated that ransition-age youth and young adults with ID who received work incentives benefits counseling (treatment group) had significantly higher rates of employment (58.9%) than the no-work incentives benefits counseling control group (47.17%).

Demand-Side Employment

Disability-employment researchers have been advocating for the integration of the supply-side employment approach with the demand-side employment approach to improve the employment outcome and quality of employment of people with disabilities receiving services from state vocational rehabilitation agencies (Chan et al., 2020, 2021; Gilbride & Stensrud, 1992). **Supply-side employment** has a focus on providing medical, psychological, educational, and vocational services to improve functioning, stamina, and job skills of people with disabilities, without considering the role of organizational behaviors, employer needs, stigma, and the changing labor economy (Strauser et al., 2010). On the other hand, the focus of **demand-side employment** is on workplace cultures and employers' disability inclusion practices (and the interaction of employer demand and the environment, e.g., the COVID-19 pandemic and the post-pandemic job economy) as predictors of employment outcomes for people with disabilities (Chan et al., 2021). Chan et al. (2021) developed and validated the *Disability Inclusion Profilers* to identify empirically supported disability inclusion policies, procedures, and practices that are associated with the inclusion of people with chronic health conditions and disabilities in the workplace. They found that disability inclusion practices could be classified into two major domains based on their relationships with disability employment: (a) Level 1 executive/senior management–level practices and (b) Level 2 mid-level management and staff-level practices. Disability inclusion practices for both levels were significantly associated with employment of people with disabilities in the workplace. The sum of these disability inclusion practices was significantly associated with employment of people with disabilities in the workplace ($r = .32$, $p < .001$; medium effect size; Chan et al., 2021). However, executive-level practices had a stronger association with employment than mid-level management and staff practices, supporting the importance of the top-down approach for disability inclusion in the workplace. Level 1 and Level 2 disability inclusion practices are described next.

Level 1 Disability Inclusion Practices

- Have an accommodations budget line item to cover costs for accommodations for employees.
- Have annual targets and assess performance to achieve application and employment goals for persons with disabilities.
- Have disability management personnel (in-house or contractual) who are responsible for handling issues related to the ADA and job accommodations.
- Have a hiring manager with a disability.
- Have senior leadership clearly communicate its commitment to employment of people with disabilities.
- Post statement of commitment to hiring people with disabilities on the company website.
- Have a senior executive with a disability.
- Report progress toward hiring persons with disabilities to senior management.
- Have internal and external resources to support the goals of the company's disability employment and inclusion program.
- Communicate emergency preparedness policy or procedures with specific mention of persons with disabilities.
- Include disability in the company's diversity and inclusion policies and procedures.
- Have senior leadership communicate clearly and affirmatively the company's commitment to recruiting and hiring people with disabilities.
- Have a disability accommodation policy.
- Offer an Employee Assistance program.
- Have an emergency preparedness policy or procedures in place with a specific mention of persons with disabilities.
- Offer healthcare coverage to employees.
- Have stay-at-work and return-to-work retention policies and procedures.
- Offer a health and wellness program to employees.
- Offer short-term disability benefits that are managed to promote the retention of people with disabilities in the workforce.
- Ensure the workplace is accessible to people with disabilities.

Level 2 Disability Inclusion Practices

- Participate in job fairs for people with disabilities.
- Provide disability inclusion training for company's HR recruiters.
- Have a mechanism to assess the number of people with disabilities in the company.
- Have internship and summer employment programs directed toward high school and college students with disabilities.
- Identify and select partners who can be valuable in recruiting qualified individuals with disabilities.
- Include "work and disability" as a topic in the company's diversity and inclusion training.
- Have a mentoring program to promote the advancement of diverse persons.
- Have strategies to attract qualified applications from persons with disabilities.
- Have contracts with employment agencies.
- Include "work and disability" as a topic in the company's new employee orientation training.
- Have a process for assessing the website for compliance of coding with existing law and regulations.
- Have policy to make all job interview candidates aware of the option to request an accommodation(s) for the interview.
- The Section 503 Voluntary Self-Identification of Disability Form has been implemented in the HR new employee processing system.
- Display nondiscrimination and/or equal opportunity policy language that specifically mentions disability on the company's external public-facing recruitment/career website.

Vocational Rehabilitation Services

It is not possible to conduct experimental studies for state VR services on the whole as an independent variable. However, the Rehabilitation Act Amendments have required the state-federal VR program to conduct ongoing research to demonstrate the effectiveness of rehabilitation interventions on employment rates and quality of employment outcomes of people with disabilities. Research evidence from nonexperimental studies supports the association between VR services and successful employment outcomes. For example, O'Neill et al. (2014) conducted a case-control study to examine the effect of VR services on return-to-work outcomes of SSDI beneficiaries using two administrative data sets that were matched prospectively; the longitudinal Disability Analysis File, formerly known as the Ticket Research File, from the Social Security Administration and the RSA-911 case service report data file from the Rehabilitation Service Administration. The Social Security Disability Insurance beneficiaries (treatment group, $n = 17,369$) who accessed state VR services in 2000 were matched with SSDI beneficiaries who had never applied for state VR services based on 36 demographic covariates. Propensity score matching led to balance between the treatment and control groups on 34 of the 36 variables. Logistic regression analysis results revealed the treatment groups completing the trial work period at significantly greater rates than the control groups in the 10 year period of the study. Dean et al. (2014) examined the association between the receipt of VR services and SSI/SSDI using a special panel dataset on Virginians with disabilities who applied for state VR services in 2000. They found that VR services are associated with lower rates of participation in disability insurance programs (a 2-point drop in SSDI receipt and 1-point drop in SSI receipt); VR service receipt is associated with lower take-up rates of SSI/SSDI; and social security beneficiaries receiving substantive VR services are more likely to be employed.

Dutta et al. (2008) analyzed RSA-911 data for the fiscal year 2005 using logistic regression analysis and found job placement, on-the-job support, maintenance, and other services (e.g., medical care for acute conditions) as significant predictors of employment success across all impairment groups. They found that job placement and support services could improve the odds for obtaining competitive employment: job search assistance (OR = 1.24; 95% CI [1.08, 1.43]), job placement assistance (OR = 1.89; 95% CI [1.66, 2.16]), and on-the-job support (OR = 2.20; 95% CI [1.90, 2.55]). In addition, diagnostic and treatment (D&T) services (OR = 1.57; 95% CI [1.35, 1.82]) and rehabilitation technology (RT) services (OR = 1.97, 95% CI [1.67, 2.33]) were found to contribute uniquely to employment outcomes for the sensory impairments group, as well as the physical impairments group (D&T services: OR = 1.31, 95% CI [1.15, 1.48]; RT services: OR = 1.41, 95% CI [1.13, 1.75]), but not the mental impairments group. Substantial counseling was associated with employment outcomes for the physical (OR = 1.16, 95% CI [1.02, 1.32]) and mental impairments groups (OR = 1.18, 95% CI [1.03, 1.35]). Miscellaneous training (OR = 1.31; 95% CI [1.09, 1.49]) was associated specifically with employment outcomes of the mental impairments group.

KNOWLEDGE TRANSLATION

Rehabilitation researchers face the challenge of translating the best available evidence into effective psychosocial and employment interventions for people with chronic health conditions and disabilities. The National Center for the Dissemination of Disability Research (2006) defined **knowledge translation** as the collaborative and systematic review, assessment, identification, aggregation, and practical application of high-quality disability and rehabilitation research by key stakeholders (i.e., consumers, employers, researchers, practitioners, and policymakers) to improve the lives of individuals with chronic health conditions and disabilities. In the context of EBP, knowledge translation is the process of connecting research knowledge to the actual applications of such knowledge in various practice settings and circumstances. Sudsawad (2007) suggested that, essentially, knowledge translation is an interactive process underpinned by effective exchanges between researchers who create new knowledge and clinicians who use the information. Continuing dialogues, interactions, and partnerships within and between groups of knowledge creators and users for all stages of the research process are integral parts of knowledge translation. To be effective, conceptual frameworks are recommended to apply theory and enhance implementation efforts (Field et al., 2014).

The **Knowledge-to-Action** (KTA) Framework, widely used in practice, provides a useful model for knowledge translation in rehabilitation (Field et al., 2014; Graham et al., 2006; Lui et al., 2014). It comprises two distinct but related components: (a) knowledge creation and (b) the action cycle. Each component involves multiple dynamic and mutually influencing phases. Action phases may be carried out sequentially or simultaneously, and knowledge phases may impact the action phases. The action cycle outlines a process representing the activities needed for knowledge to be applied in practice. Knowledge then is adapted to the local context, and barriers and facilitators to its use are explicitly assessed. The involvement of stakeholders, as well as tailoring knowledge to the needs of rehabilitation professionals, is crucial. The structural relationships among knowledge creation and the associated action steps in the KTA framework are depicted graphically in Figure 19.1.

Specifically, knowledge creation comprises three phases: (a) knowledge inquiry, (b) synthesis of knowledge, and (c) creation of knowledge tools. Knowledge inquiry involves the completion of the primary research. The synthesis stage requires appropriate research findings (i.e., systematic reviews) to identify common patterns. In developing tools and products, the best-quality knowledge is further synthesized and distilled into decision-making tools such as practice guidelines, aids for patient decisions, or algorithms (Straus et al., 2009). In rehabilitation counseling, toolkits including empirically validated

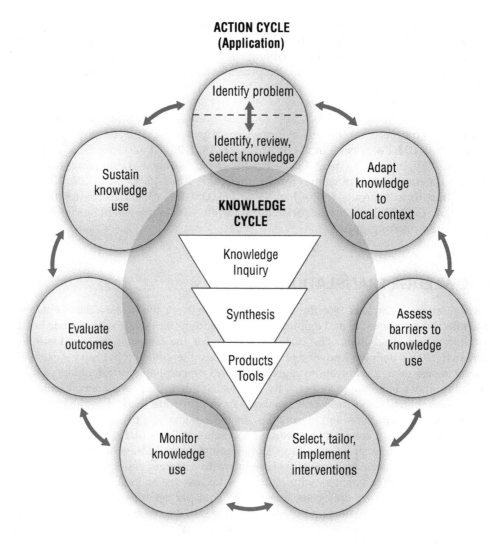

FIGURE 19.1 Knowledge-to-Action framework of knowledge translation.

assessments, planning tools, and interventions can be developed and distributed to practicing counselors.

The action cycle is composed of seven phases based on theories of planned action.
These actions can occur sequentially or simultaneously and are influenced by activities
of the knowledge phases at any point in the cycle. Included are the processes needed to
use knowledge in health care and rehabilitation settings. Specifically, these processes are
(a) identifying the problem; (b) identifying, reviewing, and selecting the knowledge to
implement; (c) adapting or customizing the knowledge to the local context; (d) assessing
the determinants (barriers) of knowledge use; (e) selecting, tailoring, implementing and
monitoring interventions related to knowledge translation; (f) evaluating outcomes or
impacts of using the knowledge; and (g) determining strategies for ensuring sustained
use of knowledge. Salient to this knowledge translation framework emphasizes on the
need to incorporate input from the various stakeholders (including patients, clinicians,
managers, or policymakers) who are the end users of the knowledge that is being implemented. The inclusion of end users of the knowledge will ensure that the knowledge and
its subsequent implementation are relevant to their needs, promoting the applications of
research and knowledge translation.

NIDILRR has made knowledge translation a high priority in all of its funded research projects. It has funded the Center on Knowledge Translation for Disability and Rehabilitation Research (KTDRR; https://ktdrr.org) to provide integrated training, dissemination, utilization, and technical assistance activities to (a) increase use of valid and relevant evidence-based research findings that inform decision-making and (b) increase the understanding and application of knowledge translation principles. It also funded the Knowledge Translation for Employment Research Center (KTER; https://kter.org) to develop and test knowledge translation strategies designed to help VR agencies and businesses find, understand, and use research related to employing people with disabilities. In addition, all NIDILRR-funded Rehabilitation Research and Training Centers, Disability and Rehabilitation Research Programs, Disability and Business Technical Assistance Centers, Traumatic Brain Injury Model Systems, and Spinal Cord Injury Model Systems are required to conduct research that meets the highest standards for inclusion in evidence-based systematic reviews. Knowledge translation must be an integral component of their systematic research program. These centers are excellent resources for best evidence information related to psychosocial and vocational interventions for people with disabilities. It can also find information about these KT-related centers in the National Rehabilitation Information Center (https://www.naric.com).

FUTURE RESEARCH DIRECTIONS

The lack of strong theory-driven research and empirical evidence to inform assessment, planning, and intervention in the rehabilitation process have been one of the most frequent criticisms of rehabilitation counseling research (Berkowitz et al., 1975; Chan et al., 2003). Current rehabilitation practices have been characterized by some scholars as "experience-based," "eminence-based," or "habit-based" (Law, 2002). In addition, rehabilitation research is frequently nonexperimental or quasi-experimental in nature (Bolton, 2004). The lack of randomized controlled trials is seen as a major barrier to the successful implementation of EBP in rehabilitation (Chwalisz & Chan, 2008). To fully adopt an evidence-based approach in rehabilitation, Dunn and Elliott (2008) proposed that rehabilitation professionals need to: (a) embrace a comprehensive theory-driven research agenda, (b) validate effective interventions based on this research agenda, and (c) facilitate the provision of empirically supported interventions based on the research evidence.

Chan et al. (2016) suggested that the evidence-based practice movement may present a window of opportunity for the rehabilitation counseling profession to promote and support a systematic agenda for theory-driven rehabilitation research. The use of scientific evidence derived from theory-driven research could improve the independent living and employment outcomes of people with chronic health conditions and disabilities, leading to overall happiness and well-being. However, the complex nature of VR makes process and outcome research challenging (Bolton, 2004; Johnston et al., 1997). Specifically, rehabilitation encompasses a broad scope of services, spans along the medical-vocational rehabilitation continuum from hospital care to community-based services, and is provided through various disciplines (e.g., occupational therapy, physical therapy, rehabilitation psychology, rehabilitation counseling, clinical rehabilitation counseling, mental health counseling) for individuals with diverse and complex impairments and disabilities. The process typically involves a range of personal and environmental processes and the interactions thereof, making it difficult to determine what aspects of service delivery contribute to what outcome. Chan, Chronister, et al. (2009), Chan, Keegan, et al. (2009), and Chan, Tarvydas, et al. (2009) advocated that the WHO's *International Classification of Functioning, Disability, and Health (ICF)* model can be used as a VR framework for conceptualizing and determining medical and VR assessment, planning, and service needs and to provide evidence-based services for people with chronic health conditions and disabilities. They also underscored the use of the *ICF* model to develop a systematic research agenda to develop and validate EBP for VR.

Specifically, the *ICF* paradigm is structured around the following broad components: (a) body functions and structure, (b) activities (related to tasks and actions by an individual) and participation (involvement in a life situation), and (c) severity of disability and environmental factors (Chan & Ditchman, 2013). Functioning and disability are viewed as a complex interaction between the health condition of the individual and the contextual factors of the environment, as well as personal factors. The *ICF* model is consistent with the holistic philosophy of rehabilitation counseling and can be an invaluable framework for case conceptualization purposes by counselors to determine the need for medical, psychosocial, and VR assessment, plan the consumer's rehabilitation program, and select empirically supported VR interventions. Using the *ICF* model to develop a systematic rehabilitation research agenda may allow researchers to quickly identify and validate a number of universal best practices (e.g., supported employment for ID/DD, IPS model of supported employment for people with severe mental illness, secondary transition, postsecondary education interventions, motivational interviewing, positive psychology interventions, self-determination interventions, work incentives benefits counseling, demand-side employment interventions, health promotion interventions, and virtual rehabilitation interventions) that can be integrated into an RC's repertoire of best practices.

Importantly, testing mediator and moderator effects should be a high priority in the rehabilitation counseling research agenda, which will further promote the use of the EBP in the field. Research questions involving moderators address when or for whom a variable most strongly predicts or causes an outcome variable, whereas mediators establish how or why one variable predicts or causes an outcome variable (Frazier et al., 2004; Hoyt et al., 2008). A mediator provides information about the underlying mechanisms for change. In contrast, a moderator effect is basically an interaction whereby the effect of an independent variable (e.g., treatment) differs at different levels of another independent variable (e.g., severity). Similar to healthcare research, the study of moderator effects in VR research is important, as what works for European American clients may not work for individuals from diverse racial and ethnic minority backgrounds, what works for men may not work for women, and what works for individuals with sensory impairments may not work for persons with psychiatric disabilities (Chan, Keegan, et al., 2009; Chan, Tarvydas, et al., 2009).

Similarly, moderators are essential in other key areas of VR research. For example, in studying the role of resiliency factors in psychosocial adjustment to disability, future research can examine whether the adjustment process is similar or different for persons with sudden onset versus chronic conditions. Therefore, rehabilitation researchers need to expend more research efforts to test moderator effects of race, gender, disability type, health status, and immunity (e.g., social support, coping skills, resilience) and vulnerability factors (e.g., stress). For theory and model building, it is equally important to study the mediator effect (i.e., the underlying mechanisms of change) to better effective design interventions (Hoyt et al., 2008). An increased emphasis on a testing mediator and moderator variables in the VR research paradigm is needed to develop effective model-driven, culturally sensitive, and evidence-based VR interventions for individuals with disabilities in the 21st century (Chan, Keegan, et al., 2009; Chan, Tarvydas, et al., 2009).

CONCLUSION

Incorporating research-based knowledge into rehabilitation counseling practice is particularly relevant in today's era of accountability, research utilization, and an EBP (Chan et al., 2016; Chronister et al., 2008; Law, 2002). As a conceptual framework or philosophy, EBP advocates that every rehabilitation and health professional should have an interest in delivering the best possible services to their clients, based whenever possible on the best clinical practices available from the strongest research evidence. Rehabilitation counseling researchers and practitioners must develop a strong focus on theory development, empirical evidence, and clinical application. Within the context of EBP, Dunn and Elliott (2008) argued for the primacy of theory and its place in rehabilitation research. Advocacy for developing theory-driven research programs that embrace methodological pluralism will advance new theory and produce meaningful research programs that inform practice in VR service delivery. The development of a systematic research agenda and conducting meaningful theory-driven research and intervention research will generate new knowledge and accumulate high-quality evidence, enhancing the ability of RCs to truly engage in EBP to improve employment outcomes and quality of life of people with disabilities (Box 19.1).

ACKNOWLEDGMENTS

The contents of this chapter were developed with support from the Rehabilitation Research and Training Center on Effective Vocational Rehabilitation Service Delivery Practices at the University of Wisconsin-Madison and the University of Wisconsin–Stout and with funding provided by the U.S. Department of Education, National Institute on Disability and Rehabilitation Research (Grant H133B100034). The ideas, opinions, and conclusions expressed, however, are those of the authors and do not represent recommendations, endorsements, or policies of the U.S. Department of Education.

CONTENT REVIEW QUESTIONS

1. How did the EBP approach to healthcare service delivery evolve within the United States?
2. What are the main conceptual bases of EBP?
3. How can rehabilitation counselors become more effective practitioners within the framework of EBP?
4. Which evidence-based methodologies and concepts are crucial in improving rehabilitation counselors' knowledge of EBP and research utilization?
5. How can the evidence-based decision-making process be illustrated?
6. Describe a hierarchical framework that emphasizes the importance of randomized controlled trials/experimental studies.
7. What is the gold standard for best scientific evidence in evidence-based medicine? How does it apply to rehabilitation counseling?

BOX 19.1 EXERCISE FOR SEARCHING EBP FROM INTERNET RESOURCES

Research on evidence-based practices is constantly evolving. Choose one of the evidence-based practices discussed in this chapter and search online for emerging research. A good place to begin is a systematic review database: (a) the Cochrane Collaboration, (b) the Campbell Collaboration (c) for Healthcare Research and Quality, (d) the American Congress of Rehabilitation Medicine, (d) the U.S. Department of Education, Institute of Educational Sciences' What Works Clearinghouse, (e) the Substance Abuse Health and Services Administration's National Registry of Evidence-based Programs and Practices, (f) the Rehabilitation Research and Training Center on Evidence-Based Practice in Vocational Rehabilitation, (g) the National Technical Assistance Center on Transition, (h) the Center on Knowledge Translation for Disability and Rehabilitation Research, (i) the Knowledge Translation for Employment Research Center, or (j) the National Rehabilitation Information Center.

8. Which elements can be considered as barriers in promoting the application of evidence-based in rehabilitation counseling?
9. Describe empirically supported strategy interventions in rehabilitation counseling.
10. How can the field of rehabilitation counseling apply, support, and advance theory-driven research?
11. Discuss how the WHO's *ICF* can be used to guide the development of a systematic research agenda in rehabilitation counseling?

REFERENCES

American Psychological Association. (2005). *Policy statement on evidence-based practice in psychology.* http://www.apa.org/practice/ebpstatement.pdf

Annual Disability Statistics Compendium. (2020). *2020 Annual disability statistics compendium.* https://disabilitycompendium.org

Arksey, H., & O'Malley, L. (2005). Scoping studies: Towards a methodological framework. *International Journal of Social Research Methodology, 8*(1), 19–32. https://doi.org/10.1080/1364557032000119616

Armstrong, R., Hall, B. J., Doyle, J., & Waters, E. (2011). Cochrane update. "Scoping the scope" of a cochrane review. *Journal of Public Health (Oxford, England), 33*(1), 147–150. https://doi.org/10.1093/pubmed/fdr015

Atkins, D., & Giusti, C. (2005). The confluence of poverty and disability. In C. Armbrister & K. Smith (Eds.), *The realities of poverty in Delaware 2003–2004* (pp. 6–8). Delaware Housing Coalition.

Bandura, A. (1982). Self-efficacy mechanism in human agency. *American Psychologist, 37*(2), 122–147. https://doi.org/10.1037/0003-066X.37.2.122

Berkowitz, M., Englander, V., Rubin, J., & Worrall, J. D. (1975). *An evaluation of policy-related research.* Praeger.

Berkowitz, M., Englander, V., Rubin, J., & Worrall, J. D. (1976). A summary of "An evaluation of policy-related research. *Rehabilitation Counseling Bulletin, 20*, 29–45.

Bezyak, J. L., Kubota, C., & Rosenthal, D. (2010). Evidence-based practice in rehabilitation counseling: Perceptions and practices. *Rehabilitation Education, 24*(1), 85–96. https://doi.org/10.1891/088970110805029886

Bolton, B. (2004). Counseling and rehabilitation outcomes. In F. Chan, N. L. Berven, & K. R. Thomas (Eds.), *Counseling theories and techniques for rehabilitation health professionals* (pp. 444–465). Springer.

Bolton, B., & Akridge, R. L. (1995). A meta-analysis of skills training programs for rehabilitation clients. *Rehabilitation Counseling Bulletin, 38*, 262–273.

Borenstein, M., Hedges, L. V., Higgins, J. P. T., & Rothstein, H. R. (2009). *Introduction to Meta-Analysis.* Wiley.

Campbell Collaboration. (2019). *Campbell Collaboration systematic reviews: Policies and guidelines (version 1.4).* https://onlinelibrary.wiley.com/pb-assets/assets/18911803/Campbell%20Policies%20and%20Guidelines%20v4-1559660867160.pdf

Campbell, K., Bond, G. R., & Drake, R. E. (2011). Who benefits from supported employment: A meta-analytic study. *Schizophrenia Bulletin, 37*(2), 370–380. https://doi.org/10.1093/schbul/sbp066

Carnevale, A. P., Rose, S. J., & Cheah, B. (2011). *The college payoff: Education, occupations, and lifetime earnings.* Georgetown University Center on Education and the Workforce.

Chambless, D. L., & Hollon, S. D. (1998). Defining empirically supported therapies. *Journal of Consulting and Clinical Psychology, 66*(1), 7–18. https://doi.org/10.1037//0022-006x.66.1.7

Chan, F., Chronister, J., & Cardoso, E. (2009). An introduction to evidence-based practice approach to psychosocial interventions for people with chronic illness and disability. In F. Chan, E. Cardoso, & J. Chronister (Eds.), *Psychosocial interventions for people with chronic illness and disability: A handbook for evidence-based rehabilitation health professionals* (pp. 3–19). Springer Publishing Company.

Chan, F., & Ditchman, N. (2013). Applying the International Classification of Functioning, Disability, and Health to psychology practice [Review of the book ICF core sets: Manual for clinical practice, by J. Bickenbach, A. Cieza, A. Rauch & G. Stucki, Eds.]. *PsycCritiques, 58*(13). https://doi.org/10.1037/a0031605

Chan, F., Keegan, J., Muller, V., Kaya, C., Flowers, S., & Iwanaga, K. (2016). Evidence-based practice and research in rehabilitation counseling. In I. Marini & M. A. Stebnicki (Eds.), *The professional counselor's desk reference* (2nd ed., pp. 605–610). Springer.

Chan, F., Keegan, J., Sung, C., Drout, M., Pai, C. H., Anderson, E., & McLain, N. (2009). The World Health Organization ICF model as a framework for assessing vocational rehabilitation outcomes. *Journal of Rehabilitation Administration*, 33, 91–112.

Chan, F., Miller, S., Pruett, S., Lee, G., & Chou, C. (2003). Research. In D. Maki & T. Riggar (Eds.), *Handbook of Rehabilitation Counseling* (pp. 159–170). Springer.

Chan, F., Rosenthal, D. A., & Pruett, S. (2008). Evidence-based practices in the provision of rehabilitation services. *Journal of Rehabilitation*, 74(2), 1–5.

Chan, F., Rumrill, P., Wehman, P., Iwanaga, K., Wu, J. R., Rumrill, S., Chen, X., & Lee, B. (2020). Effects of postsecondary education on employment outcomes and earnings of young adults with traumatic brain injuries. *Journal of Vocational Rehabilitation*, 53(2), 159–166. https://doi.org/10.3233/JVR-201093

Chan, F., Shaw, L., McMahon, B. T., Koch, L., & Strauser, D. (1997). A model for enhancing consumer-counselor working relationships in rehabilitation. *Rehabilitation Counseling Bulletin*, 41, 122–137.

Chan, F., Tansey, T. N., Iwanaga, K., Bezyak, J., Wehman, P., Phillips, B. N., Strauser, D. R., & Anderson, C. (2021). Company Characteristics, Disability Inclusion Practices, and Employment of People with Disabilities in the Post COVID-19 Job Economy: A Cross Sectional Survey Study. *Journal of Occupational Rehabilitation*, 31(3), 463–473. https://doi.org/10.1007/s10926-020-09941-8

Chan, F., Tarvydas, V., Blalock, K., Strauser, D., & Atkins, B. J. (2009). Unifying and Elevating Rehabilitation Counseling Through Model-Driven, Diversity-Sensitive Evidence-Based Practice. *Rehabilitation Counseling Bulletin*, 52(2), 114–119. https://doi.org/10.1177/0034355208323947

Chronister, J. A., Chan, F., Cardoso, E., Lynch, R. T., & Rosenthal, D. A. (2008). The evidence-based practice movement in healthcare: Iimplications for rehabilitation. *Journal of Rehabilitation*, 74(2), 6–15.

Chwalisz, K., & Chan, F. (2008). Methodological advances and issues in rehabilitation psychology: Moving forward on the cutting edge. *Rehabilitation Psychology*, 53(3), 251–253. https://doi.org/10.1037/a0013038

Chwalisz, K., Shah, S. R., & Hand, K. M. (2008). Facilitating rigorous qualitative research in rehabilitation psychology. *Rehabilitation Psychology*, 53(3), 387–399. https://doi.org/10.1037/a0012998

Cohen, J. (1988). *Statistical power analysis for the behavioral sciences* (2nd ed.). Erlbaum.

Cook, D. W. (2004). Counseling people with physical disabilities. In F. Chan, N. L. Berven, & K. R. Thomas (Eds.), *Counseling theories and techniques for rehabilitation health professionals* (pp. 328–341). Springer.

Dean, D., Pepper, J. V., Schmidt, R. M., & Stern, S. (2014). State vocational rehabilitation programs and federal disability insurance: an analysis of Virginia's vocational rehabilitation program. *IZA Journal of Labor Policy*, 3(1), 1–19. https://doi.org/10.1186/2193-9004-3-7

Delin, B. S., Hartman, E. A., & Sell, C. W. (2010). Does work incentive benefits counseling improve employment outcomes for those with serious disabilities? Preliminary evidence for the "work oriented" from two demonstration projects. In *Work Oriented" from Two Demonstratioan Projects."* APPAM Research Conference.

DePalma, J. A. (2002). Proposing an evidence-based policy process. *Nursing Administration Quarterly*, 26(4), 55–61. https://doi.org/10.1097/00006216-200207000-00010

Diette, T. M., Goldsmith, A. H., Hamilton, D., & Darity, W. D. (2012). Causality in the relationship between mental health and unemployment. In L. D. Appelbaum (Ed.), *Reconnecting to work: Policies to mitigate long-term unemployment and its consequences* (pp. 63–94). W.E. Upjohn Institute for Employment Research. http://research.upjohn.org/cgi/viewcontent.cgi?article=1828&context=up_bookchapters

Dijkers, M. (2015). What is a scoping review? *KT Update*, 4(1). http://ktdrr.org/products/update/v4n1/dijkers_ktupdate_v4n1_12-15.pdf

Dilk, M. N., & Bond, G. R. (1996). Meta-analytic evaluation of skills training research for individuals with severe mental illness. *Journal of Consulting and Clinical Psychology*, 64(6), 1337–1346. https://doi.org/10.1037/0022-006X.64.6.1337

Drake, R., Merrens, M., & Lynde, D. (2005). *Evidence-based mental health practice: A textbook*. W. W. Norton & Co.

Dunn, D. S., & Elliott, T. R. (2008). The Place and Promise of Theory in Rehabilitation Psychology. *Rehabilitation Psychology*, 53(3), 254–267. https://doi.org/10.1037/a0012962

Durlak, J. A. (1995). *School-Based Prevention Programs for Children and Adolescents*. Sage. https://doi.org/10.4135/9781483327396

Dutta, A., Gervey, R., Chan, F., Chou, C.-C., & Ditchman, N. (2008). Vocational rehabilitation services and employment outcomes for people with disabilities: A United States study. *Journal of Occupational Rehabilitation, 18*(4), 326–334. https://doi.org/10.1007/s10926-008-9154-z

Field, B., Booth, A., Ilott, I., & Gerrish, K. (2014). Using the knowledge to action framework in practice: A citation analysis and systematic review. *Implementation Science, 9*, 172. https://doi.org/10.1186/s13012-014-0172-2

Fitzgerald, S., Leahy, M. J., Kang, H. J., Chan, F., & Bezyak, J. (2017). Perceived preparedness to implement evidence-based practice by certified rehabilitation counselors: A qualitative content analysis. *Rehabilitation Counseling Bulletin, 60*(4), 203–214. https://doi.org/10.1177/0034355216659233

Flannery, K. B., Yovanoff, P., Benz, M. R., & Kato, M. M. (2008). Improving employment outcomes of individuals with disabilities through short-term postsecondary training. *Career Development for Exceptional Individuals, 31*(1), 26–36. https://doi.org/10.1177/0885728807313779

Frazier, P. A., Tix, A. P., & Barron, K. E. (2004). Testing moderator and mediator effects in counseling psychology research. *Journal of Counseling Psychology, 51*(1), 115–134. https://doi.org/10.1037/0022-0167.51.1.115

Gilbride, D., & Stensrud, R. (1992). Demand-side job development: A model for the 1990s. *Journal of Rehabilitation, 58*(4), 34–39.

Gilmore, D. S., & Bose, J. (2005). Trends in postsecondary education: Participation within the vocational rehabilitation system. *Journal of Vocational Rehabilitation, 22*(1), 33–40.

Graham, I. D., Logan, J., Harrison, M. B., Straus, S. E., Tetroe, J., Caswell, W., & Robinson, N. (2006). Lost in knowledge translation: time for a map? *The Journal of Continuing Education in the Health Professions, 26*(1), 13–24. https://doi.org/10.1002/chp.47

Grissom, R. J., & Kim, J. J. (2005). *Effect sizes for research: A broad practical approach*. Erlbaum.

Hedges, L. V., & Olkin, I. (1985). *Statistical methods for meta-analysis*. Academic Press.

Holm, M. B. (2000). Our mandate for the new millennium: Evidence-based practice. *The American Journal of Occupational Therapy, 54*(6), 575–585. https://doi.org/10.5014/ajot.54.6.575

Horvath, A. O., Del Re, A. C., Fluckiger, C., & Symonds, D. (2011). Alliance in individual psychotherapy. *Psychotherapy, 48*(1), 9–16. https://doi.org/10.1037/a0022186

Horvath, A. O., & Symonds, B. D. (1991). Relation between working alliance and outcome in psychotherapy: A meta-analysis. *Journal of Counseling Psychology, 38*(2), 139–149. https://doi.org/10.1037/0022-0167.38.2.139

Hoyt, W. T., Imel, Z. E., & Chan, F. (2008). Multiple regression and correlation techniques: Recent controversies and best practices. *Rehabilitation Psychology, 53*(3), 321–339. https://doi.org/10.1037/a0013021

Iwanaga, K., Chan, F., Tansey, T. N., Strauser, D., Ritter, E., Bishop, M., & Brooks, J. (2019). Working alliance and stages of change for employment: The intermediary role of autonomous motivation, outcome expectancy and vocational rehabilitation engagement. *Journal of Occupational Rehabilitation, 29*(2), 315–324. https://doi.org/10.1007/s10926-018-9787-5

Iwanaga, K., Wehman, P., Brooke, V., Avellone, L., & Taylor, J. (2021). Evaluating the effect of work incentives benefits counseling on employment outcomes of transition-age and young adult supplemental security income recipients with intellectual disabilities: A case control study. *Journal of Occupational Rehabilitation, 31*(3), 581–591. https://doi.org/10.1007/s10926-020-09950-7

Johnston, M. V., Stineman, M., & Velozo, C. A. (1997). Outcome research in medical rehabilitation: Foundations from the past and directions for the future. In M. J. Fuhrer (Ed.), *Assessing medical rehabilitation practices: The promise of outcomes research*. Paul H. Brookes.

Jones, M. K., Latreille, P. L., & Sloane, P. J. (2006). Disability, gender, and the British labour market. *Oxford Economic Papers, 58*(3), 407–449. https://doi.org/10.1093/oep/gpl004

Kaye, H. S. (1998). *Vocational rehabilitation in the United States* (no.20). US Department of Education, National Institute on Disability and Rehabilitation Research (NIDRR).

Kessler Foundation. (2022). *National Trends in Disability Employment (nTIDE) January 2022 Jobs Report*. https://kesslerfoundation.org/press-release/nTIDE-January-2022-Jobs-Report

Kidd, M. P., Sloane, P. J., & Ferko, I. (2000). Disability and the labour market: an analysis of British males. *Journal of Health Economics, 19*(6), 961–981. https://doi.org/10.1016/s0167-6296(00)00043-6

Kosciulek, J. F., & Szymanski, E. M. (1993). Statistical power analysis of rehabilitation counseling research. *Rehabilitation Counseling Bulletin, 36*, 212–219.

Krause, J. S., Carter, R. E., Pickelsimer, E. E., & Wilson, D. (2008). A prospective study of health and risk of mortality after spinal cord injury. *Archives of Physical Medicine and Rehabilitation, 89*(8), 1482–1491. https://doi.org/10.1016/j.apmr.2007.11.062

Kurtz, M. M., & Mueser, K. T. (2008). A meta-analysis of controlled research on social skills training for schizophrenia. *Journal of Consulting and Clinical Psychology, 76*(3), 491–504. https://doi.org/10.1037/0022-006X.76.3.491

Law, M. (2002). *Evidence-based rehabilitation: A guide to practice*. SLACK Incorporated.

Leadership for a Networked World. (2010). *The next generation of human services: Realizing the vision*. (A Report from the 2010 Human Services Summit at Harvard University). http://community.lnwprogram.org/sites/default/files/Realizing_the_Vision.pdf

Leahy, M. J., Chan, F., & Lui, J. (2014). Evidence-based best practices in the public vocational rehabilitation program that lead to employment outcomes. *Journal of Vocational Rehabilitation, 41*(2), 83–86. https://doi.org/10.3233/JVR-140704

Leahy, M. J., Chan, F., Lui, J., Rosenthal, D., Tansey, T., Wehman, P., Kundu, M., Dutta, A., Anderson, C. A., Del Valle, R., Sherman, S., & Menz, F. E. (2014). An analysis of evidence-based best practices in the public vocational rehabilitation program: Gaps, future directions, and recommended steps to move forward. *Journal of Vocational Rehabilitation, 41*(2), 147–163. https://doi.org/10.3233/JVR-140707

Leahy, M. J., Chan, F., Sung, C., & Kim, M. (2013). Empirically derived test specifications for the certified rehabilitation counselor examination. *Rehabilitation Counseling Bulletin, 56*(4), 199–214. https://doi.org/10.1177/0034355212469839

Leahy, M. J., Del Valle, R. J., Landon, T. J., Iwanaga, K., Sherman, S. G., Reyes, A., & Chan, F. (2017). Promising and evidence-based practices in vocational rehabilitation: Results of a national Delphi study. *Journal of Vocational Rehabilitation, 48*(1), 37–48. https://doi.org/10.3233/JVR-170914

Livermore, G., & Prenovitz, S. (2010). *Benefits Planning, Assistance, and Outreach (BPAO) Service User Characteristics and Use of Work Incentives (No.5ca13079097b4ae887f19a614aca2bec)*. Mathematica Policy Research.

Livermore, G., Prenovitz, S., & Schimmel, J. (2011). Employment-Related Outcomes of a Recent Cohort of Work Incentives Planning and Assistance (WIPA) Program Enrollees. *Mathematica Policy Research*.

Lui, J., Anderson, C. A., Matthews, P., Nierenhausen, E., & Schlegelmilch, A. (2014). Knowledge translation strategies to improve the resources for rehabilitation counselors to employ best practices in the delivery of vocational rehabilitation services. *Journal of Vocational Rehabilitation, 41*(2), 137–145. https://doi.org/10.3233/JVR-140706

Lundahl, B. W., Kunz, C., Brownell, C., Tollefson, D., & Burke, B. L. (2010). A meta-analysis of motivational interviewing: Twenty-five years of empirical studies. *Research on Social Work Practice, 20*(2), 137–160. https://doi.org/10.1177/1049731509347850

Lustig, D. C., Strauser, D. R., Dewaine Rice, N., & Rucker, T. F. (2002). The relationship between working alliance and rehabilitation outcomes. *Rehabilitation Counseling Bulletin, 46*(1), 24–32. https://doi.org/10.1177/00343552020460010201

Manthey, T., Brooks, J., Chan, F., Hedenblad, L., & Ditchman, N. (2015). Motivational interviewing in rehabilitation health settings. In F. Chan, N. Berven, & K. Thomas (Eds.), *Counseling theories and techniques for rehabilitation health professionals* (2nd ed., pp. 247–278). Springer.

Martin, R., West-Evans, K., & Connelly, J. (2010). Vocational rehabilitation: Celebrating 90 years of careers and independence. *American Rehabilitation, 34*(1), 15–18. https://www.aucd.org/docs/policy/employment/American%20Rehabilitation%20Summer%202010.pdf

Maslowski, A. K., Owens, R. L., LaCaille, R. A., & Clinton-Lisell, V. (2021). A systematic review and meta-analysis of motivational interviewing training effectiveness among students-in-training. *Training and Education in Professional Psychology*. https://doi.org/10.1037/tep0000363

Mays, N., Roberts, E., & Popay, J. (2001). Synthesising research evidence. In N. Fulop, P. Allen, A. Clarke, & N. Black (Eds.), *Methods for studying the delivery and organisation of health services*. Routledge.

McMahon, B. T., Shaw, L. R., Chan, F., & Danczyk-Hawley, C. (2004). Expectations and the working alliance in rehabilitation counseling. *Journal of Vocational Rehabilitation, 20*, 101–106.

Migliore, A., Timmons, J., Butterworth, J., & Lugas, J. (2012). Predictors of employment and postsecondary education of youth with autism. *Rehabilitation Counseling Bulletin, 55*(3), 176–184. https://doi.org/10.1177/0034355212438943

Murali, V., & Oyebode, F. (2014). Poverty, social inequality and mental health. *Advances in Psychiatric Treatment, 10*(3), 216–224. https://doi.org/10.1192/apt.10.3.216

Nathan, P., & Gorman, J. (Eds.). (1998). *A guide to treatments that work.* Oxford University Press.

National Center for the Dissemination of Disability Research. (2006). Overview of International Literature on Knowledge Translation. *FOCUS: A Technical Brief, 14,* 1–6. https://ktdrr.org/ktlibrary/articles_pubs/ncddrwork/focus/focus14/Focus14.pdf

Ngamaba, K. H., Panagioti, M., & Armitage, C. J. (2018). Income inequality and subjective well-being: A systematic review and meta-analysis. *Quality of Life Research, 27*(3), 577–596. https://doi.org/10.1007/s11136-017-1719-x

Norcross, J. C., & Lambert, M. J. (2011). Psychotherapy relationships that work II. *Psychotherapy, 48*(1), 4–8. https://doi.org/10.1037/a0022180

O'Neill, J., Kang, H.-J., Sanchez, J., Muller, V., Aldrich, H., Pfaller, J., Chan, F., Rumrill, P. D., & Chan, F. (2015). Effect of college or university training on earnings of people with disabilities: A case control study. *Journal of Vocational Rehabilitation, 43*(2), 93–102. https://doi.org/10.3233/JVR-150759

O'Neill, J., Mamun, A., Potamites, E., Chan, F., & Cardoso, E. (2014). *Return to work of SSDI beneficiaries who do and don't access state vocational rehabilitation agency services: Case control study.* Kessler Foundation, Rehabilitation Research and Training Center on Individual Characteristics.

Parker, R. M., & Hensen, C. E. (1981). *Rehabilitation counseling: Foundations, consumers, and service delivery.* Allyn and Bacon.

Peikes, D. N., Moreno, L., & Orzol, S. M. (2008). Propensity score matching: A note of caution for evaluators of social programs. *The American Statistician, 62*(3), 222–231. https://doi.org/10.1198/000313008X332016

Pew Research Center. (2020). *How the coronavirus outbreak has – and hasn't – changed the way Americans work.* https://www.pewresearch.org/social-trends/2020/12/09/how-the-coronavirus-outbreak-has-and-hasnt-changed-the-way-americans-work

Pfaller, J., Tu, W. M., Morrison, B., Chan, F., Anderson, C., Owens, L., Fitzgerald, S., Brooks, J., Bezyak, J., & Menz, F. (2016). Social-cognitive predictors of readiness to use evidence-based practice: A survey of community-based rehabilitation practitioners. *Rehabilitation Counseling Bulletin, 60*(1), 7–15. https://doi.org/10.1177/0034355215591779

Rehabilitation Services Administration. (2016). *Annual report Fiscal year 2013. Report on federal activities under the Rehabilitation Act.* U.S. Department of Education, Office of Special Education and Rehabilitative Services.

Rubin, S., Chan, F., & Thomas, D. (2003). Assessing changes in life skills and quality of life resulting from rehabilitation services. *Journal of Rehabilitation, 69*(3), 4–9.

Rubin, S. E., & Rice, J. M. (1986). Quality and relevance of rehabilitation research: A critique and recommendations. *Rehabilitation Counseling Bulletin, 30,* 33–42.

Sackett, D. L., Straus, S. E., Richardson, W. S., Rosenberg, W., & Haynes, R. B. (2000). *Evidence-based medicine: How to practice and teach EBM* (2nd ed.). Churchill Livingstone.

Schlegelmilch, A., Roskowski, M., Anderson, C., Hartman, E., Decker-Maurer, H., Golden, T. P., & Anderson, C. A. (2019). The impact of work incentives benefits counseling on employment outcomes of transition-age youth receiving Supplemental Security Income (SSI) benefits. *Journal of Vocational Rehabilitation, 51*(2), 127–136. https://doi.org/10.3233/JVR-191032

Schlosser, R. W. (2006). The role of systematic reviews in evidence-based practice, research, and development. *FOCUS: A Technical Brief, 15,* 1–4.

Schmidt, F., & Hunter, J. (2003). History, development, evolution, and impact of validity generalization and meta-analysis methods, 1975-2001. In K. R. Murphy (Ed.), *Validity generalization: A critical review* (pp. 31–65). Lawrence Erlbaum Associates Publishers.

Shaw, L. R., McMahon, B. T., Chan, F., & Hannold, E. (2004). Enhancement of the working alliance: A training program to align counselor and consumer expectations. *Journal of Vocational Rehabilitation, 20,* 107–126.

Smith, F. A., Grigal, M., & Sulewski, J. (2012). Think College Insight Brief, Issue no.15. In *The impact of postsecondary education on employment outcomes for transition-aged youth with and without disabilities: A secondary analysis of American Community Survey Data*. Institute for Community Inclusion, University of Massachusetts Boston.

Straus, S. E., Tetroe, J., & Graham, I. D. (2009). Knowledge to action: What is and what it isn't. In S. E. Straus, J. Tetroe, & I. D. Graham (Eds.), *Knowledge translation in health care: Moving from evidence to practice* (pp. 3–12). Wiley-Blackwell.

Strauser, D. R., Lustig, D. C., Chan, F., & O'sullivan, D. (2010). Working alliance and vocational outcomes for cancer survivors: an initial analysis. *International Journal of Rehabilitation Research. Internationale Zeitschrift Fur Rehabilitationsforschung. Revue Internationale de Recherches de Readaptation, 33*(3), 271–274. https://doi.org/10.1097/MRR.0b013e32833638e3

Sudsawad, P. (2007). *Knowledge translation: Introduction to models, strategies, and measures*. Southwest Educational Development Laboratory, National Center for the Dissemination of Disability Research.

Tansey, T. N., Bezyak, J., Chan, F., Leahy, M. J., & Lui, J. (2014). Social-cognitive predictors of readiness to use evidence-based practice: A survey of state vocational rehabilitation counselors. *Journal of Vocational Rehabilitation, 41*(2), 127–136. https://doi.org/10.3233/JVR-140705

Tansey, T. N., Iwanaga, K., Bezyak, J., & Ditchman, N. (2017). Testing an integrated self-determined work motivation model for people with disabilities: A path analysis. *Rehabilitation Psychology, 62*(4), 534–544. https://doi.org/10.1037/rep0000141

Tremblay, T., Smith, J., Xie, H., & Drake, R. E. (2006). Effect of benefits counseling services on employment outcomes for people with psychiatric disabilities. *Psychiatric Services, 57*(6), 816–821. https://doi.org/10.1176/ps.2006.57.6.816

Tucker, J. A., & Reed, G. M. (2008). Evidentiary pluralism as a strategy for research and evidence-based practice in rehabilitation psychology. *Rehabilitation Psychology, 53*(3), 279–293. https://doi.org/10.1037/a0012963

U.S. Department of Education. (2014). *The Workforce Innovation and Opportunity Act overview of Title IV: Amendments to the Rehabilitation Act of 1973*. https://www2.ed.gov/about/offices/list/osers/rsa/publications/wioa-changes-to-rehab-act.pdf

U.S. Department of Labor. (2014). *Earnings and unemployment rates by educational attainment*. http://data.bls.gov/cgi-bin/print.pl/emp/ep_chart_001.htm

U.S. Government Accountability Office. (2005). *Vocational rehabilitation: Better measures and monitoring could improve the performance of the VR program (GAO-05-865)*. https://www.gao.gov/assets/gao-05-865.pdf

U.S. Government Accountability Office. (2021). *How did state and local governments fare during the pandemic?*. https://www.gao.gov/blog/how-did-state-and-local-governments-fare-during-pandemic

Wagner, C. C., & McMahon, B. T. (2004). Motivational Interviewing and Rehabilitation Counseling Practice. *Rehabilitation Counseling Bulletin, 47*(3), 152–161. https://doi.org/10.1177/00343552040470030401

Walker, B. B., Seay, S. J., Solomon, A. C., & Spring, B. (2006). Treating chronic migraine headaches: an evidence-based practice approach. *Journal of Clinical Psychology, 62*(11), 1367–1378. https://doi.org/10.1002/jclp.20316

Wampold, B. E. (2001). *The great psychotherapy debate*. Lawrence Erlbaum Associates.

Wampold, B. E., & Imel, Z. E. (2015). *The great psychotherapy debate: Research evidence for what works in psychotherapy* (2nd ed.). Routledge. https://doi.org/10.4324/9780203582015

Wehman, P., Chan, F., Ditchman, N., & Kang, H. J. (2014). Effect of supported employment on vocational rehabilitation outcomes of transition-age youth with intellectual and developmental disabilities: A case control study. *Intellectual and Developmental Disabilities, 52*(4), 296–310. https://doi.org/10.1352/1934-9556-52.4.296

World Health Organization. (2017). *World Bank and WHO: Half the world lacks access to essential health services, 100 million still pushed into extreme poverty because of health expenses*. https://www.who.int/news/item/13-12-2017-world-bank-and-who-half-the-world-lacks-access-to-essential-health-services-100-million-still-pushed-into-extreme-poverty-because-of-health-expenses

Yaeda, J., Iwanaga, K., Fujikawa, M., Chan, F., & Bezyak, J. (2015). The use of evidence-based practice among japanese vocational rehabilitation professionals. *Rehabilitation Counseling Bulletin, 58*(2), 70–79. https://doi.org/10.1177/0034355214527323

Yamamoto, K. K., Stodden, R. A., & Folk, E. D. R. (2014). Inclusive postsecondary education: Reimagining the transition trajectories of vocational rehabilitation clients with intellectual disabilities. *Journal of Vocational Rehabilitation, 40*(1), 59–71. https://doi.org/10.3233/JVR-130662

CHAPTER 20

Psychiatric Rehabilitation

AMANDA B. TASHJIAN, CARLA KUNDERT, AND PATRICK CORRIGAN

LEARNING OBJECTIVES

After reading this chapter, you should be able to:

- *Define psychiatric rehabilitation as an approach to assist individuals with psychiatric disabilities to pursue important life goals.*
- *Recognize the principles of recovery, self-determination, and hope as facilitative conditions underlying the practice of psychiatric rehabilitation.*
- *Explain practices related to psychiatric rehabilitation that have been proved effective, including illness and wellness management, medications, family interventions, and treatments for co-occurring disorders.*

CACREP STANDARDS

CACREP 2016 Core: 2F1.a, 2F1.b, 2F1.c, 2F1.e, 2F2.b, 2F2.c, 2F2.d, 2F2.f, 2F2.h, 2F3.e, 2F3.f, 2F3.h, 2F3.i, 2F4.b, 2F4.e, 2F4.f, 2F4.h, 2F4.j, 2F5.a, 2F5.b, 2F5.c, 2F5.k, 2F5.l, 2F5.m
CACREP 2016 Specialties:
    Clinical Rehabilitation Counseling: 5D1.a, 5D1.b, 5D1.d, 5D1.e, 5D1.f, 5D2.a, 5D2.b, 5D2.c, 5D2.d, 5D2.g, 5D2.h, 5D2.i, 5D2.j, 5D2.l, 5D2.m, 5D2.o, 5D2.p, 5D2.t, 5D2.w, 5D3.b, 5D3.c, 5D3.d, 5D3.e
    Rehabilitation Counseling: 5H1.a, 5H1.b, 5H1.c, 5H1.d, 5H1.e, 5H2.a, 5H2.b, 5H2.c, 5H2.d, 5H2.e, 5H2.f, 5H2.i, 5H2.n, 5H2.q, 5H3.a, 5H3.b, 5H3.d, 5H3.e, 5H3.f, 5H3.g, 5H3.h, 5H3.j., 5H3.l, 5H3.m

INTRODUCTION

Many people are disabled by psychiatric illnesses. What we mean by this is that psychiatric illness can inhibit and limit a person's ability to engage in major life activities. Over time, rehabilitation counselors (RCs) have developed a set of specialized skills to work with individuals who experience psychiatric disabilities. Trained in either psychiatric rehabilitation or in general rehabilitation counseling programs, many RCs specialize in providing services to a large number of clients who have a psychiatric disability. In this chapter, we summarize the extensive literature on psychiatric rehabilitation, focusing especially on key principles and interventions addressed in more detail in the most recent edition of Corrigan's (2016) *Principles and Practice of Psychiatric Rehabilitation*. We begin by defining psychiatric disabilities, followed by an overview of psychiatric rehabilitation. Later, we discuss specific psychiatric rehabilitation interventions, including illness and wellness management, medications, family interventions, and treatments for co-occurring disorders. Our goal is to describe psychiatric rehabilitation as an approach to promote hope and recovery so that RCs can better assist people with psychiatric disabilities to pursue their personal, vocational, and independent living goals. A keen understanding of the psychiatric rehabilitation principles and practices contained in this chapter is crucial for all RCs, but particularly for those who seek to provide services in clinical mental health or clinical rehabilitation counseling practices.

WHO ARE PEOPLE WITH PSYCHIATRIC DISABILITIES?

Individuals with psychiatric disabilities are as multifaceted and diverse as the population in general. Henceforth, we have to understand who the person with a psychiatric disability is. People with psychiatric disabilities are individuals who, because of their illness, are unable to attain culturally and age-appropriate goals for extended periods. This definition of **people with psychiatric disabilities** contains three parts. First, psychiatric disability is based on a diagnosable mental illness. Second, the person is not able to pursue significant life goals because of the mental illness. The "appropriateness" of goals may vary by culture (e.g., Latino cultures may view familial involvement differently than White families) and age (e.g., education, employment status). Examples of important life goals relate to vocational status, relationships, physical and mental health, and recreation and spirituality. RCs need to be vigilant to context. Third, both the mental illness and its interference with the attainment of goals persist for significant periods of time, often for years. For some, there is an adaptation to the experience of mental illness, but for others there is a greater struggle. Mental health disorders impact people at varying levels. It is thus helpful to understand four conceptual domains of psychiatric rehabilitation:

1. Diagnoses: These represent the collections of symptoms and dysfunctions that cohere to form a psychiatric syndrome. Diagnoses that are typically the focus of psychiatric rehabilitation include schizophrenia, the mood disorders (such as major depression and bipolar disorder), some anxiety disorders (such as posttraumatic stress disorder [PTSD]) and obsessive-compulsive disorder), and some personality disorders.
2. Course: Psychiatric syndromes are not stable phenomena. Psychiatric disorders vary among individuals in terms of the onset and trajectory of the illness. They also vary within the individual over time in terms of the severity of symptoms and dysfunctions, such as mood disorders that may cycle over time.
3. Co-occurring disorders: Psychiatric disorders rarely occur in isolation. Instead, many people with psychiatric disabilities experience diagnoses that interact to significantly impede their life goals. Substance use disorders, in particular, frequently co-occur with serious mental illness to worsen the disease course. Psychiatric disorders also may co-occur with other physical, sensory, developmental, and cognitive disabilities.
4. Disabilities: Disabilities are defined as the inability of people to meet life goals that are appropriate for their age and culture. These goals tend to be macro-level goals that include obtaining a satisfactory job, living independently, developing intimate and mature relationships, managing one's physical and mental health needs, and participating in recreational and spiritual activities. It is important to note that it is disability per se that defines a person as being in need of psychiatric rehabilitation. People can have psychiatric diagnoses that do not interfere with their life goals. The characteristic that distinguishes psychiatric rehabilitation from other forms of mental health

psychiatric services is the focus on helping people achieve life goals that are blocked by symptoms, dysfunctions, and environmental barriers.

WHAT IS PSYCHIATRIC REHABILITATION?

Psychiatric rehabilitation is the systematic effort to help adults with psychiatric disabilities attain their personal goals. Within rehabilitation counseling, psychiatric rehabilitation is a framework that RCs can use to assist individuals with psychiatric disabilities to "achieve their personal, career, and independent living goals in the most integrated setting possible" (www.crccertification.com). Psychiatric rehabilitation is bidirectional in focus, seeking to influence an individual's strengths and challenges related to these goals *and* the community in which the person will live them out. Many different classifications of the core principles of psychiatric rehabilitation have been proposed over the years (Anthony et al., 2002; Bond & Resnick, 2000; Cnaan et al., 1988; Dincin, 1995; Hughes & Weinstein, 1997). Hence, Anthony et al. (2002) list eclecticism as one of the core principles, and Dincin (1995) refers to the pragmatism of psychiatric rehabilitation because many of its most widely practiced approaches have been developed through a trial-and-error process. In recent years, Corrigan (2013) has proposed an integrated model resting on the key structures of rehabilitation: (a) principles (the moral imperatives that guide people and society in dealing with disabilities), (b) strategies (the tools that RCs might avail to help the person), (c) settings (places where rehabilitation occurs), and (d) roles (people who support rehabilitation processes).

Central to Corrigan's (2013) integrated theory are the two guiding principles of recovery and self-determination. **Recovery** has been hailed as the primary principle of mental health services for people with psychiatric disabilities in Surgeon General David Satcher's report (U.S. Department of Health and Human Services [DHHS], 1999) to the nation, as well as President George Bush's New Freedom Commission on Mental Health (2003). Specifically, most people learn to live with psychiatric disabilities, even if they do not erase the challenges altogether. By this statement we mean that the symptoms of illness and barriers of disability diminish or disappear. At the same time, recovery is also a process in which, regardless of a person's current symptoms and disabilities, *hope* is the rule, not the exception. This belief does not mean that RCs ignore a person's worries about the future or questions of doubt and self-worth. To do so would be to ignore essential experiences. Instead, these experiences are framed in terms of hope. With a sense of recovery and hope, success in the community rests on **self-determination** (Corrigan et al., 2012). Self-determination fosters the notion that people with disabilities have the final say on the goals they wish to seek, and the supports that they might use to obtain them—supports that include the array of rehabilitation services in their community.

With recovery and self-determination in mind, the remainder of this chapter articulates specific psychiatric rehabilitation practices that have been proved effective or, when the evidence is lacking, practices that represent our best understanding of how to help in that process.

ILLNESS AND WELLNESS SELF-MANAGEMENT

An important goal of psychiatric rehabilitation is to help people learn how to manage their psychiatric disability, including understanding the nature and treatment of their mental illness and developing strategies for minimizing its impact on their lives. There are two components to this goal: **illness self-management**, so the person is better able to manage symptoms and disabilities that undermine aims, and **wellness self-management**, so the person is better able to promote health and well-being. Illness self-management includes making informed decisions about treatment, reducing the impact of distressing or problematic symptoms, and lessening relapses and rehospitalizations. The absence of illness is not enough, however. Wellness self-management centers on lifestyle choices that encourage the fullest experience of one's physical and mental capabilities. Quality of life (QOL) requires illness management as well as wellness promotion. Together, illness and wellness self-management help people with psychiatric disabilities identify and pursue personal goals to develop a physically and psychologically healthy lifestyle characterized by hope, optimism, and a sense of purpose.

Illness Self-Management

Psychiatric syndromes are sometimes similar to lifelong illnesses such as diabetes, heart disease, and asthma because they require ongoing care to minimize disruptive effects on daily living and prevent premature mortality. Increased understanding of the causes of disease and determinants of outcomes have an improved long-term prognosis of some psychiatric syndromes. Nevertheless, gains from these advances are realized only by teaching people the principles of managing their illness and helping them incorporate critical changes into their lifestyle. This approach means teaching individuals about the nature and course of those diseases, providing information about lifestyle choices that may promote better disease management, teaching them how to monitor their illness and self-administer treatments, and knowing when to contact treatment providers and others in order to address emergent concerns prior to them becoming more serious (Hanson, 1986; Lean et al., 2019). Promoting illness self-management is a critical part of helping professions that attempt to minimize the impact of a chronic disease on functioning and QOL. Furthermore, self-management has become a core concept that is taught to people with psychiatric disabilities in efforts to promote management of the psychiatric disorder (Druss et al., 2018; Mueser, Corrigan, et al., 2002). RCs help people with a psychiatric disability learn about their mental illness and how to deal with both the illness and wellness self-management more effectively.

Wellness Self-Management

The notion of wellness often is credited to Dunn (1961), who highlighted the importance of fitness, environment, and self-responsibility to fully understand health. Dunn claimed that the absence of illness does not make for a fully lived life. Scholars have begun to apply wellness to the experiences and goals of people with mental illness (O'Brien et al., 2014; Sterling et al., 2010). The goal of wellness in mental health is to integrate education, prevention, and health, while focusing on modifiable health risks such as smoking, poor diet, and little physical activity. Recently, there has been a collaborative effort between researchers and providers as a means to develop programs to remedy these health risks (Kane, 2009).

Wellness management and illness management have fundamental similarities (Salerno et al., 2011). They both use structured curricula that address coping, recovery, relapse, and social supports. These goals are furthered by attention to other factors affecting mental health problems, medication and other treatments, and personal goals development. Wellness management differs by including a focus on instruction and skills for managing practical issues associated with diet, exercise, relationships, and leisure. Wellness management is consistent with the long-standing asset-based focus of rehabilitation counseling tradition and with **positive psychology** as the study of what is "right" about people. Focused on what helps people and their communities flourish, identified practices that promote positive psychology (Kobau et al., 2011) are consistent with the goals of psychiatric rehabilitation and recovery, including shared decision-making.

Some examples of wellness recovery approaches include Wellness Recovery Action Plans (WRAPs) and The Whole Health Action Management (WHAM). WRAP was developed as a structured tool to help individuals themselves alleviate symptoms and maintain a sense of wellness. A WRAP includes (a) a daily maintenance list, (b) identifying and responding to triggers, (c) identifying and responding to early warning signs, (d) recognizing when things are getting much worse and responding in ways that will help them feel better, and (e) a crisis plan or advanced directive (Copeland, 2002). WHAM is another model for a wellness management program that has shown significantly greater improvement in participant activation for healthcare and self-assessed general health in adults with serious mental illness (Cook et al., 2020). It is a peer-led health promotion program for individuals with serious mental illness that is delivered in weekly group meetings and then followed by individual meetings. Participants of WHAM experienced improvements in participation management, self-perceived health, hopefulness, and employment status, when compared to other groups who received care as usual or a remedial illness self-management program led by peer specialists (Cook et al., 2020). Finally, peer health navigation is an additional strategy for engaging people with SMI in holistic wellness management discussed later in the section on peer support.

Shared Decision-Making

Shared decision making is critical to effective and ethical illness and wellness self-management. At all times, individuals with psychiatric disabilities are active agents in their wellness and recovery plan, having the support and guidance of professionals and anyone else who might be closely involved with the person. **Shared decision-making** is the process by which important decisions are made in active collaboration with the person, the treatment provider, and close others, such as family members. *Supported decision making* is another term and process related to shared decision-making.

Shared decision making is a movement that has been embraced by modern medicine (Campbell et al., 1996) and rapidly adopted by psychiatry (Fenton, 2003; Hamann et al., 2003; Slade, 2017). The rationale for shared decisionmaking is twofold. First, as medical technology grows, treatment decisions are less straightforward, and often depend on the personal values and preferences of the individual with the disease. The larger point is that decisions not to pursue treatments may be a source of empowerment if made for personal reasons. Shared decision-making requires an individual to learn basic information about the nature of the disorder, the treatment options, and their likely effects, both positive and negative.

Second, choosing not to follow prescriptions of recommended treatments is a problem common in modern medicine (Blackwell, 1973), including psychiatry (Coldham et al., 2002; Semahegn et al., 2018). **Psychological reactance** is a concept that refers to an individual's sensitivity to others' efforts to control the individual's behavior (Brehm, 1966). Authoritarian-based treatment recommendations may undermine some decisions because of psychological reactance (Fogarty, 1997; Moore et al., 2000). However, people may be more open to some treatment recommendations when those recommendations are posed collaboratively, respecting their right to choose which treatments they want. In order to improve adherence to recommended and effective treatments, shared decision-making involves providing people with the information they need in order to make informed decisions about treatment.

Peer Support

The historical roots of the mental health peer movement can be traced back to the Alleged Lunatic's Friend Society in England in 1845. The later publication of Beers (1923) book *A Mind That Found Itself* chronicled abuses in the name of treatment for psychiatric disabilities (Frese & Davis, 1997). In the 1970s, several influences contributed to the rise of peer services, including deinstitutionalization, widespread dissatisfaction with traditional psychiatric care, and the growth of self-help approaches for personal problems. Peer services and supports now permeate much of the formal mental health system, not as a substitute for, but as an adjunct to, the more traditional mental health services. Furthering this movement, the Surgeon General's Report on Mental Health (U.S. DHHS, 1999) hailed the importance of self-help groups and consumer-operated services. In 2003, the President's New Freedom Commission on Mental Health (2003) acknowledged consumer-operated services as an emerging best practice. Peer services emphasize the importance of people managing services for themselves in an environment where all aspects of intervention are self-determined.

The momentum of support coming from federal initiatives has driven the increase in peer services and supports. A SAMHSA survey by Goldstrom et al. (2006) found 7,500 peer support groups and organizations nationally that consisted of (a) 3,315 mutual support groups primarily providing support, (b) 3,019 self-help organizations offering education and advocacy that may sponsor and/or support mutual support groups, and (c) 1,133 consumer-operated services that included programs, businesses, or services managed and operated by recipients of mental health services. Goldstrom and colleagues reported that the mutual self-help groups reported that 41,363 individuals had attended a final meeting, self-help organizations reported having a membership of 1,005,400, and consumer-operated services noted serving 534,551 individuals in the past year. This information suggests the importance of peer support within the psychiatric rehabilitation framework in terms of an efficacious practice aligned with recovery.

Peer services also have evolved to include wellness management vis-à-vis peer health navigation. Health navigation originally emerged in the cancer treatment sphere where professionals, typically social workers or nurses, would help patients navigate complex treatments and tests (Parker et al., 2010; Wells et al., 2008). Similarly, CHWs are laypeople, often from minoritized groups to address specific health disparities, who have been effective in engaging individuals in prevention, treatment, and testing among communities in need (Jack et al., 2017; Kim et al., 2016; Lewin et al., 2005; Norris et al., 2006; Perry et al., 2014). Neither of these, however, addresses the specific needs of people with serious mental illness despite the increased risk of physical illness and reduced life expectancy experienced by this group (Druss et al., 2011; John et al., 2018). These disparities are even starker for people of color or of low socioeconomic status. Enter peer health navigators. **Peer health navigators (PHNs)** are people living in recovery from a behavioral health condition who provide in vivo support to individuals with serious mental illness in engaging with a complex and fragmented health system. This assistance may be **instrumental support** (i.e., going with the person to an appointment, helping them pick up prescriptions, following up with required labs) or **emotional/interpersonal support** (e.g., talking through anxiety about seeing the dentist, identifying coping skills that promote health). PHNs also may be matched with service users on the basis of race/ethnicity, gender, or other identity to further the connection of shared experience. Peer health navigation has demonstrated improvements in health outcomes, pain, initial diagnosis of chronic illnesses, choice of primary care services over emergency services, engagement with existing providers and services, and relationships with providers (Corrigan et al., 2017, 2018; Kelly et al., 2014, 2017, 2021)

Other Support Groups

There are other peer-driven support groups that align with a recovery framework including Self-Management and Recovery Training (SMART), the National Alliance on Mental Illness (NAMI), the Depression and Bipolar Support Alliance (DBSA), and Faces and Voices of Recovery. These groups provide individuals living with mental illness with a variety of resources that range from psychoeducation to peer support groups and crisis management strategies. SMART Recovery provides a free, self-empowering platform for individuals with substance use and co-occurring disorders (Horvath, 2000). Models like SMART Recovery, have found that individuals with co-occurring disorders who are currently in treatment responded better to SMART Recovery than to 12-step mutual help meetings (Penn et al., 2016). Local chapters of the NAMI and the DBSA strive to be accessible and often provide education, wellness resources, peer support, and opportunities for involvement for both people with mental illness and allies.

MEDICATIONS

Psychiatric medication is integral for addressing the challenges of acute episodes of severe mental illness as well as for decreasing relapses. Medications or psychosocial treatment are never one or the other. Statements such as the following examples reflect flawed clinical thinking that does not reflect evidence-based best practices: "No point in providing supported employment to Mary because she is on antipsychotics." "Don't consider antidepressants because Bobby is receiving dialectical behavior therapy." The best rehabilitation plans assist the person in integrating approaches: many people need both medication and psychosocial treatment. Although RCs do not prescribe medications, they can help people with psychiatric disabilities get proper referrals and assist in ongoing decisions about their medication.

In recent years, there has been a steady proliferation of medications for the major psychiatric disorders of schizophrenia, bipolar disorder, depression, and anxiety (Ferrando et al., 2014). Numerous effective medications are now available to alleviate the symptoms of severe mental illnesses (New Freedom Commission on Mental Health, 2003; U.S. DHHS, 1999). To be marketed in the United States, medications must be approved by the federal Food and Drug Administration (FDA). FDA approval requires that a medication be more effective than placebo ("a sugar pill") for a specific condition in at least two independent randomized controlled trials. To give a rough idea of the magnitude of the efficacy of current medications, consider that about 70% of people with symptoms of major depression respond to an efficacious antidepressant, compared to about 40% in a control group who respond to placebo (Rappa & Viola, 2013). Similarly, in 1-year follow-up, about twice as many people with schizophrenia will experience a psychotic relapse if they are taking placebo (70%) as compared to those taking an antipsychotic medication (35%). These figures vary from study to study and with regard to specific medications and situations, but findings are often in the range of a two to one or three to two for medication versus placebo.

Finding current and accurate information on specific medications and guidelines for use is often a critical, everyday task for RCs. There are widely available sources, but they must be used with caution. Online resources include the *Physicians' Desk Reference* (PDR Staff, 2017) and WebMD. Using the World Wide Web can be misleading because the rapidly proliferating health information sites are not regulated and screened for accuracy. Thus, although the internet has become a vast source of information, much of that information is anecdotal and misleading. The person's doctor and medical team are a vital resource regarding medication. We do not believe that people should just give up decisions to medical doctors; instead, they join with their doctors in coming up with the best plan. Table 20.1 summarizes the major classes of psychiatric medications, common subgroups, clinical benefits, and side effects for many medications with which RCs providing psychiatric rehabilitation should be familiar.

TABLE 20.1 The Seven Major Classes of Medications Grouped by Indications and Clinical Effects*

Indications and Clinical Effects	Subgroups	Side Effects
ANTIPSYCHOTIC MEDICATION		
Antipsychotic medication may be prescribed for disorders in the schizophrenia spectrum (e.g., schizophrenia, schizoaffective disorder) or psychoses related to affective disorders. They may relieve some of the positive symptoms of psychosis, such as hallucinations, delusions, and formal thought disorder. Some second-generation antipsychotics may relieve negative symptoms.	**Conventional** chlorpromazine (Thorazine), chlorprothixene (Taractan), droperidol (Inapsine), fluphenazine (Permitil, Prolixin), haloperidol (Haldol), mesoridazine (Serentil), molindone (Moban), perphenazine (Trilafon), pimozide (Orap), prochlorperazine (Compazine), thioridazine (Mellaril), thiothixene (Navane), trifluoperazine (Stelazine)	Wakefulness: sedation, fatigue. Cardiovascular: low blood pressure. Hormonal (endocrine): breast enlargement and increased milk production. Skin: skin rashes, skin photosensitivity. Neurological (sometimes known as extrapyramidal side effects [EPSs]): dystonia (severe muscle spasms), pseudoparkinsonism (tremor, muscle stiffness, rigidity, stooped posture, mask-like face), akinesia (reduction in spontaneous movements), akathisia (internal restlessness), tardive dyskinesia (involuntary movements, often in mouth, tongue, or fingers).
	Second Generation ("Atypical") aripiprazole (Abilify), cariprazine (Vraylar), clozapine (Clozaril), olanzapine (Zyprexa), paliperidone (Ivenga), risperidone (Risperdal), quetiapine (Seroquel), ziprasidone (Geodon)	Sedation, hypersalivation, constipation, dry mouth, obesity, metabolic changes (lipids and glucose), type 2 diabetes mellitus, pseudoparkinsonism at higher doses, agranulocytosis (sudden drop in white blood cells).
MEDICATION FOR ANTIPSYCHOTIC SIDE EFFECTS		
Medication for the side effects of antipsychotics may be prescribed for the EPSs that often result from conventional antipsychotic medication use. They relieve the various movement disorders that result from EPSs.	amantadine (Symmetrel), benztropine (Cogentin), diphenhydramine (Benadryl), propranolol (Inderal), trihexiphenidyl (Artane)	Dry mouth, blurred vision, memory problems, constipation, rapid heartbeat, loss of appetite.

(continued)

TABLE 20.1 The Seven Major Classes of Medications Grouped by Indications and Clinical Effects* (*continued*)

Indications and Clinical Effects	Subgroups	Side Effects
ANTIDEPRESSANT MEDICATION		
Antidepressant medication may be prescribed for depression and also for some anxiety disorders. They may relieve biological (e.g., insomnia and low energy), psychological (e.g., low mood and hopelessness), and behavioral (e.g., suicide) symptoms of depression.	**Tricyclic and Tetracyclic** amitriptyline (Elavil), clomipramine (Anafranil), desipramine (Norpramin, Pertofrane), doxepin (Adapin, Sinequan), imipramine (Tofranil, Janimine, SK-Pramine), nortriptyline (Aventyl, Pamelor), protriptyline (Vivactil), trimipramine (Surmontil), amoxapine (Asendin), maprotiline (Ludiomil)	Cardiovascular: orthostatic hypotension, palpitations, conduction slowing, hypertension. Central nervous system: tremor, sedation, stimulation, twitches, seizure, EPSs. Other: perspiration, weight gain, sexual dysfunction, impotence, dry mouth, constipation, urinary hesitance, esophageal reflux.
	Monoamine Oxidase Inhibitors phenelzine (Nardil), selegiline (Eldepryl), tranylcypromine (Parnate), isocarboxazid (Marplan)	Low blood pressure, high blood pressure crises (interactions with foods or medications), sexual dysfunction, insomnia, sedation, stimulation, muscle cramps, urinary hesitancy, constipation, dry mouth, weight gain, twitches.
	Selective Serotonin Reuptake Inhibitors Citalopram (Celexa), dapoxetine (Priligy), escitalopram (Lexapro), fluoxetine (Prozac), fluvoxamine (Luvox), paroxetine (Paxil), sertraline (Zoloft), vortioxetine (Brintellix)	Gastrointestinal: nausea, indigestion, diarrhea, vomiting, cramping. Neurological: insomnia, jitteriness, agitation, restlessness, headache, tremor. Other: excessive perspiration, decreased libido, delayed orgasm.
MOOD STABILIZERS		
Mood stabilizers may be prescribed for bipolar or schizoaffective disorder. They may relieve expansive mood (euphoria) and behaviors (unusual trouble with buying, sexual relations, or the police).	lithium carbonate (Eskalith, Lithane, Lithotabs, Eskalith CR, Lithobid), lithium citrate (Cibalith-S), carbamazepine (Carbatrol, Epitol, Equerto, Tegretol), valproic acid (Depakene, Depakote), lamotrigine (Lamictal), gabapentin (Horizant, Neurontin), topiramate (Qudexy, Topamax, Trokendi)	Neurological: tremor, ataxia (balance problems), sedation. Gastrointestinal: indigestion, weight gain, diarrhea. Skin: rash, hair loss. Cardiac: arrhythmia. Hematological: low blood count.

(*continued*)

TABLE 20.1 The Seven Major Classes of Medications Grouped by Indications and Clinical Effects* (*continued*)

Indications and Clinical Effects	Subgroups	Side Effects
ANTIANXIETY MEDICATION (ANXIOLYTICS)		
Anxiolytics may be prescribed for anxiety disorders (including panic) and major depression. They may relieve distress as well as related autonomic symptoms such as shortness of breath, rapid heartbeat, and profuse sweating. They may also relieve insomnia.	**Anxiolytics: Benzodiazepines** alprazolam (Xanax), chlordiazepoxide (Librium), clonazepam (Klonopin), clorazepate (Tranxene), diazepam (Valium), lorazepam (Ativan), oxazepam (Serax)	Sedation. Impaired cognitive function and judgment, amnesia. Respiratory suppression. May lead to withdrawal if terminated precipitously.
	Anxiolytics: Nonbenzodiazepines buspirone (BuSpar)	Nausea, headache, nervousness, and insomnia.
SEDATIVES/HYPNOTICS		
Sedatives and hypnotics may relieve symptoms related to insomnia.	**Hypnotics: Benzodiazepines** estazolam (Prosom), flurazepam (Dalmane), quazepam (Doral), temazepam (Restoral), triazolam (Halcion)	Sedation. Impaired cognitive function and judgment, amnesia. Respiratory suppression. May lead to withdrawal if terminated precipitously.
	Hypnotics: Nonbenzodiazepines eszopiclone (Lunesta), zalepon (Sonata), zolpidem (Ambien), zopiclone (Imovane), ramelteon (Rozerem)	Similar to benzodiazepines.
PSYCHOSTIMULANTS		
Psychostimulants may be prescribed for attention deficit hyperactivity disorder (ADHD) or narcolepsy. For ADHD, they may relieve impulsivity, promote attentiveness, and be calming. For narcolepsy, they may reduce sleepiness.	**Stimulants** amphetamine (Adderall), detroamphetamine (Dexedrine), dexmethylphenidate (Focalin), methylphenidate (Concerta, Ritalin), lisdexamfetamine (Prodrug)	Central nervous system: insomnia, headaches, nervousness, and social withdrawal. Gastrointestinal: stomach ache and appetite loss. Cardiac: elevated heart rate and blood pressure. Exacerbate psychotic symptoms.
	Nonstimulants atomextrine (Strattera), clonidine (Kapvay), guanfacine (Intuniv), armodafinil (Nuvigil), modafinil (Alertec, Provigil)	Nausea, decreased appetite, fatigue, abdominal pain, increased heart rate and blood pressure. Insomnia, irritability, and urinary retention.

*Common examples of generic and trade names (written parenthetically) are subgrouped. Significant side effects are summarized.

PSYCHOSOCIAL INTERVENTIONS

Vocational Rehabilitation

Vocational rehabilitation services are particularly beneficial for people with psychiatric disabilities and co-occurring substance use disorders (SUDs). The mental health benefits of competitive employment for people with psychiatric disabilities is well evidenced (Drake & Wallach, 2020; Gibbons & Salkever, 2019; Wallstroem et al., 2021). **Individual Placement and Support (IPS)** is an evidenced-based practice designed initially for adults with mental illness. It is a supportive employment model that incorporates competitive employment, systematic job development, rapid job search, integrated services, benefits planning, a focus on inclusion, and client-centered preferences in the job acquisition process. The rapid job search process may involve education and advocacy with both service recipients, employers, and other providers about the benefits of hiring people with disabilities, protections under the Americans with Disabilities Act, and requests for behavioral health-related accommodations. IPS aligns with a holistic approach to assessment in vocational settings, prioritizing client's long- and short-term career aspirations, current skills and strengths, and natural supports for obtaining and maintaining competitive employment. IPS teams are intended to be integrated fully into wraparound service teams in community mental health settings. While individuals with psychiatric disabilities have long been included in the provision of vocational rehabilitation (VR) services, those with SUD have often been excluded, likely attributable to the widespread use of drug screening in hiring practices. IPS has demonstrated benefits such as increased rates of competitive employment, higher wages and more hours worked, and symptom reduction for both individuals with psychiatric disabilities *and* those with co-occurring SUD (Harrison et al., 2020; Mueser et al., 2011).

People with disabilities tend to face additional barriers to education, leading to reduced rates of completion of 4-year degree programs (Coutinho & Denny, 1996; Wagner & Newman, 2012). Students with psychiatric disabilities may face cognitive, social, and adjustment-related challenges in pursuit of their education due to SMI, including challenges with organizing and retaining information, attending to tasks, interacting with peers and instructors, and dealing with stress that comes with emerging adulthood (De Silva et al., 2013; Kern et al., 2004; Rudnick & Lundberg, 2012). **Supported education**, an intervention not unlike IPS, provides practical support to college-age students with psychiatric disabilities and aims to close that achievement gap. A recent review of supported education studies by Hillborg and colleagues identified a number of components in common with IPS: person-centered approach; collaboration with educators, providers, and important others; accommodations and adjustments; reliance on natural supports; skills training; physical and psychosocial environment consideration; and long-term career counseling (2021). Although these components are defined less discretely than the principles of IPS, supported education programs demonstrate generally promising outcomes (Hillborg et al., 2021). Furthermore, IPS services may be augmented by incorporating supported education to increase the level of job opportunities, earning potential, and job tenure of people with psychiatric disabilities (Manthey et al., 2012; Murphy et al., 2005).

Supported Housing

Emerging in the 1980s from the lens of personal recovery, supported housing provided an alternative to residential housing options, often described as **custodial housing** (e.g., group living environments, living arrangements with varying levels of staff, standardized care with limited choice), where individuals could live more independently as they transitioned into the community (Rog, 2004). **Supported housing** is defined broadly as independent housing within a community that also provides mental health and other support services (Hogan & Carling, 1992). Often suppoMetrauxrted housing models include a lease agreement with a rent cap, optional support services that are unlinked to housing restrictions and the right to intensify services without risk of housing tenure (Piat et al., 2020). Since many people with psychiatric illnesses experience homelessness, individualized supported housing plans and programs aim to increase housing tenure and access to and utilization of wellness supports by providing flexibility and choice to the consumer. Supported housing has been shown to decrease rates of homelessness and hospitalization, and increase treatment adherence for those with serious mental illness (Culhane et al., 2002; Gabrielian et al., 2018; Rezansoff et al., 2017). Those individuals who participate in supported housing report better living conditions and social functioning compared to those living in high-support settings, such as hospital settings or residences within the community that have 24-hour staffing on-site (Harrison, Singh Roy, et al., 2020).

Motivational Interviewing

Many people who misuse alcohol and other drugs do not believe that the benefits of giving up the addiction outweigh the costs. Motivational interviewing (MI) originally was developed to help people make decisions about substance use (Apodaca & Longabaugh, 2009; Barnett et al., 2012). Recently, in a randomized control trial of veterans with substance use disorder, group motivational interviewing was found to be useful in increasing engagement in treatment and 12-step programming (Santa Ana et al., 2021). Generally, MI is an empirically supported, client-centered, and directive counseling approach that helps people identify the advantages and disadvantages of using drugs and alcohol (Miller & Rollnick, 2013). Someone might list advantages of alcohol use to include managing stress better and feeling more outgoing. Costs for the same person might include dealing with my angry husband and a boss who thinks partying at night gets in the way of my job performance. Note that costs and benefits of using alcohol are likely to be different for the same person using a different drug, such as cocaine. Providers rely on listening skills to help people understand the costs and benefits of a decision. This approach is not as simple as it seems: It extends much beyond a simple task of just adding up costs and benefits and moving forward when there are more benefits. Dialogue is central, creating an interactive process where people hear for themselves what underlies specific decisions. In addition, costs and benefits of giving up drugs or any other substances are not the same as costs and benefits of actively participating in a treatment program. For example, just because an individual wants to stop using alcohol or cocaine does not mean they want to spend 2 hours every day traveling across town on public transportation to get to the treatment program.

Beyond its traditional applications in substance use–related behavior change, MI has been adapted to elicit change talk among people with serious mental illness to address a number of other behaviors as well. Health promotion behaviors—including smoking cessation, weight management, and dental health—may be increased with incorporation of motivational interviewing (Billingsley & Steinberg, 2021; Park et al., 2011). MI also demonstrates potential to improve engagement and outcomes for people with SMI in working toward vocational, educational, and community participation goals (Hampson et al., 2015; Manthey, 2011). MI often is used in conjunction with other psychosocial treatments including cognitive behavioral therapy, psychotropic treatment, psychoeducation, and 12-step treatment (Hettema et al., 2005).

Cognitive Behavioral Therapy

Motivational counseling often is followed by cognitive behavioral counseling strategies, that entail helping people recognize their motives and risk factors for substance use; develop alternative strategies for dealing with motives and risk factors; and practice, and then use these new strategies (Mueser et al., 2003). **Cognitive therapy** employs a series of interactive strategies in which people learn to identify and challenge beliefs that are problematic to their functioning. For example, a person might believe he or she can only cope with job stress by drinking eight glasses of wine each night. Cognitive therapy would help him or her challenge this belief and develop a counterargument so he or she is more equipped to deal with job stress without drinking in the future. A set of studies have emerged examining the impact of cognitive therapies. One careful review, based on eight studies in the peer-reviewed literature (Cleary et al., 2008), seemed unable to find significant positive results of cognitive therapy on substance use habits of participants with co-occurring disorders. However, research in this review did suggest that the affective symptoms of participants improved. In other studies, that combined cognitive behavioral therapy with motivational interviewing suggested positive benefits in psychiatric symptoms and substance use at 9, 12, and 18 months (Barrowclough et al., 2001) and showed benefits for comorbid social anxiety and alcohol use disorders (Stapinski et al., 2021).

Care Coordination

Care coordination is essential to increasing the intensity and integration of community-based services; **assertive community treatment (ACT)** is one example. Briefly, ACT includes a multidisciplinary team with a relatively small caseload providing comprehensive and time-unlimited services covering the entire scope of challenges faced by people with psychiatric disabilities. ACT focuses on holistic, direct service by team members (rather than referrals for each need) provided in the community with 24-hour support accessible (Bond & Drake, 2015; Stein & Test, 1980). The benefits of ACT for people with serious mental illness include longer stays in the community, reduced hospitalization, symptom management, and even quality of life (Bond et al., 2001). ACT services tend to be most effective—and cost-effective—for people with more severe illness, indicated by higher rates of hospitalization (Dieterich et al., 2017).

ACT for people with co-occurring disorders considers the unique needs of people with psychiatric disabilities and substance abuse problems, and includes integrated treatment, a substance use specialist, and additional medical and pharmaceutical considerations. Numerous studies have examined ACT for this group in controlled studies (Carmichael et al., 1998; Chandler & Spicer, 2006; Drake & Brunette, 1998; Drake et al., 1997; Essock et al., 2006; Ho et al., 1999; Morse et al., 2006). Findings suggest that more intensive and integrated services had superior outcomes in some areas, but not all. However, studies differed from one another in design, clinical model, implementation, measures, and positive outcomes, making conclusions somewhat unclear (Penzenstadler et al., 2019). The most consistently positive outcomes are increased residential stability, decreased hospitalization, and decreased homelessness. Substance use outcomes are sometimes, but not consistently, improved. Substance use is difficult to assess, but at least two recent and well-done studies show that substance use treatment can be successful within various case management approaches (Essock et al., 2006; Morse et al., 2006). Substance use outcomes likely are related to quality rather than structure or quantity of substance use services (McHugo et al., 1999). None of these studies showed positive effects on incarceration outcomes, similar to other studies of ACT for people in the criminal justice field (Drake, Morrissey, et al., 2006).

FAMILY INTERVENTIONS

When a member of a family has a psychiatric disability, it affects not only the person with the disability but the family members as well. Although reactions differ by individuals as well as by their relationship to the relative with a psychiatric disability, effects of the illness are felt by parents, spouses, siblings, and children (Morey & Mueser, 2007; Tessler & Gamache, 2000). No fewer than three quarters of people with psychiatric disabilities have some sort of continuous contact with their families (Lehman & Steinwachs, 1998) and 30% to 65% are estimated to live with their families (Beeler et al., 1999). Relatives, particularly parents or guardians, assume the role of caregiver for which they are neither trained nor psychologically prepared (Doornbos, 2001). Families must learn to manage the symptoms and dysfunctions of the illness as well as the challenges and complexities of the various service delivery systems: mental health, social well-being, social security, vocational rehabilitation systems, substance abuse services, and, in some cases, the criminal justice system.

Psychoeducation

Psychoeducation has both educational and psychotherapeutic components, as the name implies. **Psychoeducation** has two primary objectives: to provide information regarding the disorder and its treatment and to teach strategies to cope with the illness, including problem-solving skills, coping and communication skills, and crisis management. Psychoeducation services are often provided in structured programs that last at least 9 months but may go as long as 5 years and are often diagnosis-specific. These programs focus primarily on information dissemination specific to the psychiatric diagnosis of the family member, and less so on the well-being of family members who are partaking in the psychoeducation process (Dixon et al., 2001; Solomon, 2000).

Psychoeducational interventions may be provided to an individual family member, a family unit, or multiple families, typically with the person with a psychiatric disability included in all, or part, of the intervention. Psychoeducational services can be facilitated in the family's home, a clinical setting, or another location. Generally, these interventions have concentrated on families with a relative with schizophrenia (Morin & Franck, 2017; Mueser & Gingerich, 2006), yet additionally have been intended for the individuals who have relatives with major depression, bipolar disorder, schizophrenia, and substance use, alcohol use, and PTSD (McFarlane et al., 2003). Current versions of psychoeducational interventions view family members as competent therapeutic agents from a strengths-based perspective. Psychoeducational interventions support collaborative relationships between the family and the practitioner (Lam, 1991).

Three prominent examples of these interventions are behavioral family management by Falloon et al. (1984), family psychoeducation by Anderson et al. (1986), and McFarlane et al. (2003) multifamily groups. In at least two randomized studies, these interventions have been determined to be effective. Falloon's et al. treatment has a sequential approach that starts with assessment, then follows to intervention strategies (including communication and problem-solving training) and ends with ongoing review. The intervention encompasses illness management strategies that employ behavior modification techniques. A behavioral analysis of the family unit and each family member is conducted in order to assess for strengths. The purpose of this approach is to aid each family member in functioning at their best given the challenges associated with having a family member with a psychiatric disability (Falloon et al., 1984).

Anderson et al. (1986) intervention is based on a family system's orientation and starts by establishing an alliance with the family at the point of the relative's admission to the hospital. Once a relationship is established, the provider will step in as a liaison with the hospital system. From there, a day-long workshop is provided to the family discussing information about the psychiatric disorder. The format of this intervention is meant to reduce isolation and stigmatization. Once the relative is discharged from the hospital, individual family sessions begin and contact is made between the family and the relative with the mental illness. Regularly scheduled sessions, phone consultations, and crisis contacts are provided as well. The duration of this type of program is open-ended and contingent on needs and negotiations among family members and the relative with a psychiatric disability. Ongoing sessions apply information from the workshop to deal with the ongoing process of social adjustment and employment for the relative with a psychiatric disability (Anderson et al., 1986).

McFarlane et al. (2003) intervention is a second-generation treatment because it combines aspects of two family psychoeducation interventions, family behavioral management and multiple family approaches. The first stage is for practitioners to meet individually with the family to build an alliance. The second stage is a workshop, similar to Anderson's intervention. The difference between Anderson's model and McFarlane's is that this approach employs problem-solving groups for both families and the relative with the mental illness. McFarlane proposes a long-term intervention with a closed format membership, where families receive support and problem-solving suggestions from other families. In addition, this intervention has the advantage of a social support group. The multifamily group, for the first year, focuses on social stabilization of the relative with a psychiatric disability; in the second year, the group shifts to accentuate social and VR for relatives with psychiatric disabilities (McFarlane et al., 2003).

CO-OCCURRING MENTAL ILLNESS AND SUBSTANCE ABUSE

Numerous people struggle with co-occurring or coexisting mental illness and substance abuse or dependence on alcohol or other drugs. First, substance use disorder is common among people with serious mental illness. There have been a number of clinical studies, along with population surveys such as the Epidemiologic Catchment Area Study (Regier et al., 1990), the National Comorbidity Study (Kessler et al., 1996), and the National Comorbidity Study Replication (Kenneson et al., 2013), that suggested approximately half of people with psychiatric disability report adequate symptoms for diagnosis of substance use disorder. This number is likely to be higher because people tend to under-report substance abuse. Screening for substance use among people with mental illness may be beneficial in better understanding the overlap between the two and by providing the appropriate interventions and referrals for integrated treatment for people with co-occurring SUD and mental illness (Yule & Kelly, 2019). Second, people with co-occurring disorders have a much greater rate of adverse outcomes than individuals who have mental illness alone (Drake & Brunette, 1998). Common adverse outcomes can include higher rates of relapse (Swofford et al., 1996), victimization (Goodman et al., 1997), violence (Steadman et al., 1998), incarceration (Abram & Teplin, 1991), hospitalization (Haywood et al., 1995), homelessness (Caton et al., 1994), and serious infections such as hepatitis and HIV (Rosenberg et al., 2001).

In the past, two systems uncoordinated between each other —mental health and substance abuse—have failed to provide effective interventions for individuals with co-occurring mental illness and substance abuse. Today, integrated care has become the standard of effective programs for people with co-occurring disorders, and interventions often are incorporated into an integrated master plan. The research literature examining the impact of interventions for people with co-occurring disorders is growing (Cleary et al., 2008; Drake et al., 2008) and has led to consensus guidelines (Ziedonis et al., 2005) summarized in the following sections.

Integrated Treatment

Interventions must be tailored to integrate both mental health and substance abuse interventions at the clinical interface (Drake et al., 2004). In spite of this definition of integration differing from administrative, financial, organizational, and physical integration, it often incorporates other concepts. *Clinical integration* refers to the same provider (or provider team) offering comprehensive mental health and substance abuse interventions that are coordinated and allow for the individual to learn about their coexisting illnesses (Bellack & DiClemente, 1999; Mueser et al., 1998; Tsai et al., 2009). It is the responsibility of the provider or providing team to successfully blend interventions that are suitable for the individual. Interventions should seem holistic and specific for the individual with dual disorders, while maintaining a consistent approach, philosophy, and set of recommendations.

Clinical integration functions on the notion that interventions should be modified and combined to meet the person's needs. The components of treatment help people to manage their co-occurring disorders by acknowledging their inseparability. For example, social skills training not only addresses the appropriateness of relationships, but also aids in the process of finding beneficial support from individuals who do not use substances and learning to avoid social situations that are associated with substance use (Mueser et al., 2003). Relapse prevention, which is often a part of integrated treatment, addresses coping strategies and risk situations related to preventing episodes of substance abuse and/or mental illness (Drake et al., 2005). Furthermore, VR focuses on employment (Becker et al., 2005), and family psychoeducation emphasizes the need to understand and cope with two (or more) co-occurring disorders (Mueser & Fox, 2002).

Stage-Wise Treatments

Programs with the greatest efficacy tailor interventions to the person's stage of treatment or recovery. Stage-wise treatment is based on the concept of stages of change (Freeman & Dolan, 2001; Prochaska & Diclemente, 1984). Although there are different ways of conceptualizing progress within recovery, commonly used stages of treatment for people with co-occurring disorders include (a) the engagement stage, where the person engages in a collaborative and trusting relationship; (b) the persuasion or motivation stage, where the professional helps the engaged person to build motivation toward recovery-oriented interventions; (c) the active treatment stage, where the person is now motivated toward acquiring new skills and supports to help manage the illness and pursue goals; and (d) the relapse prevention stage, where the person who is stable is helped to remain in remission and develop strategies for preventing relapse.

Long-Term Retention

Co-occurring disorders can lead to significant disabilities that require interventions that last for months or even years with adequate community support, as opposed to short-term intensive treatment programs (Drake, McHugo, et al., 1998). Learning how to lead a satisfying and sustainable life, either free from substances of abuse or by using harm reduction strategies to reduce negative consequences associated with drug use, often requires changing many aspects of one's life: for example, recreation, hobbies, stress management, relationships, and housing (Alverson et al., 2000). One 10-year prospective study indicates that this process takes time and often involves relapses as a part of the recovery process (Drake, McHugo, et al., 2006; Xie et al., 2005). Most research implies that longer treatment intervals are associated with better outcomes. Of course, this finding could be explained by self-selection, since people who are more motivated may elect to stay in treatment longer; or by circularity, because people who relapse are dismissed from treatment programs and therefore have shorter treatment intervals. To date, no studies have varied the length of participation in long-term retention programs systematically.

Comprehensive Services

Programs that are effective for those with co-occurring disorders provide varying individualized interventions according to the person's needs. Services include individual and group counseling, family interventions, peer group supports, vocational services, medication management, money management, housing supports, and acute trauma interventions (Mueser et al., 2003). Comprehensive programs address substance use and mental illnesses broadly as opposed to narrowly as a discrete treatment intervention (Torrey et al., 2002). For example, during acute episodes that lead to hospitalization, opportunities for accurate diagnosis, stabilization, medication changes, and linkages to other outpatient supports and services can ensue (Greenfield et al., 1995). Similarly, social, housing, and vocational programs can support people with dual diagnosis in acquiring skills and supports needed for recovery. Generally, comprehensive programs are difficult to evaluate because the interventions they provide are not discrete.

12-Step Programs

Twelve-step programs commonly are used to help people address goals undermined by substance use. These programs are peer-led, with participants benefiting from peer support in the light of 12 principles. The 12-step approach was originally embodied in Alcoholics Anonymous but has evolved to include Narcotics Anonymous and Cocaine Anonymous. For people with co-occurring disorders, 12-steps programs include Dual Recovery Anonymous (Hamilton & Sample, 1994) and Double Trouble (Vogel et al., 1998).

There has been significant research literature documenting the effects of 12-step programs on people with co-occurring disorders (Aase et al., 2008; Bogenschutz et al., 2006). Most of these studies seem to be one-group longitudinal designs showing positive benefits for people who participated in 12-step programs. Only one randomized controlled trial was found: a study with veterans challenged by major depression and substance use problems (Brown et al., 2006). In this study, participants were assigned randomly to cognitive therapy or 12-step facilitation. Results suggested that positive effects were experienced in the cognitive therapy group, whereas such benefits were not shown in the 12-step group. Although research is lacking regarding 12-step services for people with dual disorders, a comprehensive review of the research literature indicates that 12-step programs have significant and positive effects for people with alcohol abuse problems (Kelly et al., 2009). Further research should be extended to the needs of people with co-occurring disorders regarding 12-step programs and their efficacy.

Harm Reduction

In some ways, the 12-step programs reviewed suggested that personal goals are facilitated by eliminating, or at least controlling and reducing, substance use. Recent perspectives that have emerged from advocates and public health specialists suggest that substance abuse is a life choice that is not necessarily erased by abstinence. The circumstances of a person's life make specific patterns of substance use appealing to them, such that they are unlikely to engage in treatments that challenge these preferences (Marlatt et al., 2011). For these individuals the goal of **harm reduction programs** changes to reduction of harm resulting from the use of certain substances. Several programs have emerged to promote harm reduction. Needle exchange programs align with this notion and provide on-the-streets opportunities for people who use drugs intravenously to replace used needles with sterile ones for no charge or recrimination (Duplessy & Reynaud, 2014). Like needle exchange programs, safe injection sites or drug consumption rooms provide safe and sterile spaces free of victimization for people to use street drugs (Patel, 2007). Opioid replacement therapy provides people who use street opioids like heroin and fentanyl with legally prescribed medications to control cravings and stave off withdrawal symptoms (Harlow et al., 2013). Methadone is a less risky version of opioids, as well as other medication-assisted alternatives like naltrexone, buprenorphine, or a combination of the two (e.g., suboxone). Safe sex programs might also be helpful for some people with psychiatric disabilities. Ready provision of condoms for free has decreased the spread of HIV/AIDS, especially among people with low incomes (Adam et al., 2009).

Rehabilitation providers involved in harm reduction programs need to be fully aware of laws and statutes that may be relevant to these kinds of programs (Elliott, 2012). Providers are not at liberty to violate laws in promoting harm reduction; for example, they cannot purchase heroin or any other illegal drug for program participants in order to keep them from being victimized by crime. The legality of needle exchange and safe injection sites varies by jurisdiction (they also may vary by federal, state, and local city municipalities) and time period. It is crucial that providers of harm reduction remain up to date on the variety of statutes when implementing this kind of approach. In addition to provider awareness of the legal parameters of harm reduction supports, providers and those with substance use disorders can benefit from overdose prevention and reversal training (Bohnert et al., 2012). Reversal training often includes the use of naloxone which is particularly important for individuals with co-occurring disorder who are more likely to experience overdose.

There is evidence that harm reduction is being incorporated into services for people with co-occurring disorders (Laker, 2007), but the quality of this research is limited. Many of the studies found in a comprehensive review suggested that harm reduction interventions were being combined with motivational interviewing. Moreover, research has yet to address how harm reduction should be adapted for people with co-occurring disorders.

Pharmacological Interventions

Many studies have been done examining the effects of antipsychotic medication on co-occurring disorders (Smelson et al., 2008). Results imply that second-generation antipsychotic medication may have beneficial effects on the psychotic symptoms of people with dual disorders. Second-generation antipsychotic medication is also referred to as **atypical antipsychotic medication**. These medications, developed in the 1980s, have fewer motor and movement side effects compared to the first-generation antipsychotic medications (Seida et al., 2012). They may also decrease craving (as found in research on people with cocaine addiction) and decrease substance use. Benzodiazepine use is controversial in people with primary substance use disorders, but the practice appears to be common for people with dual disorders. One prospective study of people with dual disorders showed that prescribed benzodiazepines do not appear to improve outcomes and are associated with the development of benzodiazepine abuse (Brunette et al., 2003). In a meta-analysis of the treatment of co-occurring substance use and psychiatric disorders, findings suggested that clozapine may be more efficacious than other antipsychotic medications in individuals with schizophrenia and comorbid substance use disorder and valproate is preferred over lithium and quetiapine in individuals with bipolar disorders and comorbid substance use disorder (Murthy et al., 2019).

Several medications have also been examined to help people with co-occurring disorders. Anticonvulsants like valproic acid often are prescribed for people with seizure disorders, but these drugs also have mood-stabilizing capacities. Multiple studies show that valproic acid in combination with lithium is associated with improvement of alcohol disorders in people with bipolar disorders (Brady et al., 1995). Buspirone in controlled trials has demonstrated a reduction in anxiety symptoms, a reduction in the return to heavy drinking, and fewer drinking days during the follow-up period of the study (Kranzler et al., 1994). Additionally, in preliminary studies, topiramate was demonstrated to be effective in reducing alcohol use, craving, and PTSD severity and showed a tendency to reduce hyperarousal symptoms among veterans with PTSD and alcohol use disorder (Batki et al., 2014). Regarding other anticonvulsant medications, little is known about their impact on people with a dual diagnosis. The antidepressant bupropion has helped with smoking cessation in two small studies of people with schizophrenia (Evins et al., 2001; Weiner et al., 2001). To date there is no experimental evidence that antidepressants affect the use of alcohol or other drugs of abuse in people with a dual diagnosis.

Disulfiram, commonly known as Antabuse, is sometimes prescribed for people who abuse alcohol, as a way to dissuade them from using in the future. Disulfiram intensifies the "hangover effects" of alcohol consumption. As a result, people may want to avoid disulfiram in order to avoid these symptoms; usually, it is only prescribed when the person is fully informed about its effects and consents to take it. The drug has been evaluated safely in open clinical trials and was shown to decrease alcohol use in people with dual disorders (Mueser et al., 2003). Additional studies show that naltrexone, another drug, may be associated with decreased alcohol use in comorbid people with schizophrenia (Dougherty, 1997; Maxwell & Shinderman, 2000). Naltrexone has been shown to reduce alcohol cravings. In a randomized clinical trial, both disulfiram and/or naltrexone demonstrated positive effects on alcohol abuse for people with dual diagnosis (Petrakis et al., 2006). Finally, methadone replacement therapy has been used for people with schizophrenia, concurrent with psychosocial and psychiatric treatments (Miotto et al., 2001). Methadone reduces cravings related to heroin and other opioid addictions. However, methadone therapies have not been experimentally studied in people with dual disorders and are demanding in terms of time commitment. This fact makes other recovery activities difficult to engage in (e.g., attending groups, maintaining employment, upholding social roles, and adhering to dosage windows).

Legal Interventions

It is not uncommon to see interventions used that involve the legal system for people with co-occurring disorders; many are involved with the court system and are under some sort of legal control or supervision. Legal directives may include, but are not limited to; incarceration, probation and parole, outpatient commitment, involuntary hospitalization, coercive medications, and guardianships for finances. In addition, more subtle but coercive techniques also are used to shunt people into hospitals, group homes, and other supervised situations. Although many individuals experience mandatory intervention, remarkably few studies have addressed this approach. A small number of controlled studies of outpatient commitment, which include large proportions of people with dual diagnoses, do not show evidence of efficacy (Swanson et al., 2000).

More recently a focus on **Forensic Assertive Community Treatment (FACT)** has emerged as a strategy to support those with serious mental illness who are a part of the criminal justice system. FACT is a service delivery model that builds on the evidence-based assertive community treatment model for those with complex and co-occurring disorders (SAMHSA Forensic Assertive Community Treatment Action Brief). FACT programs have marked variability; however, the emphasis on both mental health and the criminal justice system makes them beneficial when the respective mental health service provider and criminal justice service provider work collaboratively to help prevent incarceration (Lamberti & Weisman, 2021). Individuals who partake in FACT programs receive a variety of services, including medication management, coordination with criminal justice entities, legal advocacy, assistance with the reinstatement of enrollment of Social Security, supportive housing, skill development in activities of daily living, occupational, vocational, and educational skill development, and cognitive behavioral therapy and motivational interviewing (SAMHSA Forensic Assertive Community Treatment Action Brief).

Ancillary Interventions

Several ancillary interventions may be helpful to individuals who do not respond well to the basic approaches mentioned earlier; these may include money management (Ries et al., 2004), intensive family interventions (Mueser & Fox, 2002), trauma interventions (Harris, 1998; Rosenberg et al., 2001), contingency management (Sigmon et al., 2000), conditional discharges (O'Keefe et al., 1997), and medications (Brunette et al., 2005). Some of these interventions might be instituted at the beginning of treatment. For example, early inclusion of family psychoeducation, which addresses mental illness and substance abuse, seems warranted for those individuals who live with their families. Long-term residential treatment is expensive but may be an effective approach for people who have

BOX 20.1 CASE CONCEPTUALIZATION

Lisa Hernandez is a young Hispanic woman who developed difficulties with depression and suicidal ideation and behavior in adolescence. Lisa's diagnosis evolved from major depression to bipolar disorder over a 10-year span and Lisa subsequently dropped out of college, was divorced three times, made several suicide attempts, was hospitalized nearly 15 times, and was seen by numerous psychiatrists and mental health practitioners. Although she has had much contact with the mental health system and practitioners, her drinking went undetected by professionals. Similarly, Lisa had entered and left substance abuse treatment programs with little change or progress; always returning back to alcohol. Lisa attended Alcoholics Anonymous without anyone detecting her bipolar disorder. She never received coordinated mental health and substance abuse treatment by the same practitioner, and remained unstable, unsatisfied, and worse off as a result.

Case Discussion Questions:

1. What are some wellness management strategies you might consider if you were working with Lisa?
2. How might family support impact Lisa's recovery journey?
3. How might you apply co-occurring disorder treatment strategies to help support Lisa?

cognitive problems or impulsive behavior and who have failed to respond to outpatient treatment. Little research has been done on these ancillary approaches to treatment, other than the previously reviewed studies of residential treatment.

CONCLUSION

We have defined psychiatric rehabilitation as systematic efforts to help adults with psychiatric disabilities move forward in their recovery process. In its evolution, the field has moved away from early assumptions related to the concepts of asylum (people are best served in enclaves apart from mainstream community life), separation of rehabilitation and medical models (psychiatric rehabilitation programs should distance themselves from mental health treatment), and transitionalism (people are best helped through gradual, stepwise programs of preparation for community living). Rather, rehabilitation has promoted an emphasis on hope, recovery, and self-determination in efforts to provide individuals with psychiatric disabilities the tools needed to accomplish the goals and pursuits they desire.

CONTENT REVIEW QUESTIONS

1. How is psychiatric rehabilitation defined?
2. What are the core principles of psychiatric rehabilitation?
3. What are some of the inventions and approaches used to promote psychiatric rehabilitation?
4. What are some of the complexities of co-occurring disorders, and how are they treated?
5. What are the roles of a rehabilitation provider with regard to psychiatric disorders and the principles of recovery and illness management?

REFERENCES

Aase, D. M., Jason, L. A., & Robinson, L. (2008). 12-step participation among dually-diagnosed individuals. *Clinical Psychology Review, 28*, 1235–1248.

Abram, K., & Teplin, L. (1991). Co-occurring disorders among mentally ill jail detainees: Implications for public policy. *American Psychologist, 46*, 1036–1044.

Adam, P. C., de Wit, J. B., Toskin, I., Mathers, B. M., Nashkhoev, M., Zablotska, I., & Rugg, D. (2009). Estimating levels of HIV testing, HIV prevention coverage, HIV knowledge, and condom use among men who have sex with men (MSM) in low-income and middle-income countries. *Journal of Acquired Immune Deficiency Syndromes, 52*, S143–S151.

Alverson, H., Alverson, M., & Drake, R. E. (2000). An ethnographic study of the longitudinal course of substance abuse among people with severe mental illness. *Community Mental Health Journal, 36*, 557–569.

Anderson, C., Reiss, D., & Hogarty, G. (1986). *Schizophrenia and the family*. Guilford Press.

Anthony, W. A., Cohen, M., Farkas, M. D., & Gagne, C. (2002). *Psychiatric rehabilitation* (2nd ed.). Center for Psychiatric Rehabilitation.

Apodaca, T. R., & Longabaugh, R. (2009). Mechanisms of change in motivational interviewing: A review and preliminary evaluation of the evidence. *Addiction (Abingdon, England), 104*(5), 705–715. https://doi.org/10.1111/j.1360-0443.2009.02527.x

Barnett, E., Sussman, S., Smith, C., Rohrbach, L. A., & Spruijt-Metz, D. (2012). Motivational Interviewing for adolescent substance use: a review of the literature. *Addictive Behaviors, 37*(12), 1325–1334. https://doi.org/10.1016/j.addbeh.2012.07.001

Barrowclough, C., Haddock, G., Tarrier, N., Lewis, S. W., Moring, J., O'Brien, R., Schofield, N., & McGovern, J. (2001). Randomized controlled trial of motivational interviewing, cognitive behavior therapy, and family intervention for patients with comorbid schizophrenia and substance use disorders. *The American Journal of Psychiatry, 158*(10), 1706–1713. https://doi.org/10.1176/appi.ajp.158.10.1706

Batki, S. L., Pennington, D. L., Lasher, B., Neylan, T. C., Metzler, T., Waldrop, A., Delucchi, K., & Herbst, E. (2014). Topiramate treatment of alcohol use disorder in veterans with posttraumatic stress disorder: a randomized controlled pilot trial. *Alcoholism, Clinical and Experimental Research, 38*(8), 2169–2177. https://doi.org/10.1111/acer.12496

Becker, D. R., Drake, R. E., & Naughton, W. J., Jr. (2005). Supported employment for people with co-occurring disorders. *Psychiatric Rehabilitation Journal, 28*(4), 332–338. https://doi.org/10.2975/28.2005.332.338

Beeler, J., Rosenthal, A., & Cohler, B. (1999). Patterns of family caregiving and support provided to older psychiatric patients in long-term care. *Psychiatric Services, 50*(9), 1222–1224. https://doi.org/10.1176/ps.50.9.1222

Beers, C. (1923). *A mind that found itself* (5th ed.). University of Pittsburgh Press.

Bellack, A. S., & DiClemente, C. C. (1999). Treating substance abuse among patients with schizophrenia. *Psychiatric Services, 50*(1), 75–80. https://doi.org/10.1176/ps.50.1.75

Billingsley, B. E., & Steinberg, M. L. (2021). Motivational interviewing produces change talk in smokers with serious mental illness. *Journal of Dual Diagnosis, 17*(2), 151–158. https://doi.org/10.1080/15504263.2021.1896826

Blackwell, B. (1973). Drug therapy: patient compliance. *The New England Journal of Medicine, 289*(5), 249–252. https://doi.org/10.1056/NEJM197308022890506

Bogenschutz, M. P., Geppert, C. M. A., & George, J. (2006). The role of twelve-step approaches in dual diagnosis treatment and recovery. *The American Journal on Addictions, 15*(1), 50–60. https://doi.org/10.1080/10550490500419060

Bohnert, A. S. B., Ilgen, M. A., Ignacio, R. V., McCarthy, J. F., Valenstein, M., & Blow, F. C. (2012). Risk of death from accidental overdose associated with psychiatric and substance use disorders. *The American Journal of Psychiatry, 169*(1), 64–70. https://doi.org/10.1176/appi.ajp.2011.10101476

Bond, G. R., & Drake, R. E. (2015). The critical ingredients of assertive community treatment. *World Psychiatry: Official Journal of the World Psychiatric Association, 14*(2), 240–242. https://doi.org/10.1002/wps.20234

Bond, G. R., Drake, R. E., Mueser, K. T., & Latimer, E. (2001). Assertive community treatment for people with severe mental illness. *Disease Management and Health Outcomes, 9*(3), 141–159. https://doi.org/10.2165/00115677-200109030-00003

Bond, G. R., & Resnick, S. G. (2000). Psychiatric rehabilitation. In R. G. Frank & T. Elliott (Eds.), *Handbook of rehabilitation psychology* (pp. 235–258). American Psychological Association.

Brady, K., Sonnes, A., & Ballenger, J. (1995). Valproate in the treatment of acute bipolar affective episodes complicated by substance abuse. *Journal of Clinical Psychology, 56,* 118–121.

Brehm, J. W. (1966). *A theory of psychological reactance.* Academic Press.

Brown, S. A., Glasner-Edwards, S. V., Tate, S. R., McQuaid, J. R., Chalekian, J., & Granholm, E. (2006). Integrated cognitive behavioral therapy versus twelve-step facilitation therapy for substance-dependent adults with depressive disorders. *Journal of Psychoactive Drugs, 38*(4), 449–460. https://doi.org/10.1080/02791072.2006.10400584

Brunette, M. F., Noordsy, D. L., Buckley, P. F., & Green, A. I. (2005). Pharmacologic treatments for co-occurring substance use disorders in patients with schizophrenia. *Journal of Dual Diagnosis, 1*(2), 41–55. https://doi.org/10.1300/J374v01n02_04

Brunette, M. F., Noordsy, D. L., Xie, H., & Drake, R. E. (2003). Benzodiazepine use and abuse among patients with severe mental illness and co-occurring substance use disorders. *Psychiatric Services, 54*(10), 1395–1401. https://doi.org/10.1176/appi.ps.54.10.1395

Campbell, M., Donaldson, L. J., Roberts, S. J., & Smith, J. M. (1996). A prescribing incentive scheme for non-fundholding general practices: An observational study. *British Medical Journal, 313*(7056), 535–538. https://doi.org/10.1136/bmj.313.7056.535

Carmichael, D., Tackett-Gibson, M., & Dell, O. (1998). *Texas dual diagnosis project evaluation report 1997–1998.* Public Policy Research Institute.

Caton, C. L., Shrout, P. E., Eagle, P. F., Opler, L. A., Felix, A., & Dominguez, B. (1994). Risk factors for homelessness among schizophrenic men: A case-control study. *American Journal of Public Health, 84*(2), 265–270. https://doi.org/10.2105/ajph.84.2.265

Chandler, D. W., & Spicer, G. (2006). Integrated treatment for jail recidivists with co-occurring psychiatric and substance use disorders. *Community Mental Health Journal, 42*(4), 405–425. https://doi.org/10.1007/s10597-006-9055-6

Cleary, M., Hunt, G. E., Matheson, S., & Walter, G. (2008). Psychosocial treatments for people with co-occurring severe mental illness and substance misuse: Systematic review. *Journal of Advanced Nursing, 65*(2), 238–258. https://doi.org/10.1111/j.1365-2648.2008.04879.x

Cnaan, R. A., Blankertz, L., Messinger, K. W., & Gardner, J. R. (1988). Psychosocial rehabilitation: Toward a definition. *Psychosocial Rehabilitation Journal, 11*(4), 61–77. https://doi.org/10.1037/h0099561

Coldham, E. L., Addington, J., & Addington, D. (2002). Medication adherence of individuals with a first episode of psychosis. *Acta Psychiatrica Scandinavica, 106*(4), 286–290. https://doi.org/10.1034/j.1600-0447.2002.02437.x

Cook, J. A., Jonikas, J. A., Burke-Miller, J. K., Hamilton, M., Powell, I. G., Tucker, S. J., Wolfgang, J. B., Fricks, L., Weidenaar, J., Morris, E., & Powers, D. L. (2020). Whole health action management: A randomized controlled trial of a peer-led health promotion intervention. *Psychiatric Services, 71*(10), 1039–1046. https://doi.org/10.1176/appi.ps.202000012

Copeland, M. E. (2002). Wellness recovery action plan: A system for monitoring, reducing and eliminating uncomfortable or dangerous physical symptoms and emotional feelings. *Occupational Therapy in Mental Health, 17*(3–4), 127–150.

Corrigan, P. W. (2013). The risk of prognostication. *Psychiatric Services, 64*(8), 719. https://doi.org/10.1176/appi.ps.640806

Corrigan, P. W. (2016). *Principles and practice of psychiatric rehabilitation: An empirical approach* (2nd ed.). Guilford Press.

Corrigan, P. W., Angell, B., Davidson, L., Marcus, S., Salzer, M., Kottsieper, P., Larson, J. E., Mahoney, C. A., O'Connell, M. J., & Stanhope, V. (2012). From adherence to self-determination. *Psychiatric Services, 63,* 169–173.

Corrigan, P. W., Pickett, S., Schmidt, A., Stellon, E., Hantke, E., Kraus, D., Dubke, R., & Community Based Participatory Research Team. (2017). Peer navigators to promote engagement of homeless African Americans with serious mental illness in primary care. *Psychiatry Research, 255,* 101–103. https://doi.org/10.1016/j.psychres.2017.05.020

Corrigan, P., Sheehan, L., Morris, S., Larson, J. E., Torres, A., Lara, J. L., Paniagua, D., Mayes, J. I., & Doing, S. (2018). The impact of a peer navigator program in addressing the health needs of Latinos with serious mental illness. *Psychiatric Services, 69*(4), 456–461. https://doi.org/10.1176/appi.ps.201700241

Coutinho, M. J., & Denny, R. K. (1996). National leadership for children and youth with serious emotional disturbance. *Journal of Child and Family Studies, 5*(2), 207–227. https://doi.org/10.1080/10511482.2002.9521437

Culhane, D. P., Metraux, S., & Hadley, T. (2002). Public service reductions associated with placement of homeless persons with severe mental illness in supportive housing. *Housing Policy Debate, 13*(1), 107–163. https://doi.org/10.1080/10511482.2002.9521437

De Silva, M. J., Cooper, S., Li, H. L., Lund, C., & Patel, V. (2013). Effect of psychosocial interventions on social functioning in depression and schizophrenia: meta-analysis. *The British Journal of Psychiatry, 202*(4), 253–260. https://doi.org/10.1192/bjp.bp.112.118018

Dieterich, M., Irving, C. B., Bergman, H., Khokhar, M. A., Park, B., Marshall, M., & Cochrane Schizophrenia Group. (2017). Intensive case management for severe mental illness. *Cochrane Database of Systematic Reviews, 2017*(1), 1. https://doi.org/10.1002/14651858.CD007906.pub3

Dincin, J. (1995). Core programs in the thresholds approach. *New Directions for Mental Health Services, 1995*(4), 33–54. https://doi.org/10.1002/yd.23319950406

Dixon, L., McFarlane, W. R., Lefley, H., Lucksted, A., Cohen, M., Falloon, I., Mueser, K., Miklowitz, D., Solomon, P., & Sondheimer, D. (2001). Evidence-based practices for services to families of people with psychiatric disabilities. *Psychiatric Services, 52*(7), 903–910. https://doi.org/10.1176/appi.ps.52.7.903

Doornbos, M. (2001). The 24-7-52 Job: Family caregiving for young adults with serious and persistent mental illness. *Journal of Family Nursing, 7*(4), 328–344. https://doi.org/10.1177/107484070100700402

Dougherty, R. J. (1997). Naltrexone in the treatment of alcohol dependent dual diagnosed patients [Abstract]. *Journal of Addictive Diseases, 16*, 107.

Drake, R. E., & Brunette, M. F. (1998). Complications of severe mental illness related to alcohol and drug use disorders. *Recent Developments in Alcoholism, 14*, 285–299. https://doi.org/10.1007/0-306-47148-5_12

Drake, R. E., McHugo, G. J., Clark, R. E., Teague, G. B., Xie, H., Miles, K., & Ackerson, T. H. (1998). Assertive community treatment for patients with co-occurring severe mental illness and substance use disorder: A clinical trial. *The American Journal of Orthopsychiatry, 68*(2), 201–215. https://doi.org/10.1037/h0080330

Drake, R. E., McHugo, G. J., Xie, H., Fox, M., Packard, J., & Helmstetter, B. (2006). Ten-year recovery outcomes for clients with co-occurring schizophrenia and substance use disorders. *Schizophrenia Bulletin, 32*(3), 464–473. https://doi.org/10.1093/schbul/sbj064

Drake, R. E., Morrissey, J., & Mueser, K. T. (2006). The challenge of treating forensic dual diagnosis clients. *Community Mental Health Journal, 42*(4), 427–432.

Drake, R. E., Mueser, K. T., Brunette, M. F., & McHugo, G. J. (2004). A review of treatments for people with severe mental illnesses and co-occurring substance use disorders. *Psychiatric Rehabilitation Journal, 27*(4), 360–374. https://doi.org/10.2975/27.2004.360.374

Drake, R. E., O'Neal, E. L., & Wallach, M. A. (2008). A systematic review of psychosocial research on psychosocial interventions for people with co-occurring severe mental and substance use disorders. *Journal of Substance Abuse Treatment, 34*(1), 123–138. https://doi.org/10.1016/j.jsat.2007.01.011

Drake, R. E., & Wallach, M. A. (2020). Employment is a critical mental health intervention. *Epidemiology and Psychiatric Sciences, 29*, 171–173. https://doi.org/10.1017/S2045796020000906

Drake, R. E., Wallach, M. A., & McGovern, M. P. (2005). Future directions in preventing relapse to substance abuse among clients with severe mental illnesses. *Psychiatric Services, 56*(10), 1297–1302. https://doi.org/10.1176/appi.ps.56.10.1297

Drake, R. E., Yovetich, N. A., Bebout, R. R., Harris, M., & Mchugo, G. J. (1997). Integrated treatment for dually diagnosed homeless adults. *The Journal of Nervous & Mental Disease, 185*(5), 298–305. https://doi.org/10.1097/00005053-199705000-00003

Druss, B. G., Singh, M., von Esenwein, S. A., Glick, G. E., Tapscott, S., Tucker, S. J., Lally, C. A., & Sterling, E. W. (2018). Peer-led self-management of general medical conditions for patients with serious mental illnesses: A randomized trial. *Psychiatric Services, 69*(5), 529–535. https://doi.org/10.1176/appi.ps.201700352

Druss, B. G., Zhao, L., Von Esenwein, S., Morrato, E. H., & Marcus, S. C, et al. (2011). Understanding excess mortality in persons with mental illness. *Medical Care, 49*(6), 599–604. https://doi.org/10.1097/MLR.0b013e31820bf86e

Dunn, H. (1961). *High level wellness.* Mt. Vernon Publishing.

Duplessy, C., & Reynaud, E. G. (2014). Long-term survey of a syringe-dispensing machine needle exchange program: answering public concerns. *Harm Reduction Journal, 11*(1), 16. https://doi.org/10.1186/1477-7517-11-16

Elliott, R. (2012). Harm reduction and international law. In R. Pates & D. Riley (Eds.), *Harm reduction in substance use and high-risk behaviour* (pp. 33–48). Wiley-Blackwell.

Essock, S., Mueser, K. T., Drake, R. E., Covell, N., McHugo, G. J., Frisman, L., Kontos, N. J., Jackson, C. T., Townsend, F., & Swain, K. (2006). Assertive community treatment versus standard case management for clients receiving integrated treatment for co-occurring severe mental illness and substance use disorders. *Psychiatric Services, 57,* 185–196.

Evins, A. E., Mays, V. K., Rigotti, N. A., Tisdale, T., Cather, C., & Goff, D. C. (2001). A pilot trial of bupropion added to cognitive behavioral therapy for smoking cessation in schizophrenia. *Nicotine & Tobacco Research, 3*(4), 397–403. https://doi.org/10.1080/14622200110073920

Falloon, I., Boyd, J., & McGill, C. (1984). *Family care of schizophrenia.* Guilford Press.

Fenton, W. S. (2003). Shared decision making: A model for the physician-patient relationship in the 21st century? *Acta Psychiatrica Scandinavica, 107*(6), 401–402. https://doi.org/10.1034/j.1600-0447.2003.00122.x

Ferrando, S. J., Owen, J. A., & Levenson, J. L. (2014). Psychopharmacology. In R. E. Hales, S. C. Yudofsky, & L. W. Roberts (Eds.), *The American psychiatric publishing textbook of psychiatry* (pp. 929–1004). American Psychiatric Publishing.

Fogarty, J. S. (1997). Reactance theory and patient noncompliance. *Social Science & Medicine (1982), 45*(8), 1277–1288. https://doi.org/10.1016/s0277-9536(97)00055-5

Freeman, A., & Dolan, M. (2001). Revisiting Prochaska and DiClemente's stages of change theory. *Cognitive and Behavioral Practice, 8,* 224–234.

Frese, F. J., & Davis, W. W. (1997). The consumer-survivor movement, recovery, and consumer professionals. *Professional Psychology, 28*(3), 243–245. https://doi.org/10.1037/0735-7028.28.3.243

Gabrielian, S., Young, A. S., Greenberg, J. M., & Bromley, E. (2018). Social support and housing transitions among homeless adults with serious mental illness and substance use disorders. *Psychiatric Rehabilitation Journal, 41*(3), 208–215. https://doi.org/10.1037/prj0000213

Gibbons, B. J., & Salkever, D. S. (2019). Working with a severe mental illness. *Administration and Policy in Mental Health and Mental Health Services Research, 46,* 474–487.

Goldstrom, I. D., Campbell, J., Rogers, J. A., Lambert, D. B., Blacklow, B., Henderson, M. J., & Manderscheid, R. W. (2006). National estimates for mental health mutual support groups, self-help organizations, and consumer-operated services. *Administration and Policy in Mental Health, 33*(1), 92–103. https://doi.org/10.1007/s10488-005-0019-x

Goodman, L. A., Rosenberg, S. D., Mueser, K. T., & Drake, R. E. (1997). Physical and sexual assault history in women with serious mental illness. *Schizophrenia Bulletin, 23,* 685–696.

Greenfield, S. F., Weiss, R. D., & Tohen, M. (1995). Substance abuse and the chronically mentally ill. *Community Mental Health Journal, 31,* 265–278.

Hamann, J., Leucht, S., & Kissling, W. (2003). Shared decision making in psychiatry. *Acta Psychiatrica Scandinavica, 107*(6), 403–409. https://doi.org/10.1034/j.1600-0447.2003.00130.x

Hamilton, T., & Sample, P. (1994). *The twelve steps and dual recovery.* Hazelden.

Hampson, M. E., Hicks, R. E., & Watt, B. D. (2015). Exploring the effectiveness of motivational interviewing in re-engaging people diagnosed with severe psychiatric conditions in work, study, or community participation. *American Journal of Psychiatric Rehabilitation, 18*(3), 265–279. https://doi.org/10.1080/15487768.2014.954158

Hanson, R. W. (1986). Physician-patient communication and compliance. In K. E. Gerber & A. M. Nehemkis (Eds.), *Compliance: The dilemma of the chronically ill* (pp. 182–212). Springer.

Harlow, W., Roman, M. W., Happell, B., & Browne, G. (2013). Accessibility versus quality of care plus retention. *Issues in Mental Health Nursing, 34*, 706–714.

Harris, M. (1998). *Trauma recovery and empowerment*. Free Press.

Harrison, J., Krieger, M. J., & Johnson, H. A. (2020). Review of individual placement and support employment intervention for persons with substance use disorder. *Substance Use & Misuse, 55*(4), 636–643. https://doi.org/10.1080/10826084.2019.1692035

Harrison, M., Singh Roy, A., Hultqvist, J., Pan, A.-W., McCartney, D., McGuire, N., Irvine Fitzpatrick, L., & Forsyth, K. (2020). Quality of life outcomes for people with serious mental illness living in supported accommodation: Systematic review and meta-analysis. *Social Psychiatry and Psychiatric Epidemiology, 55*(8), 977–988. https://doi.org/10.1007/s00127-020-01885-x

Haywood, T. W., Kravitz, H. M., Grossman, L. S., Cavanaugh, J. L., Davis, J. M., & Lewis, D. A. (1995). Predicting the "revolving door" phenomenon among patients with schizophrenic, schizoaffective, and affective disorders. *The American Journal of Psychiatry, 152*(6), 856–861. https://doi.org/10.1176/ajp.152.6.856

Hettema, J., Steele, J., & Miller, W. R. (2005). Motivational interviewing. *Annual Review of Clinical Psychology, 1*, 91–111. https://doi.org/10.1146/annurev.clinpsy.1.102803.143833

Hillborg, H., Lövgren, V., Bejerholm, U., & Rosenberg, D. (2021). Integrating interventions that can support a career-oriented recovery for young adults. *Journal of Psychosocial Rehabilitation and Mental Health, 8*(1), 35–60.

Ho, A. P., Tsuang, J. W., Liberman, R. P., Wang, R., Wilkins, J. N., Eckman, T. A., & Shaner, A. L. (1999). Achieving effective treatment of patients with chronic psychotic illness and comorbid substance dependence. *The American Journal of Psychiatry, 156*(11), 1765–1770. https://doi.org/10.1176/ajp.156.11.1765

Hogan, M. F., & Carling, P. J. (1992). Normal housing: A key element of A supported housing approach for people with psychiatric disabilities. *Community Mental Health Journal, 28*(3), 215–226. https://doi.org/10.1007/BF00756818

Horvath, A. T. (2000). Smart Recovery®: Addiction recovery support from a cognitive behavioral perspective. *Journal of Rational-Emotive and Cognitive-Behavior Therapy, 18*(3), 181–191. https://doi.org/10.1023/A:1007831005098

Hughes, R., & Weinstein, D. (1997). Introduction. In R. Hughes & D. Weinstein (Eds.), *Best practices in psychosocial rehabilitation* (pp. vi–xvi). International Association of Psychosocial Rehabilitation.

Jack, H. E., Arabadjis, S. D., Sun, L., Sullivan, E. E., & Phillips, R. S, *et al.* (2017). Impact of community health workers on use of healthcare services in the United States. *Journal of General Internal Medicine, 32*(3), 325–344. https://doi.org/10.1007/s11606-016-3922-9

John, A., McGregor, J., Jones, I., Lee, S. C., Walters, J. T. R., Owen, M. J., O'Donovan, M., DelPozo-Banos, M., Berridge, D., & Lloyd, K, *et al.* (2018). Premature mortality among people with severe mental illness - New evidence from linked primary care data. *Schizophrenia Research, 199*, 154–162. https://doi.org/10.1016/j.schres.2018.04.009

Kane, J. M. (2009). Creating a health care team to manage chronic medical illnesses in patients with severe mental illness: the public policy perspective. *The Journal of Clinical Psychiatry, 70 Suppl 3*, 37–42. https://doi.org/10.4088/JCP.7075su1c.06

Kelly, E., Duan, L., Cohen, H., Kiger, H., Pancake, L., & Brekke, J. (2017). Integrating behavioral healthcare for individuals with serious mental illness. *Schizophrenia Research, 182*, 135–141.

Kelly, E., Fulginiti, A., Pahwa, R., Tallen, L., Duan, L., & Brekke, J. S. (2014). A pilot test of a peer navigator intervention for improving the health of individuals with serious mental illness. *Community Mental Health Journal, 50*(4), 435–446.

Kelly, E. L., Hong, B., Duan, L., Pancake, L., Cohen, H., & Brekke, J. S. (2021). Service use by Medicaid recipients with serious mental illness during an RCT of the Bridge Peer Health Navigator Intervention. *Psychiatric Services, 72*(10), 1145–1150. https://doi.org/10.1176/appi.ps.201900615

Kelly, J. F., Magill, M., & Stout, R. L. (2009). How do people recover from alcohol dependence? A systematic review of the research on mechanisms of behavior change in Alcoholics Anonymous. *Addiction Research & Theory, 17*(3), 236–259. https://doi.org/10.1080/16066350902770458

Kenneson, A., Funderburk, J. S., & Maisto, S. A. (2013). Substance use disorders increase the odds of subsequent mood disorders. *Drug and Alcohol Dependence, 133*, 338–343.

Kern, R. S., Green, M. F., Nuechterlein, K. H., & Deng, B. H. (2004). NIMH-MATRICS survey on assessment of neurocognition in schizophrenia. *Schizophrenia Research, 72*(1), 11–19.

Kessler, R. C., Nelson, C. B., McGonagle, K. A., Edlund, M. J., Frank, R. G., & Leaf, P. J. (1996). The epidemiology of co-occurring addictive and mental disorders: Implications for prevention and service utilization. *American Journal of Orthopsychiatry, 66,* 17–31.

Kim, K. B., Kim, M. T., Lee, H. B., Nguyen, T., Bone, L. R., & Levine, D. (2016). Community health workers versus nurses as counselors or case managers in a self-help diabetes management program. *American journal of public health, 106*(6), 1052–1058.

Kobau, R., Seligman, M. E. P., Peterson, C., Diener, E., Zack, M. M., Chapman, D., & Thompson, W. (2011). Mental health promotion in public health: perspectives and strategies from positive psychology. *American Journal of Public Health, 101*(8), e1–e9. https://doi.org/10.2105/AJPH.2010.300083

Kranzler, H. R., Burleson, J. A., Del Boca, F. K., Babor, T. F., Korner, P., Brown, J., & Bohn, M. J. (1994). Buspirone treatment of anxious alcoholics. A placebo-controlled trial. *Archives of General Psychiatry, 51*(9), 720–731. https://doi.org/10.1001/archpsyc.1994.03950090052008

Laker, C. J. (2007). How reliable is the current evidence looking at the efficacy of harm reduction and motivational interviewing interventions in the treatment of patients with a dual diagnosis? *Journal of Psychiatric and Mental Health Nursing, 14*(8), 720–726. https://doi.org/10.1111/j.1365-2850.2007.01159.x

Lam, D. H. (1991). Psychosocial family intervention in schizophrenia: A review of empirical studies. *Psychological Medicine, 21*(2), 423–441. https://doi.org/10.1017/s0033291700020535

Lamberti, J. S., & Weisman, R. L. (2021). Essential elements of forensic assertive community treatment. *Harvard Review of Psychiatry, 29*(4), 278–297. https://doi.org/10.1097/HRP.0000000000000299

Lean, M., Fornells-Ambrojo, M., Milton, A., Lloyd-Evans, B., Harrison-Stewart, B., Yesufu-Udechuku, A., ... & Johnson, S. (2019). Self-management interventions for people with severe mental illness. *The British Journal of Psychiatry, 214*(5), 260–268.

Lehman, A. F., & Steinwachs, D. M. (1998). Patterns of usual care for schizophrenia. *Schizophrenia Bulletin, 24,* 11–20.

Lewin, S. A., Dick, J., Pond, P., Zwarenstein, M., Aja, G., van Wyk, B., Bosch-Capblanch, X., & Patrick, M. (2005). Lay health workers in primary and community health care. *The Cochrane Database of Systematic Reviews,* (1), CD004015. https://doi.org/10.1002/14651858.CD004015.pub2

Manthey, T. (2011). Using motivational interviewing to increase retention in supported education. *American Journal of Psychiatric Rehabilitation, 14*(2), 120–136. https://doi.org/10.1080/15487768.2011.569667

Manthey, T. J., Rapp, C. A., Carlson, L., Holter, M. C., & Davis, J. K. (2012). The perceived importance of integrated supported education and employment services. *Journal of Rehabilitation, 78*(1), 16–24.

Marlatt, G. A., Larimer, M., & Witkiewitz, K. (Eds.). (2011). *Harm reduction* (2nd ed.). Guilford Press.

Maxwell, S., & Shinderman, M. S. (2000). Use of naltrexone in the treatment of alcohol use disorders in patients with concomitant major mental illness. *Journal of Addictive Diseases, 19*(3), 61–69. https://doi.org/10.1300/J069v19n03_05

McFarlane, W. R., Dixon, L., Lukens, E., & Lucksted, A. (2003). Family psychoeducation and schizophrenia: A review of the literature. *Journal of Marital and Family Therapy, 29*(2), 223–245. https://doi.org/10.1111/j.1752-0606.2003.tb01202.x

McHugo, G. J., Drake, R. E., Teague, G. B., & Xie, H. (1999). Fidelity to assertive community treatment and client outcomes in the New Hampshire dual disorders study. *Psychiatric Services, 50*(6), 818–824. https://doi.org/10.1176/ps.50.6.818

Miller, W. R., & Rollnick, S. (2013). *Motivational interviewing* (3rd ed.). Guilford Press.

Miotto, P., Preti, A., & Frezza, M. (2001). Heroin and schizophrenia: subjective responses to abused drugs in dually diagnosed patients. *Journal of Clinical Psychopharmacology, 21*(1), 111–113. https://doi.org/10.1097/00004714-200102000-00022

Moore, A., Sellwood, W., & Stirling, J. (2000). Compliance and psychological reactance in schizophrenia. *The British Journal of Clinical Psychology, 39*(3), 287–295. https://doi.org/10.1348/014466500163293

Morey, B., & Mueser, K. T. (2007). *The family intervention guide to mental illness: Recognizing symptoms and getting treatment.* New Harbinger.

Morin, L., & Franck, N. (2017). Rehabilitation interventions to promote recovery from Schizophrenia: A systematic review. *Frontiers in Psychiatry, 8,* 100. https://doi.org/10.3389/fpsyt.2017.00100

Morse, G. A., Calsyn, R. J., Klinkenberg, W. D., Helminiak, T. W., Wolff, N., Drake, R. E., Yonker, R. D., Lama, G., Lemming, M. R., & McCudden, S. (2006). Treating homeless clients with severe mental illness and substance use disorder: Costs and outcomes. *Community Mental Health Journal, 42*(4), 377–404.

Mueser, K. T., Campbell, K., & Drake, R. E. (2011). The effectiveness of supported employment in people with dual disorders. *Journal of Dual Diagnosis, 7*(1–2), 90–102. https://doi.org/10.1080/15504263.2011.568360

Mueser, K. T., Corrigan, P. W., Hilton, D., Tanzman, B., Schaub, A., Gingerich, S., & Herz, M. I. (2002). Illness management and recovery for severe mental illness: A review of the research. *Psychiatric Services, 53,* 1272–1284.

Mueser, K. T., Drake, R. E., & Noordsy, D. L. (1998). Integrated mental health and substance abuse treatment for severe psychiatric disorders. *Journal of Psychiatric Practice, 4*(3), 129–139. https://doi.org/10.1097/00131746-199805000-00001

Mueser, K. T., & Fox, L. (2002). A family intervention program for dual disorders. *Community Mental Health Journal, 38,* 253–270.

Mueser, K. T., & Gingerich, S. (2006). *The complete family guide to schizophrenia.* Guilford Press.

Mueser, K. T., Noordsy, D. L., Drake, R. E., & Fox, M. (2003). *Integrated treatment for dual disorders.* Guilford Press.

Murphy, A. A., Mullen, M. G., & Spagnolo, A. B. (2005). Enhancing individual placement and support. *American Journal of Psychiatric Rehabilitation, 8*(1), 37–61.

Murthy, P., Mahadevan, J., & Chand, P. K. (2019). Treatment of substance use disorders with co-occurring severe mental health disorders. *Current Opinion in Psychiatry, 32*(4), 293–299. https://doi.org/10.1097/YCO.0000000000000510

New Freedom Commission on Mental Health. (2003). *Achieving the promise: Transforming mental health care in America.* Department of Health and Human Services.

Norris, S. L., Chowdhury, F. M., Van Le, K., Horsley, T., Brownstein, J. N., Zhang, X., Jack, L., Jr, & Satterfield, D. W, et al. (2006). Effectiveness of community health workers in the care of persons with diabetes. *Diabetic Medicine, 23*(5), 544–556. https://doi.org/10.1111/j.1464-5491.2006.01845.x

O'Brien, C., Gardner-Sood, P., Corlett, S. K., Ismail, K., Smith, S., Atakan, Z., Greenwood, K., Joseph, C., & Gaughran, F. (2014). Provision of health promotion programmes to people with serious mental illness: A mapping exercise of four South London boroughs. *Journal of Psychiatric and Mental Health Nursing, 21*(2), 121–127.

O'Keefe, C., Potenza, D. P., & Mueser, K. T. (1997). Treatment outcomes for severely mentally ill patients on conditional discharge to community-based treatment. *Journal of Nervous and Mental Disease, 185,* 409–411.

Park, T., Usher, K., & Foster, K. (2011). Description of a healthy lifestyle intervention for people with serious mental illness taking second-generation antipsychotics. *International Journal of Mental Health Nursing, 20*(6), 428–437.

Parker, V. A., Clark, J. A., & Leyson, J, et al. (2010). Patient navigation: development of a protocol for describing what navigators do. *Health Services Research, 45*(2), 514–531. https://doi.org/10.1111/j.1475-6773.2009.01079.x

Patel, K. (2007). Research note: Drug consumption rooms and needle and syringe exchange programs. *Journal of Drug Issues, 37*(3), 737–747. https://doi.org/10.1177/002204260703700312

PDR Staff. (2017). *Prescribers' digital reference (Physician's desk reference online).* http://www.pdr.net

Penn, P. E., Brooke, D., Brooks, A. J., Gallagher, S. M., & Barnard, A. D. (2016). Co-occurring conditions clients and counselors compare 12-step and smart recovery mutual help. *Journal of Groups in Addiction & Recovery, 11*(2), 76–92. https://doi.org/10.1080/1556035X.2015.1104643

Penzenstadler, L., Soares, C., Anci, E., Molodynski, A., & Khazaal, Y. (2019). Effect of assertive community treatment for patients with substance use disorder: A systematic review. *European Addiction Research, 25*(2), 56–67. https://doi.org/10.1159/000496742

Perry, H. B., Zulliger, R., & Rogers, M. M. (2014). Community health workers in low-, middle-, and high-income countries: An overview of their history, recent evolution, and current effectiveness. *Annual Review of Public Health, 35,* 399–421. https://doi.org/10.1146/annurev-publhealth-032013-182354

Petrakis, I. L., Nich, C., & Ralevski, E. (2006). Psychotic spectrum disorders and alcohol abuse: A review of pharmacotherapeutic strategies and a report on the effectiveness of naltrexone and disulfiram. *Schizophrenia Bulletin*, 32(4), 644–654. https://doi.org/10.1093/schbul/sbl010

Piat, M., Seida, K., & Padgett, D. (2020). Choice and personal recovery for people with serious mental illness living in supported housing. *Journal of Mental Health*, 29(3), 306–313.

Prochaska, J. O., & Diclemente, C. C. (1984). *The transtheoretical approach: Crossing the traditional boundaries of therapy*. Dow-Jones/Irwin.

Rappa, L., & Viola, J. (2013). *Condensed psychopharmacology 2013: A pocket reference for psychiatry and psychotropic medications*. RXPSYCH.

Regier, D. A., Farmer, M. E., Rae, D. S., Locke, B. Z., Keith, S. J., Judd, L. L., & Goodwin, F. K. (1990). Comorbidity of mental disorders with alcohol and other drug abuse. *Journal of the American Medical Association*, 264, 2511–2518.

Rezansoff, S. N., Moniruzzaman, A., Fazel, S., McCandless, L., Procyshyn, R., & Somers, J. M. (2017). Housing first improves adherence to antipsychotic medication among formerly homeless adults with Schizophrenia: Results of a randomized controlled trial. *Schizophrenia Bulletin*, 43(4), 852–861. https://doi.org/10.1093/schbul/sbw136

Ries, R. K., Dyck, D. G., Short, R., Srebnik, D., Fisher, A., & Comtois, K. A. (2004). Outcomes of managing disability benefits among patients with substance dependence and severe mental illness. *Psychiatric Services*, 55(4), 445–447. https://doi.org/10.1176/appi.ps.55.4.445

Rog, D. J. (2004). The evidence on supported housing. *Psychiatric Rehabilitation Journal*, 27(4), 334–344. https://doi.org/10.2975/27.2004.334.344

Rosenberg, S. D., Goodman, L. A., Osher, F. C., Swartz, M. S., Essock, S. M., Butterfield, M. I., Constantine, N. T., Wolford, G. L., & Salyers, M. P. (2001). Prevalence of HIV, hepatitis B, and hepatitis C in people with severe mental illness. *American Journal of Public Health*, 91(1), 31–37. https://doi.org/10.2105/ajph.91.1.31

Rudnick, A., & Lundberg, E. (2012). The stress-vulnerability model of schizophrenia: A conceptual analysis and selective review. *Current Psychiatry Reviews*, 8(4), 337–341. https://doi.org/10.2174/157340012803520450

Salerno, A., Margolies, P., Cleek, A., Pollock, M., Gopalan, G., & Jackson, C. (2011). Best practices: wellness self-management: an adaptation of the illness management and recovery program in New York State. *Psychiatric Services*, 62(5), 456–458. https://doi.org/10.1176/ps.62.5.pss6205_0456

Santa Ana, E. J., LaRowe, S. D., Gebregziabher, M., Morgan-Lopez, A. A., Lamb, K., Beavis, K. A., Bishu, K., & Martino, S. (2021). Randomized controlled trial of group motivational interviewing for veterans with substance use disorders. *Drug and Alcohol Dependence*, 223, 108716. https://doi.org/10.1016/j.drugalcdep.2021.108716

Seida, J. C., Schouten, J. R., Boylan, K., Newton, A. S., Mousavi, S. S., Beaith, A., Vandermeer, B., Dryden, D. M., & Carrey, N. (2012). Antipsychotics for children and young adults. *Pediatrics*, 129(3), e771–e784.

Semahegn, A., Torpey, K., Manu, A., Assefa, N., Tesfaye, G., & Ankomah, A. (2018). Psychotropic medication non-adherence and associated factors among adult patients with major psychiatric disorders: A protocol for A systematic review. *Systematic Reviews*, 7(1), 1–5. https://doi.org/10.1186/s13643-018-0676-y

Sigmon, S. C., Steingard, S., Badger, G. J., Anthony, S. L., & Higgins, S. T. (2000). Contingent reinforcement of marijuana abstinence among individuals with serious mental illness: A feasibility study. *Experimental and Clinical Psychopharmacology*, 8(4), 509–517. https://doi.org/10.1037//1064-1297.8.4.509

Slade, M. (2017). Implementing shared decision making in routine mental health care. *World psychiatry*, 16(2), 146–153.

Smelson, D. A., Dixon, L., Craig, T., Remolina, S., Batki, S. L., Niv, N., & Owen, R. (2008). Pharmacological treatment of schizophrenia and co-occurring substance use disorders. *CNS Drugs*, 22, 903–916.

Solomon, P. (2000). Interventions for families of individuals with schizophrenia: Maximizing outcomes for their relatives. *Disease Management and Health Outcomes*, 8, 211–221.

Stapinski, L. A., Sannibale, C., Subotic, M., Rapee, R. M., Teesson, M., Haber, P. S., & Baillie, A. J. (2021). Randomised controlled trial of integrated cognitive behavioural treatment and motivational enhancement for comorbid social anxiety and alcohol use disorders. *The Australian and New Zealand Journal of Psychiatry*, 55(2), 207–220. https://doi.org/10.1177/0004867420952539

Steadman, H. J., Mulvey, E. P., Monahan, J., Robbins, P. C., Appelbaum, P. S., Grisso, T., . . . Silver, E. (1998). Violence by people discharged from acute psychiatric inpatient facilities and by others in the same neighborhoods. *Archives General Psychiatry*, 55, 393–401.

Stein, L. I., & Test, M. A. (1980). Alternative to mental hospital treatment. *Archives of General Psychiatry*, 37(4), 392. https://doi.org/10.1001/archpsyc.1980.01780170034003

Sterling, E. W., von Esenwein, S. A., Tucker, S., Fricks, L., & Druss, B. G. (2010). Integrating wellness, recovery, and self-management for mental health consumers. *Community Mental Health Journal*, 46(2), 130–138. https://doi.org/10.1007/s10597-009-9276-6

Swanson, J. W., Swartz, M. S., Wagner, H. R., Burns, B. J., Borum, R., & Hiday, V. A. (2000). Involuntary out-patient commitment and reduction of violent behaviour in persons with severe mental illness. *British Journal of Psychiatry*, 176(4), 324–331. https://doi.org/10.1192/bjp.176.4.324

Swofford, C. D., Kasckow, J. W., Scheller-Gilkey, G., & Inderbitzin, L. B. (1996). Substance use: A powerful predictor of relapse in schizophrenia. *Schizophrenia Research*, 20, 145–151.

Tessler, R. E., & Gamache, A. (2000). *Family experiences with mental illness*. Auburn House.

Torrey, W. C., Drake, R. E., Cohen, M., Fox, L. B., Lynde, D., Gorman, P., & Wyzik, P. (2002). The challenge of implementing and sustaining integrated dual disorders treatment programs. *Community Mental Health Journal*, 38(6), 507–521. https://doi.org/10.1023/a:1020888403586

Tsai, J., Salyers, M. P., Rollins, A. L., McKasson, M., & Litmer, M. L. (2009). Integrated dual disorders treatment. *Journal of Community Psychology*, 37(6), 781–788. https://doi.org/10.1002/jcop.20318

U.S. Department of Health and Human Services. (1999). *A report of the Surgeon General*. https://profiles.nlm.nih.gov/spotlight/nn/catalog/nlm:nlmuid-101584932X120-doc

Vogel, H. S., Knight, E., Laudet, A. B., & Magura, S. (1998). Double trouble in recovery: self-help for people with dual diagnoses. *Psychiatric Rehabilitation Journal*, 21(4), 356–364. https://doi.org/10.1037/h0095288

Wagner, M., & Newman, L. (2012). Longitudinal transition outcomes of youth with emotional disturbances. *Psychiatric Rehabilitation Journal*, 35(3), 199–208. https://doi.org/10.2975/35.3.2012.199.208

Wallstroem, I. G., Pedersen, P., Christensen, T. N., Hellström, L., Bojesen, A. B., Stenager, E., White, S., Mueser, K. T., Bejerholm, U., van Busschbach, J. T., Michon, H., & Eplov, L. F. (2021). A systematic review of individual placement and support, employment, and personal and clinical recovery. *Psychiatric Services*, 72(9), 1040–1047. https://doi.org/10.1176/appi.ps.202000070

Weiner, E., Ball, M. P., Summerfelt, A., Gold, J., & Buchanan, R. W. (2001). Effects of sustained-release bupropion and supportive group therapy on cigarette consumption in patients with schizophrenia. *The American Journal of Psychiatry*, 158(4), 635–637. https://doi.org/10.1176/appi.ajp.158.4.635

Wells, K. J., Battaglia, T. A., Dudley, D. J., Garcia, R., Greene, A., Calhoun, E., Mandelblatt, J. S., Paskett, E. D., Raich, P. C., *et al*, & Patient Navigation Research Program. (2008). Patient navigation: State of the art or is it science? *Cancer*, 113(8), 1999–2010. https://doi.org/10.1002/cncr.23815

Xie, H., McHugo, G. J., Fox, M. B., & Drake, R. E. (2005). Substance abuse relapse in a ten-year prospective follow-up of clients with mental and substance use disorders. *Psychiatric Services (Washington, D.C.)*, 56(10), 1282–1287. https://doi.org/10.1176/appi.ps.56.10.1282

Yule, A. M., & Kelly, J. F. (2019). Integrating Treatment for Co-Occurring Mental Health Conditions. *Alcohol Research*, 40(1), e1–e13. https://doi.org/10.35946/arcr.v40.1.07

Ziedonis, D. M., Smelson, D., Rosenthal, R. N., Batki, S. L., Green, A. I., Henry, R. J., Montoya, I., Parks, J., & Weiss, R. D. (2005). Improving the Care of Individuals with Schizophrenia and Substance Use Disorders: Consensus Recommendations. *Journal of Psychiatric Practice*, 11(5), 315–339. https://doi.org/10.1097/00131746-200509000-00005

CHAPTER 21

Technology

MARY BARROS-BAILEY AND MICHAEL GERALD

LEARNING OBJECTIVES

After reviewing this chapter, you should be able to:

- *Evaluate important areas to consider in the use of technology within and in support of the client-counselor relationship, including tele-assessment.*
- *Discuss technology behavioral and competency issues.*
- *Describe assistive technology and its use in evaluating and meeting the needs of clients.*
- *Summarize the role of distance education in rehabilitation.*

CACREP STANDARDS

CACREP 2016 CORE: 2F1.j, 2F5.d, 2F5.e, 2F5.j
CACREP 2016 Specialties:
  Clinical Rehabilitation Counseling: 5D1.g, 5D2.q, 5D3.a
  Rehabilitation Counseling: 5H1.g, 5H2.a, 5H2.m, 5H3.b, 5H3.c

INTRODUCTION

Rehabilitation counselors are defined in the Standard Occupational Classification as those who "help people with physical, mental, developmental, or emotional disabilities live independently" (*Occupational Outlook Handbook*; U.S. Bureau of Labor Statistics, 2021). That is a very broad scope of responsibility for assessment and assistance in the development and implementation of rehabilitation interventions. Technology can help, enhance, or impede all aspects of the rehabilitation counselor's professional formation and work activity.

Technology can be used and understood in different ways. In this chapter, we use the Britannica definition of technology: "the application of scientific knowledge to the practical aims of human life or . . . to the change and manipulation of the human environment" (Augustyn, n.d., para. 1). **High technology** is defined as "scientific technology involving the production or use of advanced or sophisticated devices especially in the fields of electronics and computers" (Merriam-Webster, 2022, para. 1) while **low technology** "does not involve highly advanced or specialized systems of devices" (The Free Dictionary, 2022, para. 1). Today's existing types of technology include: 3D printing, aerospace, agriculture, artificial intelligence, assistive, biotechnology, communication, construction, education, electronics, entertainment, environmental, industrial and manufacturing, information, medical, military, robotics, sports, and vehicle (Andrea, 2022). The prevalence of technology in rehabilitation counseling is impossible to encapsulate into a single chapter. Today, technology can play a role in the manner in which the counselor professionally develops, how the client–counselor relationship is established, and every aspect of the relationship and delivery of service over the rehabilitation counselor's worklife. Thus, this chapter focuses more narrowly on assistive, communication, and education technologies in practice.

TECHNOLOGY USAGE AND ADOPTION

The COVID-19 pandemic accelerated the worldwide adoption of the types of technologies covered in this chapter, and highlighted the stark differences in technological access by various sectors of society, which were acknowledged previously but perhaps not as well understood. A 2020 survey by McKinsey and Company (LaBerge et al., 2020) found that pre-pandemic, large organizations expected it would take 454 days to increase remote working and/or collaboration, but on average, it took 10.5 days once the 2020 pandemic lockdown started; that it would take nearly two years to increase the use of advanced technologies in operations, but it took 26.5 days on average during the lockdown; and that it would take about 18 months to migrate assets to the cloud, but it took 23.2 days on average. About 90% of individuals surveyed found the internet to be essential to their lives during the pandemic shut down, and 40% of them found themselves using the internet in new ways (McClain et al., 2021). While the adoption and use of high technology have increased dramatically across the globe since 2020, other technologies—such as the fax—floundered in their performance. This result is related to the need for vastly increased volumes of information transfer; therefore, some earlier technologies were abandoned or replaced by other, more efficient means (Kassam, 2021; Kliff & Sanger-Katz, 2020; Young, 2021). Interestingly, healthcare providers are a holdout industry as about 70% of them still used faxes to remit and receive medical information (Brown, 2021).

The hyper-accelerated adoption of technology during the pandemic in 2020 and beyond has cast light on the chasms of access to high or advanced technology by individuals with disabilities, those from low socioeconomic sectors or living in rural areas, and minorities. For individuals with disabilities, the digital divide remains wide compared to those who do not identify as having a disability. Ownership of desktop or laptop computers is 62% for people with disabilities compared to 81% for the general population; smartphones, 72% versus 88%; tablet computers, 47% versus 54%; and access to broadband at home, 72% versus 78% (Perrin & Atske, 2021). In 2021 the Pew Research Center found that Americans who earned less than $30,000 annually were 33% less likely to own a desktop or laptop computer, 27% less likely to own a tablet computer, 21% less likely to own a smartphone, and 36% less likely to have home broadband. Although those in rural areas have gained a lot of ground in their adoption of technology over the past decade, they still lag behind their urban and suburban peers by 7% to 11% in their ownership of desktop or laptop computers, tablets, smartphones, and home broadband (Vogels, 2021). Based on ethnicity, Atske and Perrin (2021) found that, compared to their White peers, Blacks and Hispanics were 11% to 13% less likely to own a desktop or laptop computer and 9% to 15% less likely to have home broadband (Atske & Perrin, 2021). However, smartphone ownership was equivalent between White and Hispanic Americans, with a 2% lower difference for Blacks. The tablet computer ownership for Blacks was marginally higher by 1% in contrast to their White or Hispanic peers. Rehabilitation counselors need to be aware of not only of the prevalence and frenzied adoption of technology but also the disadvantages some of the individuals on their caseloads may have when it comes to communication, education, and assistive technologies.

COMMUNICATION TECHNOLOGY

The Counseling Relationship Online

The Commission on Rehabilitation Counselor Certification (CRCC) *Code of Professional Ethics for Rehabilitation Counselors* (CRCC, 2017) Standard J.1.b. of the CRCC Code describes the need for certificants to consider applicable laws when utilizing telecounseling technologies, including the adoption of information and communication technologies for the delivery of counseling services. Because of the increased proliferation of telecounseling services, counselors need a heightened awareness of their ethical responsibilities when providing telecounseling, as well as the potential legal and ethical issues they may encounter.

Current conversations regarding the use of technology in counseling, and the potential ethical issues that may arise, largely center on the concept of telecounseling or telerehabilitation. Telerehabilitation has been proposed as a way to improve "access for consumers, strengthening the counselor-consumer relationship, and increasing contacts with consumers" (Embree et al., 2018, p. 40), particularly for those in rural areas (Castillo & Cartwright, 2018). **Telecounseling** or **telerehabilitation** are the terms used in the present chapter and previously were referred to by a number of different names including, but not limited to, distance counseling, online counseling or online therapy; e-therapy; technology- or computer-assisted counseling; internet counseling; cyber-therapy; and remote counseling (Wheeler & Bertram, 2019). All these terms refer to counseling services that are conducted either entirely or partially through the internet, telephone, computers, hand-held devices, or other hardware or software. Despite the terms used, in general telecounseling is the delivery of mental and behavioral health services, including but not limited to, therapy by a licensed or certified practitioner to a client in a non-face-to-face setting through distance communication technologies (Rummell & Joyce, 2010). Broadly, **technology in counseling** refers to a number of different tools, strategies, and techniques that practitioners use to deliver services, communicate with clients, manage confidential case records, or assess information about clients (Reamer, 2015). Ultimately, the goal is to use technology as a medium for effective communication not a hinderance to it.

In keeping with professional ethics, **informed consent** "is the client's right to agree to participate in counseling, assessment, or other professional procedures or services" (Cottone et al., 2022, p. 117). During the informed consent process, counselors should also lay out the structure of the telecounseling services (Barnwell & Campbell, 2017). This means that prior to the initiation of telecounseling with a client, counselors should inform clients of the technologies to be used, the appropriateness of their use, where the counselor will be located, and what considerations a client should consider when selecting a location. The online setting also requires attention to other areas of informed consent normally not emphasized face-to-face.

When counselors elect to provide telecounseling using computer-based technologies, they should be aware that there are four parties involved in telerehabilitation counseling: (a) the client, (b) the counselor, (c) the software manufacturer, and (d) professional bodies (e.g., CRCC; Cottone & Tarvydas, 2016). Clients receiving computer-assisted counseling should be "intellectually, emotionally, physically, linguistically, and functionally capable of using the application and that the application is appropriate for the needs of the client" (Cottone & Tarvydas, 2016, p. 290). Counselors should explain clearly the reasons they believe clients could benefit from telecounseling and ask clients to demonstrate an ability to use the technology that will constitute telecounseling. When counselors develop materials for purposes of promoting or providing services they should ensure that materials are accessible and user-friendly (Herlihy & Corey, 2015). Counselors should be cognizant of clients with sensory differences, and work to ensure their websites or web-based materials are compliant with the Web Accessibility Initiative and Section 508 (Herlihy & Corey, 2015).

BOX 21.1 SPECIAL CONSIDERATIONS FOR ONLINE INFORMED CONSENT

- Verbally or otherwise agreeing to engage in an online session that has higher threats to privacy
- Confirmation by individuals in the session that no recording or imaging of any part of the meeting is being performed unless agreed to by the parties (which could include a discussion about the scope of the recording, any products derived from it, and its destruction)
- Confirmation of the client's identity, and identification those present at each respective site not visible off camera who may participate in or hear the client–counselor interaction.

Since 2020, it is highly likely that the majority of counselors in any practice setting in the United States have covered work activities subject to the Health Insurance Portability and Accountability Act (HIPAA) protection. The Office of Civil Rights (OCR) of the U.S. Department of Health and Human Services that oversees HIPAA enforcement, prohibits the use of public facing remote communication products such as Facebook Live and Twitch because these technologies allow wide or indiscriminate access to the communication. The OCR allows such "non-public-facing" remote communication products such as Apple FaceTime, Facebook Messenger Video Chat, Google Hangouts or Meet, Skype, and Zoom. The OCR also allows such texting applications as Facebook Messenger, iMessage, and WhatsApp. Accessibility communication tools such as closed captioning are now standard on many of these platforms and have become more accurate in speech to text. These non-public-facing platforms are allowed because they typically employ encryption technology and also require accounts and other login information, which help promote limited access to Electronic Protected Health Information (ePHI). In addition to the established guidelines to promote access to healthcare in response the COVID-19 pandemic, the OCR provided notification of discretion related to its enforcement of HIPAA noncompliance. This discretionary judgment is permitted as long as healthcare providers are deemed to be acting in accordance with the good faith provisions (U.S. Department of Health and Human Services, 2021), such as notifying clients about their medical privacy rights and procuring their written acknowledgment of that notice. Examples of acting in bad faith, under the present guidelines in response to COVID-19 are: fraud; invasion of privacy; illicit uses of data still covered under the Privacy Rule; violations of state licensing laws or professional ethics; or the use of public-facing communication products such as Facebook Live. Health and Human Services waived certain provisions of HIPAA in response to COVID-19, to allow disclosures of ePHI in situations such as treatment and coordination of care to a public health authority, persons at risk, and persons involved in a client's care. Such relaxation of the enforcement of HIPAA requirements has been extended until near the end of the current decade.

Tele-Assessment

The research on the nature and impact of the therapeutic relationship in telecounseling is limited, but what exists shows clients rate the strength of their relationship in telecounseling similar to clients receiving face-to-face counseling (Richards & Viganó, 2013). Although the relationship is critical in counseling practice, generally, relationships and boundaries with clients are a leading context of ethical dilemmas and violations among counselors (Cottone et al., 2022). Social media use perhaps represents the most significant challenge to counselors engaged in telecounseling or utilizing technology in counseling. "Both the ubiquity and synchrony, key components to social media, have made computing more like human interaction" (Herlihy & Corey, 2015, p. 253). Many people, including counselors, now engage in some form of online social media, through websites such as LinkedIn, Facebook, Instagram, and Twitter (Wheeler & Bertram, 2019). Communication with clients through social media platforms carries with it the potential for breaches of confidentiality or invasions of client privacy (Herlihy & Corey, 2015).

Communication technology impacts not only the establishment and evolution of the client–counselor relationship but also the delivery of specialized services, such as assessment. Sheperis (2020) classified computer-based assessments into five categories: computer administration of assessment instruments, automated test scoring, computer-generated reports and narratives, computer-adapted tests, and computer simulations. While all these technology-based options have been available in some fashion over the decades, they have not necessarily been the norm until the last decade starting with test developers and increasingly with assessment users since 2020. Over the last decade, as new editions of psychometric instruments were developed, some aspect of the standardized test became digitized, whether it was the instrument itself, its scoring, or its reporting. This change requires greater technological competence from the client and rehabilitation counselor if the paper-and-pencil version were no longer offered, or might be phased out in subsequent version updates. Therefore, to ensure that the technology itself does not create a threat to validity of the scores, it is recommended that a technology competency screener be administered to assist in decision-making between the use of the different paper or digital versions of an assessment. If no paper version of an instrument exists, and a screener suggests technology could impact assessment results negatively, the evaluator must disclose the mode of testing as a potential factor in the validity of the results.

The primary areas of concern for tele-assessment become the concurrent validity of digital assessments compared to paper-and-pencil versions and remote proctoring to avoid cheating or faking results. Early literature found—almost universally—no statistical differences between paper-and-pencil and digital assessments for people with and without disabilities (Brearly et al., 2017; Denscombe, 2009; Kim & Huynh, 2010; Meade et al., 2007; Öz & Özturan, 2018; Taherbhai et al., 2012). With proctoring, evolution in remote technology found that the use of webcam-based technologies was effective in staving off cheating compared to face-to-face proctoring (Grieve & de Groot, 2011; Grieve & Hayes, 2016; Hylton et al., 2016; Ladyshewsky, 2015). Because of the pressing need to move many human services including assessment online, a variety of professional organizations have provided guidelines for tele-assessment finding having found similar outcomes in the evidence-based literature compared to those from the preceding dozen years (American Psychological Association, 2020a, 2020b; National Academy of Neuropsychology, 2020; Society for Personality Assessment, 2020; Stolwyk et al., 2020; Wright, 2020; Wright et al., 2020). Many psychometric test developers now provide free training and instruction in the administration of their standardized assessments for valid and reliable outcomes (see Pearson, 2020a, Pearson, 2020b, 2020c, 2020d, 2020e; Riverside Insights, 2020; Western Psychological Services, 2020a, 2020b). Tele-assessment still is considered Plan B to a face-to-face assessment using informal and formal methods where individual and environmental observations are maximized. However, it is nonetheless a viable and valid alternative in circumstances where time, distance, public health, or other factors may necessitate a different form of administration. The contemporary literature is rife with recommendations regarding tele-assessment best practices as well as warnings as to the implications of this secondary approach to practice (Farmer et al., 2020a, 2020b).

Education Technology

The misconception that distance or remote education is a new phenomenon brought on by high technology in recent generations is false. Indeed, the Distance Education Accrediting

Commission (DEAC, 2022) was established in 1926 and accredits programs "from the secondary school level through professional doctoral degree-granting institutions" (para. 1).

Distance education in rehabilitation counseling has been around for a generation of students (Leech & Holcomb, 2004). Today, traditional and clinical rehabilitation counseling programs are like any other type of training available for many professions. It varies in the delivery of programs' accredited curriculum through a variety of synchronous and asynchronous methods.

Technology, in general, and instructional performance technology, in particular, have enhanced the ability of faculty to tailor instruction specific to the needs of each student's learning style. It also has presented the opportunity to expand practice settings for internship and practicum opportunities, monitoring, and supervision (Byrne & Hartley, 2010; Kampfe et al., 2009; Lund & Schultz, 2015; Morissette et al., 2012). Distance education also allows educators to test the efficacy of traditional counseling techniques that were once just taught in the classroom between traditional and distance education settings (Degiorgio et al., 2011; Meyer, 2015).

Since 2020, all counselor education programs likely have offered some form of distance or remote training or education, as is the experience with many educational institutions worldwide from primary school through graduate education. The impact of the forced change of delivery of teaching and training to alternative and distance formats may be too early to assess. However, early indications suggest "that for many students, the educational gaps that existed before the pandemic—in access, opportunities, achievement, and outcomes—are widening" (U.S. Department of Education, Office of Civil Rights, 2021).

For people with disabilities, access to some of the platforms may be difficult, particularly individuals with sensory, cognitive, or learning disabilities (Ting-Feng et al., 2014). Tools such as **Universal Design for Learning** that provide opportunities for all learners to access, improve, and optimize learning could enhance knowledge acquisition for all learners. Careful consideration about the delivery system and supports for the individual should occur in the decision-making process, in addition to determining whether assistive technology or educational supports exist to build the bridge for effective learning. In 2014, Quality Matters was established as a nonprofit with a mission to promote and improve the quality of online education and student learning nationally and internationally. Establishing educational standards across eight domain areas, with the last domain being Accessibility and Usability to assist teachers and faculty in all academic settings to design courses for effective online instruction for all students. Courses that are developed under these educational standards can undergo formal review and become certified as being compliant with such standards so that students of all different levels of function have greater opportunities to access learning.

Assistive Technology

The last major area of technology covered by this chapter is assistive technology. The first legal mention of assistive technology devices or services is found in the IDEA. However, it is clear that as early as 1973, in the Rehabilitation Act of 1973 (Section 504), there was an understanding that the use of assistive technology should be considered for eligible individuals with disabilities. Several other laws related to disability and technology have recognized the need for the application of specific assistive technology devices and services for people with disabilities since that first effort.

Currently, the definition of **assistive technology** in common use comes to us from the IDEA of 2004. The definition has been refined over the years to mean:

> Any item, piece of equipment or product system, whether acquired commercially off the shelf, modified, or customized, that is used to increase, maintain, or improve the functional capabilities of children with disabilities. The term does not include a medical

device that is surgically implanted, or the replacement of such device. (20 U.S.C. §1401(1)(a)(B))

Although the definition is accepted widely, it was developed specifically for an educational setting. As a result, it may have some limitations when considering the entire constellation of assistive technology devices and services used in the home or community. This definition also lacks specific examples of assistive technology. The Assistive Technology Industry Association (ATIA) definition is much more comprehensive and includes clarifying terminology and examples of technologies, stating: "Assistive technology helps people who have difficulty speaking, typing, writing, remembering, pointing, seeing, hearing, learning, walking, and many other things. People with different abilities require different assistive technologies" (ATIA, 2022, para. 5).

Individuals providing assistive technology come from multiple professions. The client is the central member of the team. The focus of the accommodation process should be on function, simplicity, and safety. Typically, the client is surrounded by a team of professionals with skills most related to the obstacle to be modified. Members of these teams should be changed as needed for the task, but may include family doctors, speech–language pathologists, rehabilitation engineers, occupational therapists, physical therapists, rehabilitation counselors, regular and special education teachers, durable medical equipment providers, and even representatives from manufacturers of assistive technology devices. The team must be careful not to ignore the housing access needs, transportation, and community access requirements that must come together to facilitate the client's participation in work. Many team members who hold credentials in one of these professions also have received training in assistive technology. RESNA brings together professionals of many disciplines around the development and use of assistive technology, and provides training and credentialing for Assistive Technology Professionals (ATPs), Rehabilitation Engineering Technologists (RETs), and Seating and Mobility Specialists (SMSs).

Assistive technology assessment is an important first step in developing an assistive technology plan, which can be performed face-to-face or remotely (Smith-Jackson & Williges, 2001). Areas assessed include wheelchair assessments (Barlow et al., 2009; Bell et al., 2020; Graham et al., 2019; Schein, Schmeler, Holm, et al., 2010; Schein, Schmeler, Saptono, et al., 2010), troubleshooting, or repairs. The most researched and cited assessment process is the Matching Person & Technology Model, which has peer-reviewed studies and forms available for free download from its website. These documents can be used individually or collaboratively to assess assistive technology needs (Scherer et al., 2002).

Appropriate assistive devices will likely be different for each person, even if those individuals have the same disabilities, experience the same obstacles, and have the same presenting need for modification. Just as each of us has our own way of completing a task, so, too, do the tools used to modify a task fit the temperament, outlook, personality, desired degree of independence, and abilities of the individual who will use the modification. Some modifications may achieve access but create new obstacles that should be explored. The need for current and future client and caregiver training, repair, maintenance, and function of the technology needs to be included in the assistive technology plan.

To achieve simplicity, the process of modification may be iterative. The team begins by trying the following:

- Step 1: the simplest, lowest technological solution first
- Step 2: more complex solutions using readily available consumer technologies are next
- Step 3: modifications using technologies developed specifically for individuals with disabilities
- Step 4: custom-built modifications if none of the previous examples suffice

Depending on the complexity of the task(s) to be modified, some combination of solutions may be used. The greatest benefit occurs if assistive technology can move someone

BOX 21.2 CASE CONCEPTUALIZATION

Jean was not diagnosed with having central auditory processing disorder and hyperacusis until early adulthood, although she was found in primary school to be dually exceptional—qualifying for an Individualized Education Program plan as well as for the gifted-talented program. Now, she is transitioning to a large university from a charter school where she recently graduated from high school and feels overwhelmed with the multiplicity of sound stimuli in the classrooms and science lab courses, which often is anxiety-provoking and tends to be cognitively fatiguing. In accommodating her learning needs, the following plan was put in place: (a) positioning her seat where she is least barraged by competing sounds, (b) providing noise-canceling headphones to allow for cognitive breaks at appropriate times, and (c) provision of bilateral hearing aids fitted to reduce background sound. Thus far, the various low and high technologies seem to help, although Jean will have access to a rehabilitation engineer to assist with more individualized technologies, if needed.

from having an obstacle in a major life area previously enjoyed to accomplishing it again, sometimes almost immediately.

The development of an assistive technology rehabilitation plan is best served by a common language. There are multiple resources available to clients, counselors, and the public to identify sources of assistive technology. The U.S. DOL's Office of Disability Employment Policy provides the Job Accommodations Network (U.S. Department of Labor, 2022a) and access to free consultation, assessment tools, and a databank of resources, such as product lists organized by disability type. The Searchable Online Accommodation Resource (U.S. Department of Labor, 2022b) is a database that contains thousands of potential low- and high-technology solutions. Locally, assistive technology projects provide directed assessments and services, professional expertise, training, lending libraries, computer laboratories, and more to help identify the best interventions to include in the rehabilitation plan to facilitate access and inclusion of people with disabilities in the workplace. These federally funded programs by the Assistive Technology Act of 2004 (Public Law 108–364) provide local communities with free or low-cost access to technical specialists who could assist with the evaluation and accommodation alternatives to meet the needs of people with disabilities.

A number of emerging technologies hold promise and may have profound effects on the field of assistive technology and people's ability to function better in their lives. Self-driving vehicles may be the most dramatic of these developments that may bridge the gap of experienced by some people in one area of major independent living engagement. Once in common use, transportation for individuals who are blind or have low vision and others who currently are unable to drive a vehicle independently will suddenly have independent access to more activities in their communities. Three-dimensional printers

BOX 21.3 ASSISTIVE TECHNOLOGY WEBSITES

- Assistive Technology Act of 2004: www.congress.gov/bill/108th-congress/house-bill/4278
- ABLEDATA: www.abledata.com
- Assistive Technology for Kids: https://at4kids.com
- Job Accommodation Network: www.askjan.orgNationalTechCenter: www.nationaltechcenter.org

are already changing many aspects of assistive technology especially in situations that require a one-of-a-kind device. For instance, prosthetists can rapidly develop and test new devices that otherwise might be too time-consuming and costly to produce. What once was costly and somewhat temperamental environment control units (e.g., lighting, heating, and door access) have become readily available consumer products now called home automation. Most commonly, these devices are voice-controlled, but other methods of operation can be added.

TECHNOLOGY IMPLICATIONS FOR REHABILITATION COUNSELORS

Professional competence is an important component of counseling ethics, as incompetent practice raises the likelihood that clients may be harmed (Welfel, 2013). **Competence** refers to the counselor's capability of performing the minimum quality of service and that the service is within the limits of their training (Cottone et al., 2022) and involved: knowledge, skill, and diligence (Welfel). Competence related to telecounseling includes both clinical and technical competence (Cottone et al., 2022). This requirement means counselors need to not only be aware of the nuances of telecounseling and how it differs from traditional in-person services, but they also need to have some knowledge about the technologies they are using—such as if it is secure, if it is user-friendly, and if it is accessible for clients. Before initiating distance counseling in their practices, counselors should seek training to develop competency in the practice of telecounseling as well as gain proficiency with the technologies they may be using (Herlihy & Corey, 2015).

Measuring technological competency—a dynamic, and a moving target—is not always easy. Someone's subjective concept of being "good" or "bad" at the use of technology sometimes has to be measured against an objective standard. This assessment is difficult to capture in an interview process. Therefore, computer and Internet assessment tools and questionnaires based on standard competencies supplement the interview process with additional information for the client and the practitioner. These instruments could assist in understanding the level of technological competencies of counselors and clients or identifying the need for computer or technological literacy classes.

Technology and Behavior

Although the last section of this chapter, awareness of the differences of behavior in the use of technology—including that of the counselor's—is likely the most important consideration. While different low and high technologies come and go, the one constant the counselor can control is behavior. Early in the study of behavior and technology, Shechtman and Horowitz (2003) tested the assumption that people interact the same with computers as in live communication. They found that when people thought they were interacting with a computer, they used less effort in the communication process. That is, people act differently when they are using technology, particularly in the online environment, than when they are in face-to-face or telephonic interactions. The immediacy of Internet communications draws on people's impulsivity (Caplan, 2002; Davis et al., 2002; Suler, 2004). Goleman (2007) explained that in the interaction with hardware, there is an absence of cues from body language and other sensory stimuli to assist in decoding communications. He stated, "the absence of information on how the other person is responding makes the pre frontal circuitry more likely to fail. Our emotional impulses disinhibited, we type [a] message and hit 'send' before [we] hit 'discard'" (para. 12).

As social media platforms capture and remit short messages (e.g., Twitter), the tendency not to control for impulsive actions that one may regret later is accentuated. Knowing that communication may be constructed socially through the influence of technology among different demographic groups making up a counselor's caseload is

BOX 21.4 REFLECTION ACTIVITY

Think of a situation when you did not use one or more the netiquette rules. What were the consequences of not following the rules? What would you have done differently to avoid such consequences?

an important insight. This information contributes to an understanding of how or why people communicate differently through the use of various platforms. For instance, someone with a hearing sensory condition might feel better communication through visual means, such as videoconferencing where they can sign, whereas another person with a vision sensory condition might prefer auditory-based technologies, such as telephones or text to speech. Beyond the lack of cues, the immediacy of the decoding process when information is received through a particular gadget or platform and the resulting response fails to allow time to mitigate impulsivity. When it comes to the use of existing and emerging technology, impulsive responses often become the norm rather than the exception. Understanding the occurrence of such behaviors is vital in the client–counselor relationship so that communication can be understood better and improved. In short, less communication effort coupled with impulsivity through the use of technology may lead to mindless communication. This type of communication may result in behaviors that otherwise would be considered improper in the more traditional forms of communication used in counseling.

If technology is a medium used in the client–counselor relationship, it should be evaluated so that it is a facilitator rather than an inhibitor of that communication. The awareness and discussion of technological options also puts a check against misinterpretation of the intent, tone, or other content of a message. The recipient's reaction to the message also may fuel the flames of the communication in a direction that the sender never originally intended. Because technology automatically creates a record of the communication that may be saved on one or multiple servers, there is documentation of the interaction to which either or both parties, and others, may have access that could be further interpreted or remitted in the future.

For nearly three decades, Shea (1994) has promoted netiquette rules. These rules are as relevant now for today's social media, texting, and other platforms operating on a variety of mobile or wireless technologies as they were when the platform was a bulletin board accessed through expensive long-distance dial-up connections. The 10 rules follow:

Rule 1: Remember the human.
Rule 2: Behave in the same way online as in real life.
Rule 3: Know where you are in cyberspace.
Rule 4: Respect other people's time and bandwidth.
Rule 5: Make yourself look good online.
Rule 6: Share expert knowledge.
Rule 7: Help keep flame wars under control.
Rule 8: Respect other people's privacy.
Rule 9: Don't abuse your power.
Rule 10: Be forgiving of other people's mistakes (Shea, 1994, p. 1).

Some form of these rules have made their way into the counseling profession ranging from guidelines on course syllabi to online group interaction norms.

CONCLUSION

Technology always has been part of the client–counselor relationship, whether when the first-known counselor Frank Parsons used low-technology quills and paper to collect data during an interview more than 100 years ago, or today using or audio, video, or other digital means for face-to-face or distance sessions. Low- and high-technology media are important tools to support the building and maintenance of the relationship and for the provision of services to our clients and evaluees. The accelerated adoption of such technology in telecounseling and telerehabilitation since 2020 has provided clients and counselors with greater knowledge of its use. It also has accentuated the prominence of the digital divide among the disability population or those with low technological literature or difficulty of access due to functional differences. Current and emerging low and high technologies should be a continued source of support and efficiency and not create barriers to any parts of the client–counselor relationship or services delivery process.

This chapter examined technology in three major areas—communication, education, and assistive technology—as well as its use in rehabilitation counseling, including salient issues in the client–counselor relationship and tele-assessment. The digital divide for people with disabilities or other minority and socioeconomic populations and the initial impacts of the accelerated adoption of high technology since 2020 were examined.

The evolution of distance technology that facilitates synchronous and asynchronous communication, education, storage, and other functions has created a dynamic medium through which people communicate and affect behavior. Rehabilitation counselors and the programs educating these professionals need to integrate awareness and understanding of low and high, software and hardware technologies impacting rehabilitation counseling practice. Equally important is the investigation of behavioral differences in the use of any technology. Measures of technological competencies of clients and counselors are vital now more than ever to help evaluate and plan employment and training needs, and maintain and accelerate the delivery of services.

A brief history of distance education, its continuum, and applications was provided. The efficacy of such a form of education and training was tempered by the advice to carefully consider convenience along with any other issues of access that may emerge.

Finally, an overview regarding technology in rehabilitation counseling would be deficient if it did not include a discussion about assistive technology. This introduction to the range of assessment, content, methodologies, content, procedures, resources, and future advances provided the reader with preliminary understanding of this vital resource to the rehabilitation counseling process.

The challenge of writing any chapter about technology is that as soon as the words hit the press, new forms of technology or the practice of its usage make some lexicon seem dated or obsolete. It is imperative that the reader focus on the essential concepts of technology use and misuse, strengths and challenges while constantly seeking information to enhance services to the client being served and to the profession.

CONTENT REVIEW QUESTIONS

1. When using technology in the client–counselor relationship, why is awareness of how technology can affect the relationship important? What considerations and expected behaviors or boundaries should be set within the relationship so that technology can assist and not inhibit it?
2. How can rehabilitation counselors assess technological competencies? Why is such assessment important? Where in the rehabilitation process can such assessment be most effective?
3. Discuss how you would assess your own technological competencies. How would you find standards specific to your practice setting or location? Would the competency standards for clients be different from those for a rehabilitation counselor?
4. Identify a hypothetical case and outline an assistive technology assessment and plan to address the needs of the individual. How do you determine what might be the best assistive technology given the physical, mental, or cognitive functional abilities and the needs of the client?

5. What resources exist to help professionals and client with assistive technology in your community? How can you empower clients to access assistive technology resources over their work lives or life spans when they are no longer receiving services from you?

REFERENCES

American Psychological Association. (2020a). *Guidelines for the practice of telepsychology.* https://www.apa.org/practice/guidelines/telepsychology

American Psychological Association. (2020b). *How to do psychological testing via telehealth.* https://www.apaservices.org/practice/reimbursement/health-codes/testing/psychological-telehealth?_ga=2.946227.381489850.1596805320-778223338.1596805320

Andrea, H. (2022). *20 different types of technology in our world.* https://www.tech21century.com/different-types-of-technology

Assistive Technology Industry Association. (2022). *What is AT?* https://www.atia.org/home/at-resources/what-is-at/

Atske, S., & Perrin, A. (2021). *Home broadband adoption, computer ownership vary by race, ethnicity in the US.* Pew Research Center. https://www.pewresearch.org/fact-tank/2021/07/16/home-broadband-adoption-computer-ownership-vary-by-race-ethnicity-in-the-u-s

Augustyn, A. (n.d.). Technology. In B. J. Habibie, W. F. Ogburn, R. Solow, A. F. C. Wallace, & F. H. Cushing (Eds.), *Britannica.* https://www.britannica.com/technology/technology

Barlow, I. G., Liu, L., & Sekulic, A. (2009). Role of telehealth in seating clinics: A case study of learners' perspectives. *Journal of Telemedicine and Telecare, 11*(3), 146–149. https://doi.org/10.1258/1357633053688750

Barnwell, S. S., & Campbell, L. F. (2017). Ethical and legal aspects of the practice of teletherapy. In S. Walfish, J. E. Barnett, & J. Zimmerman (Eds.), *Handbook of private practice: Keys to success for mental health practitioners* (pp. 492–505). Oxford University Press.

Bell, M., Schein, R. M., Straatmann, J., Dicianno, B. E., & Schmeler, M. R. (2020). Functional mobility outcomes in telehealth and in-person assessments for wheeled mobility devices. *International Journal of Telerehabilitation, 12*(2), 27–34. https://doi.org/10.5195/ijt.2020.6335

Brearly, T. W., Shura, R. D., Martindale, S. L., Lazowski, R. A., Luxton, D. D., Shenal, B. V., & Rowland, J. A. (2017). Neuropsychological test administration by videoconference: A systematic review and meta-analysis. *Neuropsychology Review, 27*(2), 174–186. https://doi.org/10.1007/s11065-017-9349-1

Brown, C. (2021). *Health care clings to faxes as US pushes electronic records.* Bloomberg Law. https://news.bloomberglaw.com/health-law-and-business/health-care-clings-to-faxes-as-u-s-pushes-electronic-records

Byrne, A., & Hartley, M. (2010). Digital technology in the 12st century: Considerations for clinical supervision in rehabilitation counseling. *Rehabilitation Education, 24*(1/2), 57–67.

Caplan, S. E. (2002). Problematic Internet use and psychosocial well-being: development of a theory-based cognitive–behavioral measurement instrument. *Computers in Human Behavior, 18*(5), 553–575. https://doi.org/10.1016/S0747-5632(02)00004-3

Castillo, Y. A., & Cartwright, J. (2018). Telerehabilitation in rural areas: A qualitative investigation of pre-service rehabilitation professionals' perspectives. *Journal of Applied Rehabilitation Counseling, 49*(2), 6–13. https://doi.org/10.1891/0047-2220.49.2.6

Commission on Rehabilitation Counselor Certification. (2017). *Code of professional ethics for rehabilitation counselors.* Author.

Cottone, R. R., & Tarvydas, V. M. (2016). *Ethics and decision making in counseling and psychotherapy* (4th ed.). Springer Publishing.

Cottone, R. R., Tarvydas, V. M., & Hartley, M. T. (2022). *Ethics and decision making in counseling and psychotherapy* (5th ed.). Springer Publishing.

Davis, R. A., Flett, G. L., & Besser, A. (2002). Validation of a new scale for measuring problematic internet use: implications for pre-employment screening. *Cyberpsychology & Behavior, 5*(4), 331–345. https://doi.org/10.1089/109493102760275581

Degiorgio, L., Moore, S. F., Kampfe, C. M., & Downey, B. O. (2011). Teaching counseling skills using interactive television: Observations from a rehabilitation counseling classroom. *Journal of Applied Rehabilitation Counseling, 42*(3), 32–38. https://doi.org/10.1891/0047-2220.42.3.32

Denscombe, M. (2009). Item non-response rates: A comparison of online and paper questionnaires. *International Journal of Social Research Methodology, 12*(4), 281–291. https://doi.org/10.1080/13645570802054706

Distance Education Accreditation Commission. (2022). *DEAC history.* https://www.deac.org

Embree, J. A., Huber, J. M., Kapp, V. A., & Wilson, J. F. (2018). Utilizing telerehabilitation to deliver vocational rehabilitation services remotely as an alternative to traditional counseling. *Journal of Applied Rehabilitation Counseling, 49*(2), 40–47. https://doi.org/10.1891/0047-2220.49.2.40

Farmer, R. L., McGill, R. J., Dombrowski, S. C., Benson, N. F., Smith-Kellen, S., Lockwood, A. B., Powell, S., Pynn, C., & Stinnett, T. A. (2020a). Conducting psychoeducational assessments during the covid-19 crisis: The danger of good intentions. *Contemporary School Psychology, 25*(1), 27–32. https://doi.org/10.1007/s40688-020-00293-x

Farmer, R. L., McGill, R. J., Dombrowski, S. C., McClain, M. B., Harris, B., Lockwood, A. B., Powell, S. L., Pynn, C., Smith-Kellen, S., Loethen, E., Benson, N. F., & Stinnett, T. A. (2020b). Teleassessment with children and adolescents during the coronavirus (COVID-19) pandemic and beyond: Practice and policy implications. *Professional Psychology, 51*(5), 477–487. https://doi.org/10.1037/pro0000349

Goleman, D. (2007). *Flame first, think later: New clues to e-mail misbehavior.* New York Times. https://www.nytimes.com/2007/02/20/health/psychology/20essa.html

Graham, F., Boland, P., Grainger, R., & Wallace, S. (2019). Telehealth delivery of remote assessment of wheelchair and seating needs for adults with children: A scope review. *Disability and Rehabilitation, 42*(24), 1–11. https://doi.org/10.2196/preprints.9914

Grieve, R., & de Groot, H. T. (2011). Does online psychological test administration facilitate faking? *Computers in Human Behavior, 27*(6), 2386–2391. https://doi.org/10.1016/j.chb.2011.08.001

Grieve, R., & Hayes, J. (2016). Employment testing online, offline, and over the phone: Implications for e-assessment. *Revista de Psicología Del Trabajo y de Las Organizaciones, 32*(2), 95–101. https://doi.org/10.1016/j.rpto.2016.04.001

Herlihy, B., & Corey, G. (2015). *ACA ethical standards casebook* (7th ed.). American Counseling Association.

Hylton, K., Levy, Y., & Dringus, L. P. (2016). Utilizing webcam-based proctoring to deter misconduct in online exams. *Computers & Education, 92–93,* 53–63. https://doi.org/10.1016/j.compedu.2015.10.002

Kampfe, C. M., Smith, M. S., Manyibe, E. O., Sales, A. P., & Moore, S. F. (2009). Coping Strategies Used by Distance Rehabilitation Counseling Interns. *Rehabilitation Education, 23*(2), 77–86. https://doi.org/10.1891/088970109805059164

Kassam, A. (2021). *The outdated machine hampering the fight against COVID-19.* https://www.bbc.com/future/article/20210903-how-covid-19-could-finally-be-the-end-of-the-fax-machine

Kim, D.-H., & Huynh, H. (2010). Equivalence of paper-and-pencil and online administration modes of the statewide English test for students with and without disabilities. *Educational Assessment, 15*(2), 107–121. https://doi.org/10.1080/10627197.2010.491066

Kliff, S., & Sanger-Katz, M. (2020). Bottleneck for US coronavirus response: The fax machine. *The New York Times.* https://www.nytimes.com/2020/07/13/upshot/coronavirus-response-fax-machines.html

LaBerge, L., O'Toole, C., Schneider, J., & Smaje, K. (2020). *How COVID-19 has pushed companies over the technology tipping point – and transformed business forever.* McKinsey & Company. https://www.mckinsey.com/business-functions/strategy-and-corporate-finance/our-insights/how-covid-19-has-pushed-companies-over-the-technology-tipping-point-and-transformed-business-forever

Ladyshewsky, R. K. (2015). Post-graduate student performance in 'supervised in-class' vs. 'unsupervised online' multiple choice tests: implications for cheating and test security. *Assessment & Evaluation in Higher Education, 40*(7), 883–897. https://doi.org/10.1080/02602938.2014.956683

Leech, L. L., & Holcomb, J. M. (2004). Leveling the playing field: The development of a distance education program in rehabilitation counseling. *Assistive Technology, 16*(2), 135–143. https://doi.org/10.1080/10400435.2004.10132082

Lund, E. M., & Schultz, J. C. (2015). Distance Supervision in Rehabilitation Counseling: Ethical and Clinical Considerations. *Rehabilitation Research, Policy, and Education, 29*(1), 88–95. https://doi .org/10.1891/2168-6653.29.1.88

McClain, C., Vogels, E. A., Perrin, A., Sechopoulos, S., & Rainie, L. (2021). *The Internet and the pandemic.* Pew Research Center. https://www.pewresearch.org/internet/2021/09/01/the-internet -and-the-pandemic

Meade, A. W., Michels, L. C., & Lautenschlager, G. J. (2007). Are Internet and paper-and-pencil personality tests truly comparable? An experimental design measurement variance study. *Organizational Research Methods, 10*(2), 322–345.

Merriam-Webster. (2022). *High technology.* https://www.merriam-webster.com/dictionary/high% 20technology

Meyer, J. M. (2015). Counseling self-efficacy: On-campus and distance education students. *Rehabilitation Counseling Bulletin, 58*(3), 165–172. https:// doi .org/10.1177/0034355214537385

Morissette, S., Bezyak, J. L., & Ososkie, J. N. (2012). A close look at distance-based supervisory relationships in master's level rehabilitation counseling programs. *Journal of Applied Rehabilitation Counseling, 43*(2), 3–8. https://doi.org/10.1891/0047-2220.43.2.3

National Academy of Neuropsychology. (2020). *Inter organizational practice committee recommendations/guidance for teleneuropsychology (TeleNP) in response to the COVID-19 pandemic.* https://www .nanonline.org/docs/PAIC/PDFs/Provisional%20Recommendations-Guidance%20for%20Te leneuropsychology-COVID-19.pdf

Öz, H., & Özturan, T. (2018). Computer-based and paper-based testing: Does the test administration mode influence the reliability and validity of achievement tests? *Journal of Language and Linguistic Studies, 14*(1), 67–85.

Pearson. (2020a). *Administering the Vineland-3 via telepractice.* https://www.pearsonassessments .com/professional-assessments/digital-solutions/telepractice/telepractice-and-the-vineland-3 .html

Pearson. (2020b). *Resources for your changing needs: Telepractice FAQs.* Pearson Assessments.

Pearson. (2020c). *Staying connected through telepractice.* https://www.pearsonassessments.com/pro-fessional-assessments/digital-solutions/telepractice/about.html

Pearson. (2020d). *Telepractice and the WISC-V.* https://www.pearsonassessments.com/professional -assessments/digital-solutions/telepractice/telepractice-and-the-wisc-v.html

Pearson. (2020e). *Telepractice no objection letter.* https://www.nebpsych.org/resources/Documents/ Pearson%20telepractice-no-objection-letter.pdf

Perrin, A., & Atske, S. (2021). *Americans with disabilities less likely than those without to own some digital devices.* Pew Research Center. https://www.pewresearch.org/fact-tank/2021/09/10/americans -with-disabilities-less-likely-than-those-without-to-own-some-digital-devices

Reamer, F. G. (2015). Clinical social work in a digital environment: Ethical and risk-management challenges. *Clinical Social Work Journal, 43*(2), 120–132. https://doi.org/10.1007/s10615-014 -0495-0

Richards, D., & Viganó, N. (2013). Online counseling: A narrative and critical review of the literature. *Journal of Clinical Psychology, 69*(9), 994–1011. https://doi.org/10.1002/jclp.21974

Riverside Insights. (2020). *Tips for remote assessment using Riverside Insights clinical products.* https:// cms.riversideinsights.com/uploads/519ab0340e984ab097cea670c02f328b.pdf

Rummell, C. M., & Joyce, N. R. (2010). "So wat do u want to wrk on 2day?": The ethical implications of online counseling. *Ethics & Behavior, 20*(6), 482–496. https://doi.org/10.1080/10508422.2010 .521450

Schein, R. M., Schmeler, M. R., Holm, M. B., Saptono, A., & Brienza, D. M. (2010). Telerehabilitation wheeled mobility and seating assessments compared with in person. *Archives of Physical Medicine and Rehabilitation, 91*(6), 874–878. https://doi.org/10.1016/j.apmr.2010.01.017

Schein, R. M., Schmeler, M. R., Saptono, A., & Brienza, D. (2010). Patient satisfaction with telerehabilitation assessments for wheeled mobility and seating. *Assistive Technology, 22*(4), 215–222. https://doi.org/10.1080/10400435.2010.518579

Scherer, M. J., Craddock, G., Gelderblom, G. J., & de Witte, L. P. (2002). Matching Person & Technology (MPT) assessment process. *Technology and Disability, 14*(3), 125–131. https://doi.org/10.3233/ TAD-2002-14308

Shea, V. (1994). *Netiquette.* http://www.albion.com/bookNetiquette

Shechtman, N., & Horowitz, L. M. (2003). *Media inequalities in conversation: How people behave differently when interacting with computers and people.* Conference on Human Factors in Computing Systems, Ft. Lauderdale, FL.

Sheperis, C. J. (2020). *Assessment procedures for counselor and helping professionals* (9th ed.). Pearson.

Smith-Jackson, T. L., & Williges, R. C. (2001). Remote measurement methods for user-centered design of telesupport systems. *Assistive Technology, 13*(2), 106–115. https://doi.org/10.1080/10400435.2001.10132041

Society for Personality Assessment. (2020). *Tele-assessment of personality and psychopathology: COVID-19 task Force to Support Personality Assessment.* https://resources.personality.org/www.personality.org/General/pdf/SPA_Personality_Tele-Assessment-Guidance_6.10.20.pdf

Stolwyk, R., Hammers, D. B., Harder, L., & Cullum, C. M. (2020). *Teleneuropsychology (TeleNP) in response to COVID-19 Practical guidelines to balancing validity concerns with clinical needs.* https://www.the-ins.org/files/webinars/20200402_covid19/INS_COVID19_Webinar-20200402.pdf

Suler, J. (2004). The online disinhibition effect. *Cyberpsychology & Behavior, 7*(3), 321–326. https://doi.org/10.1089/1094931041291295

Taherbhai, H., Seo, D., & Bowman, T. (2012). Comparison of paper–pencil and online performances of students with learning disabilities. *British Educational Research Journal, 38*(1), 61–74. https://doi.org/10.1080/01411926.2010.526193

The Free Dictionary. (2022). *Low technology.* https://www.thefreedictionary.com/low+technology

Ting-Feng, W., Ming-Chung, C., Yao-Ming, Y., Hwa-Pey, W., & Chang, S. C. H. (2014). Is digital divide an issue for students with learning disabilities? *Computers in Human Behavior, 39,* 112–117. https://doi.org/10.1016/j.chb.2014.06.024

U.S. Department of Education, Office of Civil Rights. (2021). *Education in a pandemic: The disparate impacts of COVID-19 on America's students.* https://www2.ed.gov/about/offices/list/ocr/docs/20210608-impacts-of-covid19.pdf

U.S. Department of Health and Human Services. (2021). *Notification of enforcement discretion for telehealth remote communications during the COVID-19 nationwide public health emergency.* https://www.hhs.gov/hipaa/for-professionals/special-topics/emergency-preparedness/notification-enforcement-discretion-telehealth/index.html

U.S. Department of Labor, Bureau of Labor Statistics. (2021). *Occupational outlook handbook.* https://www.bls.gov/ooh

U.S. Department of Labor, Office of Disability Employment Policy. (2022a). *Job accommodation network.* https://askjan.org

U.S. Department of Labor, Office of Disability Employment Policy. (2022b). *Searchable online accommodations resource.* https://askjan.org/soar.cfm

Vogels, E. A. (2021). *Digital divide persists even as Americans with lower incomes make gains in tech adoption.* Pew Research Center. https://www.pewresearch.org/fact-tank/2021/06/22/digital-divide-persists-even-as-americans-with-lower-incomes-make-gains-in-tech-adoption

Welfel, E. R. (2013). *Ethics in counseling and psychotherapy: Standards, research, and emerging issues* (5th ed.). CENGAGE Learning.

Western Psychological Services. (2020a). *17 assessment terms and what they mean.* https://www.wps-publish.com/17-assessment-industry-terms-and-what-they-mean

Western Psychological Services. (2020b). *Statement on tele-assessment.* https://content.wpspublish.com/Submitted-Content/pdfs/WPS%20Tele-assessment%20Statement.pdf

Wheeler, M. N., & Bertram, B. (2019). *The counselor and the law: A guide to legal and ethical practice* (8th ed.). American Counseling Association.

Wright, J. (2020). *APA guide for tele-assessment.* http://www.thetestingpsychologist.com/apa-guidelines-for-remote-assessment-w-dr-jordan-wright

Wright, J., Mihura, J. L., Pade, H., & McCord, D. M. (2020). *Guidance on psychological tele-assessment during the COVID-19 crisis.* https://www.apaservices.org/practice/reimbursement/health-codes/testing/tele-assessment-covid-19

Young, L. (2021). Death to faxes: COVID-19 highlights the need for interoperability. *Journal of AHIMA.* https://journal.ahima.org/death-to-faxes-covid-19-highlights-the-need-for-interoperability

CHAPTER 22

Clinical Supervision

JARED C. SCHULTZ, TRENT LANDON, AND ASHLEY J. BLOUNT

LEARNING OBJECTIVES:

After reading this chapter, you should be able to:

- *Apply different models of clinical supervision, including their main components and considerations for their use.*
- *Discuss the importance of the supervisory working alliance.*
- *Identify strategies for strengthening the supervisory working alliance.*
- *Discuss strategies for conducting supervision in a multicultural environment.*
- *Discuss the indivisible self-model of wellness and how it can be utilized in the supervisory process.*

CACREP STANDARDS

CACREP 2016 CORE: 2F1.g, 2F1.i, 2F1.l, 2F1.m, 2F2.c, 2F2.d
CACREP 2016 Specialties
   Clinical Rehabilitation Counseling: 5D2.a, 5D2.s, 5D2.s
   Rehabilitation Counseling: 5H1.b, 5H2.a, 5H2.q

INTRODUCTION

The process of clinical supervision plays a central role in the training of new rehabilitation counselors (RCs). Maintaining the integrity of the counseling profession, supervisors observe the work of new professionals, evaluate their performance, provide feedback, and facilitate their competency in clinical practice. It is for this purpose that clinical supervision is an expressed element of the formal education of counselors, and thus an accreditation requirement of the supervised practicum and internship experiences (Council for the Accreditation of Counseling and Related Educational Programs [CACREP], 2016). In addition to counselors in training receiving supervision as part of their graduate training, clinical supervision is a requirement of each state's counselor licensure process. Each state requires a certain amount of supervised clinical experience beyond what occurs in graduate training in order for an RC to demonstrate their ability to practice independently and obtain independent licensure as a counselor.

The requirement of clinical supervision is part of the socialization and professionalization of counselors. It is logical that those who are new to the profession will benefit from an intensive learning process focused on the implementation of one's craft. In fact, early-career counselors learn their craft by **practicing under supervision**, meaning they provide counseling services only when supervised by a more experienced counselor with advanced knowledge (Hartley & Shaheed, 2021). Furthermore, even experienced counselors tend to engage in consultation or consultation groups that involve peer supervision as a reciprocal arrangement among experienced clinicians to discuss and process clinical and ethical decisions. In this way, supervision is foundational to what it means to be a professional counselor. Having said that, there remains a significant amount of misunderstanding surrounding the clinical supervision process, and its effective implementation in practice. The purpose of this chapter is to provide the reader with a clear understanding of what clinical supervision is, how it is best implemented, and how it can play a role in attending to the wellness of professionals in the counseling field.

COMPLEXITIES OF CLINICAL SUPERVISION

Defining clinical supervision seems to be a simple task at first glance. However, as we peel back the layers of the supervisory process, a complex and often intricate process is revealed. When monitoring client safety and welfare, supervisors are expected to balance the roles of mentor and teacher with that of evaluator and gatekeeper as their supervisees learn to practice as professional counselors. Before getting into the specific definition of clinical supervision, it is important to first address the purpose of the general supervisory process.

The supervisory process can be divided into three primary functions. These include clinical supervision, administrative supervision, and professional mentorship to foster the development of the supervisee (Henderson, 2009; Schultz, 2008). Of these three functions, the clinical and administrative functions have received the most attention in the counseling literature. In contrast, an emphasis on how to foster the professional development of new counselors has received less attention. Furthermore, there continues to be a need to differentiate a clinical supervision focus on advancing the clinical competencies of the supervisee with an administrative supervision focus on supporting the supervisee to follow agency policies and protocols that are necessary within any clinical practice environment.

The role of **professional mentorship** is to foster the professional development of the supervisee. The focus of this type of mentorship is to help the supervisee to develop a sense of professional identity as they join and engage the profession, and to begin conceptualizing their professional trajectory as an RC. Professional mentorship is made up of many interactions over time, as opposed to a single event or intervention. RCs' professional identity development, goal development, and engaging the profession require that supervisees be exposed to the potential roles and functions in the profession, and current issues affecting professionals and clients. They also must have the opportunity to gain a deeper understanding of the inner workings of the profession through dialogue with an established colleague. While conversations of this sort may not have a direct impact on the administrative or clinical process with a client, they can have a significant impact on the long-term trajectory of a supervisee's career.

The intent of **administrative supervision** is to ensure that "agency needs are met, policies are understood and enforced, and that the mission of the organization is carried out at the local level" (Schultz, 2008, p. 38). Practices associated with administrative supervision may include guidance on policy activities such as documentation, program enrollment, billing, and report writing. The administrative supervision process is concerned primarily with oversight of a supervisee to ensure that all the professional requirements of the job or position are being met in an efficacious manner. Administrative supervision is necessary because it ensures that the legal and regulatory requirements of the agency are being met; however, administrative supervision on its own does not address the knowledge, skill, and dispositional development of the supervisee. For this reason, it is important that counselors receive not only administrative supervision but also clinical supervision to practice counseling ethically and effectively.

Clinical supervision is focused on counselor development and performance, rather than administrative oversight. Practices associated with clinical supervision assist the supervisee in developing their knowledge, skills, and personal dispositions that will subsequently enhance their clinical performance and development as a clinician. While clinical and administrative supervision can complement one another, it is important to note that the primary purpose of clinical supervision is to protect the safety and welfare of clients as new generations of counselors gain competence. As part of clinical supervision, the supervisor attends to not only the counseling sessions between a supervisee and client but also the developmental level of the supervisee. In this way, clinical supervisors are responsible for providing corrective feedback to support the supervisee's growth and development. This is a complex and often intricate process that is reflected in the definition of clinical supervision.

DEFINITION OF CLINICAL SUPERVISION

A common definition of clinical supervision is provided by Bernard and Goodyear (2019): "an intervention provided by a senior member to a more junior member of the profession" in a supportive and evaluative relationship that extends over time, and has "the simultaneous purposes of enhancing the professional functioning of the more junior person(s); monitoring the quality of professional services offered to the clients that she, he, or they see; and serving as a gatekeeper for the particular profession" (p. 9). The following are key components of the definition of clinical supervision.

Supervision Is Provided by a Senior Member of the Profession

Clinical supervision usually is provided by a more senior member of the profession to a junior member. This distinction is less about the amount of time the clinical supervisor has been in the field and more about the acquired experience and knowledge necessary to effectively engage in the purposes of supervision. To ensure supervision is within the supervisor's scope of clinical competence, supervisors and their supervisees must engage in ongoing discussions regarding the anticipated areas of clinical practice that will be supervised, including how to proceed when a supervisee's need for guidance exceeds the supervisor's areas of clinical competence (Hartley & Shaheed, 2021). The consideration of becoming a clinical supervisor must take into account the level of clinical competency and whether the supervisor would be effective in fostering that competence in someone else's developmental process. It is not a given that a counselor who has been in the field for a long time will be competent to provide clinical supervision. Rather, it is important to consider areas of clinical and supervisory competence.

Supervision Is Grounded in the Supervisory Relationship

The clinical supervision process is grounded in the supervisory relationship between the supervisor and the supervisee. It is within the context of that relationship that all of the purposes of the supervisory process are accomplished. The supervisory working alliance is central to the supervision process and is the most discussed and researched construct in the clinical supervision literature (Bernard & Goodyear, 2019; Borders, 2014; Schultz, 2008). The quality of the supervisory working alliance is related directly to the quality of the supervisory process, and thus a necessary part of the process of clinical supervision. The supervisory working alliance is discussed in a later section as a critical component of effective clinical supervision.

Supervision Is Evaluative

Evaluation is an essential element of clinical supervision. In order for supervisees to grow and enhance their professional functioning, they must have an understanding of their current functioning level and areas for potential improvement. Evaluations that occur in the context of clinical supervision may be both formal and informal. In other words, standardized assessment tools may be utilized to assess a supervisee's functioning in a particular area. The evaluation process also may consist of informal assessment processes, or observation and discussion regarding a particular aspect of practice. The evaluative process within supervision may be formative or summative in nature. **Formative evaluation** occurs frequently and over time to help guide the learning and development process. This process is usually more immediate and impactful on the development of the skills, knowledge, and dispositions of the supervisees as it is in closer proximity to the clinical process and specific events. **Summative evaluation** is the process utilized to assess the total growth made during a determined time. This process is best demonstrated by the midterm and final evaluations that an intern might receive from supervisors as part of their educational process or a yearly evaluation in a work environment.

Supervision Is Hierarchical

The supervisory relationship, while developmental in nature, is also hierarchical. This means that supervisors by virtue of the position they hold, have a responsibility to direct the activities of the supervisory process, and they directly influence the behaviors of those they supervise. Supervisors are responsible legally and ethically for the services being provided to the clients by their supervisees (Schultz, 2015). While the supervisory process may include a nondirective manner to maximize the supervisee's growth and development, there may be times that a directive approach becomes necessary. This recognition of the hierarchical relationship is important in establishing the roles of those participating in the supervisory process.

Supervision Extends Over Time

The supervisory process requires time to accomplish the developmental goals of the supervisee. Obtaining input on a short-term basis, or for a single case, often is referred to as professional consultation. Consultation is different from clinical supervision as the roles and relationships of the participants are significantly different. Also, within the consultation process, the hierarchical aspect of supervision does not exist, meaning that the supervisee does not have to follow the directions of the supervisor. Time is required to assess supervisees' current level of functioning and then to design interventions and supports to enhance the supervisee's functioning. Within the graduate training necessary to become a professional counselor, the amount of time may be over the course of a semester (or quarter) or two. Following graduation, the length of time one receives clinical supervision in the workplace usually will depend on the requirement for obtaining licensure as a professional counselor and the requirements of a particular agency. In some cases, agencies will continue to provide supervision to those who already have licensure with a lifelong learning approach to supervision as a best practice.

Supervision Enhances the Supervisee's Professional Functioning

The primary purpose of the supervisory process is to enhance the professional functioning of the supervisee. Professional functioning is dependent upon many different considerations, including the development of specific counseling skills, as well as the application of professional knowledge in real time with clients. Supervisees need to acquire and refine their direct counseling skills. These skills include the ability to conduct a counseling interview, tracking verbal and nonverbal behavior, and approaching clients in an empathetic manner. Those skills, however, will be ineffective unless they are paired with the professional knowledge (constructs and concepts) that is related directly to the issues being addressed in the counseling process. In addition to gaining counseling skills, supervisees must solidify their understanding of a wide range of constructs and concepts to become effective rehabilitation counselors.

In addition to counseling knowledge and skills, attention needs to be given to the personal and professional dispositions of the supervisees (Sabella et al., 2020). **Dispositions** refer to how supervisees conduct themselves in the context of the counseling relationship, and thus are directly related to their professional functioning. Professional and personal dispositions may include such qualities as being empathetic and caring, warmth, genuineness, cooperation, flexibility, and awareness of one's impact on others. While developed on a personal level, these characteristics have a direct impact on a counselor's ability to engage in a therapeutic working alliance. It has been suggested that "asking questions [using a counseling skill] without concurrent empathy [a counseling value] . . . is interrogation, not counseling" (Dollarhide, 2013, p. 221). Personal and professional dispositions reflect the values of the practitioner; thus, dispositions moderate counseling skills and help build the counseling relationship. Therefore, personal and professional dispositions that impact the quality of their counseling relationships must be addressed as well.

Supervision Monitors the Quality of Services

The clinical supervisor has an ethical and legal responsibility for the clinical services that are being provided to their supervisee's clients. To meet this responsibility effectively, the supervisor must monitor the quality of the clinical services being provided. This monitoring process may include the direct observation of services (using either live or video or audio recordings), case presentations including detailed case conceptualization, reviewing documentation, and the evaluation of supervisees' work and process. It is expected that if the quality of services is evaluated at being below the requisite level, then the supervisor will act to correct the situation. This correction is accomplished most often by utilizing didactic instruction and/or demonstration to correct deficient performance in the supervisees. There may be situations where the supervisee's skill deficiency or behavior is sufficient to warrant a more aggressive response, such as removing the person from the clinical environment until satisfactory improvement is demonstrated. This type of response is generally the exception rather than the rule.

Supervision Serves as a Form of Gatekeeping

Supervisors in both educational and agency settings serve in the role of gatekeepers for the profession. In other words, they have an influence on whether a person is allowed to enter the profession. While this approach may seem like an exclusionary practice, it is a critical role that is based on ethical and legal responsibility to the welfare of clients who receive services. Clients who receive counseling services generally are in a vulnerable position, especially psychologically. The counseling profession has an obligation to those who seek our services to provide a level of protection for them. The counseling codes of ethics (e.g., the ACA, the CRCC) acknowledge that sometimes professionals are impaired or incapacitated due to personal issues, and that they may need to step away from providing services to remain ethical in their practice. In these cases, a supervisor may play a role in helping that professional recognize the need to step away and support them in that endeavor. Individuals wishing to enter the counseling profession may demonstrate significant unresolved psychological concerns, attitudes and beliefs, or personal dispositions that interfere with their ability to form a therapeutic working alliance with vulnerable populations. When this happens, the best outcome that can be expected is an ineffective counseling process. At worst, the outcome could result in harm being done to the client. In these situations, it may prove detrimental to clients to endorse that person for entry into the profession. The gatekeeper role requires the supervisor to be honest and direct in their assessment and evaluation processes, and to identify such potential concerns in order to protect those vulnerable populations who seek counseling services.

THE SUPERVISORY WORKING ALLIANCE

Bordin (1983) was one of the early scholars to delineate the elements of the **supervisory working alliance** (SWA) as the working relationship between a supervisee and supervisor. Bordin proposed that the SWA consisted of three primary elements: (a) agreement on goals, (b) agreement on tasks, and (c) an emotional bond. In other words, an effective SWA was defined as the supervisor and supervisee having agreement on what they were going to do, how they were going to do it, and an interpersonal connection that was positive in nature. This three-part model has served as the basis for most of the research and development of SWA knowledge since its inception more than 30 years ago. Subsequent work has added detail to our understanding of the SWA to include components such as the supervisory contract.

Supervisory Contract

One of the most consistent recommendations for those engaging in clinical supervision is to develop a supervisory contract. While there is not a single method or outline of a supervisory contract, there is general agreement that its purpose is to outline the expectations for both the supervisor and supervisee, and clarify the specific details of the supervisory process. One can see how this process will make a significant positive impact on the development of the SWA as it helps to clarify the goals and tasks of supervision, and by clarifying expectations helps to foster trust in the supervisory relationship.

The supervisory contract can consist of many different components, including the frequency and duration of supervision sessions, as well as whether supervision will be in an individual or group process. In the case of clinical supervision within a counselor education program, some of these format questions are addressed by accreditation standards. CACREP (2016) accreditation allows for **individual supervision**, which is one supervisee and one supervisor, **triadic supervision** when there are two supervisees who meet with the supervisor at the same time, or **group supervision** with multiple supervisees and one supervisor. Accreditation standards also require that practicum students and interns receive at least an hour of clinical supervision from an agency supervisor each week. This standard is to ensure that students have adequate contact with an agency supervisor to facilitate their development and growth process, while also protecting the welfare of clients who receive services through the agency.

Beyond these time requirements laid out by accreditation, the question of frequency and duration are important to consider when establishing a supervisory contract. The fundamental question is whether there is an adequate opportunity for the supervisee to engage in a meaningful learning process. It is not unusual for agency supervisors to be extremely busy and adopt an "as needed" approach to clinical supervision. This approach results in the focus of supervision being on an immediate need, and reducing the amount of time available for proactive learning and reflection. It is thus a best practice for a clinical supervisor to have an open-door approach to address immediate needs that might arise, while also maintaining a consistent schedule of meeting with supervisees at regular points in time.

Beyond the format of the supervisory process, there are a number of other areas that the supervisory contract can address. For instance, it is helpful for the supervisor and supervisee to engage in discussions about the supervisor's style of supervision, the roles of both the supervisor and supervisee, and the foci of the supervisory process (Schultz, 2006). These discussions orient and address what issues will be addressed in the supervisory process, how the supervisor will approach that work, and what is expected of everyone participating. Additional topics may include the supervision theories, models, and techniques to be utilized as a part of the supervisory process. To avoid confusion and surprises when working together, it can be helpful to explore the cultural worldview of both the supervisor and supervisee as part of the supervisory contract discussion. Key concepts may include what the supervisee wants to accomplish out of the supervisory process, their values, cultural background, and general outlook on the process of professional and personal growth and how these topics fit with the supervisor's perspective.

The intent of the supervisory contract is to increase transparency in supervision. The developmental purposes of clinical supervision are best accomplished when the expectations and rules for engaging in the process are explicit and understood by all participants. While an initial supervisory contract may be written early in the supervision relationship, the complexity of all the elements of the supervisory contract requires that some of these conversations continue as part of an ongoing process.

Inherent Power Differential

The nature of the supervisory relationship contains an inherent power differential between the supervisor and supervisee. This power differential is the result of the evaluative nature of supervision, the knowledge and experience of the supervisor, and the gatekeeping function of supervision. The inherent power differential warrants attention in the supervisory relationship. It holds the potential for having either a positive impact on the supervisory relationship, or having a destructive impact on the supervisory process.

One model of power within the supervisory process that has been applied to clinical supervision (Schultz et al., 2002) divides the power bases of the supervisor into five distinct areas. Based on the original work of French and Raven (1959), the sources of power are (a) legitimate power, (b) expert power, (c) reward power, (d) coercive power, and (e) referent power. **Legitimate power** is defined as the influence one has on others as a result of the role or position one holds. For instance, a person who has the job of a manager or supervisor has a right, and even a responsibility, to direct the work of those for whom they have responsibility. **Expert power** is the influence that one has on others as a result of the expertise that individual possesses. In this way, an expert may suggest a course of action, and the recipient acts on those suggestions because of the recognition that the expert knows more about a situation than the person seeking direction. In this case, it would be unwise to not follow the suggestions of the expert. **Reward power** is the influence someone can exert based on the ability to offer the people being influenced something that is beneficial to them. In this case, a supervisor might be able to offer a raise to a supervisee for following directions. **Coercive power** then is the opposite of reward power and occurs when a manager or supervisor is able to influence another's actions due to the threat of a negative consequence for not following instructions. An example of this might be using the threat of dismissal from a job or a program if directions or instructions are not followed. The final power base in this model of supervisory power is known as **referent power**, which is the influence that a supervisor can exert within the supervisory relationship that is the result of the supervisee identifying with the supervisor and feeling connected in a personal way.

Research has found that expert power and referent power both are significantly related to the quality of the SWA (Bernard & Goodyear, 2019; Schultz et al., 2002). The significance of this finding is that the SWA benefits when the inherent power differential is addressed in a strengths-based and interpersonal manner. The SWA grows in a positive way, and the influence of the supervisor grows through activities and conversations that help the supervisor and supervisee connect in more meaningful ways. The opposite of this statement is also true. Supervisors who are overly directive and controlling may erode the quality of the SWA.

Ethical Principles and the Supervisory Working Alliance

There is an important connection between the manner in which the supervisor demonstrates ethical behavior and the quality of the SWA. The ethics of supervision are connected directly to the discussion of how power is managed within the context of the supervisory relationship. When supervisees perceive the abuse of power within the supervisory relationship, the quality of the supervisory working alliance will be impacted negatively. The perception of abuse of power is complex.

A distinction is made between mandatory and aspirational levels of ethical behavior. **Mandatory ethical behavior** refers to those professional behaviors, the violation of which can result in corrective action by the organization enforcing the professional code of conduct, usually a license or credential organization (Cottone et al., 2021). Mandatory ethical behavior is derived from the specific standards set out in a code of ethics. **Aspirational ethical behavior** refers to those professional behaviors that do not violate the specific standards in a code of ethics, but instead relate to the quality of ethical behavior above and beyond the mandatory standards. In the context of the supervisory working alliance, it is possible for a supervisor to not violate the code of ethics (mandatory ethics) and still behave in a way that is perceived as being unethical by the supervisee (aspirational ethics) and thus damage the SWA. The management of the aspirational ethical behavior of the supervisor is located in the application of the ethical principles. In other words, the supervisor who is able to fully embody the ethical principles will be perceived as being more ethical by the supervisee (Schultz, 2011).

The first of the ethical principles are beneficence and nonmaleficence (ACA, 2014). These principles are closely related, and sometimes thought to be two sides of the same coin. **Beneficence** relates to "doing good," or being of benefit to those being supervised, whereas **nonmaleficence** means to "do no harm" to those being supervised. The principle of beneficence is observed when the supervisor seeks out those opportunities to benefit supervisees, and move them along in their development in helpful and supportive ways. A key consideration for this ethical principle is that something is beneficial in as much as it helps the supervisee in their developmental journey. An example of this orientation might be confronting a supervisee on their limited self-awareness. Such a confrontation may be uncomfortable for the supervisee, and it might be perceived as not being beneficial, but it is necessary for functioning as a rehabilitation counselor and is of ultimate benefit. The path of beneficence is not always the easiest or most comfortable. The principle of nonmaleficence is observed when the supervisor consistently and constantly considers the impact of what is happening in supervision and ensures that no harm is being done. This principle of "no harm" applies to both the supervisee and clients, as the supervisor monitors the work that the supervisee is doing with clients. One challenge for the implementation of this ethical principle is the consideration of both action and nonaction. In other words, harm can be done by not acting in a particular situation, as well as acting in a harmful way. This concept can be challenging for supervisors as they need to monitor the actions that are being taken in the supervision and counseling settings, and monitor as well the potential impact of not acting. Both of these principles rely upon a continuing and open dialogue and exploration between the supervisor and supervisee, because what constitutes benefit and harm most often are dependent on individual factors that the supervisee brings to the relationship. In other words, what is beneficial to one supervisee may not be beneficial to another.

The next ethical principle to consider is justice (ACA, 2014). The principle of **justice** addresses the sense of fairness in the interactions and demands placed on supervisees. It is important for supervisors to remember that the key to determining the sense of justice in the supervisory relationship is to consider the point of view of the supervisee. Regardless of the reasons a supervisor may have for doing a particular action within the supervisory process, if the supervisee perceives the action as not being fair, then the principle of justice has been violated from the supervisee's point of view. It is for this reason that having a rationale for what is done in supervision and making that rationale transparent with the supervisee are important. Ensuring that a supervisee understands the reasons behind the activities of supervision is fundamental to ensuring the principle of justice is a positive influence in the supervisory relationship.

The principle of **fidelity** involves following through on obligations and responsibilities within the context of the supervisory relationship (ACA, 2014), in other words doing what you say you are going to do. Fidelity is one of the key components toof the process of building trust within the supervisory relationship. Building trust requires two basic elements, risk and fidelity. To build trust requires one party in a relationship to feel a sense of risk, and the other party to demonstrate fidelity in response to the risk. This process might involve asking supervisees to be vulnerable in exploring their skills, deficits in their knowledge, or an emotional response to something that happened in the counseling process. In each of these examples, the supervisee is asked to be vulnerable, or to engage in a situation in which there is some perceived risk. A number of actions will help to build trust in the supervisory relationship including the demonstration of fidelity, following through on supporting the supervisee, not passing judgment, and engaging in a developmental process that addresses concerns in a supportive manner. Conversely, if the principle of fidelity is violated, then the process of building trust is destroyed and mistrust and suspicion grow in its place.

The principle of **veracity** encapsulates the process of being accurate and honest within the supervisory relationship (ACA, 2014). It is fairly obvious that being overtly dishonest within the supervisory relationship will have a negative impact on the SWA between a supervisor and a supervisee. However, this principle plays a critical role in the entire process of supervision. Providing supervisees evaluation and feedback on their performance, actions, and emotional response to the counseling process is a critical function of supervision. Veracity, then, relates to the accuracy of evaluation and feedback, the validity of the subsequent inferences related to the supervisees' performance, and the manner in which the corrective feedback is provided. This principle then requires the supervisor to be aware of concerns related to evaluation, and the potential for bias to influence the assessment and evaluation process. It also requires a supervisor to understand how best to engage the supervisee in the corrective feedback process. Accurate and honest feedback can be delivered in a compassionate and person-centered manner, which will facilitate the growth that is the purpose of the feedback in the first place.

The ethical principle of **autonomy** highlights the importance of the individual being in control of their own life and being in control of their decision-making process (ACA, 2014). Autonomy introduces a unique challenge into the supervisory process. While supervision is fundamentally a developmental process for the supervisee, it also has an oversight element. There may be times that a supervisor needs to be very directive with a supervisee to ensure that the quality of services being provided to a client is sufficient. On its face, this approach seems to be at odds with the principle of autonomy. It is important for supervisors to remember that autonomy is foundational to the process of growth and development. In order to take responsibility for outcomes, both positive and negative, supervisees need to be in control of their decision-making processes. Therefore, while there may be times that the supervisor needs to step in and be more directive, it is critical for the supervisor to educate the supervisee to the point that the decision of what to do is clear and facilitate the supervisee's development of the requisite skills to carry out the decision. In other words, the negative impact of the necessity of direction is reduced by collaboration, education, and inclusion of the supervisee in the decision-making process.

MODELS OF SUPERVISION

Since the inception of the field of counseling, clinical supervision has been a significant element of the training process. Early approaches to the supervisory process largely followed the theoretical orientation of the supervisors (Ancis & Ladany, 2010; Borders, 2005). For example, someone receiving supervision in the provision of a cognitive therapy approach would likely experience a primary focus on cognitive issues. As clinical supervision continued to evolve, atheoretical approaches to supervision were established that focused on the interpersonal process between supervisor and supervisee as well as the developmental needs of the supervisee (Ancis & Ladany, 2010; Ronnestad & Skovholt, 2013; Stoltenberg et al., 1998). The use of models of supervision is a foundational component of the supervisory process. Specifically, models of supervision provide the overarching framework for making sense of observations of supervisees, identifying the individual needs of the supervisee, and providing direction for how to address the needs of the supervisee effectively. There are many models of supervision, and many variations to the main approaches to supervision. In this section, we focus on three models that represent common approaches to clinical supervision.

Integrated Developmental Model

The Integrated Developmental Model (IDM; Stoltenberg & McNeill, 2010) details the developmental process that a counselor experiences through stages of their professional development and career. The developmental stages are divided into four distinct levels ranging from Level 1 to Level 3 integrated. At Level 1, the counselor is at the beginning of their professional development, which is characterized by limited counseling knowledge and experience. As a result of this lack of knowledge and experience, the Level 1 counselor is learning through focused attention on applying relationship skills and basic intervention strategies. At this stage, the Level 1 counselor generally lacks the sophistication to understand the nuances of the counseling process, relying largely on direct instruction from the supervisor. There is a preference for being told directly what to do because Level 1 counselors may still be of the belief that there is "one right way" to practice counseling. Supervisors need to be aware of this tendency as the supervisee may experience a significant level of anxiety when presented with nondirective instructions. With that said, supervisees who are in this stage of development generally are highly motivated and engaged in the counseling process.

The Level 2 counselors have gained counseling knowledge and experience and are able to shift attention from themselves toward a focus on the client's experience. Level 2 counselors tend to be less satisfied with "simple answers" and may engage the supervisor in dialogue that explores issues at a deeper level. This move towards more cognitive complexity is the result of recognizing the variation in counseling, and the uniqueness that each client may bring to the process. Level 2 counselors tend to demonstrate increased confidence, and as a result tend to strive for more autonomy in the counseling process. However, this attempt at more autonomy occurs at a developmental stage where there is still a fair amount of professional ignorance. At this stage, the supervisees are still mastering the body of literature that informs the counseling process and are becoming more aware of the limits of their knowledge and understanding. In fact, this awareness grows as a result of being exposed to more clients and more complex client issues. The result is that Level 2 counselors tend to demonstrate both certainty and uncertainty in their approach to counseling. Supervisors need to be aware of this tendency and facilitate learning processes that help the supervisee to acquire more knowledge and integrate that knowledge into their overall understanding. It is during this level as well that counselors make significant strides in formulating a cohesive theoretical approach to counseling.

Level 3 counselors have achieved a level of stability in the context of their professional identity, counseling skills, and theoretical orientation. Counselors at this level tend to be reflective regarding their practice and seek regular improvement, and are able to contextualize their professional deficiencies as areas of potential improvement without devaluing the work they are accomplishing. This reflection leads to an increased desire for professional development and growth. Counselors at this level also tend to experience increased confidence in dealing with unique and novel situations. Their problem-solving skills have developed sufficiently that they can independently address concerns that might arise in the counseling process. This growing sense of capacity in the counseling process leads them to seek a greater level of autonomy.

The final level of development is referred to as Level 3 Integrated. At this stage, counselors have become proficient across multiple domains and modalities, and may expand their professional practice beyond a single counseling theory or approach. At this stage, there is stable intrinsic motivation for continuous improvement as a counselor and strong desire for autonomy.

The value of a developmental model for the process of clinical supervision is that it helps the supervisor and supervisee to conceptualize the developmental nature of become a counselor. For example, it is important to consider that a Level 1 counselor may require more directive instruction, and to not do so may result in anxiety and confusion on the part of the supervisee. Thus, for Level 1 counselors, supervisors often engage in education and discussion around the counseling skills and techniques being implemented, including concrete examples. In this way, the needs of a counselor at that developmental level are met, and the requisite work for advancing to the next level in the model is addressed simultaneously.

The Discrimination Model

The Discrimination Model originally was proposed by Bernard (1979) to integrate the functions of supervision as attending to the supervisee's (a) process skills, (b) conceptualization skills, and (c) personalization skills. **Process skills** are those skills that can be observed directly in the interaction between the counselor and client. These skills would include the use of counseling micro-skills, ability to facilitate a counseling interview, the ability to form a therapeutic working alliance, and the implementation counseling interventions. **Conceptualization skills** are those covert behaviors and processes that the counselor utilizes in the context of the counseling process. These skills include understanding and following the client's communications regarding their experiences, identifying themes in the client's experience, applying theories and frameworks to the case, making appropriate observations of verbal and nonverbal behavior, and the ability to take all of the relevant information regarding the client and create a comprehensive representation of the concerns being addressed by that client. Finally, **personalization** includes the behaviors that are the more idiosyncratic experiences that the counselor has within the counseling process. These include comfort level in the counselor role, ability to hear challenges by the client, being comfortable with differences between the client's worldview and that of the counselor and having and demonstrating fundamental respect for the client.

Depending upon the needs of the supervisees, the roles that the supervisor may take are those of teacher, consultant, and counselor (Bernard, 1997). While in a **teacher role,** the supervisor may focus on providing more instruction to the supervisee in relation to the knowledge or skills being utilized in the counseling process. Instruction focused on presenting or reteaching knowledge is referred to as didactic instruction, and may include activities such as teaching concepts, discussing readings, or reviewing principles or concepts. Instruction focused on implementing knowledge into a therapeutic activity is skills-based instruction, and may include activities such as role-play, demonstration, or practice exercises. In contrast to the teaching role, the **consultant role** involves the supervisor fostering exploration with the supervisee to better understand and clarify the needs of the client. When supervisors recognize and validate the emotional response of the supervisee in engaging in the counseling process, they are functioning in the **counselor role**. It is important to recognize that the role of counselor is not to be the supervisee's personal counselor and work on their individual issues. In fact, that type of dual relationship is considered unethical. Rather, the role of counselor acknowledges the impact of the counseling process on the affective domain of the counselor, and the challenge that adjusting to this type of professional relationship can create.

The effective use of the Discrimination Model of Supervision is demonstrated when the supervisor is addressing the functions of supervision (process, conceptualization, personalization), and adopting the role that is most beneficial to the supervisees given their development and need. It is important to recognize that the supervision roles of teacher, consultant, and counselor may be a fairly fluid process. It is reasonable to assume that more time may be spent in a specific supervisor role with a particular supervisee (e.g., a new counselor needing more teaching, or a more experienced counselor benefiting from more time in the consultant role). It also is likely that counselors will require multiple roles at all stages of their development. For example, an experienced counselor who begins working with a new clientele or population may benefit from a supervisor taking on more teaching and counselor roles as the counselor acclimates to the new work environment. The role selection of the supervisor should be based on the immediate needs of the supervisee.

Systems Approach to Supervision

Holloway's (1995) Systems Approach (SA) incorporates more complexity into the supervisory process. According to the SA model, the supervisory relationship between the supervisor and supervisee is the central organizing component of the supervisory process. The supervisory relationship is composed of three primary elements, including the contract (a set of mutually established expectations), the interpersonal structure (power and involvement of the participants), and the phase (the manner in which the relationship develops over time) of the relationship. Factors that influence the supervisory relationship include the contextual factors of the institution, the supervisor's characteristics, the supervisee's characteristics, and the client's characteristics. Each of these contextual factors will have an influence on the contract, structure, and phase of the supervisory relationship. In addition to the supervisory relationship and contextual factors, the two remaining components of the SA model of supervision include the functions of supervision and the tasks of supervision.

The **functions of supervision** include (a) monitoring and evaluating, (b) instructing and advising, (c) modeling, (d) consulting, and (e) supporting. To complete these functions, the **tasks of supervision** are the professional activities of include (a) counseling skill, (b) case conceptualization, (c) professional role, (d) emotional awareness, and (e) self-evaluation. The utility of this model of supervision is manifest when the functions and tasks of supervision are combined in a process matrix. The matrix of supervision in Exhibit 22.1 provides a visual representation of what topics or issues need to be addressed in supervision (Tasks) and the manner in which they can be addressed (Functions). For example, to organize the process of supervision a supervisor and supervisee could sit down together and fill out activities that would go into each cell of the process matrix. Specific strategies are designated to monitor and evaluate topics such as counseling skills, and case conceptualization. As each cell is filled in the plan for supervision emerges. As the supervisee develops over time, it is necessary to revisit the process matrix to update

EXHIBIT 22.1 Systems Approach to Clinical Supervision Matrix

Tasks of Supervision

Functions of Supervision	Counseling Skills	Case Conceptualization	Professional Role	Emotional Awareness	Self - Evaluation
Monitoring / Evaluating					
Advising / Instructing					
Modeling					
Consulting					
Supporting					

Exhibit 22.1 Tasks of Supervision

Source: Modified from Holloway, E. (1995). *Clinical supervision: A systems approach*. Sage. (p. 35)

the strategies, as strategies for a new counselor may not be effective with a more developed counselor.

While there are many approaches and models for providing clinical supervision, we have discussed the IDM (Stoltenberg & McNeill, 2010), the Discrimination Model (Bernard, 1979, Bernard, 1997), and the SA (Holloway, 1995). Regardless of the approach, models of supervision play an important role in the supervisory process as they provide a conceptual framework for understanding what is occurring in the supervisory process, and outlining a process for moving forward. In other words, they are descriptive and prescriptive for the supervisory process.

MULTICULTURAL SUPERVISION

The inclusion of multicultural considerations in the supervisory process is paramount, and the importance of this focus cannot be overstated. Wilson et al. (2020) stated, "All interactions are multicultural" (p. 11), even when working with individuals from apparently similar backgrounds. Integrating multicultural considerations into the supervisory process entails much more than a set of skills, or a type of approach. To demonstrate multicultural sensitivity and competence in the supervisory process requires the clinical supervisor to be aware of and concerned with the manner in which they are interacting with their supervisees. In this section, we emphasize that multicultural competencies are required of every supervisor (and every counselor). This development is a part of a lifelong effort of understanding one's own cultural background, the impact of that background on one's current place in society, the experience of others from different backgrounds, and a constant effort to engage others in an inclusive and equitable way.

Multicultural competence increasingly has been a focus of clinical supervision. Early on, there was very little focus on the impact of culture on the supervisory process (Bernard & Goodyear, 2019). That situation has been changing over the last few decades, and more attention has been given to this issue. Research has found that the multicultural competence of the clinical supervisor has a direct influence on the quality of the supervisory working alliance (Crockett & Hays, 2015; Inman, 2006; Tsong & Goodyear, 2014). Wilson et al. (2020) indicated that when working with individuals from diverse backgrounds and populations, it is critical to provide validation of their cultural experience and worldview. The need for validation is brought into focus when consideration is given to the myriad ways that an individual's experience may be invalidated in society and in their communities. Validating another's experience will contribute significantly to the quality of the supervisory working alliance. Wilson et al. (2020) stated that "validation is giving truth to what another person is communicating and experiencing from their perspective or viewpoint" and "can be viewed as acknowledging the humanity of another person" (p. 41).

Bernard and Goodyear (2019) outlined four dimensions to which multiculturally competent supervisors attend as part of the supervisory process. The first dimension is the **intrapersonal identity** and the way in which different identities that the person has intersect and impact that person's sense of self. Second is the **interpersonal dimension**, which includes the expectations and prejudices toward another person based on their membership is specific (or multiple) groups. The third dimension is **interpersonal cultural identity and behavior**, whichincludes understanding the cultural influences that impact an individual's understanding of their world, and how they interpret normative social behavior. The fourth dimension is the **sociopolitical**, which is an understanding of the privilege or oppression that an individual experiences based on a number of different factors (e.g., race, gender, sexual orientation, etc.). These four dimensions provide a starting place for supervisors to begin a self-reflective practice. The self-reflective process is critical as these four dimensions require authenticity from the participants of supervision. Inauthenticity in this process will break the potential trust between supervisor and supervisee. It will destroy efforts of validating the experiences of others, and will impact the supervisory working alliance negatively, potentially to the point of being a traumatic experience for those who hold less power within that relational dynamic.

Ancis and Marshall (2010) conducted a qualitative study to explore and identify behaviors in which the supervisor can engage that will have a beneficial impact on the multicultural experience of the supervisees. They identified six domains of multicultural behaviors that facilitated a positive experience for those receiving supervision:

A. Supervisor—Focused Personal Development
    a. Demonstrates strengths and limitations of multicultural knowledge.
    b. Proactively introduces multicultural issues in supervision.
    c. Self-discloses cultural biases, cultural background, values, and/or experiences.
    d. Demonstrates awareness of the clinical significance of racism and oppression.
E. Supervisee—Focused Personal Development
    a. Facilitates discussions of the impact of supervisee's cultural background on clients.
    b. Encourages increased multicultural awareness via discussions and activities.
C. Conceptualization
    a. Encourages consideration of cultural assumptions and counselor stereotyping.
    b. Actively engages supervisee in an exploration of the client's perspective.
C. Interventions
    a. Encourages consideration of the client's role in goal setting.
    b. Encourages supervisee to facilitate the client's awareness regarding social issues.

C. Process
   a. Conveys acceptance of cultural differences in supervisory relationships.
   b. Facilitates a safe and open supervisory climate in which the supervisee can be vulnerable and take risks.
   c. Initiates and engages in discussions about power dynamics.
D. Evaluation
   a. Identifies the supervisee's multicultural strengths and weaknesses.
   b. Multicultural discussions positively affected client outcomes.

Foundational to the process of growing in one's multicultural awareness and competence is the approach one takes towards growth in this area. The concept of cultural humility is an emerging construct in the discussions on multicultural and cross-cultural counseling and supervision. Zhu et al. (2021) noted that cultural humility "has been proposed to entail both intrapersonal and interpersonal dimensions. Intrapersonally, humble individuals have an accurate view of self, and interpersonally, they maintain an other-oriented stance, characterized by respect, openness, and lack of superiority" (p. 73). Supervisors should work on the development of cultural humility, as the acquisition of that trait will influence all aspects of their supervisory practice. They will be able to engage in authentic interactions with their supervisees and be able to model for them the manner in which they can engage their clients in similar exchanges in the therapeutic environment (see Box 22.1).

ADDRESSING WELLNESS IN SUPERVISION

The concept of wellness has been receiving increased attention in the counseling literature, and has been identified as an integral element of the helping professions (Blount & Lambie, 2018; Myers & Sweeney, 2005). While much of the focus in the professional literature may be on how to assist clients in achieving desired wellness outcomes, more attention has been turning toward the wellness practices and experiences of professionals in the counseling field. El-Ghoroury et al. (2012) found that over 70% of the graduate students surveyed in their study ($n = 387$) experienced a "stressor that interfered with their optimal functioning" (p. 122). Not only are psychology graduate students entering a challenging interpersonally based field where there is the potential for secondary trauma, compassion fatigue, and burnout (Blaylock, 2019), but they also experience the stressors of meeting the demands of graduate studies programs. Practitioners who have graduated similarly are faced with the challenges of working in an emotionally intense setting. They need to maintain their own psychological health in order to be optimally engaged in the counseling process. It is for this reason that counselors should be attending to their own wellness process.

Supervisors have an ethical and legal responsibility for the welfare of both the clients who are receiving services, and for the counselors they supervise (Schultz, 2015). Part of this responsibility is monitoring the performance of the counselor. If stressors potentially can interfere with a professional's optimal functioning, then an important component of the supervisory process is to facilitate a supervisee's engagement in wellness practices which will help to reduce the negative impact of stressors on daily function. To accomplish this end, it is helpful to have a working understanding of the model of wellness, and how to include it in the supervisory process.

While there have been many different models of wellness proposed over the years, the empirical evidence most strongly supports two models (Myers & Sweeney, 2008), the wellness wheel model (Myers et al., 2000) and the **indivisible self (IS) model** (Myers & Sweeney, 2005). The IS model was developed by conducting advanced statistical analysis of data collected to measure the wellness wheel model of wellness, and resulted in rearranging the relationships between the factors being studied. The result is that the IS

BOX 22.1 CASE CONCEPTUALIZATION

Maria is a new rehabilitation counselor who was hired to work in your agency two months ago. She recently graduated with her graduate degree in clinical rehabilitation counseling and was hired after completing her practicum and internship with your agency. During her practicum and internship, you served as her clinical supervisor, and continue to provide clinical supervision as she accumulates postgraduate hours for state licensure and a national certification. Maria was an excellent student and was very successful in her internship.

Maria immigrated to the United States from Honduras with her parents and grandparents when she was years old, and grew up in a small southern town in Texas. She went to schools that were predominantly White and was very aware of the differences between her family and her friends' families. The biggest difference that she noticed in comparison to her white friends was the structure of her family. She lived with her parents, two brothers, and her grandparents. Her grandparents played a significant role in her upbringing, while many of her friends had limited contact with their grandparents. In fact, she relied heavily on her grandparents when she was in high school and trying deal with many of the challenges of adolescents. She remembers her grandfather consoling her on one occasion and saying, "It will be okay. Our family can make it through anything."

During your last supervision session with Maria, she mentioned a concern about one of her clients. She goes on to describe her client, Megan, who is an adolescent female seeking treatment for depression and anxiety. Megan was raised in the Dallas area. She lives with both of her parents but doesn't have any siblings. She reports that before she turned 11, her father worked and her mother stayed home. But 3 years ago her mother got a job selling real estate in the Dallas area, and Megan spends a lot of time alone at home. In a previous session, Maria suggested that it would be good to include the client's parents in a counseling session. Upon reflection, Maria acknowledged that her client seemed somewhat uncomfortable with the idea. However, Maria strongly encouraged that a family session would be important for the client. The client's mother attended the next session but reported that the father was too busy to come. She went on to say, "I am not sure he would be much help anyway. He works and watches football, that is about it." During the counseling session, the mother talked about all the things that were wrong with the client, encouraging Maria to "work your magic." Maria wasn't comfortable interrupting the mother, who would talk for a long time. When Maria tried to talk, the mother would interrupt and start talking again.

Maria shared that during the next one-on-one session, her client was "distant" and would not engage in conversations. When Maria asked her what was wrong, she said, "Nothing really. This just doesn't seem to be helping very much. My life still stinks." Maria tried to console and reassure the client, but these attempts to reassure seemed to not be heard.

In the supervision session, Maria reflected: "I know something has changed, but I am not sure what it is. We have gotten off track, and the client seems to be worse now than before. I am worried that I may have done something to hurt her. It has been keeping me up at night. What do you think? What should I do?"

Case Discussion Questions

1. What does Maria's openness with you tell you about the quality of the supervisory working alliance?

(continued)

> ## BOX 22.1 CASE CONCEPTUALIZATION (*CONTINUED*)
> 2. What developmental level does Maria seem to be at, and what does she need to help her progress?
> 3. What are possible cultural influences that may be impacting Maria's interactions with this client? What are some specific strategies that a supervisor might use to explore these cultural influences?
> 4. Maria seems to have been affected personally by this experience. What are some wellness considerations you might discuss with her to help her manage the stressors she is experiencing?
> 5. What supervisory roles might you assume to help Maria deal with this situation? What specifically would you address from the position of each role?

model closely resembles and actually evolved from, the Wellness Wheel model. It represents the more empirically based approach to wellness (Hattie et al., 2004).

The IS model fundamentally is based on the Adlerian principle that the self is unified and indivisible (Myers & Sweeney, 2008). This holistic approach recognizes the interrelatedness of the various aspects of a person's life. In this respect, all the components of the model are necessary and require attention, and ignoring any particular part of a person's life will have an impact on the other aspects of their life. In the IS model, the self is composed of five second-order factors, including the creative, coping, social, essential, and physical. Each of these is then made up of third-order factors. Creative consists of thinking, emotions, control, work, and positive humor. Coping is made up of leisure, stress management, self-worth, and realistic beliefs. The social factor includes friendship and love. The essential element includes spirituality, gender identity, cultural identity, and self-care. Finally, the physical factor consists of exercise and nutrition. The IS model also recognizes that the individual experiences these factors in a variety of contexts. These contexts include local—safety (e.g., family, neighborhood, community), institutional—policies and laws (e.g., education, religion, government, business/industry), global—world events (e.g., politics, culture, global events, environment, media, community), and chronometrical—life span (e.g., perpetual, positive, purposeful). The level of wellness that an individual experiences is dependent on the manner and extent to which the individual attends to these factors in a holistic manner.

These constructs can be helpful to the supervisory process. One of the consistent foci of supervision is working with supervisees to increase their self-awareness and self-evaluation, and helping them to take responsibility for their own well-being. This evaluation can be done by utilize a four-step process that includes the following: recognize, plan, implement, and evaluate.

Step 1: Recognize

This step may be the most challenging part of the process of improving wellness. Supervisees benefit from direct conversations about their wellness, and how they are handling the emotion and stress of the counseling process. Supervisors need to be aware that even though direct questions may help to introduce the topics, supervisees may be hesitant to disclose any concerns for fear of being misunderstood or judged. Appropriate levels of self-disclosure by the supervisor can assist in reducing this concern. Additionally, the supervisees may be feeling that they are the only individuals who experience life balance and wellness challenges. Normalizing and validating their experiences will help reduce the stress related to disclosure and help strengthen the supervisory working alliance. In some cases, a wellness assessment tool, such as the Helping Professional Wellness Discrepancy Scale (Blount &

Lambie, 2018), may help to externalize the experience and assist supervisees in obtaining some level of insight into their own experience.

Step 2: Plan

Once recognition is achieved, and the supervisees have an understanding of the challenges they are experiencing related to their wellness, then the planning process can begin. It will be helpful to review the second- and third-order factors of the model and identify the areas that the supervisee currently may be ignoring or is less diligent in attending to them. Discussion regarding the factors, and how the supervisee defines and values each of them, can be productive. Included in this conversation can be topics such as past experience, cultural expectations, and familial values. This is a process that will help the supervisee generate a personal vested interest in pursuing an individually determined goal related to their wellness. Finally, in the planning process it is helpful to outline specific goals, remembering to keep them simple, attainable, and measurable and to account for adequate time to accomplish them.

Step 3: Implement

The implementation of the plan is the next step. During this phase, the role of the supervisor is to be supportive and empowering rather than demanding or providing "oversight." In extreme cases in which supervisees may be experiencing significant events that impair their ability to perform their counseling duties, they require more intensive intervention by the supervisor. In other cases the supervisor will benefit by remembering that this is a personal process of growth in which the supervisee has voluntarily engaged. As such, it is the supervisee's responsibility, and the supervisor's role is to be supportive to the extent that the supervisee requests support. It may be helpful to remember that significant changes in personal habits require time and often involve failure to follow through or reverting to one's previous behaviors. In cases where the supervisee has not accomplished the goal, or reverted back to previous behaviors, the supervisor can be of assistance by providing a reframe of "failure." The supervisor can assist in contextualizing the event in terms of positive growth and encourage the supervisee to start again.

Step 4: Evaluate

The final stage is the evaluation stage. The process of reviewing with supervisees how the process worked, what was accomplished, what next steps may be, and how they responded emotionally to the process is beneficial. The evaluation process should refer to the original goals that were set, what the expectations were at the beginning of the process, and what strategies were helpful in realizing progress. It is at this stage that future growth goals can be identified and discussed.

While wellness plays an important role in the emotional stability and experience of supervisees, focus on this process should be kept in the context of the entire supervisory enterprise. Supervisors should keep in mind that there are many things to accomplish in the limited amount of time that is allotted for supervision. They may benefit from tempering their efforts in addressing wellness so that it does not overshadow other priorities in supervision. A key consideration in this process of determining the extent to which wellness should be addressed is the ethical principle of autonomy. The role of the supervisor in this process is to be supportive, not to mandate wellness. The ability to choose the path and manner of addressing wellness should rest with the supervisees. If not, they will not be able to take responsibility and realize growth and development in those areas on which they are focusing.

CONCLUSION

The process of clinical supervision is foundational to the growth and development of new and emerging professionals. It is potentially a very rewarding and stimulating experience that benefits everyone who participates. It is a complex process that relies heavily on the quality of the supervisory working alliance for success, and requires the supervisor and supervisee to be dedicated to realizing the intent of supervision through the establishment of structure in the process. When clinical supervision is done well, the immediate benefit is a higher functioning clinician. The secondary benefits include higher job satisfaction, an increased sense of efficacy in the counseling process, and ultimately improved outcomes in the counseling process.

CONTENT REVIEW QUESTIONS

1. The supervisory working alliance is central to the clinical supervision process. What are the three primary components of the supervisory working alliance, and why is each important to the process of establishing a positive working relationship between the supervisor and supervisee?
2. Define the inherent power differential in supervision. Why does it exist in the supervisory relationship? What are some strategies a supervisor can use to reduce it in the supervisory relationship?
3. List the ethical principles that are related to the supervisory process. For each principle, provide an example of a supervisor implementing it in practice.
4. Describe the benefits for a supervisor utilizing a model of clinical supervision in their supervisory practice.
5. What are some specific examples of how a supervisor having multicultural competence will facilitate the supervisory process?
6. What are the primary factors for a supervisor and supervisee to consider related to the supervisee's wellness? What are some strategies that you would recommend for supervisees to try to improve their wellbeing?

REFERENCES

American Counseling Association. (2014). *2014 ACA code of ethics.* https://counseling.org/knowledge-center

Ancis, J. R., & Ladany, N. (2010). A multicultural framework for counselor supervision. In N. Ladany & L. J. Bradley (Eds.), *Counselor supervision* (pp. 53–95). Routledge.

Ancis, J. R., & Marshall, D. S. (2010). Using a multicultural framework to assess supervisee's perceptions of culturally competent supervision. *Journal of Counseling & Development, 88*(3), 277–284. https://doi.org/10.1002/j.1556-6678.2010.tb00023.x

Bernard, J. M. (1979). Supervisor training: A discrimination model. *Counselor Education and Supervision, 19*(1), 60–68. https://doi.org/10.1002/j.1556-6978.1979.tb00906.x

Bernard, J. M. (1997). The discrimination model. In C. E. Watkins (Ed.), *Handbook of psychotherapy supervision* (pp. 310–327). Wiley.

Bernard, J. M., & Goodyear, R. K. (2019). *Fundamentals of clinical supervision* (6th ed.). Pearson.

Blaylock, E. L. (2019). *Identity development of counseling students: Empathy, mindfulness, and compassion as predictors of countertransference, secondary traumatic stress, and client-related burnout.* Publication No. 979860732107) [Doctoral dissertation, Trevecca Nazarene University]. ProQuest Dissertations and Theses Global(.

Blount, A. J., & Lambie, G. W. (2018). Development and factor structure of the helping professional wellness discrepancy scale. *Measurement and Evaluation in Counseling and Development, 51*(2), 92–110. https://doi.org/10.1080/07481756.2017.1358060

Borders, L. D. (2005). *Tracing the development of clinical supervision* [Conference Plenary Session]. First International and Interdisciplinary Conference on Clinical Supervision. https://doi.org/10.1300/J001v24n01_02

Borders, I. D. (2014). Best practices in clinical supervision: Another step in delineating effective supervision practice. *American Journal of Psychotherapy, 68*(2), 151–162. https://doi.org/10.1176/appi.psychotherapy.2014.68.2.151

Bordin, E. S. (1983). A working alliance model of supervision. *The Counseling Psychologist, 11*(1), 35–42. https://doi.org/10.1177/0011000083111007

Cottone, C. C., Tarvydas, V. M., & Hartley, M. T. (2021). *Ethics and decision making in counseling and psychotherapy* (5th ed.). Springer. https://doi.org/10.1891/9780826135292

Council for the Accreditation of Counseling and Related Educational Programs. (2016). *2016 CACREP standards*. https://www.cacrep.org/for-programs/2016-cacrep-standards

Crockett, S., & Hays, D. G. (2015). The influence of supervisor multicultural competence on thesupervisory working alliance, supervisee counseling self-efficacy, and supervisee satisfaction with supervision: A mediation model. *Counselor Education and Supervision, 54*(4), 258–273. https://doi.org/10.1002/ceas.12025

Dollarhide, C. T. (2013). Using a values-based taxonomy in counselor education. *Counseling and Values, 58*(2), 221–236. https://doi.org/10.1002/j.2161-007X.2013.00035.x

El-Ghoroury, N. H., Galper, D. I., Sawaqdeh, A., & Bufka, L. F. (2012). Stress, coping, and barriers to wellness among psychology graduate students. *Training and Education in Professional Psychology, 6*(2), 122–134. https://doi.org/10.1037/a0028768

Hartley, M. T., & Shaheed, C. (2021). Ethics of counseling supervision. In C. C. Cottone, V. M. Tarvydas, & M. T. Hartley (Eds.), *Ethics and decision making in counseling and psychotherapy* (5th ed., pp. 331–150). Springer.

Hattie, J. A., Myers, J. E., & Sweeney, T. J. (2004). A factor structure of wellness: Theory, assessment, analysis, and practice. *Journal of Counseling & Development, 82*(3), 354–364. https://doi.org/10.1002/j.1556-6678.2004.tb00321.x

Henderson, P. G. (2009). *The new handbook of administrative supervision in counseling*. Routledge. https://doi.org/10.4324/9780203887301

Holloway, E. (1995). *Clinical Supervision: A Systems Approach*. Sage. https://doi.org/10.4135/9781452224770

Inman, A. G. (2006). Supervisor multicultural competence and its relation to supervisory process and outcome. *Journal of Marital and Family Therapy, 32*(1), 73–85. https://doi.org/10.1111/j.1752-0606.2006.tb01589.x

Myers, J. E., & Sweeney, T. J. (2008). Wellness counseling: The evidence base for practice. *Journal of Counseling & Development, 86*(4), 482–493. https://doi.org/10.1002/j.1556-6678.2008.tb00536.x

Myers, J. E., & Sweeney, T. J. (2005). *Wellness in counseling: Theory, research, and practice*. American Counseling Association.

Myers, J. E., Sweeney, T. J., & Witmer, J. M. (2000). The wheel of wellness counseling for wellness: A holistic model for treatment planning. *Journal of Counseling & Development, 78*(3), 251–266. https://doi.org/10.1002/j.1556-6676.2000.tb01906.x

Ronnestad, M. H., & Skovholt, T. M. (2013). *The developing practitioner: Growth and stagnation of therapists*. Routledge.

Sabella, S. A., Landon, T. J., McKnight-Lizotte, M., & Bernacchio, C. P. (2020). How do supervisors assess and develop professional dispositions among counselors in vocational rehabilitation agencies? A qualitative inquiry. *The Clinical Supervisor, 39*(1), 106–127. https://doi.org/10.1080/07325223.2020.1729919

Schultz, J. C. (2006). Implementing clinical supervision in rehabilitation agencies. *Directions in Rehabilitation Counseling, 17*(10), 109–119.

Schultz, J. C. (2008). The tripartite model of supervision for rehabilitation counselors. *Journal of Applied Rehabilitation Counseling, 39*(1), 36–41. https://doi.org/10.1891/0047-2220.39.1.36

Schultz, J. C. (2011). Construction and validation of a supervisor principle ethics scale. *The Australian Journal of Rehabilitation Counselling, 17*(2), 96–105. https://doi.org/10.1375/jrc.17.2.96

Schultz, J. C. (2015). Ethical practice in human services administration. In C. Flowers, J. Soldner, & S. Robertson (Eds.), *Clinical Supervision and Administrative Practices in Allied Health Professions*. Aspen.

Schultz, J. C., Ososkie, J. N., Fried, J. H., Nelson, R. E., & Bardos, A. N. (2002). Clinical supervision in public rehabilitation counseling settings. *Rehabilitation Counseling Bulletin, 45*(4), 213–222. https://doi.org/10.1177/00343552020450040401

Stoltenberg, C. D., & McNeill, B. W. (2010). *IDM supervision: An integrative developmental model for supervising counselors and therapists.* Routledge.

Stoltenberg, C. D., McNeill, B. W., & Delworth, U. (1998). *IDM supervision: An integrated developmental model for supervising counselors and therapists.* Jossey-Bass.

Tsong, Y., & Goodyear, R. K. (2014). Assessing supervision's clinical and multicultural impacts: The supervision outcome scale's psychometric properties. *Training and Education in Professional Psychology, 8*(3), 189–195. https://doi.org/10.1037/tep0000049

Wilson, K. B., Chao, S. Y., & Lusk, S. L. (2020). *Clinical supervision: Understanding diversity and interpersonal dynamics – Nuances and outcomes.* Aspen.

Zhu, P., Luke, M., & Bellini, J. (2021). A grounded theory analysis of cultural humility in counseling and counselor education. *Counselor Education and Supervision, 60*(1), 73–89. https://doi.org/10.1002/ceas.12197

APPENDIX A

Acronyms for Common Terms in Rehabilitation Counseling

BY CATEGORIES

Selected Organizations

ACA	American Counseling Association

Subdivisions of the ACA

ACES	Association for Counselor Education and Supervision
AGLGBTIC	Association for Lesbian, Gay, Bisexual, and Transgender Issues in Counseling
ARCA	American Rehabilitation Counseling Association
IAMFC	International Association for Marriage and Family Counseling
MRECC	Multiracial/Ethnic Counseling Concerns Interest Network
NCDA	National Career Development Association
NRA	National Rehabilitation Association

Subdivisions of the NRA

NAMRC	National Association of Multicultural Rehabilitation Concerns (formerly National Association of Non-White Workers [NANRW])
RCEA	Rehabilitation Counselors and Educators Association

Other Organizations

AAMFT	American Association for Marriage and Family Therapy
ABVE	American Board of Vocational Experts
ACCD	American Coalition of Citizens with Disabilities
ADAPT	American Disabled for Adaptive Public Transportation
ADARA	Professionals Networking for Excellence in Service Delivery with Individuals who are Deaf or Hard of Hearing (formerly American Deafness and Rehabilitation Association)
AMCHA	American Mental Health Counselors Association
APA	American Psychological Association
APGA	American Personnel and Guidance Association (became the American Counseling Association)
APRIL	Association of Programs for Rural Independent Living

ASCA	American School Counseling Association
ATIA	Assistive Technology Industry Association
ATP	Assistive Technology Professionals
CMSA	Case Management Society of America
CSAVR	Council of State Administrators of Vocational Rehabilitation
IARP	International Association of Rehabilitation Professionals (formerly National Association of Rehabilitation Professionals in the Private Sector)
NAMI	National Alliance on Mental Illness
NCIL	National Council on Independent Living
NCRE	National Council on Rehabilitation Education
NRCA	National Rehabilitation Counseling Association
RCC	Rehabilitation Counseling Consortium
RCLF	Rehabilitation Counseling Leadership Forum
RESNA	Rehabilitation Engineering and Assistive Technology Society of North America
RET	Rehabilitation Engineering Technologists
SDS	Society for Disability Studies
SMS	Seating and Mobility Specialists
UN	United Nations

Specialized Agencies of the UN/Acronyms

ClinFIT	Universal ISPRM Clinical Functioning Information Tool
CRPD	Convention on the Rights of Persons with Disabilities
CSDH	Commission on Social Determinants of Health
ICBDSR	International Clearinghouse for Birth Defects Surveillance and Research
ICD	International Classification of Diseases and Related Health Problems
ICF	International Classification of Functioning, Disability and Health
ICF-CY	Children and Youth Version of the International Classification of Functioning, Disability and Health
ICIDH	International Classification of Impairments, Disabilities and Handicaps
ILO	International Labour Organization
ISPRM	International Society of Physical and Rehabilitation Medicine
MDG	Millennium Development Goals
UNAIDS	UN Programme on HIV/AIDS
UNDP	United Nations Development Programme
UNESCO	United Nations Educational, Scientific and Cultural Organization
UNICEF	United Nations International Children's Emergency Fund
WHO	World Health Organization
WHODAS	World Health Organization Disability Assessment Schedule

CERTIFICATION BODIES/CREDENTIALS/LICENSURE

AASCB	American Association of State Counseling Boards
CFT	Certified Family Therapist
CCM	Certified Case Manager
CCMC	Commission for Case Manager Certification
CCMHC	Certified Clinical Mental Health Counselor
CDMS	Certified Disability Management Specialist
CRC	Certified Rehabilitation Counselor
CRCC	Commission on Rehabilitation Counselor Certification
CVE	Certified Vocational Evaluator
CRCE	Certified Rehabilitation Counselor Examination

LCPC	Licensed Clinical Professional Counselor
LCMHC	Licensed Clinical Mental Health Counselor
LMHC	Licensed Mental Health Counselor
LMHP	Licensed Mental Heal Practitioner
LPC	Licensed Professional Counselor
LPCC	Licensed Professional Clinical Counselor
MAC	Master Addiction Counselor
NBCC	National Board for Certified Counselors
NCA	National Credentialing Academy
NCC	National Certified Counselor
NCCA	National Commission for Certifying Agencies
NCE	National Counseling Examination
NCLEP	National Counselor Licensure Endorsement Process
NCMHCE	National Clinical Mental Health Counseling Examination
NCSC	National Certified School Counselor

ACCREDITATION BODIES

ASPA	Association of Specialized and Professional Accreditors
CACREP	Council for Accreditation of Counseling and Related Educational Programs
CAAHEP	Commission on Accreditation of Allied Health Programs
CHEA	Council for Higher Education Accreditation
CoRA	Committee on Rehabilitation Accreditation
CORE	Council on Rehabilitation Education (became a corporate affiliate of CACREP)
CORPA	Commission on Recognition of Postsecondary Accreditation (formerly Council on Postsecondary Accreditation [COPA])
CUSA	Commission on Undergraduate Standards and Accreditation (formerly Committee on Undergraduate Education)
DEAC	Distance Education Accrediting Commission
IRCEP	International Registry of Counselor Education Programs
URR	Undergraduate Rehabilitation Registry (CACREP Registry)

GOVERNMENTAL/LEGISLATIVE

ACA	Patient Protection and Affordable Care Act
ACTKIT	Assertive Community Treatment Knowledge Informing Transformation
ADA	Americans with Disabilities Act
ADAAA	ADA Amendments Act
AHRQ	Agency for Health Care Research and Quality
ARP	American Rescue Plan
BLS	Bureau of Labor Statistics
CDC	Centers for Disease Control and Prevention
CIL	(or ILC) Center for Independent Living
CMHC	Certified Mental Health Counselor (designated independent practitioner under TRICARE)
CSPD	Comprehensive System of Personnel Development
DBTAC	Disability and Business Technical Assistance Center
DHHS	Department of Health and Human Services
DOL	Department of Labor
DOT	Dictionary of Occupational Titles
DRRP	Disability and Rehabilitation Research Program
EEOC	Equal Employment Opportunity Commission

EHB	Essential Health Benefits
EN	Employment Network
FMLA	Family and Medical Leave Act
GINA	Genetic Information Nondiscrimination Act
HIPAA	Health Insurance Portability and Accountability Act
HITECH	Health Information Technology for Economic and Clinical Health Act
HPSA	Health Provider Shortage Area
HRSA	Health Resources and Services Administration
HUD	Housing and Urban Development
IDEA	Individuals with Disabilities Education Act
IEP	Individual Educational Plan
IOM	Institute on Medicine
IPE	Individual Plan of Employment (formerly Individualized Written Rehabilitation Plan [IWRP])
IPR	Individual Plan for Retirement
KTDRR	Knowledge Translation for Disability and Rehabilitation Research Center
KTER	Knowledge Translation for Employment Research Center
MHPAEA	Mental Health Parity and Addiction Equity Act
NIDILRR	National Institute on Disability, Independent Living and Rehabilitation Research
NIMH	National Institutes on Mental Health
NSDU	National Survey on Drug Use and Health
OCR	Office of Civil Rights
ODEP	Office of Disability Employment Policy
OFCCP	Office of Federal Contract Compliance Programs
OIS	Occupational Information System
O*Net	Occupational Information Network
OOH	Occupational Outlook Handbook
OSERS	Office of Special Education and Rehabilitative Services
PHI	Protected Health Information
RRTC	Rehabilitation Research and Training Center
RSA	Rehabilitation Services Administration
SAMHSA	Substance Abuse and Mental Health Services Administration
SMHC	Supervised Mental Health Counselor (designated under TRICARE)
SSA	Social Security Administration
SSDI	Social Security Disability Insurance
SSI	Supplemental Security Income
TRICARE	Military Health Care Insurance System
TWWIIA	Ticket to Work and Work Incentives Improvement Act
USERRA	Uniformed Services Employment and Reemployment Rights Act
VA	Veterans Administration
VEVRAA	Vietnam Era Veterans Readjustment Assistance Act
VRTAC-QE	Vocational Rehabilitation Technical Assistance Center for Quality Employment
WIA	Workforce Investment Act
WIOA	Workforce Innovation and Opportunity Act

CANADIAN ACRONYMS

CARP	Canadian Association of Rehabilitation Professionals
CCRC	Canadian Certified Rehabilitation Counselor

MISCELLANEOUS

AKSA	Attitudes and Beliefs, Knowledge, Skills and Action
AT	Assistive Technology
BIPOC	Black, Indigenous and People of Color
BLS	Basic Listening Sequence
BPS	Biopsychosocial Model
CBR	Community-Based Rehabilitation
CBRO	Community-Based Rehabilitation Organization
CBT	Cognitive Behavioral Therapy
C–C–C	Counseling–Coordinating–Consultation Model of Rehabilitation Counseling
CCI	Career Construction Interview
CCT	Career Construction Theory
CCT	Cognitive Coping Therapy
CDT	Critical Disability Theory
CET	Coping Effectiveness Training
CHW	Community Health Workers
CID	Chronic Illness and Disability
CIP	Cognitive Information Processing Theory
DALY	Disability-Adjusted Life Year
DBSA	Depression and Bipolar Support Alliance
DJ	Disability Justice
DRCC	Disability-Related Counseling Competencies
DSM	Diagnostic and Statistical Manual of Mental Disorders
EBP	Evidence-Based Practice
EMR	Electronic Medical Record
FACT	Forensic Assertive Community Treatment
FAVOR	Faces and Voices of Recovery
FIM	Functional Independence Measurement System
FRC	Forensic Rehabilitation Counselor
HMO	Health Maintenance Organization
HR	Human Resources
IDM	Integrated Development Model
IL	Independent Living
IPS	Individual Placement and Support
IS	Indivisible Self Model
JTA	Job-Task Analysis
KTA	Knowledge-to-Action Framework
LCP	Life Care Planning
LGBTQ	Lesbian, Gay, Bisexual, Transgender and Queer
LGBQQIA	Lesbian, Gay, Bisexual, Queer, Questioning, Intersex, and Ally
MDE	Major Depressive Episode
MPT	Matching Person and Technology Assessment
MHID	Multiple Heritage Identity Development
MSJCC	Multicultural and Social Justice Counseling Competencies
MTWA	Minnesota Theory of Work Adjustment
OJT	On-the-Job Training
PDR	Physicians Desk Reference
PFA	Psychological First Aid
PHN	Peer Health Navigator
POS	Point of Service
PPO	Preferred Provider Organization
Pre-ETS	Pre-Employment Transition Services

PSR	Psychosocial Rehabilitation
PWD	Persons with Disability
QOL	Quality of Life
RC	Rehabilitation Counselor
RCE	Rehabilitation Counselor Education
RCT	Randomized Clinical Trials
REBT	Rational Emotive Behavioral Therapy
RIASEC	Realistic, Investigate, Artistic, Social, Enterprising, and Conventional
SA	Systems Approach
SCI	Spinal Cord Injury
SFBT	Solutional Focused Brief Therapy
SGA	Substantial Gainful Activity
SMART	Self-Management and Recovery Training
SMI	Serious Mental Illness
SOAR	Searcheable Online Accommodation Resource
SUD	Substance Use Disorder
SWA	Supervisory Working Alliance
TIC	Trauma Informed Care
TRA	Transracial Adoption
TrAKN	Transracial Adoption Kinship Network
VR	Vocational Rehabilitation
WHAM	Whole Health Action Management
WRAP	Wellness Recovery Action Plan

ALPHABETICALLY

AAMFT	American Association for Marriage and Family Therapy
AASCB	American Association of State Counseling Boards
ABVE	American Board of Vocational Experts
ACA	American Counseling Association
ACA	Patient Protection and Affordable Care Act
ACCD	American Coalition of Citizens with Disabilities
ACE	Adverse Childhood Experience
ACES	Association for Counselor Education and Supervision
ACT	Acceptance and Commitment Therapy
ACT	Assertive Community Treatment
ACTKIT	Assertive Community Treatment Knowledge Informing Transformation
ADA	Americans with Disabilities Act
ADAAA	ADA Amendments Act
ADAPT	American Disabled for Adaptive Public Transportation
ADARA	Professionals Networking for Excellence in Service Delivery with Individuals who are Deaf or Hard of Hearing (formerly American Deafness And Rehabilitation Association)
ADL	Activities of Daily Living
AGLGBTIC	Association for Lesbian, Gay, Bisexual, and Transgender Issues in Counseling
AHRQ	Agency for Health Care Research and Quality
AKSA	Attitudes and Beliefs, Knowledge, Skills and Action
AMCHA	American Mental Health Counselors Association
AMI	Any Mental Illness
APA	American Psychological Association
APGA	American Personnel and Guidance Association (became the American Counseling Association)

APRIL	Association of Programs for Rural Independent Living
ARP	American Rescue Plan
ARCA	American Rehabilitation Counseling Association
ASCA	American School Counseling Association
ASL	American Sign Language
ASPA	Association of Specialized and Professional Accreditors
AT	Assistive Technology
ATIA	Assistive Technology Industry Association
ATP	Assistive Technology Professionals
BIPOC	Black, Indigenous and People of Color
BLS	Basic Listening Sequence
BLS	Bureau of Labor Statistics
BPS	Bio-Psycho-Social Model
CAAHEP	Commission on Accreditation of Allied Health Programs
CACREP	Council for Accreditation of Counseling and Related Educational Programs
CAP	Client Assistance Program
CARP	Canadian Association of Rehabilitation Professionals
CBR	Community-Based Rehabilitation
CBRO	Community-Based Rehabilitation Organization
CBT	Cognitive Behavioral Therapy
C-C-C	Counseling-Coordinating-Consultation Model of Rehabilitation Counseling
CCI	Career Construction Interview
CCM	Certified Case Manager
CCMC	Commission for Case Manager Certification
CCMHC	Certified Clinical Mental Health Counselor
CCRC	Canadian Certified Rehabilitation Counselor
CCT	Career Construction Theory
CCT	Cognitive Coping Therapy
CDC	Centers for Disease Control and Prevention
CDMS	Certified Disability Management Specialist
CFT	Certified Family Therapist
CHEA	Council for Higher Education Accreditation
CIL	(or ILC) Center for Independent Living
ClinFIT	Universal ISPRM Clinical Functioning Information Tool
CMHC	Certified Mental Health Counselor (designated independent practitioner under TRICARE)
CoRA	Committee on Rehabilitation Accreditation
CORE	Council on Rehabilitation Education
CORPA	Commission on Recognition of Postsecondary Accreditation (formerly Council on Postsecondary Accreditation [COPA])
CRC	Certified Rehabilitation Counselor
CRCC	Commission on Rehabilitation Counselor Certification
CRCE	Certified Rehabilitation Counselor Examination
CRPD	Convention on the Rights of Persons with Disabilities
CSDH	Commission on Social Determinants of Health
CSPD	Comprehensive System of Personnel Development
CUSA	Commission on Undergraduate Standards and Accreditation (formerly Committee on Undergraduate Education)
CVE	Certified Vocational Evaluator
DALY	Disability-Adjusted Life Year
DBSA	Depression and Bipolar Support Alliance
DBTAC	Disability and Business Technical Assistance Center
DEAC	Distance Education Accrediting Commission

DHHS	Department of Health and Human Services
DJ	Disability Justice
DOL	Department of Labor
DOT	Dictionary of Occupational Titles
DRCC	Disability-Related Counseling Competencies
DRRP	Disability and Rehabilitation Research Program
DSM	Diagnostic and Statistical Manual of Mental Disorders
EBP	Evidence-Based Practice
EEOC	Equal Employment Opportunity Commission
EHB	Essential Health Benefits
EMR	Electronic Medical Record
EN	Employment Network
FACT	Forensic Assertive Community Treatment
FAVOR	Faces and Voices of Recovery
FIM	Functional Independence Measurement System
FMLA	Family and Medical Leave Act
FRC	Forensic Rehabilitation Counselor
GINA	Genetic Information Nondiscrimination Act
HIPAA	Health Insurance Portability and Accountability Act
HITECH	Health Information Technology for Economic and Clinical Health Act
HMO	Health Maintenance Organization
HPSA	Health Provider Shortage Area
HR	Human Resources
HRSA	Health Resources and Services Administration
HUD	Housing and Urban Development
IAMFC	International Association for Marriage and Family Counseling
IARP	International Association of Rehabilitation Professionals
ICBDSR	International Clearinghouse for Birth Defects Surveillance and Research
ICD	International Classification of Diseases and Related Health Problems
ICF	International Classification of Functioning, Disability and Health
ICF-CY	Children and Youth Version of the International Classification of Functioning, Disability and Health
ICIDH	International Classification of Impairments, Disabilities and Handicaps
IDM	Integrated Development Model
IL	Independent Living
ILO	International Labour Organization
IDEA	Individuals with Disabilities Education Act
IEP	Individual Educational Plan
IOM	Institute on Medicine
IPE	Individual Plan of Employment (formerly Individualized Written Rehabilitation Plan [IWRP])
IPR	Individual Plan for Retirement
IPS	Individual Placement and Support
IRCEP	International Registry of Counselor Education Programs
IS	Indivisible Self Model
ISPRM	International Society of Physical and Rehabilitation Medicine
JTA	Job-Task Analysis
KTA	Knowledge-to-Action Framework
KTDRR	Knowledge Translation for Disability and Rehabilitation Research Center
KTER	Knowledge Translation for Employment Research Center
LCP	Life Care Planning
LCPC	Licensed Clinical Professional Counselor
LCMHC	Licensed Clinical Mental Health Counselor
LGBTQ	Lesbian, Gay, Bisexual, Transgender and Queer

LGBQQIA	Lesbian, Gay, Bisexual, Queer, Questioning, Intersex, and Ally
LMHC	Licensed Mental Health Counselor
LMHP	Licensed Mental Health Practitioner
LPC	Licensed Professional Counselor
LPCC	Licensed Professional Clinical Counselor
MAC	Master Addiction Counselor
MDE	Major Depressive Episode
MDG	Millennium Development Goals
MHID	Multiple Heritage Identity Development
MHPAEA	Mental Health Parity and Addiction Equity Act
MPT	Matching Person and Technology Assessment
MRECC	Multiracial/Ethnic Counseling Concerns Interest Network
MSJCC	Multicultural and Social Justice Counseling Competencies
MTWA	Minnesota Theory of Work Adjustment
NAMI	National Alliance on Mental Illness
NAMRC	National Association of Multicultural Rehabilitation Concerns (formerly National Association of Non-White Workers [NANRW])
NBCC	National Board for Certified Counselors
NCA	National Credentialing Academy
NCC	National Certified Counselor
NCCA	National Commission for Certifying Agencies
NCDA	National Career Development Association
NCE	National Counseling Examination
NCIL	National Council on Independent Living
NCLEP	National Counselor Licensure Endorsement Process
NCMHCE	National Clinical Mental Health Counseling Examination
NCRE	National Council on Rehabilitation Education
NCSC	National Certified School Counselor
NIDILRR	National Institute on Disability, Independent Living and Rehabilitation Research
NIMH	National Institutes on Mental Health
NRA	National Rehabilitation Association
NRCA	National Rehabilitation Counseling Association
NSDU	National Survey on Drug Use and Health
OJT	On-the-Job Training
OCR	Office of Civil Rights
ODEP	Office of Disability Employment Policy
OFCCP	Office of Federal Contract Compliance Programs
OIS	Occupational Information System
O*Net	Occupational Information Network
OOH	Occupational Outlook Handbook
OSERS	Office of Special Education and Rehabilitative Services
PDR	Physicians Desk Reference
PFA	Psychological First Aid
PHI	Protected Health Information
PHN	Peer Health Navigator
POS	Point of Service
PPO	Preferred Provider Organization
Pre-ETS	Pre-Employment Transition Services
PSR	Psychosocial Rehabilitation
PWD	People (or Persons) with Disability
QOL	Quality of Life
RC	Rehabilitation Counselor
RCC	Rehabilitation Counseling Consortium

RCE	Rehabilitation Counselor Education
RCEA	Rehabilitation Counselors and Educators Association
R/CID	Racial/Cultural Identity Development
RCLF	Rehabilitation Counseling Leadership Forum
RCT	Randomized Clinical Trials
REBT	Rational Emotive Behavioral Therapy
RESNA	Rehabilitation Engineering and Assistive Technology Society of North America
RET	Rehabilitation Engineering Technologists
RIASEC	Realistic, Investigate, Artistic, Social, Enterprising, and Conventional
RRTC	Rehabilitation Research and Training Center
RSA	Rehabilitation Services Administration
SA	Systems Approach
SAMHSA	Substance Abuse and Mental Health Services Administration
SDS	Society for Disability Studies
SFBT	Solutional Focused Brief Therapy
SGA	Substantial Gainful Activity
SMART	Self-Management and Recovery Training
SMHC	Supervised Mental Health Counselor (designated under TRICARE)
SMI	Serious Mental Illness
SMS	Seating and Mobility Specialists
SOAR	Searcheable Online Accommodation Resource
SSA	Social Security Administration
SSDI	Social Security Disability Insurance
SSI	Supplemental Security Income
SUD	Substance Use Disorder
SWA	Supervisory Working Alliance
TIC	Trauma Informed Care
TRA	Transracial Adoption
TrAKN	Transracial Adoption Kinship Network
TRICARE	Military Health Care Insurance System
TWWIIA	Ticket to Work and Work Incentives Improvement Act
UN	United Nations
UNAIDS	UN Programme on HIV/AIDS
UNDP	United Nations Development Programme
UNESCO	United Nations Educational, Scientific and Cultural Organization
UNICEF	United Nations International Children's Emergency Fund
URR	Undergraduate Rehabilitation Registry (CACREP Registry)
USERRA	Uniformed Services Employment and Reemployment Rights Act
VA	Veterans Administration
VEVRAA	Vietnam Era Veterans Readjustment Assistance Act
VR	Vocational Rehabilitation
VRTAC-QE	Vocational Rehabilitation Technical Assistance Center for Quality Employment
WHAM	Whole Health Action Management
WHO	World Health Organization
WHODAS	World Health Organization Disability Assessment Schedule
WIA	Workforce Investment Act
WIOA	Workforce Innovation and Opportunity Act
WRAP	Wellness Recovery Action Plan

Scope of Practice for Rehabilitation Counseling

ASSUMPTIONS

- The Scope of Practice Statement identifies knowledge and skills required for the provision of effective rehabilitation counseling services to persons with physical, mental, developmental, cognitive, and emotional disabilities as embodied in the standards of the profession's credentialing organizations.
- Several rehabilitation disciplines and related processes (e.g., vocational evaluation, job development and job placement, work adjustment, and case management) are tied to the central field of rehabilitation counseling. The field of rehabilitation counseling is a specialty within the rehabilitation profession with counseling at its core and is differentiated from other related counseling fields.
- The professional scope of rehabilitation counseling practice is also differentiated from an individual scope of practice, which may overlap, but is more specialized than the professional scope. An individual scope of practice is based on one's own knowledge of the abilities and skills that have been gained through a program of education and professional experience. A person is ethically bound to limit his or her practice to that individual scope of practice.

UNDERLYING VALUES

- Facilitation of independence, integration, and inclusion of people with disabilities in employment and the community.
- Belief in the dignity and worth of all people.
- Commitment to a sense of equal justice based on a model of accommodation to provide and equalize the opportunities to participate in all rights and privileges available to all people and a commitment to supporting persons with disabilities in advocacy activities to achieve this status and empower themselves.
- Emphasis on the holistic nature of human function, which is procedurally facilitated by the utilization of techniques, such as:
  - interdisciplinary teamwork,
  - counseling to assist in maintaining a holistic perspective, and
  - a commitment to considering individuals within the context of their family systems and communities.
- Recognition of the importance of focusing on the assets of the person.
- Commitment to models of service delivery that emphasize integrated, comprehensive services, which are mutually planned by the consumer and the rehabilitation counselor.

Scope of Practice Statement

Rehabilitation counseling is a systematic process that assists persons with physical, mental, developmental, cognitive, and emotional disabilities to achieve their personal, career, and independent living goals in the most integrated setting possible through the application of the counseling process. The counseling process involves communication, goal setting, and beneficial growth or change through self-advocacy, psychological, vocational, social, and behavioral interventions. The specific techniques and modalities utilized within this rehabilitation counseling process may include, but are not limited to,

- assessment and appraisal;
- diagnosis and treatment planning;
- career (vocational) counseling;
- individual and group counseling treatment interventions focused on facilitating adjustments to the medical and psychosocial impact of disability;
- case management, referral, and service coordination;
- program evaluation and research;
- interventions to remove environmental, employment, and attitudinal barriers;
- consultation services among multiple parties and regulatory systems;
- job analysis, job development, and placement services, including assistance with employment and job accommodations; and
- the provision of consultation about and access to rehabilitation technology.

Selected Definitions

The following definitions are provided to increase the understanding of certain key terms and concepts used in the Scope of Practice Statement for Rehabilitation Counseling.

Appraisal

Selecting, administering, scoring, and interpreting instruments designed to assess an individual's aptitudes, abilities, achievements, interests, personal characteristics, disabilities, and mental, emotional, or behavioral disorders, as well as the use of methods and techniques for understanding human behavior in relation to coping with, adapting to, or changing life situations.

Diagnosis and Treatment Planning

Assessing, analyzing, and providing diagnostic descriptions of mental, emotional, or behavioral conditions or disabilities; exploring possible solutions; and developing and implementing a treatment plan for mental, emotional, and psychosocial adjustment or development. Diagnosis and treatment planning shall not be construed to permit the performance of any act that rehabilitation counselors are not educated and trained to perform.

Counseling Treatment Intervention

The application of cognitive, affective, behavioral, and systemic counseling strategies includes developmental, wellness, pathologic, and multicultural principles of human behavior. Such interventions are specifically implemented in the context of a professional counseling relationship and may include, but are not limited to, appraisal; individual, group, marriage, and family counseling and psychotherapy; the diagnostic description and treatment of persons with mental, emotional, and behavioral disorders or disabilities; guidance and consulting to facilitate normal growth and development, including educational and career development; the utilization of functional assessments and career counseling for persons requesting assistance in adjusting to a disability or handicapping condition, referrals, consulting, and research.

Referral

Evaluating and identifying the needs of a client to determine the advisability of referrals to other specialists, advising the client of such judgments, and communicating as requested or deemed appropriate to such referral sources.

Case Management

A systematic process merging counseling and managerial concepts and skills through the application of techniques derived from intuitive and researched methods, thereby advancing efficient and effective decision making for functional control of self, client, setting, and other relevant factors for anchoring a proactive practice. In case management, the counselor's role is focused on interviewing, counseling, planning rehabilitation programs, coordinating services, interacting with significant others, placing clients and following up with them, monitoring progress, and solving problems.

Program Evaluation

The effort to determine what changes occur as a result of a planned program by comparing actual changes (results) with desired changes (stated goals), and by identifying the degree to which the activity (planned program) is responsible for those changes.

Research

A systematic effort to collect, analyze, and interpret quantitative or qualitative data that describe how social characteristics, behavior, emotions, cognition, disabilities, mental disorders, and interpersonal transactions among individuals and organizations interact.

Consultation

The application of scientific principles and procedures in counseling and human development to provide assistance in understanding and solving current or potential problems that the consultee may have in relation to a third party, be it an individual, group, or organization.

Index

Printed in the USA
CPSIA information can be obtained
at www.ICGtesting.com
LVHW051949260923
759374LV00007B/688